AF843473

# PRESCRIPTION IN TORT LAW

# PRESCRIPTION IN TORT LAW

## Analytical and Comparative Perspectives

*Edited by*
Israel GILEAD
Bjarte ASKELAND

INTERSENTIA
Cambridge – Antwerp – Chicago

Intersentia Ltd
8 Wellington Mews
Wellington Street | Cambridge
CB1 1HW | United Kingdom
Tel: +44 1223 736 170
Email: mail@intersentia.co.uk
www.intersentia.com | www.intersentia.co.uk

*Distribution for the UK and*
*Rest of the World (incl. Eastern Europe)*
NBN International
1 Deltic Avenue, Rooksley
Milton Keynes MK13 8LD
United Kingdom
Tel: +44 1752 202 301 | Fax: +44 1752 202 331
Email: orders@nbninternational.com

*Distribution for Europe*
Intersentia Publishing nv
Groenstraat 31
2640 Mortsel
Belgium
Tel: +32 3 680 15 50
Email: mail@intersentia.be

*Distribution for the USA and Canada*
Independent Publishers Group
Order Department
814 North Franklin Street
Chicago, IL 60610
USA
Tel: +1 800 888 4741 (toll free) | Fax: +1 312 337 5985
Email: orders@ipgbook.com

Prescription in Tort Law. Analytical and Comparative Perspectives
© The editors and contributors severally 2020

The editors and contributors have asserted the right under the Copyright, Designs and Patents Act 1988, to be identified as authors of this work.

No part of this book may be reproduced, stored in a retrieval system, or transmitted, in any form, or by any means, without prior written permission from Intersentia, or as expressly permitted by law or under the terms agreed with the appropriate reprographic rights organisation. Enquiries concerning reproduction which may not be covered by the above should be addressed to Intersentia at the address above.

Artwork on cover: Gelb-Rot-Blau, Kandinsky Vassily (1866–1944) © Centre Pompidou, MNAM-CCI, Dist. RMN-Grand Palais / image Centre Pompidou, MNAM-CCI

ISBN 978-1-78068-963-0
D/2020/7849/56
NUR 822

British Library Cataloguing in Publication Data. A catalogue record for this book is available from the British Library.

*In Memory of Pierre Widmer*
(1938–2020)

# ACKNOWLEDGEMENTS

The editors acknowledge with gratitude the financial and the administrative support provided by ECTIL, the University of Girona and the University of Wroclaw in hosting EGTL meetings on the topic of prescription.

We thank Intersentia, in particular Ann-Christin Maak-Scherpe and Rebecca Moffat, for their contribution to the quality and coherence of the project and for creative solutions in coping with the diversities and complexities of this project.

Finally, we are most sincerely thankful and indebted to our dear colleagues, the members of EGTL, for many, many hours of inspiring and thought-provoking discussions and for their labour, patience and cooperation in producing the various versions of their reports.

# CONTENTS

# LIST OF AUTHORS

*Bjarte Askeland*
Appeal Court Judge, Gulating Lagmannsrett, Bergen, Norway; Former, until 2019, Professor of Private Law, University of Bergen, Norway

*Ewa Bagińska*
Professor of Civil Law, University of Gdańsk, Poland

*Nina Baranowska*
Former Researcher, University of Wrocław, Poland

*Jean-Sébastien Borghetti*
Professor of Private Law, University Paris II Panthéon-Assas, France

*Giovanni Comandé*
Professor of Comparative Law, Sant'Anna School of Advanced Studies, Pisa, Italy

*Eugenia Dacoronia*
Professor of Civil Law, National and Kapodistrian University of Athens, Greece

*Isabelle Durant*
Professor of Private Law, Université catholique de Louvain, Belgium

*Israel Gilead*
Emeritus Professor of Law, Hebrew University of Jerusalem, Israel; Professor of Law, Sha'arey Mada Umishpat Academic Center, Israel

*Michael D Green*
Williams Professor of Law, Wake Forest School of Law, United States

*Ernst Karner*
Professor of Civil Law, University of Vienna, Austria; Director of the Institute for European Tort Law and the European Centre of Tort and Insurance Law, Austria

*Anne LM Keirse*
Professor of Private Law, Utrecht University, the Netherlands; Judge at the Court of Appeal, Amsterdam, the Netherlands

*Bernhard A Koch*
Professor of Civil and Comparative Law, University of Innsbruck, Austria

*Frédéric Krauskopf*
Professor of Law, University of Bern, Switzerland

*Piotr Machnikowski*
Professor of Civil Law and Head of the Civil Law and Private International Law Department, University of Wrocław, Poland

*Ulrich Magnus*
Emeritus Professor of Law, University of Hamburg, Germany; Affiliate Researcher, Max Planck Institute for Comparative and International Private Law, Hamburg, Germany

*Miquel Martín-Casals*
Professor of Civil Law, University of Girona, Spain

*Johann Neethling*
Research Fellow of Private Law, University of the Free State, Bloemfontein, South Africa; Emeritus Professor, University of South Africa, Pretoria, South Africa

*Elena Occhipinti*
Adjunct Professor of Civil Procedural Law, University of Pisa, Italy

*Ken Oliphant*
Professor of Tort Law, University of Bristol, United Kingdom

*Albert Ruda*
Associate Professor in Civil Law and Dean of the Faculty of Law, University of Girona, Spain

*Stefan Rutten*
Professor of Civil Procedure, University of Antwerp, Belgium

*Luboš Tichý*
Professor of European, International Private Law and Civil Law, Charles University, Prague, Czech Republic

*Vanessa Wilcox*
Secretary General, European Law Institute, Austria; Former Assistant to the European Group on Tort Law, Austria

*Bénédict Winiger*
Professor of Law, University of Geneva, Switzerland

# PART I

# THEORETICAL AND COMPARATIVE ANALYSES

# ANALYTICAL AND COMPARATIVE REPORT

Israel GILEAD and Bjarte ASKELAND

## I. INTRODUCTION

1 This project of the European Group on Tort Law (EGTL) aims to explore how the passage of time on a tort law claim can affect, actually affects and should affect, through the defence of *prescription* (limitation of actions), the claim, the parties (plaintiff P and defendant D) and other parties.[1] For the purpose of this project, claims for professional malpractice, although considered as contractual claims in some jurisdictions, are treated as tort claims to the extent that they are based on grounds of tortious conduct (such as breach of a standard of care).

2 Notably, this report focuses on the *general* law of prescription of tort liability. *Special* rules of prescription that apply to specific contexts, such as prescription in cases of sexual abuse, prescription under European Council Directives and their national implementations, or of tort claims for harms caused by

1 Hereinafter, the following two-letter codes are used in citing the reports: AT (Austria); BE (Belgium); CH (Switzerland); CZ (Czech Republic); DE (Germany); ES (Spain); EW (England and Wales); FR (France); GR (Greece); IT (Italy); NL (the Netherlands); NO (Norway); PL (Poland); US (the United States); ZA (South Africa); EU (European Union); EA (economic analysis of prescription). Reference is made to paragraph numbers.

atomic installations, are discussed, when relevant, only in the national reports and the European Union report.[2] It is also emphasised that this project does not discuss legal arrangements under which rights (such as *legal powers*) exist from the outset for a limited period of time after which they expire 'from the inside' rather than by the operation of prescription law.[3] Neither does it discuss *acquisitive* prescription as a way to acquire property rights in immovable and movables.[4]

The discussion of each of the following topics starts with a theoretical analysis, based on the first round of EGTL discussions, and then proceeds to a comparative report and its conclusions, based on the second round of EGTL discussions. It should be emphasised, though, that the analysis, the observations and the suggestions made in this report, as well as the final conclusions (Section XIII) reflect the views of the authors and not of the EGTL. 3

## II. DEFINITION OF PRESCRIPTION

*Prescription in tort law is a legal institution that prevents the plaintiff (P) from enforcing a tort claim against the defendant (D) because of P's failure to file an action on the claim during the running of a specified period of time on the claim.*

### A. ANALYSIS

The subject of prescription, as can be seen from the above definition, is usually the right of P to tort remedy from D, namely the right, the claim,[5] to damages for harm caused. This right to remedy can only come into being once a right protected by tort law, such as the right to bodily and property integrity, or the right to reputation, is breached. To the extent that one conceives of the latter right (not to be harmed by tortious conduct) as a *primary* right, and 4

2 The EU report discusses prescription in product liability law (EU 62), prescription of competition damages claims (ibid 63) and prescription periods for liability of states for violation of EU law (ibid 67). For prescription in cases of sexual abuse see *R Zimmermann and J Kleinschmidt*, Prescription: General Framework and Special Problems Concerning Damages Claim, in: H Koziol and BC Steininger (eds), European Tort Law 2007 (2008), 26.

3 Eg the legal institution of 'caducity' discussed in the report for Spain – ES 5–7.

4 See AT 2, ES 4.

5 'Right to remedy' and 'claim' are used interchangeably as the claim (in its substantive meaning) is based on the right to remedy. The term 'action' is used for the procedural 'dress' of the claim – the complaint filed.

of the former right (to tort remedy) as a *secondary* right, it is the *secondary* right which is the subject matter of prescription.

### B. COUNTRY REPORTS

5 The suggested definition complies with the definition and/or the perception of prescription law in all reported countries.[6]

## III. THE NATURE OF PRESCRIPTION AND ITS EFFECTS

### A. ANALYSIS

6 There are different ways by which prescription prevents P from enforcing a claimed right of remedy against D. Its effect may be: (a) to extinguish P's right to remedy; (b) to provide D with a *substantive* defence that prevents P from enforcing the right to remedy although the right is not extinguished; and (c) to provide D with a *procedural* defence that bars P's ability to enforce the claimed right to remedy through *judicial proceedings before an authorised court.*

7 To illustrate the difference between the effects of prescription that extinguishes the right (a) and of prescription that only provides substantive defence against enforcement of the prescribed right (b), assume that D mistakenly compensates P for damage tortiously caused by D, although the prescription period elapsed and the claim has been prescribed. Under the extinction effect (a) D would have the right to restitution under the law of unjust enrichment because P's right to compensation was extinct before payment. In contrast, under the substantive defence effect (b) D will have no right of restitution because P's right to compensation still exists.

8 To illustrate, on the other hand, the difference between the substantive effect of prescription (b) and its effect as a procedural bar (c), assume that P can enforce the claimed right to tort compensation upon D *without judicial proceedings*, for example by way of set-off, or by other ways of self-help (such as selling or confiscating D's property). Could P do that after the prescription period elapsed? The answer would be negative under prescription as a substantive defence (b) because P's substantive right to *any* remedy becomes unenforceable. In contrast, under the procedural bar concept of prescription (c) the answer would be in the affirmative because only enforcement through

[6] AT 4; BE 6; CH 3; CZ 10; DE 3; ES 8; EW 3; FR 4; GR 2; IT 3; NL 3–4; NO 2; PL 5; US 3–6; ZA 2.

*judicial proceedings* in court is barred by prescription, while P can enforce the right outside the court.

## B. COUNTRY REPORTS

In most reported jurisdictions the general rule is that prescription operates as a substantive defence (b), which on the one hand does not extinguish the right to remedy (a), but on the other hand is not just a procedural bar to the tort claim (c).[7] The prescribed right is accordingly described as being an 'imperfect' or 'natural right'.[8] Yet, there are some exceptions to the general rule in these jurisdictions, under which prescription either extinguishes some rights (a) or serves only as a procedural defence against other rights (c).[9] 9

In Italy and South Africa, the effect of prescription under the law is to extinguish the prescribed right (a). However, the reporters for Italy observe that 'actual practice with regard to the doctrine has led to the widely-held scholarly view that prescription does not actually extinguish rights'.[10] Along the same lines, the reporter for South Africa comments that this concept 'create[s] anomalies' and that the option of substantive defence (b) should be preferred.[11] In France '[i]t is not yet fully settled if prescription extinguishes the claimant's right [...] or if it simply creates a defence for the defendant.'[12] 10

In England and Wales (E&W) prescription (limitation of actions) 'operates as a procedural defence that bars judicial remedy' but does not prevent P from pursuing lawful self-help means (c).[13] This is also the general rule in the US,[14] although '(s)ome jurisdictions regard statutes of limitation as a mix of both procedural and substantive.'[15] In the Czech Republic prescription the procedural aspects of prescription are emphasised despite its classification as a substantive defence.[16] 11

The nature of the defence is still discussed in Belgium: while in the past it was perceived as substantive defence the trend seems to have turned toward its perception as procedural defence.[17] 12

---

7 AT 5; CH 6; DE 5–6; FR 6; ES 10; GR 3–4; NL 5; NO 4–5; PL 7–10.

8 AT 5; BE 8; GR 3; PL 8. In Spain it is characterised as 'counter-right' – ES 10.

9 See eg CH 7.

10 IT 7.

11 ZA 4–5.

12 FR 5.

13 EW 10. An exception is the tort of conversion where prescription extinguishes D's proprietary claim on the good – ibid.

14 US 10.

15 US 13.

16 CZ 9.

17 BE 8.

13 As to non-contractual claims against the EU, it is yet unsettled whether prescription extinguishes the right, or is a substantive or only procedural defence.[18]

## C. OBSERVATIONS

14 As the effect of prescription of tort claims depends on and varies with the perceived nature of the defence (a, b, c), and given the differences among jurisdictions in this regard, what can and should be done to promote harmonisation?

15 It is suggested that as a rule, and subject to exceptions, the middle-ground should be embraced, namely the defence should be perceived as *a substantive defence against all kinds of enforcement* (b), a defence that neither extinguishes the right (a) nor is only a procedural defence effective solely against court's proceedings (c).[19] At one end of the spectrum it is unclear why the ability to enforce a prescribed right should depend on the kind of enforcement (option a). If a right prescribes, any kind of enforcement should be barred as a rule, not only enforcements by courts. At the other end, it is unclear why as a rule the right to tort remedy should be extinguished even in cases where D does not deny its existence and even performs the corresponding duty. Indeed, even in jurisdictions where prescription is perceived as extinguishing the right (a), D who paid a prescribed debt nevertheless has no claim for restitution,[20] as in jurisdictions where prescription is a substantive defence (b).

16 The proposed general rule, however, may have exceptions where policy considerations, discussed below,[21] justify either extinction of the right (option a) or limiting the effect of the defence only to the court's proceeding (option c). Arguably, *it is not the nature of the defence that should determine its effects*, but, vice versa, *it is the desirable effects that should determine the nature of the defence in the relevant context.* Hence, questions such as whether a prescribed right can support a claim of set-off, whether statutory changes in prescription laws apply retroactively or only prospectively,[22] should be

[18] EU 5.

[19] See *Zimmermann and Kleinschmidt*, *supra* fn 2, 30 ('it is internationally widely recognized that that prescription does not extinguishes the creditor's right. The debtor is merely granted a right to refuse performance').

[20] ZA 4.

[21] Section IV.

[22] The question which law of prescription should apply on torts which are actionable under the law of more than one jurisdiction is not discussed here. For the choice of law applicable to prescription of tort claims see, eg EW 95.

decided according to the desirable outcome and not by a rigid classification of the nature of prescription which varies among jurisdictions and within a jurisdiction.

## IV. CONSIDERATIONS FOR AND AGAINST PRESCRIPTION OF TORT CLAIMS[23]

### A. AGAINST

Prescription of a tort claim, as defined above, prevents P from enforcing a tort claim against D because of the running of a specified period of time on P's claim. That may deprive Ps from pursuing and enforcing their claimed rights against Ds,[24] or unjustly weaken their claims.[25] To the extent that the claims barred by prescription are 'good claims', namely, meritorious claims that should be recognised and enforced to promote the goals of tort law, prescription of such claims may frustrate the attainment of these goals: it denies compensation from victims of tortious conduct and relieves tortfeasors from incurring the costs of such a conduct, thereby impairing both the justice and deterrence goals of tort law.[26] It can be seen as a kind of appropriation and a breach of legal ethics.[27] Moreover, prescription actually closes the doors of courts and may significantly constrict Ps' right to 'open courts',[28] which is perceived by many as a *constitutional* right that should be cherished and well protected.[29] Prescription law may restrict and erode this constitutional right. Moreover, as the ability to vindicate rights in courts empowers individuals and strengthen their trust in the state and in society, closing the doors of courts may undermine this empowerment and trust[30] and even encourage people to bypass the legal system by pursuing methods of 'self-help'.[31] 17

23 'Thus, it is obvious that the law of prescription is based on a delicate balance of conflicting interests' – *Zimmermann and Kleinschmidt*, *supra* fn 2, 31.

24 EW 11 ('[t]he right to a fair trial entails a right to have one's case heard'); GR 5; NO 9.

25 CH 9; PO 13 (claims for personal injury are therefore not subjected to prescription – ibid 14).

26 See EA Section II.

27 AT 9; DE 8 ('expropriation of property without compensation').

28 NL 7.

29 ES 10, 15 (prescription violates constitutional values).

30 DE 11 ('dissatisfaction and disappointment if an entirely valid claim cannot be enforced merely because of the lapse of the prescription period'); US 21 ('barring legitimate claims, may leave some claimants disillusioned with the legal process').

31 US 21.

## B. FOR

### 1) *An Overview*

18 Given these negative effects of prescription on 'good', meritorious, claims, what are the considerations that nevertheless counterbalance the negative and justify prescription law? It appears that the major consideration that justifies the operation of prescription law is the protection of Ds, *potential* and *actual*, from the costs associated with the threat of belated future claims, and the costs, and even wrongs, of actually filed belated claims. Such protection, it should be emphasised, is the cornerstone of prescription law not only because it benefits Ds, potential and actual, but also because it serves important communal, collective interests such as the promotion of fairness, the reduction of uncertainty that may hinder the flow of commercial activity and the use of judicial resources in an adequate manner.

19 One should also bear in mind that not all claims are meritorious, 'good claims'. Some claims may be 'bad', non-meritorious claims: either *bona-fide* claims based on misconception of facts and/or mistakes of law, or *mala-fide* claims which are false, vexatious, or extortionate. To the extent that prescription law may help screening 'bad claims' that Ds may fail to defend because of the passage of time, it preforms another important function from the perspectives of Ds and the common good.[32]

20 That the major role of prescription law is to protect Ds echoes in the rule embraced by all jurisdictions which basically allows only actual Ds to plead prescription: in all jurisdictions the court cannot raise the claim *ex officio*.[33]

21 The following is a more detailed discussion of the considerations that support prescription and should play a major role in its design and application.

### 2) *Goal – Protection of Potential Ds and the 'Multiplier'*

22 A major goal of prescription law, as stressed,[34] is to protect *potential* Ds against the uncertainty, burden and costs of exposure to the risks of future claims.[35]

---

32 AT 8 ('[p]rescription primarily serves as a protection for potential Ds against unfounded claims'); CH 10 ('the plaintiff's lack of action over a longer period of time makes it seem likely that the claim is unfounded'); DE 13 ('Prescription is also regarded as necessary because claims can be, and not infrequently are, unjustified for what reasons ever'); FR 8; NL 8. The US reporter, in contrast, argues that the passage of time may not impair courts' ability to distinguish between good and bad claim – US 19.

33 AT 7; CH 3; CZ 8; DE 5; FR 90; GR 111; IT 85; NO 137; NL 6; PL 10–11 (with the exception of claims against consumers); NO 10.

34 See *supra* 18.

35 US 22 ('Stability of transactions and relationships are important to society, and these are affected by looming potential litigation').

These costs are directly related to the length of the effective time of prescription – the longer the period in which this exposure continues the higher are these costs. Basically, there are three kinds of related costs:

- Costs of preserving evidence required to meet future claims.[36] It is an empirical question whether in the digital era these costs have decreased (less need for storage space, shelves, paper) or have increased (servers, computers, software, maintenance, cyber protection). That may also depend on rules of evidence admissibility. In any case, these costs are high and will remain high, and are directly related to the length of the effective time of prescription.
- Costs of preserving financial reserves required to meet future claims. The need to keep such reserves limits the ability of corporations and individuals to use their financial resources in an optimal manner and restricts their ability to plan ahead.[37]
- Risks of looming legal claims generate uncertainty regarding the future, uncertainty which increases with the length of the effective time of prescription. Such uncertainty may be most detrimental to potential Ds as it distorts their decision-taking process and may cause psychological and emotional harm (due to risk-aversion) that frustrates their 'peace of mind.'[38] This uncertainty limits the ability of insurance markets to properly spread the risks of liability: insurers may be reluctant to insure indeterminate, open-ended risks or ask for unaffordable premiums.[39]

It should be stressed, and constantly kept in mind, that the above costs to 23
potential Ds, costs which prescription law aims to reduce, are of a large scale and magnitude. It is so because of the actually indeterminate numbers of potential Ds. For example, producers are exposed to numerous tort claims of consumers, and the same applies to medical institutions and their patients, employers and employees, insurance companies and their insureds and so on. Actually, every one of us is a potential D. In contrast, the numbers of *actual* Ds which are protected by prescription law, and the number of *actual* Ps who are negatively affected by prescription, is much smaller. In other words, the weight attached to the protection of *potential* Ds in the overall balance between the conflicting considerations should be multiplied by many times with comparison to considerations regarding *actual* Ds and actual Ps. This enhanced normative weight is referred to as the 'multiplier'.

---

36 AT 8; CH 10; DE 14; ES 2; EW 14; US 22.

37 AT 8; DE 14; ES 2; NO 7; NL 8; PO 18; US 22.

38 ES 2 (prescription 'guarantees everyone a state of peace and tranquillity in which the person at stake can feel free of the possibility of being claimed against by another').

39 ES 2.

### 3) *Goal – Protection of Actual Ds*

24 Another important goal of prescription law is to protect *actual* Ds from the undesirable and often unfair outcomes of belated claims.

- Bad claims may be enforced upon Ds due to a failure to defend caused by the deterioration of evidence over time.[40] Although the burden of proof usually lies upon Ps, actual Ds are often in an inferior position in the evidential respect. It is so because potential Ds often have no indication of who may sue them and for what, and,[41] being left in the darkness,[42] they may be unable to collect and preserve all the relevant evidence.[43] Ps, in contrast, are well aware of the details of their own personal claim, and may be in a much better position to collect and preserve relevant evidence.[44] A failure to fend-off claims due to evidential inferiority may do injustice to the failing D, and make her substantially worse-off in financial and psychological terms,[45] leading to frustration and distrust in the system.[46]
- Similar negative effects may ensue from enforcement of claims that were 'bad' at the time in which the claim should have been filed, and because of changing legal and social norms during the delay may be unfairly considered a 'good' claim in retrospect.
- Even if an actual D succeeds in fending-off bad claims, the time, money and other resources invested in the defence are very costly in both financial, psychological and emotional terms.
- Even if P's belated claim is a good one, and much more so if it is a bad claim, the unexpected belated filing of P's claim interrupts the *status quo* that was formed during the long period of P's inaction, and thereby frustrates D's legitimate expectations that the now stabilised state of affairs would not be disturbed by 'ghosts of the past'.

### 4) *Goal – Promoting Collective Interests*

25 The interests of potential and actual Ds to be protected, by prescription law, against the mischiefs of belated claims (costs, unfairness, uncertainty and

---

40 BE 61; CH 10 ('the further in the past the relevant facts lie, the more difficult it becomes to reliably establish and assess them (because evidence is difficult or impossible to obtain)'); EW 14; IT 10, 12; NL 8 ('witnesses are untraceable, memories become blurred, and written documents get lost or are thrown away'); PO 19; US 22; ZA 14. In contrast it is argued that 'evidence remains fresh and indeed may have improved with the passage of time' – US 21.

41 AT 8.

42 DE 13 ('the darkening force of time').

43 Ibid ('remembrance fades; witnesses may have died or cannot be reached'); GR 6.

44 US 22. For the opposing view that Ps are not in a better position than Ds in this regard see US 19.

45 *Supra* 6–7.

46 EW 12 ('long dormant claims have often more of cruelty than justice to them'); NO 8; NL 8.

frustration of legitimate expectations) are not only *private* interests of Ds, but to a large extent also *collective*, *societal*, interests.[47] In other words, the financial and emotional costs and harms to Ds are not only *private* costs to Ds but also a *social* cost to society at large. The difference between private costs and social costs is that a social cost is a reduction of the overall well-being enjoyed by society at large, whereas a merely private cost is a cost to one individual or group which is offset by an ensuing benefit to another individual or group so that the overall well-being of society is *not* reduced.[48] Given the huge number of potential Ds (the 'multiplier'[49]), it is evident that the private benefits of belated claims to actual Ps, given their relatively small numbers, do not offset the private costs to potential Ds, given their large numbers. From society's perspective, to sum up, prescription law, if properly designed and applied, may enhance the overall well-being of society as its benefits to Ds far exceed its costs to Ps.[50]

In addition to the above well-being cost/benefit analysis that supports prescription because its benefits to Ds far exceed its costs to Ps, there are specific societal interests that are promoted by a well-designed prescription law: 26

- By screening bad claims and allowing good claims, a well-designed prescription law contributes significantly to the ability of tort law to achieve its goals: just and fair reparation of past harms and avoidance of future tortious activity. This is obviously a presiding consideration. Enforcement of belated bad claims in the absence of screening by prescription law may undermine the goals of tort law.
- The uncertainty that indeterminate exposure to legal risks creates may lead to malfunction of capital and insurance markets due to difficulties in assessing market value of bodies exposed to future claims and in estimating the solvency of corporations and individuals.[51] Given the vast numbers of potential Ds (the 'multiplier') that are exposed to such uncertainty, it may well distort market prices and interrupt the flow of commerce and economic activity.[52]
- The interruption of a stabilised *status quo* established by a long period of P's inaction does not only frustrate D's legitimate expectation but also may threaten 'public peace.'[53]

---

47 AT 10 ('prescription serves general interests such as legal certainty, practicability, economic efficacy and off-loading of pressure on the court system'); BE 61 ('the concept of prescription exists in the general interest: it improves legal certainty and safeguards social peace'); CH 10; GR 6; PO 17 (public policy supports prescription as means for legal certainty and stability).

48 See EA Section II.

49 See *supra* 23.

50 See EA 21.

51 BE 9 (goal of prescription is to 'ensure *legal certainty*'); NL 10–12 (stressing the importance of certainty); EU 8 (protecting the finance and the budget of the EU).

52 EW 13; US 22.

53 BE 9 ('prevent *social unrest*'); CH 8; DE 15; FR 8; GR 6; NL 10; EU 8 ('protection of public order').

- It is a societal interest that society's limited judicial resources should not be spent on stale, 'rusty' claims that are more costly to adjudicate, 'more problematic for the judge to construct historical reality',[54] and may well be bad claims.[55]
- It is the interest of society to promote fairness between Ds and Ps.[56] With the passage of a long period on Ps' claim the balance of fairness as to whether to allow a delayed claim gradually shifts towards Ds. On the one hand the delay on Ps' part may be a kind of neglect,[57] or an indication of waiver, or even an intentional misuse of right, that weakens their late claim to enforce a right.[58] On the other hand this delay may do injustice to Ds who are unable to defend due to the passage of time, whose legitimate expectations are frustrated and who may be judged by norms other than those which prevailed at the time of their conduct.[59] Moreover, the passage of time may indicate that D has already fulfilled the obligation to P.[60]

27 The relative weight attached to collective interests in the design and operation of prescription law, when compared to the weight attached to the parties' interests, can be deduced from the degree of the law's readiness to allow the parties to stipulate the effective time of prescription: reluctance to allow such stipulation testifies to a greater weight attached to collective interests.[61]

### 5) *Prescription may Promote the Interests of Ps as well*

28 Although the prescription defence bars Ps' claims to their apparent detriment, prescription law, in some respects, may also protect Ps and benefit them. Firstly, it incentivises Ps to file their claims within reasonable time and thereby protects them against failure of good claims to succeed due to the deterioration of Ps' evidence over time.[62] It should be borne in mind that the timing of

---

54 IT 9.

55 CH 10 ('prescription of claims spares courts from having to assess facts that have happened a long time ago'); DE 15 ('prescription saves public costs and resources'); EW 16 ('[c]ourts are ill-suited to determine stale demands [...] deciding them is more likely to be time-intensive'); ZA 14 ('judicial economy and smooth functioning of the legal system is best served when parties are obliged to bring their disputes to the courts promptly').

56 The Court of Justice of the EU (CJEU) observed that 'the limitation period gives protection to both the aggrieved party and the individual liable for the damage'– EU 6.

57 GR 6; PO 18; ZA 14.

58 BE 9 (P 'has to face the consequences of his negligence'); ES 8; US 22.

59 US 22 ('Society's legal standards and expectations change over time, so without a limitations period, judges and juries might apply modern legal standards to events that took place when different legal standards and sensibilities prevailed').

60 BE 10 ('sometimes, the prescription rule is founded on a deemed payment').

61 See *infra* Section XII.A.

62 AT 8 ('prescription is also an educational form of pressure to avoid negligence of Ps in exercising their legal rights'); BE 61 ('a limitation period also protects the interest of the

the initiation of proceeding is often determined not by Ps but by the P's attorney who may delay the filing for reasons that do not serve the client's interests. Secondly, earlier proceedings lead to earlier remedy to Ps. Thirdly, prescription also promotes fairness among Ps as adjudication of belated claims may often consume more judicial resources than timely filed claims. Such allocation of resources is unfair where Ps who act reasonably are deprived of societal resources consumed by other Ps who act unreasonably.

# V. ELEMENTS OF PRESCRIPTION – AN OVERVIEW

## A. ANALYSIS – THE FOUR ELEMENTS

Analytically, there are four elements – four sets of rules – that together comprise the essence of prescription law: the starting point, the prescription period, rules of prolongation and rules of upper-time-limit. These elements are presented here briefly and discussed later on in details at the following sections. 29

### 1) *The Starting Point*

The starting point[63] is the date on which P's cause of action against D, P's claim which is the subject matter of prescription, matures so that the prescription period starts to run on this claim (unless its running is postponed by a rule of prolongation[64]). In terms of the common law, the starting point is *the date on which the cause of action accrues*. 30

### 2) *The Prescription Period*

The prescription period[65] is the statutory period of time that after its running (from the starting point – from the date of accrual) the cause of action is prescribed. 31

### 3) *Rules of Prolongation*

Rules of prolongation[66] are rules that prolong the actual time that passes between the starting point (accrual) and the expiry of the prescription 32

plaintiff. The plaintiff must be given a reasonable time limit in which to submit his claim'); CZ 16; EW 15 (claimants are encouraged 'not to go to sleep on their rights'); NO 7.

63 Discussed *infra* Section VI.

64 The third element of prescription.

65 Discussed in Section VII.

66 Discussed in Section VIII.

period on P's cause of action. There are four kinds of rules of prolongation: *postponement*, *suspension*, *renewal* and *extension*. When these rules apply, the *effective time of prescription*, namely, the actual time that passes from the starting point (accrual) to expiry of the prescription period, is longer than the prescription period.

33 Rules of prolongation usually apply in situations where P's delay to file a claim against D originates in contingencies that caused the delay, such as P's unawareness of relevant facts, mental disabilities, special relation between P and D, *force majeure* and so on. When such reasons for delay render it justified from the perspective of prescription law, the effective time of prescription is accordingly prolonged by rules of postponement, suspension, renewal and extension.

- Rules of *postponement* postpone the running of the prescription period, *before it starts to run*, beyond the starting point (beyond the accrual of cause of action), until the reason for postponement ceases to exist. For example, to the extent that D's mental disability at the starting point and afterwards is recognised as justifying postponement of the running of the prescription period, the period does not start to run (is postponed) until this mental disability ends.
- Rules of *suspension* suspend the running of the prescription period as long as the reason for suspension exists. For example, to the extent that arbitration proceedings between P and D, that began after the starting point, justify the suspension of the prescription as long as they are conducted, the prescription will cease to run while these proceedings are conducted. The difference between rules of *postponement* and rules of *suspension* is discussed below.[67]
- Rules of *renewal* (also referred to as *rules of interruption*[68]) restart the running of the prescription period in the sense that a new period of prescription starts to run afresh when the reason for renewal presents itself. For example, where D admits P's right to torts compensation from D, this admission, if recognised as a rule of renewal, 'deletes' the period that ran until admission, and a new count of the period begins.
- Rules of *extension*, unlike the former rules, do not affect the running of the period, but rather *extend the period itself*.[69] For example, if the victim of a

---

67 See *infra* 156.

68 BE 16 ('when the running of time is broken […] The time that has already elapsed is lost and the count of the prescription period starts afresh'); GR 15; ZA 12.

69 Therefore, rules of extension should not be equated with rules of postponement – cf BE 29 and *Zimmermann and Kleinschmidt*, *supra* fn 2, 32 (referring to extension as 'postponement of expiry').

tort (V) dies six months before the period expires vis-à-vis D, and the law provides that the derivative claim of the heirs (the estate) against D shall not prescribe within one year after V's death, this is a rule of extension that in this case extends the prescription period by six months.

#### 4) *The Upper Time Limit*[70]

The above rules of prolongation may indeterminately prolong the effective time of prescription[71] to an extent that frustrates the goals of prescription law.[72] To avoid such indeterminate prolongation the law may set upper limits to the effective time of prescription, a 'ceiling' period, that after its running the cause of action is prescribed even though the prescription period has not yet expired because of rules of prolongation. This *upper time limit*, the 'ceiling', also referred to as 'long-stop' or 'overriding time limit', should be distinguished from the *prescription period*. As later explained,[73] it may, and actually should, start earlier than the prescription period, namely, before the starting point (date of accrual), and it may and actually should be much less susceptible to rules of prolongation, if at all. 34

## B. COUNTRY REPORTS

The analysis of prescription law as being composed of the above four elements (starting point (date of accrual), prescription periods, rules of prolongation and upper time limit) is compatible with the perception of prescription law in the reported jurisdictions,[74] although these elements may have different titles.[75] There is only one noteworthy exception: in a few jurisdictions the fourth element of upper time limit is missing.[76] 35

---

70 Discussed in Section IX.

71 See, eg BE 27 ('one could assume that in some cases there is a huge difference between the basic and the effective limitation period').

72 See Section IV.

73 See Section IX.

74 AT 12 (although commenting that the prescription period and the ceiling are part of two separate notions of prescription – see *infra* 259 regarding that view); BE 11; CH 11; CZ 19–22; DE 18–20; EW (discussing all four elements); GR 7–17; NL 14–18; NO 12–15; PL 21–39; US 24.

75 See, eg ES 13.

76 ES 13; IT 13–21; ZA 8–13. With regard to prescription of non-contractual claims against the EU, the reporters for the EU observe that in general it is perceived as composed of only two elements – the starting point and the prescription period. The exceptions are rules of prolongation in few cases of late discovery and of applications for legal aid – EU 11, 42–48.

# VI. THE STARTING POINT OF THE PRESCRIPTION PERIOD

## A. THE MEANING OF 'ACTION' AND OF 'CAUSE OF ACTION'

### 1) *An Overview*

36 The first element of prescription, the starting point (the date of the 'accrual of the cause of action' in the terms of the common law) is the date on which P's cause of action against D, claim (right) which is the subject matter of prescription, matures so that the prescription period may *potentially* start to run on this claim[77] (*potentially*, because its running may be postponed by rules of prolongation).[78]

37 It stands to reason, given the goals and justifications of prescription law, that the starting point should not precede the date on which all the substantive requirements that constitute P's cause of action against D, the essentials of the claim, come into being. Before that date P's claim, if filed, would be dismissed for being premature, and it makes no sense to start counting the prescription period against P where P's claim is immature.

38 What are the essentials, the substantive requirements that constitute P's cause of action against D, which should come into being for the starting point to be reached (for the cause of action to accrue)? The response to this question is complex as the following enquiries should be made along the way:

- What is an action?
- Given the definition of an action, what is *a cause* of action?
- How broad should the cause of action be? In other words, should different factual and legal bases of a claim be considered as belonging to the same (and broad) cause of action, or as belonging to different (and narrow) causes of action?
- In a claim for damages for harm caused by D to P, should the occurrence of harm be the starting point (date of accrual) or rather the preceding D's tortious conduct?
- Where harm is a part of the cause of action, what should be considered as the *occurrence* of harm?
- What is the starting point (date of accrual) when a tort is *continuous*?

---

77 It 'means the moment when the claim becomes enforceable' – *Zimmermann and Kleinschmidt*, *supra* fn 2, 34.

78 See *supra* 29 and *infra* Section VIII.

- Is the late discovery rule[79] a rule of the starting point (first element), or rather a rule of prolongation that postpones the running of the period after the starting point (third element)?

The following discussion presents the various answers to the above questions, trying to identify the answers that best suit the goals and justifications of prescription law. It should be stressed, at the beginning of the discussion, that it examines the notion of *cause of action* only in the context of prescription of claims, focusing on tort claims (including contractual claims of malpractice based on negligence[80]). Notably, the notion of *cause of action* may have different roles and accordingly different meanings and interpretations in other contexts, such as *res judicata*, where the question is not whether the cause of action was prescribed before adjudication, but whether it was already adjudicated in the past.[81] Given these differences, it is most important to interpret and apply the concept of cause of action in the context of prescription law in conformity with the latter's roles and goals, without 'borrowing' from other contexts, such as *res judicata*[82] or civil procedure,[83] as such undesirable 'borrowing' may lead to undesirable outcomes.[84] 39

*2) The Meaning of 'Action'*

An action in tort alleging a claim to tort remedy for harm caused[85] should usually contain the following ingredients: (a) facts regarding D's tortious conduct (act or omission) and its surrounding circumstances;[86] (b) harm caused in fact to P by D's conduct; (c) applicable tort that renders D's conduct tortious and entitles P to tort remedy against D for the harm caused.[87] Every combination of these facts, harm caused and applicable tort constitutes a particular action in tort. 40

79 Discussed at length *infra* Section VIII.B.

80 See *supra* 1.

81 The concept of 'cause of action' in the law of *res judicata* is discussed extensively in the E&W report as being relevant to the corresponding concept in prescription law – EW 21–25. The US report also discusses *res judicata* (the 'single judgment rule' – US 30).

82 The reporter for the US observes that the definition of cause of action for prescription is often assumed to be co-extensive with that of *res judicata* – US 28.

83 In this context the question is whether P's statement of facts (complaint) reveals a cause of action in the sense that these alleged facts, if established, may constitute a successful claim.

84 For such undesirable outcome where prescription law 'borrows' from *res judicata* law see the discussion of Case 1 *infra* 50, 69.

85 An *action* is the procedural dress of the substantive *claim* – see *supra* fn 5.

86 *Fait générateur* – FR 12.

87 'A factual situation the existence of which entitles one person to obtain from the court a remedy against another person [...] where all the essential elements needed to support an enforceable claim have arisen'– EW 19; '[A] set of facts sufficient to justify a plaintiff's right to file an action against the defendant' – GR 18.

### 3) The Meaning of 'Cause of Action'

41 The *cause of action*[88] is the source, the root, of a particular action. Usually a particular action (claim) arises from, or originates in, *an event* such as an accident, professional malpractice, defaming publications, etc. When an event contains a multiplicity of conducts which are tortious under tort law and/or of caused harms, it may produce a variety of particular tort claims, which differ from each other in the facts regarding D's conduct, and/or in the harms caused and/or in the applicable torts. Yet, when a group of particular claims has a common factual/legal source it is said that all these particular actions belong to the same source, the same cause of action. So the cause of action may be the event as a whole or part of it.[89]

42 This is exemplified by the following illustration. Physician D treats patient P negligently and performs three mistakes on the treatment's day: A, B and C. Mistake A causes harm X after a year. Mistake B causes harm Y after two years. Mistakes A and C together cause harm Z after three years. The *event* is the medical treatment. This event contains a multiplicity of facts regarding D's conduct (three different mistakes A, B, C) and a multiplicity of harms (X, Y, Z). It accordingly raises a multiplicity of particular actions, particular claims (for harms X, Y and Z). Yet, to the extent that these actions, or some of them, have a common factual/legal source, they may be regarded as originating in the same *cause of action* – the medical treatment in this case.[90]

## B. BROAD OR NARROW CONCEPTION OF 'CAUSE OF ACTION'?

### 1) The Question

43 The subject of prescription, it should be stressed, is not *a particular* action, *a particular* claim, but rather its *cause of action*, the source from which the

[88] The notion of 'cause of action' is not used or known in all jurisdictions; see, eg CH 13 and FR 11. On the other hand, the E&W reporters note that 'the Limitation Act 1980, makes nearly 50 references to a "cause of action"' – EW 18.

[89] The distinction between a particular action based on a particular claim and the broader cause of action is nicely summarised in the US report. It explains that '[t]he scope of a cause of action for statute of limitations purposes is that it generally encompasses all injuries suffered in a transaction or occurrence or a series of transactions and occurrences and any consequential future harms. Moreover, it includes all different legal theories that might be asserted to provide a remedy for those injuries' – US 28.

[90] In Poland, for another example, the Supreme Court held in 2015 that all claims stemming from wrongful death belong to the same cause of action. The reporter concludes that this ruling 'supports the conclusion that the subject of prescription is not *a particular* action *or particular* claim, but rather its source.'

particular claim originates. Once a cause of action prescribes with a particular claim that originates from it, all other particular claims that originate in the same cause of action also prescribe. In the above illustration, if all three particular claims belong to the same cause of action, when this cause of action prescribes because the particular claim for harm X prescribed, then the other particular claims for harms Y and Z would also prescribe. But if claims for harms X, Y and Z each belong to a different cause of action, then the prescription of the claim for X would not lead to the prescription of the other claims. The prescription period has to run separately on each cause of action before it prescribes.[91]

It therefore follows that a *broad* conception of a cause of action, namely, one that includes many particular claims (eg harms X, Y and Z belong to the same cause of action),[92] would be detrimental to Ps and beneficial to Ds because prescription of one particular claim would lead to the prescription of all claims belonging to the broadly defined cause of action.[93] In contrast, a *narrow* conception of a cause of action, namely, one that includes few particular claims or just one (eg X, Y and Z belong each to a different cause of action) would be beneficial to Ps and detrimental to Ds because prescription of one particular claim would not lead to the prescription of other claims, although emerging from the same event, because they belong to narrowly defined different causes of action. 44

Note that under the narrowest sense of the notion *cause of action* any change in any of the above ingredients of an action – facts regarding D's conduct, caused harms, applicable torts – may be perceived to be a different cause of action.[94] In contrast under a broader sense of the notion different claims 45

---

91 In South Africa the broad concept of cause of action is known as the 'single cause theory' while the narrower concept is known as *facta probanda* – ZA 17. 'In terms of the single cause theory, it is accepted that all the different claims consequent upon an unlawful act fall within one cause of action. In accordance with the *facta probanda* approach, the requisites of two or more claims are compared to establish whether there is a substantial difference despite possible overlapping. If there is no substantial difference, the two claims are regarded as falling within a single cause of action' – ZA 18.

92 This broad approach corresponds with the 'Unitary-Damage' concept suggested in *Zimmermann and Kleinschmidt*, *supra* fn 2, 38–43.

93 '[A] cause of action arises at the earliest date when all the requirements for delictual liability are present' – ZA 19. Therefore 'when a cause of action has arisen because some damage has already occurred, the plaintiff must [...] institute an action in which he claims damages for all damage already sustained as well as that expected in future' – ZA 20.

94 See, eg the reporter for the Czech Republic who observes that '[T]he Czech courts incline toward the narrow concept of cause of action' – CZ 29. He also claims that where 'damage to health gives rise to a number of partial claims [...] These are separate claims that are subject to prescription separately as well' – 31. See also the reporter for Norway who observes that 'the Norwegian system definitely operates with a *narrow* conception of a claim' (NO 18) and that the 'system featuring a narrow conception of a claims functions well' (ibid 19). The French

may be considered as belonging to the same cause of action although they differ in facts, and/or in harms and/or in applicable torts. The range between the narrowest conception of cause and the broadest conception allows for much flexibility in between.[95]

46 Since the decision as to how broad or narrow the cause of action should be defined for each particular claim is vested with the courts, it appears that courts have a wide discretion in deciding whether a particular claim has prescribed with other claims or not. In the above illustration, they would have a wide discretion to decide, where claim for X prescribed, that claims for Y and Z also prescribed (broad conception of cause of action), that Y and Z did not prescribe with X (narrow conception), or that only Z prescribed with X because mistake A caused both X and Z (intermediate conception).

*2) Cases 1–3 – Analysis and Country Reports*

47 To further illustrate the differences between the broad and the narrow conception of *cause of action*, and to present and compare the law in this regard in reported jurisdictions, the following three hypothetical cases are discussed below.

a) Case 1

*D, a ski instructor, negligently fails to make sure that all skiers in her 'off-piste' group wear helmets. P, a skier in the group, hits a tree. P immediately suffers head injury X, and years later another head injury Y that developed from the same accident.*

48 *Analysis*: The event here is the ski accident and the relevant question is whether this event constitutes one cause of action to which harms X and Y belong (broad conception), or whether it constitutes two different causes of action, one for harm X and one for harm Y (narrow conception). Under the broader conception harm Y would prescribe with harm X (favouring D) while under the narrow conception prescription of harm X would not affect the prescription of harm Y (favouring P).

---

reporter notes as well that 'If one adopts the cause of action language, it can thus be said that French law adopts a narrow conception of cause of action, since each item of loss constitutes a distinct cause of action, regardless of its origin' – FR 17.

95 See, eg the German report which notes that to 'term this concept either broad or narrow does not fully meet the German concept. It may be regarded as relatively broad though with exceptions which narrow it' – DE 27.

It appears that as a rule the broad approach should prevail in such cases. The reason is that the claim for harm X and the claim for harm Y differ from each other only in the harm sued for and otherwise are based on the same facts regarding D's tortious conduct and on the same tort/s. There is obviously one common factual/legal root to harms X and Y, indicating they belong to the same cause of action. Moreover, a narrow approach in such cases cannot be reconciled with the essence and goals of prescription law. If each new harm that results from the same tortious conduct would constitute a different cause of action, D would indeterminably be exposed to a risk of claims, undermining and frustrating the very basic goals of prescription law. 49

Should the outcome be different if under rules of *res judicata* a judgment deciding P's claim for harm X would *not* bar P's later claim for harm Y?[96] It is suggested that the outcome should remain the same. True, for the purposes of *res judicata* X and Y may be considered different causes of action and not as belonging to the same cause of action. Yet such preference of the narrow conception of cause of action, assuming that it serves the goals of *res judicata*, does not necessarily serve the goals of prescription law, where the broader conception of cause of action should be preferred.[97] It is so because of the different functions and goals of prescription on the one hand and the law of *res judicata* on the other hand. Rules of *res judicata* aim to avoid artificial division of the same legal issue into different costly judicial proceedings, to avoid conflicting decisions that may follow, and to secure the finality of judgments. Prescription law aims to avoid unjustifiably belated claims. Different goals could and often should lead to different decisions regarding the broadness of the 'cause of action' in each context. It may be broader for prescription than for *res judicata* or vice versa – broader for *res judicata* than for prescription. 50

On the other hand, some flexibility should supposedly remain for cases where harm X and harm Y are on a quite different scale: harm X is relatively and absolutely small and harm Y is relatively and absolutely of a large scope. In such cases, so goes the argument, P's reluctance to sue for the first and small harm is reasonable and P should not be 'punished' when a much greater harm occurs, nor should P be incentivised to sue for small harm just because of the fear that future greater harm would thereby prescribe. 51

Moreover, where P cannot sue for harm X alone because the harm has not yet been stabilised,[98] which happens only with the occurrence of harm Y, there is 52

96 That may be the case if harm Y is unforeseeable, or causally unrelated to harm X, or the court allowed P in her claim for X to file a later action for a later harm.
97 See *supra* 39.
98 See *infra* 86.

only one possible action and consequently only one cause of action, one which accrues with the harm of the occurrence of Y.

53 *Country reports*: The country reports reveal three approaches regarding the broadness/narrowness of the cause of action in case 1.

54 The broad approach, with minor exceptions applies, as recommended by the above analysis, in E&W,[99] the Netherlands,[100] the US[101] and South Africa:[102] harm X and harm Y are considered as belonging to the same cause of action, so that harm Y would prescribe with harm X subject to specific exceptions which justify a narrower approach.

55 The lesser broad approach, with more substantial exceptions to the rule that harm Y prescribes with harm X, applies in Austria,[103] Belgium,[104] Greece[105] and Germany:[106] harm Y is considered as belonging to a different cause of action than harm X where harm Y is unforeseeable and/or is causally unrelated to harm X ('independent harm').[107]

---

99 EW 27 (noting that P's plea that harm Y constitutes a new and independent cause of action for prescription purposes will certainly not succeed), and EW 26 observing that if A 'in one and the same fight break B's nose and knock out some of his teeth, then B has only one cause of action'.

100 NL 23 ('these two harms would prescribe on the same day as their cause of action – the negligent conduct – is the same').

101 US 29 ('if P missed filing the claim for injury X in timely fashion, a claim for injury Y would also be barred on prescription grounds'). A specific exception applies in cases where harm Y is a latent disease caused by the same exposure to toxic materials or to tobacco use that caused harm X but is casually unrelated to harm X – US 31, 33.

102 ZA 22 ('The cause of action arises with X (first harm) and P must then [...] before the prescription is concluded, institute an action in which she claims damages for X as well as for harm expected in future (once and for all rule) [...] It does not seem to matter whether one injury is much more severe than the other. It also does not seem to matter whether Y is causally connected to X or causally independent of X, since both arose from the same negligent act of D').

103 AT 17, 26.

104 DE 22.

105 GR 18.

106 DE 27 ('The German courts apply in principle the concept of unity of damage (Schadenseinheit): this means that the prescription period covers all consequences which the damaging event immediately and later on causes; the prescription period for the primary injury thus refers to, and includes, also all later consequences. However, the courts accept an important exception from this rule: if a reasonable person could not foresee the later (often secondary) consequence then a new prescription period starts for this further consequence').

107 See also NL 47 ('there is a decision from the Dutch Supreme Court from which it can be inferred that when one event causes separate damages, and a later occurring damage was not unexpected at the time the first damage that was caused by the damaging event occurred, then the later occurring harm should be considered as part of the harm that occurred first').

The narrow approach is applied in France,[108] Italy,[109] Norway,[110] Poland[111] and Spain:[112] harm X and harm Y belong to different causes of action so that harm Y would prescribe independently of harm X.[113] 56

### b) Case 2

*Physician D treats patient P negligently and performs three mistakes on the day of the treatment: A, B and C. Mistake A causes harm X after a year. Mistake B causes harm Y after two years. Mistakes A and C together cause harm Z after three years.*

*Analysis*: The event here is the medical treatment which, like the accident in Case 1, took place on a single day. Yet, unlike Case 1, the different harms X, Y and Z do not emerge from the same facts that constitute D's tortious conduct. Here each harm is related to different facts or different sets of facts. As mentioned,[114] under a broad conception of the cause of action in this case, all three harms would be considered as parts of the same and one cause of action, so that Y and Z would prescribe with X, favouring D. In contrast, a narrow conception would consider each harm, because of the different facts or set of facts from which it originates, as an independent cause of action that would prescribe regardless of the prescription of other harms, favouring P. Under an intermediate approach harm Z, for one example, would prescribe with harm X because both originate in the same mistake (A) and therefore allegedly belong to the same cause of action despite the fact that harm Z also originates in mistake C. Harm Y, however, would prescribe independently as it is the only harm that originates in fact B. 57

*Country reports*: While in Case 1 the different harms were caused by the same facts, in Case 2 there is also a difference between the facts that led to each harm. Does this difference in the facts that caused each harm justify a shift from a broad conception of cause of action to a narrower one in jurisdictions which would embrace a broad conception in Case 1?[115] 58

---

108 FR 18 ('P undoubtedly has two distinct rights to compensation, and thus two distinct causes of actions, for head injury X [...] and head injury Y [...], meaning that different personal injuries will lead to different actions, whose prescription period may not start at the same moment').

109 IT 30.

110 NO 22.

111 PL 49.

112 ES 20.

113 For the Swiss approach see CH 15.

114 See *supra* 44.

115 Including jurisdictions with minor and more substantial exceptions to the broad conception – see *supra* 57.

59 Such a shift would not take place in E&W,[116] Greece[117] or South Africa[118] which are reported as adhering to the broader conception of cause of action despite the difference in the facts that underlie each harm. The cause of action remains one because all harms, although caused by different mistakes, nevertheless have a common factual/legal source and are therefore considered as belonging to the same cause of action. Under German law, in Case 2 there would only be a shift to a narrower approach, when compared to Case 1, if the three mistakes were made independently of each other; then, there could run a separate period for each.[119] The Austrian reporters, though, suggests that there would be a shift to the narrower conception in Case 2 because of these factual differences.[120] The Dutch and the Belgian reporters as well suggest that the narrower approach would be applied in their jurisdictions.[121]

60 Obviously, countries which would apply the narrow approach in Case 1 (although all harms caused by the same facts) would do so in Case 2 (different facts causing different harms). This is indeed the case in France,[122] Italy[123] and Spain.[124] In Switzerland and Belgium the narrow approach would apply as well.[125]

c) Case 3

*Builder D lays down defective foundations for a building thereby creating the risk of future collapse. As a result, the value to the owner of the building (P)*

---

116 EW 26 ('As one is told that injury A *caused* harm X a year after the treatment, it is at that point that the cause of action accrues. Time does not start afresh in respect of harms Y (caused by mistake B) and Z (caused by mistakes A and C combined) since they relate to a single act, the negligent treatment').

117 GR 20 (harms Y and Z belong to the same cause of action as harm X). Yet, unforeseeable harms 'form a different cause of action and a new prescription period begins'; see *supra* 55 and fn 105.

118 ZA 22 (single event giving rise to single cause of action: Y and Z prescribe with X).

119 DE 29 (each harm constitutes a different cause of action 'unless the whole treatment could be regarded as one act; then, the prescription period would start with the first damage and include the further consequences. It is therefore decisive whether the three mistakes were three independent acts or elements of one single act').

120 AT 24–25.

121 BE 22 ('three limitation periods will run'); NL 22 ('damages X, Y and Z belong to different causes of action as each of the mistakes constitute an individual tort – they are caused by different sets of facts').

122 FR 19 ('Each harm gives rise to a distinct right to compensation, and thus to a distinct cause of action. The prescription for each one of these causes of action will start running at the moment when the harm that underpins it stabilises').

123 IT 31.

124 ES 21.

125 BE 22; CH 17. In Poland 'personal injury is typically an indivisible harm' (PL 50) which means there would be only one claim and one cause of action.

*decreases (harm A). Two years later the foundation subsides and requires fixing paid by P (harm B). Three year later cracks appear in the building fixed by P (harm C). Four years later the building collapses (harm D).*

*Analysis*: The question here, again, is whether each of the four harms constitutes an independent cause of action (narrowest conception), or whether all four harms belong to the same cause of action (broadest conception), or whether there are two or three causes of action (intermediate conception). 61

Application of the broadest conception in this case may be justified on the ground that the tortious activity of laying down defective foundation has a common factual/legal basis for all the four harms and ensuing claims, therefore all belonging to the same cause of action. If so, then harms B, C and D would prescribe with harm A. The opposite, narrowest, conception, can be justified on the ground that each harm has a different factual basis: laying the foundation (A), failure to fix the subsidence (B), failure to fix the cracks (C) and combination of all the above (D). An intermediate conception may determine, for example, that as A is pure economic loss it belongs to a different cause of action than the physical damage (B, C and D), or that that only the failure to fix subsidence and cracks (harms B and C) belong to a same cause of action (same kind of omission) and so on. 62

Whatever approach is actually taken it should reflect the court's best judgement as to which conception best promotes the goals of prescription law. 63

*Country reports*: Case 3 involves four harms (A, B, C, D) and three distinguished factual acts or omissions that caused them (laying the foundations and two failures to fix foundations and cracks). So, one may assume that the tendency would be to liken Case 3 to Case 2, namely, to embrace a narrower conception of cause of action. Yet, it appears that most reporters liken Case 3 to Case 1 and adopt a narrower approach than to Case 2. This can be explained by the dominance of the fact of laying defective foundations, that seems to overtake consequent omissions to fix, and is conceived as the actual source of all harms. 64

E&W,[126] the US[127] and South Africa,[128] according to reporters, would adhere to the broad approach, as in Cases 1 and 2, under which all harms prescribe with the prescription of the earlier compensable harm: harms B, C, D prescribe with harm A (or with harm B if there is no tort liability for harm A[129]). They are joined by the Dutch reporter,[130] who in Case 2 favoured the narrower 65

126 EW 40.
127 US 38.
128 ZA 24.
129 As in EW (40) and US (38).
130 NL 24.

approach, and by the reporters for Switzerland[131] who favour the narrower approach in Cases 1 and 2.

66 The Austrian,[132] German and the Polish[133] reports suggest, as in Case 1, that the intermediate approach of Case 1 would apply to Case 3 (all harms belong to the same cause of action, but if later harms are unforeseeable and/or are causally unrelated to the former harms, they are considered as independent causes of action).

d) Cases 1–3 – Further Observations

67 One may be puzzled by the diversity of the reporters' opinions as to broadness or narrowness of the cause of action in each of the three cases. Can this diversity be justified?

68 Starting with Case 1, where harms X and Y originate in exactly the same facts, it appears that the broadest approach should apply. If, as suggested by the narrow approach, any new harm, although caused by the same facts as former harm/harms, is considered a new cause of action, triggering a new prescription period, then claims for conduct that causes repeated harms could succeed numerous years after the conduct took place, thereby frustrating the goals of prescription law, leading to uncertainty. The same applies to the other, less narrow, intermediate, approach, that regards later harms, caused by the same facts as former harms, as constituting independent causes of actions if unforeseeable and/or not causally related to former harms. Why do the foreseeability of later harms and/or their causal relations to former harm matter? Analysis has shown that later harm should prescribe with former harm, if originating in the same facts, because of P's unjustified failure to sue for the former harm. Therefore, it seems irrelevant whether or not the later harm is foreseeable or causally related to former harm. All harms should be considered as belonging to the same cause of action if originating in the same facts. In principle, only in unique circumstances should different harms originating in the same facts deem as constituting different causes of harm, such as where the earlier harm is small enough or provisional to justify reluctance to sue for it, and the later harm is by far more severe.[134]

69 So how can the adoption of the narrow and the intermediate approaches be explained where there are no unique circumstances that justify them?[135]

131 CH 19.

132 AT 27.

133 DE 30 ('the prescription period for the first injury applies also to later consequences of the same occurrence'); PL 51.

134 Eg where the earlier harm is small and hardly justifies a claim while the later harm is substantially bigger – see *supra* 51.

135 Ibid.

It appears that in at least some jurisdictions the answer may well lie in the tendency to 'borrow' the meaning of the term 'cause of action' from the context of *res judicata* and apply it to the context of prescription. Courts may conclude that if a judicial decision regarding harm X does not bar a later claim for harm Y (harms belonging to different causes of action for *res judicata*), it follows that harm Y should not prescribe with harm X (different causes of action for prescription). But according to the above analysis such a 'borrowing' is mistaken as the meaning of 'cause of action' in each context should be determined according to the different roles and goals of each context.[136]

Moving to Cases 2 and 3, the adoption of the reported narrow and intermediate approaches is more plausible: in these cases different harms originate in different facts and not in the same facts as in Case 1. Yet, as all harms in each case emerge from the same major event (medical treatment in Case 2 and foundation laying in Case 3), it appears that regarding different harms as different causes of action despite their origin in the same event may also frustrate the goals of prescription law. 70

The major conclusion, to sum up, is that in deciding the broadness/narrowness of the cause of action for prescription purposes, the court should focus on the goals of prescription law and accordingly refrain from blind 'borrowing' of the meaning of cause of action from the rules of '*res judicata*' without checking their suitability to prescription law. 71

## C. THE STARTING POINT – D'S TORTIOUS CONDUCT OR OCCURRENCE OF HARM?

### 1) *The Question*

The question of how broad or narrow the concept of cause of action is, and should be, has another aspect – torts that generate liability only on the basis of D's tortious conduct, regardless of any harm caused.[137] Such torts are known in common law jurisdictions as torts *actionable per se* (such as trespass, and defamation).[138] The question of broadness or narrowness in this regard is illustrated by Case 4. 72

---

136 See *supra* 39, 50.

137 Torts that generate liability only when the tortious conduct results in harm, do not raise this question, as the cause of action does not accrue before the harm occurs. That is why the question of what the starting point is in case of *omissions* does not raise practical difficulties in most torts: cause of action accrues with the harm and not with the omission. See *F Fusco*, Commencement of the Prescription Period in Cases of Damage Caused due to Omissions, in: H Koziol and BC Steininger (eds), European Tort Law 2007 (2008), 79.

138 See, eg EW 20 and US 39.

*2) Cases 4 – Analysis and Country Reports*

*D enters P's premises without P's permission, thereby committing a tort of trespass, but without causing any damage. P can file a claim against D asking for the remedy of D's eviction but fails to do so. A year later D causes physical harm to P's premises. P files a claim to compensation for the loss.*

73 *Analysis*: The question in Case 4 is whether the starting point (day of accrual) of P's claim to compensation for the loss caused is the earlier date of trespass or the later date of damage.

74 Supporters of a broad conception of cause of action would argue that the claim for eviction and the claim for compensation belong to same cause of action, even if originating from different branches of law (property law and tort law). Having common factual and legal basis (or at least common factual basis), the starting point (accrual) should be the trespass. The claim for compensation should prescribe with the claim for eviction.

75 Supporters of the narrow conception would argue that the claim for eviction and the claim for compensation constitute each an independent cause of action, and therefore have two different starting points. The reason, arguably, is that these remedies, eviction and compensation, are different *types* of remedies, and that this difference in the nature of the remedies justifies viewing them as different causes of action. The claim for compensation should *not* prescribe with the claim for eviction because the starting point for the latter is the damage while the starting point for the former is the tortious activity.

76 Which approach should be preferred? Which one better promotes the goals of prescription law? Supposedly, as a rule, and subject to exceptions justified by the goals of prescription law, the narrow approach (which benefits P) should prevail. Usually the difference between the remedy of *enforcing P's right* and the remedy of *compensating P for harm caused by the infringement of the right* is indeed a substantial one that justifies treating claims for these different types of remedies as different causes of action. A decision not to sue for one type of remedy should not be 'punished' by predating the starting point (accrual) of a claim for a different type of remedy.

77 Arguably, and most importantly, the same rule should apply to contractual claims. Where the breach of a contract by D entitles P to sue for specific performance (enforcement) before any harm is caused, and later on harm actually occurs and P becomes entitled to compensation, the two kinds of remedy should be considered distinct causes of action: the later claim for compensation should prescribe independently and not with the earlier claim to specific performance.

78 *Country reports*: All reporters conclude that the claim for eviction on the one hand and the claim to compensation on the other hand belong to different causes of action, so that the claim for compensation would prescribe after and independently from the claim for eviction. This outcome fits the above analysis. Yet, the reported arguments leading to this conclusion vary and not all of them conform with the above analysis.

79 One argument is that the claim for eviction originates in property law while the claim for compensation originated in tort law.[139] But that the two claims, being identical in all respects, originate in different fields of law, does not necessarily mean they belong to different causes of action for prescription.

80 Another unconvincing argument is that although the rule is that prescription starts to run from the day of the tortious conduct and not the day of harm, trespass is a kind of exception because it is a continuous, recurrent tort, so that every harm is a new tort.[140] The weakness of this argument is that a new tort does not necessarily mean a new cause of action for prescription. The new tort may belong to the same cause of action as a former tort if both originate in a common factual/legal source.

81 The more convincing argument, which is in line with the above analysis, is that the narrow approach is justified here because eviction and compensation are *different kinds of remedy* and P should have the discretion, with no 'sanctions' of prescription law, to choose not to sue for one kind of remedy but sue for another one.[141] P's preference not to sue D for trespass unless this trespass caused harm to P is reasonable, avoids unnecessary litigation and should be respected.

82 The latter argument, it is worth reiterating, applies to contract law as well: a claim to compensation for harm caused by a breach should not prescribe with the claim to enforce the breached contract, given the differences between these two kinds of remedy.[142] If P is not interested in enforcing the contract but only in compensation for its breach once she suffers loss, which is reasonable,

---

139 AT 28; CH 22; CZ 36; ES 23; FR 25; IT 34; PO 54; ZA 25.

140 NL 25; NO 27–31; US 39.

141 DE 36 ('German courts would separate the two events and apply the prescription period separately for each: for the mere trespass when it occurs and for the damages claim when the damage occurred. Insofar, German law applies a narrow standard of cause of action which regards the second event and respective legal action (damages claim) as different from the first one (claim for omission). Not only the facts differ for both – damage vs. no damage – also the legal remedies are not identical); GR 26 ('The difference between the remedy of *enforcing P's right* and the remedy of *compensating P for harm caused by the infringement of the right* is a substantial that justifies treating claims for these different types of remedies as different causes of action'). See also the E&W report noting that 'where damage is the gist of the action, the cause of action accrues upon the damage occurring' – EW 20.

142 See *supra* 77. But when different harms are caused by exactly the same breach, later harms should prescribe with the initial harm: being the same *kind* of remedy they all originate in the same cause of action.

the prescription period for compensation should not run before the loss occurs. Each kind of remedy belongs to a different cause of action.

## D. WHAT IS/SHOULD BE CONSIDERED 'HARM' AND 'OCCURRENCE OF HARM' FOR PRESCRIPTION PURPOSES?

83 When P's harm, inflicted by D's tortious conduct, is a part of P's cause of action, which is usually the case, two questions have to be answered regarding the prescription of this cause of action. The first question is 'what is and should be considered a harm'? The second question is 'when does the harm occur'?

### *1) What should be Considered 'Harm' for Prescription Purposes?*

#### a) The Question

84 Quite often the infliction of harm on P by D's conduct is not an isolated event that causes a fixed harm but rather an ongoing process: initial first harm that later develops, gradually or otherwise, to a greater harm. For example, bodily injury caused by the damaging conduct may deteriorate over the time, and so is damage to property. Pure economic loss may also develop as where the fall in the value of P's shares, caused by D's negligent advice to buy these shares, deepens over time.

85 This process of 'harm development' requires a policy decision by prescription law: where the starting point (date of accrual) is the infliction of harm, should the starting point be the earliest 'signs' of harm caused (initial harm), or rather a more developed harm that would incentivise a reasonable person to sue for compensation (substantial harm), or alternatively, the harm at the end of its development process (stabilisation).[143] The difference between the three answers – initial (signs of) harm, substantial harm and stabilised harm – is that in the same case the starting point under each would be different: earliest if initial harm is sufficient for the starting point and latest if stabilised harm is required. This is exemplified by Case 5.

#### b) Case 5 – Analysis and Country Reports

*In an accidental event, D negligently caused an explosion that damaged P's ears. During the first two years P has to raise the volume to enjoy music. During the following three years P needs a hearing device. After a further five years P becomes deaf.*

---

143 For the stabilisation approach, titled 'unitary-damage' concept, see *Zimmermann and Kleinschmidt*, *supra* fn 2, 43–47.

*Analysis*: Under the *initial harm* approach – signs of harm – the starting point (date of accrual) would be the accident. Under the *substantive harm* approach the starting point would be the need to buy a hearing device. Under the *stabilisation* approach the starting point would be the deafness. 86

Given the goals of prescription it appears that the end approaches – initial (signs of) harm and stabilised harm – are inadequate. The initial (signs of) harm approach would incentivise Ps to sue for harms that in their view do not justify litigation given the scope of harm, just because of concerns that if the harm develops they may lose their claim due to an early starting point. The stabilised harm approach, on the other hand, exposes Ds to the risk of belated claims that should have been filed long ago and are allowed only because the harm has developed slowly and keeps developing. Such an indeterminate and even endless exposure (where the harm never stabilises) is unjustified in terms of the goals of prescription. It is rightly observed that the 'stabilisation' approach may lead to uncertainty and to 'great oppression' of Ds.[144] Indeed, the reporter for France acknowledges that 'in cases of personal injury or medical liability, the fact that the prescription starts only with the stabilisation of the harm means that, for many serious injuries or diseases, claims are in fact imprescriptible'.[145] 87

That leaves the intermediate approach of 'substantial harm' which makes more sense than the alternatives. More accurately, harm should be characterised as sufficiently developed to trigger the starting point (accrual) where its scope is such that a reasonable person would consider filing a claim for compensation (given the existence of the other essentials of this claim). 88

The stabilisation approach, however, may be justified and should be applied where under law P cannot in fact file a claim for the whole harm until the harm stabilises. Yet such a restriction on the ability to sue for harms is questionable. If substantial harm already occurred, why should P wait until its stabilisation and be left with no redress in the meantime? 89

*Country reports*: Three jurisdictions, according to reporters, embrace the *stabilisation* approach, at least with regard to personal injuries: France,[146] Poland[147] and Spain.[148] In these countries prescription in Case 5 would start to run only with deafness. No explanation for that approach is provided. 90

144 EW 21.

145 FR 49.

146 FR 27 ('the prescription of P's right of action starts to run as of the stabilisation of his harm. In the present case, stabilisation occurs at the soonest when P becomes deaf').

147 PL 58.

148 ES 24 ('prescription will not start running until the whole extent of damage – deafness, in the hypothetical – can be determined'). See also ES 17 ('case law states that prescription starts provided that the whole damage has taken place according to the stabilisation approach (so-called *consolidación de las secuelas*)').

91 All the other jurisdictions seem to embrace the intermediate approach, according to which prescription starts to run where the harm is substantial in the sense that it would incentivise a reasonable P to sue for compensation, although views may differ as to when a given harm becomes substantial as opposed to just 'signs of harm'.[149] In Case 5 the harm of decreasing hearing is considered substantial by most reporters.

*2) When does a Given Harm Occur?*

a) The Question

92 Where the starting point of P's cause of action is the *occurrence* of harm, whether the harm is initial, developed or stabilised, what exactly is considered as occurrence?[150] Obviously, *actual materialisation* of the risk to P satisfies the requirement of occurrence, but can the *mere creation of a yet unrealised risk* by D be considered as harm occurrence? If so, the starting point (accrual of cause of action) would be set earlier than the materialisation of the risk, favouring Ds.

93 There are several options in this regard:

- *Probability: the creation of risk* of harm per se would be considered as harm occurrence when the probability of its future materialisation into harm becomes sufficiently significant (eg it is more probable than not that the risk will materialise). Obviously a remote and speculative probability that a risk of harm may materialise cannot be considered as occurrence of this harm.
- *Certainty*: only risk of *certain* future harm (100% probability) will be deemed as occurrence of that harm for accrual purposes.

[149] AT 29 (as soon as the reduced hearing becomes a medically recognised illness/injury and deafness in the future is foreseeable); CH 25 (not just signs of harm); CZ 37; DE 35 (the starting point is 'major hearing problems […] Germany thus follows an approach which expects legal steps of the victim as soon as a reasonable person would initiate such steps'); EW 46 (harm has 'to be serious enough for him to justify instituting proceedings'. See also EW 36; IT 37 ('from the moment the damage occurred, becoming objectively perceptible and recognisable, and not from the time of a subsequent aggravation'); NO 35 ('The general attitude is that the question is whether there is a such a degree of development that one has sufficient information for stating that there is a claim'. This means that the Norwegian solution 'fits very well with the intermediate developed harm approach'; at 37); NL 45 ('For the running of the subjective prescription period, the materialisation of damage is – generally – considered as "harm"'); US 43 (loss must be one that is legally cognisable/visibly detectible); ZA 27.

[150] The harm referred to is the direct harm to the protected interest (eg bodily injury) as opposed to its consequential manifestation (eg loss of earning).

- *Materialisation*: only actual materialisation of the risk of harm can be considered occurrence of this harm.

It should be noted that a *future risk* of one kind of harm may be considered an *already materialised* risk of harm of another kind. For example, defective foundations of a building generate a future *risk* of physical harm but also cause *materialised* pure economic loss if the value of the building diminishes.[151] 94

So what should the preferred option be given the goals of prescription? Arguably, risk of future harm, even if it can be characterised as certain (100% probability), should *not* be considered as occurrence of that harm for prescription purposes where such probability is insufficient to support and establish a successful claim in court. As reiterated, the starting point (date of accrual) should not precede the date in which all the necessary substantive essentials of P's claim exist.[152] Where a claim for risk of future harm cannot succeed before that harm actually materialises, there is no justification to set a starting point for prescription earlier than actual materialisation. Moreover, even where claims for unmaterialised risk of harm can succeed in court, it is doubtful whether the starting point should precede actual materialisation. That may incentivise Ps to file claims for risk of harm, although the harm is not yet certain or has not yet materialised, thereby leading to premature and costly litigation that could be avoided by setting the materialisation of risk as the starting point. The autonomy of Ps to wait, before suing, until the future risk of harm materialises into actual harm, should be respected. 95

b) Case 6 – Analysis and Country Reports

*Builder D lays down defective foundations for a bridge, thereby creating the risk of future collapse if heavy rain falls. Two years later heavy rain indeed falls and the collapse becomes only a matter of time, as indeed happens four years after the laying of foundations.*

*Analysis*: Assuming that the occurrence of harm is the starting point (accrual) of P's cause of action against D, the question is when did the harm occur for prescription purposes? Under the *probability* option the harm occurred with the laying of foundations that created the *risk* of collapse. Under the *certainty* option the harm occurred with the rains that render the future collapse *unavoidable*. Under the *materialisation* option only the *actual collapse* should be considered occurrence of harm. Evidently, the *probability* option benefits D, 96

151 See Case 3, *supra* 61–63.
152 See *supra* 37.

while the materialisation option benefits P (difference of four years between the starting points).

97 The above analysis suggests that where P's claim cannot succeed before the actual collapse, the starting point should not precede this date.[153] But even if P's claim can succeed on the basis of *probability* or future *certainty* of the collapse, the materialisation option should in principle be preferred, to avoid unnecessary litigation and infringement of P's autonomy to avoid litigation before any risk of harm actually materialises.

98 *Country reports*: In conformity with the above analysis reporters for most jurisdictions suggest that as a general rule, that applies to Case 6, the starting point for the prescription period is the day in which the risk actually materialises, and not the earlier date where there is only a sufficient probability or certainty that the risk will materialise.[154]

99 In E&W though, there is an exception, limited to non-personal injury, which applies to defects in products: where it is *certain* that the defect would lead to imminent future physical damage (where the product is '*doomed from the start*'), or at least there is an extremely high risk of such damage, prescription would start to run from the day the future materialisation of the risk becomes certain or highly probable, and not from the date of actual materialisation.[155] Yet, it appears that this exception would not apply to Case 6 'given the lack of immediacy between defect and damage'.[156]

100 Only reporters for two jurisdictions, Austria and Norway, suggest that the applicable trigger for the running of the prescription period in general and in Case 6 is not the materialisation of the risk into actual harm but rather *certainty* or sufficient *probability* that the risk will materialise in the future.[157] The US reporter also suggests that in Case 6 the defective construction constitutes the harm, rather than the actual damage that occurs due to the defect, but notes that in cases of personal injury the materialisation of the risk would be the starting point and not the risk per se.[158]

---

153 See *Zimmermann and Kleinschmidt*, *supra* fn 2, 38 ('occurrence of damage […] determine the earliest possible moment when prescription commences to run').

154 CH 27; BE 19–21; CZ 37; DE 39; ES 25; EW 36 ('the presence of a risk of damage, even where this is established and could give rise to significant injury, does not constitute the requisite damage so that no cause of action can be made out'. See also ibid 41); GR 29 (but time will not run as long as the omission to repair lasts); IT 38; NL 46 ('for prescription purposes the damage occurs from the moment it materialises. In 'Case 6' this is the moment the defective foundation subsided'. *Certainty* that harm will occur is insufficient); PL 59; ZA 28. Special rules apply in France – FR 38. In the EU as well, the starting point is 'the materialisation of the effects of unlawful action' – EU 14–19.

155 EW 37–40.

156 Ibid 40.

157 AT 30; NO 38 (when the heavy rain falls).

158 US 45.

Interestingly, claims against the EU for *future* damage can be filed where 'the damage is imminent (coming or likely to happen very soon) and there is a high degree of certainty that it will occur',[159] but the 'running of the period of limitations for claims in damages should still be calculated from the moment in which the damage materialised'.[160] This divergence between harm *probability* (sufficient for filing a claim) and *materialisation* (required to start the period counting) aims to incentivise early challenging of illegal actions and to encourage preventive legal measures. 101

## E. THE STARTING POINT (ACCRUAL) IN CONTINUOUS TORTS

### 1) *The Question*

Quite often P claims that D's tortious conduct and its ensuing harms are not a one-day event but rather continue over a period of time. Continued exposure of employee P to harming hazardous materials at the workplace by employer D is an example and so are trespass, nuisance and false imprisonment,[161] as well as defamation, invasion of privacy, and environmental torts.[162] In such cases there is a tendency to refer to this sequence of conducts and ensuing harms as a *continuous* tort. If so, what is, and what *should* be, the starting point of P's claim in continuous torts? There are four options in this regard.[163] 102

The first option is to disregard, for prescription purposes, the continuous nature of D's conduct and its ensuing harms and to treat each daily harm ensuing from tortious conduct as an independent cause of action,[164] namely, consider it a '*recurrent*' cause of action that is reborn on each day the tortious conduct causes harm. Under this model, (the *recurrence* model), which splits a continuous tort into its constituting parts, actually disregarding the continuation aspect, there is multiplicity of starting points (dates of accrual) according to the number of causes of action.[165] 103

The second option is to embrace the concept of continuous tort also in prescription law by regarding the sequence of D's periodical tortious activities 104

159 EU 23.

160 Ibid 24.

161 EW 28.

162 US 46. 'It includes not only a continuous tortious act, but also a series of distinct yet related tortious acts that are together treated as one, as might occur with intentional infliction of emotional distress in the employment context' – ibid.

163 For difficulties in determining the starting point for continuous torts see *Zimmermann and Kleinschmidt, supra* fn 2, 37.

164 Provided that it not part of another, broader, cause of action – see Section VI.B.

165 In the US recurrence is referred to as the 'rule of separate accrual' – US 48.

and ensuing harms as one continuous tort – *as a single cause of action*. Under this concept there is only one starting point for the whole sequence, and that is the date on which the last harm in the sequence occurred (or the last tortious conduct took place). This model actually 'condenses' the sequence of the periodical tortious events into one day *at the end* of the relevant period (the *forward condensing* model), favouring Ps over Ds (late starting point: last harm or last tortious conduct).

105 The third option is like the second one but with a major difference: the sequence of tortious events (harms or tortious conduct) is 'condensed' not into the date of the *last* harm (or last tortious conduct), but rather into the *first* date of harm (or conduct). Under this model (the *backward condensing* model) the starting point for the whole sequence is the *first* harm (or the first tortious conduct). Obviously, this model favours Ds over Ps (early starting point).

106 The fourth model is a kind of 'compromise' between the former two: the continuous tort (the single cause of action) is condensed into an *interim date* between the first and the last harm (or tortious conduct), into a kind of 'average' date. Under this model (the *interim condensing* model) the starting point lies 'in the middle' between the starting points of the other two condensing models, and as such strikes a balance between the interests of Ps (late start) and Ds (early start).

### *2) Analysis*

107 Prior to the discussion of the four options regarding the starting point (date of accrual) in continuous torts, the concept of *continuous tort* itself has to be clarified. The concept, as mentioned, applies where it is claimed that D's tortious conduct and its ensuing harms are not a daily event but rather continue over a period of time. However, for a sequence of events (conducts and harms) to be considered *continuous*, there should be at least some degree of *resemblance* between the successive tortious conducts and also resemblance between the ensuing harms, and they should be sufficiently *frequent*. The required degree of resemblance and frequency in the repeated conducts and repeated harms is for the court to determine, and in their absence the sequence of events does not constitute continuous tort but rather multiplicity of sequential different torts. Accordingly, the Greek report describes continuous tort as 'cohesive units of action' that are 'produced in proximity'.[166] The Swiss report refers to the 'same' tortious activity that 'is constantly repeated over a period of time'.[167] The E&W report alludes to 'repetitions of acts or omissions of the

---

166 GR 30.
167 CH 29.

same kind',[168] stressing that there must be 'a quality of continuance in both the breach and the obligation'.[169]

Assuming that the sequence of events (tortious conducts and sequence of ensuing harms) is indeed considered a continuous tort committed by D against P, given the degree of resemblance and frequency, the first question is when and why the law should embrace the concept of recurrence (multiplicity of causes of action) or rather prefer the concept of condensing (one single cause of action). Where the latter is preferred, the second question is which kind of condensing should be embraced (*forward*, *backward* or *interim condensing*). 108

The suggested analytical answer is that as a rule the *recurrence model* should prevail. That a sequence of events (tortious conducts and ensuing harms) is characterised as continuous should not in principle interfere with the ordinary operation of prescription law under which each cause of action prescribes at its time regardless of other causes of action. Combining different causes of action into one single-cause, thereby favouring either Ps (*forward condensing* option) or Ds (*backward* condensing option), requires special justifications. Such a justification, for example, could be continuous *intentional* harm infliction by D. Arguably, D should be 'punished' by prescription law by delaying the starting point (accrual) to the end of this intentional harm infliction – applying the *forward condensing* model. Another justifiable exception could be to apply the *backward condensing* model in torts of trespass and conversion where D holds/possesses P's property and P's failure to challenge D's adverse possession should be counted against P from the *first* day of the adverse possession. Still, it is debatable whether such kind of justifications sufficiently support the single-cause concept even in exceptional cases. The counter argument is that prescription law should not be employed to promote goals other than its own goals, such as 'punishing' D or P for improper conduct, by deviating from the principle that every independent cause of action has its own starting point (date of accrual). Instead, other, and more suitable tools of prescription law can be used, such as a rule of prolongation that suspends the running of the period prolongation as long as the intentional infliction of harm by D continues. 109

### 3) *Country Reports – An Overview*

In line with the above analysis reporters for six countries state that their jurisdictions embrace the recurrence option for continuous torts rather than the concept that in a continuous tort all the causes of actions should be combined 110

[168] EW 28.
[169] Ibid.

into a single cause with one starting point (date of accrual). These countries are Austria,[170] E&W,[171] France,[172] Italy,[173] Norway[174] and South Africa.[175] Reporters from three other countries provide that in their jurisdictions recurrence is the rule and that the concept of one single cause of action is applied, as an exception, only to limited kinds of cases: Germany,[176] Greece[177] and the Netherlands.[178] The question remains open in Belgium.[179]

111 A mix of recurrence on the one hand and *forward condensing* on the other hand is reported for two countries: Poland[180] and the US.[181]

112 Only two reporters suggest that as a rule continuous torts are perceived as a single cause of action with forward condensing: Switzerland[182] and the Czech Republic.[183]

113 All in all, it appears that a clear majority of the reported countries embrace the view that in cases of continuous torts the preferred option, possibly subject to exceptions, is that of recurrence, as proposed by the analysis.

---

170 AT 31 ('prescription starts to run for each newly caused harm individually').

171 EW 28 ('a fresh cause of action accrues every day in the case of a single act or omission that continuously invades the claimant's interest(s)').

172 FR 29 (the concept of continuous tort is actually not used).

173 IT 41.

174 NO 39 ('There is no concept or notion of continuous torts within the Norwegian law').

175 ZA 29 ('The harm pertaining to each cause of action is independently subject to extinctive prescription').

176 DE 40 ('the German Federal Court in civil matters now tends to deny the possibility to distinguish repeated torts for which the prescription starts anew with each act and a continued tort for which prescription starts only at the end of the continued act. It is thus likely that the court practice accepts the institute of "continuous tort" if at all only in very rare situations').

177 The rule is recurrence – GR 30. Only in cases of continuous omission is there forward condensing so that 'the prescription of the claim is impeded whilst the omission continues to exist and starts from the moment the tortfeasor undertakes the omitted act' – ibid 31. But even this exception was criticised for being 'artificial and uncertain' – ibid 34.

178 NL 26 ('In Dutch law, a notion of continuous tort is only recognised for damage that is the result of the effects of hazardous materials, or of air, water or soil pollution').

179 BE 23 ('legislator did not answer to this question and it seems that there is no case-law on this topic').

180 PL 60–61 (forward condensing but the recurrence approach is also applied sometimes).

181 US 47–48 (recurrence 'has been applied to statutory antitrust claims as well as common law nuisance and trespass claims and occupational injury claims' – ibid 48). The reporter for the US notes that 'significant body of commentary critical of the continuous tort doctrine has developed'– ibid 46.

182 CH 28 ('distinct (separate) tortious acts trigger separate and independent prescription periods for every claim that arises from each act').

183 CZ 38 (starting point of the prescription period is 'the end of the tortious activity').

### 4) Cases 7–9 – Analysis and Country Reports

#### a) Case 7

*Every week, during a month, D1 publishes a defamatory article on P1, each time in another newspaper and on a different topic. During the same period D2 publishes a defamatory article on P2, every second day, on the same topic and in the same newspaper.*

*Analysis*: This case deals with the preliminary question regarding the degree of resemblance and frequency that renders a sequence of events (tortious conducts and ensuing harms) a continuous tort. In D2's defaming publications the degree of resemblance and frequency is much higher than in D1's defaming publications. Does it follow that D2 committed a continuous tort while D1 committed four different torts? Or maybe D1's publications meet the requirements of resemblance and frequency that render the whole sequence a continuous tort as well? Or perhaps the other way around, namely, that D2's publications did not meet these requirements and D2 committed 15 different torts as well? It appears that any attempt to provide general and clear guidelines as to the degree of resemblance and frequency that transform a series of consecutive torts into a single continuous tort may fail to be convincing, as it depends on the circumstances of each case. 114

*Country reports*: Most reporters do not consider the defamation by D1 and by D2 in Case 7 to be a continuous tort.[184] The same applies to the US, but 'while the newspaper examples would likely not be considered continuous torts, defamation actions relating to social media pages have been considered continuous torts in at least one jurisdiction'.[185] The Polish and Swiss reporters suggest that while defamation by D2 is not continuous tort, defamation by D1 is or may be considered as such.[186] Only in South Africa would defamation by both D1 and D2 possibly be conceived as continuous.[187] 115

---

184 AT 32; CZ 39; DE 41; ES 26; EW 35; FR 30–31 (referring to the criminal offence of defamation); GR 25; IT 44; NL 27; NO 42.

185 US 53.

186 PL 62 ('the first situation would likely be considered a series of separate torts, unless the plaintiff was able to establish the continued, same intent to do harm. The second scenario could more easily be treated as a continuous tort due to the frequency and similarity of wrongful conduct. The degree of *resemblance* between the successive defamatory acts is a matter for the court to determine'); CH 31.

187 ZA 32 ('The repetition of a defaming article on P each time in another newspaper can be regarded as a continuous tort because it involves a series of repeated acts causing a similar kind of harm [...] giving rise to a fresh cause of action with each publication. It probably would not matter if D publishes the same defamation every week in the same newspaper owned by him or defames P differently in different newspapers each time in the same jurisdiction').

### b) Case 8

*D, a landowner, negligently exposes P, a neighbour, to unreasonable noise for three years. P's hearing is thereby weakened on a daily basis, gradually restricting P's ability to communicate and enjoy music.*

116 *Analysis*: In this case it is evident that the requirements of resemblance and frequency are met so that the exposure and the ensuing harms can be classified as a continuous tort case. If so, which of the four models should be embraced? Arguably, as a rule, the recurrence model should be embraced rather than any of the three single-cause models.[188] But is it an exceptional case that justifies the application of the forward condensing single-cause model in order to 'punish' D and provide stronger protection to the neighbour P? Such 'punishment' may be justified, if at all, where D is not just a neighbour but an employer of P given the employer/employee special relations. Yet, it would be better, following the above analysis, to achieve such 'punishment' by a rule of prolongation that suspends the running of the period as long as employment relations continue.[189]

117 *Country reports*: According to the reports, countries would differ in their treatment of the continuous loss of hearing in Case 8. Seven reports suggest that the recurrence option would apply: Austria, Czech Republic, E&W, Germany, the Netherlands, Norway and South Africa.[190] US courts may apply either the forward condensing or recurrence model.[191] Four countries would reportedly embrace the forward condensing option: Greece,[192] Poland,[193] Spain[194] and Switzerland.[195] Only the reporters for Italy suggest that backward condensing would apply.[196]

### c) Case 9

*A waste management company digs bins of toxic content into the soil. Toxic substance leaks into the soil and ground water, causing apparent damage to crops*

188 See *supra* 109.

189 See, eg CH 44.

190 AT 33 (requiring, however, that the reduction of P's hearing capacity is foreseeable to her); CZ 39; DE 42; EW 30; NL 27; NO 46 ('the recurrence model is the closest to the Norwegian solution'); ZA 33.

191 US 54–55.

192 GR 37 (D's tort is not 'completed' before the exposure ends).

193 PL 63 (at least where P is D's employee).

194 ES 27 (at least where P is D's employee).

195 CH 33 ('The prescription period starts at the end of the damaging act').

196 IT 45 ('aggravation of the disease will then only affect the quantification of the damage'). According to the French report, cause of action accrues only with the stabilisation of harm – FR 32.

*and expenditure on cleaning on a daily basis. After two years the bins are removed from the soil.*

*Analysis*: The difference between this case and Case 8 is that the damage here is not bodily injury but property damage and pure economic loss. Does this difference affect the tendency to apply the single-cause model? 118

*Country reports*: According to most reporters the same approach which would apply in their countries in Case 8 (bodily injury) would also apply in Case 9 (property damage).[197] There are, however, some exceptions. France would apply the recurrence approach in Case 9, as opposed to one cause of action approach in Case 8, because property damage can be sued for before it stabilises.[198] In the Netherlands, while the rule is recurrence (Case 8), in cases of pollution (Case 9) the forward condensing approach would apply.[199] 119

### 5) *Final Observation*

All in all the majority of country reports substantiate the claims made in the analytical analysis.[200] Firstly, as a rule it is the recurrence approach which should apply to continuous torts.[201] Secondly, the application of the concept of one cause of action requires justification where it benefits Ps (forward condensing) or Ds (backward condensing). 120

## F. IS THE LATE DISCOVERY RULE A RULE OF THE STARTING POINT (ACCRUAL) OR A RULE OF PROLONGATION?

### 1) *The Question*

Almost all jurisdictions now apply, at least to some extent, a rule of *late discovery*, which provides that the prescription period should not start to run until P has objective or subjective knowledge of the facts that constitute P's cause of action. The rule is discussed in detail below.[202] 121

197 See, eg Spain who applies forward condensing in both cases – ES 28 ('the mere fact that damage consists in property damage instead of personal injury would not be relevant *per se* as regards prescription') and Greece 38 ('that there is not bodily injury but property damage and pure economic loss does not affect the answer).'

198 FR 34.

199 NL 26 ('the prescription period starts to run the moment after the bins have been removed from the soil because then the continuous fact has ceased to exist').

200 See *supra* 110.

201 Which meet the requirements of resemblance and frequency of the different causes of action – see *supra* 107.

202 See Section VIII.B.

122 But to which element of liability does this important rule belong? Is the *late discovery* a rule of the *starting point* (accrual of cause of action) which belongs to the first element of prescription discussed in this Section, or is it a rule of *prolongation* which is part of the third element of prescription discussed below in Section VIII? In other words, in the absence of the required discovery, is the running of the prescription period denied because the cause of action has not yet accrued (starting point not yet reached), or, alternatively, because the running of the prescription period is delayed for lack of discovery although the cause of action has accrued (the starting point reached)?

*2) Analysis*

123 Given the nature and the effect of the late discovery rule it appears to the authors, for the following reasons, that the late discovery rule *should* be regarded as a rule of prolongation which belongs to the third element and not a rule of the starting point (accrual) of the first element. The required discovery *should* not be conceived of as a constituent of the cause of action/starting point, but as a rule that delays the running of the prescription period after the accrual of cause of action/the emergence of the starting point.[203]

124 To start with, P's knowledge is not part of the substantive requirements, the essentials, that constitute P's cause of action against D. Theoretically, when these requirements are met (D's conduct, ensuing harm and applicable tort),[204] P can file a claim and succeed. As this *potential* ability to succeed, a *potential* that triggers *the starting point*,[205] does not depend on P's knowledge, it follows that the late discovery rule is not a rule of the starting point (accrual of cause of action) but a rule of prolongation.

125 Secondly, the late discovery rule can in principle be applied *after* the prescription period has begun to run, namely after the emergence of the starting point. This may happen when the right to the claim is transmitted by law from the original claimant, who has the required knowledge, to P who lacks this knowledge.[206] In such cases the discovery rule, if it applies to P, clearly operates as a rule of *suspension*, and not as rule of *postponement*.[207] Obviously, such suspension of an already running period can take place only *after* the starting point (accrual) and therefore the late discovery rule cannot be considered as a rule of starting point.

203 See the definition of the starting point (*supra* 30, 36) as 'the date on which P's cause of action against D [...] matures so that the prescription period starts to run on this claim (unless its running is postponed by a rule of prolongation)'.

204 See *supra* 40.

205 See *supra* 36.

206 See *infra* 295.

207 For the difference see *infra* 156.

Thirdly, the late discovery rule operates in the same ways (postponement and suspension) and for the same reasons (P's delay is justified) as other rules of prolongation,[208] and there is no apparent reason or justification to sever it from its 'natural' environment (third element) relocating it within the first element. 126

Fourthly, and relatedly, there is the issue of burden of proof.[209] In general, the burden of proof lies on D, who pleads the defence, to establish that *prima facie* the prescription period has already elapsed on P's cause of action. Then, the burden of proof is shifted to P to establish, *inter alia*, that for some reason the prescription period in her case was prolonged and therefore did not expire. It is so because the reasons that justify prolongation lie in P's sphere. This is obviously so with regard to P's knowledge. Whether P knew, ought to have known or had no knowledge of the essentials of her claim is a personal matter known much better to her than to D who usually does not possess the relevant information and who often lacks any ability to establish P's state of knowledge.[210] Hence, in this evidential respect as well the late discovery rule is a rule of prolongation (burden of proof lies upon P) than a rule of the starting point (burden of proof lies upon D). But even if the initial burden lies upon D (to establish awareness), this burden can easily be shifted to P (to establish unawareness) as this knowledge lies in her sphere, so that the same analysis applies.[211] 127

Fifthly, and most importantly, it is desirable that the concept of the starting point (accrual), the trigger that activates the running of the prescription period in all causes of action,[212] would have clear and general meaning across all causes of action The characterisation of the starting point as the point in time in which all the substantive requirements (essentials) are met so that a claim can potentially succeed,[213] meets this requirement. Not so where the late discovery rule is perceived as a rule of starting point, as this rule has not been applied to all causes of action or applies only to some,[214] and is applied 128

---

208 See *infra* Section VIII.C.

209 See *supra* Section XII.E.

210 See *Zimmermann and Kleinschmidt*, *supra* fn 2, 62 ('if the onus of proof were on the debtor [...] he would face an unreasonable difficult task').

211 See, eg the German report who notes that although the burden to establish P's awareness as required by the discovery rule lies upon D, it is actually P who has to 'state and, if necessary, prove facts that occurred in his or her own sphere' – DE 46. In Belgium the burden lies on D but P 'has to cooperate in the provision of evidence' – BE 32.

212 Subject to rules of prolongation.

213 See *supra* 36.

214 See, eg the reporters for Switzerland who note that '[u]nawareness basically does not influence the prescription, neither its onset nor its duration' although some 'prescription periods, however, only start once the plaintiff becomes aware of the damage he/she suffered and of the person who is liable for this damage' – CH 36.

differently by different jurisdictions to different causes of action, being sometimes subjective, sometimes objective, and requiring different degrees of knowledge.[215]

129 Finally, it appears that some of those who argue that the late discovery rule is a rule of the starting point do so because the prescription period does not start to run before P has the required knowledge. But the same can be said about other rules that are conceived of as rules of prolongation. For example, that the prescription period does not start to run where P is a minor or mentally incapacitated does not render infancy and mental incapacity rules of the starting point. They are rightly conceived of as rules of prolongation. The same should apply to the late discovery rule.

### 3) *Country Reports*

130 As the analytical distinction in this report between rules of the starting point (first element) and rules of prolongation (third element) is not always developed, in the applicable statutes/Codes and in case law, the answer to the question whether the late discovery rule is a rule of the starting point or a rule of prolongation is not always clear and is open to interpretation.[216]

131 Under express statutory law in Austria, however, the late discovery rule is not a rule of prolongation but rather of the starting point.[217] For Germany as well it is suggested, based on the interpretation of the applicable provision, that the late discovery rule is a rule of the starting point.[218] Yet the reporter notes, relying on the literature, that '[o]n the other hand, it has to be admitted that the knowledge rule could easily be regarded as a prolongation rule that extends merely the prescription period which "actually" starts when the cause of action accrues'.[219] Along the same lines, the reporter for South Africa suggests that although the rule of late discovery 'is thus a rule of the starting point but much can be said in favour of considering it as a rule of prolongation'.[220]

132 The Spanish report also classifies the discovery rule as a rule of the starting point (accrual),[221] but on the other hand suggests the subject matter of awareness

---

215 See *infra* Section VIII.B.

216 See, eg comments made by reporter for France ('the question does not seem to have received much doctrinal attention' – FR 38) and the reporter for the US ('this is not a question for which the author has found US courts or commentators to have given much (any?) thought' – US 57).

217 AT 13–14.

218 DE 44.

219 Ibid 45.

220 ZA 35.

221 ES 29, 45.

under the Civil Code is 'the cause of action'.[222] This suggestion implies that the cause of action may accrue before its discovery, namely, that the discovery rule is a rule of prolongation.

That the discovery rule is a rule of the starting point is also suggested by the reporters for Belgium,[223] and, although briefly/implicitly, by reporters for Italy[224] and Switzerland.[225] 133

Mixed approaches are reported for Greece, France and the US. In Greece the discovery rule is usually a rule of prolongation but considered a rule of the starting point in exceptional cases.[226] The French reporter notes that although the wording of the present law indicates that the discovery rule is a rule of the starting point and not of prolongation, it was considered a rule of prolongation before 2008.[227] Moreover, 'at least one decision by the *Cour de cassation* can be cited, in which the Court implicitly adopted the postponement approach' and 'treated the late discovery as a prolongation rule, and not as a rule on the starting point' by stating that the burden to prove lack of knowledge lies upon P.[228] The reporter then suggests that this is the way it should be. The reporter for the US notes that 'most courts describe the discovery rule as delaying "accrual"', but that 'in none of these cases was the implication between delayed accrual and tolling addressed by the court nor did it make any difference in the resolution of the case'.[229] All in all the reporter finds the prolongation argument persuasive.[230] 134

Reporters for the following countries suggest that in their countries the late discovery rule is a rule of prolongation: the Czech Republic,[231] E&W,[232] Norway[233] 135

---

222 Ibid 16.

223 BE 30.

224 IT 47.

225 CH 36 ('Unawareness basically does not influence the prescription, neither its onset nor its duration. Some (short) prescription periods, however, only start once the plaintiff becomes aware of the damage he/she suffered and of the person who is liable for this damage').

226 GR 44 ('the knowledge or ignorance of the existence of the claim does not, as a rule, affect the starting of the prescription. As an exception, special provisions make the starting of the prescription also dependent on other facts, such as the knowledge of the damage').

227 FR 35–36.

228 Ibid 38.

229 US 57.

230 Ibid.

231 CZ 40 ('Since the knowledge of the harm does not belong to the substantive requirements of the tortious liability and, with other words, is not part of the essentials which constitute the victims course of action, it is actually part of the rule of prolongation').

232 EW 44, 46 ('applying a discoverability approach, the claimant will still need to have an accrued cause of action'), 77, 81.

233 NO 49 ('it seems clear that the late discovery rule belongs to the third element of prescription').

and Poland.[234] For the Netherlands too the reporter refers to 'postponement because of unawareness,'[235] namely, as a rule of prolongation.

*4) Comment on Country Reports* – De Lege Ferenda *and* Lex Lata

136 The above analysis concluded that *de lege ferenda* the late discovery rule should be classified as a rule of prolongation and not as a rule of the starting point/accrual. Most reporters agree with that conclusion, or at least do not find it less desirable than the opposite conclusion, even if the *lex lata* in their jurisdictions is interpreted differently.

137 The major support for the classification of the late discovery rule as a rule of the starting point/accrual, contrary to the above analytical conclusion, seems to come from the reporters for Austria.[236] In contrast, the Limitation Act 1980 (E&W), refers explicitly to this question and provides that action may accrue before the required knowledge is acquired,[237] namely, that the discovery rule is a rule of prolongation. As to *de lege ferenda*, no counter-arguments are provided to refute the arguments supporting the analytical conclusion that the discovery rule should not be considered a rule of accrual. Other scholars reached the same conclusion as well.[238]

## VII. PRESCRIPTION PERIODS

138 The prescription period is the second element of prescription law, defined as the statutory period of time that after its running from the starting point (accrual) the cause of action is prescribed.[239]

### A. ANALYSIS – THE PRESCRIPTION PERIOD AND THE EFFECTIVE TIME OF PRESCRIPTION

139 The running of the prescription period on P's cause of action from the starting point (accrual) may be postponed or otherwise suspended by rules of

234 PL 65 ('It appears that in the absence of the required discovery the running of the prescription period is delayed by a rule of prolongation that suspends its ending').

235 NL 41.

236 See *supra* 131.

237 See, eg s. 11(4) of the limitation Act 1980 which provides that the prescription period starts to run from '(a) the date on which the cause of action accrues; or the date of knowledge (if later) of the person injured' – see *Zimmermann and Kleinschmidt*, *supra* fn 2, 30.

238 *Zimmermann and Kleinschmidt*, *supra* fn 2, 61–62.

239 See *supra* 29.

prolongation that apply where P's delay to file a claim is considered justified.[240] For the same reason the prescription period itself may be extended or even renewed by other rules of prolongation.[241] These rules of prolongation – postponement, suspension, extension and renewal – may stretch the *effective time of prescription*, namely, the actual span of time that elapses from the starting point (accrual of cause of action) until the prescription period runs out and the cause of action is prescribed.

The various rules of prolongation that open a gap between the *effective time of prescription* and the *prescription period* are discussed in the next section.[242] The discussion in this section centres on the prescription period. It should be stressed, though, that rules of prolongation on the one hand, and the length of the prescription period on the other hand, are closely related and affect each other. These are actually two different ways to provide sufficient time to Ps to file their actions where their delay to do so is considered justified: one way is a long prescription period that allows for, contains, such justified delays; the other way is rules of prolongation triggered by these delays. There is an inverse relation between these two ways: with a sufficient set of rules of prolongation that cover all justified delays, especially delay caused by late discovery of the essentials of the claim (the late discovery rule), the prescription period should be relatively short, adjusted only to the time reasonably required to file claims.[243] In contrast, in the absence of sufficient rules of prolongation the prescription period should be long enough to allow for these justified delays. 140

Arguably, the preferable way to provide sufficient time to Ps who are late in filing claims due to justified delays is by rules of prolongation and not by long periods of prescription. The reason is simple: while rules of prolongation are activated only where a justified delay actually occurs, a long prescription period may benefit Ps where there are no justifications for delays, unfairly prejudicing Ds and possibly undermining other goals of prescription law. All in all, the combination of prescription periods and rules of prolongation (which together determine the effective time of prescription) should abide with the 'unwritten rule that the creditor must be granted a reasonable time so that he has a fair chance to pursue its claim'.[244] 141

---

240 Ibid.
241 Ibid.
242 See *supra* Section VIII.C.
243 See *infra* fn 254 below discussing the French 2008 reform.
244 DE 47.

## B. ANALYSIS – OPTIMAL LENGTH OF THE GENERAL PERIOD OF PRESCRIPTION

142 Given the difference between the prescription period and the effective time of prescription, and assuming that all justified reasons for delays on Ps' part are taken care of by the proper mixture of rules of prolongation, it appears that the adequate length of the *general* prescription period is in the range of between three and five years.[245] It is a period that fairly enables Ps to file mature and well-considered actions after gathering sufficient information and evidence. Longer periods are required where existing rules of prolongation do not allow for all justified delays so that an extended period is needed to that end.

143 To this *general* period for tort claims there may be justified exceptions such as longer periods for intentional (criminal) torts (P deserves greater protection against the offender D), or shorter periods, such as for defamation (given the importance of freedom of speech).[246]

## C. ANALYSIS – ON THE DISTINCTION BETWEEN 'OBJECTIVE' AND 'SUBJECTIVE' PRESCRIPTION

144 Some jurisdictions distinguish between periods of 'subjective' prescription (usually short) and periods of 'objective' prescription (usually long).[247]

145 Arguably, this distinction between subjective and objective prescription should better be avoided. The characterisation of prescription as 'subjective' originates in and is associated with the application of the late discovery rule that postpones the running of the prescription period until awareness to the essentials of the claim can be established.[248] In some jurisdictions the test for awareness that tolls the late discovery rule is a subjective one, and hence the characterisation of prescription as 'subjective'. Where the late discovery rule does not apply, prescription is characterised as 'objective'. Yet, this difference in characterisation does not hold for other jurisdictions where the test for awareness that tolls the late discovery rule is objective rather than subjective. Under this objective test, if a reasonable person would have been aware of the essentials of P's claim, the discovery rule is tolled even though P subjectively lacked the required awareness. Given the above, it seems farfetched to characterise the whole complex of prescription law (whether subjective or

245 'A period of three years appears to be regarded, internationally, as most appropriate', *Zimmermann and Kleinschmidt, supra* fn 2, 30.

246 See *infra* 154.

247 See, eg AT 47; CZ 43; DE 50, 57; NL 30-32, 35.

248 See *infra* Section VIII.B and *supra* Section VI.F.

objective) according to the nature of the late discovery rule. This rule, after all, is only one of many rules of prolongation, it usually does not apply to all causes of action, and in some jurisdictions it is considered an objective rule. As such, it cannot and should not support a distinction between 'subjective' and 'objective' prescription.[249]

The distinction between 'subjective' and 'objective' prescription periods may also be misleading because sometimes the so-called 'objective' or 'long' prescription period is not actually a *prescription period* (the second element of prescription) but rather the *upper time limit* (the fourth element of prescription – the 'ceiling')[250] which runs independently of the prescription period.[251] Referring to an upper time limit as being an 'objective' prescription is confusing and better be avoided.[252] 146

## D. ONE, FEW OR MANY PRESCRIPTION PERIODS?

A major question regarding the prescription period is whether there should be a uniform general period that applies equally to the variety of torts and related contractual claims or, instead, specific, differentiated periods, each tailored for a different kind of causes of action. Should there be, for example, different periods for different torts, for different kinds of harm (bodily injury, damage to property, pure economic loss), for different types of Ds' conduct (intentional, simple negligence) or for tort claims on the one hand and related contractual claims (such as malpractice claims) on the other hand? 147

The pros of diversified periods adjusted to different torts, harms, types of conduct and so on are basically a better adjustment of the periods to the goals of prescription law: the length of the prescription period that best promotes these goals may be different for different kinds of claims. The cons of diversified periods are complexity and uncertainty resulting from the need to classify causes of action according to prescription periods, and from a phenomenon of 148

---

249 It should also be kept in mind that in most countries rules of late discovery are not *truly* subjective: knowledge is *imputed* to P although P lacks *actual* knowledge – see *infra* 185–189. The reporter for the Netherlands rightly distinguishes between a discovery rule which is 'truly subjective' and other discovery rules which are not 'truly subjective' as they allow knowledge imputation where there is no actual awareness – NL 43.

250 For the four elements see *supra* 29–35.

251 See *infra* 259.

252 Another problematic distinction is between 'relative' and 'absolute' periods of prescription; see, eg BE 18, 25 and CH 38. To the extent that this distinction parallels the 'subjective/objective' distinction, the above criticism of the later applies to the former. That the running of the period depends on the discoverability criterion does not make it 'relative' (as argued in *Zimmermann and Kleinschmidt*, *supra* fn 2, 30): there are other factors, unrelated to discoverability, on which the running of the period depends.

'period shopping' by Ps trying to anchor their claim in a cause of action with a longer prescription period.[253]

## E. COUNTRY REPORTS

### *1) The Prescription Periods and the Effective Time of Prescription*

149 The above conclusion, that the better way to allow for justified delays in filing actions is not by long prescription periods but rather by the combination of shortened periods accompanied by rules of prolongation, mainly by the late discovery rule, is in line with direction taken by many jurisdictions, sometimes as the result of law reforms.[254] The desirable effects of this approach are shortening of the effective time of prescription for belated actions where the delay is unjustified, and tailoring different prolongations of the effective time of prescription where delays are justified.[255]

### *2) Length of Prescription Periods*

150 The prevalent general periods for prescription of tort actions, when accompanied by the late discovery rule, are *three* years (Austria, Czech Republic, E&W, Germany, Norway, Poland, US and South Africa)[256] and five years

---

[253] It should be stressed that theoretically there could be no 'forum shopping' between the prescription period and the upper time limit (cf BE 28) as these are not alternative periods but rather two different elements of prescription – see Section V.

[254] The reporter for France, for example, notes that the 2008 reform 'has drastically shortened the normal prescription period, which has been reduced to five years. This shortening has come along with an official endorsement of the late discovery rule. This should come as no surprise, since it is the late discovery rule that makes the five-year period acceptable and limits the risk that a claimant should be time-barred even before he became aware of his right' – FR 39. The reporter for Germany notes that while prescription periods governed by the late discovery rule are usually three years, for other tort claims they range up to 30 years – DE 57. See also: AT 34; FR 44; ES 33 ('Traditionally there has been a major difference concerning prescription in tort and in contract […]. In 2015, the legislature passed a reform of several statutes […] which shortened the general period of prescription sensibly'. Reforms of prescription law are reported in Czech Republic (2012 – CZ 2); E&W (1980s – EW 1–2); France (2008 – FR 66); Germany (2002 – DE 48), the Netherlands (1992 – NL 1); Poland (2007 – PL 4); Spain (2015 – ES 33). For reforms in prescription law see also *Zimmermann and Kleinschmidt*, *supra* fn 2, 26–29.

[255] The long periods replaced by shorter periods with the discovery rule were in some countries sometimes transformed into upper time limit periods ('ceiling') or treated as a 'second' prescription periods – see *supra* Section VII.C and *infra* 244.

[256] See respectively: AT 37; CZ 40; EW 70; DE 49; NO 53; PL 73; US 60 (between two and three years); ZA 39.

(Belgium, France, Greece, Italy and the Netherlands).[257] A general period of only one year applies in Spain[258] and Switzerland.[259] There are various exceptions to the general period.[260] The period for non-contractual claims against the EU is five years.[261]

The prevalent general prescription periods for tort actions where the late discovery rule is not applied are much longer, mainly 10, 20 and 30 years. In France, for example, the period for personal injury and medical liability is ten years and for environmental damage 30 years (no late discovery rule).[262] A long period of 30 or 20 years often applies to torts which are also criminal, or at least intentional torts.[263] An exceptionally short general period for tort claims (absent the discovery rule) is the six-year period in E&W.[264] Interestingly, in E&W, there are two general periods for latent harms other than bodily injury: six years regardless of discovery and three years after discovery – the longer period decides.[265] 151

Some countries apply very short periods on claims for defamation.[266] The French reporter explains in this regard that the 'extremely short period applicable to defamation claims also illustrates the value which the legislator attaches to freedom of speech'.[267] 152

---

257 See respectively: BE 25; FR 44; GR 43; IT 54; NL 29.

258 ES 30. It is considered to be too short. But the period for defamation, and harm to privacy and honour, is four years – ES 32.

259 CH 37 (but three years as of 1 January 2020).

260 The reporters for Belgium note that a 'thorough research of all statutes of limitation under Belgian law, came to the conclusion that more than 1000 different statutes of limitation exist' – BE 26. In Austria, for example, the period for claim against auditors and for unfair competition is five years rather than three – AT 45–46. In Greece, for another example, the period for automobiles collisions claims and claims of state employees is two rather than five years and only 18 months for unfair competition claims – GR 49–51. In the US there are special periods for fraud and trespass – US 60.

261 EU 26.

262 FR 70.

263 AT 39 (30 years); BE 18; CH 37 and 40 (special rules for criminal torts); DE 52 (30 years); FR 44 (20 years for harm caused by torture or acts of barbarism, or by violence or sexual aggression committed against a minor); NL 31 (as long as the right to criminal proceedings exist. For changes in the length of the prescription periods: see ibid 64–65); PL 73 (20 years). Interestingly, in the US the period for such torts is shorter than the general period. The reporter reasons that perhaps 'this is because most intentional torts are 'snapshot torts' in which all relevant events occur in a short period of time and the victim is acutely aware of those events' – US 50.

264 EW 70.

265 Ibid.

266 AT 43 (one year); EW 70 (one year); FR 44 (three months). For comparison, in Germany the period for defamation is the general period of three years (DE 57) and in Spain it is four years while the general period is one year (ES 35).

267 FR 43.

### 3) *Multiplicity of Periods and 'Period Shopping'*

153 The reforms of prescription law, which shortened the general periods (where a discovery rule applies),[268] also unified to a large extent the prescription periods for tort claims and for torts and contractual claims, thereby mitigating the problem of 'period shopping'.[269] But even in other countries where a multiplicity of prescription periods is prevalent[270] and considered a problem,[271] 'period shopping' per se is not always considered to be a part of that problem. The reason seems to be that 'period shopping' favours Ps over Ds by allowing Ps to choose the longest period, and that is considered just.[272] Yet, such protection of Ps may lead to distorted classification of causes of action in order to help Ps enjoy longer periods.[273]

---

268 See *supra* fn 254.

269 See, eg: CZ 47 (no 'period shopping'); DE 48 ('Since the reform of 2002 more or less unified the prescription periods for all civil claims [...] "period shopping" which was usual before the reform has become unnecessary'); FR 41 (no more 'period shopping'); NL 36; NO 58 (noting that 'period shopping' in Norway 'does not in practice cause any problems worthy of mentioning').

270 See, eg CH 41 ('Numerous legal provisions regarding non-contractual liability set the beginning and duration of the prescription period (ranging from two to 30 years)'. In the US the problem is not 'period shopping' but also 'forum shopping', given the difference in prescription periods between states; see US 60 ('many states have specific statutes of limitations periods for different types of professional malpractice').

271 The E&W reporters observe that 'while a uniform limitation period across the board would promote certainty and to that extent suit the convenience [...] the adoption of such an approach without exceptions would produce greater injustice. Nonetheless, the current catalogue of prescription periods applicable to tort claims in England and Wales has been labelled as "needlessly complex", and it has been said to be "a shameful indictment of the operation of statutes within our legal system that Parliament has created such a mess."' 'The Law Commission recommend that the uniform limitation period within the "core regime" should be three years from the date of discoverability. However, a draft bill to simplify the rules came to nought' – EW 57.

272 The E&W reporters, after criticising the 'mess' caused by multiple periods (ibid), observe that 'in the case of concurrent actions for damages for personal injury in contract and tort and for personal injuries and property damage, the more favourable regime for personal injuries [...] prevails' – EW 73. The Greek reporter acknowledges that '"period shopping" may give rise to disputes' but observes that 'there is no reason why different legal basis of claims should deprive the plaintiff from the advantages that each one of them provides' – GR 53. The reporter for the US also notes that although 'period shopping' exists, this is not considered to be a problem as 'the plaintiff may choose his or her claims and recover when at least one claim is not barred by the statute of limitations and the plaintiff is successful on the merits of that claim'– US 61.

273 The reporter for Poland observes in this regard that '(c)ourts have played a primary role in "dressing" contractual breaches for torts especially in order to award compensation of non-pecuniary loss' – PL 72.

## F. A NOTE ON THE UNIFICATION OF PRESCRIPTION PERIODS

Given the major differences among European countries in the length of the prescription periods, would unification of prescription periods achieve harmonisation in prescription laws? The above analysis indicates that it would not because what should be harmonised is the *effective time of prescription* which is composed of prescription periods and also of rules of prolongation.[274] Unifying the former but not the latter would not achieve the goal of harmonisation of prescription law. For one example, it is obvious that the same periods of prescription, where one is accompanied by the late discovery rule and the other is not, would lead to quite a different effective time of prescription. 154

# VIII. RULES OF POSTPONEMENT, SUSPENSION, RENEWAL AND EXTENSION

## A. INTRODUCTION

The third element of prescription law are rules of prolongation. Sometimes Ps fail to file a claim in time and yet present reasons for the delay such as: being unaware of the claim, mental disability, special relations with D, D's absence from the jurisdiction, previous litigation between the parties, admission by D, *force majeure*, etc. Where reasons for delay render the delay justified, the role of the third element is to allow Ps to file such delayed claims. This is done, as explained,[275] by rules of prolongation of four kinds: postponement, suspension, extension and renewal.[276] 155

Rules of *postponement*, to reiterate, postpone the running of the prescription period, before it has begun, past the (potential) starting point until the reason for postponement, the contingency, ceases to exist. Rules of *suspension* suspend the running of the prescription period as long as the reason for delay exists regardless of whether the period has begun to run or not. The difference between a rule of postponement and a rule of suspension is the following. A rule of postponement applies, where its reason exists, only where the period *has not yet started to run*. In contrast, a rule of suspension applies, where the reason for suspension exists, regardless of whether the period has not yet started to run or *after* it has begun to run. To illustrate, assume that the prescription period 156

274 See *supra* 29–31.

275 Ibid.

276 For the corresponding terms in Austrian law see AT 52.

is five years, that at the starting point (date of accrual) P suffers from mental disability for one year, then becomes mentally able for two years, and then again becomes mentally disabled for an additional four years until regaining ability. P's claim is filed seven years after the starting point (accrual). If mental disability is considered a rule of *postponement*, P's claim would be prescribed since a period of six years ran over P's claim (assuming no other rules of prolongation apply). But if mental disability is considered a rule of *suspension*, P would have three years to sue as only two years ran over P's claim. In such cases a rule of suspension actually 'swallows', overtakes, the parallel rule of postponement and is accordingly more favourable to Ps. Another illustration is E&W law, which states that once the prescription period starts to run, its running cannot be stopped.[277] This statement means that E&W's law allows only rules of postponement but not rules of suspension.

157 Rules of *renewal* (also referred to as rules of *interruption*[278]) restart the running of the prescription period in the sense that a new period of prescription starts to run afresh from the date of the contingency.

158 Rules of *extension*, unlike the former rules, do not affect the running of the period, but rather extend the prescription period itself for a period that secures P's ability to file a claim within a reasonable time after the contingency, which is the reason for delay, ceases to exist.

159 Combinations of different rules of prolongation are possible (eg postponement or suspension followed by extension).

160 All rules of prolongation, as emphasised,[279] open a gap between the *prescription period* and the *effective time of prescription*. Therefore, the actual period of time that passes between accrual and prescription may be longer than the prescription period. For example, if the prescription period is five years, but the running of this period is postponed for three years because of a justified reason for delay in the specific case, the effective time of prescription would be eight years.

161 Which rule of prolongation should be applied to which contingency that justifies delay? The answer lies in the delicate balance between the goals of prescription law and between the competing interests. For example, as rules of suspension usually prolong the effective time of prescription more than rules

---

277 EW 75 ('There is no reference to "suspension" in the Limitation Act 1980. This is consistent with the general position under English law that "where an action has once accrued, and the statute has begun to run, there being then a capacity of suing and of being sued, the statute continues to run" unless "ousted [...] by a statutory provision"').

278 See, eg BE 16 ('when the running of time is broken [...] The time that has already elapsed is lost and the count of the prescription period starts afresh').

279 See *supra* 140.

of extension,[280] the former should apply where the balance tilts more to P's side, and the latter where it tilts to D's side.

162 The following discussion enumerates the contingencies that may be considered as justifying delays, ponders which rule of prolongation, if at all, should apply to which contingency, and presents the different national laws in this regard.

163 The first contingency to be discussed, and definitely the most important one, is the subject matter of the *late discovery rule* which applies in cases where P's delay in filing a claim results from P's unawareness to one or more of the essentials required to constitute a mature claim against D, as explained below.

## B. UNAWARENESS – THE LATE DISCOVERY RULE

164 The cause of action, as we have seen,[281] matures for prescription purposes when all the substantive requirements, the essentials, of P's claim against D exist: D's tortious conduct that caused P's harm. At this point in time P's claim can succeed, and this potential ability to succeed marks the starting point – the accrual of P's cause of action.[282]

165 Sometimes P is unaware for a while that she has a mature cause of action against D, and therefore files a belated claim only after awareness is attained. Where such delay is considered justified, prescription law applies a *late discovery rule* in order to allow P to file the claim despite the delay. As explained, this rule should be perceived of as a rule of prolongation (the third element of prescription) rather than a rule of the starting point (the first element).[283] The late discovery rule is the major and the most important rule of prolongation.

166 To determine the scope and effect of the late discovery rule several issues require examination and resolution. Firstly, what are the *essentials of liability*[284] that P's unawareness of them triggers the late discovery rule? Secondly, what kind of unawareness is required to trigger the rule? Is it subjective (P was unaware) or objective (a reasonable person would have been unaware) or some

---

280 Assume that the prescription period is five years and the contingency exists for four and a half years after the starting point. A rule of suspension would prolong the effective time of prescription by four and a half years. A rule of extension that allows one year after the contingency ceases would prolong the period by only by six months.

281 See *supra* 36.

282 It is the starting point (accrual) of the cause of action, provided that no other claim *that belongs to the same cause of action* had already matured. The cause of action accrues with the maturation the first claim which belongs to it – see *supra* Section VI B.

283 See *supra* Section VI.F.

284 Namely, the substantive requirements that must be met to constitute a cause of action – see *supra* 36.

hybrid test? Thirdly, what exactly should be the subject matter of awareness to each essential and its degree? Is it sufficient to be aware of 'signs' or 'preliminary' manifestation of these essentials or more than that? Fourthly, how onerous is and should be the burden on P to conduct inquiries in order to discover whether she has a mature claim against D? Fifthly, which rule of prolongation should be applied to late discovery (postponement, suspension or extension)? Finally, is and should the late discovery rule apply to all tort causes of action or only to some of them?

### 1) *Unawareness of which Essentials of Liability?*

#### a) The Question

167 The substantive requirements that have to be met to constitute a mature cause of action are those that establish that P's harm was caused by D's tortious conduct. Therefore, to be fully aware of a mature cause of action against D, P needs to know that she suffers harm, that the harm was caused by identified D, the relevant facts regarding D's conduct and that the law provides a tort remedy in the case. So there are five essentials: D's identity, D's conduct, P's harm, causation (P's harm was in fact caused by D's conduct) and the legal norm (that makes D liable to P). Hence, what are the essentials of liability that P's unawareness to them triggers the late discovery rule in P's favour?

#### b) Analysis

168 At first sight the rationale behind the late discovery rule seemingly points toward the conclusion that unawareness to *any* of the five essentials should trigger the operation of the late discovery rule. After all, where there is unawareness of the existence of a mature claim, unawareness that justifies the delay, it does not matter which essential was missing – unawareness to each should justify the delay. It makes no sense, for example, to postpone the running of the prescription period where P is unaware of the damage but to allow it to run where P is unaware of the fact that her damage was caused by D or of the facts concerning D's conduct.

169 Yet, it does make sense in this regard to treat the fifth essential – the legal norm – differently. Unlike the other four essentials, which are *facts of the physical world*, the legal norm is a 'virtual' fact open to interpretations and changes. In common law jurisdictions court decisions, for example, may change legal norms retrospectively. Exposing Ds to prolongation by the late discovery rule, just because the law has changed, or because P or P's attorney misinterpreted the law, may distort the proper balance that prescription law seeks to achieve given its goals. In addition, that the maxim *error juris semper nocet* is applied in

many jurisdictions, suggests that unawareness of the law may not be a justified reason for delay in suing.

c) Country Reports

The overwhelming majority of the reports support the above conclusion that: (a) where the late discovery rule applies and postpones the running of the prescription period it should apply to all the four *factual essentials* of P's claim: D's identity, D's conduct, harm caused to P and causal link between D's conduct and P's harm; (b) that the rule should not apply where the only unawareness is of the *legal norm/s* that render D's conduct tortious. These reports pertain to Austria,[285] Belgium,[286] the Czech Republic,[287] Germany,[288] Greece,[289] E&W,[290] France,[291] Italy,[292] the Netherlands,[293] Norway,[294] Poland,[295] South Africa[296] and Spain.[297] 170

Only two countries limit the application of the late discovery rule by not applying it, as a rule, to all four factual essentials: Switzerland and the US. 171

---

285 AT 18.

286 BE 30 (although 'the Civil Code only requires knowledge of the plaintiff's harm and of the defendant's identity to start the prescription period running, it is generally accepted that also knowledge of the defendant's tortious conduct and awareness of the causal link between the harm and the tortious conduct is necessary').

287 CZ 50 (noting that with regard to the fifth (legal) essential that the legal norm 'does not belong to the essentials of cause of action and does not play any role in prescription law').

288 DE 59.

289 GR 63 ('Apart from the awareness of *D's identity*, *D's conduct* and *P's harm* [...] also awareness of *causation*, ie that P's harm was in fact caused by D's conduct, is necessary. So, the late discovery rule applies where there is unawareness to those four elements. Unawareness of the legal norm does not hinder the running of the prescription').

290 EW 45. Section 14 of the Limitation Act 1980 enumerates the four factual essentials to which the discovery rule applies and then provides that 'knowledge that any acts or omissions did or did not, as a matter of law, involve negligence, nuisance or breach of duty is irrelevant'.

291 FR 45 (rule applies to all four factual elements) and 47 ('actual knowledge of the legal rule enabling compensation is not to be taken into account').

292 IT 59 ('ignorance of the law is relevant not in and of itself, but only if it is the result of an intentional act undertaken to conceal the existence of a right').

293 NL 43 (Supreme Court ruled that unawareness to the legal norm does not justify postponement). As to awareness to the relation between D's conduct and P's harm, it is described as 'less stringent criterion than knowing about the causal link between the damage and the tortious act' – ibid 40.

294 NO 63–69 (rule applies to four factual elements). Usually the rule does not apply to the legal norm (ibid 68) but there are exceptions (ibid 69).

295 PL 74–76.

296 ZA 41–42 (rule applies to all four essentials) and 43 (but rule does not apply to awareness 'that the facts afford him legal remedy').

297 ES 16 ('it is not required that the claimant is aware or knows that such an event entitles her to file a claim in compensation') and 45.

172 As to Switzerland, the rule is that discoverability 'basically does not influence the prescription, neither its onset nor its duration'.[298] In those exceptional cases where the rule does apply, it applies only to awareness to the essentials of damage and of D's identity.[299]

173 In the US, courts do not always apply the discovery rule to all the four factual essentials but sometimes to part of them.[300] 'Some versions of the discovery rule only require knowledge of injury. For those, unawareness of other facts supporting the claim would be irrelevant to the invocation of the discovery rule. Some versions of the discovery rule do, in addition, require knowledge of both the injury and the causal connection to the source of that harm [...]. Finally, the most demanding version of the discovery rule requires knowledge of both injury and cause as well as the facts that would support a claim of tortious conduct by the defendant'. One suggested explanation for excluding essentials from the rule's application is 'reluctance by courts to embrace an "all elements" discovery rule because of concern that such an extension of the time for suit would unfairly burden defendants'.[301] The rule does not usually apply to awareness of the legal norm (the fifth essential)[302] but the reporter cites an observation that there is 'a subtle difference between knowing the facts of defendant's actions and knowing that they amount to a breach of duty that will support a legal claim, and in some more extreme cases the difference may disappear'.[303]

#### d) Case 10 – Analysis and Country Reports

*Chemical plant D negligently exposes bordering lands to toxic substances. As a result P, a nearby resident landowner, contracts a lung disease. P failed to sue in time because his former lawyer told him that the exposure was not tortious, and only his new lawyer told him, after the running of time, that it was tortious.*

174 *Analysis*: In this case the subject of P's unawareness is the fifth essential – the legal norm. It is doubtful whether D should incur the price of the mistake made by P's first lawyer or of changes in the interpretation of the law. Moreover, P may

298 CH 48.

299 Ibid. 'The awareness of the legal situation has no incidence on the prescription of the claim' (ibid 50).

300 US 66.

301 Ibid 67. Another suggested explanation is that the discovery rule originates in medical negligence cases where the only relevant unawareness was of D's carelessness (such as leaving a foreign object in P's body after surgery) but not D's identity or the causal link – ibid).

302 Ibid 68–69. But some jurisdictions may apply the rule on knowledge of legal responsibility – ibid 70.

303 Ibid 69.

have an alternative remedy: suing the first lawyer for the negligent legal advice that prevented P from suing on time.

*Country reports*: All the reports suggest that as unawareness in this case is of the legal norm and not of any of the four factual essentials, the claim would prescribe although P reasonably relied on his lawyer's misrepresentation.[304] P indeed has an alternative claim: suing her lawyer for the loss caused by the prescription of the claim. 175

### 2) *Objective or Subjective Unawareness?*

#### a) The Question

What kind of unawareness is required to trigger the late discovery rule?[305] The test may be *subjective*, focusing on what the *individual P* actually knew, or could or should have known *given P's individual skills and abilities*. Alternatively, the test may be *objective*, focusing on whether or not a *reasonable person* could and should have gained awareness, regardless of P's subjective unawareness.[306] 176

The *subjective* test, as indicated, may have at least two versions. Under the less demanding, relaxed, version (from P's perspective) the late discovery rule applies whenever P was *actually* unaware of the essentials of her claim or at least did not 'shut one's eye' to their existence. The rule applies even if P subjectively could have and should have been aware of the essentials of her claim, given her skills and abilities, but failed to acquire the necessary knowledge and awareness. Under the more demanding version of the subjective test, the rule does not apply where P actually lacks awareness but subjectively could have and should have acquired the necessary knowledge and awareness, given her skills and abilities. 177

The *objective* test may also have at least two versions. Under the less demanding, relaxed, version (from P's perspective), the late discovery rule applies whenever P was not *grossly* negligent in failing to acquire the knowledge and awareness that a reasonable person could have and should have acquired. Under this relaxed version of the objective test the rule applies even if P was negligent 178

304 AT 18; BE 31; CH 50; CZ 50; DE 64; ES 46; EW 45 (see fn 281); FR 48; GR 64; IT 59; NL 44; PL 77; US 70 (but some jurisdictions may apply the rule to knowledge of legal responsibility); ZA 45.

305 The *actual* unawareness of P is a pre-condition to the application of the late discovery rule.

306 See, eg NL 41 ('major question about postponement because of unawareness – in Dutch law, the subjective prescription period – is whether this ground is subjective or objective. In case it is subjective the running of time is postponed until the plaintiff actually – subjectively – becomes aware of the facts constituting the claim, and in case it is objective, the running is postponed or suspended only until a reasonable person would have discovered the relevant facts, even if the plaintiff did not').

in failing to acquire knowledge but was not *grossly* negligent. Under the more demanding (ordinary) version of the objective test the late discovery rule applies only where P's failure to acquire awareness was objectively reasonable: it does not apply where P's failure to acquire knowledge and awareness was negligent, regardless of whether it was *simple* negligence or *gross* negligence.[307]

179 The first question, to sum up, is whether the test for applying the late discovery rule is and should be subjective or objective. Once an objective or a subjective test is chosen, the second question is whether it should be the relaxed, less demanding version, or the more demanding version, given that:

- Under the relaxed *subjective* version, the late discovery rule applies whenever P lacks actual knowledge.
- Under the more demanding *subjective* test the rule does not apply where P subjectively could and should have acquired awareness.
- Under the relaxed *objective* version, the rule applies unless P was *grossly* negligent in failing to acquire knowledge and awareness.
- Under the more demanding (ordinary) objective version the late discovery applies only where P's failure to acquire information was reasonable.

b) Analysis

180 As to the first question, whether the test for acquiring knowledge and awareness should be objective or subjective, it is suggested that as a rule the answer should correspond with the jurisdiction's general conception of negligence liability, or preferably with its conception of *contributory negligence.*[308] Where the general law of negligence/contributory negligence employs a *subjective* test to decide the question of carelessness, the subjective test should be the default choice for the discovery rule as well. Equally, where the general law of negligence/contributory negligence employs an *objective* test, the default test for the discovery rule should also be objective. A consideration that may support a 'deviation' from this default guidance, by adopting an objective test where the general law of negligence/contributory negligence is governed by a subjective test, is that the objective test is much easier to implement than the subjective test: while the objective test employs one standard (that of the reasonable person) the subjective test has to take into account in each case P's individual idiosyncrasies.[309]

---

307 Note that where P has skills and abilities that transcend those of the reasonable person the subjective test may be less favourable to P than the objective test.

308 The test for contributory negligence seems to be a more adequate test as it examines P's conduct, not D's, which is also the case with the discovery rule.

309 See AT 16 ('it is ultimately almost impossible to prove what she actually knew at which point in time, and whether or not she possibly misinterpreted what she saw and heard').

Once an objective or subjective test is chosen, the second question comes to the fore: which version of the chosen test should be preferred? Should it be the relaxed version (whether subjective or objective) or the more demanding (ordinary) version? 181

Starting with the *subjective* test, it appears that the more demanding version (from P's perspective) should be preferred. The relaxed subjective version, which applies the late discovery even where P could have and should have acquired the necessary awareness given her skills and abilities, is unfair and counter-productive. It is unfair because it allows P, at D's expense, to benefit from her unjustified failure to acquire actual knowledge and awareness, although subjectively she could have and should have acquired it given her skills and abilities. It is counter-productive because it encourages Ps not to seek for information that they could and should have acquired regarding their claims, thereby frustrating a major goal of prescription law which is incentivising Ps to seek information they can acquire in order to avoid unjustified delays in filing actions. 182

Now to the *objective* test, and to the choice between the relaxed version (application of the rule denied only where P's failure to acquire knowledge and awareness amounts to objectively *gross* negligence) and the more demanding (ordinary) version (rule applies only where P's failure was reasonable). It is suggested that this choice should depend on how stringent the ordinary reasonable person standard is. Where the standard of the ordinary test is stringent in the sense that relatively few individuals can meet it, the relaxed version should be chosen (only gross negligence of Ps justifies non-application of the discovery rule). But where the reasonable person standard is not stringent, so that average Ps can meet it, the ordinary objective test should apply (the late discovery rule does not apply unless P's unawareness is reasonable). 183

The conclusions, to sum up, are: 184

- The choice between objective and subjective test for the late discovery rule should be made taking into account, as a major factor, the jurisdiction's general perception of negligence/contributory negligence as being subjective or objective.
- If a subjective test is chosen, it should not be the relaxed version but the more demanding version. The rule should not apply where P failed to acquire awareness although subjectively she could have and should have acquired it given her skills and abilities.
- If the objective test is chosen, the decision whether to embrace the relaxed version or the ordinary version depends on the stringency of the objective standard that governs negligence/contributory negligence law. The relaxed

version may be appropriate where the general law of negligence applies a stringent standard. Otherwise the ordinary objective test should apply.

c) Country Reports

185 Three countries, Belgium, the Netherlands and Switzerland, are reported as applying a relaxed subjective test, under which the discovery rule always applies where P lacks actual awareness, although subjectively P could and should acquire awareness.[310] As noted, this version of the subjective test is unfair and counter-productive. Indeed, it appears that at least in the Netherlands the test is not really such a relaxed one. The reporter notes that 'If the identity of the liable person is very easy to find out with a simple act of research, the plaintiff may not sit still and cannot call on his subjective not knowing. Some sort of effort to find out who is responsible for the harm can be expected'.[311] That sounds like the more demanding subjective test.

186 Four countries are reported to apply the more demanding version of the subjective test which applies the late discovery rule only where it is established that the individual P, given her skills and abilities, was subjectively unable to acquire the awareness that she actually lacked. These countries are Austria,[312] the Czech Republic,[313] Greece[314] and Italy.[315]

187 E&W seem to employ a more demanding subjective test with regard to the significance of the harm[316] and an ordinary objective test regarding the ability to acquire knowledge.[317]

188 Germany applies a *relaxed* objective test under which 'it suffices that under an objective perspective it would have been grossly negligent not to know, or to take

---

310 BE 31; CH 38; NL 43.

311 NL 50. See also BE 31 ('some authors argue that this approach does not exempt the plaintiff of a duty to investigate when it is obvious that questions need to be asked').

312 AT 16 ('Awareness' is also imputed if the victim could easily have learned about all these relevant facts without any noteworthy effort).

313 CZ 27 ('The prescription period starts once the victim knows or should have known (actual or imputed knowledge) of all facts which meet the requirements of the wrongdoer's liability'). Personal characteristics are taken into account – ibid 51.

314 GR 65.

315 IT 63 (prescription 'does run from the moment in which the individual has acquired knowledge – or has been able to acquire knowledge [...] using ordinary diligence and taking into account available scientific knowledge').

316 Section 14(2) of the Limitation Act 1980 provides that 'an injury is significant if the person whose date of knowledge is in question would reasonably have considered it sufficiently serious to justify his instituting proceedings for damages against a defendant who did not dispute liability and was able to satisfy a judgment'.

317 Section 14(3) of the Limitation Act 1980 provides that 'a person's knowledge includes knowledge which he might reasonably have been expected to acquire-

(a) from facts observable or ascertainable by him; or

knowledge of, the relevant facts'.[318] Norway probably embraces a similar test as it employs an objective but lenient version of the test.[319]

The ordinary objective test rather than a relaxed one is applied in France,[320] Poland,[321] the US,[322] South Africa[323] and probably in Spain[324] as well as to claims against the EU.[325] 189

### 3) *What should be the Degree of Awareness for Each Essential?*

#### a) The Question

We have seen that P's unawareness of the essentials of her claim, whether subjective or objective, triggers the late discovery rule that postpones the count of the prescription period. Where awareness exists at the outset, the late discovery rule does not apply. Where awareness is gained only after the late discovery rule was triggered by P's unawareness, the late discovery rule is tolled and the postponed count of the prescription period begins. But what should be considered as 'awareness' that a given essential exists? P may have only limited knowledge about the essential or different degrees of belief in its existence and its probability. For example, where the essential is *harm*, does it suffice that P has knowledge of 'preliminary', 'signs of', or 'significant' harm, or should the 190

---

(b) from facts ascertainable by him with the help of medical or other appropriate expert advice which it is reasonable for him to seek; but a person shall not be fixed under this subsection with knowledge of a fact ascertainable only with the help of expert advice so long as he has taken all reasonable steps to obtain (and, where appropriate, to act on) that advice'.

The reporters for E&W explain that the 'difference between secs 14(2) and 14(3) turns on what the claimant ought reasonably to have done. Unlike sec 14(3), the test in sec 14(2) (on significance) is external to the claimant and involves no inquiry into what P could reasonably have been expected to do' – EW 55.

318 DE 65.

319 NO 71.

320 FR 46 ('article 2224 of the *code civil* makes it clear that ignorance of the facts enabling the claimant to exercise his right is an objective justification, as it is the time at which the claimant knew or *should have known* the facts enabling him to exercise his right that is decisive').

321 PL 79 ('revision of the starting point rule in 2017 employs the objective yardstick – "knew or should have known" for all non-personal injury claims – which works in favour of the defendant').

322 US 73 ('the test is whether P "should have discovered, by reasonable diligence, the requisite facts"').

323 ZA 41 (the Prescription Act provides 'that a creditor shall be deemed to have such knowledge if he could have acquired it by exercising reasonable care').

324 ES 47 ('Spanish law seems to leave this question in the open, although it may be guessed that a court would probably apply an objective standard. Therefore, if a reasonable victim should have known the particular victim may be deemed to have known as well and therefore prescription would be triggered').

325 EU 46 (it has to be noted, however, that the CJEU only exceptionally takes unawareness into account).

knowledge include further development of the harm for qualifying as 'awareness'. For another example, regarding the essential of *causation*, is it sufficient that P believes that there is only a *chance* of a causal link? That there is *high probability* of causal link? Or something in between?

b) Analysis

191 The rationale behind the late discovery rule indicates that awareness (which tolls the operation of the rule or prevents it from applying at the outset) should be recognised only where the knowledge about the existence of an essential, or the degree of belief in its existence, should be such that *a reasonable person would have considered to file a claim based on this knowledge*. Mere 'signs' of harm, or belief in a slim chance of causal link, for example, should not be considered as awareness of these essentials. That would unfairly prejudice Ps who have no sufficient basis for filing suits, and yet the prescription period starts to run against them. On the other hand, it is also unjustified to require awareness of the full development of harm or a strong belief that the probability of causal link is very high. That would unfairly prejudice Ds by unjustifiably delaying the running of the prescription period.

192 Analytically, there is close correlation between the required kind or degree of awareness, on the one hand, and the requirements for the accrual of cause of action (for the starting point), on the other hand. Awareness of facts that are insufficient for the starting point, for the cause of action to accrue, should not deny or toll the operation of the late discovery rule. For example, where the cause of action accrues only with the stabilisation of the harm,[326] P's awareness of harm which has not yet stabilised should be insufficient to prevent or toll the operation of the late discovery rule. The same applies to facts regarding the basis of D's liability: awareness of facts that are insufficient for P's cause of action against D to accrue (for the starting point) should also be insufficient to prevent or toll the operation of the late discovery rule.

c) Country Reports

193 In accordance with the above analysis, all reporters suggest, explicitly or implicitly, that the required degree of knowledge/awareness that prevents or tolls the operation of the late discovery rule is such *that enables P to file a claim against D with a reasonable chance to succeed*.[327] The reporter for Norway, however, points out that the subject matter of knowledge/awareness

326 See *supra* 90.

327 AT 15 ('it is commonly understood that the victim further has to "be aware" of all the relevant facts needed to file a claim'). P's 'knowledge does not have to extend to any imaginable

are not only *facts* of the essentials of liability but also the *evidence* sufficient for the claim to succeed.[328] Arguably, the ensuing delay of the running of the prescription period (until sufficient *evidence* becomes known) is unjustified and may frustrate goals of prescription law. The time needed for collecting evidence is and should be provided by the *prescription period* and not by *a rule of prolongation* such as the late discovery rule.

### *4) How Onerous should the Burden to Acquire Knowledge be?*

#### a) The Question

The kind and degree of awareness that prevents or tolls the operation of the late discovery rule depends on how heavy P's burden is to inquire whether the essentials of their potential claim exist. For example, where P *suspects* that she suffered harm, or that her harm is causally related to D's misconduct, should she try to substantiate this suspicion by conducting inquiries? Which kind of inquiries, which degree of efforts and at what cost should be considered adequate in this regard? Where the burden is heavy, failure to meet it means that a knowledge that could and should have been acquired would be imputed to P and prevent or toll the operation of the late discovery rule. This applies not only to an *objective* test of awareness that imputes to P objective awareness but also to the *subjective* test which imputes to P awareness that she could have 194

details' – ibid 52; CH 38 ('Sufficient awareness of the person liable for the damages can be assumed once the plaintiff is aware of the elements necessary to assert the claim. The mere assumption that a person could potentially be held liable does not suffice to establish awareness of the identity of the person'); CZ 52 ('The threshold of the awareness is eg the reasonable likelihood of the existence of a harm or reasonable belief of the existence of the causation'); DE 66 ('The claimant is aware of an element of liability […] if he or she knows facts from which a reasonable person in the situation of the claimant would infer that there was some wrong behaviour and/or violation of the owed care. This should be sufficient for institution legal proceedings in order to pursue the claim'); ES 16; EW 46 (it was 'held that the date of knowledge […] was that of the first of the physical injuries the claimant knew to be serious enough for him to justify instituting proceedings'). Awareness to the essential of causation means 'reasonable belief' in the 'real possibility of a causal link' between exposure and injury (ibid 55); FR 51 ('It is suggested that prescription should start to run when the victim has good reasons to suspect that his harm was caused by a *fait générateur*, and when he has identified a possible *fait générateur* and the defendant who should answer for it'); GR 60 ('it is considered that P is aware of the person bound to pay damages when he knows those facts that allow him to file an action with hopes of success. Simple suppositions, suspicions or unawareness due to negligence do not suffice'); IT 65; NL 49; PL 80; US 72; ZA 44. In Belgium the 'court does not specify which degree of certainty suffices' – BE 32.

328 NO 72 ('As for the degree of awareness the Supreme court has taken the stance that the plaintiff must have had evidence in such a degree that he could have taken the case to the court. Hence the damage must have developed to such a degree that it is more likely than not that all the elements of liability may be proved').

acquired given her subjective skills and abilities.[329] Yet, being more lenient to Ps than the objective test in most cases, the subjective test tends to require less effort from Ps to inquire and to acquire knowledge.

b) Country Reports

195 As expected, countries which apply the ordinary objective test for the discovery rule tend to impose upon Ps a relatively more onerous burden of inquiry which corresponds with the burden imposed under the general test of the reasonable person. These countries are the Czech Republic,[330] E&W,[331] France,[332] Italy,[333] Poland,[334] South Africa,[335] Spain[336] and the US.[337]

196 At the other end, Austria and the Netherlands, which embrace a relaxed subjective test, impose, if at all, a very light burden of inquiry.[338]

---

329 See *supra* 177, 182.

330 CZ 52 ('The threshold of the awareness is eg the reasonable likelihood of the existence of a harm or reasonable belief of the existence of the causation').

331 EW 109 ('a person's knowledge includes knowledge which he might reasonably have been expected to acquire from facts observable or ascertainable by him or from facts ascertainable by him with the help of medical or other appropriate expert advice which it is reasonable for him to seek but a person shall not be fixed with knowledge of a fact ascertainable only with the help of expert advice so long as he has taken all reasonable steps to obtain'). See also ibid 55.

332 FR 52 ('Very often, the victim will acquire such knowledge through a preliminary inquiry ordered by a judge').

333 IT 68.

334 PL 81 ('P should be diligent in own matters and try to find out reliable information about facts essential to the liability for her damage').

335 ZA 46 ('if P could have acquired the knowledge by exercising reasonable care [...] he will be deemed to have such knowledge').

336 ES 48.

337 In the US, where the plaintiff 'does not have sufficient information to know a matter but has a reasonable basis for suspicion, she must conduct an investigation into the facts' (US 73). When 'a plaintiff knows or should know of facts that would lead an ordinarily prudent person to investigate the matter further or inquire into whether actionable conduct was involved', this is considered to be an inquiry notice (ibid 74). 'To avoid inquiry notice ending discovery-rule tolling, it is the plaintiff's burden to show that he either (1) diligently investigated his symptoms or injury and was unable to discover the cause, or (2) that he didn't perform due diligence, but even if he had, the cause of the injury would still have been unknown' (ibid 76).

338 AT 16 ('"Awareness" is also imputed if the victim could easily have learned about all these relevant facts without any noteworthy effort, but still failed to take notice'. However, 'this duty to inquire is not very strict – a layperson typically does not have to hire an expert, for example, in order to find out about all the necessary details, unless special circumstances dictate otherwise'); NL 50 ('If the identity of the liable person is very easy to find out with a simple act of research, the plaintiff may not sit still and cannot call on his subjective not knowing. Some sort of effort to find out who is responsible for the harm can be expected').

In between there are two countries: Germany and Norway. Germany, which applies the relaxed objective test,[339] accordingly imposes a burden of inquiry which is not that light as in Austria and the Netherlands, but is also not as demanding as the reasonable person standard applied in most countries.[340] Norway imposes 'modest' duty to investigate[341] although it applies the ordinary objective standard.[342] 197

c) Case 11 – Analysis and Country Reports

*Chemical plant D negligently exposes bordering lands to toxic substances. As a result P, a nearby resident landowner, contracts a lung disease, but is unaware of the causal link between exposure and disease because his physician fails to detect it. P does not seek a second opinion. After the prescription period runs on the disease P consults his new physician that tells him about the link. Did P's claim against D prescribe?*

*Analysis*: The question here is whether P incurs the burden of seeking 'second opinion' as to the cause of P's harm. If so, the knowledge that could and should have been acquired by this 'second opinion' would be imputed to P and toll the late discovery rule. The more onerous the burden to conduct inquiries is, the more likely it is that failure to seek a second opinion would toll the discovery rule. 198

*Country Reports*: Predictably, the two countries which probably would not impose on P a duty to seek for 'second opinion', and hence would not toll the discovery rule in Case 11, are those who apply the relaxed subjective test: Austria[343] and the Netherlands.[344] No 'second opinion' would be required according to the reporter for Norway, as the duty to investigate is 'modest' 199

339 See *supra* 188.

340 DE 67 ('the claimant need not be sure that, for instance, causation is given; relative certainty suffices. On the other hand, mere first signs and a suspicion of damage do not constitute knowledge. But where the signs have become so serious that a reasonable person would react this is also expected of the victim of the tort').

341 NO 76 ('there must occur such circumstances that makes it "natural" for the victim to try to find out whether or not she has a claim [...] this may be done with a "reasonable effort" [...] Commentators have, based on the practice of the Supreme Court, suggested that the duty to investigate with regard to personal injuries is rather modest. There is support for such a stance also in preparatory works regarding amendments of the prescription act. This tendency has been criticised for undermining the rules on prescription').

342 See *supra* 188.

343 AT 19 ('There is no need for P to question his first doctor's opinion unless there are further objective criteria which have already raised his suspicion that he incurred the disease at his workplace').

344 NL 50 ('the fact that the plaintiff did not seek a second opinion would not preclude the application of the late discovery rule [...] Only when another physician tells him about the link, possibly many years later, will the subjective prescription period start to run. After all there is no subjective awareness and that is the test to be applied according to Dutch law').

despite the objective test applied.[345] The reporter for the US reaches a similar conclusion.[346]

200 Reporters for other countries which apply either the more demanding subjective test or the relaxed or the ordinary objective test, suggest that whether there exists a duty to ask for a 'second opinion' depends on the unspecified circumstances of the case. These countries are E&W,[347] Germany,[348] Greece,[349] Italy,[350] Poland,[351] South Africa[352] and Spain.[353]

201 As to France, in cases of personal injury the discovery rule does not apply. Interestingly, however, the lack of awareness may be considered *force majeure* which corresponds with the discovery rule. If so, the question is whether 'the fact that P did not seek a second opinion fails to meet the reasonable man standard'.[354]

### 5) *Which Rule of Prolongation is and should the Late Discovery be?*

#### a) The Question

202 The late discovery rule as a rule of prolongation may be either a rule of *postponement* or a rule of *suspension*.[355] The difference between postponement

345 NO 76 ('if a doctor, who is not a specialist, concludes that there is nothing wrong with the patient, she is not obliged to seek a second opinion from a specialist') and 77 ('It is not expected that the plaintiff ought to have consulted a specialist').

346 US 77 ('the tolling would begin when P consulted the new physician, who informed P of the causal link').

347 EW 109. See also fn 317 (statutory duty to consult an expert in E&W).

348 DE 68 ('Whether the courts would expect that P seeks a second opinion would depend on the circumstances. If there were clear and serious reasons for P to suspect that there was a causal link between his disease and his employment the courts will probably hold P obliged to seek expert advice on this question. The prescription would then start running at the time when P should have received such correct advice').

349 GR 67 ('The Courts, however, depending on the circumstances [...] might expect that P seeks a second opinion. In such a case, the prescription will start running from the point P should have sought the second opinion').

350 IT 68 ('using ordinary diligence and taking into account the existing scientific knowledge [...] the lack of knowledge has depended on a further circumstance, that is, the doctor's expertise').

351 PL 82 ('There is no clear-cut rule on the need to seek second opinion. The information must come from competent and reliable sources').

352 ZA 46 ('if P could have acquired the knowledge by exercising reasonable care (in seeking a second opinion which could have detected it) he will be deemed to have such knowledge').

353 ES 49 ('As to whether the victim has a burden to ask a second medical opinion, that depends on the circumstances. If for instance an average person would realise that the physician was acting negligently – eg she failed to examine the victim or have any tests done – the victim could be deemed to "know"').

354 FR 53.

355 For the different rules of prolongation see *supra* 33, 156–159. The other two options are making the discovery rule: (a) a rule of *renewal*, but that would unfairly prejudice Ds;

and suspension, as explained,[356] is that postponement may take place only where the prescription period has not yet begun to run, while suspension may also take place after the running began. This difference is usually irrelevant for the discovery rule because once awareness is acquired by P it is not lost later. It follows that the late discovery rule would usually be a rule of postponement. Yet, the discovery rule may also be a rule of suspension. Assume, for example, that the original P had sufficient knowledge about his claim so that the period started to run, but then P died and his heir lacks the necessary awareness. Should the heir's unawareness trigger the discovery rule? If so, then the rule is not just one of postponement but also a rule of suspension.

### b) Analysis

It is suggested that the discovery rule should be a rule of postponement rather than a rule of suspension. As a rule of postponement the discovery rule already opens a significant gap between the prescription period and the effective time of prescription,[357] a gap that increases uncertainty among potential Ds regarding their exposure to potential claims, and may therefore threaten to undermine the goals of prescription law. It is especially so where the unawareness that triggers the rule is governed by the relaxed subjective/objective test of awareness.[358] Making the discovery rule a rule of suspension would aggravate the uncertainty problem. 203

### c) Country Reports

For countries reported as classifying the late discovery rule not as a rule of prolongation but rather as a rule of the starting point (accrual), the discovery rule is by definition a rule of postponement. It postpones the accrual of the cause of action until P gains the required awareness. After accrual no 'disaccrual' can take place if awareness is lost. These countries are Austria, Germany, Greece, Italy, South Africa, Spain and Switzerland.[359] 204

---

(b) a rule of *extension* which guarantees that Ps would have a short but reasonable period to file a claim after awareness is gained, a rule which is less favourable to Ps than a rule of postponement.

356 See *supra* 156.

357 For this gap see *supra* 140 and 160.

358 See *supra* 176–179.

359 See *supra* 130–135. The reporter for Germany notes that 'In cases where the claimant who had actual or imputed knowledge transfers the claim to another person without such knowledge or is succeeded by such a person, the knowledge of the original claimant remains decisive if the prescription period had already begun to run before the transfer or succession' – DE 69.

205 In countries where the late discovery rule is a rule of prolongation it is perceived, in line with the above analysis, as a rule of postponement, not of suspension.[360] Only in Poland is it considered a rule of *extension*.[361]

### 6) *The Scope of the Late Discovery Rule*

#### a) The Question

206 The discovery rule may apply only to selected causes of action, namely, only to some torts, to some kinds of harm (eg bodily injury) or to some kinds of conducts (eg intentional). In contrast it may be applied across the board to all or most causes of action in tort law. So what should be its scope?

#### b) Analysis

207 There are conflicting considerations regarding the adequate scope of the late discovery rule. On the one hand this rule does justice to Ps who are late in filing their actions due to *justified* unawareness of their claim, and that applies to all tort causes of action. On the other hand the rule generates a high degree of uncertainty which negatively affects all *potential* Ds, and therefore may frustrate the certainty goal of prescription law.[362] This concern becomes even greater where awareness is determined by a relaxed subjective/objective test.[363] From this perspective the rule should be limited to kinds of claims where the injustice to Ps absent the rule counterbalances the high price of uncertainty that the rule generates. It may be limited, for example, only to cases of bodily injury.

#### c) Country Reports

208 The late discovery rule has a general application in all tort claims according to reporters for Austria, the Czech Republic, Greece, Italy, Poland, Norway and South Africa.[364] Specific limited exceptions to the general application of the

[360] See CZ 53 (includes the discovery rule with other rules of postponement); EW 75 ('There is no reference to "suspension" in the Limitation Act 1980. This is consistent with the general position under English law that "where an action has once accrued, and the statute has begun to run, there being then a capacity of suing and of being sued, the statute continues to run" unless "ousted […] by a statutory provision"'); FR 53 ('it is quite clear that this rule is only a postponement rule, and not a suspension one. Therefore, if a claim, whose prescription has started to run, is transmitted to a new creditor, who is unaware of its existence or of the elements of it, the latter will not be allowed to rely on the late discovery rule'); NO 61; NL 37; US 69–70; ZA 40.

[361] PL 83. For rules of extension see *supra* 33.

[362] See *supra* 22 and 23.

[363] See *supra* 177–178, 182.

[364] See, respectively: AT 13; CZ 52; GR 62; IT 53; NO 73; ZA 40.

rule are reported for Germany,[365] the Netherlands,[366] Poland,[367] Spain[368] and the US.[369]

Partial application of the discovery rule is reported for other countries. In E&W the rule applies mainly to bodily injury.[370] In France, in contrast, the rule does *not* apply to personal injury, medical liability and environmental damage.[371] 209

## C. OTHER RULES OF PROLONGATION

### 1) *D is to Blame for the Delay – Misleading P, Threatening P and the Like*

#### a) Analysis

Sometimes P's delay to file a claim is caused by D's misconduct: concealments of facts, misleading, threatening, vacuous promises, etc. In such cases there is good reason to prolong the effective time of prescription to allow for the delay, as no legitimate interest of D justifies such conduct against which P deserves the law's protection. To that end a rule of suspension, being more favourable to Ps than rules of postponement or extension, seems appropriate. Suspension should proceed until D's misconduct is ceased and its effect on P is ended. 210

It may be argued that where D's misconduct is by way of deliberate concealing facts or misrepresentation, the late discovery rule already provides for prolongation of the effective time of prescription. Yet, the discovery rule may not suffice here because where P's lack of awareness is caused by D's concealment or misrepresentation, only P's *actual* awareness should toll the prolongation, while in most jurisdictions the late discovery is tolled by *imputed* awareness. 211

Notably, where D's misconduct is the cause of P's delay there are other legal ways, outside prescription law, to prevent D from raising the defence (eg 'promissory estoppel') or dismiss D's defence (for example for lack of good faith). Yet, these 212

365 DE 57 (rule does not apply to intentional torts).

366 NL 35 (rule does not apply to damage caused by a criminal offence).

367 PL 37 (rule does not apply to intentional torts).

368 ES 35 (rule does not apply to defamation).

369 US 64 ('Courts, generally, have embraced the discovery rule across most tort claims [...] However, there are specific courts for specific types of claims that have declined to adopt a discovery rule').

370 EW 70, 81 (the rule applies to 'actions in respect of personal injuries following negligence, nuisance or breach of duty; action in respect of defective products [...]; actions by a deceased's estate and actions under the Fatal Accidents legislation [...] and actions in respect of latent damage not involving personal injuries').

371 FR 44. The reporters for Switzerland note that the rule is an exception which applies 'to some (short) prescription periods'– CH 48.

alternative ways do not always cover the whole range of misconducts that justify a prolongation, and a designated explicit provision specific to prescription law is preferable.

b) Country Reports

213 Determined protection of Ps from deliberate concealment and misrepresentation by Ds that caused delays in filing is provided in E&W by the Limitation Act 1980: (a) by a special rule of postponement that lasts until *actual* discovery by P;[372] (b) by authorising courts to disapply the defence in cases of personal injury.[373]

214 Greece applies a special rule of *extension* where D intentionally prevents P from pursuing the claim,[374] and so does the Netherlands in cases of deliberate concealment.[375]

215 Italy and South Africa apply a rule of *postponement* until *actual, subjective*, discovery of the facts concealed or mispresented.[376]

216 In other countries general doctrines outside prescription law are employed. The doctrine of 'abuse of right' is used to reject the prescription defence, where D improperly caused the delay, in Belgium,[377] the Czech Republic,[378] Poland[379] and Switzerland.[380] Germany uses the 'lack of good faith' for the same purpose.[381]

372 EW 83 ('Parliament was unambiguous as to the fact that deliberate concealment on the defendant's part at the time the cause of action accrues postpones the running of time').

373 Ibid ('a claimant can petition the court to disapply the ordinary time limit' on the basis of 'the conduct of the defendant after the cause of action arose, including the extent (if any) to which he responded to requests reasonably made by the plaintiff for information or inspection for the purpose of ascertaining facts which were or might be relevant to the plaintiff's cause of action against the defendant').

374 GR 68.

375 NL 52.

376 IT 71; ZA 41.

377 BE 34. See also BE 26 ('the principle of good faith may in some cases prevent a party to pursue performance or to file a lawsuit even though the statute of limitation has not expired. This will be the case if the plaintiff exercises his right after he gave the false impression that he would not exercise his right').

378 CZ 54 ('Depending on the specific situation, specifically on the nature of the misconduct, the problems are resolved based on the prohibition of abuse of right or by the mechanism of good morals').

379 PL 84.

380 CH 53 ('If, however, the defendant (intentionally or involuntarily) induced the plaintiff to refrain from proceeding within the prescription period or from taking the adequate measures to interrupt the prescription, then the court may qualify the calling of the expiry of the prescription period by the defendant as an abuse of law and disregard it').

381 DE 70 ('If the debtor made the creditor believe that the defence would not be raised and the creditor in reliance omitted to take legal action and the debtor then raises the defence, according to §242 BGB the court must disregard the defence because such behaviour offends the principle of good faith'). See also DE 84.

In the US the doctrines of 'equitable estoppel' and 'fraudulent concealment' are used.[382] In France the prescription period may also be suspended where D's misconduct amounts to *force majeure* from P's perspective.[383]

In Norway[384] and Spain[385] no special rules are employed to protect Ps. Protection of Ps from deliberate concealment and misrepresentation is provided only by the discovery rule. 217

*2) Admission by D of P's Right or Partial Performance of P's Right by D*

Admission by D of P's right, or partial performance of it, may be considered as *a creation of a new cause of action* (*de novo*),[386] which originates in D's admission or partial performance, and as such justify a rule of *renewal* (*interruption*) – the period starts to run afresh on the 'new' cause of action.[387] 218

This reasoning, however, is embedded with difficulties, such as the following. To start with, the admission may be accompanied by D's statement that the obligation to P was fulfilled. Secondly, partial performance may mean not only that D considers it to be the first payment of the entire alleged debt (which justifies a renewal), but also that D denies the rest of the alleged obligation (which does not justify renewal).[388] Thirdly, where there are many Ps or Ds it is difficult to determine whether admission by D1 to P1 also applies to other Ds and Ps.[389] Along the same line, where P has many claims against D it is unclear whether admission of one claim applies to other claims (whether they belong to the same cause of action). Finally, that D admitted her obligation to P should encourage P to file the claim in time as it eases the burden of proof, not to prolong the effective time of prescription by renewal. It is therefore doubtful whether admission or partial performance justify prolongation, especially by way of renewal. 219

---

382 'Equitable estoppel tolling prevents the defendant from employing the statute of limitations defence when that defendant took active steps to prevent the plaintiff from suing in a timely manner' – US 79. As opposed to fraudulent concealment, 'equitable estoppel may apply even when the defendant's conduct was unintentionally deceptive' – US 80.

383 FR 55.

384 NO 81.

385 ES 50.

386 Admission 'as the creation of a new obligation' – DE 71.

387 Admission or partial payment not within the prescription period but *after* P's claim has already prescribed may: (a) be considered 'as a waiver of the prescription defence' – AT 69; (b) restore the prescribed claim – CZ 56; or (c) have no effect.

388 See, eg AT 68; DE 73; ES 51.

389 See, eg AT 70 ('in the case of multiple tortfeasors, the fact that one of them admitted liability does not impact upon the prescription of the claims against the others').

220 Despite the above difficulties, admission/partial performance result in renewal/interruption of the running of the prescription period in the reported jurisdictions.[390] In the US, though, '[a]dmission by D of P's right [...] does not toll the statute of limitations. Partial performance, however, has been recognised as a basis for tolling'.[391]

### 3) *Special Relations between D and P*

#### a) Analysis

221 Where the reason behind P's delay in filing an action against D are special relations between D and P, and such delays are considered justified given the nature of the relations and their effects, rules of prolongation may and should be called for to prolong the effective time of prescription in order to protect Ps.

222 There are two major kinds of such special relations: relations of *trust/loyalty* and relations of *dependency*.

223 Special relations of *trust/loyalty* (meaning that D owes P duties of trust/loyalty) exist mainly between: trustee and beneficiary; agent and principal; attorney and clients; partners in partnerships; directors/officers and their corporations; administrator of an estate and the heirs; liquidator in bankruptcy and the creditors. Given the nature of these relations and the duties owed by D to P (contractual or statutory), P has no reason to suspect that D commits a tort against her, thereby breaching D's duties and frustrating P's legitimate expectations. Therefore, a special rule of discovery may be required, a rule which suspends the running of the prescription period as long as P has no *actual subjective knowledge* that D breached her duties of trust/loyalty to P.[392]

224 Special relations of *dependency* exist mainly between parents and offspring; spouses; custodian/guardian and ward; employer and employee; physicians and patients. In such relations P may be reluctant to file an action against D fearing a negative reaction from D that may harm P who depends on D. Therefore, a special rule of suspension that suspends the running of the prescription period as long as dependency exists, or at least a rule of extension,[393] may be required to protect Ps.

---

390 AT 68; BE 35; CH 54; DE 70; ES 51; FR 56; GR 69; IT 72; NO 82; NL 53; PL 85; ZA 48. Acknowledgement also triggers renewal for claims against the EU – EU 37.

391 US 81.

392 Such a *specific* rule of discovery is more favourable to Ps than the *general* rule of discovery as it does not impute awareness to Ps and is a rule of suspension rather than a rule of postponement.

393 A rule that guarantees that P will have a sufficient but minimal period of time to sue P after dependency is over.

## b) Country Reports

Most jurisdictions apply some rules of prolongation to some kinds of special relations between P and D. However, as clearly indicted by the table below,[394] the overall impression is of a multifaceted picture with no clear pattern. There are diverse approaches as to: which special relationships justify a rule of prolongation,[395] how general or specific the rule should be, and whether it should be rule of postponement, suspension or of extension. 225

**Table 1. Rules of Prolongation Applied to Special Relations**

| Relations | Rule of suspension | Extension | No prolongation |
|---|---|---|---|
| Parents/children | AT, CH, DE, FR, GR, IT, PL | NO | BE, CZ, ES, US, ZA |
| Spouses | AT, BE, CH, CZ, DE, FR, GR, IT, PL, ZA | NL, NO | ES, US |
| Guardian/ward | AT, BE, CZ, DE, FR, GR, IT, PL, ZA | NL, NO | ES, US |
| Attorney/client | | | AT, BE, CH DE, ES, FR, GR, IT, NL, NO, PL, US, ZA |
| Partners in partnership | AT, DE and FR (registered partnership) CH, NO, ZA | | BE, CZ, ES, GR,IT, NL, PL, US |
| Legal entity/ organs | IT, ZA | NO, NL | AT, BE, CH, CZ, DE, ES,FR, GR, PL, US |
| Administrator/ heirs | IT, ZA | GR, NL | AT, BE, CH, CZ, DE; ESP, FR, NO, PL, US |
| Liquidator/ debtors | ZA | NL, NO | AT, BE, CH, CZ, DE, ES, FR, GR, IT, PL, US |
| Employer/ employee | BE, ZA, GR | | AT, CH,[396] CZ, DE, ES, FR, IT, NL, NO, PL, US |
| Physician/ patient | GR | | BE, CH, CZ, AT, DE, ES, FR, IT, NL, NO PL US, ZA |

### 4) *P's Lack of Legal Capacity*

## a) Analysis

P may lack the mental abilities to handle her legal matters either being a minor, or due to unsound mind. Do these disabilities justify a rule of prolongation 226

394 Where the relevant relations are listed to the left and the existence of special rules are presented in the other columns.

395 In Spain, for example, no rules of prolongation are applied on special relationships, although theorists suggest that the law should be changed in this direction, especially with regard to family relations – ES 52. In the US, for another example, legal relations between D and P are no grounds for prolongation – US 82.

396 There is a special rule of suspension for employees living in the same household as the employer – CH 46.

such as suspension during disability or extension of the prescription period after disability ends? An important factor in this regard is whether P has a legal representative who is supposed to take care of P's legal affairs. Without such a representative the case for rules of prolongation is stronger than where P has a legal representative. Yet, even where P has a legal representative, rules of prolongation may be justified if there are concerns that the representative would fail to protect P's interests. In this regard it seems impossible to generalise as to whether 'natural' representatives (mainly parents) provide better or worse protection of P's interests than a non-family appointed representative.

227 There are differences in this regard between minors and adults with unsound mind. Minors usually have 'natural' representatives – their parents – which are usually also their legal representatives. Adults with unsound minds may have no representative or have a legally appointed representative who is not necessarily a relative. Another difference is that P's minority and its relevant length (from the starting point to majority) are evident, while it is much more difficult to determine whether P suffers from unsound mind and the beginning and end of this disability.

b) Country Reports

228 Like the diversity of prolongation rules applying to 'special relations' between P and D, rules of prolongation that apply to claims of minors and of the mentally disabled also differ substantially among jurisdictions.

229 Reported as least favourable to Ps are Spain and Switzerland, which do not protect minors or mentally disabled Ps by rules of prolongation.[397] Ps whose claim has prescribed may have a claim against the person who failed to appoint a representative or against a representative who failed to sue in time.[398]

230 Reported as most favourable to Ps are Belgium, France and South Africa which apply rules of postponement or even suspension during minority or mental disability regardless of whether P has a legal representative or not.[399] In the US

---

397 ES 55–59 (no rules of prolongation apply to minors or mentally disabled Ps regardless of whether they had a representative or not); CH 56 ('Minority does not influence prescription. The question whether a minor has a legal representative or not is not relevant for prescription').

398 See, eg ES ibid.

399 BE 45–46 (but with regard to minors, suspension does not apply to specific short periods); FR 59 ('Unemancipated minors or adults in tutorship [...] (due to their limited or reduced intellectual faculties) therefore enjoy a suspension or postponement of prescription as long as they remain under this special status, even though they always have a legal representative'); ZA 50.

as well some jurisdictions apply rules of prolongation although Ps have legal representatives.[400]

231 None of the other jurisdictions apply rules of prolongation where P had a legal representative, with the specific exception of the Netherlands and Poland which apply rules of suspension or extension to personal injuries suffered by minors *even if they had legal representatives.*[401]

232 Where P has no legal representative (frequently Ps who are mentally disabled[402]), almost all countries apply rules of prolongation which vary in their application, mixture and length.

233 Austria and the Czech Republic apply, where P has no legal representative, a rule of postponement if the prescription period has not yet started to run, but a rule of extension if its running has begun.[403] The prescription period starts to run (in case of postponement) or is extended from the date P reached majority/ gains capacity or from the date a representative is appointed.[404]

234 Germany, Greece and Italy apply a rule of extension that extends the prescription period up to six months after the entry of majority, the end of the mental handicap or the institution of a representative.[405] E&W and Norway apply a rule of postponement.[406] In the US some jurisdictions apply rules of postponement and some apply rules of extension.[407]

### c) A Note on Harmonisation – The *De Lege Ferenda*

235 Balancing the need to protect Ps who are minors or mentally disabled on the one hand and the goals of prescription law on the other hand, and taking into account the prevalent arrangements in the reported countries in this regard, it appears that the following unification can and should take place. Firstly, no prolongation should apply where P has a legal representative, with a possible exception where P is a minor who suffers bodily injury. Secondly, in the absence of a representative, a 'generous' rule of extension should apply. 'Generous' in this regard means extension of the prescription period up to two or three years after P reaches majority or gains full capacity or after the appointment of a representative.

---

400 US 85.

401 NL 55 (otherwise no rules of prolongation apply to minors or the mentally disabled); PL 85.

402 Minors are usually represented by their parents. In Norway, for example, all minors have legal representatives – NO 89–90.

403 For Austria see AT 61 (the extension period is up to two years). For the Czech Republic see CZ 59 (the extension period is up to one year).

404 Ibid. In Austria, the estate of a deceased is a legal person in need of a representative – AT 62.

405 DE 86-88; GR 75–77; IT 74. In Poland the extension is up to two years – PL 85.

406 EW 90–93 (with a prescription period of six years after postponement ends); NO 89–90.

407 US 83–84.

### 5) *Absence of Parties from the Jurisdiction*

#### a) Analysis

236 D's absence from the jurisdiction, a cause of delay not in P's sphere, may justify a rule of prolongation if such absence renders the filing of a claim by P pointless due to inability to serve the claim or to conduct any meaningful litigation. This may be the case, for example, where D is in a country which is in a state of war with P's country. The prolongation may be by way of suspension or by way of extension.

237 In contrast, P's absence from the jurisdiction, a cause of delay which is usually in P's sphere, may justify a rule of prolongation only in those rare cases where P's absence is involuntary and/or in special circumstances that justify prolongation (for example when being a political prisoner in another country). In this regard a rule of extension, if at all, seems adequate.

#### b) Country Reports

238 In most countries the absence of D and/or P from jurisdiction does not trigger a rule of prolongation.

239 In Austria absence of P *for public service* (eg serving as an ambassador or a soldier) triggers a rule of suspension.[408] A similar but more restricted rule applies in Italy where P serves in the military in times of war.[409]

240 Absence of D from the jurisdiction may trigger a rule of suspension in Germany ('if there are additional circumstances which make it impossible for the plaintiff to pursue the claim in time'),[410] in the US[411] and in South Africa.[412] Norway applies a rule of extension (up to one year) after D's return to the country.[413]

### 6) *Former Proceedings between the Parties – Legal and Other*

#### a) Analysis

241 Where P's belated claim against D (X) was already litigated in court against D in the past (within the prescription period), and this past litigation ended with

408 AT 55.
409 IT 75.
410 DE 89.
411 US 87.
412 ZA 51.
413 NO 93.

no binding decision (no *res judicata*), a rule of prolongation for claim X may be considered justified.[414] The past litigation of claim X testifies (a) that P did not sit idle and (b) that D became aware, within the prescription period, of P's determination to sue for X. The same applies where P's later claim (Y) differs in some respects from the claim litigated in the past (X), but both claims belong to the same cause of action.[415] The rule may be one of suspension (period does not run during the past proceedings) or one of extension (securing sufficient time for P to sue for X or Y after the past proceedings ended).

For the same reasons, where P filed a claim for X within the prescription period, and during the ongoing proceeding wishes to add claim Y by amending the statement of claim, P should be allowed to do so if X and Y belong to the same cause of action. 242

Is it justified to apply such a rule of prolongation where past proceedings were not before a court but rather ADR proceedings or administrative proceeding? That may depend on how quasi-judicial ADR proceedings are perceived in the jurisdiction. Anyhow, a rule of extension seems more appropriate then a rule of suspension. The case for a prolongation in case of settlement negotiations seems weaker as these are not quasi-judicial proceedings. 243

### b) Country Reports

Former proceedings before authorised *courts*[416] regarding the same cause of action,[417] trigger, according to most reports, rules of renewal in some countries[418] rules of suspension in other countries,[419] and also a rule of extension.[420] At least with regard to suspension, it begins with the initiation of judicial proceedings[421] and ends with the end of these judicial proceedings, or six months later.[422] In the 244

---

414 As explained in the Austrian report, although filing of a claim within the prescription period 'interrupts' prescription in the sense that the defence cannot be raised, it is so 'only if the action is pursued in an ordinary manner,' but if 'the claimant is unsuccessful or fails to pursue the action properly, the (original) prescription period […] will continue to run […] since the interrupting effect of the filing is thereby retroactively invalidated' – AT 71.

415 See the discussion of the broadness of cause of action in Section VI.B.

416 The effect of mistakenly filing actions in unauthorised courts is not discussed here.

417 Which ended with no final ruling (no *res judicata*).

418 ES 63; FR 62 ('Proceedings between the parties that have not resulted in *res judicata* therefore lead to a renewal of the prescription period, with the new delay starting to run as of the end of these proceedings'). The prescription period is also suspended if a judge issues a measure of inquiry – FR 63; GR 79–81 (renewal from the end of proceedings unless the P abandons the action or it is dismissed not on the merit and P fails to file within six months); IT 76; PL 86.

419 DE 92; NO 95 (but no prolongation after the passage of three years from the end of former litigation).

420 CH 60–61 (only in some specified procedures before a court); US 89.

421 See *infra* 332–334 (regarding what is considered initiation of proceedings).

422 DE 92.

Netherlands, though, no rule of prolongation applies where former litigation ends without a final ruling.[423]

245 Former *ADR* proceedings (including arbitration) trigger (with regard to a later claim): rules of *renewal* in Italy, Poland and Spain;[424] combined rules of *suspension* and *extension* in Belgium, France and Germany;[425] rule of *postponement* in Norway and South Africa;[426] rules of *extension* in Austria and E&W.[427]

246 Only in a few countries are *negotiations* between the parties toward a settlement considered as justifying prolongation. The Czech Republic, Germany and Spain apply a rule of suspension,[428] and Austria and E&W apply rules of extension.[429,430]

### 7) *Victim's Death and Bankruptcy*

#### a) Analysis

247 Where the victim (V) of D's tortious conduct dies before a claim is filed, and most of the prescription period had already run on the claim, the prescription period may expire before the heirs (estate) are able to file the claim, as the transmission of V's estate to them takes time.[431] A rule of prolongation may therefore be deemed justified, either suspension during the legal proceedings required for the transmission of the estate or a rule of extension up to a period that would enable the heirs to prepare an action against D. Otherwise 'it may happen that an heir acquires the inheritance and prescription has taken place between the death and the acceptation of the inheritance'.[432]

248 Similar considerations may apply where P is bankrupt, and it takes some time for the liquidator to learn about P's unfiled actions.

---

423 NL 58.

424 IT 76; PL 86; ES 63.

425 BE 50; FR 64; DE 94–95. In both countries the extension (after ADR ends) is up to six months.

426 NO 96; ZA 56. In the Netherlands no prolongation rule applies to ADR proceedings subject to specific exceptions – NL 59.

427 AT 59 (extension up to 18 months in special ADR procedures regarding medical liability cases); EW 107 (extension in case of cross-border disputes).

428 CZ 62; DE 96 (suspension during negotiations and also extension up to three month after their end); ES 66.

429 AT 63 (extension up to three months); EW 99 (extension up to four months if the court issues a protective writ).

430 There are also some specific rules of prolongation for claims such as claims against insurers (AT 58, 64), claims against the State (CZ 63–64) and claims brought before administrative boards.

431 The claim of the *dependants* which differs from that of the *heirs* (see, eg US 91) is discussed *infra* 315–320.

432 ES 68.

### b) Country Reports

It is reported that most jurisdictions do not apply rules of prolongation in favour of V's heirs (the estate), despite the inability or difficulties that they may face after V's death in suing D (having to wait for the appointment of a representative or until the transmission of the estate, or finding out that V had a mature claim against D). Jurisdictions who do so mostly do it by rules of *extension* that allow for a sufficient time for the heirs to sue after the difficulties can be overcome (appointment of representative, the actual transmission of the estate, etc).[433] The discovery rule, if applied to successors of V,[434] may also be used for prolongation.[435] 249

As to P's bankruptcy, almost no reports mention rules of prolongation that favour P's creditors. The Greece report, though, refers to a rule of renewal in this regard.[436] 250

## 8) *Other Contingencies*

### a) Analysis

Contingencies other than the above may also be considered as justifying prolongation in some jurisdictions (but not necessarily in others). They may be either statutory (specified in the statute of prescription) or recognised by courts under general concepts such as *force majeure*, concepts that may be interpreted either broadly (long list of contingencies) or narrowly (short list). The prolongation may be by way of postponement, suspension, extension or renewal. Some contingencies (such as closed courts) justify prolongation only if they occur at the end of the prescription period.[437] The list of 'other' contingencies that may justify prolongation is long and includes natural disasters, wars, closed courts, P's military service, P's imprisonment, P's illness, legal inability to sue, P's financial or evidential difficulties. 251

Analytically, prolongation is more justified with regard to contingencies that are public and evident (such as natural disasters, pandemics like the coronavirus, wars or closed courts). It is so because potential Ds can expect delays when these contingencies occur. Not so with regard to '[p]roblems within the claimant's own 252

---

[433] AT 62, 83 (extension up to two years); CZ 66 (six months); DE 97–98 (six months); EW 66 (three years from the date of death or the date of the personal representative's knowledge, whichever is the later); GR 86 (six months); US 92 (only in some states); ZA 53 (one year).

[434] See *supra* 125.

[435] NO 103.

[436] GR 87.

[437] See, eg CZ 68, GR 88.

sphere […], such as a temporary illness that does not affect her capacity, lack of resources to pursue the claim, difficulties with gathering evidence or the like'.[438] Prolongation in such personal contingencies generates a high degree of uncertainty which may frustrate the goals of prescription law.[439] P's financial or evidential difficulties, for example, do not justify prolongation.[440]

b) Country Reports

253 The broadest characterisation of these 'other' contingencies under a general formula is in French law which provides that prescription 'does not run or is suspended against one for whom it is impossible to act following an obstacle resulting from the law, from an agreement, or from force majeure'.[441] In Greece, for another example,[442] '*force majeure* is defined (as) any unforeseeable event, which renders the pursuing of the claim impossible, even though the utmost care and diligence has been demonstrated'.[443] In contrast, in Spain '[s]uspension of prescription is therefore a very exceptional phenomenon, which takes place only in the cases provided for by the legislature under unusual circumstances'.[444] A middle ground can be found in Belgium where on the one hand in principle '*force majeure* does not lead to suspension of prescription outside the statutory cases of suspension', but on the other hand 'the highest courts in Belgium seem willing to accept *force majeure* as a ground for postponement of time limits'.[445]

254 All in all, country reports testify that the 'other' contingencies to which prolongation applies and its kind (postponement, suspension, extension, renewal) vary across the different jurisdictions. These contingencies are enumerated in the country reports.[446] It is difficult to explain the major differences in this regard among the different jurisdictions, for example, why unexpected natural disasters justify prolongation in one jurisdiction but not

---

438 AT 72.

439 See *supra* 25.

440 Yet, personal contingencies such as financial or evidential difficulties may be taken into account in E&W where the court is authorised to disapply the defence of prescription by its discretion – EW 109–111.

441 FR 65 (citing art 2234 of the Civil Code).

442 GR 88–93.

443 GR 88. It applies to natural disasters, wars, sudden imprisonment and closed courts, but not to long imprisonment or military service.

444 ES 70–77. It applies to wars and legal inability to sue but not to military service.

445 BE 55. In addition, 'in principle prescription is suspended in any case where someone is hindered by law to exercise one's rights' – BE 58.

446 In Germany, for example, *force majeure* (as a rule of suspension) includes unforeseeable natural disasters, legal impediments to file a claim, closed courts, sudden illness at the end of the period and imprisonment – DE 101–107. See also CH 65; ES 70–77; EW 96; IT 79–80; NL 61; NO 105–108; PL 88; US 95–100; ZA 54.

in another.[447] Obviously, harmonization of the law in this regard would be a very challenging task …

# IX. CEILINGS ON THE EFFECTIVE TIME OF PRESCRIPTION

## A. THE ROLE AND ORIGINS OF THE UPPER TIME LIMIT – THE FOURTH ELEMENT

Rules of postponement, suspension, renewal and extension, which prolong the effective time of prescription,[448] may prolong it for many years, for decades or even forever, thereby limiting the scope and effect of the prescription defence or practically annulling it. This is especially so with regard to the late discovery rule, the major rule of prolongation, particularly when the relaxed version of the subjective test for awareness is applied. Under this version, which imposes a light burden of inquiry upon P,[449] a claim may actually become 'prescription-proof' despite P's unjustified failure to acquire awareness of her mature claim against D. For another example of an unreasonable prolongation, if P claims that she was harmed at birth by D's negligence, and the running of time is postponed until majority (18), and the prescription period is six years, the effective time of prescription would be 24 years after birth! 255

Obviously, prolongation to such an extent can undermine the goals of prescription law.[450] As to *potential* Ds, the largest group protected by prescription law, such prolongation may generate a very high degree of uncertainty regarding risks of distant future claims, resulting in high costs of evidence preservation and 'frozen' financial reserves to meet these menacing future claims. Insurance premiums may also skyrocket. As to *actual* Ds, if sued after decades, their ability to defend against baseless ('bad') claims would be substantially reduced. The public interests in certainty, fairness and adequate functioning of the judiciary may also be offended. 256

To reduce these negative effects of unchecked prolongation, restoring a reasonable degree of certainty, the law of prescription may apply an 'upper time limit', a '*ceiling period*'.[451] Under this limit a claim prescribes after the ceiling is reached even if the prescription period has not yet lapsed because 257

---

447 Compare DE 101 (prolongation) with BE 57 and ES 71 (no prolongation).

448 See *supra* 29–34.

449 See *supra* 177.

450 For these goals see Section IV.

451 Also referred to as 'long-stop' or 'overriding time limit' – see *supra* 34.

of rules of prolongation.[452] If the ceiling, for example, is 15 years, D's claim, in the above case of harm caused at birth, would prescribe 15 years after birth rather than after 24 years. Such an upper time limit reduces uncertainty and its negative effects, not only protecting potential and actual Ds but also promoting collective interests.

258 Being a balancing factor vis-à-vis rules of prolongation (in particular vis-à-vis the late discovery rule[453]), the upper time limit should in principle be a part of a 'package' composed of three parts: (a) rules of prolongation (the discovery rule in particular); (b) shortened prescription periods given the effect of rules of prolongation; (c) upper time limit on the potential of rules of prolongation to unreasonably prolong the effective time of prescription. In this role and context the upper time limit ('ceiling'/'long-stop'/'repose') functions, and is rightly perceived, as the independent fourth element of prescription, and not as an alternative, second-layer, prescription period which belongs to the second element.

259 Yet, in some reports the upper time limit is conceived of as being a second-layer prescription period which, in comparison with the first layer of the prescription period,[454] is 'objective' rather than 'subjective' and 'long' rather than 'short'. As explained,[455] this distinction between 'objective' (long) prescription periods and 'subjective' (short) prescription periods may be confusing and better be avoided. The limits on the effective time of prescription, which counter-balance unchecked prolongation, are in fact and in theory not prescription periods (the second element of prescription) but upper time limits (the fourth element of prescription).

260 That the major aim of the upper time limits, under all its names, is to counter-balance the negative effect of unchecked prolongation, mainly to restore or secure some certainty, should serve as major guide in the design of this of this element of prescription. There are five aspects to this design of the upper time

452 Another way to avoid uncertainty that may last forever (*ad infinitum*) due to rules of prolongation, is to grant Ds who are exposed to this uncertainty a 'declaration of no liability'. This unique technique is used in E&W in cases of severe disability of Ps (EW 94).

453 See BE 60 (the long period (ceiling) is 'a counter-balance' for the discovery rule). 'Such long-stops can be found in about all legal systems embracing, either partially or completely, what has been termed "subjective" prescription regime. They are in fact one of the defining features of a modern prescription regime'– *Zimmermann and Kleinschmidt, supra* fn 2, 49.

454 See, eg AT 73 (referring to the upper time limit as 'alternative prescription periods'); BE 60 ('no "ceiling periods" […] It is more accurate to describe the Belgian system as a two tier system […] a relative period of limitation and an absolute 20 years period of limitation'); BE 25 ('claims are subject to a double statute of limitation […] a relative […] as well as a so-called absolute'); GR 17, 96 (no 'ceiling' but an additional prescription period of 20 years); NL 62 ('In Dutch law, the objective prescription period functions as a "ceiling period"').

455 See *supra* 144–146.

limit: the scope of its application; date of its commencement; the length of the time limit; the application of rules of prolongation (if any); and its effect on the prescribed claim. All these aspects are discussed below.

## B. DIFFERENT ASPECTS OF THE UPPER TIME LIMIT

### 1) *Scope*

#### a) Analysis

The major aim of the upper time limit where it exists – to restore or secure some certainty for Ds to mitigate the uncertainty generated by rules of prolongation – is relevant in principle to all kinds of causes of action where rules of prolongation create such uncertainty, especially the late discovery rule. It follows that the causes of action to which rules of prolongation do not apply do not require upper time limits. Non-application of upper time limits may also be justified in cases in which the risk of damage remains latent for a very long period and public policy considerations justify allowing tort claims once these risks materialise, despite the passage of a very long time since D's tortious conduct. Latent diseases caused by exposure to hazardous materials or latent defects in the foundations of buildings and bridges are prominent examples.[456] The case for excluding any bodily injury from the scope of the upper time limit is much weaker. Such a broad exception may conflict with the rule's goal of providing minimal certainty to potential Ds. 261

#### b) Country Reports[457]

General application of the upper time limit on tort claims is reported for Austria, Germany and Greece.[458] Some specific exceptions to the limit's general application are reported for Norway.[459] A major exception to the upper time limit application – the exclusion of bodily injury from its scope of application – is 262

[456] See, eg *Howald Moor v Switzerland*, ECHR 069 (2014) (acknowledging that the systematic application of the prescription defence 'to persons suffering from diseases which could not be diagnosed until many years after the triggering events deprived those persons of the chance to assert their rights before the courts').

[457] For the scope of application of the upper time limit see *Zimmermann and Kleinschmidt, supra* fn 2, 48–56.

[458] AT 73; DE 109; GR 69.

[459] NO 109, 112 (excluding personal injury caused by businesses to employees and personal injury to a minor).

reported for the Czech Republic, France, Netherlands and Poland.[460] Restricted application of the limit is reported for E&W and for Spain.[461] The upper time limit does not exist in Italy, South Africa and Switzerland.[462] In the US the scope of the limit's application varies among the different states from non-application to a general limit for negligence claims.[463]

### 2) *Commencement*

#### a) Analysis

263 As the major aim of the upper time limit is to restore or secure some certainty for *potential* Ds, it is preferable that this limit should start running from a point in time known to or ascertainable by potential Ds. The starting point of *the prescription period* (date of accrual of cause of action) does not meet this requirement: usually this starting point is the occurrence of harm to P, and a potential D is often unaware and may not be aware of P's harm or even of P's existence. It therefore appears that the running of the upper time limit should commence on the date of D's tortious conduct,[464] a date which is known to potential Ds or can be ascertained by them.[465] For example, in product liability cases while the prescription period starts to run (unless postponed) from the date P was harmed by the product (accrual), the upper time limit should better run from the day the product was marketed by D. In cases of medical treatment causing harm later on, the starting point of the prescription period is the occurrence of harm, but the upper time limit should better start to run on the date of the medical treatment. That the running of the upper time limit starts prior to the starting point of the prescription period (accrual), namely, before P can file a claim, poses no real difficulty if this limit is long enough, as discussed below.[466]

---

460 CZ 71; FR 66; NL 32, 62 ('there is no longer a prescription period for undiscovered damage that is the result of injury or death' – ibid 65. The Dutch Supreme Court decided 'that under certain circumstances it is contrary to the principles of reasonableness and fairness to invoke the objective prescription period of 20 or 30 years' – ibid 66); PL 65.

461 EW 115 (only for latent damage not involving personal injury); ES 78 ('such ceiling rules are alien to the Spanish legal culture and result from the influence of international conventions or European Directives only').

462 IT 82; ZA 56; CH 67 (although there are 'forfeiture deadlines' for some tort claims).

463 US 101 ('Statutes of repose have been passed in some states relating to claims for products liability […] against those making improvements to real estate […] for medical malpractice, and generally for negligence').

464 As to the date of commencement where D's conduct is *continuous* see the discussion of continuous tort *supra* Section VI.E.

465 The same conclusion is reached by *Zimmermann and Kleinschmidt*, *supra* fn 2, 62–63.

466 See *infra* 266.

### b) Country Reports

In conformity with the above analysis, in most of the reported jurisdictions the day of commencement – the day from which the upper time limit starts to run – is the day of D's tortious conduct. These jurisdictions are Belgium, E&W, Germany, Greece, Netherlands, Norway, Poland and the US.[467] As the day of D's conduct often precedes the day it caused P's harm, and as P's harm is a pre-condition to the accrual of P's cause of action, the running of the upper time limit on P's claim may commence, *or even end*, before P's cause of action accrues.[468] 264

Only in the Czech Republic, and probably in Austria and France, does the upper time limit start to run from the day of harm occurrence.[469] 265

### 3) *Length*

### a) Analysis

The upper time limit, especially when it commences to run with D's conduct and not with the harm caused by it, may lead to the prescription of P's claim before the expiry of the prescription period,[470] and in some cases to prescription before the latter has started to run,[471] or even before P's cause of action accrues.[472] Therefore, to avoid injustice to Ps, the length of the upper time limit should be significant. It may also change with the nature of the claim. For example, the length may be shorter for claims regarding pure economic loss or property damage and longer for bodily injury. The relevant range seems to be between ten years and 30 years.[473] Shorter limits may bar meritorious ('good') claims,[474] while longer limits would fail to achieve the major goal of the upper time limit of securing minimal degree of certainty to potential Ds. 266

---

467 BE 60; EW 115; DE 110; GR 96; NL 32, 62; NO 110; PL 90; US 102 ('The critical feature of statutes of repose is that they begin to run at a time other than when the claim accrues […] In the case of medical malpractice, it would be at the time of the negligent act by the physician').

468 See, eg US 102 ('Because these events occur before any claim has accrued, they can bar claims before the victim has been injured').

469 AT 63; CH 67; FR 67 (time counts starts with 'the birth of the right')

470 Because of the operation of rules of prolongation.

471 For example, where P did not or could not discover that she has a mature claim.

472 Where no harm was yet caused (latent diseases or latent defects in constructions).

473 See *Zimmermann and Kleinschmidt*, *supra* fn 2, 30 ('long-stop of between ten and thirty years may be chosen').

474 See *supra* 17.

b) Country Reports

267 In Belgium, France, Greece, the Netherlands and Norway the length of the upper time limit is 20 years.[475] In other countries the time range is between ten to 30 years and the length varies not only among countries but also within countries, depending on the cause of action. A general limit of 30 years applies in Austria,[476] while a general period of ten years applies in the Czech Republic[477] and Poland.[478] In E&W the time limit is 15 years,[479] in Germany between ten and 30 years.[480] The upper time limit also varies between jurisdictions in the US.[481]

*4) Applying Rules of Prolongation?*

a) Analysis

268 Since the basic idea behind the upper time limit is to counterbalance and mitigate the uncertainty generated by rules of prolongation, it would obviously be self-defeating to apply these rules of prolongation to the upper time limit.[482] Yet, it makes much sense to subject the upper time limit to one rule of prolongation: suspension or extension where D's misconduct is the cause of P's delay.[483] D should not be allowed to rip the fruits of misconduct aimed to bar P's claim.

b) Country Reports

269 In conformity with the above analysis, rules of prolongation usually[484] do not apply to the upper time limit rule in the Czech Republic, France, Norway

---

475 BE 60; FR 67; GR 96; NL 32, 62 (30 years for harm caused by pollution and hazardous materials). Notably, 'there is no longer a prescription period for undiscovered damage that is the result of injury or death' – ibid 65. The Dutch Supreme Court decided 'that under certain circumstances it is contrary to the principles of reasonableness and fairness to invoke the objective prescription period of twenty years' – ibid 66; NO 109.

476 AT 73 (but only ten years for state liability).

477 CZ 71 (15 years for intentional torts).

478 PL 90 (20 years for 'criminal' torts).

479 EW 115.

480 DE 111.

481 US 101.

482 See, eg FR 66 ('Article 2232, 1st §, of the code civil now provides: "The deferral of the starting point, the suspension or the interruption of the prescription cannot have the effect of extending the period of the extinctive prescription beyond twenty years from the day of the birth of the right"'). See also *Zimmermann and Kleinschmidt, supra* fn 2, 62 (the discovery rule does not apply to the long-stop as it is 'the very purpose of the long-stop to serve as a counterbalance'.

483 See *supra* 210–217 above regarding D's misconduct.

484 Which may be subjected to specific exceptions.

and probably the US.[485] In contrast, rules of prolongation, *other than the late discovery rule*, apply to the upper time limit in Austria, Belgium, Germany, Greece and the Netherlands.[486] In practice, the difference between these two approaches regarding the application of prolongation rules to the upper time limit is less significant than it may seem given that the late discovery rule, which is the major and the most prevalent rule of prolongation, does not apply to the upper time limit in all jurisdictions.

### 5) *Effect on P's Claim*

#### a) Analysis

The expiration of the upper time limit, like the expiration of the prescription period, may either extinguish P's right, or provide a substantial defence against its enforcement, or serve as a procedural defence in judicial proceedings.[487] Which effect should be preferred? One should bear in mind that the prescription period (which is subject to prolongation) and the upper time limit (which is not or only partially subjected to prolongation[488]) are different elements of prescription law, with different functions, so that their effect on P's claim may or even should differ. 270

As the major aim of the upper time limit is to notify potential Ds when they will no longer be exposed to legal risks that accompany a given activity, it appears that the effect of crossing the upper time limit should either be the extinction of P's right or at least a substantive defence. A mere procedural defence would be insufficient to provide the required assurance that the legal risk is over. 271

#### b) Country Reports

In the US the effect of the upper time limit is indeed to extinguish P's right regardless of the effect of the expiry of the prescription period.[489] In continental Europe it appears that the distinction between the effect of the prescription period and that of the upper time limit is not always sufficiently noticed, especially where the upper time limit is perceived as a second-layer prescription period.[490] Notably, however, under the European Directive of Product Liability 272

485 CZ 73; FR 68; NO 111; US 101.

486 AT 76; BE 60; DE 112; GR 96; NL 62.

487 See Section III regarding the different effects of prescription.

488 See *supra* 268–269.

489 US 101 ('right is no longer available').

490 See *supra* 259.

and its implementations the effect of the upper time limit is to extinguish P's right.[491]

# X. STATUTE INTERPRETATION, JUDICIAL DISCRETION AND LACHES

## A. THE QUESTION

273 Given the pros and cons of prescription and its goals, both the legislature and the courts are required to seek for what they view as the right balance between the diversified and often conflicting considerations that underlie prescription law. This complicated balancing should be made with regard to each of the four elements of prescription, and, most importantly, with regard to their combined effect. The legislature strikes this balance while enacting the statutory rules of prescription and amending them. The courts strike this balance when interpreting the statutory rules and applying them to specific cases. They do it also while exercising judicial discretion to the extent that such discretion, explicit or implicit, is vested in them when deciding the specific case.

274 Focusing on judicial balancing, the following questions are of special interest. As to *interpretation* of statutory provisions, the question is whether judges tend and should interpret these provisions in ways that restrict the scope of the defence (favouring Ps), in ways that expand the scope of the defence (favouring DS), or in a 'neutral' way with no pre-determined tendency to restrict or expand the scope of the defence. As to judicial *discretion*, the questions are: (a) what is the difference between explicit and implicit discretion in this regard; (b) to what extent, if at all, discretion is and should be granted to courts by the legislature or 'taken' by courts by their own initiative; (c) do judges and should judges exert their discretion in ways that favour Ps, favour Ds, or in 'neutral' ways?

## B. THE ANSWERS

### *1) Interpretation and Judicial Inclination*

#### a) Analysis

275 From the analytical perspective statutory provisions should be interpreted by judges without any pre-determined inclination to restrict the scope of the

[491] See, eg AT 73 and FR 69.

defence (attaching heavier weights to considerations *against* prescription) or to expand it (attaching heavier weights to considerations *supporting* prescription). Once this kind of balancing has been made by the legislature and embedded in the statutory provisions, courts should interpret the statutory provisions in a 'neutral' way without preliminary prejudice for or against prescription. Yet, such a neutral, functional approach to prescription law, even if embraced by the legislature, may conflict with the natural tendency of judges, faced with the actual effects of prescription, to favour the 'weak' over the 'strong'. Quite often, especially with regard to claims for personal injuries and claims by minors, Ps are the 'weak' and Ds are the 'strong', and judges may well favour the former in the way they interpret and apply the law (and even more so when they exert judicial discretion).

### b) Country Reports

276 The majority of country reports stress that there is no declared policy, no apparent clear and systematic judicial inclination, of favouring Ps over Ds in the application of prescription law or vice versa. In that regard courts are 'neutral', interpretation is strict and narrow, and rejection of a claim on ground of prescription is not considered unethical. Yet, some of these reports do suggest, as expected, that judges do tend, especially in claims for bodily injury and claims of minors, to favour Ps.[492]

277 A different approach is reported for Spain where the traditional point of view has been that prescription is contrary to natural law, and should therefore be handled from a restrictive stance. Case law has stressed the apparently unjust nature of prescription in cases of tort liability claim. Yet, as legal scholarship insists on the importance of prescription, recent case law seems to be abandoning the theory of the restrictive interpretation of prescription and adopting a more neutral stance.[493] At the other end the reporter for Greece observes that 'judges are quite sympathetic toward prescription'.[494]

---

492 AT 77, 79, 80; CH 68; CZ 76 (usually neutral, sometimes favouring Ps); DE 113 (courts are 'principally neutral' but 'in certain aspects a modest preference for ways to avoid prescription may become apparent'); FR 71 ('courts are usually quite claimant-friendly when the claimant is the victim of a bodily injury or when there is significant imbalance between the economic and social weight of the parties'); NL 63 ('there are no concrete indications that Dutch judges are in practice either hostile, neutral, or sympathetic towards prescription'); NO 116 ('Judges are neutral to prescription' but 'there may be a certain tendency to interpret the rules so that prescription does not apply in cases where it would deprive a plaintiff of damages for personal injury'); PL 92 (interpretation is 'strict and neutral' but courts inclined in favour of Ps in cases of bodily injury and it may be considered unethical to raise the defence against a seriously injured minor); US 103 (no 'tilt' in any direction); ZA 57.

493 ES 80–83.

494 GR 97.

278 For E&W, the only jurisdiction that grants broad judicial discretion to disapply the prescription defence,[495] the reporters observe that judges 'differ in their approach to the law of limitations, with some being more willing than others to rule in favour of claimants'.[496]

### *2) Explicit and Implicit Discretion Distinguished*

279 Judicial discretion in prescription law is *explicit* where the statute or statutes that directly regulate the prescription defence *explicitly* authorises the court to accept or reject (disapply) the defence of prescription on a case-by-case basis. The discretion can be limited to types of damage (eg bodily injury), to types of Ps (eg minors) or to types of conduct (eg intentional or reckless wrongdoing). The discretion may be either fully unfettered or guided by statutory guidelines and considerations that should be accounted for and balanced by the court.

280 *Implicit* judicial discretion exists where the prescription statutes use open terms or broad *standards* rather than detailed *rules*. Although the borderline between *interpretation* of rules and *discretion* in applying standards and inserting meaning into open terms is not always clear, the above analysis shows that prescription law is embedded with standards that implicitly call for judicial discretion. With regard to the first element, for example, judges are actually vested with discretion to determine how broad the cause of action is and when it accrues,[497] whether torts should be considered continuous for prescription purposes[498] and when the damage occurred.[499] Another example, regarding the third element, is the court's explicit discretion to determine whether the non-discovery of the essentials of the claim by P is objectively reasonable or subjectively acceptable so that it triggers the late discovery rule.[500] Yet other examples are the classification of a claim as being in tort or in contract where there are different prescription periods to each,[501] or the scope of '*force majeure*' that justifies the P's delay in filing a claim.[502]

---

495 See *infra* 286.

496 EW 118.

497 See Section VI.B. For such implicit discretion regarding the 'cause of action' see AT 79; ZA 59; US 103 ('In "grey areas" judges may exercise discretion, such as determining when a claim accrues').

498 See Section VI.E.

499 See Section VI.D.

500 See Section VIII.B.

501 See, eg IT 92–93.

502 See, eg PL 93.

A different kind of implicit discretion exists where courts are able and willing to restrict the scope of prescription law by 'exogenous' general concepts of law, such as 'lack of good faith', 'abuse of right' or 'unfairness'. The decision to dismiss the defence of prescription on grounds of such concepts is discretionary by its nature. 281

### 3) *Explicit Discretion?*

#### a) Analysis

At first sight, granting courts explicit statutory discretion to disapply the prescription defence on a case-by-case basis may seem attractive. If prescription law aims at seeking the right balance between the interests of the litigating parties, one may wonder why the desired balance should be struck by pre-determined and general statutory rules and not be left to judicial discretion which takes into account the special circumstances of the case at bar. After all, is it not preferable that the court will strike the desired balance in the specific context of the litigating parties, and then decide whether to accept or reject the defence? Assume, for example, that the court finds that in the circumstances of the case at bar D's ability to defend and introduce evidence was increased by the passage of time rather than diminished, that P's claim looks like a meritorious one ('good claim'), and that P did not neglect her claim. Is it not preferable that the court will be authorised to reject the prescription defence rather than obliged under the statutory rules to accept it? 282

The counter argument, much more persuasive, is that the major goal of prescription law is not to do justice between the *litigating parties*, but rather to protect the vast groups of *potential* Ds,[503] and society at large, from the costs of preserving evidence and financial reserves indefinitely, and from the other private and social costs of pending uncertain legal risks. Granting wide discretion to courts to accept or reject the defence on a case-by-case basis will unavoidably generate such a degree of uncertainty that it may undermine and frustrate the goals of prescription.[504] Moreover, statutory rules reflecting statutory balancing should be preferred to discretionary judicial balancing because the perspectives behind the design of statutory rules are broader and more balanced than the judicial perspectives in a case-by-case decision. While the court naturally concentrates on doing justice between the few litigating parties, the legislature 283

---

[503] See *supra* 22.

[504] See *Zimmermann and Kleinschmidt, supra* fn 2, 57 ('judicial discretion produces uncertainty which is in direct conflict with the policy considerations underlying the law of prescription').

is more sensitive to the interests of the large group potential Ds, and the (often overlapping) interests of society at large.[505] Another consideration against explicit judicial discretion of a large scale are the costs to courts and the parties of litigating the discretion issue.[506]

b) Country Reports

284 In accordance with the above analysis, reports for almost all jurisdictions provide that they refrain from empowering their courts to disapply the statutory provisions regulating prescription by exerting wide judicial discretion under any explicit statutory provisions.

285 A recent grant of limited, and yet explicit, judicial discretion to disapply the defence, took place in 2018 in Poland with regard to consumer protection claims. In exerting this discretion the court has to balance considerations of justice and the interests of the parties.[507]

286 The major exception to the rule of 'no explicit discretion' is E&W where the Limitation Act 1980 allows for discretionary exclusion of time limit for actions in respect of personal injuries or death and for defamation or malicious falsehood. Regarding bodily injury, it is 'open to the court [...] if it appears equitable to do so to allow an action to proceed after the expiry' of the applicable limitation period.[508] 'In exercising this discretion, a court will take several factors into consideration including on the one hand the length of, and the reasons for, the delay on the part of the claimant [...] and the extent to which he acted promptly and reasonably once he knew whether or not the act or omission of the defendant, to which the injury was attributable, might be capable at that time of giving rise to an action for damages [...] and on the other hand the degree to which such a decision would prejudice the defendant'.[509] It is unclear whether this mix of statutory provisions and wide judicial discretion to disapply them is considered successful. The reporters, however, note that this discretion 'inevitably places defendants in great difficulty' and observes that 'the remedy is exceptional'.[510] Obviously, courts have to labour hard in deciding if and how to exert this explicit discretion.

---

505 See *supra* 25.

506 An argument in favour of judicial discretion is that it may solve the problem of missing rules of prolongation. See, eg E&W where discretion is used to help Ps who are unable to sue due to a statutory bar – EW 46. The counter argument is that it is much simpler to enact the missing rules of prolongation.

507 PL 95.

508 EW 27.

509 Ibid.

510 Ibid 119.

### 4) *Implicit Discretion?*

#### a) Analysis

The above analysis distinguished between two kinds of judicial implicit discretion: (a) discretion which is built into and comes with statutory open notions and standards, such as the discretion in deciding what exactly the cause of action is;[511] (b) judicial discretion as to whether to apply to prescription law general conceptions *exogenous* to it such as 'abuse of right', 'good-faith' or fairness.[512] While the first kind of discretion is unavoidable (courts must apply the statutory open notions on the case at bar), the exertion of the second kind of discretion can be avoided. Should it be avoided? On the one hand, discretionary resort to such general notions, exogenous to prescription law, that restrict the application of the defence on a casual basis, may erode the effect of the defence by generating undesirable uncertainty. It is most difficult, for example, to predict whether a court would reject the defence on the grounds that it was not raised in good faith. On the other hand, resorting to such exogenous notions may fill in the blanks in prescription law, substituting for missing rules of prolongation. It has been seen, to illustrate, that while in some jurisdictions D's misconduct that caused P's delay in filing a claim is regulated by a rule of prolongation, in other countries, where such rule is absent from prescription law, courts resort to exogenous notions of 'abuse of right' or 'good faith' to reject the defence. Still, it is advisable that resorting to such exogenous notions should be cautious and limited in scope. 287

#### b) Country Reports

Where statues of prescription use open terms and standards,[513] the exertion of implicit judicial discretion is unavoidable.[514] As noted by the reporters for E&W, 'various terms in the statute, eg "reasonable", "good faith", etc necessarily import the need to weigh conflicting considerations and as such confer courts with indirect discretion'.[515] 288

---

511 See Section VI.

512 See *supra* 216.

513 Some jurisdictions do not use such terms or standards in statutes of prescription. See, eg CH 68; GR 99; PL 96; US 104.

514 See *supra* 287.

515 EW 119. See also BE 62 ('courts have an implicit discretion when applying the open and broad standards used in the Civil Code: the "cause of action" has to be assessed case by case'); DE 115 ('The prescription provisions contain some – rather limited – interpretative range by using a few open terms'); FR 70 ('terms such as "should have known the facts" [...], or "impossible", or "*force majeure*" [....] grant the courts a fair amount of discretion'); NO 118 (inherent discretion in deciding the meaning of 'ought to').

289 Some jurisdictions do apply, to various extents, *exogenous* general standards/ concepts of law, to fill in the blanks in prescription law (such as absent rules of prolongation[516]) and to avoid injustice. Reports refer to 'abuse of right',[517] '*bones mores*',[518] fraud,[519] reasonableness and fairness,[520] 'good faith'[521] and 'equitable tolling'.[522] Other jurisdictions refrain from resorting to such exogenous notions.[523]

### 5) *Laches*

#### a) Analysis

290 The passage of time on P's cause of action may trigger defences other than prescription. A major such defence in common law jurisdictions is the defence of *laches*. This defence is based on the theory that equity aids the vigilant and not those who procrastinate when it comes to exercising their rights. If a person is slow to assert a right or claim such that the lapse of time harms the other party, the person may lose that right. A 'sister' defence is that of *estoppel*. *Estoppel* may be found where the party to be estopped has by false language or conduct led another to do that which he or she would not otherwise have done and as a result thereof that he or she has suffered injury. Another 'sister' is the defence of 'acquiescence'[524] and in Greece 'deactivation of rights'.[525]

291 Where the doctrine of laches (or estoppel) is applied in areas such as equity law[526] or administrative law, in which prescription law does not apply, there is no conflict between prescription on the one hand and laches or similar doctrines on the other hand. The question is whether it should also apply in civil cases *alongside* prescription, namely, whether it may be raised to dismiss P's claim before the expiration of the prescription period. In principle, application of such an additional defence seems undesirable as it undermines prescription law and frustrates P's legitimate expectations to be able to file a claim within the prescription period. It should be employed only in rare cases as where P remained passive and indifferent to the obvious detrimental

516 Eg where P's delay in filing was caused by D's misconduct – *supra* 210–217.
517 CH 69; FR 70; PL 92; ZA 58.
518 CZ 76.
519 FR 70.
520 NL 67.
521 CZ 79; DE 116; ZA 58.
522 US 104.
523 AT 81; DE 115; ES 84; GR 97.
524 For a detailed discussion of laches and acquiescence as equitable defences see EW 120–124 and US 105–107.
525 GR 100. It does not apply to prescription – ibid 101.
526 As is the case in E&W – EW 120.

effects of the delay in filing on D. If at all, it should be applied in exceptional cases.

### b) Country Reports

Only five countries are reported to apply rules of laches (or the like) *alongside* prescription, so that it may bar claim because of the passage of time[527] although it has not yet prescribed. This is done under the title of 'forfeiture' in Germany and the Netherlands,[528] 'renunciation' or 'abuse of right' under Belgian law,[529] and 'disloyal delay' in Spain.[530] In conformity with the above analysis the reporter for Norway stresses that the threshold for the rule is high and that actually it has not been applied in tort.[531] In the Netherlands it is also applied only in exceptional cases.[532] 292

# XI. CHANGE OF PARTIES

## A. THE PLAINTIFF IS A TRANSFEREE OF THE VICTIM'S CLAIM

### *1) The Question*

It may often happen that the actual P is not the original victim who suffered harm (V) but another person to whom V's claim against D was effectively transmitted by law or transferred otherwise.[533] P may be, for example, V's heir who substitutes V through inheritance, or V's insurer who after repairing V's harm under the insurance contract is subrogated to V's rights against D. 293

In such cases two questions have to be answered. The first question is whether such change in parties should be deemed as a new cause of action of the superseding P, so that a new count of the prescription should start. The second question is whether rules of prolongation applicable to V should also apply to the superseding P. For example, if V was aware of the essentials of his claim but the heir P is unaware of these essentials, should the late discovery rule apply to P? And if V is an adult and the heir P is a minor, should the rule of suspension during minority (if exists) apply to P? 294

---

527 And the other elements required to establish laches– see *supra* 290.

528 DE 117; NL 69–70.

529 BE 64.

530 ES 85.

531 NO 121.

532 NL 69–70.

533 Hereinafter the word 'transfer' is used both for voluntary transfer of right and for transmission of right by law.

### 2) *Analysis*

295 As to the first question (new cause of action?), where P is a transferee of V's claim (as an heir or an insurer or otherwise), the change of parties should not be considered a new cause of action which starts a new count of the prescription period. The subject matter of prescription is the claim, not the person, and where the claim remains the same but is only transferred from one person (V) to another (P) who has the same claim there is no justification for a new count. 'This follows from a general civil law principle saying that the successor may not gain a better position than his predecessor'[534] as both of them are 'in the same shoes'. Notably, that the transfer of the claim from V to P should not constitute a new cause of action does not derogate from the need to apply rules of prolongation in P's favour where such transfer leads to a justified delay in filing P's transferred claim.[535]

296 The answer to the second question (application of rules of prolongation on P?) is more complex where P is the transferee of V's claim. On the one hand, from P's perspective, if P, for example, is unaware of the essentials of the claim (although V was aware), or if P is a minor (although V was an adult), there is no reason to deny the application of the prolongation rule (if it exists). On the other hand, applying prolongation rules on P although they did not apply to V may prolong the effective time of prescription to an unreasonable period from D's perspective as well as from society's perspective, and frustrate the goals of prescription law. It is especially so where D knows that rules of prolongation do not apply to V and is unable to know that the claim was transferred to P and/or that rules of prolongation apply to P.

297 The conclusion is that applying prolongation rules on the transferee (P) should be done cautiously, taking into consideration the nature of the specific rule applied, its effects, and the goals of prescription law. For example, it is suggested that the late discovery rule should not apply to P if it did not apply to V on the day of the transfer of V's claim to P. Given the high degree of uncertainty that this rule generates, this may lead to 'over-prolongation'. In contrast, if both V and P were misled by D, it is justified to apply a relevant rule of prolongation[536] to both. Obviously, rules of prolongation that are relevant to V but not to P should cease to apply once the claim is transferred from V to P. For example, if V is disabled but P is not, a rule of prolongation in cases of disability should cease to apply with the transfer, although V remains disabled.

---

534 NO 126.

535 See *supra* 247–249.

536 See *supra* 210–217.

### 3) *Country Reports*

Asked whether the transfer of V's claim to P (insurer or heir or another transferee) is considered as constituting a new cause of action which triggers a new period of prescription, all reporters, in conformity with the above analysis, answered in the negative. In the words of the French reporter 'change of parties, whatever the cause, is not regarded as creating a new cause of action and the running of the prescription period is normally not affected by it. A change of creditor (by inheritance or subrogation, for example) therefore does not affect prescription'.[537] As observed, if P's filing was justifiably delayed because of the transfer, rules of prolongation may apply.[538] 298

As to application of rules of prolongation on P in the same way that they apply to V, focusing on the late discovery rule six reports provide, in accordance with the above analysis, that this rule would not apply to P if it did not apply to V on the date of the transfer.[539] Only two reports suggest otherwise: according to the Swiss report where P is social insurance the late discovery rule applies on P;[540] According to the Norwegian report the discovery rule may apply on P being a heir of V.[541] For the US it is reported that the prolongation rule in cases of minority would apply to heirs who are also minors.[542] 299

## B. THE DEFENDANT IS A TRANSFEREE OF THE TORTFEASOR'S OBLIGATION

### 1) *The Question*

The change of parties may occur not only where V's *right* is transferred to P, but also where the *obligation* of tortfeasor (T) to compensate P is transferred to another person (D) who becomes the defendant. Such a change may often occur where T dies and T's liability to P is transferred by inheritance law to D's estate/heirs who become the actual defendant (D) in P's claim. 300

This change of a liable party (from T to D), like the change in the entitled party (from V to P), raises two questions similar to those discussed above. Firstly, should such change of the liable party be considered as a new cause of action so that a new count of the prescription period should start? Secondly, should 301

537 FR 73. See AT 83; BE 65; CH 71–72; CZ 84; DE 118; ES 86–88; GR 102; IT 106; NL 71; NO 122–123; PL 100, 102; US 108–109; ZA 61–63.

538 See *supra* fn 535 and eg: AT 83; DE 118; FR 73; ZA 63.

539 DE 118; ES 87; FR 77; IT 114–115; NL 71; PL 100.

540 CH 71.

541 NO 125.

542 US 110, 112.

the rules of prolongation applicable to T also apply to the superseding D? For example, should the running of the period be prolonged because D, unlike T, resides in another country where service is impossible or difficult?[543]

### 2) *Analysis*

302 As to the first question (new cause of action?) the answer regarding the effect of the transfer of liability is the same as the answer regarding the transfer of a right: the subject matter of prescription is the liability, not the person, and where liability remains the same but only transferred from T to D there is no justification for starting a new period as no new cause of action accrued. As with the transfer of right from V to P,[544] the transfer of obligation from T to D does not derogate from the need to apply rules of prolongation in P's favour where such transfer leads to a justified delay in filing by P.

303 As to the second question (application of rules of prolongation to D the transferees) the answer seems to be easier where the transfer is of liability rather than of a right. In principle the change in the identity of the liable person should not prejudice P. For example, if T was not absent from the jurisdiction and D is, the relevant rule of prolongation (if it exists) should apply once the obligation is transferred from T (not absent) to D (absent). For another example, if T did not cause delay in filing by misleading P, but D did, the relevant rule of prolongation (if it exists) should apply to D, the transferee.

### 3) *Country Reports*

304 No report refers to the transfer of the obligation from T to D as constituting a new cause of action which triggers a new prescription period.[545] Relevant rules of prolongation, though, apply where the transfer causes justified delay in P's filing.[546]

305 As to the application of rules of prolongation where the obligation is transferred from T to D, it seems that there are no specific or clear rules in this regard. The reporters for Spain, for example, note that 'the same rules of prolongation which were applicable to the deceased person will be applicable to the heir',[547] and in the Netherlands the statute provides laconically that 'the transmission of a claim does not affect the obligor's defences'.[548]

543 Assuming that there is such a relevant rule of prolongation.
544 See Section XI.A.
545 Unless the right of the 'transferee' is actually an independent one – see BE 66.
546 AT 85; CH 73; CZ 84; DE 119; ES 89; GR 103; US 111.
547 ES 89.
548 NL 71.

## C. CONTRIBUTION CLAIMS

### 1) *The Question*

When more than one D is liable to P for the same harm, and the liability of the Ds to P is joint and several (*in solidum*), it may often happen that one D (D1) compensates P for the whole harm, or for more than D1's relative share of liability, and therefore files a claim of contribution against D2 to retrieve D2's part of liability paid by D1. The question is whether there are special rules of prescription that apply to D1's contribution claim against D2.[549] 306

### 2) *Analysis*

The prescription of contribution claims among tortfeasors (Ds) seems to depend on the nature of these claims: whether they are perceived as *derivative* claims or *independent* claims. D1's contribution claim against D2 is considered *derivative* if it originates in P's tort claim against D2. When D1 compensates P for D2's share of liability, P's right in tort against D2 is transferred by law to D1 who sues D2 using the tort claim of P. In contrast, D1's contribution claim against D2 is considered *independent* if it originates not in P's transferred right, but rather in the law of *unjust enrichment*, namely, based on the principle that D2 should not benefit from the fact that D1 was forced to pay to P all or part of D2's share of liability. 307

If D1's contribution claim is perceived as *derivative*, based on P's tort claim against D2 transferred to D1, then D1's claim against D2 is supposed to prescribe with P's tort claim against D2, having the same starting point (like claims of heirs and subrogated insurers that prescribe with the victim's claim). If D1's contribution claim is perceived as an *independent* claim based on unjust enrichment law, it is supposed to prescribe independently of P's claim against D2, and the starting point (date of accrual) of the contribution claim is the date of D1's payment to P (or the day on which D1 was held liable to P). 308

From the perspective of prescription law both alternatives raise difficulties. If the contribution claim is derivative, the prescription period for the claim may be very short. For example, if payment by D1 was made three years after the harm had been caused by the D1 and D2, and the prescription period is four years, D1 would have only one year left to sue contribution from D2. If, on the other hand, the contribution claim is independent, then D2 is exposed, 309

[549] For a detailed discussion of this question see *B Askeland*, Plurality of Liable Persons and Prescription of Recourse Actions in: H Koziol and BC Steininger (eds), European Tort Law 2007 (2008), 94.

for the same tortious conduct that harmed P, to a 'second' prescription period that starts when D1's contribution claim is borne.[550] In the above example D2 is exposed to a claim of contribution seven years after causing the harm to P, almost doubling the prescription period to which D2 is exposed for causing harm to P. It is questionable whether the fact that there are two tortfeasors liable *in solidum* is in itself sufficient justification for nearly doubling the possible prescription period for D2.

310 To cope with these difficulties, a rule of extension may prolong the period for D1 if the claim is derivative, and an especially short period for contribution claims may shorten the period for D2 if the claim is independent.[551]

311 Arguably, where D1 paid P despite the prescription of P's claims against both Ds, D2 should not pay for D1's 'generosity' and should not be exposed to D1's contribution claim.[552]

### 3) *Country Reports*

312 In most countries, where D1 and D2 are joint and several tortfeasors liable to P, D1's contribution claim against D2 is considered an *independent* claim and not a *derivative* claim.[553] The starting point (date of accrual) for this independent claim is either the date of D1's payment to P,[554] or the earlier day on which D1 was found liable to P.[555] The prescription period for this independent claim varies: two years in E&W,[556] five years in Spain,[557] 20 years in Greece and Italy[558] and 30 years in Austria.[559]

313 In Norway and South Africa D1's contribution claim against D2 is considered as a *derivative* claim of P's claim against D2.[560] This means that D1's cause of action against D2 accrues with P's cause of action against D2, although D1 cannot sue D2 before D1 is found liable to P. To avoid injustice to D1 (very short prescription

---

550 See ibid 95.

551 For the suggestion to apply a shortened period of one year to contribution claims (subject to the late discovery rule) see *B Askeland*, ibid 110. Another justification for such a short period is that in some jurisdictions D1 has to notify D2 about P's claim and if so D2 would not be surprised by D1's contribution claim.

552 For this outcome see AT 88, IT 129 and NL 73.

553 AT 86 (the reporters, though, suggest that it should be considered derivative – ibid 87); CH 74 (although often reinforced by a claim of subrogation); CZ 85; DE 120; ES 90; EW 61; GR 105; IT 119; NL 72; PL 105; US 113.

554 See, eg AT 86; GR 105; IT 125; PL 105; US 113 (most states).

555 See, eg EW 61; PL 105; US 113 (some states).

556 EW 61.

557 ES 90 (for some claims only one year).

558 GR 105; IT 125.

559 AT 86 (which in practice means no prescription).

560 NO 129; ZA 64.

period if at all[561]), the prescription period is extended up to one year after D1 pays P.[562] Such extension is missing in the Belgian law where 'joint tortfeasors can raise the running or acquired prescription against the contribution claim, the same way they could raise it against the plaintiff's claim'.[563]

In France P has two claims against D: 'one based on subrogation [...] and another, independent one'.[564] The independent claim accrues with D1's payment to P and its prescription period is five years.[565,566] 314

## D. DEPENDANTS' CLAIM

### 1) *The Question*

Where the victim of a tort (V) dies due to the injury caused by the liable D, and the law provides that V's dependants (Ps) are entitled to compensation from D for loss of financial support that P would have otherwise provided, the question is whether there are special rules of prescription that that apply to the Ps' claim as dependants against D. 315

### 2) *Analysis*

The dependants' claim is in principle not a *derivative* claim but an *independent* one – they sue for their personal loss of support and not as transferees of V's claim. This means that the starting point of the dependants' claim (date of accrual) is V's death and not V's injury (unless both happen on the same date). Yet, the dependants' claim has derivative features. It is based on the same facts as V's claim against D. Actually, from D's perspective the dependants' claim clearly substitutes V's claim: their claim for loss of support supersedes V's claim for lost earnings that would have been used for such support. If conceived of as derivative claim for prescription purposes, the starting point of the dependants' claim would be V's injury and not V's death. 316

As with contribution claims, both alternatives raise difficulties. If the dependants' claim is perceived as fully independent, the starting point being V's death, that may expose Ds to unreasonably long periods. For example, if V dies 317

---

561 See *supra* 309.

562 NO 130; ZA 64.

563 BE 67.

564 FR 80.

565 FR 79.

566 In Italy 'acts by which the creditor interrupts prescription against one of the joint and several debtors [...] shall have effects with respect to the other debtors' – IT 119. '[T]he interrupting effect acts also in favour of the defendant with regard to her right to act in recourse against her co-debtors' – ibid 122.

ten years after the injury, and the prescription period is five years, D may be sued by the dependants 15 years after V's injury, ten years after V's claim against D prescribed. On the other hand, it is difficult to define the dependant's claim, which comes into being only with V's death, as a derivative one only for prescription purposes, violating the principle that the starting point should not precede the date in which all the essentials of liability (in this case V's death) are present. But even if P's claim can be perceived as a derivative of V's claim, that may expose P to a too short period. Where, for example, V dies four years after injury, and the prescription period is five years, that would leave only one year to P. Moreover, if V's claim prescribes before V's death, P's claim against D would prescribe before it accrued (with V's death)!

318 There are various ways to mitigate these difficulties: a rule of extension that will provide sufficient but limited time for the dependants' claim after V's death; short period for such claim; denial of the dependants' claim if V dies after V's claim against D prescribed; short upper time limit for such claims.

#### 3) *Country Reports*

319 Reports for all countries confirm that the dependants' claim is considered an independent claim against D and not a derivative claim based on V's claim. Accordingly, the starting point (accrual of cause of action) is V's death.[567]

320 So how is the problem of too long a prescription period from D's perspective solved? Only two reports refer to solutions.[568] In Switzerland the prescription period for the dependants' claim is the general short period of one year (starting from V's death).[569] In E&W 'no action can be pursued [...] if the death occurred when the person injured could no longer maintain an action and recover damages in respect of the injury'.[570]

## XII. OTHER ASPECTS OF PRESCRIPTION LAW

### A. STIPULATION AND WAIVER

#### 1) *The Question*

321 Should the parties to potential proceedings be allowed *in advance* to validly agree on rules of prescription different from the statutory rules, such as longer

567 AT 89; BE 68; CH 75; CZ 85; DE 121; ES 91; EW 67; FR 82; GR 106; NL 74; NO 131; PL 108; US 113; ZA 65.
568 For the various solutions see *supra* 318.
569 CH 75.
570 EW 67.

or shorter periods, different rules of prolongation, or even agree to disapply the defence? In the tort context this question is relevant only to situations where potential D and potential P are able to enter a contract which regulates the prescription of future tort claims (such as situations of professional malpractice). It does not arise, for example, in situations of accidents where the parties are strangers to each other.[571] A related question is that of *waiver*. Should D be able to effectively waive the defence *in advance* by a unilateral act or bilateral agreement?

### 2) *Analysis*

The answer to the question whether contractual stipulation in advance should be allowed depends on the jurisdiction's perception regarding the goals of prescription law.[572] 322

If the dominant goal is to protect public interests (such as securing minimal degree of certainty, protecting courts from stale claims, keeping the public peace), then stipulations that *prolong* the effective time of prescription (longer periods, additional rules of prolongation) should be prohibited (although such prohibition may be easily bypassed if D decides not to raise the defence before the time agreed upon). On the other hand, public policy considerations, if dominant, should deny the validity of stipulations that *shorten* the effective time of prescription where P's claim is based on D's intentional, reckless or even grossly negligent harm-causing conduct. 323

If the dominant goal is to find the optimal balance between the interests of Ds and Ps, rather than the protection of public interests and values, stipulation should be allowed based on the freedom of contract.[573] If both parties benefit from stipulations why not allow it? However, stipulation should be restricted or disallowed where there is unequal bargaining power that may unfairly prejudice Ps who may actually have no real choice and would reluctantly agree in advance to shorten the effective time of prescription (shorter periods, omitting rules of prolongation) or may prejudice Ds by extremely extended prescription periods. 324

---

571 See DE 122 ('agreements on prescription seem to be rare in tort law already for the factual reason that the parties often had no opportunity to agree before the tort and are unwilling to do so afterwards').

572 See Section IV.

573 'It is increasingly recognized today that the parties are free by agreement to facilitate prescription and to render prescription more difficult' – *Zimmermann and Kleinschmidt*, *supra* fn 2, 33.

325 As to *waiver* of the prescription defence, in advance, by D, the above analysis applies as well: focusing on the public interests, waiver, full or partial,[574] should be prohibited, but if the focus is on the parties' interests, waiver should be allowed. Waiver *after P's claim prescribed* should always be allowed as long as the decision whether to raise the defence or not (which equals waiver) is D's and not the court's (*ex officio*).[575]

### 3) *Country Reports*

326 Two countries, Greece and Poland, do not allow *any* stipulation, which according to the above analysis means that prescription in these jurisdictions focuses on the public interest rather than on the parties' interests.[576] Interestingly, the reporters for Spain note that although all prescription rules are mandatory and parties 'lack autonomy to modify or exclude them'[577] (focus on public interests), in practice courts allow stipulations[578] (attaching greater weights to the parties' interests).

327 As to consensual *prolongation* of the effective time of prescription, Austria, Belgium and the Netherlands do not allow it at all,[579] a prohibition probably derived from the focus on public interests.[580] Few countries have limits on the extension of the prescription periods: the Czech Republic (15 years), France (10 years), Germany (30 years), Switzerland (10 years).[581]

328 Consensual *shortening* of the effective time of prescription, according to most reports, is allowed, and in some jurisdictions not only by agreement to shorten prescription periods but also by agreement to restrict rules of prolongation.[582] Yet, shortening is not allowed where it may be unfair to Ps: who agree to it because of weaker bargaining power, who had no real opportunity to negotiate (standard contracts), who are unaware that such shortening may impede their

---

574 'Full' waiver means that D undertakes not to raise the defence. 'Partial' waiver means undertaking to narrow its scope.

575 See DE 123 ('Yet, a defendant is never hindered not to raise the defence of prescription in court and thereby actually to waive the defence').

576 GR 107 ('Prescription is a legal institution of public order as it serves the public interest of legal certainty […] Therefore a contract between parties is null'); PL 112.

577 ES 92.

578 Ibid 124.

579 AT 93; BE 69; NL 75.

580 AT 90; BE 69; NE 75.

581 CZ 88; FR 85; DE 123; CH 76 (but as of 1 January 2020, the law will provide that from 'the beginning of the prescription period, the debtor may waive the plea of limitation for a maximum of ten years' – ibid 77.

582 CZ 89; DE 125; ES 94; FR 85; ZA 66.

ability to succeed (especially in claims for bodily injury), or who otherwise need protection.[583] The validity of shortening may also be denied, this time for reasons of public policy, where harm was inflicted by D intentionally, recklessly or even with gross negligence.[584]

Regarding *waiver* made *in advance* by D, who undertakes not to raise the prescription defence or to limit it, all reports state that it is invalid, with the exception of E&W and South Africa which allow it,[585] as well as the EU in non-contractual claims against the EU.[586] Interestingly, though, three reporters, for Austria, Germany and Spain, observe that courts may in practice ignore the invalidity and enforce the waiver.[587] 329

## B. MEANING OF 'FILING A CLAIM' FOR PRESCRIPTION PURPOSES

### 1) *The Question*

What is the procedural act by P that stops the running of the prescription period? Is it the filing at the court's office or site of an action (statement of claim/complaint) by P? A written notice or demand sent by P to D, or some other act? 330

### 2) *Country Reports*

All countries require a formal filing of an action by P (sometimes with service to D[588]) to stop the running of the prescription period.[589] In some countries there are also other procedural acts that stop the running of the period.[590] 331

583 AT 94–95; CH 76; CZ 91–92; DE 124; ES 94; EW 127; FR 86; NL 75; NO 134; ZA 66.

584 AT 95; CZ 92; DE 124.

585 EW 131; ZA 66.

586 EU 39–41.

587 AT 90 (pleading invalidity is abuse of right by D); DE 15 (pleading the waiver is lack of good faith); ES 93 (invalidity 'is deemed a merely blurry limit') and 108.

588 See, eg US 115 and ZA 68.

589 AT 96; BE 70; CH 78; CZ 93; DE 128; ES 40; EW 131; FR 88; GR 109; IT 134–138; NL 77; NO 135; PL 115; US 115; ZA 68. See also EU 30–35 regarding submission of claims against the EU in the CJEU.

590 See, eg CH 78 (application for conciliation); CZ 93–95 (criminal/administrative procedures); DE 128 (several procedural acts); ES 41 (out-of-court claim known as 'extrajudicial claim'); GR 110 (a plea of set off); IT 139–146 (valid written notice); PL 116 (initiation of mediation).

## C. WHEN SHOULD THE DEFENCE BE RAISED AND DECIDED?

### 1) *The Question*

332 At which procedural stage of the litigation should the defence of prescription be raised? On the one hand, the prescription defence is a threshold defence in the sense that if accepted it becomes unnecessary to litigate the case, thereby saving private and public costs. It should therefore be raised at an early stage of litigation, to avoid unnecessary litigation. On the other hand, this does not mean that the court's decision on prescription must be given at a preliminary stage. Sometimes the claim has to be litigated, partially or fully, in order to ascertain the facts required to decide the prescription defence.

### 2) *Country Reports*

333 As to the procedural stage at which the defence has to be raised by D, the reports reveal two different approaches. One approach favours an early pleading of the defence and requires either inclusion in the statement of the defence,[591] or pleading 'as soon as possible',[592] incentivising Ds to do so by mandatory or discretionary rejection of the defence if pleaded later.[593] The other approach is to allow Ds to raise the defence at any stage of proceedings,[594] sometimes even on appeal.[595] Still, even under this approach the defence may be rejected 'if the delay is not sufficiently excused'[596] or lead to imposition of expenses on D.[597] In the US it depends on the stage in which the facts can be ascertained by the jury.[598] In claims against the EU the defence should be raised in response to a claim 'no later than in the second exchange of briefs'.[599]

334 As to the stage in which the court should decide whether to accept or reject the defence, in some countries this should be done by an interim decision judgment[600] and in other only with the final judgment.[601]

---

591 CH 79; GR 112; IT 147; US 116.

592 AT 97; NO 136.

593 See, eg AT 97.

594 CZ 96; DE 130; EW 131; FR 89; NL 77; PL 118; ZA 70.

595 BE 71; NL 77; PL 118.

596 DE 130.

597 CZ 98.

598 US 117.

599 EU 58.

600 AT 98 (prescription 'has to be decided upon by means of an interim judgment if the judge wants to allow the claim' but if 'the judge wants to reject the claim on the basis of prescription, he has to reject the claim immediately'); CH 80.

601 BE 71; CZ 97; DE 131; GR 112; IT 148 ('prior to turning to the merits of the claim'); PL 119 ('not a preliminary issue'); US 118. See also EU 60 (defence decided during the formal stage of proceedings).

## D. WHO MAY RAISE THE DEFENCE?

### 1) *The Question*

Is it only D that can raise the prescription defence? Arguably, as prescription law promotes societal goals, such as avoiding 'bad claims', the court as well could be allowed to raise the defence *ex officio*. Another question is whether the defence can be raised by third parties, eg creditors of D or D's guarantors who argue that P has no enforceable claim against D. 335

### 2) *Country Reports*

No jurisdiction is reported as allowing *courts* to raise the defence *ex officio* if D refrains from doing so.[602] Most jurisdictions allow *third parties*, intervenors, to raise the defence where they have real interest in its success (such as D's creditors or guarantors).[603] Only Poland and the US do not allow it.[604] 336

## E. BURDEN OF PROOF

According to a well-established common principle, a party to litigation who makes a factual allegation incurs the evidential burden to establish that allegation.[605] Hence, it is D who should establish that the prescription period ran and expired on P's cause of action or that the upper time limit was transcended. For the same reason it is P who should establish that the running period has been postponed/suspended or renewed, or that the period has been extended, by one or more of the rules of prolongation.[606] All jurisdictions, according to the reports, follow this 'division' of the burden of proof.[607] 337

602 The same applies to claims against the EU in the CJEU – EU 56.

603 AT 99 (D's guarantor and intervener); BE 72; CZ 100 (intervenor on D's side); CH 81; DE 132 (party who benefits from the defence); FR 90 ('creditors and any other person with an interest in that the prescription be acquired may raise it or invoke it even if the debtor renounces it'); GR 114; IT 50; NO 138; ZA 69.

604 PL 121; US 118.

605 See, eg BE 74 ('the burden of proof weighs on the party who invokes the existence of a fact or a right') and GR 115 ('each litigant incurs the burden of proof regarding facts that constitute prerequisites for the application of rules of law favourable towards him'). See also EU 59.

606 As to whether the late discovery rule is a rule of accrual (burden of proof on D) or a rule of prolongation (burden on P) see *supra* 108–116.

607 AT 101 (the burden lies on the party 'to whom the facts to be proves are favourable'); CH 82 ('It is the defendant who has to establish that the prescription period passed since the accrual of the plaintiff's right to remedy and it is the plaintiff who has to establish that the running of time was or has been postponed, renewed or that the period has been extended'); CZ 103; DE 134; EW 132; ES 107; FR 91; GR 115; IT 151–153; NO 140; PL 122; US 119; ZA 71. This seems to be the case in the Netherlands as well – NL 80.

# XIII. CONCLUSIONS AND CONSIDERATIONS FOR REFORM

## A. DEFINITION OF PRESCRIPTION[608]

338 Prescription in tort law is a legal institution that prevents the plaintiff (P) from enforcing a tort claim against the defendant (D) because of P's failure to file an action on the claim during the running of a specified period of time on the claim.

## B. NATURE AND EFFECT OF PRESCRIPTION[609]

339 As a general rule prescription should be a substantive defence that neither extinguishes the right nor is a mere procedural defence limited to judicial proceedings. Exceptions are justified only where promoting the goals of prescription.

## C. GOALS OF PRESCRIPTION[610]

340 Prescription law should endeavour to strike an adequate balance between the basic and constitutional right of Ps to 'open courts' on the one hand, and on the other hand the need to protect Ds, potential and actual, as well as collective interests, from the detrimental effects of unjustifiably belated claims, in terms of injustice, uncertainty and costs.

## D. ELEMENTS OF PRESCRIPTION[611]

341 To achieve the goals of prescription law, the legislature (in enacting) and courts (in applying the statutory provisions) should look for the best available mixture of the four elements of prescription law which are closely interrelated:

- *The starting point*: the day on which a cause of action accrues so that *potentially* the prescription period can start running.
- *The prescription period*: the period that after it running from the starting point P's claim prescribes.

608 See *supra* Section II.
609 See *supra* Section III.
610 See *supra* Section IV.
611 See *supra* Section V.

- *Rules of prolongation*: rules that postpone, suspend or renew the running of the prescription period or extend it, to allow for justified delays in filing claims. These rules open a gap between the length of prescription period and the *effective time of prescription*.
- *The upper time limit*: to cope with the uncertainty generated by rules of prolongation, and to keep the effective time of prescription in reasonable boundaries, the upper time limit serves as 'ceiling' that when reached the claim prescribes although the prescription period has not yet expired.

## E. THE STARTING POINT/ACCRUAL OF CAUSE OF ACTION[612]

The main conclusions/observations on the starting point/accrual of cause of action can be summarised as follows: 342

- The subject matter of prescription is not the specific claim pleaded in the action but rather the *cause of action* to which the specific claim belongs. Once a specific claim prescribes, all the claims that belong to the same cause of action prescribe with it. Whether different claims belong to the same cause of action or to different ones (the broadness or narrowness question) should be decided by the courts with the goals of prescription law in mind.
- Where the cause of action accrues with the harm, the starting point should be the *occurrence* of the harm, its *materialisation*, neither the earlier date in which it became probable or certain, nor the later day of its stabilisation.
- tort which is classified as *continuous*, given the repetition and the frequency of D's tortious conduct and of the ensuing harm, should nevertheless be perceived for prescription purposes as a multiplicity of recurrent daily causes of action rather than a single 'stretched' cause of action. Exceptions should be allowed only if promoting the goals of prescription law, or, cautiously, on basis of public policy (eg 'punishing' intentional wrongdoing).

## F. THE PRESCRIPTION PERIOD[613]

The main conclusions/observations on the length and generality of the prescription period can be summarised as follows: 343

- The length of the prescription period should be inversely related to the extent that rules of prolongation allow for justified delays in filing. In fact, the

612 See *supra* Section VI.
613 See *supra* Section VII.

embracement of the late discovery rule, the major rule of prolongation, rightly led to a significant shortening of the period.

- Assuming that most justified delays are allowed by rules of prolongation the adequate prescription period for tort claims seems to be at the range of three to five years, as indeed is the case in most jurisdictions.
- To avoid complexities, uncertainties and 'period shopping', one general prescription period for tort claims should be preferred to a multiplicity of 'adjusted' periods. Exceptions require convincing justifications.

## G. THE LATE DISCOVERY RULE[614]

344 The main conclusions/observations on the nature, essentials and the scope of the late discovery rule can be summarised as follows:

- The late discovery rule should be perceived as a rule of prolongation (that usually postpones the running of the period) and not as a rule of the starting point, as it is actually perceived in some jurisdictions. This conclusion emerges from the analysis of the nature, characteristics and goals of the rule and its comparison to other rules of prolongation.
- The essentials of the claim that P's unawareness of them triggers the late discovery rule are and should be: D's identity; the facts regarding D's tortious conduct and surrounding circumstances; harm suffered; factual causal link between D's conduct and P's harm. Awareness to the legal implications of the above facts is not and should not be such an essential.
- To achieve a fair balance between Ds and Ps, awareness should be imputed to P, in the absence of actual awareness, where it would have been acquired by a reasonable person (the objective test), or where P, given her personal skills and abilities, could have acquired awareness (the subjective test).
- Postponement under the late discovery rule should be tolled where the awareness gained or imputed under the objective or subjective test, is such that would incentivise a reasonable person to file an action.
- The late discovery should apply to all torts and harms as opposed to partial application of the rule.

## H. OTHER RULES OF PROLONGATION[615]

345 Two kinds of decisions have to be made with regard to the other rules of prolongation. Firstly, which contingency that caused delay in instituting

614 See *supra* Section VIII.A.
615 See *supra* Section VIII.B.

proceedings justifies a rule of prolongation in P's favour? Secondly, what kind of prolongation (postponement, suspension, renewal, extension) is most suitable to each contingency? Both decisions require cautious weighing of the benefits of prolongation in terms of fairness to Ps against its various costs: unfairness to Ds, eroding certainty and consumed judicial resources.

Major points made regarding other rules of prolongation are: 346

- Delay caused by *D's misconduct* justifies a rule of prolongation. Such a rule should substitute for concepts exogenous to prescription law, such as 'good faith' or 'abuse of right' used by most jurisdictions.
- Not any *acknowledgement* by D of P's claim, or *partial performance* of it, should trigger a rule of renewal (interruption) – only those which render P's delay justified.
- *Special relations* between the parties justify prolongation if they are relations of *trust* (eg between partners) or of *dependency* (eg guardian/ward), and even more so if they are of both trust and dependency (eg parents/children).
- *Lack of legal capacity* (mental disability, minority) justifies prolongation, as a rule, only in the absence of legal representative.
- *Former legal proceedings* between the parties that ended without resolution (no *res judicata*) justify prolongation of the effective time of prescription for renewed proceedings for claims belonging to the same cause of action as the former unresolved claims.
- *Transfer of right* (eg death, bankruptcy) justifies in principle a short prolongation for the transferee, by way of extension, to cope with delays caused by the transfer.
- Other contingencies that come under the title of '*force majeure*', to the extent they justify prolongation, should, for the sake of certainty, be specified in prescription law.

## I. THE UPPER TIME LIMIT[616]

The main conclusions/observations as to the role, features, effect and scope of the upper time limit are: 347

- The role of the upper time limit is to counterbalance the operation of rules of prolongation by putting a 'ceiling' to the effective time of prescription, in order to provide minimal certainty to potential Ds. As such it should: (a) commence with D's conduct and not with the harm it caused; (b) range

[616] See *supra* Section IX.

from 10 years to 30 depending, *inter alia*, on the latency of the kind of harm; (c) not be subjected to rules of prolongation (other than the one which applies to D's misconduct).

- In some jurisdictions upper time limits are perceived as a *second* period of prescription, that unlike the *first* period, which is 'short', 'subjective' or 'relative', are 'long', 'objective' or 'absolute' second periods. Arguably, this perception is confusing, misleading and should be avoided. The upper time limit has a different role and different characteristics than the prescription period.
- Non-application of an upper time limit may/should be considered justified: (a) in cases of latent damage (including damage to the environment); (b) for causes of action which are not subjected to prolongation rules that are the '*raison d'etre*' of the upper time limit.

## J. INTERPRETATION, DISCRETION AND LACHES[617]

348 - There is a natural judicial tendency to interpret statutory rules in P's favour especially in cases of bodily injury. In principle, however, interpretation should be 'neutral' in the sense that it favours neither Ps nor Ds. Interpretation should endeavour to promote the goals of prescription law, including protection of potential Ds and collective interests, goals not always sufficiently conspicuous at the courthouse.
- *Implicit* judicial discretion is inherent in broad statutory concepts of prescription law such as 'cause of action' or 'reasonableness'. This discretion should be exerted in ways that promote the goals of prescription. Resorting to 'exogenous' broad concepts such as 'good faith' or 'abuse of right' should be done cautiously as it may undermine the certainty which prescription law aims to secure.
- *Explicit* judicial discretion to reject or limit the prescription defence on a case-by-case basis, although it may promote fairness and justice between the litigating parties, has a clear potential to frustrate the goals of protecting potential Ds and collective interests and should be restricted, if not altogether avoided. The E&W experience with such discretion provides no contradictory findings.

617 See *supra* Section X.

- Application of the defence of laches *alongside* prescription, so that a claim may be denied for laches before its prescription, is undesirable for the same reasons that judicial discretion on a case-by-case is.

## K. CHANGE OF PARTIES

349 Neither the transfer of a tort claim from V (victim) to P, nor the transfer of tort liability from the tortfeasor (T) to D, should be considered as constituting a new cause of action and as justifying renewal of the running of the prescription period. As to application of rules of prolongation on the transferee, this should be done cautiously, taking into consideration the nature of the specific rule applied, its effects, and the goals of prescription law.

## L. CONTRIBUTION CLAIMS AND DEPENDANTS' CLAIM

350 A contribution claim among tortfeasors should be perceived as *independent* cause of action that triggers independent prescription period, rather than a *derivative* of P's claim. Yet, being in essence a claim that originates in P's claim from D's perspective, a specific short period is called for to reduce the effective time of prescription from D's perspective as D is actually exposed to two cumulative periods of prescription for the same tort and same harm.

351 The same applies to a dependant's (P's) claim against tortfeasor D for the indirect loss suffered by P due to causing V's death. Although P's claim is independent as she sues for her loss, not for the transferred V's loss, from D's perspective it originates in V's claim. There are various legal ways to reduce the effective time of prescription of P's claim against D who is actually exposed to two cumulative periods of prescription for the same tort and same harm.

## M. CONTRACTING

352 Contractual agreements between the parties concerning changes in the statutory effective time of prescription should in principle be allowed subject to equal bargaining power and to prevailing public policy considerations against voluntary extension or shortening.

## N. OTHER PROCEDURAL ASPECTS

353 – Prescription as a preliminary defence should be raised by D at an early stage of the proceedings, and decided by the court as soon as possible.
– Third parties with legitimate interest should also be allowed to raise the defence but not the court *ex officio*.
– The burden to prove the elements of prescription should lie on D or others who raise the defence, with the exception of the element of rules of prolongation: the application of these rules to the litigated case has to be established by P.

# ECONOMIC ANALYSIS

Israel GILEAD



## I. INTRODUCTION

An initial inquiry into the economic analysis of prescription law, made more than a decade ago,[1] led the author to the recognition that this kind of analysis is most complicated and that: 1

> Given this complexity, it is doubtful whether substantiated conclusions can be reached regarding the efficiency of a given time limit or rule of prescription. Such a conclusion requires complex analysis of information of a kind and scope which is unattainable, "the stuff that dreams are made of" as Ronald Coase once said with regard to complex economic analysis.[2] When such dreams do not come true, one can only hypothesize about the efficiency of time limits and rules of prescription.[3]

1 *I Gilead*, Economic Analysis of Prescription in Tort Law, in: H Koziol and BC Steininger (eds), European Tort Law 2007 (2008), 112.

2 *R Coase*, The Firm, the Market and the Law (1988), 185.

3 *Gilead, supra* fn 1, 129.

2 The preceding Analytical and Comparative Report[4] (ACR) has strengthened and corroborated this recognition. It further highlights the complexity of prescription law given its goals and the parties affected by it, complexity which actually renders it unsusceptible to accurate, meaningful and reliable economic analysis.[5]

3 After reiterating the very basics of economic analysis of law (Section II), this report, highlights, on the background of the ACR, the welfare *measurement problems* that plague the economic analysis of prescription law (Section III). It then focuses on the *intricate interrelations and cross-effects between the legal variables that constitute prescription law*, as analysed in the ACR, and the ensuing difficulties for reliable economic analysis (Section IV). At the same time, it is argued (Section V) that the very basic economic analysis nevertheless suffices to support two related claims made in the ACR: the claim that a major goal of prescription law should be the protection of *potential* Ds, and the consequential claim that broad judicial discretion in the application of the defence should be avoided. A short comment on prescription law and the fair distribution of wealth concludes (Section VI).

## II. ON THE BASICS OF ECONOMIC ANALYSIS OF PRESCRIPTION LAW

### A. WELFARE AND EFFICIENCY OF LEGAL RULES

4 Economic analysis of law focuses on the effects of legal rules on the aggregate well-being, welfare,[6] in a given society. A legal rule which enhances net aggregate welfare is considered a more desirable rule than an alternative legal rule which generates less net aggregate welfare. In economic terms, the former is more 'efficient' than the latter. A rule is absolutely efficient (economically most desirable) when it generates more net aggregate welfare than any alternative rule.

5 Economic analysis of prescription law should accordingly identify the welfare affected by the present provisions of prescription law, and then examine the welfare effects of changes on the aggregate welfare, in order to trace provisions/sets of provisions that are more or most welfare enhancing (efficient).

---

4 *I Gilead and B Askeland*, Prescription: Analytical and Comparative Report (in this volume). References are to paragraph numbers.

5 This may well be the reason why 'a general look at the literature on the economic analysis of prescription law reveals that this topic has so far attracted relatively little interest, and that its discussion tends to be either very general or to focus on only some of the relevant aspects'; *Gilead, supra* fn 1, 131.

6 'Well-being' and 'welfare' are used here as synonyms which originate in the term 'utility'.

## B. WHOSE WELFARE IS AFFECTED BY PRESCRIPTION LAW?

6 The discussion of the goals of prescription law in the ACR identifies the following as being affected, in terms of welfare, by prescription law: actual plaintiffs (Ps), actual defendants (Ds), potential Ds and other members of society at large.[7] It is emphasised that the group of *potential* Ds is by far larger than the groups of *actual* Ds and Ps, as it includes many large groups exposed to the risk of tort claims, such as producers, service providers and insurers.[8] The remaining welfare effects, positive and negative, on society at large, are the effects of prescription law on members of society who are neither actual nor potential Ds or Ps, and yet are *indirectly* affected by prescription law.

## C. WHAT KINDS OF WELFARE ARE AFFECTED BY PRESCRIPTION LAW?

7 The discussion in the ACR of the policy considerations for and against prescription law[9] provides a detailed chart of the kinds of welfare affected by prescription law.

8 *On the positive side*, the welfare gained by *potential Ds* thanks to prescription, that shortens the period of their exposure to legal risks, includes: reduced costs of preserving evidence; reduced costs of keeping financial reserves; reduced welfare losses caused by the psychological effects of exposure to the risk of being held liable (risk aversion).[10] As to *actual Ds*, prescription law bars 'bad', unmeritorious claims, that otherwise would have succeeded due to Ds' inability to defend stale claims,[11] and thereby avoids welfare losses by actual Ds' caused by the success of such 'bad' claims and by Ds' loss of trust in the fairness of the legal system.[12] As to *society at large*, prescription law, as mentioned, bars 'bad' claims, thereby avoiding the negative welfare effects that such claims have on the efficiency goals of tort law (efficient deterrence, loss spreading and reduction of administrative costs).[13] From society's perspective prescription also avoids the welfare losses caused by uncertainty that obstructs the efficient functioning of markets, and welfare losses due to the additional resources consumed by

7 ACR, *supra* fn 4, Section IV.B.
8 Ibid 23 and *infra* fn 35.
9 Ibid Section IV.
10 Ibid 22–23.
11 Ibid 24.
12 *Gilead, supra* fn 1, 121–122.
13 Ibid 114–121.

adjudication of stale claims.[14] From *Ps'* perspective prescription adds to their welfare by incentivising them to *timely* file 'good' claims that would have failed if filed with delay.[15]

9 *On the negative side*, prescription leads to losses of welfare for those Ps whose 'good' claims are barred because of prescription, and who are frustrated by loss of their right to 'open courts.'[16] Failure of 'good' claims barred by prescription also leads to loss of welfare from society's perspective as it erodes the positive effect of 'good' claims on the efficiency of tort law (in terms of deterrence and loss spreading).[17]

## III. ON WELFARE MEASUREMENT DIFFICULTIES

10 As stressed,[18] information difficulties in assessing the effect of prescription law on the net aggregate welfare (efficiency) are a major obstacle in conducting a meaningful and reliable economic analysis of this law. There are two major problems in this regard: the multiplicity of affected parties, and the related problem of assessing the welfare that is gained or lost by prescription because of the nature of this welfare.

### A. WHOSE WELFARE IS AFFECTED?

11 As to the multiplicity of affected parties, it is useful, in order to understand the difficulties, to compare the economic analysis of *tort law* to that of *prescription law*. Under the famous 'Hand Formula', in tort claims the economic analysis focuses on the welfare of *two parties*: actual P and D. In contrast, the economic analysis of prescription law should take into account the effect of prescription on the welfare of *thousands/millions* of affected parties: not just *actual* Ps and Ds (as is the focus of tort law), but that of all *potential* Ds and all other members of society whose welfare is *indirectly* affected by prescription. These include, for example, the welfare gained by consumers who pay lower prices for goods and services because prescription reduces the costs to producers and suppliers of these products and services. Obviously, the number and identity of all these affected parties cannot be ascertained.

---

14 ACR, *supra* fn 4, 26.
15 Ibid 28.
16 Ibid 17.
17 See *supra* fn 12.
18 See *supra* 1.

### B. CAN THE RELEVANT WELFARE BE ASSESSED?

12 As to the assessment of the welfare effects of prescription on all affected parties, there seems to be no realistic ways to do so in a reliable manner, even if the number and identity of the affected parties could be ascertained. This difficulty exists also where the welfare effects of prescription can in theory be quantified in monetary terms. It is very difficult, for example, to assess the extra costs of preserving evidence that are saved by prescription law for all affected activities, and it is even harder to assess the costs of preserving financial reserves for all affected activities. This difficulty of assessment becomes actually unsurmountable for welfare effects which in practice cannot be monetised or quantified on a common yardstick, such as the toll of risk aversion that plagues all potential Ds, frustration and mistrust felt when 'good' claims are rejected or 'bad' claims succeed. On top of that, there is no way to assess the welfare effects of prescription of tort claims on the achievement of the goals of tort law in terms of deterrence and loss spreading, effects which are positive where prescription bars 'bad' claims, but are negative where prescription bars 'good' claims.

## IV. ON THE IMPOSSIBILITY OF ISOLATING THE WELFARE ANALYSIS (EFFICIENCY) OF A GIVEN PART OF PRESCRIPTION LAW

### A. THE PROBLEM: COMPLEX INTERRELATIONS

13 Assuming, despite the above analysis, that all parties whose welfare is affected (directly and indirectly) by prescription could be identified, and that any welfare change could be reliably measured and compared on a common yardstick, there still exists another kind of difficulty which renders efficiency analysis of prescription law most complicated and practically impossible. This difficulty is the complex interrelations, cross-effects, between the different legal norms that constitute prescription law.[19]

14 As explained in the ACR, prescription law in each jurisdiction is composed of four main elements: the starting point of prescription (accrual of cause of action); the prescription periods; rules of prolongation (postponement, suspension, renewal and extension); and the upper time limit ('long-stop').[20] Each element

[19] See *Gilead*, *supra* fn 1, 128 ('the efficiency of any rule of prescription cannot be properly evaluated in isolation. It should be evaluated in its context, and this context is all the other rules that together construct the time limit').

[20] ACR, *supra* fn 4, Section V.A.

(in each jurisdiction) contains a variety of rules, such as a rules that determine the starting point (broadness of cause of action, continuous torts, occurrence of damage),[21] and the long list of rules of prolongation (dealing, *inter alia*, with late discovery, disabilities, special relations between the parties).[22] Many such rules are composed of sub-rules: the late discovery rule, for example, is composed of sub-rules regarding the test for discovery (objective or subjective), the subject matter of discovery, the burden of inquiry and the scope of the rule.[23] Thus, the efficiency of the final product of prescription law, the *effective time of prescription*,[24] depends on the efficient composition of all elements, rules and sub-rules, namely, on many variables that are interrelated and affect each other. Therefore, the efficiency of each sub-rule, rule or element, cannot be assessed in isolation but only on the background of all the other relevant sub-rules, rules and elements.

## B. INTERRELATIONS ILLUSTRATED

15 To illustrate the above complex of interrelations/cross-effects, and the consequential difficulties in assessing in isolation the efficiency of elements, rules and sub-rules of prescription law, let us examine one rule which belongs to the fourth element of liability: the upper time limit (that after its lapse a claim prescribes although the prescription period has not expired).[25] From the economic analysis perspective, the upper time limit, being an additional bar to belated claims, may enhance welfare by reducing legal uncertainty and its related cost, and by barring 'bad' claims.[26] On the other hand, it may reduce welfare by barring 'good' claims. To determine the efficiency of this element (its net contribution to the aggregate welfare), the rules that compose this element should be examined. These rules determine the *length* of the time limit, its *commencement* and its *scope*.[27]

16 Focusing on one of these rules, what should be the efficient *length* of this time limit? The answer depends on the other rules of this element. It depends on the rule of *commencement*: the time limit should probably be shorter if it starts to run not from the harm caused, but longer if it starts to run from the much earlier date of the tortious conduct.[28] The efficiency of the length of the time limit also

---

21 Ibid Section VI.
22 Ibid Section VIII.
23 Ibid Section VIII.B.
24 Ibid 34, 140.
25 Ibid 34, Section IX.
26 Ibid Section IX.A.
27 Ibid Section IX.B.
28 As in the case of defective product that causes harm years after its marketing.

depends on the rule which determines the *scope* of the time limit application: it stands to reason that if the time limit applies to bodily injury it should be longer than if it applies only to property damage, and that it should also be longer if it applies to latent damage and not just to damage that manifests itself much earlier.[29]

Moreover, the efficiency of the rule that determines the length of the upper time limit also depends on a rule – the late discovery rule – that belongs to another element of prescription: rules of prolongation.[30] As explained,[31] the main role of the upper time limit is to counterbalance the uncertainty generated by rules of prolongation, mainly the late discovery rule. The degree of uncertainty produced by the late discovery rule depends, *inter alia*, on a sub-rule of the discovery rule that determines what kind of unawareness to the essentials of the claim triggers the late discovery rule.[32] If *subjective actual* unawareness is sufficient to trigger the late discovery rule, the latter would have very broad application and generate a high degree of uncertainty that may justify a *shorter* upper time limit. But if only *objectively justified* unawareness triggers the discovery rule, it would have narrower application and generate less uncertainty, and therefore a *longer* time limit may be more efficient. 17

These interrelations between rules of the upper-time-limit *inter se*, and between each of them and a variety of rules and sub-rules of other elements, are only one example of the actual inability to assess in isolation the efficiency of a sub-rule, a rule and elements of liability, due to their intricate interrelation and cross-effects.[33] It is most difficult to assess the efficiency of a multifaceted body of law composed of various interrelated elements, rules and sub-rules. 18

## V. STILL IMPORTANT INSIGHTS

Although allegedly unable, for the above reasons, to lead to reliable conclusions regarding the efficiency of a given sub-rule, rule or element of prescription, economic analysis does provide general important insights into prescription law. 19

29 ACR, *supra* fn 4, 262.

30 Ibid 32–33, Section VIII.

31 Ibid Section IX.A.

32 Ibid 175–189.

33 See *Gilead*, *supra* fn 1, 130 referring to the second element ('given the above complexities and in the absence of reliable information, one can only speculate as to whether the optimal general period of prescription in a given jurisdiction is three or five years, or any other relatively short period') and to the fourth element ('it is hard to tell whether the optimal long-stop period is 12 years, 15 or 18, or any other period').

20 Viewing prescription law from the welfare enhancement (efficiency) perspective, the economic analysis, like the ACR,[34] but more strongly, identifies the enhancement of the welfare of *potential* Ds as a major goal that prescription law should promote. It is so because potential Ds are by far the largest group whose welfare is affected (positively) by prescription law.[35] Moreover, enhanced welfare of potential Ds often corresponds with the enhanced welfare of society at large, as both benefit from reduced legal uncertainty and its various related costs.[36] In comparison, the effect of prescription on the welfare of *actual* Ps and actual Ds is indeed minor in terms of aggregate gained/lost welfare. Furthermore, the positive and negative effects of prescription on the welfare of actual Ps and Ds may offset each other,[37] thereby having an even smaller effect on the net aggregate welfare.

21 For the same reason the economic analysis of prescription law strengthens the ACR's suggestion that broad judicial discretion to disapply the prescription defence on a case-by-case basis should be avoided.[38] The reason, again, is that such discretion generates uncertainty that reduces the welfare of many: potential Ds and society at large. This massive loss of welfare exceeds by far the net welfare that such discretion generates for the few that are actually parties to prescription litigation.[39]

## VI. A CONCLUDING REMARK: ECONOMIC ANALYSIS OF PRESCRIPTION AND THE JUST DISTRIBUTION OF WELFARE

22 A major characteristic of the economic analysis of law is that in its aggregate welfare calculus, seeking for efficiency, it attaches the same weights to the welfare of the poor and the rich, the weak and the strong. This 'neutral' approach may be rightly criticised for being unjust as it disregards considerations of fair and

34 ACR, *supra* fn 4, 22–23.

35 Ibid 23 ('the weight attached to the protection of potential Ds in the overall balance between the conflicting considerations should be multiplied by many times with comparison to considerations regarding actual Ds and actual Ps. This enhanced normative weight is referred to as the "multiplier"').

36 Ibid 25.

37 D's welfare gain from dismissal of P's claim is offset by P's welfare loss.

38 Ibid 282–292.

39 See ACR 283. See also *Gilead*, *supra* fn 1, 131 ('Judicial discretion leads to added uncertainty which, as we have seen, significantly diminishes the efficiency of tort law in its various aspects. While this added uncertainty has a negative effect on all potential defendants, it benefits only a relatively small number of actual plaintiffs whose actions are "saved" by the discretionary powers').

just distribution of welfare that justify attaching heavier weights to the welfare of the poor and the weak than to the welfare of the rich and the strong. Applied to prescription, the argument is that in the welfare calculus heavier weights should be attached to lost welfare of actual Ps (assuming they are relatively poor and weak) than to the welfare of Ds (assuming they are relatively rich and strong).

Well, not all Ds are strong and rich and not all Ps are weak and poor. But 23
assuming that this is indeed the case, and heavier weights should be attached to the welfare of Ps than to the welfare of Ds,[40] this does not seem to change the above analysis. The reason, again, is that the number of Ps that are negatively affected by prescription is only a fraction of the number of potential Ds that benefit from it.[41] Therefore attaching heavier weights to the welfare of the few Ps than those attached to the welfare of the many potential Ds would not change the conclusions reached in the ACR and strengthened in this report. Firstly, that the interests of potential Ds should play a major role in the design and evaluation of prescription law. Secondly, that broad judicial discretion should be avoided due to the consequent uncertainty that ensues and negatively affects the welfare of potential Ds and society at large.

---

40 Which will worsen the measurement difficulties; see Section III.

41 See *supra* fn 35.

# PART II

# PRESCRIPTION IN TORT LAW OUTLINED

# CASE SCENARIOS

**Case 1**

*(Failure to ensure the wearing of a ski helmet): D, a ski instructor, negligently fails to make sure that all skiers in her 'off-piste' group wear helmets. P, a skier in the group, hits a tree. P immediately suffers head injury X, and years later another head injury Y that developed from the same accident.*



**Case 2**

*(Three mistakes during one treatment): Physician D treats patient P negligently and performs three mistakes on the day of the treatment: A, B and C. Mistake A causes harm X after a year. Mistake B causes harm Y after two years. Mistakes A and C together cause harm Z after three years.*

**Case 3**

*(Consecutive harms from one injury): Builder D lays down defective foundations for a building thereby creating the risk of future collapse. As a result, the value to the owner of the building (P) decreases (harm A). Two years later the foundation subsides and requires fixing paid by P (harm B). Three years later cracks appear in the building fixed by P (harm C). Four years later the building collapses (harm D).*



**Case 4**

*(Trespass case): D enters P's premises without P's permission, thereby committing a tort of trespass, but without causing any damage. P can file a claim against D asking for the remedy of D's eviction but fails to do so. A year later D causes physical harm to P's premises. P files a claim to compensation for the loss.*



**Case 5**

*(Developing ear damage): In an accidental event, D negligently caused an explosion that damaged P's ears. During the first two years P has to raise the volume to enjoy music. During the following three years P needs a hearing device. After a further five years P becomes deaf.*

**Case 6**

*(Defective foundations of bridge): Builder D lays down defective foundations for a bridge, thereby creating the risk of future collapse if heavy rain falls. Two years later heavy rain indeed falls and the collapse becomes only a matter of time, as indeed happens four years after the laying of foundations.*



**Case 7**

*(Continuing defamation): Every week, during a month, D1 publishes a defamatory article on P1, each time in another newspaper and on a different topic. During the same period D2 publishes a defamatory article on P2, every second day, on the same topic and in the same newspaper.*



**Case 8**

*(Noise from the neighbour): D, a landowner, negligently exposes P, a neighbour, to unreasonable noise for three years. P's hearing is thereby weakened on a daily basis, gradually restricting P's ability to communicate and enjoy music.*

**Case 9**

*(Toxic bins): A waste management company digs bins of toxic content into the soil. Toxic substance leaks into the soil and ground water, causing an apparent damage to crops and expenditure on cleaning on a daily basis. After two years the bins are removed from the soil.*


| | | | | | |
|---|---|---|---|---|---|
| An. and Comp. Report | 46 | Germany | 354 | Poland | 532 |
| Austria | 152 | Greece | 392 | South Africa | 565 |
| Belgium | 189 | Italy | 425 | Spain | 593 |
| Czech Republic | 228 | Netherlands | 459 | Switzerland | 631 |
| France | 320 | Norway | 495 | United States | 673 |


**Case 10**

*(Lung disease I): Chemical plant D negligently exposes bordering lands to toxic substances. As a result P, a nearby resident landowner, contracts a lung disease. P failed to sue in time because his former lawyer told him that the exposure was not tortious, and only his new lawyer told him, after the running of time, that it was tortious.*


| | | | | | |
|---|---|---|---|---|---|
| An. and Comp. Report | 64 | Germany | 362 | Poland | 537 |
| Austria | 147 | Greece | 399 | South Africa | 570 |
| Belgium | 194 | Italy | 429 | Spain | 600 |
| Czech Republic | 231 | Netherlands | 467 | Switzerland | 637 |
| France | 326 | Norway | 499 | United States | 679 |


**Case 11**

*(Lung disease II): Chemical plant D negligently exposes bordering lands to toxic substances. As a result P, a nearby resident landowner, contracts a lung disease, but is unaware of the causal link between exposure and disease because his physician fails to detect it. P does not seek a second opinion. After the prescription period runs on the disease P consults his new physician that tells him about the link.*


| | | | | | |
|---|---|---|---|---|---|
| An. and Comp. Report | 73 | Germany | 363 | Poland | 538 |
| Austria | 147 | Greece | 400 | South Africa | 570 |
| Belgium | 193 | Italy | 431 | Spain | 601 |
| Czech Republic | 231 | Netherlands | 469 | Switzerland | 637 |
| France | 327 | Norway | 501 | United States | 681 |

# PRESCRIPTION IN TORT LAW: AUSTRIA

Ernst KARNER and Bernhard A KOCH

## I. INTRODUCTION

1 The Austrian general rules on prescription can be found in the fourth chapter ('Hauptstück') of the third part of the Austrian Civil Code (*Allgemeines Bürgerliches Gesetzbuch*, ABGB), therefore in the code's last substantive segment. It is entitled 'Von der Verjährung und Ersitzung' ('Of extinctive and acquisitive prescription') and therefore combines the possible effect of the passage of time on rights and claims combined.[1] §§1451 ff ABGB therefore not only address the

---

[1] This has to be seen in light of the more general approach of the codification at the time to merge what is now distinguished as property law on the one hand and the law of obligations on the other into one big part on 'rights in things' ('Von den persönlichen Sachenrechten'), defining things in its very first section as 'everything that is distinct from the person and serves the use of humans' (§285 ABGB).

loss of a claim (as will be the prime focus in the following), but also the accrual of a right by another after fulfilling certain criteria over a specific period of time.

§1451 ABGB defines prescription as 'the loss of a right which has not been exercised over a period defined by law'.[2] If this loss coincides with the passage of the right to another due to the latter's qualified possession, the ABGB speaks of acquisitive prescription, thereby making it a mere sub-category of the former (§1452 ABGB).[3] This sub-category is addressed in §§1453–1477, whereas §§1478 ff ABGB focus on cases where someone 'just' loses a right, but no-one else acquires it instead (extinctive prescription, or – as §1478 ABGB calls it – 'eigentliche Verjährung', which literally translates as 'actual prescription'). Still, this second part of the rules on (extinctive) prescription include references to the former, and both types of prescription are addressed in the third part of the ABGB rules thereupon (§§1493 ff ABGB), which *inter alia* deal with general aspects such as postponement and the effect of prescription. 2

The ABGB addresses the prescription of tort claims specifically in §§1489 f ABGB.[4] Other statutes with tort law content either refer back to these provisions[5] or include specific rules on prescription, which either essentially mirror the ABGB provisions (eg §20 AtomHG, §17 para 1 EKHG, §55 ForstG, §8 RHPflG)[6] or include at least partial deviations therefrom (eg §6 AHG, §37h KartellG, §5 OrgHG, §13 PHG, §5 PolBEG).[7] 3

2 The term 'right' in this context is meant to include the notion of 'claim'.

3 The drafters of the ABGB therefore saw acquisitive prescription as a two-step process: First, the original owner loses his right due to his failure to exercise it properly, and this in turn results in the accrual of the right by another. This is not how it is being understood today, however – property rights are not extinguishable by the mere passage of time, and rights can be acquired over time that have never existed before (such as servitudes). See *G Iro and O Riss*, Sachenrecht (7th ed, 2019), no 6/85.

4 These provisions equally apply to claims arising under contractual liability, since the ABGB deals with both contractual and delictual liability in one chapter. This was somewhat disputed, though, until an amendment to §1489 ABGB in 1916 clarified this expressly. However, the specificities of contractual liability claims will not be addressed in the following in light of the focus of this report.

5 This is either done by general reference to the rules of the ABGB in general where the statutes do not foresee deviations therefrom, which is understood to include the provisions on prescription (eg §14 PHG) or by specific reference to the ABGB rules on prescription (eg §337 para 2 ASVG, §17 para 2 EKHG).

6 *Atomhaftungsgesetz* (Act on liability for damage caused by radioactivity, AtomHG), *Eisenbahn- und Kraftfahrzeughaftpflichtgesetz* (Act on liability for railroads and motor vehicles, EKHG), *Forstgesetz* (Forest Act, ForstG), *Reichshaftpflichtgesetz* ('Reich' liability Act, RHPflG).

7 *Amtshaftungsgesetz* (Act on liability for public authorities, AHG), *Kartellgesetz* (Act against cartels and other infringements of competition law, KartellG), *Organhaftungsgesetz* (Act on liability of representatives of public authorities, OrgHG), *Produkthaftungsgesetz* (Product liability Act, PHG), *Polizeibefugnis-Entschädigungsgesetz* (Act on compensation for the exercise of police authority, PolBEG).

## II. DEFINITION OF PRESCRIPTION

4 Despite the wording of §1451 ABGB quoted *supra* 2, prescription does not lead to the loss of a right, but rather bars its enforcement, so the definition given by the general report would be accepted under Austrian law.[8]

## III. THE NATURE OF PRESCRIPTION AND ITS EFFECTS

### A. THE EFFECT OF PRESCRIPTION

5 The effect of prescription also under Austrian law is that a claim for remedy can no longer be pursued in court. The underlying right is not extinguished, however, but merely reduced to a so-called 'Naturalobligation' (*obligatio naturalis*, literally translated as 'natural obligation'), a right stripped of its possibility to be enforced. Consequently, if the debtor (voluntarily or erroneously) compensates the victim *after* the passage of the prescription period, for example, she cannot claim it back from the recipient afterwards, since the latter is not deemed unjustly enriched thereby.[9] Equally, set-off remains possible both with and against a prescribed claim.[10]

6 The only exception thereto was imposed upon Austrian law by art 11 EC Product Liability Directive,[11] which foresees that 'that the *rights* conferred upon the injured person pursuant to this Directive shall be *extinguished* upon the expiry of a period of ten years from the date on which the producer put into circulation the actual product which caused the damage, unless the injured person has in the meantime instituted proceedings against the producer' (emphasis added).

---

8 See, eg *M Bydlinski*, in: P Rummel (ed), Kommentar zum ABGB$^3$ (2002, in the following: Rummel$^3$), §1451 no 1. See also the singular exception mentioned *infra* 6.

9 This is spelled out in §1432 ABGB: 'Payments of a time-barred debt [...] cannot be claimed back as in the case where someone makes a payment despite knowing that he does not owe it.'

10 While it is undisputed that the creditor can cancel or reduce his own (non-prescribed) claim by setting it off against an already prescribed claim by the debtor, recent academic opinion holds that a debtor cannot use a prescribed claim that she herself has against the creditor to offset her duty vis-à-vis the latter. A recent decision of an enlarged panel of the Austrian Supreme Court (*Oberster Gerichtshof*, OGH) leaves this question unanswered (OGH 1.12.2015 6 Ob 179/14p), but it remains unclear whether this might indicate a change of the court's opinion in this respect. An even more recent decision of one chamber of the Supreme Court has confirmed its earlier position in favour of set-off (OGH 19.7.2016 10 Ob 51/16x), however. There is common accord, though, that a claim that is already prescribed before the counterclaim arose cannot be used for set-off against the latter.

11 Council Directive 85/374/EEC of 25 July 1985 on the approximation of the laws, regulations and administrative provisions of the Member States concerning liability for defective products, OJ L 210, 7.8.1985, 29–33, as amended by Directive 1999/34/EC of the European Parliament and of the Council of 10 May 1999, OJ L 141, 4.6.1999, 20–21.

This was ultimately[12] implemented by §13 PHG, even though its wording deviates therefrom and speaks of '*claims* for damages' ('Ersatzansprüche') that 'lapse after ten years' (emphasis added). The ten-year period in product liability cases therefore leads to a so-called preclusion ('Präklusion') of the right to compensation, leaving not even an *obligatio naturalis*. However, this is a singular exception and indeed an aberration in the eyes of Austrian lawyers.

### B. PRESCRIPTION AS A DEFENCE[13]

Prescription is a defence that has to be introduced by the debtor.[14] If she fails to do so, it will not be raised *ex officio* by the court even if all facts evidencing the requirements of prescription are proven (§1501 ABGB). Arguments against the effect of prescription, eg a postponement of the passage of time, have in turn to be raised by the claimant, which is but a consequence of the fundamental rule that each party has to bring forward and prove arguments in favour of her respective position.[15] Whether or not the requirements of §1489 ABGB or its counterparts in other statutes are met is a matter of substantive law and not procedure. 7

## IV. CONSIDERATIONS FOR AND AGAINST PRESCRIPTION OF TORT CLAIMS

Prescription primarily serves as a protection for potential Ds against unfounded claims.[16] In this regard it is also relevant that Ds are protected from difficulties in gathering evidence: the further removed in time the relevant facts to be proved are, the more difficult the reliable establishment of these facts becomes.[17] Moreover, it has to be considered that even if the facts of a certain case can be 8

---

12 Initially, the Austrian statute had avoided to transform this rule into Austrian law and converted it into a mere prescription period leaving an *obligatio naturalis* intact after ten years; see *BA Koch*, Product Liability in Austria, in: P Machnikowski (ed), European Product Liability. An Analysis of the State of the Art in the Era of New Technologies, (2016), 111 (no 88).

13 See also *infra* Section XII.B.1.

14 The defence may be disregarded if the debtor had raised it against good faith, eg if she had failed to disclose facts to the claimant that would have supported the latter in filing her claim sooner; OGH RIS-Justiz RS0034537, RS0014838.

15 *L Rosenberg*, Die Beweislast[5] (1965), 98 f, 100 f, 108; *E Karner*, The Function of The Burden of Proof in Tort Law, in: H Koziol and BC Steininger (eds), European Tort Law 2008 (2009), 68 ff; OGH RIS-Judikatur RS0037797. See also *infra* Section XII.B.2.

16 *K Spiro*, Die Begrenzung privater Rechte durch Verjährungs-, Verwirkungs- und Fatalfristen (1975), Vol I 10 ff; followed by *H Koziol*, Basic Questions of Tort Law (2010), no 9/1.

17 *H Koziol*, Basic Questions, no 9/4.

proved without difficulty, Ds sometimes need protection against claims which they do not know about and often even cannot know about.[18] The security of Ds in planning their affairs is also protected.[19] Finally, it is argued that, concerning the Ps, prescription is also an educational form of pressure to avoid negligence of Ps in exercising their legal rights.[20]

9 In spite of all these arguments mentioned in favour of prescription, it should not be overlooked that there are also substantial arguments against prescription. In particular, F Bydlinski[21] mentions the protection of acquired rights, the principle of freedom and the postulate of justice: against their will, Ps lose their rights and the assets connected with them without the loss being justified within the relationship to the Ds alone. Ds obtain an advantage without having given anything in return and against the will of the Ps.[22] Therefore prescription is seen as a kind of expropriation.[23] Looking only at the considerations mentioned above, prescription could therefore be seen as constituting a breach of legal ethics.[24]

10 An examination of the mutual interests shows that prescription regularly cannot be justified by only weighing up the parties' individual interests (*inter partes*), but that this institute greatly serves general interests, which are the requirements of legal certainty, practicability and economic efficacy.[25] Furthermore, social interests such as quick enforcement through and the off-loading of pressure on the court system can be mentioned in favour of prescription.[26]

11 As argued elsewhere,[27] it has to be considered that a claim can only prescribe when other interests prevail, which is always – as R Zimmermann[28] emphasises – a delicate weighing up of opposed interests.[29]

---

18 *H Koziol*, Basic Questions, no 9/5.

19 *H Koziol*, Basic Questions, no 9/6 f.

20 OGH 5 Ob 606/89 JBl 1990, 115 *(E Eypeltauer)*; OGH 2 Ob 58, 59/91 JBl 1993, 726 *(Ch Huber)*; OGH 5 Ob 557/93; OGH 8 Ob 244/98k ÖBA 1999, 552 *(P Apathy)*.

21 *F Bydlinski*, System und Prinzipien des Privatrechts (1996), 167 f, followed by *H Koziol*, Basic Questions, no 9/1.

22 *F Bydlinski*, System, 167 f; accord *R Welser and A Kletečka*, Bürgerliches Recht I$^{15}$, no 710; *S Meissel*, in: H Koziol, P Bydlinski and R Bollenberger (eds), Kurzkommentar zum ABGB (6th ed, 2020, in the following: KBB), §1451 no 1; *H Koziol*, Basic Questions, no 9/2; *P Vollmaier*, Verjährung und Verfall (2009), 66 ff.

23 See for example *R Zimmermann and J Kleinschmidt*, Prescription: General Framework and Special Problems Concerning Damages Claims, in: H Koziol and BC Steininger (eds), European Tort Law Yearbook 2007, 31.

24 *F Bydlinski*, System, 167 f.

25 *F Bydlinski*, System, 167 f.

26 *P Vollmaier*, Verjährung und Verfall, 50 ff.

27 *BA Koch*, Verjährung im österreichischen Schadenersatzrecht de lege lata und de lege ferenda, in: H Koziol and J Spier (eds), Liber amicorum for Pierre Widmer (2003, in the following: FS Widmer), 174.

28 *R Zimmermann*, '... ut sit finis litium', JZ 2000, 857.

29 For a detailed weighing up of interests see *H Koziol*, Basic Questions, no 9/4 ff.

# V. ELEMENTS OF PRESCRIPTION – AN OVERVIEW

As shown in more detail below, the Austrian statutory rules on prescription combine the standard elements thereof that can also be found in other jurisdictions: §1489 ABGB, for example, specifies each point in time when the subjective and the objective prescription start to run respectively (which is often not simultaneous), and defines the respective period that needs to pass until the claim is deemed prescribed under either of the two regimes. The objective (longer) period of prescription thereby effectively serves as a ceiling to the shorter (subjective) period irrespective of the claimant's knowledge of the key elements of her claim which triggers the running of the latter period. However, both the short as well as the long period are part of two separate notions of prescription that coexist (rather than the latter simply curtailing the former); they are only linked to each other inasmuch as the lapse of the first period cuts off the enforcement of the claim even though the respective other period may still not have expired yet.[30] The general rules on prescription *inter alia* add rules of prolongation which equally apply to the prescription of tort claims, but are not peculiar for these. 12

# VI. THE STARTING POINT OF THE PRESCRIPTION PERIOD

## A. THE STARTING POINT OF PRESCRIPTION UNDER AUSTRIAN LAW

### *1) Short (Subjective) Prescription Period*

Prescription as a rule cannot start before a claim has arisen, if only because one cannot start losing something which one has not yet acquired. However, the standard rule of tort law prescription in Austria (§1489 ABGB, first sentence) foresees one further element required to trigger the running of prescription: 13

> Compensation claims prescribe within three years starting from the time *when the person harmed becomes aware of the damage and the identity of the injurer*, whether the damage was caused by the breach of a contractual duty or independently of any contract. [...] (emphasis added).[31]

---

[30] Austrian law would therefore not perceive the long-stop period as a separate (here: fourth) element of prescription; see *infra* Sections VI.A.2 and IX.

[31] Translation by *BC Steininger*, in: E Karner, K Oliphant and BC Steininger (eds), European Tort Law: Basic Texts (2nd ed, 2018).

14 In light of the express statutory wording, the late discovery rule is therefore clearly an element of the starting point of prescription and does not come into play as a rule of prolongation.

15 Despite the statutory wording, it does not suffice that the injured party[32] merely knew both of her loss as well as of the injurer's identity per se.[33] First of all, the victim not only needs to know the injurer but also the person liable if separate, such as in cases of vicarious liability.[34] Moreover, it is commonly understood that the victim further has to 'be aware' of all the relevant facts needed to file a claim,[35] therefore have at least a basic knowledge and understanding of the essential facts such as those establishing a causal link between the harm and the defendant as well as the latter's conduct (in case of fault liability). Her knowledge does not have to extend to any imaginable details as long as she is in a position to successfully file a complaint, allowing her to allege sufficient facts that support every element of her claim. However, she must not wait until she has collected the last bit of evidence before proceeding to court.[36]

16 'Awareness' is also imputed if the victim could easily have learned about all these relevant facts without any noteworthy effort, but still failed to take notice.[37] However, this duty to inquire ('Erkundigungsobliegenheit') is not very strict – a layperson typically does not have to hire an expert, for example, in order to find out about all the necessary details, unless special circumstances dictate otherwise.[38] The standard is therefore very low – the victim should just not have 'shut her eyes before the truth',[39] but she does not have to actively investigate the matter. Still, requiring awareness of the claimant is not entirely subjective as it seems at first sight since it is ultimately almost impossible to prove what she actually knew at which point in time, and whether or not she possible misinterpreted what she saw and heard.[40]

---

32 If the victim is a minor or otherwise incapacitated, it is her legal representative whose awareness is relevant: OGH RIS-Justiz RS0034452. In the case of legal persons harmed, it is the awareness and knowledge of its organs and representatives that counts: *P Vollmaier*, in: A Fenyves, F Kerschner and A Vonkilch (eds), Großkommentar zum ABGB – Klang-Kommentar[3] (2012, in the following: Klang-Kommentar), §1489 no 16 ff.

33 OGH 1 Ob 98/56 JBl 1956, 505 ZVR 1956/127; see also *H Koziol*, Österreichisches Haftpflichtrecht I[3] (1997), no 15/11 ff; *M Leitner*, Zur kurzen Verjährungsfrist des §1489 ABGB, ÖJZ 2014, 45 ff.

34 *P Vollmaier*, in: Klang-Kommentar, §1489 no 27.

35 The legal implications of these facts are for the court to assess.

36 Eg OGH 10 Ob 25/05g.

37 OGH 8 Ob 243/79 ZVR 1980/347; 1 Ob 632/90 JBl 1991, 654; *H Koziol*, Haftpflichtrecht I[3], no 15/11 ff.

38 Cf, eg OGH 7 Ob 54/14p Zak 2014, 295, RIS-Justiz RS0034327.

39 Cf OGH 1 Ob 64/00v SZ 74/14.

40 *R Madl*, in: A Kletečka and M Schauer (eds), ABGB-ON[1.06] (2018, in the following: ABGB-ON), §1489 no 7.

**Case 1** – *D, a ski instructor, negligently fails to make sure that all skiers in her 'off-piste' group wear helmets. P, a skier in the group, hits a tree. P immediately suffers head injury X, and years later another head injury Y that developed from the same accident.*

If injuries X and Y were both caused by the same encounter with the tree, preceded by D's failure to monitor compliance with the helmet requirement, and if Y is already foreseeable at the time P sues with respect to X, she must combine her claim for compensation with an action for declaratory relief with respect to future loss Y. If, however, Y develops independently from X and only shows later in time, a separate period of prescription starts to run once P learns about Y and the fact that it can be traced back to D's omission. 17

**Case 10** – *Chemical plant D negligently exposes bordering lands to toxic substances. As a result, P, a nearby resident landowner, contracts a lung disease. P failed to sue in time because his former lawyer told him that the exposure was not tortious, and only his new lawyer told him, after the running of time, that it was tortious.*

The prescription in this case starts to run as soon as P should have known of his potential claim against D, even if misled by his former lawyer. While courts are rather generous in this respect, it is still the objective possibility to learn of the damage and of its link to D's sphere which may trigger liability that counts. In this case hypothetical, P obviously knows of the harm and even of the facts that may lead to D's liability, which fulfils the requirements of §1489 ABGB.[41] The fact that the lawyer gave the wrong advice (ie misinterpreted the known fact legally) is relevant for the latter's malpractice insurance and no longer for D. 18

**Case 11** – *Chemical plant D negligently exposes bordering lands to toxic substances. As a result, P, a nearby resident landowner, contracts a lung disease, but is unaware of the causal link between exposure and disease because his physician fails to detect it. P does not seek a second opinion. After the prescription period runs on the disease P consults his new physician who tells him about the link. Did P's claim against D prescribe?*

This depends upon the answer to the question at what point in time the causal link became objectively detectable by P. As explained above, courts tend to be generous with victims in this respect and do not apply any expert standards to their imputed knowledge. There is no need for P to question his first doctor's opinion unless there are further objective criteria which have already raised his suspicion that he incurred the disease at his workplace. 19

---

41 Cf OGH RIS-Justiz RS0034547: Subjective error by the plaintiff irrelevant.

### 2) *Long-Stop (Objective) Prescription Period*

20 The victim's knowledge of the key facts supporting her claim is irrelevant for triggering the second prescription period foreseen in §1489 ABGB (second sentence):

> [...] If the person harmed has not become aware of the damage or the identity of the injurer or if the damage arose from one or more criminal offences, which can only be committed intentionally and are punishable with imprisonment of more than one year, the claim only expires after 30 years.

21 The trigger of this long-stop period, at least as expressed by the legislator at the time, is not the full cause of action, but merely the cause of harm, even if the latter has not yet materialised within 30 years after the cause was set.[42] However, this is being increasingly criticised by academic writers and some more recent court rulings, arguing that while the awareness of the victim may be dispensable here, still the full cause of action must have arisen, ie at least a first damage must already have occurred. Otherwise, the fundamental principle enshrined in §1478 ABGB that a claim cannot prescribe before it can be enforced would be violated.[43] This would obviously make a difference with latency periods extending beyond 30 years, as is possible with asbestos-related harm, for example.

### 3) *Multiple Torts and/or Multiple Tortfeasors*

22 In case of (actual or potential) multiple tortfeasors, the claim against each and every one of them is treated separately with regard to prescription. Therefore, if for example two people harm the victim, but on different days (or if the victim learns about the second tortfeasor later), the claim against the first person may be prescribed, while the victim may still enforce her claim against the second one, even if the latter is jointly and severally liable with the former for the whole loss. This is not seen differently if the two causes of harm share the same factual and/or legal background.

---

42 *R Welser*, Schadenersatz statt Gewährleistung (1994), 87 f; *R Rebhahn*, Zur neuen Regelung der Verjährung im BGB und zur langen Verjährung von Schadenersatzansprüchen, in: C Fischer-Czermak et al (eds), Festschrift Rudolf Welser (2004, in the following: FS Welser), 868 ff; OGH 4 Ob 57/78 DRdA 1980, 27 (*H Koziol*); OGH 4 Ob 76/81 DRdA 1983, 186 (*P Bydlinski*); OGH RIS-Justiz RS0034502; OGH RIS-Justiz RS0034504.

43 *H Koziol*, Haftpflichtrecht I$^3$, no 15/19; *H Koziol*, Basic Questions, no 9/21 ff; *H Koziol*, Der Beginn schadenersatzrechtlicher Verjährungsfristen, in: M Wandt et al (eds), Versicherungsrecht, Haftungs- und Schadensrecht: Festschrift für Egon Lorenz zum 80. Geburtstag (2014, in the following: FS Lorenz), 653, 658 ff; *R Madl*, Beginn der langen Verjährung nach §1489 Satz 2 ABGB unabhängig vom Eintritt eines Schadens? in: P Apathy et al (eds), Festschrift für Helmut Koziol (2010, in the following: FS Koziol), 774 ff. For more references and details see *infra* Section IX.

23 Recent Supreme Court cases deal with incidents of investments going wrong: In case of various failures to properly inform the victim about the risks of the investment, the victim can claim compensation triggered by each of these omissions independently until prescription regarding the last relevant misconduct in time (or regarding the last one she learned about) has expired.[44]

24 This is also true for multiple actions attributable to the same person: In the example of a physician performing three mistakes, which all would have caused the same loss individually, the victim can wait with claiming compensation until the period starting last expires (which may be later even for simultaneous wrongdoings if the victim initially only knows about one possible cause, but not the others).[45] If these three mistakes lead to different injuries, each harm will be treated separately with regard to prescription.

**Case 2** – *Physician D treats patient P negligently and performs three mistakes on the day of the treatment: A, B and C. Mistake A causes harm X after a year. Mistake B causes harm Y after two years. Mistakes A and C together cause harm Z after three years.*

25 X, Y and Z are treated separately (also) for prescription purposes. The short prescription period for P's claim against D regarding harm X therefore starts as soon as P learns about X (which must have already started to show), that A might have caused X and that it was indeed a mistake, which is correspondingly true for mistake B causing harm Y as well as for harm Z caused by A and C jointly.

## B. OCCURRENCE OF THE HARM

26 When it comes to knowledge of the damage as one prerequisite for the short prescription period to start running, Austrian court practice has undergone a change of perspective: Initially, the Austrian Supreme Court had taken the view that the three-year period commences when the occurrence of the harm is (merely) foreseeable.[46] In the middle of the 1990s, however, a different view – the so-called 'moderate theory of unity' (*gemäßigte Einheitstheorie*) – began to gain the upper hand: for prescription to run, the victim must have sustained

44 See in particular OGH 21.03.2017 10 Ob 70/15i.

45 See, eg OGH 4 Ob 144/11x: The patient sued for two potential flaws of his treatment by the same doctor – either the surgeon had overlooked a previous infection, or the infection occurred during the operation. If the patient became aware of these two possibilities at different points in time, prescription runs for both causal theories separately and independently, even though the patient sues the same defendants because of the same injuries (the consequences of the infection) sustained in one and the same operation.

46 OGH 8 Ob 27/87 ZVR 1988/83; for further references see *A Riedler*, Judikaturwandel in der Frage der Verjährung von Entschädigungsforderungen nach §1489 ABGB?, ZVR 1993, 44.

(and must or should easily be aware of) at least a first partial loss, which was confirmed by an enlarged panel of the Supreme Court.[47] Once the first damage has occurred and the victim became (or should have become) aware of it, however, the prescription period also runs for all other consequential losses, which is why it is necessary to combine the claim for compensation of the first damage with an action for a declaratory judgment (*Feststellungsklage*) with regard to future consequential losses. If the injured party fails to do so, claims in respect of all such consequential loss prescribe within three years from the (actual or imputed) knowledge of the first partial loss, unless such future harm was not at all foreseeable[48] for the injured party.[49]

**Case 3** – *Builder D lays down defective foundations for a building thereby creating the risk of future collapse. As a result, the value to the owner of the building (P) decreases (harm A). Two years later the foundation subsides and requires fixing paid by P (harm B). Three years later cracks appear in the building fixed by P (harm C). Four years later the building collapses (harm D).*

27 Assuming that this pure economic loss is compensable at all (which is more likely under contractual rather than in delictual liability), the key question in this case is from when onwards P had sufficient reason to predict the occurrence of harms A to D. As soon as P learns about the first harm A (the depreciation of the building because of the flaws of its foundations) – and not before then – can she sue for that loss (presuming she knows whom to turn to and why). If at that point in time it is already clear that harms B to D will occur (though it is not yet clear when), P has to combine her suit for compensating loss A with an action for declaratory relief regarding D's liability for losses B to D.

**Case 4** – *D enters P's premises without P's permission, thereby committing a tort of trespass, but without causing any damage. P can file a claim against D asking for the remedy of D's eviction but fails to do so. A year later D causes physical harm to P's premises. P files a claim to compensation for the loss.*

28 Austrian law does not recognise damage per se, the problem of trespass of this hypothetical scenario would merely trigger remedies in property law, including injunctive relief. The first tort claim arises once P's property is actually harmed, and it is only from then onwards that prescription would start to run.

---

47 OGH 1 Ob 621/95 SZ 68/238.

48 Foreseeability is assessed from the *ex ante* perspective of the injured party and not through the eyes of an expert looking at the case *ex post*.

49 *H Koziol*, Haftpflichtrecht I³, no 15/13; *F Bydlinski*, Schadensentstehung und Verjährungsbeginn im österreichischen Recht, in: E Deutsch et al (eds), Festschrift für Erich Steffen zum 65. Geburtstag (1995, in the following: FS Steffen), 65. See also *BA Koch*, FS Widmer, 173.

**Case 5** – *In an accidental event, D negligently caused an explosion that damaged P's ears. During the first two years P has to raise the volume to enjoy music. During the following three years P needs a hearing device. After a further five years P becomes deaf.*

Prescription starts to run as soon as P realises that her hearing impairment is a medical condition and that this can be traced back to D's negligence. If future deafness is already predictable at this point, she also has to ask for declaratory relief in advance, otherwise her claim for this additional harm will be time-barred once the deafness actually occurs. 29

**Case 6** – *Builder D lays down defective foundations for a bridge thereby creating the risk of future collapse if heavy rain falls. Two years later heavy rain indeed falls and the collapse becomes only a matter of time, as indeed happens four years after the laying of foundations.*

Even though this will typically be a case of contractual rather than delictual liability, the trigger for prescription is the same:[50] As soon as the bridge owner learns about the defect in the foundations (which as such already reduces the value of the construction even before it is actually ruined) and can trace this to D's negligence, the three-year prescription period starts to run even though it may not yet be clear whether and to what extent it will indeed collapse in the future. She also has to seek declaratory relief for such future losses at this point in time already. 30

## C. CONTINUOUS TORT

The victim does not have to file for declaratory relief regarding future harm, even when already foreseeable, if such harm is caused by a continuous or recurring tort.[51] This includes pollution cases, where a factory continues to emit toxic fumes or fails to stop poisonous liquids from reaching groundwater, or dangerous installations which those responsible for it neglect to alleviate over time. In all such cases, prescription starts to run for each newly caused harm individually, even though the victims may know from day one onwards that they will incur future injuries until the harmful situation is stopped. 31

**Case 7** – *Every week, during a month, D1 publishes a defamatory article on P1, each time in another newspaper and on a different topic. During the same period D2 publishes a defamatory article on P2, every second day, on the same topic and in the same newspaper.*

---

50 See also *infra* 37.

51 *P Vollmaier*, in: Klang-Kommentar, §1489 no 26. This is only the case for ongoing wrongdoing, but not if a single harmful conduct triggers damage that increases over time.

32 Each publication starts an independent period of prescription, even if it contains the identical defamatory content, irrespective of whether it is in the same newspaper or not.

**Case 8** – *D, a landowner, negligently exposes P, a neighbour, to unreasonable noise for three years. P's hearing is thereby weakened on a daily basis, gradually restricting P's ability to communicate and enjoy music.*

33 Prescription starts to run on every day of the continued exposure to noise, presuming P at that point already knows about the ensuing reduction of her hearing capacity, and that this is due to the ongoing noise.

**Case 9** – *A waste management company digs bins of toxic content into the soil. Toxic substance leaks into the soil and ground water, causing an apparent damage to crops, and expenditure on cleaning on a daily basis. After two years the bins are removed from the soil.*

34 Ongoing omissions such as failure to recall a defective product or to remove toxic agents from the environment are considered to be recurring torts for prescription purposes, therefore triggering prescription periods on every day until the product is recalled or the toxic bins are removed.

# VII. PRESCRIPTION PERIODS

## A. OVERVIEW

**Table 1. Short-stop prescription periods**

| Cause of action | Discovery rule | Prescription period | Statutory basis | Notes |
|---|---|---|---|---|
| General tort claim | Yes | 3 years | §1489 ABGB[52] | Also applies to contractual claims for compensation |
| Intentional crime | No | 30 years | §1489 ABGB | Only if punishable with at least one year's imprisonment |
| Defamation by word, writing or conduct | Yes | 1 year | §1490 ABGB | |
| Torts by auditors | Yes | 5 years | §275 para 5 UGB | |
| Infringement of competition law | Yes | 5 years | §37h KartellG | |

52 Equally applies for other torts, either by direct reference to §1489 ABGB or by copying the rule, see *infra* 37, 41 f.

## B. PRESCRIPTION PERIODS IN THE ABGB

In Austrian private law, there is a general prescription period of 30 years for all civil claims, including claims for unjust enrichment[53] (§1478 ABGB). 35

However, for certain civil claims there are special rules setting shorter periods. §§1480 ff ABGB address, for example, claims arising out of contracts in everyday life, such as payments for the delivery of goods or the performance of services in the context of a commercial business (§1486 ABGB), or the payment of interest and other recurring performances (§1480 ABGB). 36

Two of these special provisions (§§1489–1490 ABGB) concern tort law. As already mentioned above, tort claims generally prescribe three years after P became aware of the damage, the identity of the tortfeasor and all facts needed in order to enforce her claim (§1489 ABGB, first sentence).[54] This period applies to all compensation claims, regardless of whether liability lies in tort or contract law, as expressly stated by §1489 ABGB, which is why there are no problems of 'period shopping' in Austria. 37

In addition, §1489 ABGB in its second sentence foresees a long-stop period of 30 years, which applies irrespective of whether P has already learned about the elements triggering the three-year period.[55] They are linked inasmuch as the claim is prescribed as soon as the first of the two periods has lapsed. 38

The same 30-year period applies according to §1489 ABGB to claims for compensation of damage arising from one or more criminal offences which can only be committed intentionally and are punishable with imprisonment of more than one year. It is thereby irrelevant whether the tortfeasor was actually criminally convicted, or even whether there was a criminal trial at all.[56] Over the last few years, this rule has become particularly important in practice with regard to cases of child abuse that date back several decades.[57] 39

---

53 OGH 1 Ob 182/92s ecolex 1999, 319 (*G Wilhelm*); OGH RIS-Justiz RS0119861; *P Rummel*, Zur Verjährung von Bereicherungsansprüchen: noch ein Appell an den Gesetzgeber, FS Koziol, 377 ff; *R Madl* in: ABGB-ON, §1489 no 5 ff; *P Vollmaier*, in: Klang-Kommentar, §1478 no 72.

54 *Supra* Section VI.A.1.

55 While §1485 ABGB extends the general 30-year prescription period of §1478 ABGB to 40 years if the claimants are legal persons (and therefore in their favour), the Supreme Court has made clear that this extension does not apply in the special case of §1489 ABGB: OGH 1 Ob 120/10v SZ 2010/94. This is still subject to criticism in academic writing, see, eg *P Vollmaier*, in: Klang-Kommentar, §1489 no 3.

56 *P Vollmaier*, in: Klang-Kommentar, §1489 no 46.

57 For the discrepancies between the prescription of civil and criminal claims in the case of child molestation see *M Spitzer and F Kernbichler*, Kindesmissbrauch und §1489 ABGB – Brüche zwischen strafrechtlicher und zivilrechtlicher Verjährung, ÖJZ 2010, 330.

40 A project to reform Austrian tort law proposed to shorten the long-stop period of §1489 ABGB to ten years, but only in respect of claims for pure economic loss.[58] However, the fate of said reform is yet unclear.

41 The periods foreseen by §1489 ABGB are generally independent from the legal basis of the claim, the degree of fault[59] or the object of compensation.[60] Therefore this provision also applies to claims made on an equitable basis, as the ones foreseen by §1310 ABGB in case of minors and other tortfeasors lacking full capacity.[61]

42 Additionally, the scope of §1489 ABGB extends to no-fault claims by way of reference in the statutes introducing these.[62]

43 §1490 para 1 ABGB contains an exception for certain types of defamation: If the victim is insulted 'by words, writing or conduct', her claim prescribes already one year (and not three years) after the victim learns about the insult and the defamer. This does not apply if the conduct included physical conduct, so this exception is limited to mostly verbal abuse whose effects are deemed to 'cool off' after a shorter period of time.[63]

## C. PRESCRIPTION PERIODS IN OTHER STATUTES

44 There are some further particular rules on prescription periods in special statutes, such as, for example, in public liability law (§6 para 1 AHG, *Amtshaftungsgesetz*, Public Liability Act),[64] where the long-stop prescription period is ten years from the occurrence of the damage if the injured party does not become aware of the damage, whereas the short-stop period remains three years, but does not apply if the tortious conduct amounted to a crime sanctioned with at least one year of imprisonment.[65]

---

58 See *H Koziol*, Gedanken zur österreichischen Schadenersatzreform, in: BMJ (ed), 200 Jahre ABGB 2012, 333.

59 Except in the aforementioned case of certain criminal acts for which only the 30-year period applies.

60 *R Madl*, in: ABGB-ON, §1489 no 5.

61 OGH 1 Ob 201/05y, JBl 2006, 183; further LG Klagenfurt 1 R 129/91 EvBl 1991/198. In detail *F Kerschner*, Freiwillige Haftpflichtversicherung als 'Vermögen' iS des §1310 ABGB?, ÖJZ 1979, 289 and *M Nademleinsky*, Wann beginnt die Verjährungsfrist in den Fällen des §1310 ABGB?, EF-Z 2008, 52 ff.

62 See *supra* 3.

63 *R Madl*, in: ABGB-ON, §1490 no 1.

64 *R Madl*, in: ABGB-ON, §1489 no 5.

65 See also §27 para 1 KHVG (*infra* fn 86), which reduces the long-stop period of direct claims against the motor vehicle liability insurer to ten years after the accident, while the short three-year period applies correspondingly.

Another exception applies for compensation claims against auditors, with §275 para 5 UGB (*Unternehmensgesetzbuch*, Commercial Code) setting the short-stop period at five rather than three years.[66] The start of that period is still disputed, though. The courts recently stated that claims based on §275 para 5 UGB prescribe five years after the occurrence of the damage, because they see this rule as a *lex specialis* to §1489 ABGB, and that the long-stop 30-year rule does not apply.[67] 45

§37h KartellG, which implements art 10 of Directive 2014/104/EU,[68] foresees a five-year subjective prescription period for compensation claims based on the infringement of competition law (starting with the victim's awareness of the key facts constituting her claim as required by art 10 para 2 of the Damages Directive) coupled with a ten-year[69] long-stop period triggered by the occurrence of the harm. However, neither prescription period can start as long as the anti-competitive conduct is still ongoing. 46

As mentioned earlier,[70] product liability claims are precluded ten years after the product was put into circulation, which replaces the long-stop period of 30 years of §1489 ABGB, while its shorter (subjective) three-year period also applies here, whichever ends first.[71] 47

## D. PRESCRIPTION OF ADJUDICATED CLAIMS

If the tortfeasor is required to pay damages, the claim arising from the judgment (*Judikatsschuld*) can be enforced for 30 years.[72] However, if the injured party filed for a declaratory judgment alternatively or cumulatively (see above), the tortfeasor is obliged to compensate the injured party for all consequential loss arising from the damaging event. This judgment makes a determination 48

---

66 *R Madl*, in: ABGB-ON, §1489 no 5.

67 OGH 1 Ob 44/06m ecolex 2006, 895. Critically *C Völkl and A Lehner*, in: M Straube, T Ratka and RA Rauter (eds), UGB – Wiener Kommentar zum Unternehmensgesetzbuch[4] (2016), §275 UGB no 81 ff.

68 Directive 2014/104/EU of the European Parliament and of the Council of 26 November 2014 on certain rules governing actions for damages under national law for infringements of the competition law provisions of the Member States and of the European Union, OJ L 349, 5.12.2014, 1–19.

69 While not foreseen in the Directive (though permitted by recital 36), the ten-year long-stop period was chosen in order to put it in line with the time during which the competition authorities can sanction the anti-competitive behaviour with fines according to §33 KartellG.

70 *Supra* 6.

71 See further *R Madl*, FS Koziol, 775 ff.

72 JMV (*Justizministerialverordnung*) RGBl (*Reichsgesetzblatt*) 1858/105, which is still binding according to §4 para 1 *Erstes Bundesrechtsbereinigungsgesetz* (BGBl I 1999/191).

on the legal basis of the tort claim without any temporal restriction, which is why another action for a declaratory judgment is not necessary.[73] However, this rule is not applicable to judgments concerning recurrent payments, such as annuities.[74]

49 In addition to making a determination on the legal basis of the claim without any temporal restriction, declaratory judgments also exclude the prescription defence as against claims for consequential loss for a period of 30 years according to the courts.[75] So, for example, if damage occurs five years after the declaratory judgment, the injured party has 25 more years until this claim is prescribed. A different view is taken in Austrian literature: here it is stated that the injured party has only three years after becoming aware of the damage and the tortfeasor, according to the short-stop period in §1489 ABGB.[76] In the most recent decision, however, the Austrian Supreme Court stated that the short three-year period in §1489 ABGB applies to damage occurring later than 27 years after the declaratory judgment becomes legally binding. It did not go further into details concerning this problem, because the injured party in the specific case had taken action against the tortfeasor after more than 30 years and therefore the claim was prescribed in any case.[77] This solution leads to the strange result that there are different prescription periods for subsequent items of damage, dependent on the time of their arising. However, independently from that, it still has to be concluded that claims for consequential loss that arises later than 30 years after the declaratory judgment came into effect can be enforced within three years, especially because the enforcement of these claims is not possible before the damage arises.[78] This is why the defendant – when there is a declaratory judgment – cannot trust in not being held responsible for the damage caused.

---

73 OGH 2 Ob 116/16x JBl 2016, 797; OGH RIS-Justiz RS0049165.

74 OGH2 Ob 316/70 EvBl 1971/162 and others; OGH 2 Ob 246/04x; OGH 2 Ob 46/05m ecolex 2006, 125; OGH 2 Ob 100/10k; OGH RIS-Justiz RS0034202.

75 OGH 2 Ob 58, 59/91 JBl 1993, 726 *(Ch Huber)* and others; especially OGH 2 Ob 254/98m JBl 1999, 605 (*A Riedler*); OGH 2 Ob 170/05x ecolex 2006, 285 (*G Wilhelm*).

76 *H Koziol*, Haftpflichtrecht I[3], no 15/12 fn 48; *G Ertl*, Die Verjährung künftiger Schadenersatzansprüche, ZVR 1993, 39; *A Riedler*, Judikaturwandel in der Frage der Verjährung von Entschädigungsforderungen nach §1489 ABGB? – Ein Beitrag wider die Verjährung künftiger Ansprüche, ZVR 1993, 52 f; *F Bydlinski*, FS Steffen, 69; *P Apathy*, Verjährung von Schadenersatzansprüchen, JBl 1996, 315; *P Vollmaier*, in: Klang-Kommentar, §1478 no 72; *R Madl*, in: ABGB-ON, §1489 no 16.

77 OGH 2 Ob 116/16x EvBl 2017/17 (*U Frauenberger-Pfeiler*).

78 This is correctly concluded from §1478 2nd sentence ABGB by *R Madl*, in: ABGB-ON, §1489 no 16.

# VIII. RULES OF POSTPONEMENT, SUSPENSION, RENEWAL AND EXTENSION

## A. MODIFICATIONS OF PRESCRIPTION PERIODS UNDER AUSTRIAN LAW IN GENERAL

Since the default prescription period in tort law does not start to run unless the claimant has become aware of the key facts supporting her claim (see *supra* Section VI.A.1), there is already a flexible element included in the general concept of prescription, so unawareness does not lead to a 'modification' of the prescription period, but prevents the ordinary start thereof. However, since this is a statutory element defining that start, it is dealt with above already.[79] 50

Other deviations regarding the start, the running or the end of a prescription period are governed by general rules of prescription law which also apply outside of tort law. 51

There are two main types of modifications of the prescription period, which are referred to as 'Hemmung' (suspension, §§1494–1496 ABGB) and 'Unterbrechung' (interruption, §1497 ABGB) of prescription. There are two variations of the former, the so-called 'Fortlaufshemmung' ('suspended continuance of prescription', where the running of the prescription period itself is paused, either from the start or in between) and the 'Ablaufshemmung' ('suspended expiry of prescription', where the prescription period runs normally, but its ending is being postponed). In both variations, prescription continues to run (or comes to an end) after the reason for the 'Hemmung' is over. If prescription is 'interrupted', on the other hand, it starts completely anew after the reason for this 'Unterbrechung' has fallen away, no matter how long the prescription period until then has already run, so it is more of a full reset rather than a mere interruption as the literal translation would indicate. 52

## B. 'FORTLAUFSHEMMUNG' (SUSPENDED CONTINUANCE OF PRESCRIPTION)

### 1) *Special Relations between P and D*

Prescription does not run as long as the parties to the claim are married or in a registered partnership, or while a relationship of custody persists between 53

[79] *Supra* Section VI.A.1.

them, such as between parents or guardians on the one hand and children on the other, or between legal representatives of certain handicapped adults[80] and the latter (§1495 ABGB). If children claim to have been harmed by their parents, for example, prescription does not even start while the children are minors, whereas in the hypothetical case of a claim between two spouses where prescription has already started to run before they got married it is temporarily put to a halt while the marriage lasts and continues for the remainder of the time after divorce.

54 There are no further special rules providing for modifications of the prescription period between certain specific parties, such as in case of some medical treatment relationship such as between doctors and patients or between employers and employees.

*2) Physical Absence of Certain Creditors*

55 According to §1496 ABGB, the running of prescription is also temporarily stayed as long as the creditor (but not the debtor)[81] is abroad serving in the military or in some civil servant function (such as an ambassador) and continues after her return to Austria. This is not extended to other creditors (let alone debtors) absent from the jurisdiction for other reasons, however.[82]

*3) Closed Courts*

56 §1496 ABGB also foresees a pause during a 'Stillstand der Rechtspflege' (standstill of legal practice), as long as there is no way for the creditor to pursue her claim before the competent court of law, such as in times of war.[83] This is the only *force majeure* recognised as impacting upon prescription, though only insofar. Obstacles that only concern the creditor personally (such as lack of resources or an illness preventing the timely filing of the claim) are irrelevant in that respect.[84]

---

80 According to new terminology introduced in 2017, the ABGB now speaks of 'Erwachsenenvertreter' (representatives of adults, previously referred to as 'Sachwalter'), who can be assigned to represent someone who is incapable to conduct all or parts of her matters herself due to a mental handicap or illness (§§239 ff ABGB).

81 OGH 6 Ob 57/60 JBl 1960, 640.

82 *M Bydlinski*, in: Rummel³, §1496 no 1.

83 This includes also situations where war or turmoil prevents contacting a court, as was presumed during the civil war in former Yugoslavia.

84 It is therefore convincingly argued that war (only) at the domicile of the claimant abroad does not fall under this exception: *R Madl*, in: ABGB-ON, §1496 no 4.

*4) Deferment of Payment*

57 As long as a creditor grants the debtor extra time to fulfil her obligations under the former's claim, it cannot start to prescribe, since the creditor could not enforce it earlier.[85]

*5) Filing Direct Claims Against an Insurer*

58 According to §27 KHVG, the direct claim of a traffic accident victim against the insurer of the vehicle's keeper is subject to the same rules of prescription as her claim against the insured.[86] The running of that prescription period is temporarily halted, however, from the time the victim files her claim with the liability insurer until the latter denies the claim in writing, after which prescription continues.

*6) Special ADR Procedures in Medical Liability Cases*

59 According to §58a of the Law regulating the medical profession (*Ärztegesetz*, ÄrzteG), the prescription of medical liability claims is suspended as soon as the alleged tortfeasor, her representative, her liability insurer or the carrier of the hospital where she was employed (if applicable) has confirmed in writing that she is willing to negotiate the matter out of court. This is also true if either patient or doctor or their representatives ask the patient ombudsman (*Patientenanwalt*)[87] or the mediation panel of the chamber of medical doctors[88] to intervene in handling the claim. The suspension ends as soon as either of the parties or the aforementioned ADR institutions declare in writing that the attempts to settle the claim have failed. At the very latest, however, suspension ends in such cases 18 months after it started (§58a para 3 ÄrzteG).

*7) Suspension of Public Authority Liability Claims*

60 According to §6 para 1 AHG, the prescription of liability claims against a public authority is temporarily suspended as soon as the victim has filed a formal demand for compensation with that authority as required by §8 AHG, until the victim receives a written response.[89]

---

85 OGH 4 Ob 2265/96h; RIS-Justiz RS0017597, RS0034405; *R Madl*, in: ABGB-ON, §1496 no 7.

86 However, the long-stop period vis-à-vis the insurer is capped at ten years after the accident (§27 para 1 KHVG).

87 *BA Koch*, Medical Liability in Austria, in: BA Koch (ed), Medical Liability in Europe (2011), 1 (no 98).

88 *BA Koch*, Medical Liability in Austria, no 99 f.

89 *BA Koch*, The Liability of Public Authorities in Austria, in: K Oliphant (ed), The Liability of Public Authorities in a Comparative Perspective (2016), 19 (no 11).

## C. 'ABLAUFSHEMMUNG' (SUSPENDED EXPIRY OF PRESCRIPTION)

### 1) *Lack of Representative in Case of Incapacity*

61 If someone is incapable of conducting her own affairs (such as minors or certain mentally handicapped persons), prescription cannot start before they are assigned a legal representative (such as a guardian in case of children). If prescription had already started to run before someone lost full capacity, it continues to run, but it cannot end before two years after the person has regained capacity or was assigned a representative. Therefore, if two out of three years of the short prescription period had already expired before the claimant fell mentally ill, for example, and she was assigned a legal representative not before one year later, the prescription period is effectively prolonged for two more years.

62 §1494 ABGB is applied by analogy to situations where there is a conflict of interest between the parties,[90] but also where legal persons lack a capable representative, such as in the case of a claimant who passes away while prescription is running. In this case, the claim becomes part of the estate, which is deemed a legal person in need of a representative. Here as well, prescription continues to run in the meantime, but cannot lapse before two years after that representative has been installed.[91]

### 2) *ADR and Settlements Proceedings*

63 If and as long as both parties show the intent to settle the claim (eg if the tortfeasor pledges to consider it without denying it altogether),[92] it cannot prescribe. Once attempts to resolve the matter out of court have failed, the creditor must proceed to file an action in court without unreasonable delay, which is commonly understood to leave her some three months at maximum (subject to special circumstances of the case).[93] If she fails to do so, prescription will lapse as if no settlement attempts had been made, so these merely postpone the end of the limitation period rather than prolong it.

---

[90] For example, if the victim and the tortfeasor share the same guardian or other legal representative, in which case so-called 'Kollisionskuratoren' (ad hoc representatives of the parties for that specific claim) need to be appointed by the court. For claims between victim and guardian herself, see *supra* 53.

[91] *M Bydlinski*, in: Rummel[3], §1494 ABGB no 1. This is also the only instance where the death of the claimant has an impact upon the running of prescription.

[92] There is no need for any formalised initiation of ADR proceedings. However, the debtor must show at least willingness to settle the claim instead of simply putting the victim off. See *R Madl*, in: ABGB-ON, §1496 no 8.

[93] See, eg OGH RIS-Justiz RS0034450.

If the tortfeasor responds to the victim's claim that her liability insurer will handle the loss adjustment on her behalf, the limitation period cannot expire before the liability insurer has denied the claim,[94] even if the loss should exceed the cover under the policy.[95] In this case as well, the victim has an 'adequate' amount of time left to litigate her claim after she was informed of the denial.[96] 64

In case of a crime, where the victim demands compensation in an adhesion claim accompanying the criminal trial, prescription is only suspended with respect to what the victim asks (or could have asked) for in such ancillary proceedings, so if she only seeks damages for her personal injury, the prescription of her claims regarding property losses inflicted by the same crime will not be affected.[97] 65

### 3) *Competition Law*

According to §37h paras 2 and 3 KartellG, the prescription of damages claims for the infringement of competition law are suspended as soon as either the competition authorities have launched proceedings or at least taken measures to investigate the matter, or while the parties try to settle the claim according to §37g KartellG. Once the authorities have ended the investigation or proceedings, prescription cannot lapse before one year thereafter.[98] 66

## D. 'UNTERBRECHUNG' (INTERRUPTION OF PRESCRIPTION)

There are essentially two prime contingencies which lead to a complete restart of the prescription period. 67

### 1) *Admission of Liability*

Any unilateral statement of or conduct by the defendant (be it explicit or implicit) that objectively has to be interpreted as (or can only be based on)[99] an admission of liability leads to a complete halt of prescription, which means that it starts completely anew (and will not just be continued) should the defendant revoke her admission. Full payment of compensation alone suffices, whereas in the case of partial payments one needs to find out whether this was really meant to be 68

---

94 OGH RIS-Justiz RS0034942, RS0119595.

95 OGH 7 Ob 219/04p SZ 2004/188.

96 See, eg OGH 2 Ob 664/86 (five months too long).

97 OGH RIS-Justiz RS0115181, RS0115182. Cf *infra* Section VIII.D.2 (interruption of prescription if the claimant herself initiates an action against the tortfeasor).

98 *R Madl*, in: ABGB-ON, §1496 no 6/1.

99 Examples include the tortfeasor's request for a deferred payment of the amount claimed by the victim without explicit mentioning of liability.

just a first instalment or only an admission with respect to the corresponding part.[100] Similarly, an admission of liability as such is enough, even if the amount of compensation remains in dispute, as long as this dispute is only about the assessment of the loss and not about the extent of liability. Mere preparedness to enter into settlement negotiations does not suffice, however, even though such talks may lead to a suspension of prescription (*supra* Section VIII.C.2).[101]

69 An admission of liability after the prescription period has lapsed does not lead to a 'reactivation' of the already prescribed claim; it is instead interpreted as a waiver of the prescription defence.[102]

70 In the case of multiple tortfeasors, the fact that one of them admitted liability does not impact upon the prescription of the claims against the others.[103]

*2) Filing a Claim*

71 Once and to the extent[104] a claim has been filed with a court,[105] prescription is 'interrupted',[106] but only if the action is pursued in an ordinary manner,[107] leading to a final decision in favour of the claimant. It is therefore rather this ruling than the filing per se that leads to an interruption.[108] If the claimant is unsuccessful or fails to pursue the action properly, the (original) prescription

---

100 OGH RIS-Justiz RS0034464.

101 *R Madl*, in: ABGB-ON, §1497 no 16.

102 *M Bydlinski*, in: Rummel³, §1497 no 4.

103 OGH RIS-Justiz RS0017363.

104 Suing for only part of the loss has no impact upon the prescription of the remainder, which may already have started to run even if not yet materialised (*supra* Section VI.A.1): *R Madl*, in: ABGB-ON, §1497 no 20; OGH RIS-Justiz RS0019184.

105 Even a foreign court, if it has jurisdiction. A final ruling abroad leads to a restart of the prescription period: OGH RIS-Justiz RS0045270. If the foreign court dismisses the case, eg based on *forum non conveniens*, and the claimant subsequently files the case in Austria without undue delay, the interruption of prescription continues in the meantime: 17 Ob 9/11i JBl 2011,793 (*Kogler*).

106 This also applies to lodging a claim in insolvency proceedings, but only if the claim is confirmed. Prescription starts anew if these proceedings are terminated (cf §9 *Insolvenzordnung*, Austrian Insolvency Act). However, if the claim is contested in the examination hearing, the expiry of the prescription period is only suspended until the end of the time granted to challenge this decision: OGH RIS-Justiz RS0108885.

107 This is subject to a case-by-case analysis; any unusual delay with actively pursuing the case (though to be proven by the defendant) will be held against the claimant: *M Bydlinski*, in: Rummel³, §1497 ABGB no 10. If the court where the claim was originally filed denies international jurisdiction, the case is still pursued in an ordinary manner as long as the claimant refiles the case in the competent jurisdiction without delay: OGH RIS-Justiz RS0123216.

108 *R Madl*, in: ABGB-ON, §1497 no 3, 39 (on the academic dispute at what point in time prescription is really interrupted – at the time of the favourable ruling or retroactively at the filing).

period (whose expiration is temporarily suspended during trial) will continue to run (or its expiration in the interim become effective) since the interrupting effect of the filing is thereby retroactively invalidated.

### E. CONTINGENCIES WHICH HAVE NO IMPACT UPON THE RUNNING OF PRESCRIPTION

Problems within the claimant's own sphere other than those already addressed, such as a temporary illness that does not affect her capacity, lack of resources to pursue the claim, difficulties with gathering evidence or the like, have no impact upon the running of prescription.[109] 72

## IX. CEILINGS ON THE EFFECTIVE TIME OF PRESCRIPTION

While they effectively serve as ceilings on the effective time of the short-stop period, the long periods under Austrian law are deemed to be alternative prescription periods rather than exceptions or limitations to the short one, which is why the long periods are already dealt with *supra* Section VI. Here is an overview of the periods addressed there: 73

**Table 2. Long-stop prescription periods**

| Cause of action | Commencement | Length | Statutory basis | Notes |
|---|---|---|---|---|
| General tort claim | Cause of harm | 30 years | §1489 ABGB | Also applies to contractual claims for compensation. Start disputed in academia |
| Public authority liability | Occurrence of harm | 10 years | §6 para 1 AHG | |
| Product liability | Circulation of product | 10 years | § PHG | |
| Infringement of competition law | Occurrence of harm | 10 years | §37h KartellG | Does not start before end of the anti-competitive conduct |
| Torts by auditors | – | – | §275 para 5 UGB | No long stop according to jurisprudence |

109 *R Madl*, in: ABGB-ON, §1497 no 32.

74 The 30-year prescription period in the second sentence of §1489 ABGB[110] applies to all tort and contractual liability claims alike[111] and is seen as an absolute limitation on the admissibility of a legal action by some authors,[112] while others point out correctly that this corresponds to the general rule in §1478.[113]

75 There are also different opinions amongst authors concerning the question of the beginning of the long-stop prescription period for tortious and contractual liability claims. Some claim it begins to run with the damaging act committed,[114] others say it depends on the occurrence of the damage,[115] which has also become the opinion of the Austrian Supreme Court.[116]

76 The rules of postponement[117] also apply to the ceiling period in §1489 ABGB.[118]

## X. STATUTE INTERPRETATION, JUDICIAL DISCRETION AND LACHES

### A. JUDICIAL ATTITUDE TOWARDS PRESCRIPTION

77 As the courts see one main reason for the existence of prescription rules in the requirement of legal security, prescription periods are interpreted rather strictly. This can specifically be seen when looking at the rules in §§1486, 1487 ABGB (prescription period of three years as an exception to the general rule), which are considered to be exhaustive[119] and are interpreted narrowly, due to the fact that

---

110 *Supra* Section VII.B.

111 *M Bydlinski*, in: Rummel³, §1489 ABGB no 2. On exceptions, see *supra* 44 ff.

112 *R Welser*, Schadenersatz statt Gewährleistung (1994), 88; *R Rebhahn*, FS Welser, 869; pro 'ceiling period' also *P Mader and S Janisch*, in: M Schwimann (ed), ABGB Praxiskommentar³ (in the following: Schwimann³), §1489 no 2.

113 *H Koziol*, Probleme aus dem Grenzbereich von Schadenersatz- und Sozialversicherungsrecht, DRdA 1980, 34; *H Koziol*, Haftpflichtrecht I³, no 15/19; *P Bydlinski*, DRdA 1983, 191; *R Madl*, FS Koziol, 774 ff.

114 *R Welser*, Gewährleistung, 87 f; *R Rebhahn*, FS Welser, 868 ff; *M Spitzer and F Kernbichler*, Kindesmissbrauch und §1489 ABGB, ÖJZ 2010, 330.

115 *H Koziol*, Haftpflichtrecht I³, no 15/19, Basic Questions, no 9/21 ff; *H Koziol*, FS Lorenz, 658 ff; *R Welser and A Kletečka*, Bürgerliches Recht I¹⁵, no 728; *F Bydlinski*, FS Steffen, 74, 75 fn 15; *M Bydlinski*, in: Rummel³, §1489 no 6; *P Mader and S Janisch*, in: Schwimann³, §1489 no 25; *P Vollmaier*, in: Klang-Kommentar, §1489 no 48; *BA Koch*, Verjährung im österreichischen Schadenersatzrecht de lege lata und de lege ferenda, FS Widmer (2003), 190 f; *R Madl*, FS Koziol, 774 ff.

116 OGH 2 Ob 58/91 JBl 1993, 726 (*Ch Huber*).

117 *Supra* Section VIII.

118 See for example OGH 5 Ob 175/14t iFamZ 2015/139 (*F Parapatits*).

119 See EB RV 2 BlgHH 21. Session 160; HHB 428. Contra *G Call*, Die Verjährung der Ansprüche eines gewerbsmäßigen Verwalters einer Wohnungseigentumsanlage, ÖJZ 1978, 203.

they are exceptions to the general rule of 30 years.[120] Therefore, the courts could be seen as particularly respectful of the requirement of legal clarity and legal security.

However, on the other hand, there are better reasons to apply these rules analogously to other cases not explicitly regulated by law.[121] This less strict approach is also more in line with the necessity of a weighing up of the mutual interests mentioned in Section III. The courts have taken this approach in some cases.[122] One example was the case of a claim for the return of excessive bank interest. Generally, as this case is not mentioned in §§1486 ff ABGB, which regulate the exceptions from the general 30-year rule, these claims should prescribe in 30 years. However, in 2003 the Austrian Supreme Court decided to apply some other rules, which set a shorter period of three years analogously to this case.[123] 78

Concerning tort law, there has not been such a development of analogous application of shorter periods yet, but there has been a less strict approach in another way through a less strict interpretation concerning the beginning of the prescription period. For example, in a case of child abuse committed by a cleric in the 1980s, the Austrian Supreme Court decided that the prescription period for the tort claim against the monastery where the cleric was employed only started to run in 2012. In this year, the victim had learned that the cleric in question had had a history of child abuse known by the monastery even before the beginning of his employment. The Supreme Court concluded that only in 2012 had the victim gained knowledge of all the relevant facts to enforce his claim and therefore, even if his claim against the cleric was prescribed, his claim against the monastery was not prescribed.[124] 79

Rejecting a claim on the basis of rules of prescription is not seen as unethical. 80

## B. USE OF OPEN TERMS

As already mentioned, in Austria the prescription rules are seen as rather technical and exhaustive rules that have to be interpreted narrowly. This can also be seen when considering the fact that Austrian prescription law does 81

---

120 OGH 7 Ob 192/72 EvBl 1973/87; further OGH 8 Ob 516, 517/92 JBl 1993, 314; OGH 10 Ob 504/94 JBl 1995, 175; OGH RIS-Justiz RS0033210.

121 *M Bydlinski*, in: Rummel³, §1486 no 1; *P Mader and S Janisch*, in: Schwimann³, §1486 no 1; *W Dehn*, in: KBB⁶, §1486 no 1; *P Vollmaier*, in: Klang-Kommentar, §1486 no 6.

122 OGH 8 ObA 220/98f RdW 2000, 299; OGH 9 ObA 157/98y ZAS 2000, 26 (*R Bollenberger*); OGH 9 ObA 61/02i DRdA 2003, 439 (*B Schwarz*); and many more; last for example OGH 4 Ob 218/13g immolex 2014/68 (*M Cerha*); OGH RIS-Justiz RS0034265.

123 OGH 4 Ob 73/03v ecolex 2004, 262 (*M Leitner*). See also *R Madl*, Ausgewählte Rechtsfragen zur Rückforderung zuviel bezahlter Zinsen bei mangelnder Bestimmtheit einer Zinsanpassungsklausel ÖBA 2003, 722.

124 OGH 1 Ob 124/13m ÖJZ 2014, 45 (*M Leitner*).

not use any such terms as 'reasonableness' or 'good faith' – those are explicitly mentioned by neither the ABGB nor other statutory rules; nor is the use of such terms recommended in the Austrian literature.

### C. LACHES

82 'Laches' as a concept is unknown in Austrian prescription law, even though its Germanic predecessor knew a similar concept referred to as 'Verwirkung'.[125] However, as explained above regarding the short-stop period in §1489 ABGB,[126] the courts do not allow Ps to just stay passive. If they are able to gain knowledge of the necessary requirements without noteworthy effort, the prescription period starts to run at the moment where they could have learned of the damage and/or the tortfeasor.[127] Also, if the victim shows no sign of intention to enforce her claim over time, her conduct may exceptionally be interpreted as an implied waiver if in light of an objective assessment it leaves no doubt that this was her intention, though courts are reluctant to go that far. Mere non-enforcement alone will never suffice.[128]

## XI. CHANGE OF PARTIES

### A. TRANSFER OF THE CLAIM FROM THE ORIGINAL VICTIM TO ANOTHER

83 If the original victim dies and her claims are transferred to her heirs, this does not affect the running of the prescription period if already started against the victim before her death. The only exception thereto is the interim period between the victim's death (when her estate temporarily becomes a legal person of its own) and the devolution of the estate to the heirs by decision of the probate court:[129] According to Austrian courts (in analogy to §1494 ABGB), prescription is postponed in the interim while the estate is unrepresented.[130]

---

125 OGH RIS-Justiz RS0014221.

126 *Supra* Section VI.A.1.

127 OGH 1 Ob 535/90 JBl 1990, 653 *(R Reischauer)* and many more; last OGH 5 Ob 22/15v Zak 2015/398; OGH 7 Ob 56/15 h; OGH RIS-Justiz RS0034327; *H Koziol*, Haftpflichtrecht I$^3$, no 15/10; *R Madl*, in: ABGB-ON, §1489 no 18; contra *M Leitner*, Schadenersatzverjährung: Kann aus dem Gesetz eine Nachforschungsobliegenheit abgeleitet werden?, ÖJZ 2016, 581 (negating the existence of such a duty).

128 See also *infra* Section XII.A.1.

129 See *C Fischer-Czermak and K Windisch*, Chapter 9: Law of Succession, in: C Grabenwarter and M Schauer (eds), Introduction to the Law of Austria (2015), 168, 187 f.

130 *Supra* 62. OGH 5 Ob 606/89 JBl 1990, 115 (critically *E Eypeltauer*) following *Ch Huber*, JBl 1985, 474 f; see also OGH 5 Ob 212/04v JBl 2005, 460; OGH 8 Ob 41/06x MietSlg 58.194; OGH 1 Ob 3/10p ecolex 2010, 748.

If the victim's claim against the tortfeasor is subrogated to an insurer that compensated the victim, neither does a new claim arise, nor does the running of time on (now) the insurer's derivative subrogation claim start afresh, but simply continues to run.[131] 84

## B. CLAIM DIRECTED AGAINST ANOTHER DEFENDANT THAN THE ORIGINAL TORTFEASOR

Also, in the mirror-image scenario of a change of parties, the transfer of a claim against a new defendant does not start a new prescription period. Apart from the case of an unrepresented estate as mentioned before (which may also apply if the tortfeasor dies), there is no prolongation or postponement of the prescription period in the case of a claim transferred by inheritance law. 85

## C. CONTRIBUTION CLAIMS BETWEEN TORTFEASORS

If one of several jointly and severally liable tortfeasors fully compensates the victim (or beyond her individual ultimate share), her contribution claims against the remaining tortfeasors are seen as independent claims of unjust enrichment and as originating from her payment to the victim, according to Austrian court practice[132] and some authors.[133] This approach would lead to the application of the general 30-year rule in §1478 ABGB and therefore, as the prescription period would start with her payment, the contribution claim would not be prescribed. 86

However, the correct approach is to see the payor's claim against the other tortfeasors as the victim's original claim now ceded to the tortfeasor once she indemnifies the victim.[134] Therefore, her derivative contribution claim is a substitute for the victim's claim for prescription purposes, and the prescription period which began for the victim's original claim continues to run as against the paying tortfeasor. However, the latter should be granted reasonable time to enforce her claim against the remaining tortfeasors and therefore the prescription period in this case may exceptionally be prolonged.[135] 87

---

131 *M Lukas*, Zession und Synallagma (2000),114; for further references see *W Thöni*, in: Klang-Kommentar, §1394 ABGB no 9.

132 OGH 4 Ob 2017/96p ecolex 1996, 668; OGH 9 ObA 107/12v; OGH RIS-Justiz RS0104512.

133 *H Gamerith and C Wendehorst*, in: P Rummel and M Lukas (eds), AGBG[4], §896 no 10; *F Kerschner*, Kommentar zum Dienstnehmerhaftpfichtgesetz[3] (2019), §6 no 14; *P Bydlinski*, in: KBB[6], §896 no 5.

134 *Ch Huber*, Die Verjährung von gesetzlichen Rückersatzansprüchen, JBl 1985, 395; *H Koziol*, Haftpflichtrecht I[3], no 15/23.

135 *M Bacher*, Ausgleichsansprüche zwischen mehreren Sicherern einer fremden Schuld (1994), 98 ff; *H Koziol*, Haftpflichtrecht I[3], no 15/23.

88 If one of the tortfeasors indemnifies the victim after the latter's tort claim has already prescribed (which renders it an imperfect obligation),[136] the remaining tortfeasors are not enriched (since they can no longer be sued by the victim anyhow). The paying tortfeasor therefore does not have a contribution claim against them. In this constellation, it would be easier to follow the opinion of those authors who say that the payor's contribution claim is a substitute for the victim's claim for prescription purposes, which would consequently be transferred to the payor in the exact same state that it was in when it was still the victim's claim,[137] and since it was prescribed already then, it remains prescribed also after the compensation payment by one of the tortfeasors.

### D. DEPENDANTS

89 According to §1327 ABGB,[138] dependants of a deceased victim have an independent tort claim of their own against those who tortiously killed the victim, to which the ordinary rules of prescription apply as these claims only arise with the latter's death. The prescription period cannot start before that time.[139]

## XII. OTHER ASPECTS OF PRESCRIPTION LAW

### A. STIPULATION

#### *1) Waiver of Prescription*

90 According to §1502 ABGB, the parties cannot waive the prescription defence in advance, therefore any purported waiver is not valid. However, if the party who sought to waive the prescription defence in advance later raises the defence of prescription in the court proceedings, this is seen as an abuse of legal right according to §1295 para 2 ABGB and is therefore not permitted.[140] Furthermore,

---

[136] See *supra* 5.

[137] *Ch Huber*, JBl 1985, 395; *S Perner*, in: Klang-Kommentar, §896 no 91. At least for the claim regulated in §1042 ABGB, the Austrian Supreme Court has adopted this view, see OGH 4 Ob 15/05t EvBl 2005/159; *S Perner and M Spitzer*, Unterhaltserhöhung nach Körperverletzung und Regress – kein Problem des Bereicherungsrechts, EF-Z 2006, 36.

[138] This provision reads: 'If bodily injury results in death, not only must all expenses be compensated, but also what is lost thereby by the surviving dependants for whose maintenance the deceased was obliged to provide by law.'

[139] This is also coherent with the general rule that, for tort claims, prescription starts with the damage occurred, see *supra* Section VI.

[140] OGH 4 Ob 124/55 EvBl 1956/36 and others; last see for example OGH 3 Ob 183/10y; OGH RIS-Justiz RS0014828. See also *P Mader*, Verjährung und außergerichtliche Rechtsdurchsetzung, JBl 1986, 1; *R Madl*, in: ABGB-ON, §1502 no 3.

the parties cannot agree to a longer prescription period than that provided by the statutory rules. This rule (§1502 ABGB) applies to the long and the short prescription periods.

However, the effect of this strict rule is ameliorated by others. For example, it is generally accepted that settlement negotiations postpone the prescription periods.[141] 91

On the other hand, to waive the prescription defence after the end of the prescription period is seen as valid.[142] This waiver does not have to be explicit but can also occur in an implied way.[143] Once stated, this waiver cannot be withdrawn unilaterally.[144] 92

### 2) *Modification of the Prescription Periods*

It is not only forbidden to prolong the statutory prescription periods but also to create any cases of postponement or renewal of the period other than the statutory ones by agreement between the parties, because this would also lead to a restriction of the prescription rules.[145] 93

Shortening the prescription periods is generally allowed,[146] but only if this shortening takes place between approximately equal partners. If it is agreed upon by means of standard terms and conditions, the general limitations for terms and conditions apply.[147] For example, §879 para 3 ABGB forbids the use of collateral agreements that are grossly disadvantageous for one of the parties. Whether a collateral agreement is grossly disadvantageous for one of the parties has to be evaluated by considering the specific facts of the individual case and by weighing up criteria such as the degree of fault, the nature of the damage (personal injury, loss of property or pure economic loss) or if there was a situation of duress or a power imbalance between the parties.[148] 94

---

[141] *P Mader and S Janisch*, in: M Schwimann (ed), ABGB Praxiskommentar³, before §§1494–1496 no 3; *P Vollmaier*, in: Klang-Kommentar, Vor §§1494–1496 no 6; *supra* Section VIII.C.2.

[142] OGH 1 Ob 158/74 SZ 47/104; OGH 2 Ob 356/74 EvBl 1976/66 and others; OGH 5 Ob 269/97p wobl 1998, 210 (*P Mader*); OGH RIS-Justiz RS0034734.

[143] OGH 1 Ob 642/77 SZ 50/110; OGH 3 Ob 524/87; OGH 2 Ob 616/90 and many more; *P Vollmaier*, in: Klang-Kommentar, §1502 no 11.

[144] OGH 5 Ob 269/97p wobl 1998, 210 (*P Mader*); *P Vollmaier*, in: Klang-Kommentar, §1502 no 13.

[145] OGH 2 Ob 336/55 EvBl 1956/189; OGH RIS-Justiz RS0034798; *P Vollmaier*, in: Klang-Kommentar, §1502 no 20.

[146] *R Madl*, in: ABGB-ON, §1502 no 9.

[147] OGH 1 Ob 1/00d EvBl 2001/49 and others; especially OGH 1 Ob 88/14v JBl 2015, 372; see also OGH 5 Ob 286/08g RdW 2009, 519.

[148] For further information see *H Koziol*, Haftpflichtrecht I³, no 18/5 ff.

95 Within the scope of application of the Austrian consumer protection law (*Konsumentenschutzgesetz* or KSchG), liability for personal injury cannot be limited; furthermore, in the case of loss of property, liability for gross negligence or intent cannot be excluded, even if it is specifically negotiated (§6 para 1 no 9 KSchG) and therefore the prescription period for these claims also cannot be restricted.[149]

## B. SOME PROCEDURAL ASPECTS

### 1) *Pleadings by the Parties*

96 The act that stops the running of the prescription period is the formal filing of a complaint.[150] Prescription is a defence that has to be pleaded by D; the court may not raise it at its own initiative.[151] The prescription defence can be raised up until the end of the oral pleadings in the adjudication at first instance.[152]

97 The parties, according to their duty to bring matters to court in good time (*Prozessförderungspflicht*),[153] should raise the prescription defence as soon as possible. If they do not do so, they risk the rejection of their plea as stated in §179 ZPO (*Zivilprozessordnung*, Civil Procedure Act). According to this rule, the court can reject the plea if the parties negligently failed to raise the prescription defence earlier and if the acceptance of the plea would delay the court proceedings considerably.

98 As the prescription defence is relevant for the legal basis of the claim, it has to be decided upon by means of an interim judgment if the judge wants to allow the claim, and cannot be the subject of subsequent proceedings concerning the exact amount of compensation.[154] If the judge wants to reject the claim on the basis of prescription, he has to reject the claim immediately.[155]

99 According to settled case law, the prescription defence can also be raised by D's guarantor (*Bürge*)[156] and by his intervener (*Nebenintervenient*).[157]

---

149 *P Apathy*, in: M Schwimann and G Kodek (eds), ABGB Praxiskommentar[4], §6 KSchG no 43.

150 See §1497 ABGB, *R Madl*, in: ABGB-ON, §1497 no 2 ff.

151 *Supra* 7.

152 OGH RIS-Justiz RS0034726; OGH 7 Ob 11/04z ecolex 2004, 704; see *R Madl*, in: ABGB-ON, §1501 fn 20.

153 See §178 para 2 ZPO (*Zivilprozessordnung*, Civil Procedure Act).

154 OGH 5 Ob 175/58 ZVR 1959/49 and others; OGH 10 Ob 110/05g; OGH RIS-Justiz RS0034934. See also *P Vollmaier*, in: Klang-Kommentar, §1501 no 7.

155 *G Kodek*, Budgetbegleitgesetz 2011 – die justiziellen Bestimmungen im Überblick, Zak 2011, 5; also *B Köck*, Das Zwischenurteil zur Verjährung, Zak 2011, 167; OGH 1 Ob 65/14m. See also ErläutRV 981 BlgNR 24. GP 86.

156 *W Dehn*, in: KBB[6], §1501 no 1.

157 OGH 2 Ob 108/74 SZ 48/67; OGH RIS-Justiz RS0035487.

A joint tortfeasor with D could refuse to pay a contribution to D if the latter indemnified the victim after the prescription period had lapsed, since after that point in time, D was no longer obliged to pay. 100

*2) Burden of Proof*

In Austria, as elsewhere, each party must prove the facts that support their case and, therefore, the burden of production (the burden of going forward with the evidence) and the burden of persuasion (relates to the question of who must bear the risk of failing to prove a fact) is on the party to whom the facts to be proved are favourable.[158] As prescription is a defence in favour of the defendant, it is the defendant who has to prove when the prescription period began and ended if he raises this defence.[159] 101

158 *W Rechberger*, in: H Fasching and A Konecny (eds), Kommentar zu den Zivilprozessgesetzen³, Vor §266 no 32; *H Fasching*, Lehrbuch des österreichischen Zivilprozessrechts² (1990), no 882; OGH 2 Ob 163/58 JBl 1959, 135; OGH 2 Ob 86/98f JBl 1998, 724; OGH 6 Ob 95/04w JBl 2006, 182.

159 Eg OGH 1 Ob 26 27/86 SZ 59/129; OGH 7 Ob 11/04z ecolex 2004, 704; OGH 1 Ob 13/10h; OGH 4 Ob 116/14h; OGH 1 Ob 197/14y. See also *P Vollmaier*, in: Klang-Kommentar, §1501 no 9.

# PRESCRIPTION IN TORT LAW: BELGIUM

Isabelle DURANT and Stefan RUTTEN

## I. INTRODUCTION

1 The aim of the present report is 'to explore how (and why) the passage of time on an alleged tort claim affects (and should affect) the claim, the parties and other parties through the defence of prescription' under Belgian law. The report refers exclusively to extinctive prescription (or, rather, liberating prescription)[1]

[1] *Infra* 7 and fn 22.

and nothing will be said about acquisitive prescription (*prescription acquisitive/ verkrijgende verjaring*).[2]

In Belgium, prescription is primarily regulated by the Civil Code (arts 2219 ff). Furthermore, a few special prescription provisions have been adopted by the legislator (eg art 26 of the preliminary title of the Code of Criminal Procedure;[3] art 8*bis* of the Act of 30 July 1979 on fire and explosion prevention;[4] art 23 of the Act of 22 July 1985 on civil liability in the field of nuclear energy;[5] art 12 of the Act of 25 February 1991 concerning liability for defective products;[6] arts 12 and 13 of the Act of 31 March 2010 concerning compensation for damage resulting from healthcare;[7] art 88, §2 of the Act of 4 April 2014 on insurances applicable to the claims covered by art 29*bis* of the Act of 21 November 1989 on compulsory motor vehicle liability insurance, which concerns the compensation of vulnerable victims of traffic accidents by the insurer who insure the liability of the owner, driver or holder of the implied motor vehicles).[8] 2

The last substantial reform in the field of prescription took place in 1998. It was the occasion for the legislator to reduce drastically the prescription period (of 30 years until 1998) as regards claims *in personam* (*actions personnelles/ persoonlijke rechtsvorderingen*)[9] and, within these claims, to introduce a distinction between two regimes of prescription: on the one hand the common regime (any claim *in personam* prescribes after ten years) (art 2262) and on the other hand the regime specifically applicable to claims aiming at compensating damage founded on non-contractual liability (art 2262*bis*). 3

---

2 Also called in French *usucapion*, which is a means of acquiring a thing or a right as the effect of possession.

3 Loi du 17 avril 1878 contenant le titre préliminaire du Code de procédure pénale/Wet van 17 april 1878 houdende de voorafgaande titel van het Wetboek van Strafvordering.

4 Loi du 30 juillet 1979 relative à la prévention des incendies et des explosions ainsi qu'à l'assurance obligatoire de la responsabilité civile dans ces mêmes circonstances/Wet van 30 juli 1979 betreffende de preventie van brand en ontploffing en betreffende de verplichte verzekering van de burgerrechtelijke aansprakelijkheid in dergelijke gevallen.

5 Loi du 22 juillet 1985 sur la responsabilité civile dans le domaine de l'énergie nucléaire/Wet van 22 juli 1985 betreffende de wettelijke aansprakelijkheid op het gebied van de kernenergie.

6 Loi du 25 février 1991 relative à la responsabilité du fait des produits défectueux/Wet van 25 februari 1991 betreffende de aansprakelijkheid voor produkten met gebreken.

7 Loi du 31 mars 2010 relative à l'indemnisation des dommages résultant de soins de santé/ Wet van 31 maart 2010 betreffende de vergoeding van schade als gevolg van gezondheidszorg.

8 Loi du 4 avril 2014 relative aux assurances/Wet van 4 april 2014 betreffende de verzekeringen. In this case, the victim's claim is not founded on tort law liability rules, but on the Act of 21 November 1989 which set up a free-standing compensation system released from liability rules. Cf for instance Pol Brugge 12 October 2004, Rechtspraak Antwerpen, Brussels, Gent (RABG) 2005, 67, cmt *G Jocqué*.

9 As distinct from the claims *in rem* – actions involving possession or property rights – which still prescribe after 30 years in accordance to art 2262 of the Civil Code (*actions réelles/ zakelijke rechtsvorderingen*).

A few more punctual changes have also been made since 1998. For example, art 2277*bis* was introduced in 2007. This provision implements the Directive 2004/35/EC on environmental liability with regard to the prevention and remedying of environmental damage and concerns the limitation period in which the cost recovery proceedings have to be initiated.[10] More recently, in 2013 new rules concerning the interruption of the limitation period were introduced and art 2244 has been modified (on these points, cf *infra* 16).[11]

4 The present report will focus on liability in tort law to say when non-contractual liability is concerned. As a rule of thumb, contractual liability rules, not tort law rules, shall be applied when the author of the damage and the aggrieved party are bound by a contract (eg a contractor or an architect and his client). Tort law rules are also excluded as a rule of thumb between the aggrieved party and the subcontractor called to help one of the contracting parties, with the consequence that the latter is almost granted immunity.[12] The third case presented in the Case Scenarios may serve as an example, given that the builder and the owner of the building were bound by a contract for the construction of it (**Case 3** – *defective foundations and risk of future collapse*). Tort law rules should be applicable in the case where the collapse of the building should cause death or injuries. On the contrary, the damage to the built complex should be considered to be a contractual damage, with the consequence that contractual liability rules should find application.

The primacy of contractual rules is subject to two exceptions. Firstly, when the breach of contract is a criminal offence or when the damage is the consequence of a criminal offence, a claim based on tort law (non-contractual rules) can be brought by the aggrieved contracting party against another contracting party or against the subcontractor (and even more broadly against an executing agent such as a worker).[13] This exception finds application especially in case of bodily injuries. Secondly, a tort law claim may be brought by a contracting party against another party when the damage is not purely contractual (damage typical of the contract). Between parties which are bound by a contract, tort law rules may only be applied if the damaging event may be analysed both as a breach of a contractual duty and as a tortious fault and if the damage is

---

10 *IC Durant*, Belgium, in: H Koziol and BC Steininger (eds), European Tort Law (hereinafter ETL) 2007 (2008), 173, no 12 ff.

11 *IC Durant*, Belgium, in: E Karner and BC Steininger (eds), ETL 2013 (2014), 29, no 5 ff.

12 Cour de cassation/Hof van Cassatie (Cass), 24 March 2016, C.14.0329.N; Revue de Droit Commercial Belge/Tijdschrift voor Belgisch Handelsrecht 2017, 200, cmt *R Steennot*. Most of the decisions delivered by the Supreme Court are to be found on the official website of the Ministry of Justice (<http://jure.juridat.just.fgov.be/>).

13 Cass, 26 October 1990; Arresten van het Hof van Cassatie (Arr Cass) 1990–91, 244; Pasicrisie (Pas.) 1991 I, 216; Revue critique de jurisprudence belge (RCJB) 1992, 497, cmt *RO Dalcq*.

different from this resulting from the non-performance of the contract.[14] Tortious fault is traditionally defined as 'any breach, however slight, whether voluntary or involuntary, by act or omission, of a pre-existing standard of behaviour'.[15]

Although the present report focuses on non-contractual claims, just a few words about contractual claims should be given. Such a claim prescribes, as a rule of thumb, after ten years (art 2262 of the Civil Code). The prescription period starts from the day after the cause of action arose, which is the moment the obligation is due.[16] It is irrelevant whether the creditor is aware of this moment or not. In certain areas, this rule is overlooked in favour of a special regime. For instance, a tenant's claim aiming to recover unduly paid amounts prescribes after one year from the despatch of the demand for reimbursement to the lessor by registered letter (art 2273 of the Civil Code).

On the basis of the foregoing, it has to be pointed out here that a *medical* 5
*contract* presents a special feature: when a criminal infringement within the meaning of arts 418 and 420 of the Criminal Code is committed in the course of contract performance, ie when harm is caused due to lack of caution or prudence but with no intention to endanger another's life (manslaughter or involuntary injury), the victim of the medical malpractice may found his/her claim against the doctor (aiming at compensating damage) on contractual rules *or* on non-contractual rules (tort law rules); he/she has the choice. This is because the lack of caution or prudence in the meaning of the Criminal Code matches the negligence or carelessness required by art 1382 of the Civil Code (which is the statutory provision of liability based on fault).[17] Therefore, it is not unusual that tort law rules find application when harm is caused in the course of performance of a medical contract. Readers should not be surprised to find examples from the medical field in the present report.

As far as *notaries* are concerned, most trial judges adopt a dualistic approach when they have to decide on the nature of the relationship between them and

---

[14] Cass, 29 September 2006, C.03.0502.N; Arr Cass 2006, 1863; Pas 2006, 1911; Nieuw juridisch Weekblad (NjW) 2006, 946, cmt *I Boone*; Rechtskundig Weekblad (RW) 2006–07, 1717, cmt *A Van Oevelen*; RABG 2007, 1256; Revue générale de droit civil belge/Tijdschrift voor Belgisch Burgerlijk Recht (RGDC/TBBR) 2008, 557; Tijdschrift voor Bouwrecht en Onroerend Goed (TBO) 2007, 66, cmt *K Vanhove*.

[15] Free translation of *J Dabin and A Lagasse*, Examen de jurisprudence (1939–1948). La responsabilité délictuelle et quasi-délictuelle, Revue critique de jurisprudence belge (RCJB) 1949, 50, no 10.

[16] *I Durant*, Le point de départ des délais de prescription extinctive et libératoire en matière civile, in: P Jourdain and P Wéry (eds), La prescription extinctive. Etudes de droit comparé (2010), 264, no 38.

[17] Cass, 26 October 1990, *supra* fn 13.

their clients: When the notary draws up a notarial act, he could engage his non-contractual liability towards his client while in other cases (for instance when he assists somebody in drawing up a private agreement), he could engage his contractual liability.[18] In a decision delivered in 2013 however, the Supreme Court considered that nothing prevents a judge from applying the rules governing contractual liability to a notary who draws up a deed, according to the circumstances. Nevertheless, it did not raise to the status of general principle that a notary asked to draw up a deed is necessarily contractually liable to his client.[19]

## II. DEFINITION OF PRESCRIPTION

6 Extinctive prescription is a legal institution that is well known under Belgian law, the rules for which, as said, are laid down in the Civil Code. Pursuant to art 2219 of this Code, 'prescription is a mean [...] to be released after a period of time has passed and in accordance with conditions established by the law'.[20] As defined by the Supreme Court (*Cour de cassation/Hof van Cassatie*), prescription is a means of extinction of the action, arising from the non-exercise of this action before the expiry of the time limit stipulated by the law.[21]

## III. THE NATURE OF PRESCRIPTION AND ITS EFFECTS

7 Although the legislator says that prescription is a manner in which an obligation may be extinguished (art 1234 of the Civil Code), most scholars consider that it does not result in the extinguishment of the debt but consists in a means for the defendant (ie the debtor) to be discharged of it.[22]

---

[18] *D Sterckx*, La prescription de l'action en responsabilité notariale devant la Cour constitutionnelle et la Cour de cassation, Journal des tribunaux (JT) 2013, 623.

[19] Cass, 6 June 2013, C.12.0224.F; JT 2013, 629; Notarieel en Fiscaal Maandblad 2014, 41, cmt *H Casman*; Revue du notariat belge (Rev not b) 2014, 268, cmt *D Sterckx*. On this decision, *Durant*, *supra* fn 11, no 49 ff.

[20] Free translation of art 2219 of the Belgian Civil Code.

[21] Cass, 18 March 2013, S.12.0084.F; Arr Cass 2013, 777; Pas 2013, 723; JT 2013, 343; Journal des tribunaux du travail (JTT) 2013, 259; Jurisprudence de Liège, Mons et Bruxelles (JLMB) 2013, 922; Chroniques de droit social/Sociaalrechtelijke kronieken (Chron DS/Soc Kron) 2014, 89.

[22] *V Sagaert*, Les effets de la prescription en droit belge, in: P Jourdain and P Wéry (eds), La prescription extinctive. Etudes de droit comparé (2010), 105, no 2.
That is the reason why, in French, the institution is better named 'prescription libératoire' than 'prescription extinctive' (*M Marchandise*, La prescription. Principes généraux et

It is the result of this point of view that prescription does not have effect automatically. On the contrary, it is obligatory for prescription to be invoked by the defendant for having effect. Therefore, it is generally said that prescription consists of a *defence* (*exception/exceptie*). The defendant is not obliged to invoke it. He may waive his right.[23]

If it can be said that prescription provides the defendant with a defence, it remains that the nature of this defence is a matter for discussion.[24] The question is whether the defence is a *substantive* defence or a *procedural* defence. If most authors were of the opinion, in the past, that prescription was a substantive defence,[25] the trend seems to have turned in favour of the other qualification.[26] Therefore, it is said that prescription extinguishes legal action but does not affect the right to remedy itself (cf however *infra* 10, the case in which the prescription rule is founded on a *deemed payment* and not on the plaintiff's inaction).[27] If prescription is invoked successfully by the defendant, the plaintiff's claim will be said to be inadmissible by the judge. When litigation in court is barred because the prescription period elapses, the victim's right to obtain compensation does still exist; the tortfeasor's debt still exists, as has been stated by the Supreme Court for many years (*Cour de cassation/Hof van Cassatie*). 8

According to this Court, 'extinctive prescription does not affect the existence of the debt but only the fact that it is due'.[28] By inference, 'When a debt is prescribed, and therefore is no longer due, offsetting can not be operated on. The passing of limitation period prevents the debtor from taking advantage of offsetting when the conditions of it were not met before the prescription is acquired'.[29]

If it is true that the time-barred debt continues to exist, it is no longer subject to enforcement proceedings. That is why it is said that its nature is changing

---

prescription libératoire (2014), no 7; *P Wéry*, Droit des obligations. Vol 2 (2016), no 867 and fn 967 and no 875).

23 In matters of public policy however, prescription has obligatorily to be invoked.

24 *Marchandise*, *supra* fn 22, no 6.

25 *G Block*, Les fins de non-recevoir en procédure civile (2002), no 70; *J Linsmeau*, L'action en répétition d'une dette prescrite, RCJB 1972, 7, no 15; *ME Storme*, Perspectieven voor de bevrijdende verjaring in het vermogensrecht met ontwerpbepalingen voor een hervorming, Tijdschrift voor Privaatrecht (TPR) 1994, 1977, 1984.

26 *I Claeys*, De nieuwe verjaringswet: een inleidende verkenning, RW 1998–99, 377, no 24; *J Leclercq*, Réflexions sur un principe général de droit: la répétition de l'indu, JT 1976, 105, no 23; *Marchandise*, *supra* fn 22, no 7; *W Wilms*, De betaling van een verjaarde schuld, RGDC/TBBR 1988, 156, no 11.

27 *Wéry*, *supra* fn 22, no 873.

28 Cass, 13 June 2014, C.11.0595.F-C.11.0673.F; RW 2014–15, 1542; JLMB 2016, 151 (free translation).

29 Ibid (free translation).

once it is time-barred. From that moment, natural obligation is spoken about (*obligation naturelle/natuurlijk verbintenis*). In its turn the natural obligation becomes a civil obligation when it is voluntarily executed or recognised. But the execution under constraint of a natural obligation does not deprive the debtor from bringing a claim for repayment.[30]

## IV. CONSIDERATIONS FOR AND AGAINST PRESCRIPTION OF TORT CLAIMS

9 In view of the preparatory works of the Civil Code, it is generally said that the goals of the prescription mechanism are to ensure *legal certainty* and to prevent *social unrest*.[31] After a certain period of time, the (presumed) debtor must know that he/she is released. Time eventually consolidates things. But other justifications are also put forward by legal scholars, such as the fact that the *means of proof* are deteriorating over time and eventually disappear over the years. One may add that in a certain way prescription reeks of the *idea of sanction*: the plaintiff has to face the consequences of his negligence.

10 A number of other considerations come into play when some of the particular prescription regimes are applicable, ie regimes in which the prescription periods are very short. Two ideas must be mentioned.

Firstly, sometimes, the prescription rule is founded on a *deemed payment* and not on the plaintiff's inaction. This happens on the issue of debts that, as a rule of thumb, are not evidenced in writings due to the fact that it is common to pay them without any delay (eg according to art 2272 of the Civil Code, a merchant's action prescribes in one year for the payment of goods sold to consumers). When a prescription regime founded on a deemed payment is successfully invoked, the plaintiff's right is said to be extinguished, and not only his legal action (on this point, cf *supra* 8). In this case, when he invokes the prescription argument, the defendant does not only say that the litigation no longer has to be looked into, but just that he has paid his debt and that the plaintiff may not ask for a second (undue) payment.[32] Should the debt have been recorded in a written document, the particular prescription regime would be set aside and common rules should regain the upper hand, which does in fact happen often. Habits have indeed changed since the adoption of the

30 Cass, 29 November 2013, C.12.0540.F-C.12.0544.F; Pas 2013, 2406; RGDC/TBBR 2017, 468.

31 *M Regout-Masson*, La prescription des actions en matière de responsabilité. Vol 1, in: JL Fagnart (ed), Responsabilités. Traité théorique et pratique (2014), 6, no 2; *A Van Oevelen*, Algemeen overzicht van de bevrijdende verjaring en de vervaltermijnen in het Belgisch privaatrecht, TPR 1987, 1755, no 7; *Wéry*, *supra* fn 22, no 872.

32 *Marchandise*, *supra* fn 22, no 417.

Civil Code. Moreover, prescription regimes founded on deemed payments find application under contractual agreements. Therefore, no further details will be given on them.[33]

Secondly, sometimes, the prescription is founded on the idea that the debtor's ruin must be avoided. This idea explains the rule contained in art 2277: All actions for payment of sums payable by the year or on shorter periodic terms prescribe in five years. This provision applies especially on default interests.[34]

## V. ELEMENTS OF PRESCRIPTION – AN OVERVIEW

According to art 2262*bis* (1) of the Civil Code, any claim aiming at compensating damage founded on non-contractual liability prescribes after five years from the day that follows the one on which the injured party is aware of the damage or of its aggravation and of the identity of the liable person. Such a claim prescribes anyway after 20 years from the day that follows the one on which the event having caused the damage occurred. All four traditional elements of prescription are present under Belgian law. 11

### A. RULES OF ACCRUAL

With regard to non-contractual liability claims, the prescription starts to run from the day that follows the one on which the injured party is aware of the damage (or its aggravation) and of the identity of the liable person. In short, the knowledge must be about two elements ('double' knowledge): the damage and the tortfeasor's identity. The fourth case presented in the Case Scenarios may serve as an example (**Case 4** – *tort of trespass having caused harm to P's premise*). In this case, a claim for damages based on tort law shall prescribe five years after the victim is aware of the damage and of the identity of the tortfeasor. 12

Authors discuss the *meaning* of this knowledge. Does one have to consider that time is running from the moment the injured party has an actual knowledge of both elements (in this case, one speaks about subjective knowledge),[35] or 13

---

[33] Details can be found in *Wéry*, *supra* fn 22, no 818.

[34] *Wéry*, *supra* fn 22, no 891.

[35] In favour of a subjective approach (actual double knowledge): *E De Kezel*, Problematiek van verborgen letselschade en verjaring: reflectie over een speciale vergoedingsregeling n.a.v. zgn. 'asbestschadevorderingen', TPR 2004, 107, no 11; *G Velghe*, 'Daadwerkelijke

is it sufficient that the injured party ought reasonably to have this knowledge (in this case, one speaks most generally about objective knowledge or normative approach)? In that approach, a certain duty to investigate rests with the victim. Should this second option be selected, a new question arises: what should the reference be in order to come to the conclusion that the injured party ought to have the knowledge? One solution could be to use the standard of the reasonable and prudent person in the same circumstances.[36] Another solution could be to take into account the victim's personal characteristics to decide whether he/she ought to have knowledge of the damage and the identity of the tortfeasor.[37]

In a decision delivered on 5 September 2014, the Supreme Court clearly opted for the subjective approach (actual double knowledge) by reference to the drafting history of the law.[38] According to the Court,

> [i]t results from the drafting history of [art 2262*bis* of the Civil Code] that the legislator took as a starting point of the period of limitation the day on which the injured party has actual knowledge of all necessary elements to bring a liability action suit. The injured party must really have knowledge of the damage and identity of the person who could be held liable, which implies that he/she is able to establish causation between the damaging event and the damage.[39]

According to some authors, the subjective approach does not imply that the tortfeasor has to obtain a confession on the part of the victim. The one who invokes that the claim is time-barred (ie the tortfeasor) will however have to establish that the claimant (ie the victim) had the required actual knowledge for too long by means of objective evidence (documents, facts, etc).[40] In other words, a judge's decision should not be guided by the victim's subjective

kennisname' als aanvangspunt van de vijfjarige verjaringstermijn (art 2262*bis*, §1, tweede lid BW). De schermerzone tussen 'kennen' en 'behoren te kennen', RW 2012–13, 945, no 4.

36 In favour of an objective approach (normative concept, referring to the *bonus pater familias* standard): *Marchandise*, *supra* fn 22, no 317; *T Vansweevelt*, De verjaring van buitencontractuele vordering (art 2262*bis* BW), in: H Vuye and Y Lemmens (eds), Springlevend aansprakelijkheidsrecht (2011), 293, no 16.

37 *I Claeys*, Opeisbaarheid, kennisname en schadeverwekkend feit als vertrekpunten van de verjaring, in: I Claeys (ed), Verjaring in het privaatrecht. Weet de avond wat morgen brengt? (2005), 31, no 81.

38 Cass, 5 September 2014, C.12.0605.N; Pas 2014, 1744; RGDC/TBBR 2015, 379, cmt *E Verjans*. Previously: Cass, 26 April 2012, C.11.0143.N; Pas 2012, 922; RABG 2012, 1013; RW 2012–13, 944, cmt *G Velghe*; RGDC/TBBR 2013, 50, cmt *E Verjans*; RCJB 2015, 55, cmt *P Wéry*.

39 Free translation.

40 *I Boone*, De verjaring van de vordering tot schadeherstel op grond van buitencontractuele aansprakelijkheid en van de burgerlijke vordering uit een misdrijf, in De herziening van de bevrijdende verjaring door de Wet van 10 juni 1998. De gelijkheid hersteld? (1999), 93, no 143.

statements.[41] From the moment the tortfeasor should have to prove the knowledge by means of objective evidence, the subjective and the normative approaches are getting closer.[42] It should for instance be the case if it results from the facts that it was impossible that the victim could not have had the required knowledge.[43]

Concerning the *extent* of the knowledge, despite the fact that the legal provision speaks only about the knowledge of the damage and tortfeasor's identity (the abovementioned 'double knowledge'), it is generally said that the limitation period begins to run when the victim possesses all the elements needed to bring a lawsuit.[44] 14

The Supreme Court subscribes to that view, stating explicitly in the abovementioned decision of 5 September 2014 that having knowledge of the damage and the identity of the person who could be held liable implies that the victim can establish causation between the damaging event and the damage. Nevertheless, the Court also said that causation does not have to be proven with certainty in order for the time limit to start to run. This can be explained by the fact that causation is only certain once the proceedings are complete.[45] Therefore, it is generally admitted that the victim must at least be aware that causation is possible between the damaging event and the sustained damage; it may reasonably be understood by the victim that the defendant might be liable due to a fault or other damaging event.[46] More recently, the Supreme Court deduced from art 2262*bis* of the Civil Code that the prescription period starts to run when the victim has at his/her disposal the elements that would allow him/her to consider that the alleged tortfeasor would be liable for the damage.[47]

As far as the damage is concerned, the Court has been saying for many years that to become aware of the existence of damage does not imply that one has become aware of its extent (cf *infra* 21).[48]

---

41 *E Verjans*, Enkele verduidelijkingen omtrent het vertrekpunt van de vijfjarige verjaringstermijn voor buitencontractuele rechtsvorderingen uit artikel 2262*bis* BW, RGDC/TBBR 2015, 380, no 5 ff.

42 *Marchandise, supra* fn 22, no 317; *Velghe, supra* fn 35, no 6.

43 According to Regout-Masson (free translation), '[t]he decision of the Supreme Court of 26 April 2012 does not imply […] that the judge might not take into account the fact that on a given moment the injured party had or was able to have at his/her disposal information needed to remove any doubt about the existence of damage and the identity of the person'. *Regout-Masson, supra* fn 31, 25, no 49.

44 *Marchandise, supra* fn 22, no 315.

45 *IC Durant*, Belgium, in: E Karner and BC Steininger (eds), ETL 2015 (2016), 21, no 11.

46 *Durant, supra* fn 16, no 52; *Regout-Masson, supra* fn 31, no 54; *Verjans, supra* fn 41, no 12.

47 Cass, 30 March 2017, C.16.0111.F-C.16.0286.F; Pas 2013, 2406; RGDC/TBBR 2017, 468.

48 Cass, 9 December 2010, C.09.0607F; JLMB 2011, 196; Cass, 9 December 2010, C.10.0306.F; Arr Cass 2010, 2936; Pas 2010, 3171; NjW 2011, 135, cmt *I Boone*; Revue générale des

## B. THE PRESCRIPTION PERIOD

15 With regard to non-contractual liability claims, the regular period of prescription in Belgium is five years. This period is shorter than where contractual liability claims are concerned (cf *supra* 4). It shall apply unless the legislator has provided for a special regime. For instance, a limitation period of three years shall apply to the action grounded on the Act of 25 February 1991 concerning liability for defective products, beginning to run from the day on which he should reasonably have become aware (art 12).

## C. RULES OF PROLONGATION

16 There are various events, provided for by the Civil Code, that interrupt or suspend the running of the prescription period.[49]

It is said that the limitation period is *interrupted* when the running time is broken by the exercise or by the recognition of the right to which it applies (ie the right to be compensated). The time that has already elapsed is lost and the count of the prescription period starts afresh. The main causes for interruption are: (1) a court order, notice of summons or seizure notified to the party that one wishes to prevent from invoking prescription; (2) a formal legal demand; and (3) the recognition by the debtor (ie the tortfeasor) of the victim's right (art 2244 ff of the Civil Code). Prescription may be interrupted several times. Every time, the interrupting act must be performed before the expiration of the running prescription period.

The limitation period is *suspended* when the passage of time is not taken into account for a while. When the suspending cause has disappeared, time runs anew. The effect of the suspension is to prolong the initial prescription period with the number of days, months or years, the suspension lasted. According to art 2251 of the Civil Code, time runs against any person, except otherwise provided for by law. For instance, prescription does not run against minor children (art 2252) or between spouses (art 2253).[50]

17 The limitation period may also be *prolonged* by the law, most of the time due to any circumstance preventing bringing an action in due time. Prorogation

---

assurances et des responsabilités 2011, no 14750; Circulation, Responsabilité, Assurances/Verkeer, Aansprakelijkheid, Verzekering 2011, 415; JLMB 2012, 201; Cass, 13 October 2017, C.16.0454.F.

49 *M Regout-Masson*, La prescription des actions en matière de responsabilité. Vol 2, in: JL Fagnart (ed), Responsabilités. Traité théorique et pratique (2014), 5 ff.

50 The limitation period is suspended between spouses during marriage: Cass, 16 April 2015, C.14.0466.F; Arr Cass 2015, 1017; Pas 2015, 988; JLMB 2015, 1956; Rev not b 2015, 686.

consists of a general and objective measure in favour of everybody being in the conditions provided for in the law. Prolongation extends the period of time in an indeterminate manner.[51]

A striking example of legal prorogation – maybe even the only one – is provided for in art 26 of the Preliminary Title of the Code of Criminal Procedure. According to this provision, '[c]ivil action arising from an infringement prescribes in accordance with the rules of the Civil Code or specific legislations applicable to the action for damages. However, this action may not prescribe before the public action'.[52] This provision shall apply in respect to any claim seeking an order based on facts disclosing the existence of an infringement.[53] It is of public order.[54] The civil judge who makes a decision on a claim based on an infringement has to find that the facts that are at the basis of this claim fall within the scope of the criminal legislation. He has to establish the elements constituting the infringement having an impact on the prescription.[55] To decide whether the civil action is prescribed or not, one has to determine each period of prescription separately (with regard to civil rules and with regard to criminal rules). For civil purposes, the latest date of expiry shall be considered. Claims that are introduced up until the date of expiry shall not be declared to be time-barred[56] and when a claim for damages is brought before the criminal court by the victim before the expiration of the running criminal prescription period, the civil prescription period shall stop running until the day of delivery of the decision that puts an end to the litigation.[57]

One of the cases presented in the Case Scenarios may serve as an example (**Case 7** – *defamatory articles published in newspapers*). As far as tort law is concerned, each publication should be considered to be an autonomous faulty conduct. For each fault, the prescription period shall start from the day that follows the one on which the injured party is aware of the damage and of the identity of the liable person (cf *supra* 12). Pursuant to the abovementioned

---

51 *Marchandise*, *supra* fn 22, no 220.

52 Free translation.

53 Cass, 23 October 2006, S.05.0010.F; Pas 2006, 2112; Revue régionale de droit 2006, 229, cmt *R Capart*; JLMB 2007, 698; JTT 2007, 227; Chron DS/Soc Kron 2007, 270, cmt *S Remouchamps*; Cass, 22 January 2007, S.04.0088.N-S.04.0169.N; Pas 2007, 128; JTT 2007, 481, cmt *F Lagasse and M Palumbo*; RCJB 2008, 168, cmt *F Kéfer*; Chron DS/Soc Kron 2008, 443; Cass, 7 April 2008, S.07.0058.F; Pas 2008, 821; JLMB 2009, 628; JTT 2008, 285; Chron DS/Soc Kron 2008, 448; Cass, 20 April 2009, S.08.0015.N; Pas 2009, 967; JTT 2009, 427; RW 2009–10, 876.

54 *Marchandise*, *supra* fn 22, no 228.

55 *Marchandise*, *supra* fn 22, no 226. Cass, 25 October 2004, S.99.0190.F; Pas 2004, 1656; Cass, 9 February 2009, S.08.0067.F; Pas 2009, 392; JTT 2009, 211; JLMB 2010, 633.

56 *Marchandise*, *supra* fn 22, no 229.

57 Cass, 7 September 2016, P.16.0362.F.

art 26, the civil action may however not prescribe before the public action. The public action prescribes after five years in the case of defamation (art 21 of the Preliminary Title of the Code of Criminal Procedure and art 443 of the Criminal Code). *A priori*, there will be as many offences as articles have been published.[58] If by any chance it should be decided that the numerous offences constitute the sign of the same criminal intention, the prescription period of five years would start from the last occurrence of those committed with the same mental intention (art 65 of the Criminal Code).[59]

## D. CEILING ON THE EFFECTIVE TIME OF PRESCRIPTION

18 The manner with which the starting point of the five-year period of limitation is set is favourable to the victim. To balance the system, the legislator has introduced another rule: the claim prescribes anyway after 20 years from the day that follows the one on which the event having caused the damage occurred, regardless of the awareness, externalisation or even existence of damage.

One speaks sometimes about the *relative* period of limitation as far as the five-year period is concerned as opposed to the *absolute* period, which refers to the 20-year period of limitation. However, indeterminate prolongation is not really avoided by this long stop, because the running of this 'ceiling period', which is therefore perhaps not really a long stop, may be interrupted or suspended according to the abovementioned rules.[60] The 20-year period of time is also a prescription period. The tortfeasor could potentially answer for the consequences of the damaging event for much longer than 20 years.

The ceiling of 20 years may also be torn by application of art 26 of the Preliminary Title of the Code of Criminal Procedure (cf *supra* 17).[61] In certain circumstances, the starting point of the limitation period with regard to criminal rules is established when the victim attains the age of majority. This is the case when a child under the age of ten is the victim of a rape. Taking this

---

58 *F Discepoli*, La prescription de l'action publique, in: B Compagnion (ed), La prescription (2011), 309, 318; *L Verslyppe*, De verjaring van de strafvordering, Nullum Crimen (2018), 1, no 63.

59 *Discepoli*, *supra* fn 58, 319; *Verslyppe*, *supra* fn 58, no 79.

60 *Durant*, *supra* fn 16, no 28; *A Jacobs*, La loi du 10 juin 1998 modifiant certaines dispositions en matière de prescription, RGDC/TBBR 1999, 10, 29; *Marchandise*, *supra* fn 22, no 229; *T Vansweevelt*, De verjaring van de buitencontractuele vordering (art 2262*bis* B.W.): de kennis van de schade, de identiteit van de aansprakelijke persoon én van het causaal verband tussen fout en schade ? Revue de droit de la santé/Tijdschrift voor gezondheidsrecht 2008–09, 206, no 3.

61 *Durant*, *supra* fn 16, no 6.

rule into account, it is possible that the public action should be time-barred for more than 20 years after the facts (art 21 of the Preliminary Title of the Code of Criminal Procedure and art 375 of the Penal Code). The preparatory works of the Act of 10 June 1998 give the following example.[62] A six-year-old child is raped; the public action will be time-barred when it is 28 years old (because public action prescribes after ten years in case of a crime),[63] which means 22 years after the facts; civil action will be prescribed at the same time.

## VI. THE STARTING POINT OF THE PRESCRIPTION PERIOD

In a lot of cases, a damaging event, existence, externalisation and awareness 19
by the victim of the damage, as well as identification of the tortfeasor are concurrent. It is not however necessarily the case. Externalisation of the harmful consequences may for instance occur years after the damaging event. One need only to think of soil or water pollution causing health problems over the long term, to bodily injuries appearing several years after a traffic accident or a medical intervention.

This point should not be confused with the idea that damage must be certain to be compensated, but it is not necessary for it to be current and existing. If it was only possible or hypothetical, it could not be compensated. It should be noted that anxiety about dying, fear of being harmed or anguish over bad feelings could be seen in itself as certain, current and existing damage, and so deemed to be compensated. As a rule of thumb, the risk of damage is however not sufficient to lead to compensation of the not yet certain damage (cf **Cases 3** and **6** – *risks of collapse*).

Before 1998, the prescription period started from the day after the one on 20
which the damaging event became a source of obligation and thus produced harmful consequences, irrespective of awareness by the victim.[64] Since 1998, not only do the liability conditions have to be fulfilled to make the meter run, but it is also required that the victim has a knowledge of these conditions.

However, as far as the damage is concerned, it must be stressed that the victim 21
must only be aware of the existence of it but not of its extent. Once the victim

---

62 Report drawn up on behalf of the Justice commission, Parliamentary Documents, Sénat de Belgique/Belgische Senaat, 1997–1998, Doc no 1-883/3, 26.

63 According to art 21 of the Preliminary Title of the Code of Criminal Procedure, public action prescribes after ten years, five years or six months from the day on which the infringement is committed, depending on whether this infringement is a serious crime (felony), a major offence (misdemeanour) or a minor offence (infraction).

64 *Marchandise*, *supra* fn 22, no 312.

is aware of the existence of the damage (and of the other factual data about the liability conditions), time is running.[65] It results from this rule that the plight of *foreseeable damage* is bound to this present damage. Two situations may be distinguished here. On the one hand, the foreseeable future damage could be certain; in this case, it may be compensated without any delay. On the other hand, if it is uncertain, it could be the subject of reservations. In addition, according to art 2262*bis*, para 2 of the Civil Code, a claim aiming at compensating a damage reserved by a judgment which has become final prescribes after 20 years from the delivering of the judgment having admitted reservation. It can be recalled that only *certain* damage may be compensated and not uncertain damage.[66] Should the final judgment not have formulated any reservation, it will be the responsibility of the victim to establish that this judgment did not concern the damage for which it is now asking for compensation, for fear of hearing the force of *res judicata* raised.

22 The unforeseeable aggravation of the initial damage is treated in a different manner. In this regard, the Belgian legislator has made the choice to provide for a specific period of limitation. According to art 2262*bis* of the Civil Code, any claim aiming at compensating the aggravation of the (initial) damage, prescribes after five years from the day that follows the one on which the injured party is aware of the aggravation. The claim aiming at compensating the aggravation is considered to be autonomous. The preparatory works of the Act of 10 June 1998 define the aggravation as the unexpected increase of the damage not within the sphere of the reasonably foreseeable evolution of the initial damage.[67] Under aggravation, one therefore has to include not only the unforeseeable consequences of the initial damage but also, more extensively, distinct damage unknown at the time of the first procedure.[68] This explains why authors wrote that when a damaging event occurs, a distinct limitation period runs with regard to each damage, the starting point of which is linked to the victim's awareness.[69]

That is why, with regard to the situation described in the Case Scenarios in which three mistakes were committed during the same medical treatment (**Case 2** – *three mistakes during one treatment*), each of them (A, B and C) having caused a distinct harm (X, Y and Z), it is likely that three limitation

---

65 *Marchandise, supra* fn 22, no 314; *M Marchandise*, La prescription libératoire en matière civile (2007), no 51; *T Vansweevelt and B Weyts*, Handboek Buitencontractueel Aansprakelijkheidsrecht (2009), no 93.

66 *Vansweevelt and Weyts, supra* fn 65, no 1017.

67 Report drawn up on behalf of the Justice commission, Parliamentary Documents, *Chambre des représentants/Kamer van volksvertegenwoordigers*, 1997–1998, Doc no 1087/7, 9.

68 *Ibidem. Jacobs, supra* fn 58, 22.

69 *Boone*, fn 40, no 138; *Claeys, supra* fn 37, no 57; *Vansweevelt and Weyts, supra* fn 65, no 93.

periods will run. Each starting point of the five-year period will be determined depending on the awareness by the patient of the liability conditions, and especially the existence of the damage (not its extent) and the identity of the tortfeasor.

With regard to the situation described in the Case Scenarios in which a ski instructor was negligent with the consequence that a skier, not wearing an helmet, hits a tree (**Case 1** – *consecutive harms from one injury*), the first thing to say is that the claim basis could be the contract, if it is considered that this includes a security obligation to people. Nevertheless, as already mentioned, when the violation of his obligation by a contractor involves violence to the physical integrity of the other party, courts generally accept a claim based on tort law.[70] Considering that it would be the chosen solution in this case, a distinction should be made depending on whether the second injury was foreseeable or unforeseeable. The foreseeable but uncertain damage could and should be the subject of reservations. In the latter case, the claim prescribes 20 years from the delivering of the judgment having admitted reservations. Unforeseeable damage in the abovementioned meaning should lead to an autonomous claim. In this latter case the five-year limitation period starts to run the day after the day on which the injured party is aware of the new damage. The same can be said about the case concerning the damage caused to P's ears following an explosion (**Case 5** – *damage to P's ears is worsening over time*) or following exposure to unreasonable noise (**Case 8** – *damage to P's hearing weakening on a daily basis*). Uncertain but foreseeable damage has to be the subject of reservations; unforeseeable aggravation is an autonomous damage.

Taking into account these principles, how can one grasp the situation in which 23
damage is generated by a continuous fact and appears gradually? Pollution generated by industrial activity grows and grows as toxic products are discharged into a stream (cf **Case 9** – *toxic bins*). The legislator did not answer this question and it seems that there is no case law on this topic. Two approaches as developed by Claeys are conceivable: a global approach of the phenomenon or a sequential approach.[71] In the first approach, the limitation period begins to run once the victim becomes aware of the continuous damaging event (for instance, the dumping of toxic products) and its consequences (for instance, the river pollution). In the second approach, the victim should be aware of a new damage each day and prescription should begin to run with regard to this

---

70 *B Dubuisson*, Responsabilité contractuelle et responsabilité aquilienne. Comparaison n'est pas raison, in: S Stijns and P Wéry, De raakvlakken tussen de contractuele en de buitencontractuele aansprakelijkheid/Les rapports entre les responsabilités contractuelle et extracontractuelle (2010), 1, no 16.

71 *Claeys*, *supra* fn 37, no 59.

damage. This means that that victim might claim damages for the damage having occurred in the five years before he took legal action.

Should the tortfeasor's conduct also constitute an infringement, civil action for damages may not prescribe before the public action (cf *supra* 17), it being understood that in case of continuing infringement, the starting point of the limitation period is the day on which the infringement came to an end.[72]

## VII. PRESCRIPTION PERIODS

24 The statute of limitations that applies to civil lawsuits was radically changed by the law of 10 June 1998. Since then, the main principles applicable in regard to statutes of limitations are the following.

Personal claims, except for tort claims, are statute-barred after a period of ten years. For example, the ten-year statute of limitation applies to claims for the performance of a contract or claims to obtain damages for breach of contract. The ten-year statute of limitation period begins to run from the time when the debtor has to effect performance (or, in other words, from the time when the personal claim has become actionable (*opeisbaar/exigible*).[73]

This ten-year statute of limitation is also the general statute of limitation, which is applied in all matters where no specific statute of limitation exists (eg in procedural law).

Claims *in rem* become statute-barred after a period of 30 years. This 30-year statute of limitation applies to claims to recognise, modify or abolish limited rights *in rem*, such as usufruct (*vruchtgebruik/usufruit*), long lease (*erfpacht/bail emphytéotique*), etc.

25 Tort claims are subject to a double statute of limitation. The Civil Code provides for a relative five-year statute of limitation as well as a so-called absolute 20-year statute of limitation for tort claims.

The relative five-year statute of limitation begins to run when two cumulative requirements are met: (1) the plaintiff knows of the facts giving rise to the right to damages or knows of the aggravation of the damage; and (2) the plaintiff knows of the identity of the liable party. It is required that the prejudiced person has effective knowledge both of the facts and the existence of the damage on the one hand and of the identity of the liable party on the other hand.

---

72 *Discepoli, supra* fn 58, 319; *Verslyppe, supra* fn 58, no 79.

73 *H de Page and R Dekkers,* Traité élémentaire de droit civil belge, VII, (1957), 1047, no 1148; *Claeys, supra* fn 37, no 28–29.

The absolute 20-year statute of limitations applicable to tort claims begins to run from the time of the act giving rise to the right to damages ('injury rule'). After the 20-year statute of limitation has expired, no claim can be brought before the court, even when the plaintiff did not know of the facts giving rise to the right to damages or did not know of the identity of the liable party. The absolute 20-year statute of limitations is a limitation period, not a ceiling period (see *infra* Section IX).

The abovementioned statutes of limitations are applicable to civil claims in general. However, specific laws also provide for particular statutes of limitations. Different periods for different torts within tort law exist, eg in the Law on product liability,[74] in the Insurance Law,[75] liability claims against the directors of a company,[76] recourse of governmental agencies in cases of environmental damage,[77] etc. A thorough research of all statutes of limitation under Belgian law came to the conclusion that more than 1,000 different statutes of limitation exist.[78] 26

Additionally, likewise prescription, the principle of good faith may in some cases prevent a party from pursuing performance or from filing a lawsuit even though the statute of limitation has not expired. This will be the case if the plaintiff exercises his right after he gave the false impression that he would not exercise his right. The principle of good faith precludes the plaintiff from exercising a claim or right when the exercise of the claim is objectively irreconcilable with the prior position that the plaintiff had taken with regard to that claim or right.

To the authors' knowledge, no empirical data exist on the difference between the basic and the effective limitation periods in Belgium. From a theoretical point of view one could assume that in some cases there is a huge difference between the basic and the effective limitation period, because, as explained under Section IX, in Belgian law there is no ceiling period. 27

---

74 Article 12, §2 Law on product liability (a three-year prescription period and a ceiling period of ten years).

75 A specific statute of limitation applies to the direct claim of the plaintiff against the insurance company of the defendant (art 88, §2 of the Insurance Law: a two-tier prescription period consisting of a relative five-year prescription period and a ten-year absolute prescription period).

76 Article 2:143, §§1-2 of the Code of Companies and Associations (a single-tier five-year prescription period).

77 Article 2277*ter* of the Civil Code (a two-tier prescription period: a relative five-year prescription period combined with an absolute prescription period of 30 years).

78 *I Claeys, M De Ruysscher and L Wermoes*, Verjaringsbepalingen in het Belgisch recht. Een overzicht van alle verjaringsbepalingen in het Belgisch recht! Ubi lex distinguit, debemus distinguere (2011).

28 In private law cases 'period shopping' between the general ten-year statute of limitation and the specific double statute of limitation for tort claims could be an issue. It could be an issue because the ten-year statute of limitation begins to run from the time when the debtor has to effect performance, whereas in tort claims the 'discovery rule' applies. Notwithstanding the importance of the accrual point, the distinction between contract and tort is quite clear. Moreover, in general there is a prohibition on the 'cumulative application' of contract and tort. Only exceptionally, when non-performance constitutes a criminal offence or an infringement on a general non-contractual duty, can the plaintiff choose between the contract or the tort track.

## VIII. RULES OF POSTPONEMENT, SUSPENSION, RENEWAL AND EXTENSION

29 According to Belgian prescription law, suspension and interruption/renewal are the main legal techniques used to prolong the effective limitation period. Moreover, some statutory or judge-made rules on the lengthening of prescription could be interpreted in the sense of a postponement or respite. For the sake of clarity, each concept is first defined.

Suspension (*schorsing/suspension*): the running prescription is halted during the period that the circumstances that give rise to suspension exist. After the suspension period, the time already elapsed is not cleared and the remaining time of the prescription period starts running.

Interruption or renewal (*stuiting/interruption*): the time of prescription already elapsed is not taken into account. Instead a new period runs afresh starting on the day that the circumstances that gave rise to renewal have ended. Although 'interruption' is the term used in the Napoleonic Code, the less confusing term 'renewal' is preferred in a comparative context.

Postponement, respite or extension (*verlenging/prorogation or prolongation*): postponement in contrast to suspension does not take into account the time elapsed, but provides the plaintiff an additional, usually short, period of time to act after the circumstances that gave rise to the postponement have ended.

### A. UNAWARENESS – THE LATE DISCOVERY RULE

#### 1) *Unawareness of what Elements of Liability?*

30 Under Belgian law, unawareness in general does not renew or suspend prescription. The five-year relative statute of limitation applicable in torts is an

application of the late discovery rule, however. In the Belgian two-tier system of prescription, the late discovery rule is regarded as defining the starting point of the relative prescription period. The five-year relative prescription period only begins to run when two cumulative requirements are met: (1) the plaintiff knows of the facts giving rise to the right to damages and (2) the plaintiff knows of the identity of the liable party.

Although art 2262*bis*, §1, sub 2 of the Civil Code only requires knowledge of the plaintiff's harm and of the defendant's identity to start the prescription period running, it is generally accepted that knowledge of the defendant's tortious conduct and awareness of the causal link between the harm and the tortious conduct is also necessary.[79] In a recent judgment, the Supreme Court expressly confirmed that knowledge of the plaintiff's harm and of the defendant's identity requires that the plaintiff is able to apprehend the causal link between the tortious conduct and the harm (**Case 11** – *lung disease II:* the relative prescription period begins running when the new physician tells P about the causal link between the exposure and the lung disease).[80]

Moreover, knowledge of the harm does not require that the plaintiff has knowledge of the extent of the harm or that the exact proportions of the harm are established by an expert. It is sufficient that the plaintiff is aware of any harm or loss.[81]

Knowledge of the identity of the defendant only exists when the plaintiff obtained all information necessary to sue the defendant: besides first name and surname, an address of the defendant is also required. What if the wrong person is sued? It is generally accepted that if the plaintiff knew the identity of all possible liable parties, but sued the wrong party, the limitation period ran in favour of the party that was not sued.[82]

*2) Objective or Subjective Unawareness?*

Initially, the question of whether the relative prescription period begins to 31
run only when the plaintiff has effective knowledge of the facts or also runs when a reasonable person would have discovered the relevant facts (normative knowledge) was debated.[83] The Supreme Court (*Cour de cassation/Hof van*

---

79 *Verjans, supra* fn 41, no 12–13.
80 Cass, 5 September 2014, C.12.0605.N.
81 *Vansweevelt, supra* fn 36, no 19–20.
82 *Vansweevelt, supra* fn 36, no 29–31.
83 Some jurisprudence was of the opinion that actual knowledge was required: *I Boone*, De verjaring van de vordering tot schadeherstel op grond van buitencontractuele aansprakelijkheid en van de burgerlijke vordering uit een misdrijf, in: H Bocken, I Boone and B Claessens et al (eds), De herziening van de bevrijdende verjaring door de wet van

*Cassatie*) ended the discussion by ruling that the prescription period only begins to run when the plaintiff has effective knowledge of the damage. The prescription does not begin to run the moment the plaintiff is presumed to have had knowledge of the damage.[84] Although Belgian law takes a subjective approach to the question of awareness, in the sense that the prescription period does not commence until the plaintiff factually has knowledge of the specified elements of liability, some authors argue that this approach does not exempt the plaintiff of a duty to investigate when it is obvious that questions need to be asked.[85]

Awareness of the fact that tort law provides remedy in the plaintiff's case is not an additional condition for the start of the primary limitation period. However, some authors and some case law take the legal knowledge of the plaintiff into account when assessing the moment that the plaintiff had effective knowledge of the harm. The specific skills of the plaintiff are then regarded as an element of proof that can be used by the defendant to argue that the plaintiff had knowledge (**Case 10** – *lung disease I:* normally the prescription period begins running after P is informed by the second lawyer that the exposure was tortious, although an opposite assessment is arguable).[86]

### *3) What is Considered Awareness of an Element of Liability and how Heavy is the Burden to Acquire Knowledge?*

32 The Supreme Court specified in its judgment of 5 September 2014 that it is not required for the plaintiff to have absolute certainty regarding the causal link between the harm and the tortious conduct.[87] However, the Court does not specify which degree of certainty suffices to start the limitation period. Some legal scholars suggest that the limitation period starts when the plaintiff had enough information to seriously consider a causal link between the harm and the tortious conduct.[88] In the example of Case 11 (unawareness of the causal link between exposure and disease because the physician of the plaintiff

10 juni 1998 (1999), 113; *E De Kezel*, Problematiek van verborgen letselschade en verjaring: reflectie over een speciale vergoedingsregeling n.a.v. zgn. 'asbestschadevorderingen', TPR 2004, 107, 118–119: *A Van Oevelen*, Recente ontwikkelingen inzake de bevrijdende verjaring in het burgerlijk recht, RW 2000–01, 1433, 1438. However, other authors argued that a normative knowledge should suffice: *Claeys, supra* fn 37, 77; *Durant, supra* fn 16, 287; *Marchandise, supra* fn 65, 63; *Vansweevelt, supra* fn 36, 304; *Vansweevelt and Weyts, supra* fn 65, no 67.

84 Cass, 26 April 2012, C.11.0143.N; Cass, 5 September 2014, C.12.0605.N.

85 *Verjans, supra* fn 41, no 8–11.

86 Labour Court Liège, 19 October 2004, JLMB 2005, 1267; *Vansweevelt, supra* fn 36, no 18; *Verjans, supra* fn 41, no 7.

87 Cass, 5 September 2014, C.12.0605.N.

88 *Verjans, supra* fn 41, no 18.

fails to detect it), a Belgian judge probably will consider that the plaintiff did not have sufficient certainty about the causal link. The relative five-year prescription period will only start to run from the moment the second physician detects the causal link and informs the plaintiff.

The burden of proof of the awareness of the relevant elements lies on the defendant who invokes the prescription of the claim.[89] However, the claimant has to cooperate in the provision of evidence.[90] When there remains doubt regarding the awareness of the claimant, the claimant will be given the benefit of the doubt.[91]

## B. OTHER RULES OF PROLONGATION

### 1) *D is to Blame for the Delay*

As with *force majeure*, the applicability of the maxim '*fraus omnia corrumpit*' on the rules regarding prescription is debated in Belgium. 33

Some authors argue that if the defendant committed fraud that led to the occurrence of the prescription, the defendant cannot rely on his own fraudulent conduct. Two conditions have to be fulfilled: the conduct of the defendant must infringe on the rights of the plaintiff and the defendant must have committed fraud by using 'devious tricks'.[92]

Other authors point out that the application of this principle would undermine one of the rationales of prescription, namely legal certainty. After a certain period of time it is impossible for the judge to make a sensible decision, due to the lack of reliable proof. Allowing the application of the '*fraus omnia corrumpit*' principle would in fact make the claims not subject to limitation.[93]

Although '*fraus omnia corrumpit*' is considered a general principle of law by the Belgian Supreme Court, its application on the prescription remains uncertain. Furthermore, the authors that do agree on the applicability of

---

89 Court of Appeal Gent, 22 January 2015, RW 2016–17, 664; Court of Appeal Antwerp, 19 January 2015, Not.Fisc.M. 2016, 37; Court of Appeal Gent, 25 April 2014, TBO 2014, 151.

90 *Durant*, *supra* fn 16, no 12.

91 *I Claeys*, Overzicht van rechtspraak bevrijdende verjaring (1992–2017), TPR 2018, 743, no 57.

92 *E Verjans*, Correctiefiguren op de onbillijke gevolgen van de bevrijdende verjaring, TBBR 2014, 162-157-158.

93 *S Somers*, De objectieve onkenbaarheid of de onmogelijkheid om een vordering in te stellen als criterium voor een mensenrechtelijke toets van verjaringsregels bevestigd, TBBR 2015, 448, 456; *Verjans*, *supra* fn 92, 162-156-157.

*'fraus omnia corrumpit'* do not share the same vision on the consequences of the fraud. Some authors defend that the fraud suspends the prescription for as long as the defendant commits fraud. Other authors defend that the prescription period is extended for a short period of time after the plaintiff has discovered the fraudulent behaviour.[94]

34 With regard to the applicability of the doctrine of abuse of rights, the opinions are less divided. Most authors agree that the defendant abuses his right when he invokes the prescription after his behaviour made it impossible for the plaintiff to file his claim within the time limit, or after his behaviour hindered the plaintiff to interrupt the running prescription period.[95] If the defendant blocked the plaintiff to file his claim, the prescription period can be extended for a short period of time so that the plaintiff can file his claim. In some cases, the restoration of *status quo ante* can only be achieved by denying the defendant the right to invoke the prescription.[96]

*2) Admission by D of P's Right or Partial Performance of P's Right by D*

35 Extinctive prescription is renewed if the debtor acknowledges the claim which is subject to prescription (art 2248 of the Civil Code). Similarly, extinctive prescription is also renewed when D consents to waiver of the obtained prescription (art 2220 of the Civil Code) or to waiver of the already acquired part of the prescription period.[97]

Acknowledgement of P's right renews prescription, even if the claim is only acknowledged partially or with certain restrictions.[98]

36 The acknowledgement by D can be tacit or explicit, but the acknowledgement must be certain.[99] The (partial) performance by D can, but will not necessarily, constitute proof of such acknowledgement. If payment is not made voluntarily, but as the result of the execution of a judicial decision, there is no

---

94 *Verjans*, *supra* fn 92, 162-158-159.

95 Court of First Instance Brussels, 28 November 2011, RABG 2012, 1064; Commercial Court Brussels, 27 November 2007, RW 2010–11, 1010; *Verjans*, *supra* fn 92, 162–163.

96 *C Lebon*, Stuiting, schorsing en verlenging van verjaringstermijnen, in: I Claeys (ed), Verjaring in het privaatrecht. Weet de avond wat de morgen brengt? (2005), 119–120; *Verjans*, *supra* fn 92, 162–165.

97 Cass, 23 October 1986, Arr Cass 1986–87, 268, Pas. 1987, I, 250, RW 1986–87, 2093, TBBR 1988, 207, noot A. Van Oevelen and Rev. Not. B. 1987, 39, noot J.E; *M De Ruysscher*, Burgerlijke stuiting van de bevrijdende verjaring: een stand van zaken, RW 2013–14, 843, 853–854.

98 *ME Storme*, Extinctive Prescription in Belgian Private Law – Old Questions and recent Developments, in: E Hondius (ed), Extinctive prescription, On the limitation of actions, Reports to the 14th international Congress of the international Academy of comparative law (1995), no 10.

99 Cass, 7 November 2011, Pas. 2011, 2443; *De Ruysscher*, *supra* fn 97, 853.

acknowledgement of debt that interrupts the limitation period. On the other hand, voluntary performance under the threat of enforcement of a judicial decision does not necessarily imply that the acknowledgement is involuntary and can result in the interruption of the prescription period. The precise circumstances of the case will determine whether or not the (partial) performance constitutes an acknowledgement by D of P's right.[100]

### 3) *Special Relations between D and P*

#### a) Parents/Children

In general, family relations do not give rise to suspension or extension of the 37
prescription period. However, prescription is suspended in favour of minors (art 2252 of the Civil Code). Other family relations (eg between parents and children of age) do not give rise to suspension or extension of the prescription period.

#### b) Spouses

Prescription is suspended between spouses (art 2253 of the Civil Code), without 38
any exceptions.[101]

#### c) Guardian/Ward

Article 2252 of the Civil Code prescribes in general that the prescription 39
vis-à-vis minors and persons under judicial disability is suspended. Other legal provisions can however deviate from this general rule.[102] In addition, claims lodged by the minor vis-à-vis his/her guardian and related to the financial management of the guardian, only lapse five years after the minor becomes of age (art 419 of the Civil Code).[103]

#### d) Attorney/Client

In principle, the attorney-client relation is governed by contract law, not tort law. 40
In cases of legal malpractice, the client generally has a claim for breach of contract against his attorney. The existence of an attorney-client relationship does not

---

100 *De Ruysscher*, *supra* fn 97, 853–854.

101 Eg Cass, 16 April 2015, C.14.0466.F.

102 Cass, 1 June 1995, Arr Cass 1995, 561.

103 *S Mosselmans*, Art. 419 B.W., in: P Senaeve, F Swennen and G Verschelden (eds), Personen- en familierecht. Artikelsgewijze commentaar met overzicht van rechtspraak en rechtsleer (2002).

formally constitute grounds for a suspension of the prescription. The information asymmetry between client and attorney is compensated by the commencement of prescription. The Civil Code contains a specific five-year prescription period for legal malpractice claims against attorneys (art 2276*bis* of the Civil Code). This specific prescription period commences only after the appointment of the attorney is terminated, irrespective of the moment the attorney committed the malpractice.[104] This specific five-year prescription period is applicable for contract and tort claims. Although commencement and suspension of the prescription period both concern the same question, namely whether prescription runs or not, they have to be considered different doctrines.

e) Partners in (Business) Partnership

41 The mere fact that a business partnership exists between plaintiff and defendant does not postpone, suspend or renew the prescription of a tort claim between the partners.

f) Legal Entity/Organs

42 In company law the statute of limitations for all actions brought against the board of directors, the supervisory board and/or the auditors in relation to the execution of their task is five years from the date of the contested act or omission. In cases where facts have intentionally been concealed, prescription only starts from the date the act or the omission was discovered (art 2:143, §§1-2 of the Code of Companies and Associations). This specific prescription period applies for contract and tort claims in company law. Claims between other legal entities and their organs are governed by the general rules of prescription.

g) Employer/Employee

43 Employment relations do not influence the extinctive prescription in tort law. There is no statutory provision that allows the prescription period to be suspended or renewed in case of such relations. Therefore, the general prescription periods in tort law apply.[105]

---

104 When an attorney committed a mistake in first instance in 2014, but the same attorney continued to handle the case in appeal, so that his appointment lasted until 2018, when the Court of Appeal decided upon the appeal, the prescription of the client's claim will only run after the attorney-client relation is terminated in 2018. The legislator deliberately did not define 'termination of the appointment'; the termination can be deducted from the circumstances, for example when the attorney returns the evidence used in court to his client and charges his final fee.

105 *I Vanden Poel, A Van Eeckhoutte, S Heyndrickx, G De Maeseneire and E De Kezel,* Overzicht van rechtspraak. Arbeidsovereenkomsten (2005–2012), TPR 2014, 113, 540.

### h) Physician/Patient

44 Medical treatment relations do not influence the extinctive prescription in tort law. In general, family relations, similarly to employment and medical treatment relations, do not give rise to suspension or extension of the prescription period. The relative prescription period of five years will start running as soon as the patient is aware of the malpractice of his physician, irrespective of whether the patient/physician relation was ended.

### *4) P's Lack of Legal Capacity*

### a) Minor with or without Representative

45 Prescription is also suspended in favour of minors and those who are deemed mentally incapacitated, even if they have a legal representative (art 2252 of the Civil Code).[106] By suspending the prescription, these persons without legal capacity are protected against negligence by their legal representatives.[107] Surprisingly enough, this rule only applies for the general prescription periods (including the general prescription period applicable in tort claims) but not for many shorter prescriptions (the so-called 'specific' prescription periods) (art 2252 of the Civil Code).[108]

### b) Adult with Mental Disability with or without Representative

46 Similarly to the situation of minors, the prescription is suspended vis-à-vis persons deemed mentally incapacitated. In other words, if the mental disability results in a legal incapacity, the prescription will be suspended, irrespective of whether the plaintiff has a legal representative (art 2252 of the Civil Code).[109]

### *5) Absence of Parties from the Jurisdiction*

47 The plaintiff's and/or defendant's physical absence from the jurisdiction does not suspend the running prescription period.

---

106 Cass, 30 June 2006, C.04573.F.; *M Regout-Masson*, La prescription libératoire en matière civile. Examen de la jurisprudence publiée de janvier 2007 à juin 2012, JT 2012, 697, 706.

107 *C Lebon*, Verjaring, in: E Dirix and A Van Oevelen (eds), Bijzondere overeenkomsten. Artikelsgewijze commentaar met overzicht van rechtspraak en rechtsleer (2004), 84.

108 *Van Oevelen*, *supra* fn 31, 1819.

109 *Vansweevelt*, *supra* fn 36, no 68.

### 6) *Former Legal and Other Proceedings between the Parties*

#### a) Before a Court

48 In case of the introduction of the demand before the court, the prescription is only renewed in relation to the parties involved in the procedure. Ongoing litigation between the same parties regarding similar claims or ongoing litigation between different parties regarding comparable claims does not interrupt the prescription.[110]

49 Nevertheless, the Class Actions Act provides three grounds of suspension in case of collective redress procedures. Under Belgian law a class action can only be used when a group of consumers has suffered harm resulting from a company's breach of contract or violation of certain specified (European or Belgian) laws or regulations (arts XVII.36 and XVII.37 of the Code of Economic Law).

First of all, if the class action is declared admissible, the prescription period in respect of the consumer who opted out is suspended between the publication of the admissibility decision in the Belgian Official Gazette ('*Moniteur Belge*'/'*Belgisch Staatsblad*') and the day he notifies his decision to opt out to the court registry (art XVII.63, §1 of the Code of Economic Law).

Secondly, there is a specific suspension ground in case the procedure has to be put on hold due to the fact that the group representative is no longer apt, and a new group representative cannot be found. In this case the prescription period regarding the individual claims of the group members is suspended between the publication of the admissibility decision in the Belgian Official Gazette ('*Belgisch Staatsblad*'/'*Moniteur Belge*') and the day on which the decision is taken to close the collective redress procedure (art XVII.63, §2 of the Code of Economic Law).

Lastly, the prescription period in respect of the individual consumer is suspended for the consumer who has been excluded from the final list of the consumers who are part of the group that can claim redress.[111] The prescription is suspended between the publication of the admissibility decision in the Belgian Official Gazette ('*Belgisch Staatsblad*'/'*Moniteur Belge*') and the day on which the consumer is notified that he is not included on the final list (art XVII.63, §3 of the Code of Economic Law).

---

110 *Lebon, supra* fn 96, 104.

111 The act on collective redress actions entrusts the practical handling of the reparation of damage to a loss administrator ('*schadeafwikkelaar*'/'*liquidateur*'), appointed by the court (both in cases where a settlement has been reached and ratified, and in the case of judicial proceedings) (art XVII.57 Code of Economic Law).

### b) ADR

Contrary to arbitration, which leads to a renewal of the prescription period, the introduction of a mediation procedure only causes the suspension of the prescription period. Both court-ordered mediation (ie mediation ordered by a judge during the judicial procedure) and out-of-court mediation suspend the running of prescription.[112] 50

As a court-ordered mediation presumes the claim is pending before a court, which entails the suspension of the prescription period and the running of a new prescription period from the day of the final court decision, it is logical that prescription remains suspended during a court-ordered mediation.

Also, an out-of-court mediation suspends prescription when certain requirements are fulfilled. Firstly, a formal proposition to introduce a mediation made by one party to another party by registered mail is required. Secondly, the proposition suspends the prescription period for the duration of one month (art 1730, §§2-3 of the Judicial Code). Only if a mediation protocol is signed within that month, will the prescription be further suspended during the time of the mediation (art 1731, §3 of the Judicial Code).[113]

The prescription starts running again one month after the notification by one of the parties or by the mediator expressing their will to end the mediation process. The notification ending the mediation must be done by registered mail (art 1731, §4 of the Judicial Code).

### c) Arbitration

Under Belgian law, the introduction of an arbitration procedure has the same consequences as the introduction of a procedure before the national courts by a subpoena.[114] By issuing a request for arbitration to the other party, either in accordance with art 1678 of the Judicial Code (arbitration *ad hoc*) or in accordance with the rules of the arbitration institution, the prescription period will be renewed.[115] 51

---

112 *JF Van Drooghenbroeck and M Marchandise*, Les causes d'interruption et de suspension de la prescription libératoire. Rapport belge, in: P Jourdain and P Wéry (eds), La prescription extinctive. Etudes de droit comparé (2010), 467.

113 Some authors add a third condition: the condition that the out-of-court mediation is led by a mediator licensed by the federal Conciliation Committee (*Van Drooghenbroeck and Marchandise, supra* fn 112, 467).

114 *De Ruysscher, supra* fn 97, 848; *D Philippe*, CESL: Change of circumstances and prescription, in: I Claeys and R Feltkamp (eds), The Draft Common European Sales Law: Towards an Alternative Sales Law? A Belgian Perspective (2013), 299 and 315; *M Storme and B Demeulenaere*, International Commercial Arbitration in Belgium (1989), 74, no 32.

115 *De Ruysscher, supra* fn 97, 848; *Philippe, supra* fn 114, 315.

The running of prescription is halted from the moment the arbitration has been initiated, more precisely, the moment the request for arbitration was issued (art 1702 of the Judicial Code) or the moment the parties appear voluntarily before the arbitrators.[116] In case of an arbitration *ad hoc* this request does not have to comply with any formalities (art 1678 of the Judicial Code). In case of institutional arbitration, the request must be issued in accordance with the applicable arbitration rules.[117]

A new prescription period will start to run the day after the interruption has ended, ie the day after the arbitrators have rendered their arbitral award and/or the day after their mandate has ended.[118]

d) Negotiations

52 Although some authors argue that negotiations should interrupt statutes of limitation, under Belgian law negotiations generally do not suspend or interrupt statutes of limitation.[119] However, some specific provisions prescribe the suspension of prescription during negotiations. This is the case, for example, regarding consumer sales. During the negotiations between the seller and the consumer the prescription will be suspended (art 1694*quater* of the Civil Code). Specific rules concerning negotiations can also be found in insurance law.[120]

As of 1 January 2019 collaborative negotiations conducted with the assistance of collaborative attorneys[121] suspend the running limitation period. The suspension of the limitation period starts from the day the agreement to start collaborative negotiations is signed between the parties (art 1741, §2 of the Judicial Code). The suspension of the prescription ends one month after one of the parties notifies the other party of its intention to end the collaborative negotiations (art 1741, §3 of the Judicial Code). This rule of suspension only applies when all formal requirements enumerated in art 1738 of the Judicial Code are met. The general principle that negotiations do not suspend prescription is not altered.

---

116 Court of First Instance Brussels, 16 October 2003, DCCR 2005, 74; *De Ruysscher, supra* fn 97, 848; *Van Drooghenbroeck and Marchandise, supra* fn 112, 412–414 and 432–433.

117 *De Ruysscher, supra* fn 97, 848; *Van Drooghenbroeck and Marchandise, supra* fn 112, 412–414 and 432–433.

118 Arbitral Award, 10 March 1967, RHA 1967, 103; *Lebon, supra* fn 96, 106.

119 *Vansweevelt, supra* fn 36, no 44.

120 *Philippe, supra* fn 114, 316–317.

121 Collaborative attorneys are attorneys who followed a minimum of training in collaborative negotiation techniques and are officially licensed by the Bar as collaborative attorneys.

### 7) *Victim's Death*

The victim's death never suspends a running prescription period. When the inheritance is accepted without liability beyond the assets descended, prescription runs against the inheritance even during the reflection period for the heirs to decide whether to accept or to renounce the inheritance (art 2259 of the Civil Code). Even when the victim dies intestate, with apparently no living heirs, prescription keeps running (art 2258 of the Civil Code). In such a case, any interested party can ask for the appointment of a trustee, who can act on behalf of the inheritance.[122] 53

### 8) *Victim's Bankruptcy*

After the victim is declared bankrupt, only the liquidator can act as a claimant or defendant in court. However, there are exceptions to this principle. The victim can still exercise personal claims, such as a claim for moral damages. In so far as the tort claim is a mere patrimonial claim, the liquidator must act as claimant.[123] When the interests of the victim conflict with the interests of his creditors, the bankrupt victim can act without being represented by the liquidator.[124] Taking into account that after the victim is declared bankrupt he or the liquidator can exercise the claim, the bankruptcy does not suspend or renew the running limitation periods. 54

### 9) Force Majeure

Article 2251 of the Civil Code clearly states that prescription can only be suspended in case there is a statutory provision that provides a ground for suspension or interruption of prescription. The old maxim '*contra non valentem agere non currit praescriptio*' has no legal basis and is not accepted as a general principle under Belgian law,[125] although legal scholars and case law do refer to it. In principle *force majeure* does not lead to the suspension of prescription outside the statutory cases of suspension.[126] When one is prevented in fact (eg unavoidable error or *force majeure*) to exercise one's rights, prescription is not suspended.[127] *Force majeure* is a factual impediment to the 55

---

122 *R Dekkers and E Dirix*, Handboek burgerlijk recht, Vol III (2005), 523, no 1254.

123 *J Caeymaex*, L'accès du failli au prétoire, Jurisprudence, JLMB 1990 1514.

124 *I Verougstraete*, Manuel de la continuité des entreprises et de la faillite (2011), 434–435.

125 Cass, 30 June 2006, C.04573.F.

126 *Lebon, supra* fn 107, 83; *Claeys, supra* fn 37, no 32; *Philippe, supra* fn 114, 318; *Van Oevelen, supra* fn 31, 1820–1821.

127 *Lebon, supra* fn 107, 82–83; *Storme, supra* fn 98, no 31; *Vansweevelt, supra* fn 36, no 61; *Verjans, supra* fn 92, 160.

plaintiff to exercise his right and therefore it is not considered to be a ground for suspension or interruption under Belgian law.[128] However some changes in this assumption are noticeable.

First of all, the Belgian legislator has introduced the notion of *force majeure* in some statutory provisions in order to bring the Belgian legislation into accordance with the case law of the European Court of Human Rights regarding access to justice. Article 89 §2 of the Insurance Act,[129] for example, speaks about a postponement or respite of prescription in case of *force majeure* of the claimant.[130] In some other cases, case law has recognised that prescription is 'suspended' in case of *force majeure* or impossibility to exercise the claim, but a closer analysis shows that, in reality, no suspension, but a respite is meant: the so-called suspension is only granted if there was an impossibility during the last part of the prescription period.[131]

Secondly, the highest courts in Belgium seem willing to accept *force majeure* as a ground for postponement of time limits. With regard to the time limits in the Belgian Code of Civil Procedure, the Belgian Supreme Court has accepted the notion of *force majeure*. In case of *force majeure* the time limit will be extended with the time necessary to complete the action or formality and not with the duration of the impediment.[132] The Belgian Constitutional Court took into account the case law of the European Court of Human Rights with regard to access to justice, to allow postponement of a running prescription period.[133] It is therefore possible that the Belgian Supreme Court will also take into account this case law in its future judgments regarding the question of whether *force majeure* causes postponement of the prescription period.[134]

56 After both World Wars it was accepted that prescription was suspended during war time. In accordance with the principle that *force majeure* does not lead to suspension of prescription outside the statutory cases of suspension, after both wars a Royal Decree was enacted that suspended the prescription of all claims in civil matters for all plaintiffs who lived in or should have filed their claim in occupied territory.[135]

---

128 Cass, 25 January 1962, Pas. 1962, I, 610; *Lebon, supra* fn 107, 82–83; *Storme, supra* fn 98, no 31; *Van Drooghenbroeck and Marchandise, supra* fn 112, 471; *Vansweevelt, supra* fn 36, no 61; *Verjans, supra* fn 92, 160.

129 Act of 4 April 2014 on Insurance, *BS* 30 April 2014.

130 *Somers, supra* fn 93, 455.

131 *Storme, supra* fn 98, no 32.

132 Cass, 24 September 2012, Pas. 2012, 1722; Cass, 9 November 2011, JT 2011, 733.

133 Constitutional Court, 6 November 2014, 164/2014.

134 *Somers, supra* fn 93, 455–456.

135 *de Page and Dekkers, supra* fn 73, no 1233.

In so far as no general statutory provisions prescribe the suspension of prescription in case of natural disasters, military service or imprisonment, those circumstances do not interrupt a running prescription period. 57

Although prescription can only be suspended in case there is a statutory provision that provides a ground for suspension or interruption of prescription, Belgian case law has further refined this by adding that in principle prescription is suspended in any case where someone is hindered by law to exercise one's rights.[136] Legal inability to file a claim is thus accepted as a sperate ground for suspension, not as an application of *force majeure*. 58

It is important to note that the prescription period is not postponed until the first working day of the courts when a prescription period ends on a weekend day or in a vacation.[137] Closed courts do not constitute *force majeure*, as the renewal of prescription is obtained through the issue of summons by a bailiff and neither the collaboration of the court, nor the collaboration of the Registry is required to renew prescription. 59

## IX. CEILINGS ON THE EFFECTIVE TIME OF PRESCRIPTION

There are no 'ceiling periods' *sensu stricto* according to Belgian law (*supra* 18). It is more accurate to describe the Belgian system as a two-tier system: a five-year relative period of limitation and an absolute 20-year period of limitation. 60

The absolute prescription period for tort claims follows the same rationale as the enactment of a ceiling period, but it remains a prescription period that can be prolonged, so indeterminate prolongation is not avoided. The absolute limitation period of 20 years is a counterbalance for the 'discovery rule' applied regarding the relative five-year prescription.[138] The absolute limitation period makes sure that the plaintiff's claim prescribes within a reasonable period of time, even when the plaintiff gains very late knowledge of the elements that entail the running of the relative five-year limitation period. If the damaging event occurred in 2010 and the plaintiff only becomes aware of the damage in 2028, the plaintiff will only have two years left to exercise his claim. According to the absolute prescription period, the claim of the plaintiff is barred in 2030, notwithstanding the fact that the plaintiff was only aware of the damage for two years.

136 Cass, 13 November 1997, Arr Cass 1997, 1125, Pas. 1997, I, 1178.

137 *Dekkers and Dirix*, *supra* fn 122, 507, no 1215.

138 *Vansweevelt*, *supra* fn 36, no 35.

The absolute prescription period starts running from the damaging event.[139]

During the Parliamentary proceedings the question of whether the absolute limitation period for tort claims was a 'ceiling period' or expiration term was expressly addressed and answered negatively. It was expressly stated that the rules regarding suspension and interruption of prescription fully apply to the absolute prescription period.[140] When the damaging event occurred in 2010 and prescription was suspended until 2015 (eg due to the minority of the plaintiff), the absolute prescription period ends in 2035.

The absolute 20-year prescription period does not apply to tort claims which are subject to a specific statute of limitation.

## X. STATUTE INTERPRETATION, JUDICIAL DISCRETION AND LACHES

### A. STATUTE INTERPRETATION

61 Any statutory provision regarding prescription has to be interpreted in light of the general purposes of the concept of prescription (purposivist theory of interpretation). The purposes of the legal concept of prescription are three-fold. First of all, a limitation period protects the interest of the defendant. The defendant is protected against a situation of lack of documentary evidence. Secondly, the concept of prescription exists in the general interest: it improves legal certainty and safeguards social peace. Prescription prevents a party from being wrongfully convicted to performance of a debt. Thirdly, a limitation period also protects the interest of the plaintiff. The plaintiff must be given a reasonable time limit in which to submit his claim. Any statutory provision has to be interpreted in such a way that it balances those three interests.[141]

### B. JUDICIAL DISCRETION

62 Under Belgian law, the court has no discretion to disapply the limitation period in tort claims. Neither in claims in respect of personal injuries nor in claims for defamation can the courts disapply the primary or the long-stop limitation periods.

139 *Vansweevelt*, *supra* fn 36, no 36.

140 Explanatory Memorandum, Parliamentary Documents, *Chambre des représentants/Kamer van volksvertegenwoordigers*, 1996–97, Doc no 1087/1, 7–8.

141 *Claeys*, *supra* fn 37, no 4–7.

On the other hand, courts have an implicit discretion when applying the open and broad standards used in the Civil Code: the 'cause of action' has to be assessed case by case. Judges have a discretion in assessing when the plaintiff had sufficient knowledge of the causal link between the plaintiff's harm and the tortious conduct of the defendant ...

Article 2251 of the Civil Code determines that the prescription rules are applicable to all persons, unless the law provides an exception. Therefore, the judge cannot suspend or extend the prescription period based on the principles of equity (however cf *supra* 55–59 on *force majeure*, *'fraus omnia corrumpit'* and no 34 and 64 on abuse of rights). 63

The suspension of the prescription period in certain circumstances is such an exception provided by law. The suspension of the prescription is based on grounds which make it unreasonable to expect the plaintiff to exercise his rights or to perform an act of renewal.[142]

## C. LACHES

Could one say that the plaintiff runs a risk when he takes a long time to bring a lawsuit (although the prescription period has not yet expired), and even more so when by his inaction he creates the legitimate expectation on the part of the defendant that he will not enforce his right to tort remedy? The answer to this question is affirmative.[143] Two dangers are awaiting him. 64

On the one hand, the judge could infer from the plaintiff's inaction his renunciation to his right (right to tort remedy in the present case) according to the circumstances. Renunciation may indeed be implied. However, it has to be unequivocal. The judge may therefore not conclude renunciation if it is not certain that the plaintiff had the will to waive his right voluntarily.[144]

On the other hand, the *théorie de l'abus de droit/theorie van misbruik van recht* can possibly be invoked. Should the judge consider that the plaintiff's behaviour clearly exceeds the limits of the normal exercise of the right (to tort remedy) by a prudent and careful victim, there would be a situation of *abuse of right*.[145] In this case, the judge will decide on the best way to impose sanction

---

142 *Storme, supra* fn 98, no 30; *Vansweevelt, supra* fn 36, no 61.

143 *Wéry, supra* fn 22, no 874.

144 *S Stijns and I Samoy*, La prescription extinctive: le rôle de la volonte et du comportement des parties, in: P Jourdain and P Wéry (eds), La prescription extinctive Etudes de droit comparé (2010), 341, no 25.

145 *Marchandise, supra* fn 22, no 235; *Stijns and Samoy, supra* fn 144, no 27; *Vansweevelt and Weyts, supra* fn 65, no 253; *Wéry, supra* fn 22, no 874.

on them; this sanction may consist of the deprivation of the possibility to enforce the right to tort remedy, at least during a certain period of time, which leads to a kind of prolongation of the initial limitation period.[146]

# XI. CHANGE OF PARTIES

## A. THE PLAINTIFF IS A TRANSFEREE OF THE VICTIM'S CLAIM

65 The insurer,[147] the health insurance fund or the social security institution who compensated the injured party are subrogated by operation of law into the legal position of the injured party.[148] Subrogation is a doctrine that allows one party (the subrogee) to 'step into the shoes' or 'stand in the shoes' of another party (the subrogor) for the purpose of recovering the money that the subrogee has paid to the subrogor. The technique of subrogation has both advantages and disadvantages from the point of view of the subrogee. The main advantage is that the subrogee may take advantage of any security which the creditor enjoyed in relation to performance of the obligation; but the disadvantages include the possibility of being met with a defence or right of set-off which the debtor enjoyed against the creditor (the subrogor) and the possibility of the right expiring according to the prescription period applicable to the creditor's claim.[149] The 'step into the shoes' principle entails that the doctrine of the relativity of the prescription is disregarded. The subrogee benefits from any act of renewal or interruption that the subrogor accomplished before the subrogation took place. On the contrary, the subrogee does not benefit from any act of renewal or interruption of the limitation period accomplished after the subrogation.[150] No specific limitation period exists regarding the subrogated claim. The subrogation of the victim's claim does not change the legal status of this claim with regard to the running,[151] the renewal or the interruption of the limitation period.

---

146 *Marchandise*, *supra* fn 22, no 235.

147 According to art 95 of the Insurance Act the insurer who paid compensation is subrogated in the rights that the insured or the beneficiary has against the tortfeasor.

148 For a detailed enumeration of the cases and legal provisions of subrogation by operation of law see: *I Boone*, Verjaring van subrogatoire en zelfstandige verhaalsvorderingen, in: I Claeys (ed), Verjaring in het privaatrecht. Weet de avond wat morgen brengt? (2005), 244–246, no 3; *Vansweevelt*, *supra* fn 36, no 54.

149 *Boone*, *supra* fn 148, 246, no 4.

150 *Vansweevelt*, *supra* fn 36, no 55.

151 Eg the prescription of the subrogated claim starts running from the moment the injured party had knowledge of the damage and the identity of the tortfeasor. The moment the insurer (as subrogee) acquired this knowledge has no influence on the prescription (*Boone*, *supra* fn 148, 251–252, no 11).

## B. THE DEFENDANT IS A TRANSFEREE OF THE TORTFEASOR'S OBLIGATION

The most common hypothesis in which the tortfeasor's obligation is 'transferred', is the situation in which the plaintiff has a right of direct action (*action directe/ rechtstreekse vordering*) against the tortfeasor's liability insurer. According to art 150 of the Insurance Act 2014 the plaintiff has a personal and autonomous right against the insurance company, although no privity of contract exists between the injured party and the tortfeasor's liability insurer. Under Belgian law a direct action is not regarded as the transfer of the policyholder's obligation to his liability insurer, nor is it related to the concept of joint liability. The right of direct action finds its basis within the law and only exists in so far as it is created by an express law. The direct action is a separate claim, completely autonomous from the tort claim the plaintiff has against the tortfeasor.[152] The prescription of the right of direct action is regulated by the Insurance Act. According to art 88, §2 of the Insurance Act the right of direct action of the plaintiff against the insurer is subject to a limitation period of five years. The prescription period starts running from the damage-causing event or, when a criminal offence was committed, from the day of the offence. When the plaintiff proves he only became aware of his right of direct action against the insurer later, the five-year limitation period starts running from the day of his awareness. In case the plaintiff is not immediately aware of his direct action, the Insurance Act provides an absolute limitation period of ten years. This absolute limitation period also starts running from the day of the damage-causing event. According to the case law of the Supreme Court, the ten-year period is not a ceiling period, but an absolute prescription period, subject to suspension or renewal.[153] Compared with the absolute prescription period of 20 years for tort claims, the prescription of the right of direct action is stricter than the prescription of the tort claim itself. 66

## C. CONTRIBUTION CLAIMS

The joint and severally liable or *in solidum* liable defendant who alone compensated the plaintiff is by law subrogated in the rights of the plaintiff (art 1251, 3° of the Civil Code). The defendant has a right of subrogation in 67

[152] Beneluxhof 21 December 1990, <http://www.courbeneluxhof.be>, concl. H Lenaerts; *T Vansweevelt and B Weyts*, De verjaring van de rechtstreekse vordering in het verzekeringsrecht, in: N Carette and B Weyts (eds), Verantwoord aansprakelijkheidsrecht. Liber amicorum Aloïs Van Oevelen (2017), 616–619.

[153] Cass, 7 October 2005, NJW 2006, 74, noot GJ, TBH 2006, 752, noot C Van Schoubroeck and T Verz. 2007, 33, noot P Fontaine; Cass, 6 April 2006, AR C.0500.40.N, concl. P. Cornelis, RGAR 2007, no 14.319.

so far as he has compensated the injured party above his personal share in the damage. Due to the right of subrogation the defendant can exercise the rights of the plaintiff against his joint tortfeasors. The defendant is placed in the same legal position vis-à-vis the other joint tortfeasors as the plaintiff was.[154] The joint tortfeasors can raise the running or acquired prescription against the contribution claim, the same way that they could raise it against the plaintiff's claim. The defendant nevertheless benefits from any act of the plaintiff that renewed or suspended prescription. For example, when the joint liability is confirmed by a judicial decision, the defendant is subrogated in the *actio judicate* of the plaintiff, which is subject to a limitation period of ten years, starting from the date the judgment was delivered.[155]

From the application of the concept of subrogation on contribution claims follows that the payment of the damages does not start a new, distinct limitation period.[156]

### D. DEPENDANTS' CLAIM

68 Parents, spouses and/or children of the injured party can claim damages for the personal losses caused by the tortfeasor. The claim for damages caused to the dependants (loss of support, loss of services and burial expenses) is not subject to a specific prescription period. This tort claim is regarded as an autonomous claim and is subject to the general prescription regime. There is no interaction between the suspension or renewal of the limitation period of the claim of the injured party and the dependants' claim.

When the dependants, as heirs, exercise the claim of the injured party they step into the shoes of the injured party.

## XII. OTHER ASPECTS OF PRESCRIPTION LAW

### A. STIPULATION

69 In Belgian law, a distinction is made between prescription as a concept and prescription as a defence.[157]

---

[154] Cass, 10 July 1952, Arr Cass 1952, 650, Pas. 1952, I, 738; Cass, 17 June 1982, RCJB 1986, 680; Cass, 6 June 1994, C.93.0037.F, RW 1994–95, 914; *Claeys, supra* fn 91, 763–764, no 71.

[155] Cass, 7 April 2017, C.15.0534.N; Cass, 10 May 1957, Arr Verbr 1957, 758, RCJB 1958, 5.

[156] *Claeys, supra* fn 91, 764, no 71.

[157] *Van Oevelen, supra* fn 31, 1763–1764, no 10.

Prescription as a concept is linked to public policy, as it ascertains legal certainty and protects the defendant. Following this perspective, parties are not allowed to exclude prescription or to renounce prescription not yet acquired. Similarly, parties are not allowed to agree on a longer prescription period than the one prescribed by law.[158]

Prescription as a defence only regards private interests and a defendant is not compelled to invoke prescription. This perspective implies that renunciation in regard to the prescription already acquired is allowed. The general view taken is that parties may agree to reduce the limitation periods, unless exercise of the right would be rendered impossible, and reservation made for legislation on unfair clauses. As a last consequence, the parties can agree at any moment to suspend prescription.[159]

## B. MEANING OF 'FILING A CLAIM' THAT INTERRUPTS THE RUNNING OF PRESCRIPTION

In general, under Belgian law, extinctive prescription is renewed or interrupted 70
when the plaintiff actually makes a claim (eg the introduction of a demand before the court or a seizure) or the defendant acknowledges the right of the plaintiff.[160] Contrary to the suspension and extension grounds, the renewal of the prescription always requires a juridical act,[161] either by the plaintiff or by the defendant.[162]

## C. WHEN SHOULD THE DEFENCE BE RAISED AND DECIDED?

The defence of prescription can be raised at any stage of the proceedings 71
(art 2224 of the Civil Code). In other words, the defence can be raised until the judge takes the case under deliberation. The defence can be raised for the first time in front of the appellate judge. The defence cannot be raised for the first time in front of the Supreme Court (*Cour de Cassation/Hof van Cassatie*) as the function of the Supreme Court hinders it from deciding any new arguments, unless the argument regards public policy.[163]

---

158 *Van Oevelen, supra* fn 31, 1764–1765, no 11.

159 *Van Oevelen, supra* fn 31, 1765–1772, no 12–16; *Storme, supra* fn 98, no 36.

160 *Storme, supra* fn 98, no 9.

161 According to the DCFR: 'A juridical act is any statement or agreement, whether express or implied from conduct, which is intended to have legal effect as such. It may be unilateral, bilateral or multilateral.'

162 *Van Oevelen, supra* fn 31, 1806–1807.

163 *Dekkers and Dirix, supra* fn 122, 526, no 1263.

The defence of prescription is considered to be a plea of inadmissibility. The defence of prescription does not regard the merits of the case, nor is it a mere procedural defence.[164] The judge will normally decide regarding the admissibility of the claim after dealing with any jurisdiction issues and/or procedural defences, but before adjudicating the merits of the case. However, when the inadmissibility is raised, the Judicial Code prescribes that a judge can only order a research measure (eg the appointment of an expert witness) after adjudicating the plea of inadmissibility (art 875*bis* of the Judicial Code). The only exception to this rule is the hypothesis in which the research measure is necessary to enable the judge to decide on the plea of inadmissibility. When the defence of prescription is raised, the judge can only order any research measures after rejecting the defence of prescription. Besides this restriction, the defence of prescription will not elicit an immediate decision regarding the defence of prescription.

## D. WHO MAY RAISE THE DEFENCE?

72 In principle the prescription has to be invoked by the defendant. However, art 2225 of the Civil Code provides that the creditors of the defendant and all other persons who have an interest that prescription is acquired (eg a guarantor, a co-debtor, etc) can also invoke the defence of prescription, although the defendant himself renounces the defence of prescription.[165]

73 Article 2223 of the Civil Code provides that a judge is not allowed to invoke *ex officio* that a right is prescribed. Only when the prescription rule is of a public policy nature, is the judge allowed to raise the issue of prescription *ex officio*.[166] In general the rules regarding the prescription of tort claims are not a matter of public policy and cannot be invoked *ex officio* by the judge.

## E. BURDEN OF PROOF (OF ELEMENTS AND OF RULES OF PROLONGATION)

74 The general principles regarding the burden of proof apply on the defence of prescription. Article 8:4 of the Civil Code and art 870 of the Judicial Code formulate the principle that the burden of proof weighs on the party who invokes the existence of a fact or a right. This division of the burden of proof is generally referred to under the adage *actori incumbit probatio*. When the

164 *Van Oevelen, supra* fn 31, 1772–1774, no 17.
165 *Dekkers and Dirix, supra* fn 122, 526–527, no 1264.
166 *Stijns and Samoy, supra* fn 144, no 47.

defendant alleges prescription, he must indicate the facts that constitute prescription. In so far as the plaintiff contests these facts, the defendant will have to prove the contested facts: the defendant has to prove the plaintiff knew of the facts giving rise to the right to damages and the plaintiff knew of the identity of the liable party.[167]

When the plaintiff invokes that the defendant renounced the defence of prescription, the plaintiff has to prove the renunciation by the defendant.[168]

---

167 Cass, 16 February 2007, C.03.0572.N.

168 Cass, 29 November 2013, C.12.0540.F-C.12.0544.F.

# PRESCRIPTION IN TORT LAW: CZECH REPUBLIC

Luboš Tichý

# I. INTRODUCTION

## A. SCOPE OF APPLICATION OF THE CIVIL CODE

1 Czech civil law does not contain special provisions on prescription in tort law as it is part of prescription regulation as a whole. Despite this, the following text relates solely to prescription in tort law.

Prescription of claims for compensation of damage (tortious claims) is governed in principle exclusively by the new Civil Code ('CC/2012').[1] Only the Atomic Law[2] and the Law on State Liability[3] Act contain specific regulations. 2

## B. ORIGIN AND REFORM OF CZECH PRESCRIPTION LAW

Until 1951, Austrian prescription law (§1451 ff AGBG) applied. Following a communist coup d'état, a new civil code (CC) was introduced including the new, very short and strict rules on prescription (§§87–99), literally excluding an autonomy of parties (§99). Through the introduction of the civil code of 1964, some of the 'Austrian' provisions appeared in Czech law. In 2012, a new civil code was introduced which entered into effect on 1 January 2014, and which also reformed prescription law in the Czech Republic. 3

While CC/1964 emphasised that courts shall not reaffirm a previous creditor's claim, the law currently in force (§609 of CC/2012[4]) sees the fundamental consequence of prescription in the regulation as a debtor not being liable to perform its contract. BGB's influence (§214) is eminent not only here, but it is also reflected in the regulation of prescription by claims arising between spouses (§646 CC/2012)[5] during the duration of marriage, and also in postponement of the commencement of the prescription period in case of damage of health (personal injury) of a minor (§622 CC/2012).[6] The rule stipulated in §203 BGB was transplanted in §648 CC/201[7] which regards postponement of commencement of the prescription period in case of negotiation outside the 4

---

1 Civil Code, no 89/2012 Coll.

2 Atomic Act, no 263/2016 Coll.

3 Act no 82/1998 Coll. on Liability for Damage Based either on Maladministration or on Illegal Decision.

4 'If a right has not been exercised within a limitation period, it becomes time-barred and the debtor is not obliged to perform. However, if a debtor performed after the expiry of a limitation period, he may not claim that his performance be returned.'

5 'Between spouses, a limitation period neither commences nor runs while the marriage lasts. This applies, by analogy, to mutual rights of persons living in a common household, a person represented and his legal representative, a ward and his guardian and a person under tutorship and his tutor.'

6 'In the case of bodily harm to a minor lacking full legal capacity, the limitation period does not commence before the minor acquires full legal capacity. If he does not acquire full legal capacity, the limitation period shall not commence until his guardian is appointed upon the person reaching the age of majority.'

7 'If, within a limitation period, a creditor asserts a right against a public body and continues in duly initiated proceedings, the statute of limitations is suspended. This also applies to an already enforceable right if an application for court enforcement or private enforcement has been filed with respect to the right.'

court. Influenced by §1502 ABGB and art 141 OR, §610 CC/2012[8] governs the possibility to waive the right to invoke prescription in advance.

## II. DEFINITION OF PRESCRIPTION

5 Two changes are of fundamental importance. The short (subjective) prescription period was extended from two to three years (§629 para 1) and the late discovery rule was amended by the introduction of the imputed knowledge of the factual basis of the claim. The starting point is now outlined not just by actual knowledge of the plaintiff: he or she should have known.[9]

6 Czech law does not define prescription. It merely stipulates its major importance subsisting in effects caused by it: the debtor is relieved of its duties and provided with a possibility to defend itself from the creditor's claims with a special defence in the form of a right to invoke prescription (a defence of the debtor) in court proceedings, ie in the form of a special procedural right. This definition is, in principle, in compliance with the concept indicated in ACR.

7 The right to invoke prescription (raise the defence) as such is not subject to prescription. Simultaneously, it does not prevent creditors from fulfillment of its claim for goods as it is forbidden for debtors that have already fulfilled their obligation to reclaim the performance as an unjust enrichment (para 10).

## III. THE NATURE OF PRESCRIPTION AND ITS EFFECTS

8 In contrast to preclusion (§654 CC/2012 – not applicable in tort law), which must be examined and considered *ex officio*, the court is not allowed to take into consideration *ex officio* the fact that the claim is prescribed. In other words, a

---

8 '(1) A court shall only take into account the statute of limitations if the debtor invokes that the right has become time-barred. If a person waives his right to invoke statute of limitations in advance, the waiver is disregarded. (2) If parties are obliged to mutually return what they acquired under an invalid contract or an extinguished obligation, the court shall take the defence of statute of limitations into account only if the statute of limitations could also be invoked by the other party. This also applies if a performance was provided on the basis of a putative juridical act.'

9 '(1) Where a right is enforceable before a public body, the limitation period commences from the date on which the right could be *asserted* for the first time. (2) A right may be asserted for the first time once the entitled person became aware of the circumstances decisive for the start of the limitation period or when he should and could have learnt thereof.' (§619 CC/2012.)

court may deny a claim raised after the expiry of the prescription period only if a debtor asserts its right to invoke prescription (prescription defence). This procedural step thus has a consequence in the field of substantive law.

Preclusion is an institute of substantive law which is applied in the form of a preclusion defence within proceedings before a court. In other words, prescription provides the defendant with procedural defence. That bares the ability of the plaintiff to enforce the alleged right to remedy through judicial proceedings before an authorised court. The right of the plaintiff does not extinguish but cannot be enforced. 9

If the debtor performs after the prescription period elapses, his performance cannot be regarded as unjustified enrichment and cannot be restituted. 10

Czech law does not actually share the concept of prescription that effects a substantive defence that prevents the claimant from enforcing the right to remedy after the prescription period elapsed. If he tries to enforce his claim, for example by way of set-off, this can be invalidated in court proceedings based on the defendant's defence. 11

As already mentioned above, the right to invoke prescription as such is not subject to a prescription period. However, the period in which this right may be asserted is another issue that is subject to a persisting discussion. It is the prevalent opinion that the right to raise the prescription defence may be asserted until the adoption of the decision on appeal. This is unless the nature of the decision on merits is so specific that it effectively excludes the possibility to assert the right to invoke the prescription.[10] 12

The prescription defence can be rejected by the court if it contradicts good morals. These are exceptional cases of abuse of right to the detriment of the other party that did not cause expiration of the prescription period, and to which the extinction of a claim to performance resulting from expiration of the prescription period would be a disproportionately harsh sanction.[11] It also includes cases among closest relatives when the right to invoke prescription is seen as an abuse of law.[12] 13

The so-called proper middle ground concept is fully acceptable. In order to reflect differences among the variety of tort claims there are tools for making the basically rigid legal institute (prescription) slightly more flexible (see the starting point of the prescription period, prolongation, etc). 14

---

10 *K Svoboda*, in: Švestka, Dvořák, Fiala (eds), Občanský zákoník, Komentář (Civil Code, Commentary), Vol I (2014) 1530 and Krajský soud (Regional Court) Brno 16 Co 579/87.

11 Supreme Court 25 Cdo 1839/2000.

12 Ústavní soud (Constitutional Court) I. ÚS 643/04.

## IV. CONSIDERATIONS FOR AND AGAINST PRESCRIPTION OF TORT CLAIMS

### A. AGAINST

15 The fact that a creditor is not deprived of its rights either is also occasionally mentioned.[13] 'The closing the doors' effect can very often be completed even at the end of court proceedings, namely as result of the appellate court's ruling.

### B. FOR

16 Czech legal theory typically enumerates two major purposes of prescription. Firstly, it is stated that prescription is primarily to give an incentive to entitled subjects, ie to creditors, to claim their rights at an early stage. Secondly, prescription is to protect debtors that would otherwise be subject to possible enforcement claims for an uncertain period of time.[14]

17 It is also considered a public interest in the form of legal certainty preventing the existence of long-term rights.[15]

18 Prescription as a tool for preventing collective societal costs and protection of the actual defendants has only limited importance (relevance) in Czech legal culture.

## V. ELEMENTS OF PRESCRIPTION – AN OVERVIEW

19 Object and consequences of prescription (§§609 and 610 CC/2012[16] – relevance of prescription), object of prescription (§§611 et seq. CC/2012),[17] particularly §611 CC/2012 on proprietary rights as an object of prescription and right to restitution of immaterial damage with respect to life, dignity, name, health, reputation, privacy or similar personal rights (§612 CC/2012).

---

13 *J Švestka*, in: Švestka and Dvořák (eds), Občanské právo soukromé (5th ed., 2009) 255.

14 *J Švestka*, in: Švestka et al (eds), *supra* fn 10, 312.

15 Ibid.

16 See *supra* fn 4 and 8.

17 'All property rights are subject to limitation except as provided by a statute. Other rights are subject to limitation where provided by a statute.'

Commencement (starting point) of prescription period – in general §§619 et seq. CC/2012,[18] §620 CC/2012 for commencement of prescription period in tort law.[19] 20

Length of prescription period (§§629 et seq. CC/2012,[20] §636 CC/2012[21] and §637 CC/2012[22] for tort law).

Prolongation of prescription, including its suspension (§§646 et seq. CC/2012).[23] 21

Postponement, renewal and extension of prescription period (§653 CC/2012).[24]

The general rule stipulates ten years as the ceiling (long-stop) from the date that the damage was incurred (§636 para 1 CC 2012).[25] The exception to this is 22

---

18 'In the case of the rights to life and dignity, name, health, respect, honour, privacy and similar personal rights, only the rights to remedy harm caused to these rights are subject to limitation.'

19 '(1) Circumstances decisive for the commencement of a limitation period for a right to compensation for damage include knowledge of the damage and the person liable to provide the compensation of damage. This also applies, by analogy, to the remedy of harm. (2) Circumstances decisive for the commencement of a limitation period for a right to compensation for damage caused by a defective product under Section 2939 include knowledge of the damage, the defect and the identity of the producer'. (§620 CC/2012.)

20 '(1) The length of a limitation period is three years. (2) A property right becomes time-barred no later than after ten years from the date on which it became due unless a statute specifically provides a different limitation period.'

21 '(1) A right to compensation for damage or other harm becomes time-barred no later than ten years after the date the damage or harm was incurred. (2) Where damage or harm has been caused intentionally, the right to its compensation becomes time-barred no later than fifteen years after the date on which the damage or harm occurred. This also applies in case of damage or harm resulting from a breach of a duty due to bribery consisting in offering, promising to provide or providing a bribe by a person other than the aggrieved person or in directly or indirectly soliciting a bribe from the aggrieved person. (3) Subsections (1) and (2) do not apply to a right arising from harm to freedom, harm to life or bodily harm.'

22 'The right to compensation for damage caused by a defective product under Section 2939 becomes time-barred no later than ten years after the date on which the producer placed the defective product on the market.'

23 'Between spouses, a limitation period neither commences nor runs while the marriage lasts. This applies, by analogy, to mutual rights of persons living in a common household, a person represented and his legal representative, a ward and his guardian and a person under tutorship and his tutor.'

24 '(1) If a right has been time-barred and the debtor has acknowledged his debt, a claim is renewed and a new limitation period commences on the date on which the debt was acknowledged. However, if the debtor specifies in the acknowledgement a period within which he will discharge his debt, the right becomes time-barred ten years after the last day of the period specified. (2) If a right, although already time-barred, has been granted by a decision of a public body, Subsection (1) applies by analogy.'

25 See *supra* fn 14.

the ceiling of 15 years that applies to intentional damage as well as in cases of corruption (§636 para 2 CC/2017).[26]

## VI. THE STARTING POINT OF THE PRESCRIPTION PERIOD

23 This institution can be understood as the basis of a subjective right (claim). Courts examine the merit of the right to invoke prescription in relation to the claim raised in the action. It is irrelevant how contractual parties qualify the claim as well as grounds on which the right to invoke prescription was asserted.[27]

### A. THE MEANING OF 'ACTION' AND 'CAUSE OF ACTION'

24 Czech law distinguishes between a short (so-called subjective) prescription period and long (objective) prescription period (long-stop).[28] The short period starts running from the first day that the right could have been exercised for the first time (§619 para 1 CC/2012). This is the day when the creditor learned of the facts that are relevant for the beginning of the prescription period or when the creditor should and could have learned of them. These facts required for the commencement of the prescription period of right for damages include the awareness of the harm and the person of the debtor.

25 A special rule regarding the right for damages in cases of product liability provides for the beginning of the prescription period as the victim's knowledge of harm, defect of the product and identity of the producer (§620 para 2 CC/2012).

26 The notion of 'cause of action' in terms of cause of claim for damages under Czech law means the factual basis of the victim's claim. In other words, the plaintiff can substantiate his (or her) claim on facts that meet the requirements of a legal remedy. The plaintiff can claim damages once he (or she) knows the required elements of the defendant's liability.

27 The prescription period starts once the victim knows or should have known (actual or imputed knowledge) of all facts which meet the requirements of the wrongdoer's liability. Although §620 para 1 CC/2012 speaks (like §199 BGB and §1489 ABGB) only of the liable person and the harm, it follows from the case law (like under German and Austrian law) that the knowledge of the victim must also include the wrongful act, causation between the harm and the wrongful

---

26 See *supra* fn 14.
27 Supreme Court, Decisions Coll. R13/2005.
28 See *infra* Section IX.

act and, if required, also the fault. In other words, the starting point of the prescription period requires the accrual of the claim and this presupposes the actual or imputed knowledge of all relevant facts upon which the victim can base his (or her) claim.

A controversial stipulation of the commencement of the prescription period exemplifies the opinion that the moment in which the injuring party realised the damage must be decisive. It is irrelevant whether the injured party allegedly correctly assessed the information on a factual or legal basis. However, acquisition of knowledge in the form of rough knowledge about the consequences of damage is sufficient.[29] 28

## B. BROAD OR NARROW CONCEPTION OF 'CAUSE OF ACTION'

In order to accommodate a claim, all elements of the respective tort norm must be satisfied. This actually represents the cause of action which should also be applied for prescription purposes. The most important element of the tort law relationship is the damage as a consequence of the damaging event (including the wrongful act). The Czech courts incline towards the narrow concept of cause of action. This includes the worsening of the health of the victim once (years ago) he (or she) was affected by a damaging event. His (or her) claim should be regarded as a 'new' claim with a separate accrual of prescription period.[30] This case law is based on an approach of only including the immediate consequences resulting from a damaging event (tortious conduct). This may favour the victim (plaintiff) who is not under the obligation of foreseeability of later (further) consequences. On the other hand, it is the plaintiff who bears the burden of proof with regard to causality. A narrow sense of the cause of action may reflect and include different aspects compared with the broad concept where the main ingredients (elements) remain stable. 29

Two different situations must be distinguished with respect to the scope of legal basis. One cause together with the fulfilment of other elements of liability give rise to damage formed in one moment. However, fulfilment of virtually the same criteria gives rise to another claim that is formed later. Czech law is based on the presumption that these are two relatively independent types of damage and hence two separate claims with different points of commencement of prescription period.[31] 30

---

29 Ibid, 1562.

30 1 Cz 23/83, R 9/1986

31 Supreme Court 1 Cz 23/83.

31 Another problem is the fact that damage to health gives rise to a number of partial claims (components of a right to compensation of damage), which could be, for instance, treatment and medication expenses, loss of/on income, compensation for pain suffering and compensation for social decapacitation, one-off compensation in case of death, etc. These are separate claims that are subject to prescription separately as well.[32]

32 A different situation constitutes the question of damage to property in case of an indivisible whole. In such cases, the prescription period commences when the injured parties become aware of the whole damage, even though the damage was caused by two or more separate events.[33]

**Case 1** – *D, a ski instructor, negligently fails to make sure that all skiers in her 'off-piste' group wear helmets. P, a skier in the group, hits a tree. P immediately suffers head injury X, and years later another head injury Y that developed from the same accident.*

The short (subjective) period of three years would start from the date that P learns the identity of the person of the tortfeasor (be it the liability based on contract or tort) and the facts which led to the injury. In the case of a later head injury, the prescription would have a separate, new regime even if this injury had developed from the same accident. The prescription period would start to run from the date that P learned of the new injury and was able to impute it to the tortfeasor and other facts (accident) which may cause his (or her) another injury.

**Case 2** – *Physician D treats patient P negligently and performs three mistakes on the day of the treatment: A, B and C. Mistake A causes harm X after a year. Mistake B causes harm Y after two years. Mistakes A and C together cause harm Z after three years.*

Like in Austrian or German law, the resolution of this case would depend on when P learned or was grossly negligent in not learning that the improper treatment (mistake of the physician) caused personal injury (harm). If the latter situation applies, then the prescription period would start from the treatment's day. If P did not learn without being grossly negligent for this unawareness, the prescription period would start from the date that P actually became aware of the respective cause of action.

It is worth mentioning that this claim is not the subject of a 'long-stop' prescription period (§636 para 3 Civil Code). Damages for personal injury never prescribe.

---

[32] Supreme Court, Decisions Coll. R 38/1970.

[33] Supreme Court Cz 19/74.

**Case 3** – *Builder D lays down defective foundations for a building thereby creating the risk of future collapse. As a result, the value to the owner of the building (P) decreases (harm A). Two years later the foundation subsides and requires fixing paid by P (harm B). Three year later cracks appear in the building fixed by P (harm C). Four years later the building collapses (harm D).*

Provided that other requirements were evident to P, the prescription period would start from the occurrence of each respective harm (A, B, C, D). This is based on the prevailing 'separate damage' approach. Assuming that the harm was not caused intentionally, the claim would undergo the 'long-stop' period of ten years starting after accomplishment of the building.

In case of personal injury, it is inferred that the commencement of the prescription period is in the moment in which the injured party acquainted itself with the conclusion of an expert opinion.[34] 33

As to whether a risk or danger of a future knowledge may put prescription in motion, the answer is negative. This stems indirectly from stable jurisprudence which rules that only such an event which allows at least a 'frame idea' of its nature in terms of damaging consequences[35] can be regarded as a harm. Therefore, there is no need for the victim to take steps to hinder prescription since the prescription period then starts running from the first occurrence of the factual harm even if this 'new' harm was caused by the previous ('old') harm. 34

However, it is the wrongdoer (defendant) who according to rules of burden of proof must prove when the harm occurred (and subsequently also when the victim gained – or has to gain – knowledge of the harm). 35

The prescription period commences upon the outbreak of the illness by the victim and not upon acquisition of knowledge about tripled probability of suffering a contagious disease in the future. 36

## C. THE STARTING POINT – BREACH OF DUTY OR OCCURRENCE OF DAMAGE?

**Case 4** – *D enters P's premises without P's permission, thereby committing a tort of trespass, but without causing any damage. P can file a claim against D asking for the remedy of D's eviction but fails to do so. A year later D causes physical harm to P's premises. P files a claim to compensation for the loss.*

---

34 Supreme Court 25 Cdo 1891/2007.

35 Supreme Court 25 Cdo 2592/2006, 25 Cdo 308/2009.

36a From the perspective of Czech law there are two separate cases. The remedy in pure trespass is an injunction of prohibition of such a trespass. This claim is of a property law nature and therefore it is not covered by prescription, since the case is beyond its scope. In the second part of this 'story', the claim for damages underlies the prescription regime. The starting point of the prescription period is the accrual (occurrence) of a damage.

According to the conception of Czech prescription law (and other legal orders) the focus is put on the harm (damage, personal injury, etc) regardless of whether it results from the tort or the contract. Any claim (action) against a 'pure' wrongful act (tort) prescribes depending on which right should be protected. It stems from it that Czech law prefers the narrow approach based on the concept of compensation for harm caused by the infringement of a right. In other words, the occurrence of harm is the essential element when speaking of Czech prescription law with regard to tort law, which is closely associated with harm and the compensation for it.

## D. WHAT IS CONSIDERED 'HARM' FOR PRESCRIPTION PURPOSES?

37 In its majority, harm is performed (accomplished) within a short motion, within a very short period of time. And this mostly happens as a direct consequence of the damaging event, as it affects the right protected by legal order. Thus, the occurrence of the harm is generally the day of the damaging event. The terms 'initial harm', 'developed harm' and 'stabilised harm' are relative notions. All of them refer to cases which can be classified as continuous damage. But each phase of the specific 'developing' (continuous) harm should as a rule be regarded as its closed, relatively final status with an adverse input into the third party's interest. This concept is very much associated with the concept of a narrow cause of action which allows (incentivises) P to sue at a rather early starting point without any risk with regard to further development of the harm. The obligation of P to foresee future negative consequences of a damaging event practically does not exist under Czech law. Otherwise the victim may be faced with the risk of a belated filing of the lawsuit.

**Case 5** – *In an accidental event, D negligently caused an explosion that damaged P's ears. During the first two years P has to raise the volume to enjoy music. During the following three years P needs a hearing device. After a further five years P becomes deaf.*

The Czech court would – from the perspective of prescription – consider each worsening of P's capacity to hear a separate damage. For each 'stabilisation of state of health' a separate period would apply. From that respective date the prescription period would start to run.

**Case 6** – *Builder D lays down defective foundations for a bridge, thereby creating the risk of future collapse if heavy rain falls. Two years later heavy rain indeed falls and the collapse becomes only a matter of time, as indeed happens four years after the laying of foundations.*

The basis of the liability is a contract. Since the Czech prescription in cases of damage claims does not distinguish between contractual and tortious damage, the general subjective (short) period of three years and the long-stop (objective) period of ten years apply.

The starting point of the prescription period is not the risk of the future damage but the accrual (appearance) of the factual damage.

## E. THE STARTING POINT (ACCRUAL) IN CONTINUOUS TORTS

The Czech court practice apparently seems to tend not to perceive the continuous performance of tortious behaviour as one act. Accordingly, the growing harm should be regarded as only one basis for a good claim. That would mean that the starting point of a prescription period would be equal to the end of the tortious activity. In contrast,[36] the prescription period starts once the victim learns of individual harms. 38

However, in very rare situations the courts may accept the notion of 'continuous tort' and consider the harm entered as a consequence of it a unity. Then the starting point may be the day that the victim learns of the end of the tortious activity.

However, there do exist cases of harm that are undoubtedly separated. This problem has been resolved in two ways. Firstly, if there is a continuous wrongful activity, one has to wait until such activity is terminated.[37] Secondly, the courts apply the harm stabilisation doctrine which is used mainly in cases of long-lasting illness or developing bodily harm. One has to take into consideration that the continuous conduct of the tortfeasor does not matter with regard to the running (and the stopping) of the prescription period in Czech law. 39

**Case 7** – *Every week, during a month, D1 publishes a defamatory article on P1, each time in another newspaper and on a different topic. During the same period*

36 Supreme Court R 38/1975.

37 Supreme Court 2 Cz 19/74.

*D2 publishes a defamatory article on P2, every second day, on the same topic and in the same newspaper.*

The individual 'attacks' of defamation are to be treated separately. In each of them the starting point of the prescription period is independent.

**Case 8** – *D, a landowner, negligently exposes P, a neighbour, to unreasonable noise for three years. P's hearing is thereby weakened on a daily basis, gradually restricting P's ability to communicate and enjoy music.*

See the solution in Case 5.

**Case 9** – *A waste management company digs bins of toxic content into the soil. Toxic substance leaks into the soil and ground water, causing an apparent damage to crops and expenditure on cleaning on a daily basis. After two years the bins are removed from the soil.*

The short (subjective) prescription period (three years) would start from the date that the victim learns (or does not learn due to the gross negligence) of the person of the tortfeasor and other facts instituting his (or her) claim. The 'long-stop' (objective) period of the year starts with the occurrence of the harm.

### F. IS THE LATE DISCOVERY RULE A RULE OF THE STARTING POINT (ACCRUAL) OR A RULE OF PROLONGATION?

40 Since the knowledge of the harm does not belong to the substantive requirements of the tortious liability and, in other words, is not part of the essentials which constitute the victim's course of action, it is actually part of the rule of prolongation.

## VII. PRESCRIPTION PERIODS

### A. INTRODUCTION

41 In contrast to the prescription regime by different claims, in case of a claim arising from a tort, two types of prescription periods are distinguished that differ in their length and particularly in the moment of their commencement.

42 In the first case, namely in the case of the subjective or short prescription period, which is the subject of this report, the commencement of the prescription period is given subjectively, ie based on the knowledge of elements of a claim by the injured party. This type of prescription period is referred to as 'subjective' as the commencement of the prescription period is determined subjectively. In the second case the objective prescription period (long-stop rule) is the subject of Section XI.

A subjective prescription period is equal to a general prescription period amounting to three years. Negligible differences by the subjective prescription period regard the general tort regime (§620 (1) CC/2012)[38] and the regime of the prescription period to right to compensation for damage caused by a defective product (§620 (2) CC/2012).[39] Commencement of the prescription period here presupposes subjective knowledge of the injured party about damage, defect and identity of the producer. 43

A distinctive regime applies to cases of damage caused in connection with execution of public authority, a resolution or incorrectly conducted procedure or a resolution on custody, punishment or protective measure. The same applies to cases of atomic damage. 44

## B. THE PRESCRIPTION PERIOD AND THE EFFECTIVE TIME OF PRESCRIPTION

The Czech legislator also uses two methods in order to handle the delays of the victim which are regarded as justified: fixed periods of prescription and rules of prolongation. Whereas in the first case there are only two ways, namely the short and long periods, in the second case four ways, namely postponement, suspension, extension or even renewal exist. Based on this alone, the legislator has more options on how to resolve the complex environment of tortious harms. 45

## C. THE LATE DISCOVERY RULE AND THE LENGTH OF THE PRESCRIPTION PERIOD

In the Czech jurisdiction, the late discovery rule is the major rule of prolongation which extends the gap between the prescription period and actual time of prescription and gives the victim a fair chance to pursue his (or her) claim. 46

## D. ONE, FEW OR MANY PRESCRIPTION PERIODS

Traditionally, in the field of tort law the claims for damages prescribe in a three-year period (the same rule applies to the contractual damages). Therefore, no 'prescription period shopping' exists. This short period (with a subjective starting point – see late discovery rule, *infra* Section VIII.A) applies as a general 47

---

[38] See *supra* fn 13.

[39] See *supra* fn 13.

rule regardless of the nature of the claim to all tort damages (be it pecuniary or non-pecuniary loss). Within a three-year period, intentional violation of life, personal injury or negligible harms, etc prescribe. It starts once the plaintiff had actual knowledge not only of the damage and the identity of the tortfeasor (as the law explicitly indicates[40]), but also of the circumstances on which the claim is based and the required conditions (elements) of the liability of the defendant are fulfilled.[41]

## VIII. RULES OF POSTPONEMENT, SUSPENSION, RENEWAL AND EXTENSION

48 Czech law distinguishes three kinds of extension of the basic subjective (short) prescription period. First of all, it is the suspension (§§622 and 645 CC/2012) which means that the prescription period either does not start running or does not run during the time that an obstacle exists. In certain cases (§§645 in fine, §652 Civil Code) the prescription period is prolonged in order to suspend the expiry of the prescription period. The renewal means that the prescription period starts running again from the beginning.

49 These alternations of the prescription period apply only to the short (subjective) prescription period of time whereas the course of the long (objective) prescription period remains untouched. The long-stop period is never prolonged even due to unawareness (incapacity to be aware).

### A. UNAWARENESS – THE LATE DISCOVERY RULE

50 The general cause of action covers all the substantive requirements (the essentials) of a tort claim. In other words, it consists of all requirements of a defendant's tort liability, namely the person of the tortfeasor, his conduct, the damage, the causal link between the tortfeasor's conduct and the damage and, when necessary, also wrongfulness and fault. The actual or imputed knowledge includes all specific facts that the respective tort law (legal norm) requires. For example, if the law requires a tortious conduct against good morals it is necessary that the plaintiff also knows that the defendant (wrongdoer) had this lead in knowledge. Even without knowledge of these facts by the victim, the prescription of the victim's claim does not start. Legal norm does not constitute a requirement (element) of it; it does not belong to the essentials of cause of action and does not play any role in prescription law.

---

40 §620 para 1 CC/2012.

41 See *infra* Section VIII.A.

**Case 10** – *Chemical plant D negligently exposes bordering lands to toxic substances. As a result P, a nearby resident landowner, contracts a lung disease. P failed to sue in time because his former lawyer told him that the exposure was not tortious, and only his new lawyer told him, after the running of time, that it was tortious.*

Under Czech case law the mistake of an advisor (lawyer in this case) is to be imputed to the plaintiff since the lawyer was obliged to support his (or her) client. Then the solution depends on whether the lawyer was grossly negligent and, if yes, whether his (or her) gross negligence should be imputed to the plaintiff. If this question can also be answered in an affirmative way, then the plaintiff's claim against D is prescribed. However, P can sue the first lawyer since his claim against him is not prescribed yet because P learned from the second lawyer that the first lawyer advised him incorrectly.

*1) Objective or Subjective Unawareness?*

As a rule, a hybrid test applies in the Czech jurisdiction. This happens in two stages. Firstly, the objective test in the form of a reasonable man as if he were in the position of the concrete victim is used. This criterion can be adjusted by the subjective test, taking into account both the personal characteristics and specific circumstances of the case. The hybrid test applies both to the actual knowledge and to the imputed knowledge. 51

*2) What is Considered Awareness of an Element of Liability?*

As to the scope of the late discovery rule, this rule covers all kinds of causes of action. As to the degree of certainty, the Czech courts seem to go the middle way. The threshold of the awareness is, eg the reasonable likelihood of the existence of a harm or reasonable belief of the existence of the causation. This should be sufficient for institutional legal proceedings in order to pursue the claim. 52

*3) How Heavy is the Burden to Acquire Knowledge?*

As a rule, the burden corresponds to the degree of the certainty of the existence of the respective fact. However, the court practice requires that the victim has to prove the facts on the lever of the common degree of standard of proof. This means with the likelihood that almost equals the certainty. 53

**Case 11** – *Chemical plant D negligently exposes bordering lands to toxic substances. As a result P, a nearby resident landowner, contracts a lung disease, but is unaware of the causal link between exposure and disease because his physician fails to detect it. P does not seek a second opinion. After the prescription period runs on the disease P consults his new physician that tells him about the link.*

Like in Case 10, under Czech law a mistake of a doctor would be imputed to P. However, in this case, in contrast to Case 10, the information of P communicated to the first doctor plays an eminent role. If P omitted to tell the doctor about toxic substances then he could be considered to be acting grossly negligent and then his claim against D would be prescribed.

## B. OTHER RULES OF PROLONGATION

### *1) D is to Blame for the Delay*

54 According to Czech court practice the situations where a delay to file a claim is caused by D's misconduct are not dealt with by the rules of prolongation. Depending on the specific situation, specifically on the *nature* of the misconduct, the problems are resolved based on the prohibition of abuse of right or by the mechanism of good morals.

55 More serious cases are dealt with by §650 CC/2012. According to this rule, the course of the prescription period is suspended as long as a creditor prevents a debtor from raising its claim. The same also applies in cases when a creditor did not try to enforce its claim because it was misled by trickery committed by the debtor or a person close to the debtor.

### *2) Admission by D of P's Right or Partial Performance of P's Right by D (Renewal)*

56 If the claim was prescribed and the debtor acknowledged its debt, the claim of the creditor would be restored and a new prescription period commenced to run from the day in which the debt was recognised. However, should the debtor simultaneously with the debt recognition also determine a period in which the debt will be performed, the claim becomes prescribed in ten years from the last day of the period (§653 para 1 CC/2012).[42]

57 The same is true if a judicial or other official act is undertaken and recognises the claim even though it was prescribed.

58 As already mentioned in Section I, Czech law provides for several cases of postponement of commencement of prescription period or its suspension.

42 'If a right has been time-barred and the debtor has acknowledged his debt, a claim is renewed and a new limitation period commences on the date on which the debt was acknowledged. However, if the debtor specifies in the acknowledgement a period within which he will discharge his debt, the right becomes time-barred ten years after the last day of the period specified.'

*3) P's Lack of Legal Capacity*

59 Cases of a minor lacking full legal capacity pursuant to §622 CC/2012.[43]

It is necessary to have a legal representative or a custodian with the exception of the previous case of §645 CC/2012.[44]

*4) Special Relations between D and P (Suspension, Extension)*

60 Claims arising between spouses within the duration of marriage and claims between partners living in the same household, claims between the represented party and its representative, a guardian and its ward or a tutor and the person under its tutorship (§646 CC/2012).[45]

*5) Absence of Parties from the Jurisdiction*

61 There is no rule providing for this in Czech law.

*6) Former Legal and Other Proceedings between the Parties*

62 In cases of negotiation between a creditor and a debtor, the prescription period commences after the creditor or the debtor explicitly refuse to continue negotiation (§647 CC/2012).[46]

63 When an injured party raises a claim pursuant to the Law on State Liability by the Ministry of Justice, the course of the prescription period is suspended.

64 If, within a limitation period, a creditor asserts a right against a public body and continues in duly initiated proceedings, the statute of limitations is suspended. This also applies to an already enforceable right if an application for court enforcement or private enforcement has been filed with respect to the right (§648 CC/2012).

---

43 See *supra* fn 6.

44 'Where a person is required to have a legal representative or a guardian, a limitation period for a right of or against such a person commences only on the day on which the legal representative or guardian of that person is appointed. A limitation period which has already begun shall continue to run, but shall end no earlier than one year after the obstacle is removed.'

45 See *supra* fn 5.

46 'In the case of an agreement on out-of-court negotiations between the debtor and creditor concerning a right or a circumstance constituting a right, the limitation period only after the creditor or debtor has expressly refused to continue such negotiations; where a limitation period commenced earlier, it is suspended for the duration of the negotiations.'

65 Where a creditor asserts a mutual right before a public body and both rights are related to the same contract or several contracts concluded in dependence on each other with respect to their purpose, a limitation period is suspended from the date on which proceedings on the right against which the mutual right is directed were initiated. In other cases, a limitation period is suspended from the date on which the mutual right was asserted (§649 CC/2012).

*7) Victim's Death*

66 Where a duty passed to an heir, a limitation period shall expire no earlier than six months after the date on which the heir obtained a confirmation of the inheritance (§643 para 1 CC/2012).

*8) Tortfeasor's Bankruptcy*

67 Where a legal person has been restored, a limitation period for its creditors shall expire no earlier than six months after the date on which the registration of the legal person in a public register was restored (§643 para 2 CC/2012).

9) Force Majeure

68 The prescription period is suspended for the duration of *force majeure* preventing a creditor from enforcing its claim in the past six months (§651 CC/2012).[47]

*10) General Rule on Prolongation*

69 Generally, the prescription period does not end later than six months after the day that its course was renewed after some of the obstacles were removed (§652 CC/2012).[48]

## IX. CEILINGS ON THE EFFECTIVE TIME OF PRESCRIPTION

70 As mentioned *supra* (Section IV), tort prescription law is based on two kinds of prescription period: the short (subjective) period and the long (objective) period which serves as a ceiling.

---

47 'A limitation period is suspended for the duration of an event of force majeure which prevented the creditor from asserting his right in the last six months of the limitation period.'

48 'If a limitation period continues to run after any of the obstacles provided under Sections 646 to 651 have been removed, the limitation period shall end no earlier than six months after the date on which it commenced again.'

## A. LENGTH AND SCOPE OF APPLICATION

The general length of objective long-stop is ten years. The special rule in §636 para 2 CC sets forth a period of 15 years in case of intentional damage and damage as a result of corrupt behaviour. In case of harm to freedom, harm to life or bodily harm (personal injury) the objective prescription period does not apply (§636 para 3 CC). 71

## B. COMMENCEMENT

Another difference between the subjective and objective periods of time is the starting point of them. While the long-stop (objective prescription) period starts running from the time that the damage occurred (was completed), the starting point of the subjective (short) prescription period is the date of awareness or imputable unawareness. This is the difference compared with other legal orders where the trigger of the starting point lies in the act of the tortfeasor or in the event causing the damage. 72

## C. APPLICATION OF RULES OF PROLONGATION

The long-stop cannot be prolonged. Postponement, suspension, extension or even renewal are excluded. 73

# X. STATUTE INTERPRETATION, JUDICIAL DISCRETION AND LACHES

## A. INTERPRETATION

Apart from the period in which the right to invoke prescriptions must be invoked during the proceedings (see *supra*), there are no major issues. 74

It is true that courts welcome the assertion of a right to invoke prescription and treat it with generosity for a pragmatic reason – denial of the claim as time-barred is seen as the most effective and easiest way to handle the issue. 75

Generally speaking, the courts' approach towards interpretation of prescription rules is neutral. However, there are deviations in favour of the victim rather than of the tortfeasor. Instead of a continuous flow of the prescription period, the 76 courts clearly prefer to separate it by the individual occurrences of damages. In other words, the prescription periods start running individually.

77 The case law considers the action (lawsuit) for damages of the victim to be only a pure procedural act[49] in the sense that it does not represent a demanding task for the plaintiff and despite this it is able to stop the (flow of) prescription period which also shows an inclination in favour of the victim. The plaintiff does not legally need to qualify the facts indicated in his lawsuit including a reference to specific legal norm (provision of a statute). Also, the argument of good morals (*bonos mores*), even if rarely used regarding the justification and denial of the prescription defence, speaks in favour of the victim. This approach is not based on the category of laches but rather on duress, which might cause the claim, particularly among relatives. In favour of the defendant is the objective criterion for the assessment of unawareness of damage on the side of the plaintiff.[50]

## B. DISCRETION

78 The wording of the prescription rules in the CC does not allow any discretion in terms of modifying the length of the prescription or even whether to apply or not to apply the legal norms on prescription or to relax (adapt) the prescription regime otherwise. These rules are to a great extent of mandatory nature. The admission of discretion would lead to a threat of legal certainty.

## C. LACHES

79 The principle of good faith can lead to the conclusion that the claim should be disregarded since it ceased to exist, even though the lapse of a time period has not occurred yet. This is because the pursuit (enforcement) of such a claim realises (happens) in violation of good faith. The plaintiff made use of his right a relatively long time after the prescription period had already started to run and in the expectation that his right would not be enforced any longer.[51]

---

49 Constitutional Court III. ÚS 182/01, see *supra* 11.

50 Constitutional Court II. ÚS 309/95, ÚS 643/04, Supreme Court Cdo 1839/2000, *J Švestka*, in: Švestka et al (eds), *supra* fn 10, 587 n 6.

51 *L Tichý*, Obecná část občanského práva (General part of civil law) (2014) 124/3 no 300.

# XI. CHANGE OF PARTIES

## A. INTRODUCTION

A general norm of the repealed s 111 (§111) of the old CC/1964 still applies as an unwritten rule: 'a change in person of the creditor or debtor shall not affect the running of the prescription period'. 80

## B. THE PLAINTIFF IS A TRANSFEREE OF THE VICTIM'S CLAIM

If the victim's claim is assigned after the starting point of the prescription period to a third person, the flow continues to run towards the assignee (third person) as it would have run towards the original creditor (assignor). 81

The solution consists in the rules of burden of proof. First of all, the tortfeasor (defendant) when raising the prescription defence has to prove the time that the plaintiff (victim) obtained the knowledge about the tortfeasor and the damage (or as the case may be should have obtained this information). If the defendant fails to bear his burden of proof, his defence must be dismissed. 82

Only §643 CC/2012 contains a specific regulation, according to which prescription may not expire sooner than six months after the day in which the acquisition of inheritance was confirmed to the respective heir (§643(1) CC/2012).[52] 83

## C. THE DEFENDANT IS A TRANSFEREE OF THE TORTFEASOR'S OBLIGATION

In case of change of debt (liability) from an original debtor to a third person the general rule also applies here: In principle this does not affect the prescription regime. The exception represents the case of restoration of a legal entity prescription period that may not expire sooner than six months from the day in which the registration of the legal entity in the commercial register was restored (§643(2) CC/2012).[53] 84

---

52 See 'Where a duty passed to an heir, a limitation period shall expire no earlier than six months after the date on which the heir obtained a confirmation of the inheritance' (§643 para 1 CC/2012).

53 See 'Where a legal person has been restored, a limitation period for its creditors shall expire no earlier than six months after the date on which the registration of the legal person in a public register was restored' (§643 para 2 CC/2012).

### D. CONTRIBUTION CLAIMS AND DEPENDANT'S CLAIMS

85 The claims which substitute the original cause of action and serve as contribution claims among joint tortfeasors or claims for last maintenance are independent claims with their own prescription regime separated from the claim of the original victim in Czech tort law.

## XII. OTHER ASPECTS OF PRESCRIPTION LAW

### A. WAIVER AND STIPULATION

86 The tortfeasor can waive the defence of prescription only under certain conditions. He cannot waive it at any time, since his waiver 'in advance is disregarded' (§610 para 1 in fine CC). It is stated that this rule is in compliance with the Austrian (§1502 ABGB) and Czechoslovak (§574 para 2 CC/1964) law, since one may not waive his rights which have not come into existence yet.[54] Since the waiver realised after the starting point of the prescription period but before its elapse, it would mean the freedom to enforce the right of the victim without any time limitation. Therefore, the waiver can be completed only after the elapse of the long objective prescription period (10, 15 years).[55] The waiver is considered to be a one-sided expression directed to the court which is not revocable.[56]

87 Since the prescription as a legal category is a reflection of certain public interests, it is embedded to some extent in mandatory legal norms. As a consequence, the party autonomy is rather limited.

88 The stipulation may address only the subjective (short) prescription period. The parties can conclude an agreement by which they relax the length of prescription period in terms of extension or shortening it. However, they may not deviate from the starting point of the prescription period as it is set forth in the law. The parties cannot validly stipulate the length of prescription period by extension beyond 15 years and it may not be shorter than one year.[57]

89 An agreement on relaxation of statutory rules of suspension and renewal may be considered valid accordingly.[58]

---

54 *P Tégl and D Weinhold*, in: Melzer, Tégl, Občanský zákoník, Komentář (Civil Code, Commentary), Vol III (2016) 901 n 41, 42.

55 Ibid, n 45.

56 Ibid, n 41, 48 which is very disputable view (Tichý).

57 §630 para 1 CC/2012.

58 However, there is no case law and no comments in the literature on it yet.

There is no legal requirement regarding a special form of the parties' agreement. 90

Two other kinds of limits of party autonomy are codified in §630 para 2 CC. 91
Firstly, there is a personal limit represented by 'the weaker party', who is considered (under the Civil Code – §433) a person, whose autonomy is limited and therefore the party is unable to decide freely to enter into a contract.[59]

Another limit of a stipulation only regards the shortening of the prescription 92
period in case of a damage to freedom, life or health and damage as a result of intentional violation of a duty.[60]

## B. FILING, SUBMISSIONS – MEANING OF 'FILING A CLAIM' THAT INTERRUPTS THE RUNNING OF PRESCRIPTION

The Czech law acknowledges several procedural acts by which the debtor can 93
stop the running of the prescription period. First of all, it is a lawsuit by which the court proceeding will be instituted. Apart from this there is also a petition on compensation towards criminal proceedings or even administrative proceedings. All these vehicles are covered by §648 CC which considers suspension of the prescription period 'an assertion of a right against a public body'.

The institution of legal proceedings means that the lawsuit reached (was lodged) 94
the court (or other public body). A service of such a document to the defendant (debtor) is not required.

Also, a submission which does not meet all legal requirements, or even contains 95
statements which are uncertain or not understandable, can stop the running of the prescription period. The formal defects of such a lawsuit should be disregarded.[61]

## C. WHEN SHOULD THE DEFENCE BE RAISED AND DECIDED?

The prescription defence may be raised at any stage of the proceedings until the 96
appellate court issues its ruling. Prescription may not be invoked in appellation proceedings provided that prescription is not apparent from the case file, evidence or factual findings of the court of first instance.[62]

---

59 *P Tégl and D Weinhold*, in: Melzer, Tégl, Občanský zákoník, Komentář (Civil Code, Commentary), Vol III (2016) 988, n 20.

60 See *supra* and §635 para 3 CC.

61 Constitutional Court III. ÚS 182/01.

62 Nejvyšší soud (Supreme Court) 32 Cdo 4291/2007. See more on this *infra* XII.D.

97 The Czech court decides the prescription defence in its final judgment.

98 If the prescription defence is raised at the late stage of proceedings it may have an impact on the court's decision of the costs of proceedings.

## D. WHO MAY RAISE THE DEFENCE?

99 The defence of prescription is a one-sided procedural act towards a court (or other public body) with which the case is pending. It can be invoked at any stage of proceedings when the court examines the facts.[63]

100 The defence can be raised not only by the debtor or his successor, but also by the intervenor on the side of the debtor.[64]

101 The effect (consequence) of the successful defence is that the court dismisses the lawsuit in its final decision. However, in certain cases the court can even decide its decision upon the cause of action.[65] As a consequence of such a decision, the claim of the creditor ceases to exist.

102 The court itself is not allowed to deal (assert, acknowledge) with it *ex officio*. The court must not even, within its duty of advice, indicate such a defence of the debtor.

## E. BURDEN OF PROOF

103 The debtor who raises the prescription defence bears the burden of proof. He (or she) has to prove the elapse of prescription period. This duty covers the starting point of the prescription period including the possible negligent unawareness of the creditor (plaintiff). The burden of proof regarding a suspension, renewal or extension of the prescription period is with the plaintiff.

104 A different regime of starting of the long (objective) prescription period regards the claim for compensation of damage caused by defective product. In this case, the prescription period starts running at the time of the introduction of the product in the market. The claim prescribes within the general ten-year period (§637 CC).

---

63 *K Svoboda*, in: Švestka et al (eds), Občanský zákoník, Komentář (Civil Code, Commentary), Vol I (2014) 1529, 1530.

64 Supreme Court 25 Cdo 539/2008.

65 PR 12/1999, 662 – Regional Court Hradec Králové 18 Co 728/96.

The Czech special treatment exists in case of 'the claims which must be primarily asserted with the affected person' (§628 CC). In this case the general rule of the starting point as the date of the appearance of the damage (harm) does not apply. Instead, the date that the claim was enforced with this person matters. This is the case, eg in the enforcement of a compensation of a damage caused by the State. In other words, a harm resulting from an act of the government. 105

# PRESCRIPTION IN TORT LAW: ENGLAND AND WALES

Ken OLIPHANT and Vanessa WILCOX*



* Readers should note that the hypothetical cases discussed in this chapter, and the order of their discussion, are not entirely the same as in other chapters.

## I. INTRODUCTION

The limitations statutes we are familiar with today are rooted in the limitation periods of 13th-century land-related actions in England. It was not until the Limitation Act 1623, however, that the notion was extended to non-land-related claims, including torts. Under that Act, limitation periods of two years for actions on the case for words, four years for actions of assault and false imprisonment and six years for most other actions were introduced. The law of limitations was left virtually undisturbed until Parliament enacted a single limitation period of six years under the Limitation Act 1939 from when the cause of action in tort and contract, but not on a specialty, accrued. Parliament intervened more frequently thereafter among other things to reduce the limitation period for personal injury claims to three years (under Law Reform (Limitation of Actions, etc) Act 1954); to introduce an alternative period which commenced, in personal injury actions, when 'material facts' were known to the claimant (under the Limitation Act 1963); and to legislate for judicial discretion to set aside the ordinary time limit in personal injuries cases (under the Limitation Act 1975). The current principal piece of legislation on the subject, the Limitation Act 1980, entered into force on 1 May 1981[1] and applies in England and Wales only. As its Preamble notes, the statute is: 'An Act to consolidate the Limitation Acts 1939 to 1980'. Important amendments have since been made to the Limitation Act 1980, for our purposes, by the Latent Damage Act 1986 (which is also limited in its application to England and Wales),[2] the Consumer Protection Act 1987 (which applies across the UK),[3] the Administration of Justice 1

1 Limitation Act 1980, sec 41(2).
2 In force since 18 September 1986.
3 In force since 1 March 1988.

Act 1985[4] and the Defamation Act 1996 (which applies to the whole of the UK with the exception of Scotland).[5]

2 Part I of the Limitation Act 1980 (secs 1–27C) sets the ordinary time limits for different classes of action.[6] However, the latter may qualify for extension or exclusion in accordance with provisions under Part II of the Act (secs 28–33B).[7] Miscellaneous and general provisions are contained in Part III (secs 35–41).[8] By virtue of sec 37 of the Limitation Act 1980, actions involving the Crown are generally dealt with in the same way as those between private subjects.[9] Several specialised provisions also exist outside the Limitation Act 1980.[10] While most aspects of tortious claims are governed by the 1980 Act or other statutory limitation periods, with respect to some actions, eg an action for breach of copyright, no statute exists: '[I]t follows from the absence of any common law concept of limitation that in the event of a lacuna in the statutory provisions, no limitation period will apply.'[11] However, as indicated *infra* 121 ff, equity also plays a role in promoting finality through the doctrines of laches and acquiescence, either of which may operate to bar relief where a claimant tarries in pursuing his cause.

## II. DEFINITION AND STRUCTURE

### A. DEFINITION

3 'Limitation is a defence'.[12] By one account, 'a limitation period is construed as including any provision which specifies a time-limit within which legal proceedings of a particular kind must be brought or, exceptionally, within which notice of a claim or dispute must be given to another party.'[13] This encompasses statutes which do not in themselves create causes of actions.[14] Where a wrong

---

4 In force since 30 October 1985. The Act led to new secs 4A, 28(4A), 32A, etc of the Limitation Act 1980. However, those provisions were substituted by the Defamation Act 1996.

5 In force since 4 July 1996.

6 Limitation Act 1980, sec 1(1).

7 Limitation Act 1980, sec 1(2).

8 Limitation Act 1980, sec 34 has been repealed.

9 Cf sec 37(2) of the Limitation Act 1980.

10 Limitation Act 1980, sec 39 reads: 'This Act shall not apply to any action or arbitration for which a period of limitation is prescribed by or under any other enactment (whether passed before or after the passing of this Act) or to any action or arbitration to which the Crown is a party and for which, if it were between subjects, a period of limitation would be prescribed by or under any such other enactment.'

11 *A McGee*, Limitation Periods (2014), para 1.062.

12 *Birmingham City Council v Abdulla* [2012] UKSC 47, [42] per Lord Sumption.

13 *A McGee*, Limitation Periods (2014), para 1.001.

14 *T Prime and G Scanlan*, The Law of Limitation (2nd ed, 2005), 2 ff.

results in concurrent liability, eg in contract and tort,[15] the starting point is that a party may pursue his grievance under either cause and in so doing take advantage of the longer of the two limitation periods relevant for the action in question. In the case of medical malpractice leading to personal injury, however, actions against the UK's National Health Service (NHS), which provides free healthcare at the point of delivery, would necessarily have to be in tort given the absence of a contract. While a private patient can generally frame his action in either contract or tort, special rules apply in respect of personal injuries which displace the application of the limitation period ordinarily applicable for actions founded on simple contract (*infra* 26). Where a claimant elects to seek compensation for personal injury the period prescribed for such injuries applies by default.[16] In the case of (particularly) minor personal injury combined with other loss, however, a claimant may choose to abandon the personal injury aspect of the claim and sue purely in contract for the other loss.

## B. STRUCTURE OF THE REPORT

Various considerations underlie the law of limitations (Section IV), an area of law which regulates: 4

- when time starts to run (rules of accrual, Section V);
- the duration of the period (the limitation period, Section VI); and
- the consequence of the expiry of that period (the nature of prescription and its effects, Section III).

As regards the last enumeration, it may be that certain rules or discretions operate to influence the effective time limit, whether to shorten or lengthen it. In particular, English law applies: 5

- rules of prolongation: postponement, renewal or extension of the prescription period (Section VII);
- ceilings on the effective time of prescription (Section VIII); and
- statutory, judicial discretion and equitable rules (Section IX).

Procedural rules and rules regulating a change of the parties (Section X), in addition to possible reform relating to whiplash and the impact that would have, if implemented, on the law of limitations (Section XI), are also set out in this report. 6

---

15 See *Henderson v Merrett Syndicates* [1995] 2 AC 45.

16 Limitation Act 1980, sec 11(2).

## III. THE NATURE OF PRESCRIPTION AND ITS EFFECTS

7 Before elaborating on other aspects of the law of limitation, it is perhaps useful to begin with rules governing when time stops running, the effects of the statutory bar and other preliminaries. The Limitation Act 1980 is peppered with references that actions shall not be 'brought' after the expiry of certain time periods. The word is not defined in the Act itself; however, by virtue of CPR r 7.2(1), proceedings are started when the court issues a claim form at the request of the claimant. CPR r 7.2(2), adds that a claim form is issued on the date entered on the form by the court. It is on this date that time stops running against the claimant.

8 Practice Direction 7A (para 5.1) addresses the issue of where a claim form was received in the court office on a date earlier than the date on which it was issued by the court in providing that the claim is 'brought' for the purposes of the Limitation Act 1980 and any other relevant statute on that earlier date. Although later than the point at which the defendant has notice of the action against him, that the action is brought when proceedings are issued (and at that point the limitation clock stops running) is justified on the grounds that that date, as opposed to the date of service upon the defendant, promotes certainty and avoids the problem of the defendant seeking to evade service.[17] While para 5.2 of Practice Direction 7A goes on to state that the court will record the relevant date, by a date stamp either on the claim form held on the court file or on the letter that accompanied the claim form, case law confirms that bringing a claim is a unilateral act so that if the form is lost and no stamp is ever affixed on it, a claimant will not be prejudiced.[18] A claimant will, however, have to prove on the balance of probabilities that they delivered the claim form and indeed para 5.4 of Practice Direction 7A states that: 'Parties proposing to start a claim which is approaching the expiry of the limitation period should recognise the potential importance of establishing the date the claim form was received by the court and should themselves make arrangements to record the date.' A claim that expires on a particular day but is posted under the locked doors of a court which has closed for business will be considered out of time.[19]

9 To avoid computing parts of a day, the day of the occurrence of the event which founded the claim is generally disregarded from the calculation of the period within which the action should be brought. Thus, in *Marren v Dawson Bentley and Co*,[20] where the claimant was injured at work at 13:30 on 8 November 1954

---

17 Law Commission, Limitation of Actions Consultation (1998), CP 151, para 14.8.

18 *Page v Hewetts Solicitors* [2012] EWCA Civ 805.

19 *Barker v Hambleton District Council* [2011] All ER 23, albeit an action under the Planning and Compulsory Purchase Act 2004.

20 *Marren v Dawson Bentley and Co* [1961] 2 QB 135.

and issued a claim against his employers for damages arising from their negligence on 8 November 1957, Havers J held that the claim was valid since time began to run from the very first moment of 9 November 1954 and expired at the very last moment of 8 November 1957.

The effect of an expiry of a limitation period depends largely on the tort in question. With the exception of conversion and the long-stop period under the Consumer Protection Act 1987, the general rule is that the expiration of the limitation period does not extinguish a claimant's rights. As regards the former, sec 3(2) of the Limitation Act 1980 states that the title of the owner of the chattel is extinguished (and consequentially any remedy they might otherwise have been entitled to is lost) once the period prescribed for bringing the action has expired and the owner failed to recover possession of the chattel. Similarly, by virtue of sec 11A(3) of the Limitation Act 1980 (which transposes art 11 of Directive 85/374/EEC on defective products),[21] no action can be brought after the expiration of the period of ten years from the date on which the producer put its product which caused damage into circulation and the right of action shall be extinguished (*infra* 65). Limitation operates as a *procedural* defence that bars a judicial remedy. The claimant is not, however, prevented from pursuing his grievance by other lawful self-help means. 10

## IV. CONSIDERATIONS FOR AND AGAINST PRESCRIPTION OF TORT CLAIMS

The right to a fair trial entails a right to have one's case heard (fairly). It is a right which in more modern times is entrenched in the Human Rights Act 1998 (sch 1, art 6), incorporating the European Convention on Human Rights (in particular, art 6 ECHR),[22] but one which long preceded that enactment. Indeed, the 39th clause of the Magna Carta of 1215 gave all 'free men' the right to justice and a fair trial. Justice and fairness also underlie the various enactments on limitations leading up to the limitation statute currently in force. The Preamble to the 1540 Act of Limitation, while limited to land-related claims, is still instructive. It opened: 11

> Forasmuch as the time of limitation appointed for suing [...] extend and be of so far and long time past, that it is above the remembrance of any living man, truly to try and know the perfect certainty of such things, as hath or shall come in trial, or do

[21] Council Directive 85/374/EEC of 25 July 1985 on the approximation of the laws, regulations and administrative provisions of the Member States concerning liability for defective products, as amended.

[22] Rome, 4 November 1950, as amended.

> extend unto the time and times limited by the said laws and statutes, to the great danger of mens' consciences that have or shall be impanelled in any jury for the trial of the same; and it is also a great occasion of much trouble, vexation, and suits to the king's loving subjects at the common laws of his realm, so that no man, although he [...] [has] been in peaceful possession for a long season, of and in lands, tenements and other hereditaments, is or can be in any surety, quietness or rest, of and in the same, without a good remedy and reformation be had, made, and provided for the same [...]

12 The law of limitation seeks to promote finality in civil disputes and from the above Act, which was the first to set limitation periods by reference to a fixed period of time in the manner we are familiar with today, we derive three categories of subjects which this area of law seeks to protect, namely *defendants*, *claimants* and *the public*. In a consultation on the Limitation of Actions conducted in 1998, the Law Commission echoed the above sentiments by observing that: 'In general terms, limitation of actions is necessary in the interests of defendants and of the state', but added that: 'In formulating a limitation regime one must also ensure that it works fairly for plaintiffs.'[23]

## A. DEFENDANTS' INTERESTS

13 As has been observed, 'long dormant claims have often more of cruelty than justice to them'.[24] The lack of finality troubles and vexes 'the King's loving subjects' and robs them of their peace. Fairness demands that persons be put on notice, without undue delay, of any wrong they may have committed rather than harassing them with stale claims;[25] hence the reference to statutes of limitation as 'statutes of repose' or 'Acts of peace'. The revival of ancient claims also hampers parties from planning ahead since their settled expectations may be disrupted at any time; parties are consequently discouraged from dealing with those who face potential liability of ambiguous magnitude and temporal exposure, to their and indeed possibly society's loss.

14 Reference in the Preamble to a period being so long that it is *above the remembrance* of any living man to be certain of things in trial is reference to the loss, or deterioration, of evidence through the passage of time. The law does not work fairly for defendants if limitation periods are such that it is difficult and, in the worst case, impossible for them to prove their cases or if they are

---

23 *Law Commission*, Limitation of Actions Consultation (1998) CP 151, para 1.22. See also *A Burrows*, Some Recurring Issues in Relation to Limitation of Actions, in: A Dyson, J Goudkamp and F Wilmot-Smith (eds), Defences in Tort (2015), 311 ff.

24 *A'Court v Cross* (1825), 3 Bing 329, 332 per Best CJ, 130 ER 540, 541.

25 *AB v Ministry of Defence* [2013] 1 AC 78, [164] per Lady Hale.

forced to expend huge financial resources in the preservation of evidentiary records.

## B. CLAIMANTS' INTERESTS

Lawmakers are obligated to reconcile, as far as possible, the conflicting interests of each litigating party. The law of limitations encourages claimants 'not to go to sleep on their rights',[26] and in so doing urges them to settle disputes or institute proceedings at a time when the quality of evidence is relatively reliable. To that extent, claimants' and defendants' interests overlap. A delicate balance has to be struck, however, between affording claimants sufficient leeway to decide if a case should be brought against a defendant and to gather preliminary evidence on the one hand without inspiring the precipitation of litigation on the other. 15

## C. THE PUBLIC'S INTEREST

Courts are ill-suited to determine stale demands. If based on inaccurate or incomplete evidence, deciding them is more likely to be time-intensive and indeed such cases are prone to (wasteful) appeals and add to costs associated with the administration of justice, costs it might be added which are ultimately borne by taxpayers. Claimants should thus be discouraged from sitting on their rights to the extent that legal certainty, the effective administration of justice and public confidence in the justice system demand. 16

## D. THE CURRENT LEGISLATIVE APPROACH

The weight of the various considerations discussed above is reflected in the present trend which has been for the legislature to formulate shorter periods with the more flexible approaches: 17

- first, of taking account of the claimant's knowledge – eg since the Limitation Act 1963, which was enacted following the injustice in the personal injury case of *Cartledge v E Jopling & Sons Ltd*,[27] a trigger based on reasonable discoverability exists. A similar rule was also introduced for actions not involving personal injuries under the Latent Damage Act 1986 (*infra* 45); and

---

26 *Law Commission*, Limitation of Actions Consultation (1998) CP 151, para 1.35, fn 80.

27 *Cartledge v E Jopling & Sons Ltd* [1962] 1 QB 189.

- second, of conferring courts with a discretion to allow an action to proceed in certain cases despite the fact that the claim is already statute-barred (since the Limitation Act 1975, *infra* 80).[28]

# V. THE STARTING POINT OF THE PRESCRIPTION PERIOD

## A. CAUSE OF ACTION

18 Section 2 of the Limitation Act 1980, which sets out the ordinary time limit in tort, reads: 'An action founded on tort shall not be brought after the expiration of six years from the date on which the *cause of action* accrued.'[29] It was the Limitation Act 1939 that introduced the principle of a fixed limitation period running from the *accrual of the cause of action*[30] and indeed the current instrument, the Limitation Act 1980, makes nearly 50 references to a 'cause of action'. It does not, however, go on to define the term, although 'action' is taken to embrace '*any* proceeding in a court of law, including an ecclesiastical court'.[31] That said, in legal parlance 'action' is restricted to '*civil* proceedings commenced by writ or in any other manner prescribed by rules of court'.[32] Certain actions, which need not detain us here, are expressly excluded from the scope of the 1980 Act.[33]

19 For assistance on the meaning of a 'cause of action' one must therefore turn to case law which defines it as 'a factual situation the existence of which entitles one person to obtain from the court a remedy against another person'.[34] A cause of action thus exists where all the essential elements needed to support an enforceable claim have arisen, these being duty, breach, causation and damage in the case of negligence, for example. Whether one has arisen therefore requires an enquiry into substantive law. The 1980 Act makes specific reference to certain causes of action in tort – such as conversion, defamation, malicious falsehood, negligence, nuisance, breach of duty, actions under the Consumer Protection Act 1987, actions under the Fatal Accidents Act 1976, etc – subjecting them

---

28 See also *A McGee*, Limitation Periods (2014), paras 1.057 ff.

29 Emphasis added.

30 Inspired by *Law Reform Committee*, Twenty-First Report (Final Report on Limitation of Actions) (1977, Cmnd 6923).

31 Limitation Act 1980, sec 38(1). Emphasis added.

32 Senior Courts Act 1981, sec 151(1). Emphasis added.

33 By sec 38(11): actions under Part 3 of the Social Security Administration Act 1992, sec 127(c) of the Social Security Contributions and Benefits Act 1992 and Part 1 of the Tax Credits Act 2002.

34 *Letang v Cooper* [1965] 1 QB 232, 242 ff per Diplock LJ. See also *infra* 42.

to special rules. A competent claimant and competent defendant are further essential elements to ground a cause of action so that no action can be brought, for example, in the case of an injured claimant and a dissolved corporate defendant, unless the latter is restored to the register 'for the purpose of bringing proceedings against the company for damages for personal injury'.[35]

As seen *supra* 18 time begins to run, for limitation purposes, when the cause of action accrues. As mentioned, when the cause of action accrues is a question of common law. The enquiry hinges on whether the tort is one that is actionable per se, that is without proof of damage (eg trespass to the person), or one that is not actionable per se (eg negligence). In the former case, the cause of action accrues *when the wrong is committed.* Since '[n]egligence alone does not give a cause of action, damage alone does not give a cause of action: the two must co-exist,'[36] where damage is the gist of the action, the cause of action accrues *upon the damage occurring.*[37] 20

### 1) *Single Wrongful Act Precipitating Separate Incidents of Damage*

The principle of *res judicata* precludes the relitigation of already decided claims.[38] To ensure that a defendant does not answer more than once for the consequences of the same act,[39] English law imposes a general policy – referred to as the 'single action' rule – in favour of awarding damages resulting from one and the same cause of action once and for all. According to Coke this old rule is based upon the maxim *interest rei publicae ut sit finis litium* and justified by the concern that 'otherwise great oppression might be done under colour and pretence of law'.[40] Once *some* damage has occurred as a result of a single wrongful act, therefore, the cause of action has accrued. The extent or type of damage need not be known. Otherwise undesirable states of uncertainty would exist in cases where the full extent of damage cannot be ascertained long after the limitation period has expired. Rather, compensation is available for future or indeed prospective (whether certain or contingent) damage which the claimant can reasonably anticipate will arise as a result of the wrong.[41] This is especially the case with personal injury 'where every 21

---

35 Companies Act 2006, sec 1030.

36 *JR Mundy v London County Council* [1916] 2 KB 331, 334 per Reading CJ.

37 *Pirelli General Cable Works Ltd. v Oscar Faber & Partners* [1983] 2 AC 1.

38 See also *K Oliphant*, England and Wales: Tort Law, in: K Oliphant (ed), Aggregation and Divisibility of Damage (2009), no 59, 62 ff.

39 *Rothwell v Chemical & Insulating Co Ltd, Re Pleural Plaques Litigation* [2008] 1 AC 281 at [14] per Lord Hoffmann.

40 *Ferrer's Case* (1597) 6 Co Rep 7a, 9a.

41 McGregor on Damages (19th ed, 2014), para 11-025.

day damages are awarded which take into account prospective pain and suffering, prospective loss of amenities of life, prospective medical expenses and prospective loss of earnings.'[42] Thus in *Fetter v Beale*,[43] where the claimant recovered damages in an action against a defendant for injury following assault and battery and years later, 'by reason of the same battery, part of his skull was come out,' the claimant was barred from pursuing a subsequent action.

22 A corollary of the single action rule is that a claimant seeking damages for a *tort actionable on proof of damage* must do so within the relevant time limit set, that period commencing – in the case of separate incidents of damage arising from a single wrongful act – on the date the *earliest* damage was suffered. As has been observed: 'A house that has received a shock may not at once shew all the damage done to it, but it is damaged none the less then to the extent that it is damaged, and the fact that the damage only manifests itself later on by stages does not alter the fact that the damage is there.'[44] Although the earliest damage completes the cause of action, in practice establishing the starting date for torts not actionable per se can prove difficult.

23 There are exceptions to the single action rule, however, so that a single wrongful act may entitle the claimant to more than one recovery. This is the case where the wrong precipitates multiple causes of action, in particular:

- where more than one protected interest is infringed by a wrong;
- where a single act not actionable per se causes damage on two or more separate occasions in respect of the same protected interest; or
- in the case of a continuing wrong.

24 Where more than one protected interest is infringed by a wrong, eg damage to a cab driver and his vehicle, the authorities state that a separate cause of action arises in respect of each interest. Thus in *Brunsden v Humphrey*[45] the claimant was not prevented from pursuing damages for personal injury after he had already received damages in respect of the damage to the vehicle he was driving.[46] This was also the case in *Gibbs v Cruikshank*[47] where it was held that trespass to land accompanied by the seizure of property under distress

42 Ibid.

43 *Fetter v Beale* (1706) Holt KB 12, 12. Also reported as *Fitter v Veal* (1706) 12 Mod 542. The decision was approved in *Cartledge v E Jopling & Sons Ltd* [1963] AC 758.

44 *Darley Main Colliery Co v Mitchell* (1886) 11 App Cas 127, 231 per Lord Halsbury.

45 *Brunsden v Humphrey* (1884) 14 QBD 141.

46 'Nobody can doubt that if the plaintiff had recovered any damages for injury to his person, he could not have maintained a further action for fresh bodily injuries caused by the same act of negligence, merely because they had been discovered or developed subsequently': ibid, 148 per Bowen LJ.

47 *Gibbs v Cruikshank* (1873) LR 8 CP 454.

amounted to interferences with two separate protected interests giving rise to two separate causes of action. Separate causes of action exist in the case of an accident which causes injury to a person and kills their spouse, for example, since the tort gives rise to an action for personal injury caused to the former and damages for dependants[48] under the Fatal Accidents Act 1976 in respect of the death.[49] Although the foregoing remains the law in England and Wales, the practice has been criticised. While not a true case of *res judicata*, it is thought contrary to public policy and an abuse of process, subject to special circumstances, 'that matters which could have been litigated in earlier proceedings should thereafter be allowed to proceed.'[50] It was thus said in *Talbot v Berkshire County Council* that had *Henderson v Henderson*[51] been cited in *Brunsden v Humphrey* the rule in *Henderson*, that a party is estopped in subsequent litigation from raising a claim which they ought properly to have been raised in a previous action, would have prevented the subsequent recovery.[52] That the days of *Brunsden* and similar authorities are 'numbered'[53] has been noted. In *Talbot* itself, three examples were given of special circumstances in which the above rule can be set aside: ignorance of the existence of a claim, an agreement between the parties to hold a claim in abeyance and a representation relied upon by the claimant which resulted in the claim being deferred. For limitation purposes, time runs from the moment each cause of action is complete.

A single act not actionable per se may also cause damage on two or more 25
separate occasions in respect of the same protected interest. At Court of Appeal level Brett MR in *Darley Main Colliery Co v Mitchell*, a case on subsidence in consequence of the defendant's excavation work on land adjoining the claimant's, observed: 'It may be argued that the *causa causans* is not the same. The *causa causans* of the first is the excavation [ie a non-continuing act causing damage]; the *causa causans* of the second is, as a matter of fact, the excavation unremedied, or the combination of the excavation and of its remaining unremedied [ie causing new damage].'[54] On appeal, Lord Fitzgerald, whose decision supplies us with the relevant facts, ruled in the same vein that: 'There was a complete cause of action in 1868, in respect of which compensation was given, but there was a liability to further disturbance. The defendants permitted the state of things to continue without taking any steps to prevent the

---

48 As defined in sec 1(3) Fatal Accidents Act 1976.

49 *Marginson v Blackburn BC* [1939] 2 KB 426.

50 *Talbot v Berkshire County Council* [1994] QB 290, 301 per Mann LJ.

51 *Henderson v Henderson* (1843) 3 Hare 100.

52 *Talbot v Berkshire County Council* [1994] QB 290, 296 per Stuart-Smith LJ and at 301 per Mann LJ.

53 McGregor on Damages (19th ed, 2014), para 11-005.

54 *Mitchell v Darley Main Colliery Co* (1884) 14 QBD 125, 134.

occurrence of any future injury. A fresh subsidence took place, causing a new and further disturbance of the plaintiff's enjoyment, which gave him *a new and distinct cause of action*.'[55] Such a rule takes the pressure off claimants from having to litigate at the point of the initial damage for speculative future damage lest they be barred by the time that damage manifests. Admittedly, the reasoning adopted by some of the authorities on this subject is difficult to follow, especially where analogies are drawn with continuing wrongs.[56]

26 **Case 1** – *Physician D treats patient P negligently and performs three mistakes on the day of the treatment: A, B and C. Mistake A causes harm X after a year. Mistake B causes harm Y after two years. Mistakes A and C together cause harm Z after three years.*

In applying the law to a fact scenario in which D, a physician, negligently treats P, a patient, causing damage, one must first note that an action can be brought in tort (for negligence causing personal injuries) or in contract, if one existed. Personal injuries are defined under sec 38(1) of the Limitation Act 1980 as including 'any disease and any impairment of a person's physical or mental condition'. The provision adds that '"injury" and cognate expressions shall be construed accordingly'. P's action against D's mistakes A, B and C would fall within the language of 'personal injury' and the relevant limitations rule will be that of sec 11 of the Limitation Act 1980 on the special time limit for actions in respect of personal injuries. This is also the case notwithstanding the existence of an underlying contract, since sec 11 applies in respect of 'damages for negligence, nuisance or breach of duty (*whether* the duty exists *by virtue of a contract* or of provision made by or under a statute or independently of any contract or any such provision) where the damages claimed by the plaintiff for the negligence, nuisance or breach of duty consist of or include damages in respect of personal injuries to the plaintiff or any other person.'[57] Thus P cannot rely on the time limit for actions founded on simple contract under sec 5 of the Limitation Act 1980 which is six years from the date on which the cause of action accrued (ie when the breach took place; in this case, on the date of treatment). Dealing exclusively with the cause of action limb for now, by virtue of secs 11(3) and (4)(a) of the Limitation Act 1980 an action cannot be brought after the expiration of the period of three years from the date on which the cause of action accrued. It has already been seen above that in the case of negligence the date P suffered damage is the date of accrual.

[55] *Darley Main Colliery Co v Mitchell* (1886) 11 App Cas 127, 151. Emphasis added.

[56] As was the case in *Smith, Stone and Knight Limited v Birmingham* [1939] 4 All ER 116, for example. See *T Prime and G Scanlan*, The Law of Limitation (2nd ed, 2005), 15.

[57] Limitation Act 1980, sec 11(1). Emphasis added. See also sec 11(2).

As one is told that injury A *caused* harm X a year after the treatment, it is at that point that the cause of action accrues. Time does not start afresh in respect of harms Y (caused by mistake B) and Z (caused by mistakes A and C combined) since they relate to a single act, the negligent treatment. The position under English law is that if 'A assaults B today and again tomorrow, two actions lie. Should A, however, in one and the same fight break B's nose and knock out some of his teeth, then B has only one cause of action.'[58] Given that harm Y arose two years after the treatment (ie a year after cause of action accrued) and harm Z arose three years after the treatment (ie two years after cause of action accrued), however, P will not be time-barred in respect of them.

**Case 2** – *D, a ski instructor, negligently fails to make sure that all skiers in her 'off-piste' group wear helmets. P, a skier in the group, hits a tree. P immediately suffers head injury X, and years later another head injury Y that developed from the same accident.* 27

The facts in the skiing hypothetical scenario differ to the extent that P suffers an immediate head injury, X, and *years* later head injury Y developed from the same accident. As regards injury X, there is concurrency of both the date of the tort and the date on which the cause of action accrued. The position as regards injury Y is that time commences with injury X, the corollary being that an action will be statute-barred if not pursued within three years of the cause of action accruing, ie the accident. It is of course open to P to argue his claim along the lines of the claimant in *Darley Main Colliery Co*; that is, that a single act, the negligent failure of the instructor to warn P to wear a helmet, led to injury X and injury X combined with injury Y gave rise to a new cause of action and a fresh limitation period commencing on the date of harm Y. However, this will certainly not succeed. As Lord Holt CJ explained in *Fetter v Beale* (noted *supra* 21): 'Every new dropping is a *new nuisance*; but *here is not a new battery*. And in trespass, the grievousness or consequence of the battery is not the ground of the action, but the measure of the damages; which the jury must be supposed to have considered at the trial.'[59] Should P indeed be barred in respect of harm Y, he can always rely on sec 33 of the Limitation Act 1980 (*infra* 80). It is open to the court under sec 33 if it appears equitable to do so to allow an action to proceed after the expiry of the period in sec 11. In exercising this discretion, a court will take several factors

---

58 *J Murphy and C Witting*, Street on Torts (14th ed, 2015), 687.

59 *Fetter v Beale* (1706) Holt KB 12, 12.

into consideration including on the one hand the length of, and the reasons for, the delay on the part of the claimant (sec 33(3)(a)) and the extent to which he acted promptly and reasonably once he knew whether or not the act or omission of the defendant, to which the injury was attributable, might be capable at that time of giving rise to an action for damages (sec 33(3)(e)) and on the other the degree to which such a decision would prejudice the defendant (sec 33(1)(b)).

28 Returning to the exceptions to the single action rule enumerated *supra* 23, a fresh cause of action accrues every day in the case of a single act or omission that continuously invades the claimant's interest(s) by going on *de die in diem* or from day to day. Responding to the question 'What is a continuing cause of action?', Lord Lindley in *Hole v Chard Union*[60] replied that: 'Speaking accurately, there is no such thing; but what is called a continuing cause of action is a cause of action which arises from the repetition of acts or omissions of the same kind as that for which the action was brought.' The rule is that 'there is a fresh cause of action arising every day, and if the breach and resulting damage have continued for more than the period of limitation, the Limitation Act, if relied upon by the defendant, will bar the plaintiff's action for the damage occurring before the critical date but not for the damage occurring after it.'[61] Whether 'separate acts are so knit up together, so close in time and quality' as to be described as continuing wrongs is said to be a 'question of degree'.[62] What is clear, however, is that a continuing cause of action is not 'constituted by repeated breaches of recurring obligations nor by intermittent breaches of a continuing obligation.' Rather, there must 'be a quality of continuance in both the breach and the obligation'.[63] In *National Coal Board v Galley*, it was observed that: 'The general proposition that persistence in tortious conduct of particular kinds such as trespass or nuisance constitutes a continuing cause of action must be regarded as established'.[64] *Konskier v B Goodman Ltd*[65] is an example of a continuing trespass committed where a builder failed to remove rubbish that had been dumped on the claimant's property; whereas *Shadwell v Hutchinson*, a case on the obstruction of ancient lights, illustrates continuing nuisance.[66] Note, however, that trespass and nuisance need not be continuous and, conversely, continuity is by no means limited to such torts.

60 *Hole v Chard Union* [1894] 1 Ch 293, 295.
61 *Cartledge v E Jopling & Sons Ltd* (1962) 1 QB 189, 207 per Pearson LJ (as he was then).
62 *National Coal Board v Galley* [1958] 1 WLR 16, 26 per Pearce LJ.
63 *National Coal Board v Galley* [1958] 1 WLR 16, 27 per Pearce LJ.
64 Ibid.
65 *Konskier v B Goodman Ltd* [1928] 1 KB 421. See also *Holmes v Wilson* (1839) 10 A & E 503.
66 *Shadwell v Hutchinson* (1831) 2 B & Ad 97.

In *Coventry v Apsley*,[67] for example, it was held that a continuing cause of action arose out of the claimant's false imprisonment and that the defendant's benefit of the statute of limitations was ousted in respect of that part of the imprisonment that was within the limitation period. In *Clarkson v Modern Foundries Ltd*,[68] a case on pneumoconiosis, it was held that the wrong constituted continuing negligence between the period of 1940–1951 when the claimant was exposed to the offending dust while employed by the defendant.[69] A fresh action accrues anew until the tort ceases, or in the case of an omission until the defendant is no longer able to remedy his wrong.[70] As inferred earlier, when the limitation period for the final cause of action expires, only damage occurring within the applicable period is recoverable.[71]

**Case 3** – *Assuming that in Case 1 above the three treatment mistakes (A, B, C) were performed in three consecutive weeks and not on the same day – would the three mistakes be considered 'a continuous tort' rather than three individual torts (A, B, C)? And if so, what would be the accrual date of this continuous tort (harm X, harm Z or another date?).* 29

Assuming in the example given *supra* 26 that the three treatment mistakes A, B and C were performed in three consecutive weeks and not on the same day, mistakes B and C would not amount to a continuance of mistake A; they are repeated breaches of recurring obligations. In the absence of a continuing tort, a new cause of action accrues once harms X, Y and Z occur. This should leave P with ample time to lodge his claims.

**Case 4** – *D, an employer, negligently exposes P, an employee, to unreasonable noise at the workplace for three years. P's hearing is thereby weakened on a daily basis, gradually restricting P's ability to communicate and enjoy music.* 30

If D, an employer, negligently exposes P, an employee, to unreasonable levels of noise at a workplace for a period of three years and P's hearing progressively deteriorates over time, D may be found liable for failing to implement appropriate safe work practices to prevent the damage in question from arising. This is because, where risks are an inherent and inescapable feature of an industry, employers must take precautions known to be available to prevent them from materialising into harm. They must also take initiative and keep up to date with improvements in knowledge and technology in their respective fields. However, the courts are slow to blame employers 'for not

67 *Coventry v Apsley* (1691) 2 Salk 420. See also *Hardy v Ryle* (1829) 9 B & C 603.
68 *Clarkson v Modern Foundries Ltd* [1957] 1 WLR 1210.
69 See McGregor on Damages (19th ed, 2014), para 11-022 for more details.
70 *Midland Bank v Hett, Stubbs & Kemp* [1978] Ch 384.
71 *Cartwright v GKN Sankey Ltd* [1972] 2 Lloyd's Rep 242.

ploughing a lone furrow'[72] by adopting standards which are disproportionate to all likelihood of risk.[73] The question is what a prudent employer would have done in light of what he knew or ought to have known at the time of the incident. In *Thompson v Smiths Shiprepairers (North Shields) Ltd*,[74] 1963 – the year in which the Ministry of Labour published its Noise and the Worker practice guide – was considered to be the relevant date, in noise-induced hearing loss claims, from which employers should have been aware of the risks posed by their industry. Since employers in the industry ought to have provided their workers with ear protectors only from that year onwards, damage sustained before then was not actionable. The earliest dates employers can be held liable for other work-induced diseases (including dermatitis, work-related upper limb disorders and vibration white finger) have already been settled and, although these may be adjusted, eg to take the size of the employer into consideration,[75] they are likely to be admitted. In *Thompson*, the cause of action was expressly described as continuing and indeed personal injury cases involving continuing torts are most likely to be employers' liability cases concerning failure to provide safe systems in the workplace.[76] Returning to the hypothetical fact scenario, P's action would fall to be described in the same manner as that in *Thompson* and a fresh cause of action will accrue every day for as long as the breach continues, on the proviso that D was under a duty to prevent noise-induced hearing loss during the period of exposure or at least parts thereof.

31 **Case 5** – *Is a continuous failure of producer D to recall a defective product that causes harm to consumer P regarded as a continuous tort?*

Where D, a producer fails to recall a defective product that causes harm to consumer P – eg a defective pacemaker that causes damage to P's heart over a period it ought to have been recalled – one must turn to the product liability rules in force. The Consumer Protection Act 1987 does not itself provide for a producer's liability for damage caused by its failure to recall a dangerous product, but in appropriate circumstances a duty to recall and a corresponding liability for breach of that duty can arise at common law. In practice, the content of that duty is likely to be shaped by the General Product Safety Regulations 2005, reg 15 of which deals specifically with recall notices.[77] Although there has been no case on the point, such a failure does seem to be the kind of

---

72 *Thompson v Smiths Shiprepairers (North Shields) Ltd* [1984] QB 405, 415–416 per Mustill J.

73 *M Lunney, D Nolan and K Oliphant*, Tort Law: Text and Materials (6th ed, 2017), 201 f.

74 *Thompson v Smiths Shiprepairers (North Shields) Ltd* [1984] QB 405. See also *Crookall v Vickers*-Armstrong Ltd [1955] 1 WLR 659.

75 *Kellett v British Rail* (unreported, QBD, 3 May 1984).

76 See *Law Commission*, Limitation of Actions Consultation (1998) CP 151, para 3.28.

77 See *K Oliphant and V Wilcox*, Product Liability in England and Wales, in: P Machnikowski (ed), European Product Liability: An Analysis of the State of the Art in the Era of New Technologies (2016), no 79 ff.

mischief that gives rise to a continuing wrong. Criminal liability and other consequences may also ensue for the contravention of various provisions under the Regulations. However, no cause of action can be brought under the common law of negligence in the absence of damage (*supra* 20). Even where damage does arise, no continuing tort exists unless the damage in question is continuing. Where, for example, P is injured by a defective gadget and suffers minor injuries from which he recovers and five years later is injured by the same gadget, that ought to have been but is yet to be recalled, he will be barred from bringing an action outside the three-year limit in respect of the first tort (under sec 11 Limitation Act 1980).

Where a waste management company throws toxic substances in bins into holes in the ground, the contents of which seep into the soil and leak into ground water causing damage on a daily basis, such facts are on all fours with those in the continuing nuisance case of *Hole v Chard Union* where the defendant was found liable for polluting a stream running through the claimant's land with sewage.[78] P's action would, therefore, be in respect of a continuing nuisance and a fresh cause of action arises every day until D abates the nuisance two years later when the bins are removed. 32

*2) Defamation*

Generally, multiple causes of action may be pursued against a defendant that engages in a series of separate wrongful acts. The approach taken under the law of defamation, however, is fact-dependant: English law continues to draw a distinction between statements published in writing or other permanent form (libel) and statements not published in writing or other permanent form (slander). Traditionally, for libels and slanders actionable per se,[79] the cause of action was complete at the time of publication. For slander of a kind where proof of special damage is an ingredient, the cause of action is complete when the special damage is suffered. These principles are not impacted by the introduction of a new serious harm test in all defamation actions under sec 1 of the Defamation Act 2013. The new test goes only to the requirement for the statement to be defamatory, and it is enough that the publication 33

78 *Hole v Chard Union* [1884] 1 Ch 293.

79 Historically words that imputed: (a) unchastity or adultery to any woman (under sec 1 Slander of Women Act 1891); (b) that a person had a contagious or infectious disease; (c) a crime punishable with imprisonment; (c) or if they were calculated to disparage the plaintiff in any office, profession, calling, trade or business held or carried on by him at the time of the publication (under sec 2 Defamation Act 1952) were actionable per se. Section 14 Defamation Act 2013, which entered into force on 1 January 2014, repeals the Slander of Women Act 1891 and also requires special damage in the case of (b) above so that only two categories of slander per se remain.

is *likely to* cause serious harm to the claimant's reputation, even if it has not already caused such harm.

34 Under the common law, a new cause of action accrued on each publication of defamatory material, including every *republication* (the 'multiple publication rule'). Section 8 of the Defamation Act 2013, however, introduces a single publication rule where a person publishes a statement to the public and subsequently publishes (whether or not to the public) that statement or a statement which is substantially the same. This responds to problems highlighted in *Loutchansky v Times Newspapers Ltd (No 2)*[80] where the Court of Appeal reaffirmed the orthodox rule in concluding that every time material archived on the internet was accessed it was deemed to give rise to a separate cause of action, subject to its own limitation period. In a Consultation on the Draft Defamation Bill,[81] the Ministry of Justice explained that this multiple publication rule was wholly unsuitable for the modern internet age, thus leading to the proposal which in turn led to the enactment of the single publication rule. The cause of action will thus be treated as having accrued on the date of the first publication, notwithstanding the subsequent republication, unless the manner of that republication is materially different from the manner of the first publication (sec 8(3) and (4) Defamation Act 2013).

35 **Case 6** – *Every week D publishes a defaming article on P, each time in another newspaper. Is this a continuous tort? Would it matter if D publishes the same defamation every week in the same newspaper owned by him or defames P differently in different newspapers each time in the same jurisdiction?*

Where D publishes a defamatory article about P every week, whether in the same or a different newspaper, this would not constitute a continuing tort. The starting point is that the single publication rule applies so that time begins to run for the purpose of sec 4A of the Limitation Act 1980 from the date of the first publication unless it can be shown that the subsequent publications were materially different from the first. Section 8(5) of the Defamation Act 2013 provides a non-exhaustive list of considerations a court may have regard to in determining this question, including the level of prominence that a statement is given and the extent of the subsequent publication.

### *3) When does Harm Occur?*

36 Where damage is the gist of the claimant's action, for example in the case of negligence, the presence of a risk of damage, even where this is established

---

80 *Loutchansky v Times Newspapers Ltd (No 2)* [2001] EWCA Civ 1805, noted by *K Oliphant*, England and Wales, in: H Koziol and BC Steininger (eds), European Tort Law 2001 (2002), 131, nos 76 ff.

81 Consultation Paper CP 3/11, March 2011, paras 70 ff.

and could give rise to significant injury, does not constitute the requisite damage so that no cause of action can be made out. This was made clear in the conjoined appeals in *Rothwell v Chemical & Insulating Co Ltd, Re Pleural Plaques Litigation*,[82] where claimants who were exposed to asbestos while working for their respective employers developed pleural plaques which did not in themselves cause other asbestos-related disease, but indicated the presence of asbestos fibres in the lungs. The House of Lords ruled that proof of damage is an essential element in a claim in negligence and symptomless plaques were not compensable damage. Moreover, while a diagnosis of pleural plaques may cause attendant anxiety or even clinical depression, in the absence of sufficiently serious injury to found a claim there can be no recovery for such. Their Lordships also dismissed the claimant's argument that the presence of pleural plaques, the risk of future asbestos-related disease and anxiety about the onset in the future of a life-threatening disease can constitute damage so as to complete the cause of action in tort, holding that: 'The aggregation theory put forward in these appeals fails [...] not because the three elements, plaques, risk and anxiety, are in aggregation too trivial, but because none can sustain a tort action. Nought plus nought plus nought equals nought.'[83] The ruling can be contrasted with that of *Cartledge v E Jopling & Sons Ltd*[84] where the plaintiffs had undoubtedly suffered actionable injury (pneumoconiosis) as the result of toxic exposure in the workplace, but its onset was only gradual and the question was *when* the physical effects to which the plaintiffs were subjected constituted such injury. Different formulations of the relevant requirement are to be found in the opinions delivered in the House of Lords – for example, that there should be 'personal injury beyond what can be regarded as negligible'[85] or 'real damage as distinct from purely minimal damage'.[86] On the facts, the House of Lords found that the onset of pneumoconiosis consequent upon the inhalation of silica participles amounted to actionable damage, completing the plaintiffs' causes of action and triggering the relevant limitation period. It was immaterial that the plaintiffs were unaware they had the condition – which, in its early stages, could not even be detected on X-ray examination – and experienced no symptoms.[87] It seems that the factors distinguishing such injury from the pleural plaques in the previous case included its negative effects on lung capacity (which would be apparent in

82 *Rothwell v Chemical & Insulating Co Ltd, Re Pleural Plaques Litigation* [2008] 1 AC 281. See also *K Oliphant*, England and Wales, in: H Koziol and BC Steininger (eds), European Tort Law 2007 (2008), 242 ff, nos 5 ff.

83 Para 73 per Lord Scott.

84 *Cartledge v E Jopling & Sons Ltd* [1963] AC 758. See *K Oliphant*, England and Wales, in: H Koziol and BC Steininger (eds), European Tort Law 2007 (2008), 242, no 12.

85 *Cartledge v E Jopling & Sons Ltd* [1963] AC 758, 772, per Lord Reid

86 *Cartledge v E Jopling & Sons Ltd* [1963] AC 758, 774, per Lord Evershed.

87 The law of limitation has now been amended (see sec 11 Limitation Act 1980).

situations of unusual exertion), susceptibility to other conditions, and life expectancy, and its potential to advance without further exposure.[88]

37 In an action for damages for negligence other than for personal injuries, eg for a defect caused by negligent advice, design, etc (ie a risk of damage), proof of a damage-causing breach is no less essential. In *Pirelli General Cable Works Ltd v Oscar Faber & Partners*,[89] a case of a defective chimney, the House of Lords ruled that the cause of action accrued when the physical damage to the building first occurred, Lord Fraser explaining that 'damage will commonly consist of cracks coming into existence even though they may be undiscovered or undiscoverable'.[90] On the facts, the claimant's right of action was time-barred. The real-damage rule does, however, admit an exception. In *Pirelli* itself Lord Fraser went on to express the view that:[91]

> There may perhaps be cases where the defect is so gross that the building *is doomed from the start*, and where the owner's cause of action will *accrue as soon as it is built*, but it seems unlikely that such a defect would not be discovered within the limitation period. Such cases, if they exist, would be exceptional.

38 A statutory period that starts on the completion of a thing may be unjust to a claimant who, at the time of completion, was unaware of the existence of his cause of action and only becomes cognisant of the fact after the expiration of the period. The rigour of that rule is somewhat ameliorated by the fact that it facilitates a claimant's recovery of pure economic loss at an early stage.

39 Although subsequent courts have questioned Lord Fraser's ruling,[92] the exception to the requirement of damage has been applied. In *Tozer Kemsley and Millbourn (Holdings) Ltd v J Jarvis & Sons Ltd*,[93] a case in respect of an air-conditioning plant that was defective as a result of negligent design and installation, for example, Sir William Stabb QC ruled that 'a building in that defective state is a damaged building. It is a damaged article in the sense that it is not a sound one [...] a building is a manufactured thing, and if it is unsuitable or defective when it is handed over it seems to me that the cause of action arises when the person acquires it in its defective state.' The authorities

---

88 See [8], per Lord Hoffmann.

89 *Pirelli General Cable Works Ltd v Oscar Faber & Partners* [1983] 2 AC 1.

90 Ibid, 16.

91 Ibid. Emphasis added.

92 Eg in *Ketteman v Hansel Properties Ltd* [1987] 2 WLR 312, Lord Keith and Lord Brandon branded the passage in *Pirelli obiter dicta.*

93 *Tozer Kemsley and Millbourn (Holdings) Ltd v J Jarvis & Sons Ltd* (1984) 1 Const LJ 79. See also *Chelmsford District Council v TJ Evers* (1983) 25 BLR 99 and *Kaliszewska v John Clague & Partners* [1984] Construction Law Report 62 (on the facts in *Kaliszewska* the start of the period postponed on grounds of estoppel).

on the threshold for establishing whether a structure is so grossly and obviously defective that it is doomed from the start although no physical damage has yet occurred are limited: in *Jones v Stroud District Council* Neill LJ, with whom the other judges concurred, emphasised that 'Lord Fraser intended to limit his exception of "a building which is so defective as to be doomed from the start" to extreme cases where the defects were likely to be disclosed almost immediately.' Lord Fraser's words were thus not intended to apply to a case 'where the defect, though serious, might not have led to any danger to health or safety for many years'. Furthermore, his Lordship added that the exception was limited to 'gross defects and to the rare case'.[94] The house in *Jones* had been completed in 1964, purchased in 1975 and in late 1976 a corner of one of the bedrooms began to subside, cracks appeared in the roof and a wall and the house became noticeably damp. A report completed in 1977 concluded that in part this was due to a drought and in part inadequate foundations. Subsequent remedial work was carried out and completed in 1978. The Court of Appeal held that the cause of action did not arise until 1976 when the condition of the property first gave rise to a present and imminent danger to the health of its occupiers. *London Congregational Union Incorporated v Harriss and Harriss (a firm)*[95] is another instructive case. The building in that case was designed, and its construction supervised, by a firm of architects engaged in 1969. It was completed in 1970 but flooded following heavy rainfall in 1971. Further damage occurred in subsequent years and an action was eventually brought against the defendant architects in 1977, *inter alia*, for damages for negligence in the design of the surface of the water drains. Since the drains had functioned satisfactorily for some 20 months and had not produced immediate damaging effects, it followed that the defect in the drains was latent and distinct from the subsequent physical damage. Furthermore, the design could not be said to have caused the claimant's economic loss (ie the cost of putting the drains in order) at the date of completion, because the ordinary relationship of client and architect which existed between the parties was not such that liability for pure economic loss would arise on proof of negligent design without proof of damage to the property.

**Case 7** – *Builder D lays down defective foundations for a building thereby creating the risk of future collapse if heavy rain falls. As a result, the value to the owner of the building P decreases (harm A). One year later heavy rain indeed falls. Two years later the foundation subsides and requires fixing paid by P (harm B). Three years later cracks appear in the building fixed by P (harm C). Four years later the building collapses (harm D).* 40

94 *Jones v Stroud District Council* [1988] 1 All ER 5, 13.

95 *London Congregational Union Incorporated v Harriss and Harriss (a firm)* [1988] 1 All ER 15.

Where D lays down defective foundations for a building thereby creating the risk of future collapse if heavy rains fall, the question whether, by way of exception, the underlying risk will be deemed as harm for accrual purposes hinges on whether it constitutes an extremely high risk of imminent future physical damage. The exceptional nature of the rule must be emphasised and indeed one judge has clarified that it cannot be accepted that a case is: 'to be treated as within an exception to the general rule if it can be shown that "nothing practicable could be done" to save the building or that part of the building which is the subject of the action'.[96] It follows that where, as a result of D's conduct, P suffers losses A (fall in value of the building), B (subsidence five years after completion which was repaired), C (cracks eight years after completion which were also repaired) and D (collapse 12 years after completion), the exception to the general rule that the cause of action does not accrue until damage occurs would not apply given the lack of immediacy between defect and damage. Moreover, as seen *supra* 39, the pure economic loss argument (loss A), would not stand. Rather, the action accrues when the foundations subside (at the point of damage B). (The above analysis must, however, be seen in the context of the discoverability test inserted as secs 14A and 14B of the Limitation Act 1980 by the Latent Damage Act 1986 (*infra* 68).)

41 **Case 8** – *A negligent medical treatment by physician D more than triples the probability that patient P will contract a disease. P indeed contracts the disease after five years.*

Where a negligent medical treatment by D more than triples the probability that patient P will contract a disease and P indeed contracts the disease five years later, it is at that point that the cause of action accrues. (The doomed from the start exception is limited to non-personal injury cases.) Moreover, neither consequent anxiety of the risk of future disease, nor indeed any clinical depression arising out of fear, is actionable in the absence of a compensable injury (*supra* 36).

*4) Temporal Uncertainty*

42 **Case 9** – *Employer D negligently exposes employee P to toxic radiation at the workplace for ten years. It is known that during this period P's lungs were injured by the radiation, but because P is a heavy smoker, it is unknown when exactly.*

[96] Nor on the other hand should a case be treated as 'outside any exception on the ground only that the repair or correction of the defect is practicable.': *London Congregational Union Incorporated v Harris and Harris (a firm)* [1988] 1 All ER 15, 27 per Lawton LJ.

Where D, an employer, negligently exposes P, an employee, to toxic radiation at a workplace for ten years and it is known that during this period P's lungs are damaged by the radiation but because P is a heavy smoker it is not known when exactly the damage occurred, the question is one of evidence. A cause of action accrues when there exists 'every fact which it *would be necessary* for the plaintiff to prove, if traversed, in order to support his right to the judgement of the Court';[97] 'once those facts exist, it is irrelevant that the plaintiff will have great difficulty in proving them. He cannot claim that time does not run against him until he has all the evidence he requires.'[98] The cause of action thus accrues when P suffers more than minimal damage, notwithstanding he is not aware of it (as was the case in *Cartledge v E Jopling & Sons, supra* 36). This moment is to be estimated by medical experts. As regards P's habit of smoking and the difficulties that that causes in diagnosing the damage, D must take his victim as he finds him.[99] As long as the initial injury was foreseeable, D will be liable for all the harm caused by the toxic exposure.

**Case 10** – *A concert pianist is injured by a reckless cyclist during his summer holiday (1 July). His fingers are broken, and he can no longer play. His financial loss occurs only in August, at the time of the first planned concert.* 43

Where a pianist is injured by a reckless cyclist during the summer holidays (more specifically, in July) and his finger is broken, preventing him from playing, yet his financial loss only arises in August, at the time of his first planned concert, damage to his finger completes a tortious cause of action in negligence. It is at that moment – or the moment after which the damage could no longer be characterised as trivial – that the cause of action accrues. Assuming a hearing took place immediately after the incident, a claim for loss of prospective earnings (as well as pain and suffering and loss of amenity) – even despite uncertainties and imponderables – could be lodged (*supra* 21).[100]

## B. DATE OF KNOWLEDGE

The deficiencies of setting the accrual of the cause of action as a starting date for the purpose of limitations of actions were made apparent by the facts in *Cartledge v E Jopling & Sons* (*supra* 36). While the Limitation Act 1939 had 44

97 *Read v Brown* (1888) 22 QBD 128. Emphasis added.

98 *A McGee*, Limitation Periods (2014), para 5.074.

99 See further *M Lunney, D Nolan and K Oliphant*, Tort Law: Text and Materials (6th ed, 2017), 279.

100 For how this is calculated see McGregor on Damages (19th ed, 2014), paras 38-065 ff.

already provided for the postponement of the limitation period in the case of fraud and mistake until the latter were, or with 'reasonable diligence' could have been, discovered by the claimant, no such provision had been made for personal injuries so that on the facts, the claimants' cause of action accrued before the injury (pneumoconiosis caused by the inhalation of noxious dust at their place of employment) was discovered. Although their Lordships felt bound by the law as it then stood, they decried its harsh effect. The case eventually led to an alternative trigger in the limited field of personal injuries under the Limitation Act 1963 so that an action could still be brought later than three years from the date on which the cause of action accrued, provided it was brought no later than 12 months after the claimant had knowledge of the 'material facts relating to that cause of action'.[101] On the recommendation of the Law Commission, which saw merit in harmonising the law in England with that in Scotland, the 12-month period was extended to three years under the Law Reform (Miscellaneous Provisions) Act 1971 and a subsequent review prompted the introduction of a broader definition of 'date of knowledge' under the Limitation Act 1975.[102] The 1975 Act was subsequently consolidated into the Limitation Act 1980, which also provides an analogous starting point for claims under the Fatal Accidents Act 1976. It was not long, however, before Parliament was moved to respond – in the ad hoc fashion that is characteristic of this field of law – when the facts in *Pirelli* (*supra* 37) came to light. Again, the wisdom of time running before a claimant knows or could be expected to know they had suffered damage, this time in a non-personal injury context, was questioned. *Pirelli* prompted Parliament to adopt a comparable starting point for other negligence claims which run from the claimant's date of knowledge (alongside the one that ran from the accrual of the cause of action). This it did by amending the Limitation Act 1980 (through the Latent Damage Act 1986).[103] A corresponding provision was grafted onto the Limitation Act 1980 when the Consumer Protection Act 1987 entered into force.[104] Date of

---

101 Limitation Act 1963, sec 7(3), no longer in force, read: '[…] any reference to the material facts relating to a cause of action is a reference to any one or more of the following, that is to say -

(a) the fact that personal injuries resulted from the negligence, nuisance or breach of duty constituting that cause of action;
(b) the nature or extent of the personal injuries resulting from that negligence, nuisance or breach of duty;
(c) the fact that the personal injuries so resulting were attributable to that negligence, nuisance or breach of duty, or the extent to which any of those personal injuries were so attributable.'

102 By *Law Reform Committee*, Report on Limitation of Actions in Personal Injury Claims (1974, Cmnd 5630).

103 Sections 14A and 14B were inserted into the 1980 Act by the Latent Damage Act 1986.

104 Its sch 1 introduced a new sec 11A, sec 14(1A), sec 28(7), sec 32(4A) and 33(11A) to the 1980 Act, among other amendments.

knowledge (also termed the date of reasonable discovery or discoverability) is variously defined depending on the action in question. The above case studies will be looked at again in the context of the more favourable date of knowledge test.

**Case 1** (*supra* 26) – applying the sec 11(4)(b) Limitation Act 1980 limb to the case of the negligent physician, the patient would be subject to a three-year period which runs from the date of knowledge (if later than the date of accrual). The definition of date of knowledge for purposes of sec 11 is set out in sec 14(1) as the date on which the claimant had knowledge: 45

- that the injury in question was significant (sec 14(1)(a));
- that the injury was attributable in whole or in part to the act or omission which is alleged to constitute negligence, nuisance or breach of duty (sec 14(1)(b));
- the identity of the defendant (sec 14(1)(c)); and
- if it is alleged that the act or omission was that of a person other than the defendant, the identity of that person and the additional facts supporting the bringing of an action against the defendant (sec 14(1)(d)).

As has been observed, an often overlooked point is that in 'applying a discoverability approach, the claimant will still need to have an accrued cause of action' albeit the precise need to fix when the cause of action accrued will be diminished in importance.[105] Returning to the hypothetical case, the facts are similar to those in *Bristow v Grout*.[106] The claimant there sustained a leg injury and was facially scarred following a road accident. He brought an action for damages, for which he received compensation, and pursued a subsequent action when he developed significant hip problems which he alleged were caused by the accident. In line with the wording of sec 14(2) of the Limitation Act 1980, which expands on the notion of 'significant',[107] Jupp J held that the date of knowledge for the purposes of sec 11(4)(b) was that of the first of the physical injuries the claimant knew to be serious enough for him to justify instituting proceedings, and not of a separate injury that was discovered after the settlement of the initial claim, notwithstanding it arose from the same accident. This analogous application of the single action rule (*supra* 21 ff) was upheld on appeal. Since P had sec 14(2) knowledge at the time of harm X, 46

---

105 *A Burrows*, Some Recurring Issues in Relation to Limitation of Actions, in: A Dyson, J Goudkamp and F Wilmot-Smith (eds), Defences in Tort (2015), 320 ff. The paper also discusses central difficulties in applying the discoverability limb.

106 The Times, 3 November 1986.

107 Which reads: 'For the purposes of this section an injury is significant if the person whose date of knowledge is in question would reasonably have considered it sufficiently serious to justify his instituting proceedings for damages against a defendant who did not dispute liability and was able to satisfy a judgment.'

assuming the latter was significant (and that the all other facts are known), time begins to run against him in respect of all the injuries he sustained from that moment so that he will be prevented from relying on subsequent knowledge of further injuries arising from the same facts. This is the case whether or not P has recovered any damages in respect of the prior injury.[108] It is perhaps worth highlighting that scholars have opined that 'this point might be decided differently today'.[109] In any case, the courts may be willing to exercise their sec 33 discretion where a claimant is deprived of an action by the statutory bar (*infra* 79). On the facts, however, harm Y which arose two years after the treatment (ie one year after the date of knowledge) and harm Z which arose three years after the treatment (ie two years after discoverability) are within the limitation period.

47 **Case 2** (*supra* 27) – provided injury X amounted to a significant injury in a sec 14(2) of the Limitation Act 1980 sense (and assuming all the other sec 14(1) enumerations are satisfied), the answer given in the skiing hypothetical scenario would not be different since P had the requisite knowledge when injury X occurred. Harm Y is not a new cause of action. As such P will be defeated by the statute were he to bring a further action outside the period in respect of injury X in reliance on the discovery of a more serious injury caused by the same incident that gave rise to injury X.

48 **Case 3** (*supra* 29) – where three treatment mistakes A, B and C were performed in three consecutive weeks, the point at which P has knowledge that harm X is significant (and of attribution) is the point at which the period of limitation starts running in respect of mistake A but not in respect of harms Y or Z whose periods will be triggered when P discovered their respective significance.

49 **Case 6** (*supra* 35) – in the case of defamation, time runs from the date of publication or subsequent publication, if any and if materially different from the initial publication (sec 8 of the Defamation Act 2013). Knowledge that injury to reputation was significant is irrelevant for limitation purposes.

50 **Case 4** (*supra* 30) – time runs for an employee who was negligently exposed to unreasonable levels of noise at his workplace from when P had knowledge of the facts in sec 14(1) of the Limitation Act 1980, including that the injury was significant. The House of Lords in *A v Hoare*[110] ruled that 'significance' is an *entirely impersonal* standard, thus marking a decisive shift away from earlier

108 *McCafferty v Commissioner for Metropolitan Police* [1977] 1 WLR 1073; *Miller v London Electrical Manufacturing Co Ltd* [1976] 2 Lloyd's Rep 284.

109 *A McGee*, Limitation Periods (2014), para 8.034.

110 *A v Hoare* [2008] AC 844.

authorities that had adopted a partly objective, partly subjective approach.[111] Since the standard is not to be varied with the person to whom it is being applied, P's actual personal attributes such as his intelligence, aspirations and the like are to be disregarded as is the subjectively perceived effect of P's gradual loss of hearing to his private life or career.[112] For the purpose of deciding when P had knowledge of the various matters in sec 14(1), including the fact that the noise-induced hearing loss was sufficiently serious to justify his instituting proceedings for damages against his employer, D, consideration will be had not only to P's actual knowledge but also his imputed or constructive knowledge (sec 14(3)). P will probably seek legal advice at some point. Subsection (1) of sec 14 expressly states that 'knowledge that any acts or omissions did or did not, as a matter of law, involve negligence, nuisance or breach of duty is irrelevant.' In essence, it is factual, not legal, knowledge that counts. As McGee explains, reliance on expert advice is limited to questions of fact. The most important consequence of the provision, therefore, is that incorrect legal advice given by P's legal team would not aid him under the 1980 statue. Rather the remedy would be for damages in respect of such negligent legal advice[113] (see also *infra* 55).

**Case 5** (*supra* 31) – the option of commencing a limitation period from the date of discoverability is also available for actions in respect of defective products under sec 11A of the Limitation Act 1980, which tailors the definition of knowledge to the specific context (sec 11A(4)).[114] Since sec 11A applies exclusively to actions under the Consumer Protection Act 1987, and failure to recall would be actionable only under common law, sec 11 would apply to determine the time limit within which an action for such failure resulting in personal injury must be brought; if the action is exclusively for property damage, it would be squarely covered by sec 2 (time limit for actions founded on tort) or possibly sec 14A (special time limit for latent non-personal injury negligence actions (*infra* 52). Note that unlike the other sections mentioned in this paragraph, sec 2 does not incorporate a secondary limitation period (*infra* 58). 51

111 See, for example, *McCafferty v Metropolitan Police District Receiver* [1977] 1 WLR 1073, 1081, per Geoffrey Lane LJ.

112 See *McCoubrey v Ministry of Defence* [2007] EWCA Civ 17.

113 *A McGee*, Limitation Periods (2014), para 8.042.

114 'Subject to subsection (5) below, an action to which this section applies in which the damages claimed by the plaintiff consist of or include damages in respect of personal injuries to the plaintiff or any other person or loss of or damage to any property, shall not be brought after the expiration of the period of three years from whichever is the later of—

(a) the date on which the cause of action accrued; and
(b) the date of knowledge of the injured person or, in the case of loss of or damage to property, the date of knowledge of the plaintiff or (if earlier) of any person in whom his cause of action was previously vested.'

52 An action against the waste management company (*supra* 32), assuming it was a case of negligence and not intent (as to which see *infra* 68), would be dealt with under sec 14A of the Limitation Act 1980. In the case of latent damage not involving personal injuries, sec 14A(6) provides that knowledge means knowledge both of the material facts (as defined in sec 14A(7); essentially the same as sec 14(2))[115] about the damage in respect of which damages are claimed and of certain other facts relevant to the action (broadly similar to sec 14(1)(b)–(c)).[116] Indeed, the courts have 'been prepared to cite cases on the date of knowledge under s. 14 of the 1980 Act as aids to interpreting the meaning of s. 14A,'[117] albeit with some exceptions. The issue of attributability is well illustrated by the facts in *Wilson v Le Fevre Wood & Royle*, a case on damp caused by the negligent construction of a property.[118] The defendant in that case repeatedly represented that the property was not defective and only needed time to dry out thus delaying the claimant from seeking advice. The latter was considered to have had the knowledge required by sec 14A(5) for bringing an action for damages when he finally dismissed the defendant's assertions about condensation and sought advice. Since he failed to take action within three years from the relevant date, however, his action was barred. Section 14A(8)(c), the exact counterpart of sec 14(1)(d), applies where, as is likely to be the case here, the offending act or omission is attributable to an employee. In that case, P is fixed with knowledge when the identity of the employer (ie of the waste management company in this case) and any additional facts supporting the bringing of an action against the defendant company are known. As with sec 14(1), it is factual, not legal, knowledge that triggers the starting date (sec 14A(9)). Knowledge includes constructive knowledge (sec 14A(10)).

53 **Case 7** (*supra* 40) – where D lays down defective foundations, the clock starts to tick against P when he had knowledge of the facts in sec 14A(5)–(10) of the Limitation Act 1980, including that the injury was sufficiently serious to justify his instituting proceedings for damages against D. This is likely to be the date the foundations subsided (at the point of damage B).

---

115 The material facts about the damage are such facts about the damage as would lead a reasonable person who had suffered such damage to consider it sufficiently serious to justify his instituting proceedings for damages against a defendant who did not dispute liability and was able to satisfy a judgment.

116 The other facts referred to in subsection (6)(b) above are: (a) that the damage was attributable in whole or in part to the act or omission which is alleged to constitute negligence; and (b) the identity of the defendant; and (c) if it is alleged that the act or omission was that of a person other than the defendant, the identity of that person and the additional facts supporting the bringing of an action against the defendant.

117 *A McGee*, Limitation Periods (2014), para 6.014.

118 *Wilson v Le Fevre Wood & Royle* (1995) 66 Con LR 74.

**Case 8** (*supra* 41) – as regards the negligent medical treatment administered to patient P that more than tripled the probability that P would contract a disease and P indeed contracts the disease five years later, the date of knowledge under sec 11 of the Limitation Act 1980 is the date P had knowledge of the various matters listed in sec 14(1), including the fact that the injury was significant: that is, if P would reasonably have considered the injury sufficiently serious to justify proceedings (*supra* 50 and *infra* 55). 54

**Case 9** (*supra* 42) – where D, an employer, negligently exposes P, an employee, to toxic radiation at a workplace for ten years and it is known that during this period P's lungs are damaged by the radiation but because P is a heavy smoker it is not known when exactly the damage occurred, the date of knowledge under sec 11 of the Limitation Act 1980 is the date P first had knowledge that the toxic radiation has caused him significant injury (sec 14(1)(a)) and that the injury was attributable in whole or in part to the act or omission which is alleged to constitute negligence, nuisance, or breach of duty (sec 14(1)(b)). As seen *supra* 50, no account is to be taken of P's personal characteristics, either pre-existing (ie including that P is a heavy smoker) or consequent upon the injury which he has suffered.[119] As regards what the claimant needs to know, the Supreme Court in *AB v Ministry of Defence* clarified that a 'real possibility of a causal link' is sufficient for 'attributability'.[120] As regards what requisite state of mind amounts to knowledge, the court ruled that a claimant is deemed to have acquired knowledge of the facts in sec 14 'when he first came reasonably to believe them'.[121] In referring to 'reasonable belief' as part of the description of the requisite knowledge, the focus is not so much on whether or how far the belief is evidence-based, but more on whether it is held with a sufficient degree of confidence to justify embarking on the preliminaries to making a claim including collecting evidence.[122] In other words, the minimum standard of knowledge needed for P to commence the limitation period under sec 11(4) is a 'reasonable belief' in the 'real possibility of a causal link' between exposure and injury. While the facts P is required to know may be ascertainable by him only with the help of experts, the date P consults an expert is not, on its own, likely to assist the court in determining whether by then he had the requisite knowledge. Section 14(3) deems P to have acquired such knowledge only at the point at which he might, with the help of advisers, reasonably have been expected to acquire it.[123] The difference 55

119 *A v Hoare* [2008] AC 84, at [33] per Lord Hoffmann.

120 *AB v Ministry of Defence* [2013] 1 AC 78, at [35] per Lord Walker. See *A Morris and K Oliphant*, England and Wales, in: K Oliphant and BC Steininger (eds), European Tort Law 2012 (2013), 174, no 17 ff.

121 *AB v Ministry of Defence* [2013] 1 AC 78, at [11] per Lord Wilson.

122 Ibid, at [83] per Lord Mance.

123 Ibid, at [13] per Lord Walker.

between secs 14(2) and 14(3) turns on what the claimant ought reasonably to have done. Unlike sec 14(3), the test in sec 14(2) (on significance) is external to the claimant and involves no inquiry into what P could reasonably have been expected to do.[124]

56 **Case 10** (*supra* 43) – the date the pianist had the requisite knowledge of his injury for the purposes of sec 14(1) of the Limitation Act 1980 and that it was serious enough to be significant for the purposes of sec 14(2) is the date the three-year period starts to run. On the facts, this is unlikely to be later than the date on which the cause of action accrued, ie the date of the accident.

## VI. PRESCRIPTION PERIODS

57 While a uniform limitation period across the board would promote certainty and to that extent suit the convenience of the legal profession and the general public, the adoption of such an approach without exceptions would produce greater injustice. Nonetheless, the current catalogue of prescription periods applicable to tort claims in England and Wales has been labelled as 'needlessly complex', and it has been said to be 'a shameful indictment of the operation of statutes within our legal system that Parliament has created such a mess.'[125] The Law Commission recommend that the uniform limitation period within the 'core regime' should be three years from the date of discoverability.[126] However, a draft bill to simplify the rules came to nought.

### A. TIME LIMIT FOR ACTIONS FOUNDED ON TORT – SEC 2

58 Traditionally a six-year limitation period applies to a majority of actions. This goes back to the Limitation Act 1623. Yet it is difficult to 'trace any information on the reason why the six-year period was thought appropriate.'[127] The general six-year period continues to apply to actions founded on tort (sec 2 Limitation Act 1980), including actions under sec 3 of the Protection from Harassment Act 1997 (ie to recover damages for 'anxiety caused by the

124 *A v Hoare* [2008] AC 84, at [39] per Lord Hoffmann.

125 *A Burrows*, Some Recurring Issues in Relation to Limitation of Actions, in: A Dyson, J Goudkamp and F Wilmot-Smith (eds), Defences in Tort (2015), 315 ff.

126 *Law Commission*, Limitation of Actions Consultation (1998), CP 151, paras 15, 13 ff. See further *K Oliphant*, Basic Questions of Tort Law from the Perspective of England and the Commonwealth, in H Koziol (ed), Basic Questions of Tort Law from a Comparative Perspective (2015), nos 156 ff.

127 *Law Commission*, Limitation of Actions Consultation (1998), CP 151, para 1.8.

harassment and any financial loss resulting from the harassment')[128] and breach of statutory duty, unless otherwise provided. As a corollary the enforcement of European Community rights before English courts is also an action founded on tort.[129]

## B. CONVERSION AND THEFT – SECS 3 AND 4

The time limit for conversion is the same as the general time limit for actions founded on tort, namely six years from the date of the conversion, since the action lies without proof of damage (sec 2(1)). Conversion is one of the few torts, however, in which the right is extinguished after the period prescribed for bringing the action expires (sec 3(2)). Successive conversions do not restart time which continues to run from the date of the original conversion (sec 3(1)). In the case of theft,[130] however, *no* time limit applies against a person from whom a chattel is stolen (sec 4(1)). This is also the case with successive thefts (sec 4(2) and (4)). Section 4(1) does not, however, apply to the claimant's advantage in the case of a purchase in good faith or any conversion following it, even if dishonest (sec 4(2)). Rather sec 3(1) applies. 59

## C. ACTIONS FOR DEFAMATION OR MALICIOUS FALSEHOOD – SEC 4A

The time limit for defamation and malicious falsehood is uniquely short. For slander actionable per se, the Limitation Act 1623 set a period of two years. However, the drive for uniformity led to all actions in defamation and malicious falsehood falling within the general period for actions in tort (and simple contract) of six years under the Limitation Act 1939. The period prescribed for defamation was reduced to three years by the Administration of Justice Act 1985 (which led to the insertion of a new sec 4A in the Limitation Act 1980[131]) but as a quid pro quo this was coupled with a discretionary 12-month extension (under new sec 32A Limitation Act 1980[132]), both changes being based on the recommendations of the Faulks Committee on Defamation.[133] Subsequent recommendations by the Neill Committee, which cited evidentiary problems associated with the deferral of defamation actions, 60

128 Limitation Act 1980, sec 11(1A).

129 *R v Secretary of State for Transport ex parte Factortame (No 6)* [2001] 1 WLR 942.

130 As defined in sec 4(5) Limitation Act 1980.

131 Administration of Justice Act 1985, sec 57(2).

132 Administration of Justice Act 1985, sec 57(4).

133 Report of the Committee on Defamation (1975, Cmnd 5909).

ultimately led to the introduction of the Defamation Act 1996 and to the reduction of the time limit to one year for actions brought in defamation and malicious falsehood.[134] The clock starts to tick from the date on which the cause of action accrues (sec 4A Limitation Act 1980).[135] Since an action in malicious falsehood will not be admitted absent special damage, unless an exemption applies in line with sec 3 of the Defamation Act 1952, the cause of action accrues when such damage arises.[136] (Accrual rules applicable in defamatory actions have been dealt with *supra* 33 ff.) Where a claimant issues proceedings after the time limit for actions for defamation or malicious falsehood has expired, they may still succeed in persuading the court to exercise its discretion to disapply the ordinary time limit, pursuant to sec 32A of the Limitation Act 1980.

## D. SPECIAL TIME LIMIT FOR CLAIMING CONTRIBUTION – SEC 10

61 Section 10 of the Limitation Act 1980 contains a special time limit for claiming contribution. Under sec 1 of the Civil Liability (Contribution) Act 1978, a person who is liable, D1, in respect of damage suffered by another person, P, may recover contribution from any other person liable in respect of the same damage (whether jointly with him or otherwise), D2. However, sec 10(1) limits the period within which a contribution can be sought by D1 to two years from the date on which a right to recover contribution, from D2, in respect of the damage accrues (s 10(2)), namely two years from the date of a judgment or award given in civil proceedings in respect of the damage in question (s 10(3)). Section 10(3) also states that no account shall be taken of any judgment or award given or made on appeal in so far as it varies the amount of damages awarded against the person in question (D1 for our purposes). That is, the clock does not start running from the date of the subsequent decision. Where D1 makes or agrees to make any payment to P in compensation for damage caused, in other words where D1 seeks to settle the dispute with P, the relevant date

[134] Supreme Court Procedure Committee, Report on Practice and Procedure in Defamation (1991).

[135] Inserted by sec 5(2) Defamation Act 1996.

[136] 'In an action for slander of title, slander of goods or other malicious falsehood, it shall not be necessary to allege or prove special damage – (a) if the words upon which the action is founded are calculated to cause pecuniary damage to the plaintiff and are published in writing or other permanent form; or (b) if the said words are calculated to cause pecuniary damage to the plaintiff in respect of any office, profession, calling, trade or business held or carried on by him at the time of the publication.'

shall be two years from the date on which the amount to be paid by D1 is agreed between D1 and P. This is regardless of whether or not D admits any liability in respect of the damage or when the payment is actually made (sec 10(4)).

## E. SPECIAL TIME LIMIT FOR ACTIONS IN RESPECT OF PERSONAL INJURIES – SEC 11

The general six-year period under the Limitation Act 1939 also applied in personal injury cases. However, this was reduced to three years (under Law Reform (Limitation of Actions, etc) Act 1954) after the Law Revision Committee reasoned that 'the desirability of a speedy trial is probably more obvious in cases of actions for personal injuries and actions for slander than in other actions.'[137] The facts in *Cartledge v E Jopling & Sons Ltd* led to the adoption of the discoverability test under the Limitation Act 1963 (*supra* 44) and Parliament would go on to legislate for judicial discretion to set aside the ordinary time for actions in respect of personal injuries and death (under the Limitation Act 1975; now sec 33 Limitation Act 1980).The result of these and other reforms is sec 11 of the Limitation Act 1980 which provides that a claim shall be brought within a period of three years from the date on which the cause of action accrued or the date of knowledge (if later) of the person injured (sec 11(4)). Where sec 11 applies, it disapplies all other provisions (sec 11(2)) (*supra* 3 and 26). 62

Before the decision of the House of Lords in *Stubbings v Webb*,[138] it was thought that the (extendable) three-year period under sec 11(4)(a) applied even to the intentional infliction of personal injury,[139] but the House of Lords there took the contrary view. The claimant, then aged 30, commenced proceedings against her adoptive father and stepbrother in August 1987, claiming damages for sexual and physical abuse and rape amounting to trespass to the person. She claimed that the relevant incidents occurred when she was between the ages of two and 17. She sought to rely upon the latent injury provisions of sec 11 of the 63

[137] *Law Revision Committee*, Fifth Interim Report (Statutes of Limitation) (1936) Cmd 5334, para 5. In fact, the Committee went on to advocate uniformity.

[138] *Stubbings v Webb* [1993] AC 498. Noted by *A McGee* (1993) 109 Law Quarterly Review (LQR) 356, *M Jones* (1994) 110 LQR 31, and *M Lunney* (1993–94) 4 King's College Law Journal (KCLJ) 79. See further *A Mullis*, Compounding the Abuse? The House of Lords, Childhood Sexual Abuse and Limitation Periods (1997) 5 Medical Law Review (Med L Rev) 22, *J Conaghan*, Tort Litigation in the Context of Intra-familial Abuse (1998) 61 Modern Law Review (MLR) 132. See also *K Oliphant*, England and Wales, in: M Martín-Casals (ed), Children in Tort Law: Children as Victims (2007), 66 ff.

[139] *Letang v Cooper* [1965] QB 232.

Limitation Act 1980 on the grounds that, although she knew she had been a victim of abuse, she did not know until September 1984 that certain psychological conditions from which she suffered were caused by the abuse. The House of Lords ruled that, as her claim was for trespass to the person, the six-year limitation period under sec 2 applied, and no extension was permitted by the legislation; the action was therefore statute-barred. The claimant subsequently brought proceedings before the European Court of Human Rights, but the Court found no violation of the Convention.[140] Attempts to circumvent the decision in *Stubbings* by 'dressing down' an intentional tort as one in negligence were criticised by the Court of Appeal in *KR v Bryn Alyn Community (Holdings) Ltd*.[141] In a welcomed move, *Stubbings* was later unanimously overruled by the House of Lords in *A v Hoare*.[142] In 1988, the claimant in *A v Hoare* was the victim of an attempted rape for which the defendant was convicted and sentenced to life imprisonment. In 2004, the defendant won £7 million in the British national lottery whilst on day release from gaol and the claimant shortly afterwards commenced civil proceedings for damages against him. The claim was struck out[143] before trial on the ground that it was time-barred in line with the decision of the House of Lords in *Stubbings*. The claimant appealed against the striking-out, unsuccessfully, before the Court of Appeal.[144] The House of Lords ruled, however, that the limitation period correctly applied to an intentional (eg sexual) assault is not the general limitation period of six years under sec 2 of the Limitation Act 1980, which cannot be extended, but the special limitation period provided in respect of personal injury which, while of only three years, commences on 'the date of knowledge' as defined in sec 14 of the Act where this is later than the general starting point. In Lord Carswell's words, 'breach of duty' under sec 11(1) 'must be construed broadly enough to include trespass to the person.'[145]

64 On the death of a person, sec 1 of the Law Reform (Miscellaneous Provisions) Act 1934 operates to transfer all causes of action vested in him to his estate. If the person injured dies before the expiration of the period set out in sec 11(4) of the Limitation Act 1980, the period applicable as respects the cause

---

140 *Stubbings v UK* [1997] 1 FLR 105.
141 *KR v Bryn Alyn Community (Holdings) Ltd* [2003] QB 1441.
142 *A v Hoare* [2008] 1 AC 844. Noted by *D Capper* [2008] CJQ 172 and *S Tofaris* [2008] CLJ 463 and *K Oliphant*, England and Wales, in: H Koziol and BC Steininger (eds), European Tort Law 2008 (2009), 131, nos 41 ff.
143 *A v Hoare* [2005] EWHC 2161 (QB).
144 *A v Hoare* [2006] 1 WLR 2320.
145 *A v Hoare* [2008] 1 AC 844 at [63].

of action surviving for the benefit of his estate shall be three years from the date of death or the date of the personal representative's knowledge,[146] whichever is the later (sec 11(5)) (see also *infra* 67).

## F. ACTIONS IN RESPECT OF DEFECTIVE PRODUCTS – SEC 11A

Section 11A of the Limitation Act 1980 applies to actions for defective products under Part I of the Consumer Protection Act 1987 (sec 11A(1)). It displaces the time limits given in the preceding provisions of the Limitation Act 1980 (sec 11A(2)). Where damages claimed by the plaintiff consist of or include damages in respect of personal injuries to the plaintiff or any other person or loss of or damage to any property, sec 11A(4) provides that a claim shall not be brought after the expiration of the period of three years from whichever is the later of the date on which the cause of action accrued and the date of knowledge (see sec 14(1A)) of the injured person or, in the case of loss of or damage to property, the date of knowledge of the plaintiff or (if earlier) of any person in whom his cause of action was previously vested. With the exception of the ten-year long-stop period under sec 11A(3), the ordinary time limit is extendable at the court's discretion (secs 33 and 33(1A)). The overall long-stop period applies from the relevant time, within the meaning of sec 4 of the Consumer Protection Act 1987 (ie when the product was supplied to another or *put into circulation*), and operates to extinguish a right of action whether or not that right of action had accrued or time had begun to run. The italicised phrase was said to be interpreted as meaning that a product is taken out of the manufacturing process operated by the producer and enters a marketing process in the form in which it is offered to the public in order to be used or consumed.[147] 65

Where the injured person died before the expiration of the above period, the deceased's estate must bring an action for surviving claims (see sec 1 Law Reform (Miscellaneous Provisions) Act 1934) within a period of three years from whichever is the later of the date of death and the date of the personal representative's knowledge (sec 11A(5)).[148] There will be no possibility to override the time limit through recourse to sec 33 of the Limitation Act 1980 (sec 12(1)). 66

146 See sec 11(6) and (7) Limitation Act 1980.

147 *O'Byrne v Sanofi* [2006] ECR 1-1313.

148 See sec 11A(6) and (7).

## G. SPECIAL TIME LIMIT FOR ACTIONS UNDER FATAL ACCIDENTS LEGISLATION – SEC 12

67 Whereas an action by the deceased's estate falls under the ambit of sec 11(5) of the Limitation Act 1980 (*supra* 64), dependants pursuing actions under the Fatal Accidents Act 1976 come within the language of sec 12. Section 12(2) states that no action shall be brought after the expiration of three years from the date of death or the date of knowledge (*supra* 50 and 55) of the person for whose benefit the action is brought, whichever is the later. By virtue of sec 12(1), no action can be pursued under the Fatal Accidents Act 1976 if the death occurred when the person injured could no longer maintain an action and recover damages in respect of the injury (whether because of a time limit in the 1980 Act or in any other Act, or for any other reason). Section 13 contains detailed rules on the operation of the time limit under sec 12 in relation to different dependants. The court's general discretion to extend time under sec 33 applies, except where an injured person would have been barred by the time limit in sec 11 or indeed sec 11A in accordance with sec 12(1) (sec 33(2)).

## H. ACTIONS IN RESPECT OF LATENT DAMAGE NOT INVOLVING PERSONAL INJURIES – SECS 14A AND B

68 Section 14A of the Limitation Act 1980 applies to any action for damages for negligence other than damage resulting in personal injury or death. The limitation period is either six years from the date on which the cause of action accrued or three years from the date of knowledge. A long-stop period of 15 years applies (sec 14B(1)).

## I. ACTIONS TO ENFORCE JUDGMENTS – SEC 24

69 By virtue of sec 24(1) of the Limitation Act 1980, an action to enforce a judgment must be brought within six years from the date on which the judgment became enforceable. The provision does not apply to enforcement by execution, only to enforcement by suit. No arrears of interest in respect of any judgment debt are recoverable after the expiration of six years from the date on which the interest became due (sec 24(2)).

70 The following table outlines the various statutory prescription periods central to tortious actions:

Table 1. Periods Relevant to Tortious Actions under the Limitation Act 1988

| Action | Limitation Period | Trigger | Authority | Discretionary exclusion of time limit | Long-Stop | Accrual Rule | Authority |
|---|---|---|---|---|---|---|---|
| Tort (in general) | Six years | Date cause of action accrues | Section 2 Limitation Act 1980 | – | – | – | – |
| Defamation (libel or slander) and malicious falsehood (including slander of title and slander of goods) | One year | Date cause of action accrues | Section 4A Limitation Act 1980 | Yes, sec 32A Limitation Act 1980 | – | – | – |
| An action for a contribution | Two years | Date right to recover contribution from any other person accrued | Section 10 Limitation Act 1980 | – | – | – | – |
| Personal injury | Three years | Date cause of action accrued or if later, from the date of knowledge | Section 11 Limitation Act 1980 | Yes, sec 33 Limitation Act 1980 | – | – | – |
| Product liability | Three years | Date cause of action accrued or if later date of knowledge | Section 11A Limitation Act 1980 | Yes, but only in respect of personal injuries or death (sec 33(IA)(b)) | Ten years. The court has no discretion to disapply this period (sec 33(1A)(a)) | From the relevant time, within the meaning of sec 4 Consumer Protection Act 1987 | Section 11A(3) Limitation Act 1980 |
| Wrongful death | Three years | Date of death or if later, date of knowledge | Section 12 Limitation Act 1980 | Yes, sec 33 Limitation Act 1980 | – | – | – |
| Latent damage (other than that causing personal injury or death) | Six years<br>Three years | Date cause of action accrued or if later, date of knowledge | Section 14A Limitation Act 1980 | – | 15 years | Date cause of action accrued | Section 14B Limitation Act 1980 |
| An action to enforce a judgment | Six years | From the date on which the judgment became enforceable | Section 24 Limitation Act 1980 | – | – | – | – |

## J. OTHER ACTIONS

71 The general six-year period also applies to actions founded on simple contract (sec 5 Limitation Act 1980). In actions on a specialty, which includes contracts by deed, a period of 12 years applies from the date on which the cause of action accrued (unless a shorter period of limitation is prescribed by any other provision of the 1980 Act) (sec 8). In the case of restitution, no specific period exists under the Limitation Act 1980. Rather, the period hinges on the specific ground for seeking restitution (in the case of mistake, for example, it would be six years from the date on which the mistake was or could reasonably have been discovered (sec 32)). Injunctions and other equitable remedies are discussed more fully *infra* 120 ff.

72 Several statutes set out their own limitation periods (see *infra* 88–89, 95 and 104). In the case of the Human Rights Act 1998, for example, actions must be brought within a period of one year from the date on which the act complained of took place (sec 7(5)(a)). However, the period may be extended where a court or tribunal considers it equitable having regard to all the circumstances (sec 7(5)(b)).[149]

## K. CLASSIFICATION OF CLAIMS OR PERIOD SHOPPING

73 The *ad hoc* development of the law of limitations means that little thought was given to overall coherence with different periods, definitions of discoverability, etc, applying to different regimes.[150] This is exacerbated by the lingering effect of the forms of action since a number of causes of action in tort alone, and correspondingly a number of statutory periods, may apply on a given set of facts. In the case of latent damage from an adjoining piece of land, for example, whereas a six-year period would apply under sec 2 (time limit for actions founded on tort) from the date on which the cause of action in nuisance accrued, sec 14A would apply if the action is framed in negligence (the period being either six years from the date on which the cause of action accrued or three years from the time of reasonable discoverability, if later). Subject to constraints by the wording of the Act of 1980, a claimant will be advised of the merits both, from a procedural and substantive perspective, of choosing one action over another. The draftsman's intention to limit choice in respect of certain interests, however, is unambiguous. Concerned to protect claimants, in the case of concurrent actions for damages for personal injury in contract and tort and for personal injuries and property damage, the more

---

149 Human Rights Act 1998, sec 7(5) is subject to any rule imposing a stricter time limit in relation to the procedure in question.

150 *Law Commission*, Limitation of Actions Consultation (1998) CP 151, para 11.3.

favourable regime for personal injuries, which is subject to a discretionary extension, prevails (*supra* 3, 26 and 65). Yet if the personal injury aspects are minor and/or the claimant chooses to forgo a claim in respect of them, the unextendable periods prescribed for actions founded on simple contract (under sec 5) or tort (under sec 2) would apply instead.

# VII. RULES OF POSTPONEMENT, SUSPENSION RENEWAL AND EXTENSION

## A. AVENUES TO PROLONG ORDINARY TIME LIMIT

Various ways exist through which a claimant can overcome a statutory bar otherwise applicable to their claim. Section 1(2) of the Limitation Act 1980 expressly states that the ordinary time limits given in Part I of the Act are subject to extension or exclusion in accordance with the provisions of Part II of the Act. Express reference is made, under Part II, to: (a) an *extension* of limitation periods in the case of disability (discussed *infra* 76 and 90 ff);[151] (b) *fresh accrual* of action in the case of acknowledgement and part payment (*infra* 77); (c) a *postponement* in the case of fraud, concealment and mistake (*infra* 78); and (d) discretionary *exclusion* of time limit for actions for defamation or malicious falsehood and for actions in respect of personal injuries or death (*infra* 79). All these serve to prolong the effective time limit, thus operating in the claimant's interest. 74

### 1) *Suspension*

There is no reference to 'suspension' in the Limitation Act 1980. This is consistent with the general position under English law that 'where an action has once accrued, and the statute has begun to run, there being then a capacity of suing and of being sued, the statute continues to run',[152] unless 'ousted [...] by a statutory provision'.[153] However, suspension is possible under sec 13 of the Arbitration Act 1996, for example, where the period between the commencement of arbitration and the date of a court order to set it aside or to declare it to be of no effect may be excluded from the computation. Also, the parties may expressly or impliedly agree, whether before or after the expiry, that the defendant will not plead the statutory limitation period, that the cause of action will not accrue until a condition precedent occurs, that a 75

151 See also reference to extension of time limits because of alternative dispute resolution in certain cross border or domestic contractual disputes in sec 33 of the Limitation Act 1980.

152 *Rhodes v Smethurst* (1838) 4 M & W 42, 59 per Lord Abinger CB.

153 *Tito v Waddell (No 2)* [1977] Ch 106, 246 per Sir Robert Megarry V-C.

claimant's right will be extinguished under the terms agreed[154] or indeed to suspend its running (via a standstill or tolling agreement), subject to legislation on unfair contract terms (*infra* 99 ff and 125 ff).[155] Such latitude is consistent with the fact that for the defence to operate it must be asserted (*infra* 131) and for the most part that the expiry of a limitation period does not extinguish the right in question (*supra* 10). Granting the parties such autonomy may allow the defendant to fulfil his obligations or it may facilitate the extension of negotiations to settle a claim and in so doing saves courts' time and the public's purse. While it has been suggested that breach of an agreement not to plead the statute of limitations would only entitle the innocent party to an action for breach of contract, the editors of Chitty on Contracts prefer the alternative view that such an agreement would prevent the defendant from relying on the Limitation Act 1980.[156]

*2) Extension*

76 The application of Part II of the Limitation Act 1980 in the case of disability is dealt with more fully *infra* 90 ff. Suffice to say for now that the existence of disability *before* the cause of action accrues delays the starting of the clock until that disability ceases. The use of 'extension' in this context is thus not to 'extend the basic limitation period so that it will not end while justification exists or before P is given a reasonable amount of time to file a claim after the justification expires'. Rather, it is used in the sense of postponing its starting point. An extension does, however, arise in the quoted sense, for example under sec 11(5) of the Limitation Act 1980 (*infra* 64).

*3) Fresh Accrual, Reset or Renewal*

77 While not relevant to tortious actions, secs 29–31 of the Limitation Act 1980 set out a different approach to prolonging claims. A limitation period of equal length may be repeatedly (and automatically) extended by further acknowledgments or payments. However, a right of action, once barred by the Limitation

---

154 Arbitration Act 1996, sec 12 specifically contemplates this: 'Where an arbitration agreement to refer future disputes to arbitration provides that a claim shall be barred, or the claimant's right extinguished, unless the claimant takes within a time fixed by the agreement some step—
(a) to begin arbitral proceedings, or
(b) to begin other dispute resolution procedures which must be exhausted before arbitral proceedings can be begun,
the court may by order extend the time for taking that step.'

155 Unfair Contract Terms Act 1977. See Chitty on Contracts, General Principles (32nd ed, 2015), paras 28–107 ff for further details. See also para 4.1 Pre-Action Protocol for Professional Negligence.

156 Chitty on Contracts, General Principles (32nd ed, 2015), para 28–109.

Act 1980, cannot be revived by any subsequent acknowledgement or payment (sec 29(7); see also *infra* 85).

### 4) *Postponement*

By virtue of sec 32(1) of the Limitation Act 1980, where (a) an action is based upon the *fraud* of the defendant, (b) any fact relevant to the plaintiff's right of action has been *deliberately concealed* from him by the defendant, or (c) the action is for relief from the consequences of a *mistake*, the limitation period shall not begin to run until the plaintiff has discovered the fraud, concealment or mistake (as the case may be) or could with reasonable diligence have discovered it (sec 32 Limitation Act 1980). (As with disability, the effect is to delay the starting of the clock.) Suffice to say that the courts have ruled that the terms of sec 32(1)(b) are wide enough to cover both the case where the concealment is contemporaneous with the accrual of the cause of action and where it occurs at some later date.[157] Where a *subsequent* deliberate concealment of facts supervenes, the clock will therefore be turned back to zero until the concealed facts are, or ought to have been, discovered (see also *supra* 77).[158] 78

### 5) *Exclusion*

Where a claim was not brought timeously, the courts have a general discretion to allow it to proceed in respect of some causes of action, including defamation, malicious falsehood, personal injuries or death as well as actions under Consumer Protection Act 1987. The effect is to deny the defendant the defence of prescription (secs 32A and 33 Limitation Act 1980). It is perhaps worth highlighting that appeals against the use of such discretion will only succeed with difficulty (*infra* 119).[159] 79

### 6) *Other Methods*

Additionally, it might be added that other aspects of the limitations statute, very long basic limitation periods, the discoverability test, etc, all contribute to 80

---

157 *Sheldon v RHM Outhwaite (Underwriting Agencies) Ltd* [1996] AC 102.

158 Ibid, 144 per Lord Browne-Wilkinson: 'it does not seem to me absurd that a plaintiff who has been prevented by the dishonourable conduct of the defendant from learning of the facts on the basis of which to found his action should be afforded the full six-year period from the date of the discovery of such concealment to bring his action. Certainly, that consequence is far less bizarre than the result of the construction favoured by the majority of the Court of Appeal [1994] 3 WLR 999 under which a plaintiff's right of action can become time-barred before he even becomes aware of the relevant facts, his ignorance being due to the deliberate concealment of such facts by the defendant.'

159 *Yates v Thakeham Tiles Ltd* [1995] PIQR 135.

an extension of effective time limits. Indeed, in the case of theft (*supra* 59) or fraud or fraudulent breach of trust the clock never began to tick (*infra* 86).

## B. SPECIFIC CASES

### 1) *Non-Discoverability of Facts*

81 Several provisions in the Limitation Act 1980 are designed to counter the disadvantages that attach to claimants proving their cases, for example as a result of information asymmetry or other evidentiary difficulties. Among them, discoverability rules seek to ease the unfairness that may arise where damage cannot reasonably be known until after the action was barred under the cause of action limb. Such rules exist for our purposes for: actions in respect of personal injuries following negligence, nuisance or breach of duty (sec 11(4)(b)); actions in respect of defective products (sec 11A(4)(b)); actions by a deceased's estate (secs 11(5)(b) and 11A(5)(b)); actions under the Fatal Accidents legislation (sec 12(2)(b)); and actions in respect of latent damage not involving personal injuries (sec 14A(4)(b)). Among the factors relevant in determining the relevant date of knowledge in the case of personal injuries or death, for example, are the fact that the claimant knew that the injury in question was significant and/or the identity of the defendant (sec 14(1); *supra* 45 ff and 50 ff) as well as the denial of liability on the defendant's part (secs 14(1A)(a), 14(2) and in the case of non-personal injury latent damage, sec 14A(7)). The legislature has also come to claimants' aid where the latter is a victim of theft so that the right of such a person to bring an action is not subject to any time limits (*supra* 59). The rules on the postponement of limitation period in case of fraud, concealment or mistake also seek to tackle unawareness of facts constituting the cause of action. In such cases, time does not begin to run until the claimant has or could with reasonable diligence have discovered the above (*supra* 78). Courts may also exercise their discretion inherent in Part II of the 1980 Act to override limitation periods for certain causes of action (*supra* 79). In taking the matters in the round, the courts will have regard, *inter alia*, to the length of, and the reasons for, the delay on the part of the plaintiff (secs 32A(2)(a) and 33(3)(a)) which may well include the non-discoverability of facts.

### 2) *Defendant's or Claimant's Conduct*

82 There are various ways in which defendants' conduct influences limitation periods. Conduct constituting a continuing tort or conduct that infringes multiple protected interests, for example, accrues disadvantages to defendants (*supra* 23 ff). Conduct resulting in the death of a victim may also lead to the

effective extension of the applicable period to the benefit of the deceased's dependants and/or estate (*supra* 66 and 67). In the case of a joint action to which a tortfeasor is not a party, a further period is conferred should his fellow tortfeasor seek contribution (*supra* 61). The courts have also striven to interpret the language of the statute to further Parliament's objective and not frustrate it: today, claimants who suffer intentional injury benefit from 'the more favourable limitation treatment introduced by the 1975 Act for victims of injuries caused by negligence'[160] which releases the burden, in particular on sexually abused victims (*supra* 63).[161] The multiple publication rule in the case of actionable defamation that applies where the manner of a subsequent defamatory publication materially differs from that of the first publication is equally worth repeating (*supra* 34).

The 1980 Act also extends its protection to a claimant where a defendant seeks to obstruct the course of justice by not cooperating or by seeking to gain an unfair advantage through resort to delaying tactics. The effect of secs 14(1A)(a), 14(2) and 14A(7) is to delay the commencement of the clock where a defendant disputes liability. In the case of procedural delays, a claimant can petition the court to disapply the ordinary time limit in respect of personal injuries or death under sec 33 on the basis of 'the conduct of the defendant after the cause of action arose, including the extent (if any) to which he responded to requests reasonably made by the plaintiff for information or inspection for the purpose of ascertaining facts which were or might be relevant to the plaintiff's cause of action against the defendant' (sec 33(3)(c)). In this respect, it has also been shown that protective rules apply where the defendant has engaged in fraud (*supra* 78 and *infra* 86) or indeed theft (*supra* 59). Whereas Parliament was unambiguous as to the fact that deliberate concealment on the defendant's part at the time the cause of action accrues postpones the running of time, the courts have attributed a broad meaning to Parliament's intention: namely, that subsequent active concealment also gives the plaintiff the benefit of the statutory postponement (*supra* 78). 83

The desire to balance the interests of claimants with those of defendants lies behind the adoption of provisions which weigh against claimants who are not proactive in asserting their claims. Indeed the 'date of knowledge' test only affects the operation of the starting point for those claimants whose causes of action accrue *before* the moment of reasonable discovery. A claimant who is cognisant of all the required facts but sits on his claim is bound by the less favourable of the two dates. Attention is also invited to that fact that in considering whether 84

160 *A v Hoare* [2008] 1 AC 844, at [14] per Lord Hoffmann.

161 *P Handford*, Sexual abuse and personal injury limitation law – Order restored? (2008) 16 Tort L Rev 61, 63.

to exempt a claimant from failing to commence proceedings in time under sec 33, a court will take into consideration the extent to which the plaintiff acted promptly and reasonably once he knew whether or not the act or omission of the defendant, to which the injury was attributable, might be capable at that time of giving rise to an action for damages (sec 33(3)(e)); similar guidelines also exist for actions in respect of defamation and malicious falsehood (sec 32A(2)). In the former case, the steps, if any, taken by the plaintiff to obtain medical, legal or other expert advice and the nature of any such advice he may have received (sec 33(3)(f)) are also a vital consideration.

#### 3) *Admission by D of P's Right or Partial Performance of P's Right by D*

85 Cooperation on the part of the defendant will help equip the claimant with the knowledge required for discoverability (*supra* 44 ff) and the admission by the defendant of a fraud, concealment or mistake (*supra* 78) as well as liability (secs 14(1A)(a), 14(2) and 14A(7)) precipitate the running of the clock. On the other hand, following acknowledgments or payments, the clock returns to zero (*supra* 77).

#### 4) *Legal Relations between the Claimant and Defendant – Trusts and Bailment*

86 Section 21 of the Limitation Act 1980 sets a limit of six years from the date on which the right of action accrued for actions to recover trust property or in respect of any breach of trust (sec 21(3)). No period applies, however, in respect of any fraud or fraudulent breach of trust to which the trustee was a party or privy or to recover from the trustee trust property or the proceeds of trust property in the possession of the trustee or previously received by the trustee and converted to his use (sec 21(1)). Where D is a custodian of P's chattels, bailment could constitute a cause of action founded in tort under sec 2 of the Limitation Act 1980 (although this may also ground a concurrent action in contract or indeed in restitution).[162] No special rules on postponement, renewal or extension apply in the latter case unless there has been some fraud, concealment or mistake (*supra* 78).

#### 5) *Medical Treatment Cases*

87 Medical negligence may result in injuries that lie dormant for long periods of time. For actions in respect of personal injuries or death, the hardship caused to claimants by the rigour of the cause of action accruing before reasonable

162 Note that certain alternative resolution dispute methods are referred to in the 1980 Act. See sec 33A on mediation in certain cross-border disputes. The provision also makes a single reference to arbitration. See also secs 10(3)(b) and 39 on arbitration.

discovery is to some extent ameliorated by commencement at the point of discovery or imputed discovery (*supra* 44 ff). This, in addition to the effect of death, concealment, omissions, the sec 33 discretion, etc, impacts medical practitioners, actions against whom are likely to be in respect of personal injuries or death. Moreover, except in the case of actions under the Consumer Protection Act 1987, the rights of a claimant who suffers personal injury or dies are not disturbed by a long-stop rule. Apart from this, the statute does not operate to extinguish claimants' rights in such cases.

### 6) *Employment Relations*

The Employment Rights Act 1996 sets out various rights of employees and the times within which grievances arising in respect of breaches of such rights can be raised. Under sec 111, for example, a complaint may be presented to an employment tribunal against an employer by any person that he was unfairly dismissed by the employer. However, such a claim must be brought within a period of three months beginning with the effective date of termination or within such further period as the tribunal considers reasonable. The three-month period applies to most complaints under the Act.[163] Specific statutory limitation periods exist for other breaches likely to arise in the context of employment relations, including under the Sex Discrimination Act 1975, the Disability Discrimination Act 1995 and the Equality Act 2010. 88

### 7) *Family Relations*

Special time limits apply to certain family-related issues such as divorce[164] and inheritance.[165] However, these fall outside the realm of tort law. 89

### 8) *Disability and Minority*

Section 28 of the present Limitation Act offers protection to parties under disabilities. The provision dates back to the 1623 statute (sec 7). If on the date when any right of action accrued, the person to whom it accrued was under a disability, an action may be brought at any time before the expiration of six years from the date when he ceased to be under a disability or died (whichever first occurred) notwithstanding a limitation period has expired (sec 28(1) Limitation Act 1980). In the case of libel or slander, the applicable period is one year from the date on which he ceased to be under a disability (sec 28(4)); in the case of personal injury, death and actions under 90

---

163 See *A McGee*, Limitation Periods (2014), 27.030 ff for further analysis.
164 Matrimonial Causes Act 1973, secs 3 and 13.
165 Inheritance (Provision for Family and Dependants) Act 1975, sec 4.

the Consumer Protection Act 1987, three years (sec 28(6) and (7)). In the former case, however, no action can be brought after the expiry of the long-stop period (sec 28(7)(a)). Subject to the 15-year long stop (sec 28A(2)) for latent damage under sec 14A, a time limit of three years applies from the date when a claimant ceased to be under a disability or died (whichever first occurred) notwithstanding that the period mentioned in sec 14A has expired (sec 28A(1)).[166] The language of the section is clear: it only applies '*if* on the date when any right of action accrued for which a period of limitation is prescribed by this Act, the person to whom it accrued was under a disability'. Therefore, it is against a claimant whose disability arises *subsequent* to the accrual of the cause of action.[167]

91 Section 38, on interpretation, in particular its subsection (2), sets out a list of persons to be treated, for the purposes of the 1980 Act, as under a disability: that is, an infant or a person who lacks capacity to conduct legal proceedings. A person is said to attain full age on attaining the age of 18 (sec 1(1)) Family Law Reform Act 1969).[168] By virtue of sec 2(1) and (2) of the Mental Capacity Act 2005 a person is said to lack capacity in relation to a matter if at the material time he is unable to make a decision for himself in relation to the matter because of an impairment – permanent or otherwise – of, or a disturbance in the functioning of, the mind or brain. Section 38 applies in 'this Act, unless the context otherwise requires'; as such 'disability' is to be interpreted uniformly across the 1980 Act. In light of its exhaustive definition, the courts have determined that it would do too much violence to the language of the 1980 Act to treat an attack of dermatitis as a disability.[169] Physical disability can nonetheless be taken into consideration under the general clause in sec 33 which allows the disapplication of the ordinary time limit in light of the length of, and the reasons for, the delay on the part of the plaintiff (sec 33(3)(a)).[170]

92 The general rule under English law that, once time has started to run, nothing can suspend it means that no subsequent or intermittent disability, however involuntary, affects the operation of the statute. This raises no problem in the case of children, since the 'disability' that constitutes infancy is non-recurrent. The effect on the other category of disabled persons is that once an individual

166 See also the narrow rule in sec 28.

167 *Purnell v Roche* [1927] 2 Ch 142.

168 By virtue of sec 1(2), sec 1(1) applies for the purposes of any rule of law, and, in the absence of a definition or of any indication of a contrary intention, for the construction of 'full age', 'infant', 'infancy', 'minor', 'minority' and similar expressions, *inter alia*, in any statutory provision, whether passed or made before, on or after the date on which this section comes into force.

169 See *Chagos Islanders v AG* [2003] EWHC 2222 where it was unsuccessfully contended that this list was non-exhaustive.

170 *Pilmore v Northern Trawlers Ltd* [1985] 1 Lloyd's Rep 552.

ceases to be under a disability, however brief, the clock starts to run so that a subsequent disability will not stop the clock. The burden of proof lies with the claimant to show that he did not cease to be under a disability at the material time(s). While a lack of rules to suspend the operation of time may seem to produce grave hardship for individuals who suffer from intermittent disability, a statutory qualification exists under sec 33(3)(d) of the Limitation Act 1980 which applies in respect of actions for personal injuries or death.[171] The discretion, which is also relevant for actions under Part I of the Consumer Protection Act 1987, makes explicit reference to the duration of any disability of the plaintiff arising *after* the date of the accrual of the cause of action as one of several factors the courts should have regard to deciding whether to allow the claimant's action notwithstanding the expiry of time. That discretion does not, however, apply to the ten-year long-stop period for defective products (sec 33(1A)).

It is worth adding that children and persons who lack mental capacity to make certain decisions for themselves can only pursue actions though a litigation friend (eg parents or guardian, close relatives or friends, or a professional such as the Official Solicitor).[172] (A child may also conduct proceedings without a litigation friend in certain circumstances.) By virtue of sec 28(2) of the Limitation Act 1980, the sec 28 extension of the limitation period in case of disability does not apply 'where the right of action first accrued to some person (not under a disability) through whom the person under a disability claims.' A person is treated as claiming through another person if he became entitled by, through, under, or by the act of that other person to the right claimed (sec 38(5)). Section 28(1) would also not apply where a litigation friend subsequently becomes disabled. Where an action is initiated by a child or a litigation friend acting on behalf of the child or person of unsound mind and that action is abandoned, a subsequent action can be brought at a later date (as this may be more tactically prudent) provided the action is still within the prescribed period.[173] In *Tolley v Morris*,[174] where the defendant applied to strike out the action as an abuse of process, the House of Lords ruled by a majority that to do so would be to deprive the child, who was two years old at the time of the accident, of his rights. Such an approach would serve no useful purpose since a fresh action could be commenced until the time prescribed after the child ceased to be under the disability. 93

The effect of *severe disability* may be that a claim could persist forever. A court has jurisdiction under CPR r 40.20 to grant a binding declaration of 94

171 Emphasis added.

172 See Practice Direction 21.

173 See *A McGee*, Limitation Periods (2014), 19.025 ff.

174 *Tolley v Morris* (1979) 1 WLR 592. *Hogg v Hamilton* [1992] PIQR P387 where the Court of Appeal struck out the second writ.

non-liability in favour of a defendant 'whether or not any other remedy is claimed'. Such a declaration was sought in *Eidha v Toropdar*[175] against a ten-year-old boy who suffered serious personal injuries and may never have regained full mental capacity. Threats of proceedings were made without proceedings actually ever being issued on the boy's behalf. While thought of as rather unsavoury, negative declarations are a matter of discretion and can, on the right facts (eg lengthy delay with the consequence of evidence becoming stale), assist in achieving justice. In this case, the claimant bus driver, Toropdar, was granted such as declaration on the basis that there was a real danger that the case could hang over him *ad infinitum*.

### *9) P or D's Absence from the Jurisdiction*

95 Regulation (EC) No 864/2007 of the European Parliament and of the Council of 11 July 2007 on the law applicable to non-contractual obligations (Rome II)[176] states as regards torts/delicts that the law of the country in which the damage occurs shall be the applicable law, governing *inter alia* the manner in which an obligation may be extinguished and rules of prescription and limitation, including rules relating to the commencement, interruption and suspension of a period of prescription or limitation (arts 4 and 15(h)). The Foreign Limitation Periods Act 1984 sets out the position where an action or proceeding is brought before a court in England and Wales, but the law of another country falls to be taken into account in accordance with rules of private international law. The general position under sec 1(1) is that the law of England and Wales relating to limitation shall not apply. Rather, that of the other country shall. Both the law of England and Wales and the law of the other country relating to limitation may fall to be taken into account in certain circumstances (sec 1(2)), in particular in the case of double actionability. This private international law rule, which evolved from *Phillips v Eyre*,[177] provides that in order to found a suit in England and Wales for a tort committed abroad, the wrong must be of such a character that is actionable under the law of the foreign jurisdiction and would have been actionable if committed in England and Wales. While sec 10 of the Private International Law (Miscellaneous Provisions) Act 1995 abolishes this in respect of most causes of action, it is still relevant in respect of defamation claims (sec 13).[178] The general rule disapplying English law also does not apply to the extent that the application of foreign law would conflict with public policy, including hardship (sec 2 Foreign Limitation Periods Act 1984).

---

175 *Eidha v Toropdar* [2008] EWHC 1219 (QB).

176 [2007] OJ L 199.

177 *Phillips v Eyre* (1870) LR 6 QB 1.

178 See sec 13 Private International Law (Miscellaneous Provisions) Act 1995.

### *10)* Force Majeure

The well-known and settled rule that once time has started to run nothing can suspend it has already been mentioned. This was discernible as early as *Prideaux v Webber*[179] where the court adjudged against a claimant who justifiably argued that 'certain rebels had usurped the government and that none of the King's Courts were open'. In the same vein while a 'very strong case was put, that of the Courts of Justice being shut up in time of war, so that no original could be sued out', Sir William Grant MR in *Beckford v Wade*,[180] referring to *Hall v Wybourn*[181] and *Aubry v Fortesque*,[182] ruled that the statute would bar the action. The statute, he said, is 'general and must work upon all cases, which are not exempt by the exception'. That said, the exclusionary rules under Part II of the 1980 Act may be relevant in the event of *force majeure*. The presence of war may also affect the running of the limitation period: the Limitation (Enemies and War Prisoner) Act 1945 prevents the commencement of the clock against a claimant or defendant who is an enemy or is detained in enemy territory.[183] The period of limitation is not reckoned until 12 months from the date he ceases to be an enemy or to be detained (sec 1). 96

### *11) Former or Ongoing Litigation*

Former or ongoing litigation may have an impact in the case of a claim for contribution. It will be remembered that an action to recover contribution by D1 from D2 must be brought within a period of two years from the date a judgment is given against D1 in civil proceedings (*supra* 61). If D1 appeals against liability for damage and the appeal results in a variation of the amount of damages awarded against him, the two-year time limit remains unaffected. Of course, if he succeeds on the merits on appeal, he would not need to seek recourse against D2. 97

In other cases, a claimant may seek to persuade the court to exercise its discretion under secs 32A(2)(a) and 33(3)(a) of the 1980 Act. In both cases, the court will take the length of, and the reasons for, the delay on the part of the plaintiff into consideration in deciding whether to grant the claimant's request. The parties would be wiser to agree not to commence litigation pending the conclusion of negotiations or other proceedings, however (*infra* 99 ff). 98

---

179 *Prideaux v Webber* (1661) 1 Lev 31.
180 *Beckford v Wade* (1810) 17 Wes 87, 93.
181 *Hall v Wybourn* (1689) 2 Salk 420.
182 *Aubry v Fortescue* (1713) 10 Mod 206.
183 Enemy and enemy territory are defined in sec 2(1) of the Act.

### 12) *Settlements and ADR Proceedings*

#### a) Settlements

99 Where the limitation is approaching parties needing more time to settle a dispute may enter into a standstill agreement (*supra* 75 and *infra* 125 ff) or issue a protective claim or writ. The latter entails issuing proceedings (which as will be seen below stops the limitation period running), but delaying serving the defendant for a maximum duration of four months.[184] Once an agreement has been reached, the remedy for failure to honour any provision, for instance to pay compensation set out in the agreement, is usually damages for breach of contract. The time limit to enforce contractual obligations is contained in sec 5 of the Limitation Act 1980 (*supra* 26 and 71).

100 *Part 36 Offer*: should the parties choose to settle their dispute, an offer may be made pursuant to the self-contained procedure set out in Part 36 of the Civil Procedure Rules. The offer must specify a period for acceptance of not less than 21 days.[185] If a Part 36 offer is accepted, the claim will be stayed.[186] Unless the parties agree otherwise in writing, where a Part 36 offer that is or includes an offer to pay or accept a single sum of money is accepted, that sum must be paid to the claimant within 14 days of the date of acceptance.[187] If not, the claimant may enter judgment for the unpaid sum.[188] Detailed rules exist on clarifying, withdrawing and changing the terms of offers.[189]

101 Note that where a case has been fully argued, whether at first instance or on appeal, and it then settles or is withdrawn or is in some other way disposed of, the Court of Appeal in *Barclays Bank Plc v Nylon Capital LLP*[190] ruled that it nonetheless retains the right to decide whether or not to proceed to give judgment. Although an issue may no longer be live between the parties, Lord Neuberger MR ruled that a powerful reason for proceeding to give judgment would be where the case raises a point which it is in the public interest

---

184 CPR r 7.5. Note however, that the courts are taking a less indifferent stance to such claims. In *Nomura International Plc v Granada Group Ltd* [2007] 2 All ER (Comm) 404, Cooke J stated at [37]: 'The key question must always be whether or not, at the time of issuing a writ, the claimant was in a position properly to identify the essence of the tort or breach of contract complained of and if given appropriate time to marshall what it knew, to formulate particulars of claim […] If a claimant cannot do that which is necessary to prosecute the claim by setting out the basis for it, even in a rudimentary way, a claimant has no business to issue a claim form at all "in the hope that something may turn up".'

185 CPR r 36.5 and r 36.6.

186 CPR r 36.14.

187 CPR r 36.14(6).

188 CPR r 36.14(7).

189 CPR r 36.7 ff.

190 *Barclays Bank Plc v Nylon Capital LLP* [2011] EWCA Civ 826, at [74].

to ventilate in a judgment. Obvious examples of such cases, he added, are where the case raises a point of law of some potential general interest, where an appellate court is differing from the court below, where some wrongdoing or other activity should be exposed, or where the case has attracted some other legitimate public interest. Where a court hands down judgment despite the matter having been disposed of between the parties, the time limit for actions to enforce judgments under sec 24 applies instead (*supra* 69).

*Contribution*: in the context of a right of recourse against a fellow tortfeasor under sec 10, the rule is that where D1 makes or agrees to make any payment to P in compensation for damage (whether he admits any liability in respect of the damage or not), D1 must seek a contribution from D2 within two years from the earliest date on which the amount to be paid is *agreed* (not when it is made and notwithstanding other terms are to be agreed) between him and P (sec 10(4) Limitation Act 1980; *supra* 61). 102

*Additional time limit for actions for damages for late payment of insurance claims*: the Enterprise Act 2016 inserts a new sec 5A into the Limitation Act 1980 on the additional time limit for actions for damages for late payment of insurance claims. Section 5A(1) provides that where an insurer has paid all sums due in respect of an insurance claim, an action for late payment[191] may not be brought more than one year after that payment. Subsection (2) provides that the receipt of any form of payment which extinguishes the insurer's liability in respect of the original insurance claim will constitute the beginning of the one-year period for bringing a late payment claim specified in subsection (1). As the Explanatory Notes to the Act go on to add, this payment may be, for example, a payment in accordance with a court or arbitral award, or an amount agreed by the insurer and insured in a binding settlement agreement. A late payment action will be barred by the expiry of whichever period ends sooner: the one-year period after payment of all sums due in respect of the insurance claim, or the usual limitation period (contained in sec 5 Limitation Act 1980 – time limit for actions founded on simple contract (*supra* 26 and 71)) of six years from the date of breach of the implied term as to payment within a reasonable time. This provision extends to England and Wales only. 103

b) Arbitration

*Arbitration proceedings*: sec 39 of the Limitation Act 1980 explicitly provides that the Act does not apply to any arbitration for which a period of limitation is 104

---

191 Ie in breach of the term implied into a contract of insurance by sec 13A Insurance Act 2015 which was inserted by sec 28 Enterprise Act 2016. Section 13A(1) implies into every contract

prescribed by or under any other enactment (whether passed before or after the passing of the 1980 Act). Section 13 of the Arbitration Act 1996 deals with the application of Limitation Acts and states that they apply to arbitration proceedings as they apply to legal proceedings. Reference to cause of action in the Limitation Act 1980 is therefore a reference to a cause of arbitration in an arbitration context. The parties are free to agree when arbitral proceedings are to be regarded as commenced for the purposes of the Limitation Acts (sec 14(1) Arbitration Act 1996). In the absence of such an agreement, the rule where the arbitrator is named or designated in the arbitration agreement is that arbitral proceedings are commenced when one party serves on the other party or parties a notice in writing requiring him or them to submit that matter to the person so named or designated.[192] The court is given power to extend the time for beginning arbitral proceedings under sec 12 of the Arbitration Act 1996 provided the conditions in sec 12(3)[193] are met.

105 *Arbitration awards*: an action to enforce an arbitration award is of six years from the date on which the cause of action accrued (sec 7 Limitation Act), that being from the date of breach of the promise under the agreement.[194]

106 *Contribution*: as regards the special time limit for claiming contribution in respect of an award made on any arbitration, D1 must do so no later than two years from the date of the award (sec 10(3) Limitation Act 1980; *supra* 61).

#### c) Cross-Border Mediation and ADR

107 Sections 33A and 33B of the Limitation Act 1980, which will not be considered in any detail here, provide respectively for an extension of time limits because of mediation in certain cross-border disputes and because of alternative dispute resolution in certain cross-border or domestic contractual disputes.

### *13) Court Ruling or Law that Prevents P from Litigating the Claim*

108 If a claimant is barred from litigation by a decision at common law or by statute, they have no cause of action in England and Wales. However, in the

of insurance that if the insured makes a claim under the contract, the insurer must pay any sums due in respect of the claim within a reasonable time.

192 See also sec 14(4) and (5).

193 The court shall make an order only if satisfied: (a) that the circumstances are such as were outside the reasonable contemplation of the parties when they agreed the provision in question, and that it would be just to extend the time; or (b) that the conduct of one party makes it unjust to hold the other party to the strict terms of the provision in question.

194 *Agromet Motoimport Ltd v Maulden Engineering Co (Beds) Ltd* [1985] 2 All ER 436.

case of a grievance against a public authority an action may be taken to the European Court of Human Rights. Article 35 of the European Convention on Human Rights (ECHR) sets the admissibility criteria for such petitions, among other things requiring that all domestic remedies have been exhausted. The action must be brought before the Strasbourg Court within a period of six months from the date on which the final (domestic) decision was taken (art 35(1) ECHR).

### *14) Evidential Difficulties*

The Limitation Act 1980 deals with evidential difficulties both directly and indirectly. As regards the former, reference is made to the various rules on discoverability discussed above. By way of example, the definition of date of knowledge for purposes of secs 11 and 12 includes the identity of the defendant (sec 14(1)(c)). Section 14(3) adds that a person's knowledge includes knowledge which he might reasonably have been expected to acquire from facts observable or ascertainable by him or from facts ascertainable by him with the help of medical or other appropriate expert advice which it is reasonable for him to seek but a person shall *not* be fixed with knowledge of a fact ascertainable only with the help of expert advice so long as he has taken all reasonable steps to obtain (and, where appropriate, to act on) that advice (*supra* 50 and 55). Where a defendant disputes liability (secs 14(1A)(a), 14(2) and 14A(7)) or where evidence has been sought and not yet received, for example due to the complicated nature of the request, this clearly delays the commencement of the period. Section 32(5), which applies in the case of concealment is also relevant here: where a plaintiff's right of action (or the defendant's identity or the existence or significance of damage) has been deliberately concealed from him by the defendant, the effect of that provision is that the period of limitation does not begin to run until the plaintiff has discovered or could with reasonable diligence have discovered it (*supra* 78). Evidential difficulties are also a general consideration that the court must have regard to in excising its discretion to exclude the ordinary time limits in Part II (secs 32A(2)(a) and 33(3)(a)). Further, the conduct of the defendant after the cause of action arose is a crucial consideration, including the extent (if any) to which he cooperated following requests reasonably made by the plaintiff for information (sec 33(3)(c); *supra* 83) as are the steps, if any, taken by the plaintiff to obtain medical, legal or other expert advice and the nature of any such advice he may have received in an action in respect of personal injury or death (sec 33(3)(f); *supra* 84). 109

Since delay impoverishes evidence, the Limitation Act 1980 guides judicial responses to a request under secs 32A and 33 in another relevant manner: both sections state that the extent to which, having regard to the delay, the evidence 110 adduced or likely to be adduced by the plaintiff or the defendant is or is likely to be less cogent than if the action had been brought within the ordinary time is a reason not to disapply the ordinary time limits in Part I of the 1980 Act.

### *15) Financial Difficulties by P in Raising Money Required for Litigation*

111 Several avenues exist to fund litigation in England and Wales. While legal aid is available to help meet the costs of legal advice and representation in a court or tribunal, there are strict eligibility criteria. Civil legal aid is now very limited in scope, though it remains available, *inter alia*, in the case of clinical negligence where a child has suffered severe disability from a brain injury caused during pregnancy, birth or in the first eight weeks of life, subject to income and capital limits.[195] But other mechanisms exist. Before-the-event (BTE) legal expenses insurance is included in most motor insurance and household buildings and contents policies as an optional. After-the-event (ATE) cover, a first-party insurance policy against legal costs should the action prove unsuccessful, is also available and can be used in conjunction with a conditional fee agreement (CFA) (or 'no win no fee'), although these tend to predominate in certain types of injury, and are less common now for personal injury than they once were. The archaic barriers against maintenance and champerty have been lowered so that funding for litigation may be sought from third parties. Unless compelled to do so under secs 32A(2)(a) and 33(3)(b), which directs courts to have regard to the length of, and the reasons for, delay on the part of the plaintiff, a claimant who fails in his quest to obtain legal funding may lose his right to a judicial remedy. On the other hand, the Limitation Act 1980 makes several references to the financial state of a potential defendant. This is the case under secs 14(1A)(a), 14(2) and 14A(7) which all relate to the definition of knowledge. A claimant is not taken to have knowledge in respect of a defendant who is not able to satisfy a judgment. As seen above, the effect of the single action rule (*supra* 21 ff and 46) and the time limit for actions to enforce judgements under sec 24 (*supra* 69) is that a claimant may be wise to postpone an action against an impecunious defendant until such time as he is able to satisfy any judgement debt imposed on him (*supra* 63). In such a case, the limitation statute will not operate against him.

### *16) Closed Courts*

112 See *supra* 8 and 96.

[195] See the reforms to civil legal aid contained in the Legal Aid, Sentencing and Punishment of Offenders Act 2012.

*17) Prolongation by Courts on Grounds of Justice*

The exclusionary rules have already been dealt with above. See also the rules on equity *infra* 120 ff. 113

# VIII. CEILINGS ON THE EFFECTIVE TIME OF PRESCRIPTION

To counter the fact that delay impinges on the fairness of a trial and impedes the definitive resolution of claims,[196] long-stop periods exist in respect of certain causes of action. 114

## A. LATENT DAMAGE NOT INVOLVING PERSONAL INJURIES

In the case of latent damage not involving personal injuries, a long-stop period of 15 years applies from the date of an act or omission alleged to constitute *negligence* (sec 14B(1) Limitation Act 1980). Where there is more than one date, the period starts from the last of these dates. The fact that the cause of action has not yet accrued or that the claimant still does not know of his cause of action is irrelevant (sec 14B(2)). Note that the long-stop provision in sec 14B of the Limitation Act 1980 refers to negligence. Where a plaintiff's right of action (or the defendant's identity or the existence or significance of damage) has been deliberately concealed from him by the defendant,[197] sec 32(5) operates to override the long-stop period. Section 32(5) also disapplies the general limitation period in sec 14A in favour of that in sec 2 so that a period of six years applies in combination with the start date in sec 32(1), namely when the plaintiff has discovered the concealment or could with reasonable diligence have discovered it. Since the parties can contractually postpone the beginning of the limitation period, in theory this means that the effective prescription period can exceed the long-stop period (*supra* 75, 99 and *infra* 125 ff). 115

## B. CONSUMER PROTECTION ACT 1987

A long-stop period of ten years from the relevant time within the meaning of sec 4 of the Consumer Protection Act 1987 applies (sec 11A Limitation 116

---

196 *Abdulla v Birmingham City Council* [2012] UKSC 47, at [41] per Lord Sumption.

197 Or indeed, the defendant's agent and to any person through whom the defendant claims and his agent (sec 32(1)).

Act 1980). In relation to a producer, own brander or importer, the relevant time is the time the product was supplied to another or was put into circulation. The effect of the application of sec 11A(3) is to extinguish a right of action whether or not that right of action had accrued or time had begun to run. The long-stop period in sec 11A of the Limitation Act 1980 is not overridden in the case of fraud, concealment or mistake (sec 32(4A)). The courts are nonetheless conferred a narrow discretion to add a new party, under sec 35 of the Limitation Act 1980 even after the long-stop period has expired (*infra* 128 ff). It would seem given para 13.1 of Practice Direction 16 that the defendant must plead the defence even where a right has been extinguished since it cannot be raised by the courts *ex officio* (*infra* 131; see also *supra* 10 and 115, in the latter case regarding the postponement of the defence).[198]

117 Ignoring the long-stop provision, a limitation period of three years applies in England and Wales from the date on which the cause of action accrued or the date of knowledge, if later. Knowledge for the purpose of sec 11A of the Limitation Act 1980 includes such facts about the damage caused by the defect as would lead a reasonable person who had suffered such damage to consider it sufficiently serious to justify his instituting proceedings for damages against a defendant who did not dispute liability and was able to satisfy a judgment. Where a producer, P, sells a defective product which seven years later causes harm which is discovered six years later, it will not remain possible to bring a claim for as long as 16 (ie 7+6+3) years after P's sale of the product, however, because of the operation of the long-stop provision: a claim under the Consumer Protection Act 1987 will expire ten years after the product was supplied by the producer, own brander or importer to another.

## IX. STATUTE INTERPRETATION, JUDICIAL DISCRETION AND LACHES

### A. INTERPRETATION

118 Judicial interpretation in the context of the law of limitation in no different from that in other contexts. Where Parliament's intention is not explicit (*casus omissus*), judges are tasked to fill gaps. This was the case, for example in respect of *when* a cause of action accrues (*supra* 20). Similarly, where a draftsman, though having directed his mind to the point, has left a rule ambiguous, judges will strive to construe the provision 'without doing any great violence to

[198] *A McGee*, Limitation Periods (2014), para 2.030 and Chitty on Contracts, General Principles (32nd ed, 2015), para 28–108.

its wording'.[199] This may entail taking a provision literally on the one hand or minutely investigating the language of earlier Limitation Acts and decisions on such statutes on the other. Although an interpretation may be attractive, there have been times where the courts have had to concede that it is not one that could possibly be given to the perceived intention of Parliament. This was the case for example in *Cartledge v E Jopling & Sons Ltd* (*supra* 36). Yet the ruling went on to persuade Parliament to amend the law (*supra* 44). Clearly, judges in England differ in their approach to the law of limitations, with some being perceived as more willing than others to rule in favour of claimants. That this area of law is no less subject to appeals than any other confirms the difficult task that judges are faced with.

## B. DISCRETION

While the courts' discretion in Part II of the 1980 Act is wide, its exercise inevitably places defendants in great difficulty. As such, the remedy is exceptional. The onus is on the plaintiff to satisfy the court that the primary limitation period should not apply.[200] In seeking the indulgence of the court, proportionality is an important factor. It is a question which, as May LJ put it in *McGhie v British Telecommunications Plc*, 'has an eye [...] to the strength of the claimant's claim'.[201] A weak claim, owing say to inconsistencies in evidence, is likely to divert precious resources and as such militates against the exercise of the discretion.[202] Courts will also be slow to jump to the claimant's aid where the value of the claim is disproportionate to the costs of running it.[203] On the other hand 'it would be a great prejudice to a claimant who was very badly injured and likely to suffer the consequences of that injury for many years to come if, what would otherwise be a very large claim, based upon very strong evidence, were to be lost through a refusal to exercise the discretion under sec 33'.[204] While it is fair to say that the courts tend to err on the side of allowing a claim with merits to proceed (*supra* 79), and indeed are directed under secs 32A(1) and 33(1) to consider the prejudice on the claimant of barring the action, a very important matter under those subsections is also the prejudice of such a decision on the defendant. In addition to the court's Part II discretion, various terms in the statute, eg 'reasonable', 'good faith', etc, 119

---

199 *Sheldon v RHM Outhwaite (Underwriting Agencies) Ltd* [1996] AC 102, per Staughton LJ.

200 *Dale v British Coal Corporation* [1992] PIQR 373 at P382 per Stuart-Smith LJ.

201 *McGhie v British Telecommunications Plc* [2005] EWCA Civ 48, at [35].

202 *Collins v Secretary of State for Business, Innovation and Skills* [2013] EWHC 1117.

203 *Robinson v St Helens Metropolitan Borough Council* [2002] EWCA Civ 1099, at [33] per Sir Murray Stuart-Smith (as he then was).

204 *McGhie v British Telecommunications Plc* [2005] EWCA Civ 48, at [35] per May LJ.

necessarily import the need to weigh conflicting considerations and as such confer courts with indirect discretion.

## C. LACHES AND ACQUIESCENCE

120 Section 36(2) of the Limitation Act 1980 states: 'Nothing in this Act shall affect any *equitable jurisdiction* to refuse relief on the ground of acquiescence or otherwise.'[205] In addition to the equitable doctrine of acquiescence, which we will turn to in due course, the equitable doctrine of laches may bar recovery on the part of a claimant on the appropriate set of facts. As the italicised phrase in sec 36(2) emphasises, the defences only apply in equity's domain.

121 In *Partridge v Partridge* North J, quoting Coke on Littleton, observed that 'Laches, or Lasches, is an old French word for slacknesse or negligence, or not doing.'[206] The doctrine is based on the equitable maxims that 'delay defeats equity' or 'equity aids the vigilant and not those who slumber on their rights.' The claimant's undue delay may also induce a belief on the part of the defendant that the former's claim will not be asserted, hence it has been said that:[207]

> Sometimes laches is taken to mean undue delay on the part of the plaintiff in prosecuting his claim and no more. Sometimes acquiescence is used to mean laches in that sense. And sometimes laches is used to mean acquiescence in its proper sense, which involves a standing by so as to induce the other party to believe that the wrong is assented to. In that sense it has been observed that acquiescence can bear a close resemblance to promissory estoppel.

122 However, unlike laches, acquiescence is not conditional on the claimant's undue delay. All that needs to be shown is an express or implied representation on the claimant's part which might be fairly regarded as equivalent to a waiver of his rights or, though perhaps not waiving his rights, puts the other party in a situation in which it would not be reasonable to place him if the remedy were afterwards to be asserted.[208]

123 Laches and acquiescence can be invoked *firstly*, where the cause of action, although one in common law, on the facts is more appropriately remedied in equity (eg by specific performance, an injunction, or an account of profits – an equitable remedy, *inter alia*, for torts involving interference with intellectual

---

205 Emphasis added.

206 *Partridge v Partridge* [1894] 1 Ch 351, 360.

207 *Goldsworthy v Brickell* [1987] Ch 378, 410; per Nourse LJ.

208 *Lindsay Petroleum v Hurd* (1874) LR 5 PC 221, 239–240.

property rights). The doctrines have no application where statutory limitation periods apply, either expressly or analogously.[209] Thus, it can never bar a claimant's claim before the expiration of a prescribed black-letter period. It is relevant only as a bar to the equitable remedy being pursued. Indeed, sec 36(1) of the Limitation Act 1980 specifically provides that time limits under that Act – including the time limit under sec 2 for actions founded on tort and the time limit under sec 5 for actions founded on simple contract – 'shall not apply to any claim for specific performance of a contract or for an injunction or for other equitable relief [...]'. That said, for historical reasons, the court's discretion to apply limitation periods under the Limitation Act 1980 to cases in equity is preserved to some extent since the section goes on to add 'except in so far as any such time limit may be applied by the court by analogy in like manner [...]'. *Secondly*, the doctrine of laches and acquiescence can also be relied upon where the cause of action itself is in equity (eg breach of confidence (cf the new tort of misuse of private information which is rooted in breach of confidence), breach of fiduciary duty, etc). In the absence of a statutory limitation period, the issue before the courts is whether the claimant's action itself should be time-barred. While the 'equitable doctrines rest on the same basis as the law of limitation, that stale demands should not be enforced',[210] unlike the position under the Limitation Act 1980, where the period begins to run on the date on which the cause of action accrued or in some cases, if later, the date of knowledge of the facts giving rise to the cause of action, with laches and indeed acquiescence the period only begins to run from the date of knowledge of the entirety of the facts relevant to the claimant's rights. The editors of Chitty on Contracts note further that 'while statute ordinarily prescribes a fixed time limit which applies in general irrespective of the conduct of the parties, the equitable doctrines look primarily at the conduct of the claimant and its effect on the defendant or on third parties, so that the length of time which will bar the claim varies greatly in accordance with the circumstances and the type of relief sought.'[211]

The burden of asserting laches or acquiescence lies with the defendant. An extract from the judgment delivered by Lord Selborne in *Lindsay Petroleum v Hurd*[212] sets out the prerequisites of the application of both defences: 'Two circumstances, always important in such cases, are, the length of the delay and the nature of the acts done during the interval, which might affect either party and cause a balance of justice or injustice in taking the one course or the other, so far as relates to the remedy.' Each case is to be decided on its facts, 124

209 *Re Pauling's Settlement Trusts* [1963] 3 WLR 742.
210 Chitty on Contracts, General Principles (32nd ed, 2015), para 28–135.
211 Ibid.
212 *Lindsay Petroleum v Hurd* (1874) LR 5 PC 221, 239–240.

applying a broad approach, directed to ascertaining whether it would in all the circumstances be unconscionable for a party to be permitted to assert his beneficial right.[213]

## X. PARTIES AND CHANGE OF PARTIES

### A. STIPULATION AND WAIVER

125 While the Limitation Act 1980 itself is silent on the issue, parties may sensibly agree to the extension of time usually with a view to exploring the prospect of resolving their dispute (*supra* 75 and 99 ff).

126 As seen above, where a protective claim has been issued, the particulars of claim must be served within a four-month period (CPR r 7.4). CPR r 7.5 is more specific in stating that this must be done '[...] before 12 midnight on the calendar day 4 months after the date of issue of the claim form.' A problem may arise where attempts to settle a case fail and a party has failed to comply with the above rule. CPR r 7.6(2) allows for an extension of time for serving a claim form and limited circumstances for an extension after expiration of the four-month period exist under CPR r 7.6(3). A party that applies for an extension of time after the deadline but who does not qualify under CPR r 7.6(3) may seek relief from sanctions under CPR r 3.9.[214] In *Denton v White*[215] the court ruled that a judge should address an application for relief from sanctions in three stages. The Master of the Rolls and Vos LJ in their joint judgment determined that the first stage is to identify and assess the seriousness and significance of the 'failure to comply with any rule, practice direction or court order' which engages rule 3.9. If the breach is neither serious nor significant, the court is unlikely to need to spend much time on the second and third stages. The second stage is to consider why the default occurred. The third stage is to evaluate 'all the circumstances of the case, so as to enable [the court] to deal justly with the application [...]'.

127 In the case of standstill agreements, standard contract formalities apply: the agreement may be entered into orally but, in practice, the parties will usually insist on a formal written contract. Clear and unambiguous wording, or more

213 *Frawley v Neill* [2000] CP Rep 20 per Aldous LJ.

214 Paragraph 1 of which reads: 'On an application for relief from any sanction imposed for a failure to comply with any rule, practice direction or court order, the court will consider all the circumstances of the case, so as to enable it to deal justly with the application, including the need a) for litigation to be conducted efficiently and at proportionate cost; and to enforce compliance with rules, practice directions and orders.'

215 *Denton v White* [2014] EWCA Civ 906 at [24].

suitably precedent standstill agreements, should be used. In *Hyundai Marine & Fire Insurance & v Houlder Insurance Services*,[216] a question arose as to whether a standstill agreement can cover claims for unknown fraud. The court resorted to the old epithet that 'fraud unravels all' in concluding that on its proper construction the agreement simply had no application.

## B. CHANGE OF THE PARTIES

CPR r 19.1 states that any number of claimants or defendants may be joined as parties to a claim. This must be done in a timely fashion however since the effect of the provisions in sec 35 taken together is that while the parties may bring new claims or amend existing ones after the expiry of any time limit under the Limitation Act 1980, these shall be deemed to be a separate action and to have been commenced on the same date as the original action (sec 35(1)(a)). Exceptions are admitted under sec 35(4) ff which permits rules of court to provide for the addition or substitution of a new party if this is necessary for the determination of the original action. This will not be the case unless either the new party is substituted for a party whose name was given in any claim made in the original action in mistake or any claim already made in the original action cannot be maintained by or against an existing party unless the new party is joined or substituted as plaintiff or defendant in that action. CPR r 19.5 sets out special rules for the addition and substitution of parties after the end of a relevant limitation period. 128

In *Horne-Roberts v SmithKline Beecham Plc*,[217] where the claimant's solicitor made a mistake as to the name of the defendant vaccine manufacturer, it was held that substitution of the latter for the correct manufacturer, even after the ten-year long-stop limitation period had expired, was permissible within the meaning of sec 35(5)(b) and (6)(a) of the Limitation Act 1980 and CPR r 19.5(3)(a). The relevant enquiry was said to be whether the intended defendant could be identified by reference to a description which was more or less specific to the particular case. This requirement was satisfied since the claimant had intended to sue the manufacturer of a vaccine identified by reference to a batch number. It was not until *Declan O'Byrne v Aventis Pasteur MSD Ltd* that the question of whether the power under sec 35 of the Limitation Act 1980 was consistent with art 11 of the Product Liability Directive. In that case, the UK Supreme Court unanimously ruled that it was not open to the claimant to substitute a parent company, Aventis Pasteur SA, for its subsidiary, Aventis Pasteur MSD, after the expiry of the ten-year long-stop 129

[216] *Hyundai Marine & Fire Insurance & v Houlder Insurance Services* [2015] EWHC 378.

[217] *Horne-Roberts v SmithKline Beecham Plc* [2001] EWCA Civ 2006.

limitation period.[218] This was notwithstanding an ECJ ruling allowing the Supreme Court to hold that, in the proceedings instituted within the ten-year period against the wholly-owned subsidiary of the 'producer', that producer can be substituted for that subsidiary if that court finds that the putting into circulation of the product in question was, in fact, determined by that producer.[219] On the facts, the Supreme Court ruled that the fact that Aventis Pasteur MSD was a wholly-owned subsidiary was by no means decisive and that all the circumstances pointed to it being in a position to decide when the allegedly defective vaccine was to be distributed in the UK. The conclusion is that the above extinction is not watertight. It is also thought that the discretion applies in respect of the shorter three-year period.[220]

130 Cases by third parties against insurers under the Third Parties (Rights against Insurers) Act 1930 are also worth mentioning; sec 9 of the Limitation Act 1980 (time limit for actions for sums recoverable by statute) applies to such actions. In *Lefevre v White*,[221] on the bankruptcy of the insured driver, the claimant issued fresh proceedings against the insured's insurer claiming damages for personal injury suffered from a car accident. The limitation period having already elapsed, the court held that the claimant could not replace the insured in his initial action and that his only option was to commence fresh proceedings against the insurers. Unfortunately, he was time-barred from doing so in the eyes of the court.

## C. PLEADINGS BY THE PARTIES

### 1) *Pleading the Defence*

131 Paragraph 13.1 of Practice Direction 16 of the Civil Procedure Rules, on Statements of Case, states: 'The defendant must give details of the expiry of any relevant limitation period relied on.' The defence must therefore be pleaded so it is not open to a court to raise the matter *suo officio* where the latter does not elect to do so.[222] Depending on the specific details of the case, the defendant will be advised to either: (a) apply to have the claimant's

218 *Declan O'Byrne v Aventis Pasteur MSD Ltd* [2010] UKSC 23.

219 *Declan O'Byrne v Sanofi Pasteur MSD Ltd and Sanofi Pasteur SA* (C-127/04) [2006] 1 WLR 1606, 1622.

220 *A McGee*, Limitation Periods (2014), para 6.032, fn 65.

221 *Lefevre v White* [1990] 1 Lloyd's Rep 569. Cf *London Steamship Owners Mutual Insurance Association Ltd v Bombay Trading Co Ltd (The Felicie)* [1990] 2 Lloyd's Rep 21 (Note), where substitution was ordered.

222 *Kennett v Brown* [1988] 1 WLR 582.

statement of case struck out;[223] (b) raise the limitation issue as a preliminary one with a view to obtaining summary judgment[224] having filed an acknowledgement of service or a defence;[225] or (c) wait until full trial to raise the defence. A defendant may, however, agree with the claimant in a contract supported by consideration or by deed not to plead the statute (*supra* 75, 99 ff and 125 ff).[226]

*2) Burden of Proof*

If successfully pleaded, the burden then shifts to the claimant to prove that the action was brought within the prescribed time limit (*supra* 92). Since no other defence in civil law places the onus of proof on claimants, however, Burrows is of the view that 'the law has taken a wrong turn' here. This is supported, he continues, by the fact that the onus is on the defendant under the closely linked equitable doctrine of laches (*supra* 124).[227] 132

## XI. CONSIDERATIONS FOR REFORM

A focus of debate in recent years in the UK has been the rising number of claims for whiplash-related injury in road traffic accidents and concern has been expressed in particular about the rise in such claims notified *more than* 300 days after the date of the accident; these are said to have increased four-fold between 2011 and 2014 (from around 4% to 12%).[228] A specific issue for insurers is whiplash claims brought late in the limitation period. As one participant in the debate has put it, 'if you have not made a claim within two and a half years, with all the advertising and texting that goes on to say, "Why don't you make a claim?" something has gone wrong somewhere.'[229] 133

---

[223] See CPR r 3.4. See *A McGee*, Limitation Periods (2014), paras 21.001 ff.

[224] See CPR r 24.2: The court may give summary judgment against a claimant or defendant on the whole of a claim or on a particular issue if: (a) it considers that (i) that claimant has no real prospect of succeeding on the claim or issue; or (ii) that defendant has no real prospect of successfully defending the claim or issue; and (b) there is no other compelling reason why the case or issue should be disposed of at a trial.

[225] See CPR r 24.4. A court may exceptionally give permission to file for summary judgment before acknowledgement of service or a defence have been filed: CPR r 24.4.

[226] Chitty on Contracts, General Principles (32nd ed, 2015), para 28–109.

[227] *A Burrows*, Some Recurring Issues in Relation to Limitation of Actions, in: A Dyson, J Goudkamp and F Wilmot-Smith (eds), Defences in Tort (2015), 314 ff.

[228] *Frontier Economics*, Motor Insurance Compensation Systems with a Focus on Whiplash and Soft Tissue Injuries: A Report for Aviva (March 2015), 16.

[229] Nigel Teasdale of the Forum of Insurance Lawyers, in House of Commons Transport Committee, Cost of Motor Insurance: Whiplash, Fourth Report of Session 2013–14, Volume I. Available here: <http://www.publications.parliament.uk/pa/cm201314/cmselect/cmtran/117/117.pdf>.

However, while the NHS says that whiplash symptoms often take only six to 12 hours to develop, a small number of people do indeed experience delayed onset.[230] In 2013, the House of Commons Transport Committee recommended that the government explain the rationale for the three-year limitation period in the case of personal injury and bring forward recommendations for reducing it.[231] In response, the government said it had no plans to change the current long-standing period. Creating a specific road traffic personal injury limitation period would make the law more complex, 'increase the number of cases in the short term, and may front-load the expenses into a shorter period with potential cost implications for the courts and the parties. Changing the law in this way would also make claims for changes in other special cases harder to resist.'[232] Instead the government brought forward a package of measures announced in a consultation by the Ministry of Justice in November 2016 on Reforming the Soft Tissue Injury ('whiplash') Claims Process.[233] One of several measures referred to under the reform programme which purports to 'crack down on minor, exaggerated and fraudulent soft tissue injury ("whiplash") claims stemming from road traffic accidents' is the introduction of a new 'diagnosis' model. It was the government's view that mandating a medical examination at a specific time is likely to have a positive impact in tackling the issue of claims being brought at the end of the limitation period, often without medical evidence.[234]

---

230 See *A Morris and K Oliphant*, England and Wales, in: E Karner and BC Steininger (eds), European Tort Law 2013 (2014), 199, no 37 ff. See also See also *K Oliphant*, The Whiplash Capital of the World: Genealogy of a Compensation Myth, in: E Quill and R Friel (eds), Damages and Compensation Culture: Comparative Perspectives (2016).

231 *House of Commons Transport Committee*, The Cost of Motor Insurance, Fourth Report (HC 117, 2013), para 40.

232 *Ministry of Justice*, Reducing the Number and Costs of Whiplash Claims: A Government Response to Consultation on Arrangements Concerning Whiplash Injuries in England and Wales (Cm 8738, 2013), para 18.

233 Cm 9299.

234 Cm 9299, paras 46 and 51.

# PRESCRIPTION IN TORT LAW: FRANCE

Jean-Sébastien BORGHETTI

## I. INTRODUCTION

1 The French *code civil*, which was adopted in 1804 and marks the birth of modern French law, inherited the concept of prescription from Roman law and earlier French law. Prescription was the subject of title XX of the third book of the *code civil* (which deals mostly with the law of obligations, inheritance law and patrimonial relations within the family). Following the *jus commune*, prescription in the original *code civil* covered 'acquisitive' prescription (*prescription acquisitive* or *usucapion*) and 'extinctive' prescription (*prescription extinctive*).[1] As time went by, French rules on prescription grew more and more complex and the Code's provisions ceased to reflect adequately the state of the law on this issue. Quite apart from the fact that the bringing together of acquisitive and extinctive prescription was increasingly criticised,[2] a number of special (extinctive) prescription periods were created by the legislator, mostly outside the *code civil*, which resulted in an extraordinary variety of applicable prescription periods. Case law also developed a distinction, barely sketched in the Code, between 'real' prescription periods and 'foreclosure' (*forclusion*) periods, the main difference between the two being that the latter, unlike the former, cannot be suspended.

2 As a result of this complexity, and like in many other Western countries,[3] more and more lawyers called for a reform of the law of prescription at the end of the 20th century. It was initially thought that such reform would be part of a wider reform of the law of obligations, but, quite surprisingly, the French Parliament took the initiative to reform prescription law on a stand-alone basis in 2008, and not to wait for this wider reform. This has been achieved through loi no 2008-561 of 17 June 2008, which came into force immediately.

---

1 *Reinhard Zimmermann*, Verjährung, in: Jürgen Basedow, Klaus J Hopt and Reinhard Zimmermann, Handwörterbuch des Europäischen Privatrechts, Band 2 (2009), 1637.
2 *Zimmermann, supra* fn 1, 1637.
3 *Jean-Sébastien Borghetti*, Prescription, ZEuP 1/2016, 167.

This statute deals both with acquisitive and extinctive prescription but separates them more clearly than the Code formerly did. Both types of prescription are now the subject of two different titles in the *code civil* (title XX for extinctive prescription and title XXI for acquisitive prescription) and have only the name 'prescription' in common.[4] As far as extinctive prescription is concerned, the reform has tried to rationalise the law, by reducing the number of applicable periods, and has substantially reduced the length of the 'normal' prescription period, which has been brought down from 30 to five years. The simplification that was sought has only been partially achieved, though, and there are still many different prescription periods applicable, if only because most of the special periods mentioned in provisions outside the *code civil* have not been affected by the 2008 reform. 3

## II. DEFINITION OF PRESCRIPTION

Article 2219 *code civil* now defines extinctive prescription as 'a mode of extinction of a right that results from the inaction of its holder during a certain period of time'.[5] This definition is intended to be general, and therefore also applies in the context of tort law. Subject to what will be said in the next section about the nature of prescription, this definition can be regarded as a correct expression of the reality of French law. It can therefore be said that, in accordance with the conception that prevails in most Western legal systems, *prescription in tort law is a legal institution that prevents P from enforcing an alleged right against D because of the running of a specified period of time on the tort claim.* 4

## III. THE NATURE OF PRESCRIPTION AND ITS EFFECTS

The nature of prescription has long been a subject of debate in France. It is not yet fully settled whether prescription extinguishes the claimant's right (what French lawyers usually call the substantive approach), or if it simply creates a defence for the defendant (what French lawyers often call the procedural approach, even though this defence may be seen as having more to do with 5

4 Only two rules are now common to both types of prescription; see art 2259 *code civil*.

5 Article 2219: 'La prescription extinctive est un mode d'extinction d'un droit résultant de l'inaction de son titulaire pendant un certain laps de temps'. The English translation of the *code civil* articles is borrowed from Prof DW Gruning (with occasional amendments by the author of this contribution), whose English translation of the entire Civil Code is accessible on the French law official website Legifrance (<www.legifrance.gouv.fr>).

substantive law than procedure).[6] While above-mentioned art 2219 *code civil* and other provisions[7] clearly adopt the extinction approach, other provisions seem to follow the defence approach. This is especially the case of art 2224 *code civil*: 'Personal *actions* [emphasis added] or movable rights of action prescribe in five years from the day the holder of a right knew or should have known the facts enabling him to exercise his right'.[8]

6 It is generally considered, however, that the debate on the nature of prescription is mostly a theoretical one, since the two main issues on which it may have an impact are the subject of clear and well-established rules. The first question is whether a debtor who paid his debt after prescription had elapsed can claim restitution. The answer under French law has always been negative and this was confirmed in 2008 by art. 2249 *code civil*: 'A payment that has been made to extinguish a debt cannot be claimed back on the sole ground that the prescriptive period had run out'.[9] The second question is whether, from an international private law perspective, the law applicable to prescription is the same as the one applicable to the right at issue. French law traditionally offers an affirmative answer to this question, which has been confirmed in 2008 and can now be found at art 2221 *code civil*: 'Extinctive prescription is subjected to the statute governing the right that it affects'.[10] Both solutions suggest that French law in effect adheres to the (substantive) defence approach to prescription.[11]

---

6 French lawyers do not clearly distinguish between a procedural defence and substantive defence, both generally and in the context of prescription. One reason for this is probably that offset (*compensation*) is deemed to apply automatically in French law as soon as its conditions are met. Even though it can be described as a way of self-help, offset therefore does not require that the defendant takes an out-of-court initiative to happen.

7 See art 2221 *code civil*: 'La prescription extinctive est soumise à la loi régissant le droit qu'elle affecte' ('Extinctive prescription is subjected to the statute governing the right that it affects'); art 2227, 1st sentence: 'Le droit de propriété est imprescriptible' ('The right of ownership is imprescriptible'). The original *code civil* further presented extinctive prescription as a cause of extinction of obligations (former art 1234), thus apparently adhering to the extinction approach (even though it regulated extinctive prescription apart from the rest of the law of obligations). However, the recent reform of French contract and obligations law, which was adopted and entered into force in 2016, does not mention prescription among the extinction causes of obligations any more.

8 Article 2224: 'Les actions personnelles ou mobilières se prescrivent par cinq ans à compter du jour où le titulaire d'un droit a connu ou aurait dû connaître les faits lui permettant de l'exercer'. See also arts 2225, 2226 and 2226-1 *code civil*, which set specific delays of prescription for different kinds of *actions* (ie claims).

9 Article 2249: 'Le paiement effectué pour éteindre une dette ne peut être répété au seul motif que le délai de prescription était expiré'.

10 Article 2221: 'La prescription extinctive est soumise à la loi régissant le droit qu'elle affecte'.

11 'Long-stop mechanisms', as opposed to ordinary prescription delays, affect the substance of the right, at least in some cases; see eg art 1245-15 *code civil*; see *infra* 66 ff.

This never seems to have been criticised, as this approach appears as a good compromise, and less radical than the rather extreme extinction approach. It should be mentioned, however, that the solution whereby he who has paid a debt 'struck' by prescription cannot claim restitution for what he paid, is sometimes justified by the idea that prescription does not extinguish the substantive right it affects, but only the right of action, ie the possibility to bring a claim for performance. Another way to present this is to say that a debt struck by prescription becomes a natural obligation. 7

## IV. CONSIDERATIONS FOR AND AGAINST PRESCRIPTION OF TORT CLAIMS

Comparatively little attention is devoted by French lawyers to the pros and cons of prescription. The terse style of the decisions by the *Cour de cassation* (the French superior court in civil matters) further prevents that considerations on this issue be found in them. Besides, economic considerations play a small part in legal argumentation generally and are therefore not often put forward on the subject of prescription. Yet it is usually agreed that, though extinctive prescription has the obvious con of barring good claims, this con is more than counterbalanced by the addition of several considerations, such as: 8

- Late claims create social unrest, since they disturb well-established situations; *quieta non movere*, as the Latin dictum says.
- The passage of time increases the probability that what was owed has indeed been paid; and if it was not, prescription can be considered a sanction against the negligent creditor.
- A debtor should not be overburdened by old debts (this consideration is especially strong in the case of debts that accrue periodically, and therefore not so much in the context of tort law).

## V. ELEMENTS OF PRESCRIPTION – AN OVERVIEW

The original *code civil* rules on prescription dealt mostly with suspension and renewal and listed the various prescription periods applicable in different contexts. Rules on accrual were not made explicit and there was no ceiling on the effective time of prescription ('long-stop'). In the course of time, case law made clear what the starting point of the various prescription periods was, and it developed rules on accrual. 'Long-stop' periods, on the 9 other hand, were introduced quite late, sometimes as a result of European harmonisation.[12]

10 The 2008 reform marked a clear change in that respect. Like many other legal systems, French law now clearly recognises the four sets of rules that can be considered as composing prescription law: rules of accrual, prescription period, rules of prolongation, and ceiling. One chapter of the *code civil* now deals with rules of accrual and the prescription period (arts 2224–2227), while another one deals with the ceiling and the rules on prolongation (arts 2228–2246).

## VI. THE STARTING POINT OF THE PRESCRIPTION PERIOD

### A. THE MEANING OF 'ACTION' AND 'CAUSE OF ACTION'

11 French law does not really know the concept of cause of action, probably because it focuses on substantive law rather than procedure. It does distinguish, though, between the substantive right (*le droit*) and the right of action (*l'action*). The latter is dependent on the former. The right of action therefore cannot come into existence before the substantive right; but it may die out before the substantive right does, as is for example the case when the right of action becomes extinct due to prescription.

12 This intimate connection between the substantive right and the right of action means that, as far as prescription in tort law is concerned, the starting point of the prescription period depends first of all on the birth date of the substantive right to compensation. For such a right to exist, it is necessary that there is harm, a fact giving rise to liability (*fait générateur*, which is usually a tortious conduct, but not necessarily[13]), and a causal connection between these two first elements. Technically speaking, there can be no right to compensation, and thus no prescription, as long as harm has not occurred. The occurrence of *fait générateur*, which necessarily predates that of harm, if only for an instant, is therefore not sufficient to create a right to compensation, and thus to constitute the equivalent of a cause of action.[14] The *fait générateur*,

---

12 The best example is the 1985 European Directive on product liability, which sets a three-year prescription period as well as a ten-year long stop.

13 There are several strict liability regimes under French law, whereby a defendant may be made liable for harm caused by a thing, or by an accident, without regard to his or someone else's conduct.

14 The *fait générateur*, however, is enough to create a 'seed' of debt, which may be transferred by way of inheritance, so that the person who has inherited it may be made liable for the harm caused by this *fait générateur*, even if this harm occurs after the death of the person to whom this *fait générateur* should initially have been ascribed.

however, does have an impact on the right of action, since (1) the starting point of prescription normally depends on the victim's knowledge of all elements necessary to bring his claim, including the *fait générateur*, and (2) the applicable prescription period as well as the long-stop period may also depend on the basis of liability, ie on the *fait générateur*.

The right to compensation comes to life with the occurrence of harm, since it is the moment when the three conditions are met give birth to liability: *fait générateur*, harm and causation. The right of action cannot predate the right to compensation and both come to life simultaneously. It can happen, however, that the right of action cannot be exercised immediately, for example because the victim is not aware of its existence, or because of a legal or physical impossibility for him to bring a claim. This is the reason why the starting point of prescription is normally not the moment at which the right to compensation and the corresponding right of action came into existence, but the moment at which the victim, ie the creditor, became aware of the existence of his right. This rule is expressed at art 2224 *code civil*: 'Personal actions or movable rights of action prescribe in five years from the day the holder of a right knew or should have known the facts enabling him to exercise his right'.[15] This is confirmed in the case of a bodily injury by art 2226, 1st § *code civil*: 'An action in civil liability arising from an event that resulted in a personal injury, brought by the direct or indirect victim of the losses resulting from it, prescribes in ten years from the date of the consolidation of the initial or of the aggravated injury'.[16] Consolidation, in this context, is the moment at which the physical or psychological state of the claimant stabilises, after the disruption caused by the injury. 13

## B. BROAD OR NARROW CONCEPTION OF 'CAUSE OF ACTION'?

While the articulation of the substantive right to compensation, of the right of action and of the starting point of prescription is quite clear in theory, things get more complicated when several *faits générateurs* cause one same harm, or when one *fait générateur* causes distinct harms. 14

---

[15] Article 2224 *code civil*: 'Les actions personnelles ou mobilières se prescrivent par cinq ans à compter du jour où le titulaire d'un droit a connu ou aurait dû connaître les faits lui permettant de l'exercer'.

[16] Article 2226, 1st § *code civil*: 'L'action en responsabilité née à raison d'un événement ayant entraîné un dommage corporel, engagée par la victime directe ou indirecte des préjudices qui en résultent, se prescrit par dix ans à compter de la date de la consolidation du dommage initial ou aggravé.

15 In the first case (several *faits générateurs*), French law considers that the victim has one right to compensation, but with several debtors (unless all *faits générateurs* can be ascribed to the same person). Even though there is only one right to compensation the victim then has several rights of action: he has one against each debtor, and he may even have two or more rights of action against one same debtor if two or more *faits générateurs* of the harm are to be ascribed to the latter. Each one of these rights of actions may be subjected to different prescription rules, but their common basic element is the harm suffered, as there can be no right to compensation, and thus no right of action, as long as the harm has not occurred.

16 In the second case (several harms), even though the law is not totally explicit, it should be considered that the victim has a distinct right to compensation, and thus a distinct right of action, for each item of harm he suffers. One should even go one step further and consider that a victim has a distinct right to compensation for every *item of loss* resulting from the harm. As a matter of fact, French law increasingly distinguishes between the initial harm and the losses that result from it. It is normally those losses,[17] and not the harm itself, that must be compensated by the tortfeasor. As far as *res judicata* is concerned, it is well established that each item of loss gives rise to a separate cause of action,[18] and this solution must be considered as applying also to the determination of the starting point of prescription.

17 If one adopts the cause of action language, it can thus be said that French law adopts a narrow conception of cause of action, since each item of loss constitutes a distinct cause of action, regardless of its origin. This is illustrated by the cases that follows.

**Case 1** – *D, a ski instructor, negligently fails to make sure that all skiers in her 'off-piste' group wear helmets. P, a skier in the group, hits a tree. P immediately*

---

[17] See especially art 1235 of the Reform bill on civil liability, which makes the distinction explicit: 'Any certain loss is reparable where it results from harm and consists of an injury to a lawful interest, whether patrimonial or extra-patrimonial' ('Est réparable tout préjudice certain résultant d'un dommage et consistant en la lésion d'un intérêt licite, patrimonial ou extrapatrimonial'). The English version of the bill is borrowed from the translation by S Whittaker and JS Borghetti, available on the website of the French Ministry of Justice.

[18] See art 1262, paras 2–3 of the Reform bill on civil liability, which purports to confirm existing law: 'In the case of the worsening of the harm subsequent to judgment, the victim may claim supplementary compensation for the loss which results from it. In the case of personal injury, the victim can also claim a supplementary compensation for any pre-existing head of loss not included in the initial claim' ('En cas d'aggravation du dommage postérieurement au jugement, la victime peut demander un complément d'indemnité pour le préjudice qui en résulte. En cas de dommage corporel, elle peut également réclamer une indemnisation complémentaire pour tout chef de préjudice préexistant non inclus dans la demande initiale').

*suffers head injury X, and years later another head injury Y that developed from the same accident.*

Under French law, P undoubtedly has two distinct rights to compensation, and thus two distinct causes of actions, for head injury X (and the resulting losses) and head injury Y (and the resulting losses). This solution is undisputed and can be deduced from art 2226, 1st § *code civil*, which states that: 'An action in civil liability arising from an event that resulted in a personal injury, brought by the direct or indirect victim of the losses resulting from it, prescribes in ten years from the date of the consolidation of the initial or of the aggravated injury'. This provision speaks of the action in liability arising from an event that resulted in *a* personal injury, meaning that different personal injuries will lead to different actions, whose prescription period may start at different moments. 18

**Case 2** – *Physician D treats patient P negligently and performs three mistakes on the day of the treatment: A, B and C. Mistake A causes harm X after a year. Mistake B causes harm Y after two years. Mistakes A and C together cause harm Z after three years.*

Here again, the solution of the case is quite simple from a French law perspective. Each harm gives rise to a distinct right to compensation, and thus to a distinct cause of action. The prescription for each one of these causes of action will start running at the moment when the harm that underpins it stabilises, in accordance with art 2226, 1st § *code civil*. It should be noted that P can sue for Y regardless of whether he sued for X, and for Z regardless of whether he sued for X or Y. 19

**Case 3** – *Builder D lays down defective foundations for a building thereby creating the risk of future collapse. As a result, the value to the owner of the building (P) decreases (harm A). Two years later the foundation subsides and requires fixing paid by P (harm B). Three year later cracks appear in the building fixed by P (harm C). Four years later the building collapses (harm D).*

In French law, this case would be a contractual case, to be solved according to the general rules of contract law and the special rules that apply to building contracts in the *code civil*. Besides, the '*non-cumul*' rule, that forbids a claimant to rely on tort law when he has a claim in contract against the defendant, bars any claim in tort by P. 20

As far as harm A is concerned, the normal behaviour for P, if he is aware of the defective foundations when the building is completed, would be not to accept the building. If he does accept the building, despite his being aware of the defective foundations, he might be barred from seeking compensation for future losses caused by this defect. If he chooses to accept the building, however, he may probably reduce the price owed to the contractor in proportion of 21 the defect, in application of art 1223, 1st § *code civil*: 'Having given notice to perform, a creditor may accept an imperfect contractual performance and reduce the price proportionally'.[19]

22 Assuming that P is not barred from seeking compensation by his acceptance of the building, D is liable to P for harm B, ie the cost of fixing, in application of art 1792, 1st § *code civil*: 'Any builder of a work is liable as a matter of law to the owner or to the buyer of the work for the damages, even those resulting from a defect of the ground that compromises the stability of the building or that, by affecting it in one of its essential component parts or one of its complementary elements, that render it unsuitable for its purposes'.[20]

23 D is also liable to P for harm C and harm D under art 1792, 1st § *code civil*. The exact moment at which these harms appear may not be decisive, as, according to art 1792-4-1 *code civil*, a builder is relieved of liability or of warranty ten years from the date of acceptance of the works. The question is therefore whether the harm appeared before or after those ten years. The builder may be liable for a harm that appears more than ten years after the acceptance of the building if this harm is a consequence of another harm which the builder was asked to fix during the ten years of his warranty. In the present case, harms C and D might be considered as future consequences of the building's defect made manifest by harm B, so that P should be liable for them, even if they appear after the expiration of the ten-year warranty period.

## C. THE STARTING POINT – BREACH OF DUTY OR OCCURRENCE OF DAMAGE?

24 As has already been explained, the right to compensation comes to life with the occurrence of harm, since it is the moment when the three conditions

[19] Article 1223, 1st §: 'Le créancier peut, après mise en demeure, accepter une exécution imparfaite du contrat et solliciter une réduction proportionnelle du prix' (translation by J Cartwright, B Fauvarque-Cosson and S Whittaker). This provision, which sets a new rule, was introduced in French law by the contract law reform that came into force on 1 October 2016. It is not yet clear if it applies in the context of building contracts, which are regulated by specific provisions.

[20] Article 1792, 1st §: 'Tout constructeur d'un ouvrage est responsable de plein droit, envers le maître ou l'acquéreur de l'ouvrage, des dommages, même résultant d'un vice du sol, qui compromettent la solidité de l'ouvrage ou qui, l'affectant dans l'un de ses éléments constitutifs ou l'un de ses éléments d'équipement, le rendent impropre à sa destination'. It should be noted that, under French law, there may be a discussion on whether P is allowed to recover for costs which he incurred before seeking D's liability.

are met which give birth to liability: *fait générateur*, harm and causation. It is therefore clear that it is the occurrence of damage, and not the breach of duty (or any other *fait générateur*) that constitutes the starting point of the prescription period. This is illustrated by the following case.

**Case 4** – *D enters P's premises without P's permission, thereby committing a tort of trespass, but without causing damage. P can file a claim against D asking for the remedy of D's eviction but fails to do so. A year later D causes physical harm to P's premises. P files a claim to compensation for the loss.*

French law does not have an exact equivalent for the tort of trespass. The remedy of D's eviction is of course available under French law, but it is considered as pertaining to the law of property, and not to the law of torts. In the present case, the fact that P does not seek this remedy immediately would not bar him from seeking compensation for the loss caused by D's fault. The starting point of prescription for his right to damages would be the occurrence of the loss, and not D's fault, ie D's entering P's premises. 25

## D. WHAT IS CONSIDERED 'HARM' FOR PRESCRIPTION PURPOSES?

A difficulty is that there is no clear definition of harm in French law. The harm that is relevant for prescription purposes, ie the harm that kicks off prescription, will actually be defined differently depending on the context. Personal injury enjoys a privileged status in that respect, so as to make compensation easier for those who suffer it. 26

**Case 5** – *In an accidental event, D negligently caused an explosion that damaged P's ears. During the first two years P has to raise the volume to enjoy music. During the following three years P needs a hearing device. After a further five years P becomes deaf.*

This is a case of personal injury and, according to art 2226, 1st § *code civil*, the prescription of P's right of action starts to run as of the stabilisation of his harm. In the present case, stabilisation occurs at the soonest when P becomes deaf. Provided he sues within the prescription delay, he can ask compensation for any loss he suffered due to his ears being damaged, including 'temporary losses' suffered during the time in which his hearing capacity was declining. 27

**Case 6** – *Builder D lays down defective foundations for a bridge thereby creating the risk of future collapse if heavy rain falls. Two years later heavy rain indeed falls, and the collapse becomes only a matter of time, as indeed happens four years after the laying of foundations.*

28 This case is governed by the special rules applicable to building contracts (see Case 3). In this context, the question is whether the defect became manifest during the ten-year warranty period. If so, the builder is liable for any loss resulting from this defect, even if this loss happens after the end of the ten-year period.

## E. THE STARTING POINT (ACCRUAL) IN CONTINUOUS TORTS

29 Generally speaking, the concept of continuous tort has little relevance in the context of French tort law (as opposed to criminal law), and it is actually not used. This should come as no surprise, since it is the harm, and not the tortious conduct, which is decisive and determines the existence of a substantive right to compensation and of a cause of action.

**Case 7** – *Every week, during a month, D1 publishes a defamatory article on P1, each time in another newspaper and on a different topic. During the same period D2 publishes a defamatory article on P2, every second day, on the same topic and in the same newspaper.*

30 In French law, compensation for damage caused by defaming articles can only be sought on the basis of special criminal law provisions (law of 29 July 1881 on the freedom of the press), and subject to very strict procedural rules. Even if compensation claims can be brought before civil courts, it is criminal law rules that will determine if there are one or several causes of action. Unlike what normally happens in tort law, it is therefore not the harm that will determine the existence of a cause of action, but the existence of a criminal offence.

31 In the present case, the question therefore is whether the different articles constitute separate criminal offences. If D1 publishes several defaming articles on different topics, these articles should be considered as separate offences and a different action should be brought for each of them. On the other hand, the articles published by D2 would probably be considered as constituting one unique offence, which could give rise to one claim only.

**Case 8** – *D, a landowner, negligently exposes P, a neighbour, to unreasonable noise for three years. P's hearing is thereby weakened on a daily basis, gradually restricting P's ability to communicate and enjoy music.*

32 In this case, the harm suffered by P should be regarded as unique, and consists in the progressive weakening of his hearing capacity. Consequently, and in accordance with art 2226, 1st § *code civil*, there is only one cause of action, and prescription will start to run as of the stabilisation of P's state.

**Case 9** – *A waste management company digs bins of toxic content into the soil. Toxic substance leaks into the soil and ground water, causing an apparent* *damage to crops and expenditure on cleaning on a daily basis. After two years the bins are removed from the soil.*

Since this is not a case of bodily injury, the concept of stabilisation does not apply. Prescription will start to run as of the moment when the claimant 'knew or should have known the facts enabling him to exercise his right' (art 2224 *code civil*), ie as soon as the cause of the damage to the crops has been or should have been identified. If the claimant brings a claim before the removal of the bins, he may ask damages for harm that has not yet materialised, but will necessarily materialise in the future.[21] He may also demand the removal of the bins. 33

If the claimant brings a claim more than five years (the applicable prescription period) after he became aware of the initial harm and of its origin, he shall not be able to get damages for any harm that he suffered more than five years earlier. But he should be allowed to claim damages for any harm suffered since less than five years, ie for the toxic substance staining the crops and the resulting cleaning costs incurred during that period. The reason for this is that harm in this case can be considered as divisible. The daily staining of the crops constitutes a separate harm, and can thus be considered as a separate cause of action. 34

## F. IS THE LATE DISCOVERY RULE A RULE OF THE STARTING POINT (ACCRUAL) OR A RULE OF PROLONGATION?

The late discovery rule has been officialised in art 2224 *code civil*, which provides: 'Personal actions or movable rights of action prescribe in five years from the day the holder of a right knew or should have known the facts enabling him to exercise his right'. The rule is thus presented as pertaining to the starting point of prescription, and not as a rule of prolongation that postpones the running of the period after the starting point. 35

Before the 2008 reform, however, the starting point of prescription was considered as independent from the claimant's knowledge of his right, but prescription was postponed until he acquired this knowledge in application of the *contra non valentem non currit praescriptio* rule. It could thus be argued that art 2224 actually combines a rule on the starting point and a rule on prolongation. 36

[21] The problem, however, is that neither the claimant nor the judge may know at that date when the bins will be removed. But the judge may order the defendant to reimburse the claimant's cleaning costs as long as the pollution lasts.

37 The analysis one adopts has an impact on the burden of proof.[22] As a matter of fact, if the late discovery rule determines the starting point of the prescription period, then it should be for the defendant to prove that the claimant had knowledge of the facts enabling him to exercise his right more than five years before he brought his claim. On the other hand, if the rule has to do with postponement, then, if the claimant brings his claim more than five years after the birth of his right to compensation (ie after the appearance of the harm), it will be for him to prove that he was not time barred, because he acquired knowledge of all the necessary facts less than five years before the claim was initiated.

38 The question does not seem to have received much doctrinal attention, but at least one decision by the *Cour de cassation* can be cited, in which the Court implicitly adopted the postponement approach.[23] As this was a product liability case, it was not art 2224 *code civil* which was applicable, but art 1245-16, which also integrates the late discovery rule and provides that the action for reparation based on the special product liability provisions is subject to a prescription period of 'three years starting from the day on which the claimant knew or ought to have known of the harm, the defect and the identity of the producer.' In this decision, the Court said that it was for the claimant to prove that he had only had knowledge of the defect when the expert nominated by the court handed down his report, less than three years before the claim was brought. The *Cour de cassation* thus treated the late discovery as a prolongation rule, and not as a rule on the starting point. This, it is suggested, is the way it should be.

## VII. PRESCRIPTION PERIODS

39 The trend in France, as in other legal systems,[24] has been towards a shortening of the prescription periods. The 1804 *code civil* provided that the normal prescription period was 30 years (with several exceptions).[25] A 1985 statute set a shorter prescription period of ten years for tort law claims, without changing the general rule.[26] The 2008 reform has drastically shortened the normal prescription period, which has been reduced to five years.

22 The choice between these two approaches may also have an impact when the right to compensation was born before the 2008 reform came into force but the action was brought after that date, in which case the old and new rules on prescription must be combined.

23 Cass. civ. 1, 10 July 2013, n. 12-23499.

24 See *Borghetti*, *supra* fn 3, 167–182.

25 Former art 2262 *code civil*.

26 Former art 2270-1 *code civil*.

This shortening has come along with an official endorsement of the late discovery rule. This should come as no surprise, since it is the late discovery rule that makes the five-year period acceptable and limits the risk that a claimant should be time-barred even before he became aware of his right.

This five-year period applies to all types of claims, including tort and contract claims. However, there are still many special prescription periods in French law, some longer and some shorter than the normal period. But these do not apply to general areas of law, such as contracts, torts,[27] or unjust enrichment. Their field of application is generally narrower, and concerns only a certain type of contracts, or a certain tort. For example, liability actions arising out of building contracts are subjected to specific prescription periods (two or ten years, depending on the type of harm). Other examples of specific prescription periods include claims arising out of transportation contracts (art L 133-6, 1st § *code de commerce*; one year),[28] claims arising out of insurance contracts (art L 114-1, 1st and 2nd §§ *code des assurances*; two years);[29] claims for the compensation of bodily injuries (art 2226, 1st § *code civil*; ten years); product liability claims (art 1245-16 *code civil*; three years);[30] medical liability claims (art L 1142-28 *code de la santé publique*; ten years; depending on the circumstances, these claims can be in contract or in tort);[31] claims for the compensation of environmental damage (art L 152-1 *code de l'environnement*; 30 years);[32] claims for the compensation of damage 40

---

27 Between 1985 and 2008, however, tort claims were subjected to a specific ten-year prescription period.

28 Article L 133-6, 1st § *code de commerce*: 'Les actions pour avaries, pertes ou retards, auxquelles peut donner lieu contre le voiturier le contrat de transport, sont prescrites dans le délai d'un an, sans préjudice des cas de fraude ou d'infidélité'.

29 Article L 114-1, 1st and 2nd §§ *code des assurances*: 'Toutes actions dérivant d'un contrat d'assurance sont prescrites par deux ans à compter de l'événement qui y donne naissance. Toutefois, ce délai ne court:

1°En cas de réticence, omission, déclaration fausse ou inexacte sur le risque couru, que du jour où l'assureur en a eu connaissance;
2°En cas de sinistre, que du jour où les intéressés en ont eu connaissance, s'ils prouvent qu'ils l'ont ignoré jusque-là'.

30 Article 1245-16 *code civil*: 'L'action en réparation fondée sur les dispositions du présent chapitre se prescrit dans un délai de trois ans à compter de la date à laquelle le demandeur a eu ou aurait dû avoir connaissance du dommage, du défaut et de l'identité du producteur'.

31 Article L 1142-28, 1st § *code de la santé publique*: 'Les actions tendant à mettre en cause la responsabilité des professionnels de santé ou des établissements de santé publics ou privés à l'occasion d'actes de prévention, de diagnostic ou de soins et les demandes d'indemnisation formées devant l'Office national d'indemnisation des accidents médicaux, des affections iatrogènes et des infections nosocomiales en application du II de l'article L. 1142-1 et des articles L. 1142-24-9, L. 1221-14, L. 3111-9, L. 3122-1 et L. 3131-4 se prescrivent par dix ans à compter de la consolidation du dommage'.

32 Article L 152-1 *code de l'environnement*: 'Les obligations financières liées à la réparation des dommages causés à l'environnement par les installations, travaux, ouvrages et activités

caused by nuclear accidents (art 8 Paris convention; ten years).[33] A very special rule applies to claims based on defamation, intended to protect freedom of speech; they prescribe in three months (art 65 of the law of 29 July 1881 on the freedom of the press). Besides, judgments prescribe in ten years (art L 111-4 of the *code des procédures civiles d'exécution*).[34]

41 Despite this diversity of prescription periods, there is no significant problem of 'period shopping' in French law today, at least as far as tort claims are concerned. The '*non-cumul*' rule[35] prevents the risk of period shopping between contract and tort. When the prescription period was significantly different in tort and in contract,[36] the issue of whether a claim was in tort or in contract could be decisive, and this fuelled litigation as to the boundaries between liability in tort and liability in contract, but this is not the case anymore.

42 There are furthermore some cases where the existence of fault or gross negligence allows a claimant to rely on the normal prescription period, instead of a specific prescription period that would otherwise apply. This is the case, for example, in product liability, or in the field of building contracts (which belongs to contractual liability, in the French context). As far as product liability is concerned, however, this possibility does not seem to have resulted so far in a lot of period shopping, with claimants trying to rely on the existence of negligence by the producer, and not simply on the product's defect.

43 If one leaves aside the specific prescription periods set by international texts (product liability and nuclear accidents), these various periods express the French legislator's intention to mark the importance of certain interests (bodily integrity, the environment), which it believes deserve greater protection than others, or the special protection it wants to offer to some victims (children, in the case of compensation claims for harm caused by abuse against them). The extremely short period applicable to defamation claims also illustrates the value that the legislator attaches to freedom of speech.

---

régis par le présent code se prescrivent par trente ans à compter du fait générateur du dommage'.

33 Article 8, a, 1st sentence of the Convention on Third Party Liability in the Field of Nuclear Energy of 29th July 1960, as amended by the Additional Protocol of 28th January 1964 and by the Protocol of 16th November 1982: 'The right of compensation under this Convention shall be extinguished if an action is not brought within ten years from the date of the nuclear incident'.

34 Article L 111-4, 1st §, *code des procédures civiles d'exécution*: 'L'exécution des titres exécutoires mentionnés aux 1° à 3° de l'article L. 111-3 ne peut être poursuivie que pendant dix ans, sauf si les actions en recouvrement des créances qui y sont constatées se prescrivent par un délai plus long'.

35 See *supra* 20.

36 See *infra* 39.

Below is a table indicating the prescription periods for the main types of civil liability claims. 44

**Table 1. Main prescription periods**

| Cause of action | Discovery | Prescription period | Note |
|---|---|---|---|
| General rule (art 2224 *code civil*) | Yes | 5 years | |
| Personal injury (art 2226, 1st § *code civil*) | No | 10 years | Starting point: stabilisation of the personal injury |
| Medical liability (art L 1142-28, 1st § *code de la santé publique*) | No | 10 years | Starting point: stabilisation of the personal injury |
| Product liability (art 1245-16 *code civil*) | Yes | 3 years | |
| Environmental damage (art L 152-1 *code de l'environnement*) | No | 30 years | |
| Nuclear accidents (art 8 Paris convention) | No | 10 years | |
| Defamation (art 65 law 29 July 1881) | No | 3 months | |
| Harm caused by torture or acts of barbarism, or by violence or sexual aggression committed against a minor (art 2226, 2nd § *code civil*) | Unclear | 20 years | |
| Contribution claims | | 5 years | |

# VIII. RULES OF POSTPONEMENT, SUSPENSION, RENEWAL AND EXTENSION

## A. UNAWARENESS – THE LATE DISCOVERY RULE

Article 2224 *code civil* provides: 'Personal actions or movable rights of action prescribe in five years from the day the holder of a right knew or should have known the facts enabling him to exercise his right'. What the facts are which enable the claimant to exercise his rights in the context of tort law claims is not made explicit, but there is little doubt that they include the basic conditions of tort under French law: harm, a fact giving rise to liability (*fait générateur*),[37] and a causal relationship between these two elements. In the context of tort law, knowledge of a fourth fact is also necessary: the 45

[37] See *supra* 12.

identity of the person to which the *fait générateur* must be ascribed, ie of the tortfeasor.

46 As far as the nature of awareness is concerned, art 2224 *code civil* makes it clear that ignorance of the facts enabling the claimant to exercise his right is an objective justification, since it is the time at which the claimant knew *or should have known* the facts enabling him to exercise his right that is decisive.

47 On the other hand, actual knowledge of the legal rule enabling compensation is not to be taken into account. This is suggested by the formulation of art 2224, which mentions the *facts* (and not the *rules*) that enable the claimant to exercise his right. Besides, French law generally applies (albeit with some exceptions) the rule whereby citizens are presumed to know the law and cannot put forward their ignorance of it as an excuse or a defence.

**Case 10** – *Chemical plant D negligently exposes bordering lands to toxic substances. As a result, P, a nearby resident landowner, contracts a lung disease. P failed to sue in time because his former lawyer told him that the exposure was not tortious, and only his new lawyer told him, after the running of time, that it was tortious.*

48 In this case, the erroneous statement by the lawyer should have no impact on the starting point of the prescription period (which would be the stabilisation of P's personal injury). On the other hand, if this erroneous statement results in P's being time-barred to claim compensation for his personal injury (which is unlikely, given that he has ten years to do so as of the stabilisation of his harm: art 2226, 1st § *code civil*), P will have a claim against the first lawyer based on professional negligence.

49 As is made clear from the table above, the late discovery rule does not apply to all tort law claims. Quite to the contrary, all special prescription periods, except the one applicable to product liability claims, have a starting point that is independent from the victim's awareness of the elements necessary to exercise his right. But all these periods are significantly longer than the normal prescription period (they range from ten to 30 years),[38] so that the non-applicability of the late discovery rule is not so problematic. Besides, in cases of personal injury or medical liability, the fact that the prescription starts only with the stabilisation of the harm means that, for many serious injuries or diseases, claims are in fact imprescriptible.

50 The rule according to which prescription starts to run when the personal injury stabilises could also be analysed as a late discovery rule, in the sense that prescription is postponed as long as the victim is not fully aware of the

---

[38] Except the three-month prescription period applicable to defamation claims, which is precisely intended to hinder such claims.

size of his harm. Yet, once the harm has stabilised, prescription starts to run, regardless of whether the victim is aware of the other elements needed to exercise his right.

When the 'real' late discovery rule applies, it is not clear exactly what degree 51 of knowledge is required from the victim for prescription to start running. What is quite sure, however, is that prescription will not be postponed until the victim is *certain* of the existence of a *fait générateur*, of causation between this fact and his harm, and of the identity of the tortfeasor. It is suggested that prescription should start to run when the victim has good reasons to suspect that his harm was caused by a *fait générateur*, and when he has identified a possible *fait générateur* and the defendant who should answer for it. As far as harm is concerned, it is sufficient that the victim is aware that he has suffered some harm, even if the full extent of it is not yet known.[39]

Very often, the victim will acquire knowledge of the elements necessary to his 52 claim through a preliminary inquiry ordered by a judge before the formal claim is filed, in application of art 145 *code of civil procedure*, which provides: 'If there is a legitimate reason to preserve or to establish, before any legal process, the evidence of the facts upon which the resolution of the dispute depends, legally permissible preparatory inquiries may be ordered at the request of any interested party, by way of a petition or by way of a summary procedure'. In a couple of cases, the *Cour de cassation* has even accepted the view that the victim had acquired knowledge of the *fait générateur* or of causation through an expertise ordered by the judge after the formal claim had been filed.[40] This solution in effect makes the claim immune to prescription and should therefore not be generalised.

Even though this is not made explicit in the provisions (arts 2224 and 1245-16 53 *code civil*) acknowledging the late discovery rule, it is quite clear that this rule is only a postponement rule, and not a suspension one. Therefore, if a claim, whose prescription has started to run, is transmitted to a new creditor, who is unaware of its existence or of the elements of it, the latter will not be allowed to rely on the late discovery rule. He may be able to rely on art 2234 *code civil*, however. Prescription will thus be suspended if the reasons why the claimant was not aware of the claim amount to *force majeure*.

**Case 11** – *Chemical plant D negligently exposes bordering lands to toxic substances. As a result, P, a nearby resident landowner, contracts a lung disease, but is unaware of the causal link between exposure and disease because his physician fails to*

39 Things are of course different when the harm consists in a personal injury and art 2226, 1st § *code civil* applies.

40 See *supra* fn 23; Cass. civ. 1, 27 November 2019, n. 18-16537.

*detect it. P does not seek a second opinion. After the prescription period runs on the disease P consults his new physician that tells him about the link. Did P's claim against D prescribe?*

54 As this is a personal injury case, the late discovery rule embedded in art 2224 *code civil* does not apply. It is art 2226, 1st § *code civil*, that applies, and prescription will start to run as of the stabilisation of the harm. In the case of a lung disease, this stabilisation often never happens, and prescription is therefore not a problem. In the exceptional case where the lung disease would stabilise and P would bring his claim more than ten years after this stabilisation, he could try to rely on art 2234 *code civil*, which provides that 'prescription does not run or is suspended against one for whom it is impossible to act following an obstacle resulting from the law, from an agreement, or from force majeure'.[41] The question would then be if the failure of the first physician to detect the causal link amounts to *force majeure* for P. In theory, *force majeure* and the absence of negligence are two distinct standards, the former being stricter than the latter. In practice, however, the courts often regard the two as similar. The answer to the question might therefore depend on whether the fact that P did not seek a second opinion meets the reasonable man standard. If it does, then it could be considered that P was prevented by *force majeure* from becoming aware of the link between the exposure and his disease, and that prescription was thus suspended until the new physician told him about the causal link. If it does not, then P should have sought a second opinion which would presumably have made him aware of the causal link, thus enabling him to bring his claim.

## B. OTHER RULES OF PROLONGATION

### 1) *D is to Blame for the Delay*

55 There is no explicit rule in French law that directly addresses the hypothesis in which it is the defendant who is to blame for the delay with which the claimant brings the claim, because he has misled or threatened the claimant, for example.[42] In cases where the late discovery rule applies, however, the defendant's conduct will postpone the starting point of the prescription, at least when it has prevented the claimant from becoming aware of the elements necessary to exercise his right. Quite independently from the late discovery

---

41 Article 2234 *code civil*: 'La prescription ne court pas ou est suspendue contre celui qui est dans l'impossibilité d'agir par suite d'un empêchement résultant de la loi, de la convention ou de la force majeure'.

42 See however *infra* 70.

rule, art 2234 *code civil* sets a general rule whereby 'prescription does not run or is suspended against one for whom it is impossible to act following an obstacle resulting from the law, from an agreement, or from force majeure'.

### 2) *Admission by D of P's Right or Partial Performance of P's Right by D*

Article 2240 *code civil* sets out that 'the acknowledgement by the debtor of the right of the person against whom he was prescribing interrupts the period of prescription'. This acknowledgement can come under different guises. It can of course consist in a formal agreement between the parties, but it can also be a unilateral declaration by the debtor. It has always been accepted that partial performance of the debt is also a form of acknowledgement. Acknowledgement by the debtor interrupts the prescription period, ie entails a renewal of the period. 56

### 3) *Special Relations between D and P*

There is only one case in which the *code civil* provides that the existence of a special relationship between the debtor and the creditor leads to prescription being postponed or suspended. Article 2236 provides that prescription 'does not run or is suspended between spouses as well as between partners bound by a civil pact of solidarity [registered partnership]'. 57

The existence of a special relationship may however have an impact in other circumstances. First of all, a relationship may lead to a moral impossibility for the creditor to bring his claim, in which case prescription may be suspended for *force majeure*, pursuant to art 2234 *code civil*. Besides, art 2235 *code civil* provides that, except for certain types of debts (which have nothing to do with tort law), prescription 'does not run or is suspended against unemancipated minors or adults in tutorship'.[43] The result of this is that prescription cannot run between an unemancipated minor (creditor) and his parents (debtors), or between an adult in tutorship (creditor) and his ward (debtor). 58

---

[43] Article 2235 *code civil*: 'It does not run or is suspended against unemancipated minors or adults in tutorship, except for actions for payment or recovery of salaries, annuity instalments, alimony payments, rents, sharecropping payments, rental expenses, interest on loans, and generally any action for payment of sums payable by the year or on shorter periodic terms' ('Elle ne court pas ou est suspendue contre les mineurs non émancipés et les majeurs en tutelle, sauf pour les actions en paiement ou en répétition des salaires, arrérages de rente, pensions alimentaires, loyers, fermages, charges locatives, intérêts des sommes prêtées et, généralement, les actions en paiement de tout ce qui est payable par années ou à des termes périodiques plus courts').

### *4) P's Lack of Legal Capacity*

59 Disability as such is not a cause of postponement or suspension of prescription, but art 2235 *code civil* provides: '[Prescription] does not run or is suspended against unemancipated minors or adults in tutorship, except for actions for payment or recovery of salaries, annuity instalments, alimony payments, rents, sharecropping payments, rental expenses, interest on loans, and generally any action for payment of sums payable by the year or on shorter periodic terms'. Unemancipated minors or adults in tutorship (who are normally under this status due to their limited or reduced intellectual faculties) therefore enjoy a suspension or postponement of prescription as long as they remain under this special status, even though they always have a legal representative.

60 In the case where a creditor suffers from a disability, but is not in tutorship, prescription may nevertheless be suspended or postponed if this disability amounts to *force majeure* and makes it impossible for him to exercise his right (art 2234 *code civil*).

### *5) Absence of Parties from the Jurisdiction*

61 The creditor's physical absence from the jurisdiction is not a specific cause of postponement or suspension of prescription but can lead to that result if it creates an obstacle to claiming that amounts to *force majeure* (art 2234 *code civil*).

### *6) Former Legal or Other Proceedings between the Parties*

62 Article 2241 *code civil* provides: 'Judicial demand, even by way of summary proceedings, interrupts the delay of prescription and the delay of foreclosure. The same occurs when the demand is brought before a court without jurisdiction when the act of referral to the court is annulled on account of a procedural defect'.[44] Proceedings between the parties that have not resulted in *res judicata* therefore lead to a renewal of the prescription period, with the new delay starting to run as of the end of these proceedings (art 2242 *code civil*).[45]

---

[44] Article 2241 *code civil*: 'La demande en justice, même en référé, interrompt le délai de prescription ainsi que le délai de forclusion. Il en est de même lorsqu'elle est portée devant une juridiction incompétente ou lorsque l'acte de saisine de la juridiction est annulé par l'effet d'un vice de procédure'.

[45] Article 2242 *code civil*: 'The interruption resulting from the judicial demand has continuous effect until the proceedings terminate' ('L'interruption résultant de la demande en justice produit ses effets jusqu'à l'extinction de l'instance').

French law also offers the possibility to ask a judge to grant preliminary measures of inquiry.[46] In such a case, art 2239 *code civil* provides: 'Prescription is also suspended when the judge grants a measure of inquiry before any proceedings begin. The prescriptive period begins to run again, for a duration that cannot be inferior to six months, beginning from the day this measure has been carried out'. 63

Finally, art 2238 *code civil* provides: 'Prescription is suspended from the day when, after a dispute arises, the parties agree to proceed to mediation or conciliation, or, if there is no written agreement, from the day of the first meeting of the mediation or conciliation. Prescription is also suspended from the moment of the conclusion of an agreement to engage in a participatory procedure. The prescriptive period begins to run again, for a duration that cannot be inferior to six months, from the date on which either one of the parties or both, or the mediator or the conciliator, declares that the mediation or conciliation has ended. In case of a participatory procedure agreement, the prescriptive period begins to run again from the term provided in that agreement, for a duration that cannot be inferior to six months'.[47] 64

### 7) *Other Contingencies*

French law does not provide for any specific cause of postponement or suspension in relation with the victim's death or bankruptcy. Neither are closed courts, or evidential or financial difficulties, specific causes of postponement or suspension. But art 2234 *code civil* provides for a general cause of postponement or suspension, that may cover such hypotheses: 'Prescription does not run or is suspended against one for whom it is impossible to act following an obstacle resulting from the law, from an agreement, or from force majeure'. 65

---

46 See *supra* 52.

47 Article 2238: 'La prescription est suspendue à compter du jour où, après la survenance d'un litige, les parties conviennent de recourir à la médiation ou à la conciliation ou, à défaut d'accord écrit, à compter du jour de la première réunion de médiation ou de conciliation. La prescription est également suspendue à compter de la conclusion d'une convention de procédure participative. Le délai de prescription recommence à courir, pour une durée qui ne peut être inférieure à six mois, à compter de la date à laquelle soit l'une des parties ou les deux, soit le médiateur ou le conciliateur déclarent que la médiation ou la conciliation est terminée. En cas de convention de procédure participative, le délai de prescription recommence à courir à compter du terme de la convention, pour une durée qui ne peut être inférieure à six mois'.

## IX. CEILINGS ON THE EFFECTIVE TIME OF PRESCRIPTION

66 The 2008 reform of prescription has introduced a general 20-year ceiling period. Article 2232, 1st § *code civil* now provides: 'The deferral of the starting point, the suspension or the interruption of the prescription cannot have the effect of extending the period of the extinctive prescription beyond twenty years from the day of the birth of the right'.[48] However, according to the 2nd § of art 2232, this ceiling period does not apply to certain claims, especially compensation claims for bodily injuries (subjected to a special ten-year prescription period; art 2226, 1st § *code civil*), claims for harm caused by torture or acts of barbarism, or by violence or sexual aggression committed against a minor (subjected to a special 20-year prescription period; art 2226, 2nd § *code civil*). Besides, it is unclear whether this 20-year ceiling should apply to claims subjected to special prescription rules introduced before the 2008 reform and which are to be found in statutes outside the *code civil*.

67 In the context of tort law claims, the birth of the right, which constitutes the starting point of the 20-year delay, normally corresponds to the occurrence of harm. When harm increases over time, or when there is a time-discrepancy between the occurrence of harm and the occurrence of the resulting losses for the claimant, the determination of the exact starting point may be problematic. There is no case law on this issue so far, however.

68 Rules of prolongation normally do not affect the ceiling. However, art 2232, 2nd §, provides that the postponement or suspension of prescription between spouses (art 2236 *code civil*) occurs regardless of the ceiling, as does the renewal of prescription resulting from the initiation of litigation (art 2241, 1st § *code civil*), and the renewal of prescription resulting from a conservative measure taken in application of the code of civil enforcement procedures or of an act of forced execution (art 2244 *code civil*).

69 There is also a special ten-year ceiling applying to product liability claims, in accordance with the 1985 Directive.[49] This special ceiling is not affected by any prolongation rule, except the initiation of litigation.

---

[48] Article 2232, 1st §: 'Le report du point de départ, la suspension ou l'interruption de la prescription ne peut avoir pour effet de porter le délai de la prescription extinctive au-delà de vingt ans à compter du jour de la naissance du droit'.

[49] Article 1245-15 *code civil*, implementing art 11 of the Directive.

# X. STATUTE INTERPRETATION, JUDICIAL DISCRETION AND LACHES

French law does not explicitly allow judicial discretion on a case-by-case basis to accept or reject the prescription defence in tort claims. However, even though case law on this is rather scarce, it is generally accepted that fraud or abuse of right on the part of the defendant may allow the judge to dismiss the defence based on prescription. Besides, and even though legislative provisions on prescription are not as open-ended as other provisions of the *code civil*, terms such as 'should have known the facts' (art 2224 *code civil*), or 'impossible', or '*force majeure*' (art 2234 *code civil*), grant the courts a fair amount of discretion. 70

On a more general level, it is difficult to say if French judges are rather hostile, neutral or sympathetic to prescription. What can be said, though, is that French courts are usually quite claimant-friendly when the claimant is the victim of a bodily injury or when there is significant imbalance between the economic and social weight of the parties, in favour of the defendant. In such cases, courts might be more willing to interpret prescription rules in a way favourable to the claimant. Generally speaking, however, courts do not appear to regard as unethical the rejection of a claim on the basis of the rules of prescription. 71

French law does not have a laches doctrine or an equivalent for it in the field of tort law. Recently, however, the *Cour de cassation* ruled that the application of the normal prescription period could entail a violation of the right to respect for private life (art 8 of the European Convention on Human Rights), in a case where a grown-up man wanted to challenge his legally established filiation.[50] This type of reasoning – setting aside prescription when its application would violate a basic right – could eventually be applied in the field of tort law, even if French case law does not offer any example of it so far.[51] 72

# XI. CHANGE OF PARTIES

## A. THE PLAINTIFF IS A TRANSFEREE OF THE VICTIM'S CLAIM

In French law, change of parties, whatever the cause, is not regarded as creating a new cause of action and the running of the prescription period is not normally affected by it. A change of creditor (by inheritance or subrogation, 73

[50] Cass. civ. 1, 21 November 2018, n. 17-21095.

[51] But this reasoning has already been applied by the European Court of Human Rights to tort claims: see esp. *Howald Moor v Switzerland*, ECHR 069 (2014).

for example) therefore does not affect prescription. But the transferee of a right to compensation can rely on postponement or suspension causes that are specific to him, such as *force majeure* (art 2234 *code civil*) or tutorship (art 2235 *code civil*).

**Case** – *V's right against D is subrogated to insurer P that compensated V under the insurance policy for harm caused by D. Does the running of time on P's subrogation claim start afresh when P acquires the right of subrogation, or does the running on V's claim continue on P's claim?*

74 In French law, subrogation has the effect that the right of the new creditor is exactly the same right as the one of the initial creditor. Article 1346-4, 1st § *code civil* provides: 'Subrogation transfers to its beneficiary, up to the limit of the satisfaction which he has rendered, the right arising from the obligation and its ancillary rights, apart from rights which belong exclusively to the creditor personally'. As a result, the running on V's claim will continue on P's claim.[52]

**Case** – *V dies and his rights against D are transmitted by the law of inheritance to P. When V died, only one month remained of the prescription period. P sues after two months but argues, alternatively, that: a) when V died a new count of the prescription period starts afresh for P; b) That even if the running of time continues it is postponed by rules of prolongation because P was unaware of the claim against D (V was aware) or because P suffers from mental disability (V did not).*

75 P is regarded under French law as the continuator of V. As a result, his claim against D is exactly that of V and remains subject to the same prescription period. However, if P could not (reasonably) be aware of V's claim during the first month after V's death, he can rely on art 2234 *code civil*, which provides that prescription is suspended against one for whom it is impossible to act following an obstacle resulting from *force majeure*. Besides, if P suffers from mental disability, prescription will be suspended against him, on the basis of either art 2235 or art 2234 (*force majeure*) *code civil*, depending on whether he is in tutorship or not.

## B. THE DEFENDANT IS A TRANSFEREE OF THE TORTFEASOR'S OBLIGATION

76 Like a creditor's change, a debtor's change (usually as a result of the initial debtor's death and subsequent inheritance) has no impact on the course

52 While the applicable legislative provisions clearly lead to this solution, case law can be more ambiguous: see *Julie Klein*, Le Point de départ de la prescription (2013), n. 334.

of prescription. Besides, the various rules of prolongation are normally independent from the defendant's state or status, which means that, for example, the mental disability of the transferee has no impact on the prescription of the debt.

## C. CONTRIBUTION CLAIMS

77 When there are joint tortfeasors, these are jointly and severally liable to the victim (*responsabilité solidaire ou in solidum*). When a tortfeasor has compensated the victim, he may claim contribution from the other tortfeasors, subject to the rules on contribution. If this is the case, the first tortfeasor may actually rely on two different legal bases.

78 The first one is subrogation. In application of art 1346 *code civil*, the first tortfeasor is automatically subrogated in the right of the victim: 'Subrogation takes place by the sole operation of law in favour of a person with a legitimate interest in it who satisfies a debt provided that his satisfaction discharges as against the creditor another person who is subject to the final burden in respect of all or part of a debt'. If the first tortfeasor relies on this subrogation, his claim will be a derivative one and subject to the same prescription that applied to the victim's claim.

79 But the first tortfeasor also has an independent claim against the other tortfeasors, that is not explicitly mentioned by the *code civil*, but whose existence has never been disputed. Whatever the prescription period applicable to the victim's claim, this independent contribution claim is subjected to the ordinary prescription period, ie five years (art 2224 *code civil*). It starts to run as of the payment made by the first tortfeasor to the victim.

**Case** – *P and D are jointly and severely tortfeasors vis-à-vis V. A month before the prescription period on V's claims against P and D expire, P compensates V. Two months later P sues D for contribution. P argues that the running of the prescription period on her claim starts only with the payment to V. D argues that P's contribution claim substitutes V's claim for prescription purposes and is therefore prescribed. What would the court decide in your jurisdiction?*

80 As explained above, in French law, P has two claims against D: one based on subrogation in V's right; and another, independent one, based on the fact that P and D are jointly and severally liable to V. Whilst the first claim prescribes exactly as it would have if it had been brought by V, the second one must be regarded as a distinct claim, whose prescription starts to run at the moment when V sued P for compensation (as P could then immediately bring D into the case).

81 Note that if P's payment to V was made after V sued P before the courts, then the initiation of the procedure by V interrupted prescription against P, and possibly against D. It is not totally clear, though, if the interruption of prescription against one among several tortfeasors held jointly and severally also has effect as against the others.[53]

## D. DEPENDANTS' CLAIMS

82 No special rule applies under French law to claims brought by dependants of the initial victim. As far as prescription is concerned, dependants' claims are independent from the initial victim's claim and may therefore be subject to different prescription delays or rules. In practice, however, dependants' claims always arise as a result of the initial victim having suffered a personal injury. The rule of art 2226, 1st § *code civil* therefore applies, whereby: 'An action in civil liability arising from an event that resulted in personal injury, brought by the direct or indirect victim of the harm, prescribes in ten years from the date of the consolidation of the initial or of the aggravated injury'. A dependant's claim will therefore be subject to a ten-year prescription period, that starts to run as of the stabilisation of the initial victim's state (ie from his death, in many cases).

**Case** – *V dies due to injury caused by D. At his death only one month remained of the prescription period. P, a dependant, sues after two months for loss of support but argues that the running of the prescription period on her claim starts only with V's death. D argues that P's claim as a dependant substitutes V's claim for prescription purposes and is therefore prescribed.*

83 Under French law, if V dies due to injury caused by D, then his injury did not stabilise before his death, and, if art 2226, 1st § *code civil* applies, prescription did not start to run before his death, neither against V nor against P. It will therefore be assumed that D is liable under the special product liability regime, and that the three-year prescription period (art 1245-16 *code civil*) started to run before V's death, so that only one month of it remained at that moment. Assuming that P's claim is also based on the special product liability regime, as will normally be the case, its prescription depends on when the

---

[53] Article 2245, 1st §, of the *code civil* suggests so, but it can be debated whether it applies outside of a contractual context. It provides: 'The calling in of one solidary debtor by judicial demand, or by an act of forced execution, or by the acknowledgement by the debtor of the right of the person against whom he was prescribing, interrupts the period of prescription against all the others, even against their heirs' ('L'interpellation faite à l'un des débiteurs solidaires par une demande en justice ou par un acte d'exécution forcée ou la reconnaissance par le débiteur du droit de celui contre lequel il prescrivait interrompt le délai de prescription contre tous les autres, même contre leurs héritiers').

loss of support happened. If it happened immediately after V's injury, then prescription started to run when P acquired knowledge of the defect and the identity of the producer, ie probably at the same time when the prescription of V's claim started to run. In this case, P's claim is thus prescribed. On the other hand, if the loss of support only happened as a result of V's death, P's claim only started to run as of the death, and it is not prescribed when P sues.

The same reasoning applies where V dies after the expiration of the prescription period. 84

## XII. OTHER ASPECTS OF PRESCRIPTION LAW

### A. STIPULATION

Under French law, the parties are free to modify the rules of prescription that are normally applicable, subject to certain limits. Article 2254, 1st and 2nd §§ *code civil* provides: 'The duration of the prescription may be made shorter or longer by agreement of the parties. Nevertheless, it may not be reduced to less than one year nor extended to more than ten years. The parties may also, by common agreement, add other causes of suspension or interruption of prescription to those provided by legislation'. 85

Such agreements on prescription are not subjected to any specific formal requirement. In theory, the possibility to agree in advance on different rules of prescription also applies to tort law. In practice, however, such agreements will only seldom be possible in a tort law context (especially as, given the '*non-cumul*' rule, no claim in tort can arise when there is a valid contractual relationship between the parties). Besides, such agreements on prescription would probably be considered as void if agreed between a consumer and a professional (at least if they reduce the prescription delay), on the basis that they are unfair (art L. 212-1 of the consumer code). 86

Waiver of prescription is also possible, but only once prescription has been acquired. Article 2250 *code civil* provides: 'Only a prescription that has been acquired may be renounced'. Article 2251 adds: 'Renunciation of prescription is express or tacit. Tacit renunciation results from circumstances which unequivocally demonstrate the intent not to claim prescription'. 87

### B. MEANING OF 'FILING A CLAIM' THAT INTERRUPTS THE RUNNING OF PRESCRIPTION

As is made clear by art 2240 *code civil*, it is the formal initiating of court proceedings that interrupts prescription. This can be done in various ways, 88 the most common one being through a writ served by a court bailiff (*assignation par huissier*). A written notice or demand sent by the creditor to the debtor is not enough to stop the running of the prescription period.

## C. WHEN SHOULD THE DEFENCE BE RAISED AND DECIDED?

89 The prescription defence is technically a '*fin de non-recevoir*' (plea of non-admissibility), which prevents the judge examining the merits of the case. Article 122 of the code of civil procedure provides: 'A plea of non-admissibility is any ground whose purpose is to get the adversary's claim declared inadmissible, without entering into the merits of the case, for lack of a right of action, such as not being the proper party, lack of interest, statute of limitations, fixed time-limit or res judicata'. Nevertheless, the defence does not have to be raised at the beginning of proceedings, since art 123 of the code of civil procedure provides: 'A plea of non-inadmissibility may be raised at any stage of the proceeding, without prejudice to the judge's discretion to order payment of damages by those who abstained, with dilatory intent, from raising them earlier'.

## D. WHO MAY RAISE THE DEFENCE?

90 Prescription cannot be raised *ex officio* by the judge. The solution has always been accepted and is now set out by art 2247 *code civil*: 'Judges cannot on their own motion, set up a plea of prescription'.[54] But another party than the claimant can raise the defence. Article 2253 *code civil* provides: 'Creditors and any other person with an interest in that the prescription be acquired may raise it or invoke it even if the debtor renounces it'.[55]

## E. BURDEN OF PROOF

91 In accordance with the general rules on the burden of proof (see art 12 code of civil procedure), it is for the party who raises the prescription defence, namely the defendant, to prove that the prescription delay has run out. Conversely, it is for the claimant to prove the postponement or suspension, or the renewal of prescription, if he intends to rely on it.[56]

---

54 Article 2247: 'Les juges ne peuvent pas suppléer d'office le moyen résultant de la prescription'.

55 Article 2253: 'Les créanciers, ou toute autre personne ayant intérêt à ce que la prescription soit acquise, peuvent l'opposer ou l'invoquer lors même que le débiteur y renonce'.

56 On the burden of proof of late discovery, see *supra* 38.

# PRESCRIPTION IN TORT LAW: GERMANY

Ulrich Magnus

## I. INTRODUCTION

1 German prescription law is primarily regulated in the German Civil Code (BGB). The Code, originally enacted in 1900, contains the general prescription rules which always apply if no more specific provisions on prescription exist. There are some further special prescription provisions, though only a few in tort law. The special acts on strict liability regularly refer to the prescription provisions of the BGB.[1]

2 The BGB provisions on prescription were profoundly reformed in 2002.[2] The main aim of the reform was to modernise the whole prescription regime and to

1 See, eg §14 Straßenverkehrsgesetz (Road Traffic Act, StVG); §11 Haftpflichtgesetz (Liability Act, HPflG); §17 Umwelthaftungsgesetz (Environmental Liability Act, UmweltHG). A limited exception is, for instance, §32 Atomgesetz (Nuclear Energy Act, AtomG) which contains slight modifications in order to meet the requirements of the Paris Nuclear Liability Convention which Germany has ratified; but for the rest §32 AtomG refers to the BGB provisions.

2 The reform of the prescription provisions was a central part of the German reform of the law of obligations of 2002.

unify the different prescription periods as far as possible and reasonable. Smaller adaptations and amendments occurred in 2004[3] and 2013.[4] The new provisions also apply to tort claims. Tort claims as understood here are claims based on the commission of a tort which entitle to compensation, such as damages claims, or to injunctive relief against threatening damage. The following text exclusively centres on the reformed prescription provisions of the BGB.

## II. DEFINITION OF PRESCRIPTION

The BGB does not define prescription ('*Verjährung*') but describes its effects in §§214 et seq. BGB. The main effect is stated in §214 (1): 'After limitation occurs, the obligor is entitled to refuse performance.'[5] The Code thus understands prescription as a right to refuse the owed performance because of the passage of a certain period of time since the claim accrued. This is the general view of the courts[6] and legal doctrine.[7] Prescription, thus, not only constitutes a procedural bar but is a substantive defence which does not however extinguish the prescribed right.[8] This nature does not vary according to varying situations. To modify the nature of prescription due to different situations has not been ventilated or proposed thus far. 3

Generally, only a claim ('*Anspruch*') can prescribe.[9] Claims are characterised by the fact that the creditor can request a certain conduct or omission from the debtor.[10] Subjective rights such as the right to bodily integrity, to property, etc do not regularly prescribe. They exist as long as there is a holder of that right. The Code allows only few exceptions from the principal non-prescription 4

3 This adaptation aligned the prescription provisions in 19 special acts to the revised prescription provisions of the BGB; see to this Act *H Mansel and Ch Budzikiewicz* NJW 2005, 321.

4 This amendment added provisions on later prescription of claims of sexually abused minors.

5 This is the quasi-official translation authorised by the German Ministry of Justice and Consumer Protection; see <http://www.gesetze-im-internet.de/englisch_bgb>.

6 See, eg BGHZ 17, 199 (206).

7 See, among others, *J Ellenberger*, in: O Palandt (ed), BGB (78th ed, 2019) Überbl vor §194 n 4; *W Henrich*, in: H G Bamberger and H Roth and W Hau and R Poseck (eds), Beck'scher Online-Kommentar zum BGB (BeckOKBGB, 1 November 2019) §194 n 3; *F Peters and F Jacoby*, in: J von Staudinger (ed), Kommentar zum Bürgerlichen Gesetzbuch mit Einführungsgesetz und Nebengesetzen (2019) Vorbem zu §§194–225 n 1 et seq.

8 See §214 (2) BGB.

9 See expressly §194 (1) BGB.

10 See §194 (1) BGB: 'The right to demand that another person does or refrains from an act (claim) is subject to limitation.' (Quasi-official translation authorised by the German Ministry of Justice and Consumer Protection; see <http://www.gesetze-im-internet.de/englisch_bgb>.)

of subjective rights.[11] In tort law, the right to request compensation for an infringement of a person's rights or for omission of threatening conduct is always a claim in the sense of the provisions on limitation.

## III. THE NATURE OF PRESCRIPTION AND ITS EFFECTS

5 In German law, prescription does, as mentioned, not extinguish the claim but grants a defence which the debtor must raise (so called '*Einrede*').[12] The court is not allowed to take account *ex officio* of the fact that a claim is prescribed.[13] The court may not even point to that fact if the debtor has evidently overlooked the prescription of the claim.[14] Such indication would offend the commandment of neutrality of the judge. The nature as pure defence has the consequence that if he or she has satisfied an already prescribed tort claim, a debtor cannot claim restitution of the money paid.[15]

6 In German law limitation is no purely procedural remedy. The defence blocks the substantive right. The debtor can refuse performance whether the creditor claims performance in court proceedings or outside. Also, in private international law situations prescription is now qualified in all EU countries as a matter of substantive law not of procedural law.[16]

7 Besides prescription in its specific sense, German law knows of a number of cut-off rules under which the respective right is extinguished after the lapse of a certain time.[17] However, they need not be examined here in detail because they generally play no role for tort claims.[18]

---

11 See, eg §218 BGB concerning the right to terminate a contract.

12 See already Denkschrift zum Entwurf eines Bürgerlichen Gesetzbuchs (1896) 56; now, eg *K Larenz and M Wolf*, Allgemeiner Teil des Bürgerlichen Rechts (8th ed, 1997) §17 n 1; *H Mansel and M Stürner*, in: NomosKommentarBGB Bd. 1 (3rd ed, 2016) Vor §§194–225 n 45.

13 Also already Denkschrift zum Entwurf eines Bürgerlichen Gesetzbuchs (1896) 56.

14 BGH NJW 2004, 164; this solution is however disputed; see *Staudinger, Peters and Jacoby*, §214 n 15 et seq.; further *C Meller-Hannich*, JZ 2005, 656 (662).

15 See §214 (2) sent 1 BGB: 'Performance rendered in satisfaction of a claim that is now statute-barred may not be claimed back even if performance was rendered without knowledge of the limitation.' (Quasi-official translation authorised by the German Ministry of Justice and Consumer Protection; see <http://www.gesetze-im-internet.de/englisch_bgb>.)

16 See art 12 (1) (d) Rome I Regulation; art 15 (h) Rome II Regulation.

17 See for instance §§121, 124 BGB (right to declare a declaration of intent avoided because of error or fraud).

18 An exception is the exclusion period of ten years in §13 Produkthaftungsgesetz (Product Liability Act, ProdHaftG) which implemented art 11 Product Liability Directive.

# IV. CONSIDERATIONS FOR AND AGAINST PRESCRIPTION OF TORT CLAIMS

## A. AGAINST

8 There are some arguments advanced against prescription although they primarily concern the length of the prescription period. Since the creditor in fact loses his or her claim by prescription this legal institute must comply with the German constitutional principles on the protection of property. These principles (art 14 Grundgesetz [Basic Law, GG]) regard – justified – claims as property.[19] Article 14 GG does not allow an expropriation of property without compensation. However, it is no expropriation if a statute merely defines the borders of property rights. In general, prescription provisions are viewed as merely determining the borders of property. In order to fall under this category they must meet a fair balance between the interests of creditors and the interests of debtors.[20] It is common ground that prescription as such is indispensable in order to beware persons of endless claims.[21] To meet the constitutional standard, however, the period of prescription must be such that the creditor had a fair chance to pursue its claim.[22] If he or she does not use this chance it is justified to preclude the creditor's claim. In certain contrast to this argument it is not required that the creditor must know of the existence of the claim.[23] Yet, it must be remembered that generally and in particular with respect to tort claims the regular prescription period starts running only from that point of time when the creditor knows the identity of the debtor and the circumstances of the claim or was grossly negligently unaware of these facts.[24]

9 Which prescription period is adequate is largely a matter of legislative discretion. Only at the extremes is a constitutional solution clear: the period must neither be too long nor too short.

10 Not only must the prescription period find a fair balance between the interests of the creditor and the debtor; the rules according to which prescription may be suspended or renewed must also meet this fairness standard.

11 It has been doubted that prescription serves the aim of legal peace because it would cause dissatisfaction and disappointment if an entirely valid claim cannot

---

19 See BVerfGE 45, 174; BVerfGE 68, 222.

20 BVerfGE 37, 140; *Staudinger, Peters and Jacoby*, Vorbem zu §§194–225 n 8.

21 *Staudinger, Peters and Jacoby*, Vorbem zu §§194–225 n 8.

22 *Palandt, Ellenberger*, Überbl vor §194 n 10; *Staudinger, Peters and Jacoby*, Vorbem zu §§194–225 n 9.

23 See BGH NJW-RR 2006, 384.

24 See §199 (1) BGB.

be enforced merely because of the lapse of the prescription period.[25] However, between the parties the outcome cares for a final solution and legal certainty. And if the creditor had a reasonable time to pursue its claim he or she cannot complain.

## B. FOR

12 It is undisputed in German court practice and legal doctrine that there must be a time barrier within which claims must be pursued. Thus, prescription is regarded as a necessary legal institute. This is even so for claims for which it could be argued that there should be no prescription at all, as for instance for claims for murder in the strict criminal sense,[26] for sexual abuse during minority or for injuries with very long latency periods such as asbestosis. However, even in these cases a final point of time is regarded as justified after which no civil law claims can be enforced if the defence is raised. Part of the justification can be drawn from the fact that in many of these cases social or private insurance systems provide for compensating benefits. Tort law would only be invoked in redress claims of the respective insurer, often against another (liability) insurer.

13 According to common opinion prescription serves several goals. A central goal is the protection of the interests of the debtor.[27] Already the Motives to the BGB stated that the debtor must be protected against 'die verdunkelnde Macht der Zeit' ('the darkening force of time').[28] This concerns mainly difficulties of proof: the longer ago the claim arose the more difficult it becomes to establish the truth (although the debtor does not normally carry the burden of proof, it becomes more difficult to rebut any proof the creditor advances; remembrance fades; witnesses may have died or cannot be reached, etc). If claims could be brought long after they accrued this would also increase the danger that the debtor can no longer enforce eventual own redress possibilities he would have had, had the claim been brought in time. Prescription is also regarded as necessary because claims can be, and not infrequently are, unjustified for what reasons ever.[29] Prescription then blocks these claims at least where the defendant raises the defence. And the longer ago a cause of action accrued the more the justification of the claim may be doubtful.

---

25 *Staudinger, Peters and Jacoby*, Vorbem zu §§194–225 n 7.

26 In criminal law there is no prescription of murder: §78 (2) Criminal Code (Strafgesetzbuch, StGB).

27 See BGHZ 128, 74 (82 et seq.); NomosKommentar, *Mansel and Stürner*, Vor §§194–225 n 32 et seq.; *Palandt, Ellenberger*, Überbl vor §194 n 8; *Staudinger, Peters and Jacoby*, Vorbem zu §§194–225 n 5 et seq.

28 Motive zum Bürgerlichen Gesetzbuch Bd. I (1896) 512.

29 *Staudinger, Peters and Jacoby*, Vorbem zu §§194–225 n 5.

A further consideration is that the debtor should not be forced for an unlimited time to keep books or other proof and money resources for eventual risks concerning old claims and transactions. Prescription enables the debtor to freely dispose of its means that otherwise had to be held in stock as necessary precaution. The protection of debtors by a time frame is all the more necessary because the claim may only be alleged but may not exist in reality or may be unfounded. After prescription the debtor need no longer defend against the substance of the claim but can refuse it alone because of the time argument. 14

Another central goal and justification of prescription is to serve legal peace.[30] 15
After the lapse of the prescription period the possibility to come back to old claims and disputes is silenced ('*finis litium*'). The debtor of the claim, but also third persons and the public as a whole, are then entitled to rely on the fact that the old claim will and can no longer be enforced. Moreover, potential plaintiffs and potential defendants act 'in the shadow of the law' of prescription. They usually know that after a certain period of time no claim can be successfully raised anymore and they generally behave correspondingly. Potential plaintiffs regularly do not institute such claims; potential defendants can trust that such claims when raised will be unsuccessful.

It is also acknowledged that prescription – as an unintended though welcome by-product – facilitates the task of the courts which need no longer go into the substance of the dispute but can, if the defence is validly raised, easily dismiss the claim just because the time limit has lapsed.[31] Insofar prescription saves public costs and resources. 16

A further general aspect is that the rapidity and ease of commerce profits from, and may even require, – rather short – prescription periods. Again, this is said to be a mere by-product and no direct aim of prescription.[32] 17

## V. ELEMENTS OF PRESCRIPTION – AN OVERVIEW

As in many other legal systems, in German law four basic elements form the general prescription law: (1) provisions on when the prescription period starts running (§§199–201 BGB); (2) the period of time after the lapse of which a claim is prescribed (§§195–198 BGB); (3) provisions on when the lapse 18

30 BGHZ 59, 74; BGHZ 128, 74 (82); NomosKommentar, *Mansel and Stürner*, Vor §§194–225 n 34; *Palandt, Ellenberger*, Überbl vor §194 n 9.

31 NomosKommentar, *Mansel and Stürner*, Vor §§194–225 n 35; *Palandt, Ellenberger*, Überbl vor §194 n 11; *Staudinger, Peters and Jacoby*, Vorbem zu §§194–225 n 7.

32 See *Palandt, Ellenberger*, Überbl vor §194 n 11; *Staudinger, Peters and Jacoby*, Vorbem zu §§194–225 n 7.

of the prescription period is suspended and when prescription starts anew (§§203–213 BGB); (4) provisions on the effects of prescription (§§214–218 BGB).

19 The prescription period generally 'commences at the end of the year in which 1. the claim arose and 2. the obligee obtains knowledge of the circumstances giving rise to the claim and the identity of the obligor, or would have obtained such knowledge if he had not shown gross negligence.'[33] In tort law the tort claim must have accrued and the victim must know the tortfeasor, the damage and causation, and in case of fault liability the facts that constitute wrongfulness and the required degree of fault. Grossly negligent unawareness of these facts suffices.[34]

20 The regular period of prescription in Germany is three years,[35] however, it is 30 years for intentionally caused bodily harm, violation of freedom and sexual self-determination.[36] These periods apply irrespective of whether the cause of action is contract or tort.[37] Indirect intent suffices;[38] indirect intent is given if the actor is aware that the wrongful result may occur but nevertheless accepts its occurrence.[39] Since the victim may become aware of the relevant facts only many years after the tort was committed there are further periods of ten and of 30 years which apply irrespective of the victim's knowledge and set a maximum time limit.[40]

21 There are various grounds which suspend the running of the prescription period, in particular if the creditor initiates court or other formal proceedings in order to pursue the claim.[41] Suspension means that the time during the suspension does not count for the prescription period. Only on a few occasions does the prescription period start anew, namely, if the debtor acknowledged the claim or if an act of execution in favour of the creditor had been performed or applied for.[42]

22 The main effect of prescription has already been mentioned: the claim can no longer be enforced.[43] The court will dismiss a claim if the defence is raised.

---

33 §199 (1) BGB (quasi-official translation authorised by the German Ministry of Justice and Consumer Protection; see <http://www.gesetze-im-internet.de/englisch_bgb>).

34 See the text of §199 (1) BGB.

35 §195 BGB.

36 §197 (1) no 1 BGB. This provision has been in force since 30 June 2013. It was inserted in reaction to scandals concerning sexual misuse of children in German church communities and schools.

37 NomosKommentar, *Mansel and Stürner*, §197 n 3.

38 Thus far there is no case law on the new provision. However, intent generally includes indirect intent.

39 See BGHZ 7, 313; BGH NJW 1986, 180 (182).

40 §199 (2), (3) and (4) BGB.

41 See §204 BGB.

42 §212 (1) BGB.

43 §214 (1) BGB.

# VI. THE STARTING POINT OF THE PRESCRIPTION PERIOD

## A. THE MEANING OF 'ACTION' AND OF 'CAUSE OF ACTION'

German law distinguishes between the regular prescription period and specific periods. According to §199 (1) BGB the regular prescription period is three years; it starts at the end of the year during which the *Anspruch* accrued.[44] The English equivalent for *Anspruch* or sometimes *Anspruchsgrundlage* is probably the term 'claim' or 'cause of action' or sometimes 'action' (although the latter more often describes the procedural action that has to be taken). It means that a claimant can base his or her claim on facts that meet the preconditions of a legal remedy. In tort law it means that the claimant can claim – generally compensation – if the respondent has fulfilled the required elements of the tort in question. The most general German tort provision (§823 (1) BGB), for instance, requires that the respondent has caused damage to either life, body, health, freedom, property or another 'absolute' right of another person in a wrongful and negligent or intentional way. In order to set the regular prescription period of three years in motion the tortfeasor must have fulfilled all these preconditions. This includes that the damage must have happened either as a first injury to the person's integrity or as damage to property. Without any damage having occurred the regular (short) prescription period will not run.[45] To start this period it is, however, further necessary that the victim must know (or be grossly negligently unaware) of the identity of the tortfeasor and the facts that can be qualified as damage, causation, wrongfulness and fault. 23

However, where the victim has no such actual or imputed knowledge or where, for instance, damage has not yet entered, prescription nonetheless runs for 30 years from the date 'on which the act, breach of duty or other event that caused the damage occurred' if the injury concerned life, body, health or liberty.[46] For instance, for mesothelioma, it is the date of exposition to asbestos at which prescription starts. For all other claims, in particular for property damage, the starting point is, in the absence of any actual or imputed knowledge, either the date of accrual of the claim (then ten-year prescription period) or the date when 'the act, breach of duty or other event that caused the damage occurred' (then 30-year prescription period), whichever is the earlier date.[47] 24

44 The same rule applies to special prescription periods, §200 BGB.

45 *Staudinger, Peters and Jacoby*, §199 n 32.

46 §199 (2) BGB.

47 §199 (3) BGB.

25 Where the tortious act has damaged at the same time both the victim's body and property, for prescription purposes the tortious act is the relevant cause of action for which the prescription time runs. Nonetheless, it is possible in such a case that the prescription period for the bodily injury may start earlier than the period for the property damage, namely if the victim becomes aware – and could become aware – of the property damage only later. A respective case would be the situation that a person is personally attacked and injured in his or her home and discovers only considerable time later that at the same time the tortfeasor also stole a certain object. Since prescription starts only when the victim has knowledge (or grossly negligent unawareness) of the identity of the tortfeasor *and* the circumstances giving rise to the claim (in particular of the damage) it is possible that the victim knows of the bodily harm but not yet of the property damage or vice versa even though they were caused by the same act. Injury and theft committed in a close time and place would be regarded as one tortious act.

26 A special provision regulates the situation that the tortfeasor by its tort has something received from, or at the expense of, the victim.[48] The victim then can claim the return of what the tortfeasor received even if the tort claim already prescribed. The return claim prescribes separately after ten years from the date when the tort claim accrued. The effect of the regulation is that the victim may claim what still enriches the tortfeasor, although the claim for full compensation is no longer enforceable.

## B. BROAD OR NARROW NOTION OF 'CAUSE OF ACTION'

27 As a general principle that always applies, all elements of the respective tort norm must be satisfied in order to base a claim on it. This is the cause of action on which proceedings can be instituted. For prescription purposes no other notion of cause of action is used. The German courts apply in principle the concept of unity of damage ('*Schadenseinheit*'): this means that the prescription period covers all consequences which the damaging event immediately and later on causes; the prescription period for the primary injury thus refers to, and includes, also all later consequences.[49] However, the courts accept an important exception from this rule: if a reasonable person could not foresee the later (often secondary) consequence then a new prescription period starts for this

---

[48] §852 BGB.

[49] See already Reichsgericht Juristische Wochenschrift (JW) 1907, 302; RGZ 87, 306 (312); RGZ 106, 283 (285); continued by the Bundesgerichtshof: BGHZ 50, 21 (24); BGH NJW 1991, 2833 (2835); BGH Deutsches Steuerrecht (DStR) 2015, 1887; BeckOKBGB, *G Spindler*, §199 n 27; *Palandt, Ellenberger*, §199 n 14; *Soergel, Niedenführ*, §199 n 20; strongly against the concept of unity of damage: *Staudinger, Peters and Jacoby*, §199 n 47 et seq.

further consequence.[50] To term this concept either broad or narrow does not fully meet the German concept. It may be regarded as relatively broad though with exceptions which narrow it. Yet, it must be borne in mind that the regular prescription period only starts if the victim knows (or grossly negligently does not know) the identity of the tortfeasor and the circumstances giving rise to the claim including the damage (if the damage, as generally, is an essential element of the violated tort norm). This often results in a commencement of limitation much later than the date of the damaging event.

**Case 1** – *(Failure to ensure the wearing of a ski helmet)*: The regular prescription period of three years would start here with the end of the year when the accident occurred irrespective of whether the claim would be based on contract or tort and provided that the victim was not unable to pursue the claim due to the head injury. For, the victim knew the identity of the tortfeasor and the facts which led to the injury. The prescription would also cover the later head injury due to the general concept of unity of damage unless this consequence was unforeseeable. In practice, victims when claiming compensation for the first damage regularly request an additional court order stating that the tortfeasor be liable for all future consequences of the accident. The prescription period for this title is 30 years.[51] 28

**Case 2** – *(Three mistakes during one treatment)*: It shall evidently be assumed that D's three different mistakes caused bodily injury, that D acted merely negligently, and that P discovered or could have discovered the different harms one, two and three years later. In German law the solution would depend on whether and when P knew or was grossly negligent in not knowing that the treatment caused harm (damage). If P was grossly negligent in not knowing that the treatment could have the indicated different consequences, the prescription period would start on the treatment day and end three years after the close of the year of treatment.[52] If P neither knew nor was grossly negligently unaware of the different injuries at the time of treatment but became aware of them only after one, two and three years, the prescription period would start for each mistake at the date the respective damage became obvious to P[53] unless the whole treatment could be regarded as one act; then, the prescription period would start with the first damage and include the further consequences. It is therefore decisive whether the three mistakes were three independent acts or elements of one single act. In the – unlikely – case that the damage would become obvious only many years later, the 'long-stop period' that runs independently of any subjective knowledge or unawareness would start on the day of treatment for all three mistakes and then run for 30 years.[54] 29

50 See RGZ 83, 354 (360); BGHZ 50, 21 (24); BGH NJW 1991, 2833 (2835).
51 §197 (1) no 3 BGB.
52 See §199 (1) BGB.
53 This also follows from §199 (1) BGB.
54 See §199 (2) BGB.

30 **Case 3** – *(Consecutive harms from one injury)*: In German law the basis of claim in this case would be both contract and tort. Unless the contract provided for a shorter period of prescription, the period[55] would start running on the day of the first injury. Generally, in accordance with the concept of unity of damage, the prescription period for the first injury applies also to later consequences of the same occurrence.[56] However, if the secondary injury was objectively unforeseeable it would set in motion a new prescription period.[57] Thirty years after the accident all claims would be prescribed.[58]

## C. THE STARTING POINT – BREACH OF DUTY OR OCCURRENCE OF DAMAGE?

31 German prescription law has developed a differentiated system with respect to the date when the prescription period starts running. The differentiation takes account of the kind of injury (injury to the person v. injury to property and economic interests) and whether or not the victim has actual or imputed knowledge of the circumstances giving rise to a claim. Depending on this differentiation the prescription period starts either when the tort was committed or when the injury was suffered and the damage entered or when the victim had actual or imputed knowledge.

32 In order to answer the question of prescription law whether and when the harm complained of must have occurred, it must first be decided whether the harm must have already occurred or whether the risk of harm suffices to set prescription in motion. In the first line, this depends on the requirements of the respective tort. As mentioned, in German law, a tort claim for damages (the '*Anspruch*' or claim or cause of action) becomes due only if damage has occurred. The mere risk that some damage may occur does not suffice for the accrual of a damages cause of action.[59] It does not set the prescription period in motion. As also mentioned above, the ordinary prescription period starts running as soon as the victim knows the identity of the tortfeasor and the circumstances giving rise to the claim (or is grossly negligently unaware).[60] The knowledge or imputable unawareness must include the damage. However, apart from any cause of action for damages a claimant may have a right for injunctive

---

55 In this case the period is five years, §634a (1) no 2 BGB. The period starts when the customer accepted, or was obliged to accept, the building as conforming to the contract.

56 See the references *supra* fn 49.

57 See the references *supra* fn 50.

58 See §199 (2) BGB.

59 See BGHZ 73, 363 (365); BGHZ 124, 30; BGHZ 186, 152; also, eg, NomosKommentarBGB, *Mansel and Stürner*, §199 n 18.

60 §199 (1) BGB.

relief that threatened damage be avoided, in particular where its repetition is threatening. The prescription for the right to injunctive relief begins when the act that seriously threatens to cause damage is done.

A further question is when the harm has occurred that is relevant for prescription. Where a single tortious act causes a primary damage (for instance, an infection with HIV), the occurrence of the harm is generally the day of that event (eg the infection because at this time the ordinary status of the body is negatively affected). Nonetheless, the regular (short) prescription period starts only at the end of the year when the victim knew or grossly negligently did not know the damage (eg the infection). This prescription period applies to all later consequences of that event as far as they were foreseeable.[61] The underlying argument is that the victim could and should institute proceedings in order to preserve his or her rights – if necessary apply for a declaratory judgment that the tortfeasor be liable for all future damage caused by the damaging event or to achieve an acknowledgement by the tortfeasor. Only where future risks are unforeseeable does the victim need not take steps to hinder prescription because the ordinary prescription period then runs from the occurrence of that unforeseeable 'new' damage caused by the original 'old' event. 33

Where the tort consists of several acts, of which only the last one causes the damage, prescription starts running as soon as the last act has been finished.[62] Where liability rests on a strict liability provision or statute the prescription period commences when the specific risk materialises[63] that the provision or statute is designed to avoid (for instance, for the strict liability of car-holders when a car accident occurs and causes damage). In case of damage through a tortious omission the relevant starting point is the time when the tortfeasor should have acted in order to avoid the damage but did not act.[64] 34

Where the damage is caused by separate repetitions of the tortious conduct the harm occurs at each repetition anew with its own prescription period (short or long period). Where the damage is caused by a continuous tort (as far as still accepted in German law, see *supra* 32) the prescription period starts only when the tort ends, for instance the pollution stops. 35

**Case 4** – *(Trespass case)*: Under German law the plaintiff in this case would have a right for a court declaration or an injunction that the defendant omits such trespass.[65] This claim would prescribe within the ordinary prescription period. 36

---

61 See *supra* at Section IV.B.

62 BGH NJW 2008 3361 n 12 (only last refinancing transaction caused the damage complained of).

63 See, eg BeckOKBGB, *Henrich*, §199 n 44.

64 See §199 (5) BGB.

65 The legal basis is §1004 in combination with §823 BGB.

However, since this right originates from the right of ownership which as such is not subject to prescription, the plaintiff could claim again omission of the trespass each time that the defendant trespasses the plaintiff's premises. A prescription of the first trespass claim would not hinder to raise a new claim to omit the trespass when it occurs again. However, as the first trespass did not cause any damage no tort claim for damages would lie at this time. A tort claim for damages lies only after the second trespass which led to damage. German courts would separate the two events and apply the prescription period separately for each: for the mere trespass when it occurs and for the damages claim when the damage occurred. Insofar, German law applies a narrow standard of cause of action which regards the second event and respective legal action (damages claim) as different from the first one (claim for omission). Not only do the facts differ for both – damage v. no damage – the legal remedies are also not identical. However, if the plaintiff accepted the defendant's trespassing conduct over a considerable period of time, the institute of acquiescence ('*Verwirkung*') may bar any further trespass claim (though not a damages claim).

## D. WHAT IS CONSIDERED 'HARM' FOR PRESCRIPTION PURPOSES?

37 Generally, the harm relevant for prescription is the damage which all causes of action in tort require. In cases where damage merely threatens, the aggrieved party can – under certain circumstances – only claim omission of the threatened conduct or event but no damages.[66]

38 **Case 5** – *(Developing ear damage)*: German courts would hold that the regular three-year prescription period started when P began to experience major hearing problems and had reasonable ground to suspect that they were caused by the noise of the explosion. For, the regular three-year prescription starts running as soon as the cause of action came into existence (day of explosion) and the victim knew or without gross negligence should have known all relevant circumstances (including the damage) and the liable person. Germany thus follows an approach which expects legal steps of the victim as soon as a reasonable person would initiate such steps. Theoretically, the 30-year period would start with the day of the explosion (however, since the plaintiff cannot neglect without gross negligence his loss of hearing ability and its connection with the explosion, the 30-year period has no practical relevance in this case).

39 **Case 6** – *(Defective foundations of bridge)*: The contractual claim for defective work would prescribe after five years after the work had been accepted

[66] See §1004 BGB.

as conforming performance.[67] The regular (three-year) prescription[68] of D's liability in tort would start for all harms at the date when a possible victim knew or grossly negligently did not know that the damage (collapse of the bridge) occurred. The long-stop period of 30 years is most likely irrelevant in this case because any victim would know or be grossly negligently unaware of the damage.[69] The tortious prescription might thus end earlier or later than the contractual prescription period.

## E. THE STARTING POINT (ACCRUAL) IN CONTINUOUS TORTS

It was accepted court practice that a tort that lasts over some time constitutes a 40
continuous tort for which the prescription period only starts when the tortious activity ends.[70] Wrongful imprisonment may be an example.[71] However, the German Federal Court in civil matters now tends to deny the possibility to distinguish repeated torts for which the prescription starts anew with each act and a continued tort for which prescription starts only at the end of the continued act.[72] The Court argued that a continuous tort often consists of a number of single acts or omissions so that a distinction would be 'practically hardly possible'.[73] Furthermore, the aims of limitation law would militate against the delay of the commencement of the prescription period if the claimant had a reasonable earlier opportunity to pursue his or her claim.[74] It is still open whether this means a full rejection of the concept of continuous tort. The Federal Court at least denied a continuous tort in the case of the lasting failure of the Federal Republic of Germany to correctly implement certain EU-Directives.[75] On the other hand, the same decision held that there were several different actions of Germany (to correctly implement the Directives) which each started a separate prescription period.[76] Also in a more recent decision, the BGH held that a continuous tort (the unauthorised exhibition of pictures) produces

67 §634a BGB.

68 Three years from the end of the year in which the cause of action accrued.

69 See §199 (2) and (3) no 2 BGB.

70 See BGH NJW 1973, 2285; assenting MünchKommBGB, *Grothe*, §199 n 13; *Palandt, Ellenberger*, §199 n 22.

71 See, eg MünchKommBGB, *Grothe*, §199 n 13.

72 See BGHZ 181, 199 n 30 (in that case the Danish producers and dealers of pork had sued the Federal Republic of Germany for having incorrectly implemented certain EU Directives relevant for the pork trade thus hindering Danish pork imports; the claimants requested damages under European state liability law; Germany argued that the claim was prescribed; the Federal Court denied prescription); however, still differently BGH NJW 1973, 2285.

73 BGHZ 181, 199 n 30.

74 BGHZ 181, 199 n 32.

75 See BGHZ 181, 199 n 29.

76 BGHZ 181, 199 n 29, 32.

continuously new damage starting the prescription period each day anew.[77] It is thus likely that the court practice accepts the institute of 'continuous tort' if at all only in very rare situations. Where the tortfeasor commits repeated though new acts (as in the case of the failed implementation of the Directives) the courts are likely to regard each act as setting a separate prescription period in motion. Where the tortfeasor acts in the beginning and merely maintains this tortious situation without any further active conduct (as in the case of the exhibition of pictures) nonetheless the prescription starts anew on each new day. In any event, the general principle is still valid that prescription starts if in the light of the relevant facts known to the claimant the latter could reasonably be expected to institute legal proceedings with relatively sure prospects of success (even if it would be a suit for a declaration that the tortfeasor should be liable for any future damage).[78]

41 **Case 7** – *(Continuing defamation)*: German courts would most likely treat the different defamation acts as separate acts for which the prescription period starts anew with each new publication.[79] It would not matter whether the defamation was published in the same or in different newspapers.

42 **Case 8** – *(Noise from the neighbour)*: German courts would solve this case in the same way as Case 5. The prescription period would start running from the date at which even an average person could have no longer neglected that there was serious ear damage stemming from the neighbour's noise.

43 **Case 9** – *(Toxic bins)*: The tortious activity is the digging of the bins. The regular three-year prescription period would start at the end of the year during which the victim learns of the identity of the tortfeasor and the digging of the toxic bins (or neglecting these facts grossly negligently). The 30-year period would start with the digging of the bins, the competing ten-year[80] period with the entrance of the damage to the crop or with the cleaning costs.

## F. IS THE LATE DISCOVERY RULE A RULE OF THE STARTING POINT (ACCRUAL) OR A RULE OF PROLONGATION?

44 There is no easy answer to the question whether the late discovery rule should be regarded as a rule of the starting point or as a prolongation rule. As already

---

77 BGH NJW 2015, 3165 n 23.

78 BGH NJW 1973, 2285.

79 See BGH NJW 1973, 2285 (a letter by which a company wrongly pretends to own a patent on a product of a competitor was regarded as no continuous act but as a finished act. Therefore, the prescription period started with the publication of the letter although the effect of the letter continued to affect the rights of the competitor).

80 See §199 (3) no 1 BGB (accrual of claim).

mentioned above, in German law, the regular prescription period of three years starts only if the victim has actual or imputed knowledge (§199 (1) BGB). The text of the provision formulates the knowledge as a condition for the commencement of the – regular, short – prescription period together with the accrual of the claim ('[...] the standard limitation period commences at the end of the year in which 1. the claim arose and 2. the obligee obtains knowledge [...]'). Also, the heading of the provision ('Commencement of the standard limitation period and maximum limitation periods') demonstrates that the German legislator evidently regards the subjective element of knowledge as the essential starting point for the regular prescription period to be set in motion. Also seen from a practical point of view, in most cases the prescription period starts only in accordance with the knowledge rule. Under this practical view, the mere accrual of the cause of action in most cases does not determine the length of the prescription period.

On the other hand, it has to be admitted that the knowledge rule could easily be regarded as a prolongation rule that extends merely the prescription period which 'actually' starts when the cause of action accrues.[81] However, this is no compelling reason why a prescription system such as the German one should not combine the accrual of the cause of action as starting point (for the long-stop prescription period) with the knowledge rule (for the short-stop period). Therefore, for the regular short prescription period the actual or imputed knowledge is the starting point. For the long-stop periods the late discovery rule merely has the function eventually to limit their length. 45

## G. UNKNOWN DATE OF DAMAGE

Where it is known that the harm was caused but its exact date remains unknown, this problem is solved in two different ways: first, §199 (1) BGB provides that the regular prescription period of three years starts by the end of the year in which the claim arose. Insofar, it is unnecessary to specify the exact date of when the claim arose. Secondly, the rules on burden of proof help. The general rule applies that the tortfeasor who invokes prescription must prove when the victim gained the necessary knowledge of the identity of the tortfeasor and the circumstances giving rise to the claim.[82] If this remains open, the possibility cannot be excluded that the cause of action was not prescribed and the defence of prescription must be dismissed. The claimant must, however, support the finding of the truth and in particular state and, if necessary, prove facts that occurred in his or her 46

81 See, eg *Staudinger, Peters and Jacoby*, §199 n 76.
82 BGH NJW 2007, 1584 n 32, BGH NJW 2008, 2578.

own sphere.[83] For the long-stop period that applies irrespective of any actual or possible knowledge the tortfeasor also has the burden of proof that the damage occurred and the claim arose before this period.

## VII. PRESCRIPTION PERIODS

47 As already indicated, the German Civil Code provides for a combination of two general periods of prescription which in principle apply to all kinds of civil claims, a short subjective one and a subsidiary objective long one. The Code does not provide for a minimum prescription period although it is an unwritten rule that the creditor must be granted a reasonable time so that he has a fair chance to pursue its claim.

48 The prescription rules of the Civil Code do not generally differentiate according to the specific nature or field of the claim. Contractual and extra-contractual claims are generally treated alike. Therefore, for prescription purposes, there is no need for disguising a contract case as a tort case or vice versa. Since the reform of 2002 more or less unified the prescription periods for all civil claims, 'period shopping' which was usual before the reform has become unnecessary. Nonetheless, there are certain special periods for specific claims, in particular for damages claims and other claims. The distinction can be explained by the principle that the more valuable the injured right or position is, the longer the prescription period tends to be. For example: the intentional violation of life, body, health and liberty prescribes 30 years after the commission of the tort without regard to the victim's knowledge of the relevant facts; non-intentional violations of these rights can prescribe earlier (depending on the actual or imputed knowledge of the victim); damages claims concerning property or economic loss prescribe at the latest after ten years (see the details *infra*).

49 The most important and most general prescription period is the short regular period of three years.[84] It applies to almost all tort claims; its start depends on (1) that the claim arose and (2) that the claimant had actual knowledge of the identity of the tortfeasor and the circumstances on which the claim is based or was grossly negligently unaware of these facts.[85] For reasons of easier calculation and practical facilitation the three-year period commences only at the end of the year in which the required conditions are fulfilled (so-called ultimo rule).[86] In practice the short prescription period solves most cases where prescription is at stake.

83 See BGHZ 91, 260.
84 §195 BGB.
85 §199 (1) BGB.
86 See §199 (1) BGB.

In addition to the regular knowledge-based period there is a much longer objective prescription period which applies where the victim has no actual or potential knowledge of the identity of the tortfeasor and/or the circumstances giving rise to the claim. This period functions as a subsidiary maximum period for prescription (long-stop period).[87] It amounts to 30 years for damages claims concerning (non-intentional) injury to life, body, health and liberty.[88] Whether infringements of the general personality right are also covered is disputed but should be accepted since the provision intends to protect the personal sphere of the victim against too early a prescription.[89] However, claims for compensation of property damage or pure economic loss do not fall under this provision.[90] The 30-year period starts 'on the date on which the act, breach of duty or other event that caused the damage occurred.'[91] It is thus the tortious activity of the tortfeasor (including the damage) that sets the maximum prescription period in motion. Where during the course of the 30-year period the victim obtains actual or potential knowledge of the person of the tortfeasor and of the circumstances relevant for the claim the general short period commences and may end much earlier than the 30-year period. Then, this earlier end constitutes the applicable prescription period.[92] 50

For damages claims concerning other rights (property, economic loss, etc) the Civil Code contains a combined solution: in the first line the regular short period applies to these claims; if the necessary knowledge for setting this period in motion is lacking, the objective maximum prescription period comes into play. It is either ten years from the date the claim arose or 30 years 'from the date on which the act, breach of duty or other event that caused the damage occurred. The period that ends first is applicable.'[93] Since a tortious cause of action generally arises only if damage occurred, the ten-year period may not have lapsed although 30 years lapsed since the tortfeasor's activity (for instance, exposing the victim to asbestos although the damage did not yet break out). In such a case claims are statute-barred after 30 years even if the (later) victim had 51

---

87 §199 (2) BGB.

88 §199 (2) BGB.

89 Pro application of the 30-year period: BeckOKBGB, *Henrich and Spindler*, §199 n 42; *Erman, J Schmidt-Räntsch*, §199 n 33a; *Staudinger, Peters and Jacoby*, §199 n 95; contra: MünchKomm, *H Grothe*, §199 n 51; NomosKommentarBGB, *Mansel and Stürner*, §199 n 94; *Palandt, Ellenberger*, §199 n 44; *Soergel, Niedenführ*, §199 n 55.

90 MünchKomm, *Grothe*, §199 n 51; NomosKommentarBGB, *Mansel and Stürner*, §199 n 94; *Palandt and Ellenberger*, §199 n 44.

91 §199 (2) BGB (in the semi-official translation authorised by the German Ministry of Justice and for Consumer Protection on <http://www.gesetze-im-internet.de/englisch_bgb>).

92 See *Staudinger, Peters and Jacoby*, §199 n 91 and 93.

93 §199 (3) BGB (in the semi-official translation authorised by the German Ministry of Justice and for Consumer Protection on <http://www.gesetze-im-internet.de/englisch_bgb>).

no chance to know of the damage and thus of his or her cause of action. The only way to avoid this dilemma is the possibility to sue in time for a declaratory judgment if there is the suspicion that the former exposition or other activity may have led to any long-term damage or to achieve an acknowledgement by the – potential – tortfeasor that he be liable for any eventual late damage.

52 As already indicated above, a special prescription rule applies to damages claims 'based on intentional injury to life, limb, health, liberty or sexual self-determination.'[94] This provision was only inserted in 2013 after several scandals concerning the sexual abuse of minors had become public. For the prescription of the intentional violation of the listed rights the knowledge of the victim is irrelevant. The 30-year period starts in these cases when the cause of action accrues;[95] that means with the commission of the violation.

53 The 'strict' 30-year period applies also to claims which have been acknowledged by judgment, arbitral award,[96] enforceable settlement, enforceable document or recognition in insolvency proceedings.[97] In these cases the period starts running 'on the date when the decision becomes final and absolute, the enforceable instrument is executed or the claim is recognised in insolvency proceedings, but not before the claim arises.'[98]

54 For all other kinds of claims – for instance, for injunctive relief in respect of property – the objective maximum period is ten years after the cause of action arose.[99] The ten-year rule also applies where the tortfeasor received something from, or at the expense of, the victim.[100] During this period this claim can still be enforced even if the underlying tort claim already prescribed (due to the three-year period). What can be claimed is then determined by the law of unjust enrichment.

55 German law thus provides for an absolute time limit of 30 years for damages claims for personal injury while the maximum prescription period for other damages claims is ten to 30 years and for the rest of claims ten years. However, it must be borne in mind that the provisions on suspension and renewal may in fact lead to much longer prescription periods. This is particularly true for

---

94 §197 (1) no 1 BGB (in the semi-official translation authorised by the German Ministry of Justice and for Consumer Protection on <http://www.gesetze-im-internet.de/englisch_bgb>).

95 See §200 BGB.

96 Arbitral awards have the effect of a final judgment, see §1055 ZPO (Civil Procedure Code).

97 See §197 (1) no 3–5 BGB.

98 §201 BGB (in the semi-official translation authorised by the Geman Ministry of Justice and for Consumer Protection on <http://www.gesetze-im-internet.de/englisch_bgb>).

99 §199 (4) BGB.

100 §852 BGB.

claims based on sexual abuse of minors. The prescription of these claims is suspended until the minors reach the age of 21 or, if they live with the tortfeasor in a common household even thereafter, until this community ends.[101] Only then does the 30-year period start so that the claim can prescribe more than half a century after the act of the tortfeasor.

Besides the general prescription rules of the German Civil Code a number of specific provisions exist, though mainly without relevance for tort law. Examples from the field of contract law are, for instance, the two-year prescription periods for delivery of defective goods[102] or defective (movable) works.[103] In tort law the German Nuclear Energy Act (Atomgesetz, AtomG) contains a special maximum prescription period of 20 years for damage caused by nuclear material which had been stolen, lost, jettisoned or abandoned.[104] This regulation is required by art 8b Paris Convention on Third Party Liability in the Field of Nuclear Energy of 1960. Other special rules are §§12 and 13 Produkthaftungsgesetz (Product Liability Act, ProdHaftG) which implement respective provisions of the EU Directive on product liability. According to these provisions, any claim is excluded ten years after the producer put the defective product into circulation.[105] As under general German law the regular prescription period of the ProdHaftG and the Directive is three years. However, contrary to German law the period starts running not only where the claimant had knowledge (or grossly negligent lack of knowledge) of the person of the tortfeasor and the relevant circumstances; under the Act and the Directive merely negligent unawareness suffices.[106] Further, under the Act and the Directive the prescription period starts immediately at the date of knowledge or negligent lack of it, not at the end of the year in which that happened. Special prescription rules apply also in case of infringements of the provisions of the Act on Unfair Competition (Gesetz gegen den unlauteren Wettbwerb, UWG). Damages claims under this Act prescribe within six months after the cause of action accrued and the creditor gained knowledge, or was grossly negligently unaware, of the circumstances and the identity of the actor.[107] In the absence of knowledge damages claims prescribe within ten years from accrual and 30 from the damaging act.[108] 56

101 See §208 BGB.
102 §438 (1) no 3 BGB.
103 §634a (1) no 1 BGB.
104 §32 (2) AtomG.
105 §13 ProdHaftG and art 11 Product Liability Directive.
106 §12 ProdHaftG and art 10 (1) Product Liability Directive; see also *Palandt, H Sprau*, §11 ProdHaftG n 2/3.
107 §11 (1) and (2) UWG.
108 §11 (3) UWG.

57 **Table 1. Prescription periods and starting points**

| Cause of action or tort | Discovery rule | Prescription period (in years) | Notes (in years) |
|---|---|---|---|
| Bodily injury | Yes | 3–30 | 3: knowledge<br>30: without knowledge |
| Property damage | Yes | 3–10 | 3: knowledge<br>10: without knowledge |
| Defamation | Yes | 3–30 | 3: knowledge<br>30: without knowledge |
| Intentional torts | No | 3–30 | 3/10: property, economic loss<br>30: bodily, etc injury |
| Contractual claims | Partly yes, partly no | 6 months–10 years | |
| Unfair competition damages claims | Yes | 6 months–30 years | 6 mo.: knowledge<br>10/30: without knowledge |

## VIII. RULES OF POSTPONEMENT, SUSPENSION, RENEWAL AND EXTENSION

58 German prescription law acknowledges three kinds of extension of the 'normal' prescription period: suspension of prescription where the suspended time does not count for prescription;[109] suspension of expiry where in certain cases the prescription period is prolonged by six months; and the renewal of prescription where the period starts anew.[110] As mentioned above, German law does not regard the requirement of actual or imputed knowledge that is necessary to set the short prescription period in motion as a form of prolongation of the 'actual' prescription period.

### A. UNAWARENESS – THE LATE DISCOVERY RULE

#### 1) *Unawareness of what Elements of Liability?*

59 The application of this rule in German law has already been outlined above (*supra* 44 et seq.). The facts the creditor must be aware of for setting prescription in motion include the name and address of the tortfeasor, the damage, the causal link between the tortfeasor's activity and the damage, and, where necessary, the

---

109 See §209 BGB.

110 §212 BGB.

facts that constitute wrongfulness and fault. The necessary actual or imputed knowledge includes all specific facts that the respective tort norm requires. For instance, where the tortfeasor is liable for deceit ('*arglistige Täuschung*') because he failed to inform about own better knowledge it is necessary that the victim also knows that the tortfeasor had this lead in knowledge.[111] Without this knowledge the prescription of the victim's claim does not start.

With respect to the required knowledge, the claimant must know the mentioned relevant facts but not the legal position. If he or she errs in the legal qualification of the facts this does not hinder the commencement of the prescription period.[112] 60

The claimant must either actually know the relevant facts or must be grossly negligently unaware of them. The standard of the actual knowledge is a purely subjective one whereas the standard for the imputed knowledge is mainly objective. In this latter case, the claimant must have overlooked facts or considerations which no reasonable person in the same situation would have overlooked; the claimant's neglect of the reasonable care required in the situation must have been grave.[113] However, the BGH always adds that the neglect of the necessary care must also be 'subjectively entirely inexcusable'.[114] Such neglect is regularly inexcusable if almost no one would have shown it in the situation at hand. A victim of medical malpractice who does not seek further information is, for instance, grossly negligent only if there are strong indicia for such malpractice; the injury alone is not sufficient.[115] The Federal Court held that a patient who suffered from severe pain after an operation need not necessarily infer that the pain was the consequence of medical malpractice.[116] The patient is thus not necessarily grossly negligent if he or she institutes legal proceedings only 11 years after the operation when a medical expert had mentioned this possibility although the pain occurred immediately after the operation.[117] The Court indirectly held that the patient need not immediately seek further medical opinions if there are negative consequences of a medical treatment unless there are specific indications of medical malpractice of the first doctor which even a layperson can discover. 61

Where the claimant depends on the representation by another person (as minor by a parent, as ward by a guardian, as legal person by an authorised agent, etc) 62

111 See BGH BKR 2009, 372 n 20.

112 See, eg MünchKommBGB, *Grothe*, §199 n 29.

113 *Palandt, Ellenberger*, §199 n 39; *Staudinger, Peters and Jacoby*, §199 n 82; for the general definition of gross negligence see for instance BGH NJW 2009, 1482 n 34.

114 BGH NJW 2009, 1482 n 34 with references to former decisions to the same avail.

115 BGH NJW 2010, 681 n 17.

116 BGH NJW-RR 2010, 681 n 6.

117 BGH ibid., n 7.

the knowledge and imputed knowledge of the representative is decisive.[118] The same is true where the claimant employs another person, for instance a lawyer, to clear the facts and pursue the claimant's interests.[119]

63 With respect to its scope, the so-called late discovery rule covers almost all claims based on tort (or contract). Exceptions are damages claims which follow from the intentional infringement of life, body, health, freedom or sexual self-determination.[120] A further exception is the claim for the return of what the tortfeasor received through the tort and still possesses.[121] In both situations the actual or imputed knowledge of the facts and circumstances of the tort do not affect the prescription period.

64 **Case 10** – *(Lung disease I)*: Under German law, the error of the first lawyer is imputed to the claimant because the latter employed the lawyer whose task was to clear the facts and the legal position in the interest of the claimant.[122] If the lawyer's error was grossly negligent (as the case seems to imply), the plaintiff is deemed to have known all relevant facts, so that P's claim against the chemical plant is prescribed. However, a claim against the first lawyer is not yet prescribed since P learns only from the second lawyer that the first advice was erroneous and there lies a claim against the first lawyer.

### 2) *Objective or Subjective Unawareness?*

65 German law follows a mixed unawareness test. On the one hand, the subjective knowledge counts. On the other hand, if such knowledge is lacking (or cannot be proved) it suffices that under an objective perspective it would have been grossly negligent not to know, or to take knowledge of, the relevant facts.

### 3) *What is Considered Awareness of an Element of Liability?*

66 The claimant is aware of an element of liability, for instance the tortfeasor's negligence, if he or she knows facts from which a reasonable person in the situation of the claimant would infer that there was some wrong behaviour and/or violation of the owed care.

---

118 See *Palandt, Ellenberger*, §199 n 24; *Staudinger, Peters and Jacoby*, §199 n 57 et seq.

119 MünchKommBGB, *Grothe*, §199 n 34; *Palandt, Ellenberger*, §199 n 24; *Staudinger, Peters and Jacoby*, §199 n 60. An exception applies where the claim is directed against the employed person or concerns a claim that affects that person; BGH NJW 2014, 1294 n 20 et seq.

120 §197 (1) no 1 BGB.

121 §852 BGB.

122 See BGH NJW-RR 2008, 1495 n 40 (lawyer); BGH NJW 2008, 2427 n 15 et seq. (gross negligence of site manager imputed to claimant who employed him).

### 4) *How Heavy is the Burden to Acquire Knowledge?*

Actual or imputed knowledge of the relevant facts (damage, causation, wrongfulness and fault [if necessary], identity) must be so certain that a reasonable person would institute legal proceedings in order to secure the own rights.[123] However, the claimant need not be sure that, for instance, causation is given; relative certainty suffices. Likewise, knowledge is not only present if the damage has fully developed with all consequences. On the other hand, mere first signs and a suspicion of damage do not constitute knowledge. But where the signs have become so serious that a reasonable person would react this is also expected of the victim of the tort.[124] 67

**Case 11** – *(Lung disease II)*: Again, the question is whether the first doctor was grossly negligent and, if so, whether his gross negligence would be imputed to P. In contrast to Case 10, the first doctor is however not employed to discover the cause of the disease and to clear the basis for a possible claim against the chemical plant (as the first lawyer in Case 10 is) but merely to heal the disease. For this reason, even if the first doctor was grossly negligent with respect to the discovery of the cause of the disease, German courts would most likely not impute his negligence to P.[125] Whether the courts would expect that P seeks a second opinion would depend on the circumstances. If there were clear and serious reasons for P to suspect that there was a causal link between his disease and his employment the courts will probably hold P obliged to seek expert advice on this question. The prescription would then start running at the time when P should have received such – correct – advice. 68

### 5) *Transfer of Claim*

In cases where the claimant who had actual or imputed knowledge transfers the claim to another person without such knowledge or is succeeded by such a person, the knowledge of the original claimant remains decisive if the prescription period had already begun to run before the transfer or succession. Where this period had not yet started before the transfer or succession the knowledge of the new claimant becomes relevant.[126] 69

---

123 See, eg *Staudinger, Peters and Jacoby*, §199 n 71.

124 See, for instance, BGH NJW 2008, 2576 n 28.

125 *Palandt, Ellenberger*, §199 n 24 (for the comparable situation of an employed lawyer).

126 *Staudinger, Peters and Jacoby*, §199 n 56.

## B. OTHER RULES OF PROLONGATION

### *1) D is to Blame for the Delay*

70 If the debtor made the creditor believe that the defence would not be raised and the creditor in reliance omitted to take legal action and the debtor then raises the defence, according to §242 BGB the court must disregard the defence because such behaviour offends the principle of good faith.[127]

### *2) Admission by D of P's Right or Partial Performance of P's Right by D*

71 Where the debtor admits in a clear way the plaintiff's right this is regarded as the creation of a new obligation for which a new period of prescription starts running.

72 German law provides for such renewal or recommencement of the prescription period as another means of prolongation in two situations: '(1) the obligor acknowledges the claim towards the obligee by part payment, the payment of interest, the provision of security or in another way, or (2) a judicial or official act of execution is undertaken or applied for.'[128]

73 The debtor must carry out an act that qualifies as acknowledgement. The Code gives a non-exhaustive list of acts of that kind (part payment, etc). But any act from which a creditor can infer with reasonable certainty that the debtor accepts that he or she is still bound to perform and will perform suffices. For instance, the request for a further time extension for payment has been regarded as acknowledgement.[129] Where the debtor explicitly acknowledges merely a part of the creditor's claim the prescription starts afresh only for this part. Partial performance, such as a part payment, is however generally an acknowledgement of the full claim unless the debtor or the circumstances clearly otherwise indicate.

74 An act of execution can have the same effect as an acknowledgement. The prescription period also starts afresh if in respect of the claim an act of formal execution took place or had been applied for. However, this effect occurs only if the act of execution is granted and neither cancelled nor revoked.[130]

---

127 See BGH WM 1988, 128; *Palandt, Ellenberger*, Überbl vor §194 n 16 et seq.; *Staudinger, Peters and Jacoby*, §214 n 18 et seq.

128 §212 (1) BGB (in the semi-official translation authorised by the German Ministry of Justice and for Consumer Protection on <http://www.gesetze-im-internet.de/englisch_bgb>).

129 BGH NJW 1978, 1914.

130 See §212 (2) and (3) BGB.

### 3) *Special Relations between D and P*

*Parents/children*: The prescription of tort claims of a child against a parent, against a spouse of the parent or against a life partner of the parent does not start running until the child becomes 21.[131] 75

*Spouses*: The running of the prescription of claims between spouses is suspended (meaning does not count for the prescription time) as long as the marriage exists.[132] The same is true of claims between civil (life) partners as long as the civil partnership exists.[133] 76

*Guardian/ward*: The prescription of claims between a guardian/legal custodian/ curator and the ward is not running in the time during which the guardianship/ custodianship/curatorship exists.[134] 77

*Attorney/client*: The relationship between attorney and client as such does not lead to a suspension or extension of the prescription period. However, if the attorney conceals their own tort the running of the prescription period starts only when the client becomes aware (or was grossly negligently unaware) of the damage and that the attorney caused it. 78

*Partners in partnership*: Partners in partnerships other than life partnerships do not have so close a relationship that the prescription period is suspended during the partnership or otherwise prolonged. 79

*Legal entity/organs*: No suspension or prolongation of the prescription period also applies to claims between a company and its officers or shareholders. 80

*Employer/employee*: The relationship between employer and employee does not lead to a suspension or extension of the prescription period. 81

*Physician/patient*: Also, the relationship of doctor and patient neither suspends nor extends the prescription period. 82

*Other*: Since 2002 the German Civil Code provides for the suspension of prescription with respect to claims for the infringement of the right of sexual self-determination. The prescription is suspended until the victim becomes 21 or, if later, until the victim no longer lives in a common household with the tortfeasor.[135] 83

There is no specific prescription provision for the case that the tortfeasor hinders – through fraud, duress, etc – the creditor to pursue a claim before 84

---

131 §207 (1) sent 2 no 2 BGB.
132 §207 (1) sent 1 BGB.
133 §207 (1) sent 2 no 1 BGB.
134 §207 (1) sent 2 no 3–5 BGB.
135 §208 BGB.

the prescription period ends. However, such conduct can violate the good faith commandment of §242 BGB and exclude the prescription defence as long as the conduct lasts.[136]

85 It is common ground that evidentiary or financial difficulties are no reason to suspend or prolong the prescription period. The courts are also not allowed to modify the prescription periods on mere discretion.

### 4) *P's Lack of Capacity*

86 *Minor with representative*: No specific prescription rules except for claims between parent and child (see *supra* 75) apply to claims of or against minors who have a legal representative. However, if the minor has no representative (and has no partial capacity in respect to the claim)[137] any running prescription period does not end earlier than six months after the minor has reached majority (at the age of 18) or the lack of representation is remedied.[138] Where the prescription period is shorter than six months (in tort law no such short period applies so far) only this shorter period exceeds the date when majority is reached.[139]

87 *Adult with mental disability with representative*: Likewise, no specific prescription rules apply to claims of and against adults with mental disability who have a legal representative.

88 *Adult with mental disability with no representative*: If an adult who lacks legal capacity[140] has no legal representative, any prescription period running for or against him or her ends only six months after the lack of representation is remedied or the person regains full capacity.[141] Also, where the prescription period is shorter than six months only this shorter period exceeds the date when majority is reached.[142]

### 5) *Absence of Parties from the Jurisdiction*

89 The mere physical absence of the plaintiff or the defendant from the involved jurisdiction does not as such affect the running of prescription. However, if there are additional circumstances which make it impossible for the plaintiff to pursue

136 MünchKommBGB, *Grothe*, Vor §194 n 23; *Staudinger, Peters and Jacoby*, §214 n 18 et seq.
137 See §§112, 113 BGB.
138 §210 (1) sent 1 BGB.
139 §210 (1) sent 2 BGB.
140 An adult person is incapacitated if he or she 'is in a state of pathological mental disturbance, which prevents the free exercise of will, unless the state by its nature is a temporary one' (§104 no 2 BGB).
141 §210 (1) sent 1 BGB.
142 §210 (1) sent 2 BGB.

the claim in time the running of the prescription period would be suspended, for instance, if due to the defendant's absence and the necessity to discover the new address of the defendant the service of the claim comes unavoidably and despite the plaintiff's utmost care too late.[143]

*6) Former Legal and Other Proceedings between the Parties*

*Before a court*: Any form of legal proceedings in respect of the claim in dispute suspends the further running of the prescription period as long as the proceedings are pursued.[144] Six months after a final decision or other ending of the proceedings the period continues to run. If the court decision confirms the claim a separate prescription period of 30 years starts running.[145] 90

The suspension also ends six months after the court proceedings have ended even without a binding decision,[146] for instance, where the plaintiff withdraws the suit.[147] Where the parties do not further the proceedings but set them at rest without formally ending them, the six-month period begins with the last procedural act of the court or of the parties.[148] Litigation on a close matter has generally no effect on prescription of the 'actual' claim. 91

Where the parties settle the claim in court such settlement has the same effect as a judgment and prescribes after 30 years from the day of settlement.[149] 92

*ADR*: ADR proceedings (conciliation, mediation, med-arb proceedings and the like) can suspend prescription as well. The Civil Code contains a special provision on conciliation proceedings. There, it is necessary that either the claimant institutes proceedings before 'a conciliation body established or recognised by the Land justice administration authority or, if the parties seek conciliation in mutual agreement, with any other conciliation body which settles disputes.'[150] According to the prevailing view it is already sufficient that one of the parties requests conciliation, if a respective conciliation clause has been agreed upon.[151] During such conciliation prescription is suspended.[152] After the 93

143 See also *Staudinger, Peters and Jacoby*, §206 n 12a.
144 §204 BGB (para 1 of the provision contains 14 different legal actions, besides the institution of legal proceedings in a state court, also the beginning of arbitration proceedings etc).
145 §197 (1) no 3 and 4 BGB.
146 §204 (2) sent 1 BGB.
147 *Staudinger, Peters and Jacoby*, §204 n 147.
148 §204 (2) sent 2 BGB.
149 §197 (1) no 4 BGB.
150 §204 (1) no 4 BGB.
151 Sufficient: MünchKommBGB, *Grothe*, §203 n 5; NomosKommBGB, *Mansel and Budzikiewicz*, §203 n 28; *Palandt, Ellenberger*, §203 n 2; not sufficient: *Staudinger, Peters and Jacoby*, §203 n 9.
152 §203 sent 1 BGB.

end of the conciliation proceedings prescription continues to run no earlier than six months after that end.[153]

94 *Mediation*: Mediation proceedings are regarded as negotiations[154] during which the running of the prescription period is suspended.[155] Prescription then ends, unless otherwise agreed upon, three months after the end of the negotiations, respectively the mediation.[156]

95 *Arbitration*: Where the claimant has initiated arbitration proceedings concerning a tort claim the prescription is suspended as long as these proceedings are pursued.[157] Parallel to the solution in state court proceedings, the suspension ends six months after the arbitration proceedings have ended either by a binding award or even without such decision,[158] for instance, where the plaintiff withdraws the suit.[159] Where the parties do not further the proceedings but set them at rest without formally ending them, the six-month period begins with the last procedural act of the tribunal or of the parties.[160]

96 *Negotiations*: Negotiations about the claim suspend the running of the prescription period as long as they last.[161] After their end the running of the period continues and ends not earlier than three months after the end of the negotiations.[162] Furthermore, an agreement with the debtor to temporarily withhold performance also stops prescription for the agreed time.[163] Negotiations require that both sides must be prepared to talk about the claim in dispute.[164]

### 7) *Victim's Death*

97 After the victim's death all his or her claims and obligations generally pass to the heirs. A claim that by succession has thus become part of, or is directed against, an estate does not prescribe earlier than six months after the heir has accepted the estate or insolvency proceedings over the estate have been opened or a curator or executor has been instituted.[165]

---

153 §203 sent 2 BGB.
154 BeckOK-BGB, *Spindler*, §203 n 4; BeckOGK, *Meller-Hannich*, §203 n 24.
155 §203 sent 1 BGB.
156 §203 sent 2 BGB.
157 §204 (1) no 11 BGB.
158 §204 (2) sent 1 BGB.
159 *Staudinger, Peters and Jacoby*, §204 n 147.
160 §204 (2) sent 2 BGB.
161 §203 sent 1 BGB.
162 §203 sent 2 BGB.
163 §205 BGB.
164 BGH NJW 2007, 587.
165 §211 BGB.

In case the victim of the tortious conduct dies before a claim is filed but also before the prescription period has lapsed the prescription period ends no earlier than six months after the heir has accepted the heirship or after the estate has been declared insolvent or an administrator has been appointed.[166] However, if the remaining prescription period was shorter than six months that period allies instead.[167] 98

### 8) *Tortfeasor's Bankruptcy*

The insolvency of the tortfeasor as such does not affect the lapse of the prescription period. However, the running of the period is suspended if the claim is filed in the insolvency proceedings.[168] 99

The bankruptcy of the victim of a tort does not affect the running of the prescription of the tort claim. 100

### *9)* Force Majeure

*Natural disaster*: Generally, the term *force majeure* (*'höhere Gewalt'*) also includes unforeseeable natural disasters which hinder the person to approach a competent court before the prescription period lapsed. 101

*Wars*: There had been special rules during World Wars I and II which prevented the completion of the prescription period if due to wartime circumstances persons had to be absent from their regular home.[169] After the wars these provisions were abolished. However, imprisonment as a prisoner of war can still suspend the running of the prescription period.[170] 102

*Military service*: Military service as such is no unforeseeable event. In times of war it may hinder the lapse of the prescription period (see the preceding point). 103

*Imprisonment*: Innocent imprisonment is *force majeure* in the sense of §206 BGB and suspends prescription whereas justified imprisonment is not.[171] 104

*Legal inability to file a claim*: In extraordinary cases, legal impediments to file a claim have been accepted as an equivalent to *force majeure*, for instance, if under the political system (in the former German Democratic Republic) it was dangerous to file specific claims.[172] 105

---

166 §211 sent 1 BGB.

167 §211 sent 2 BGB.

168 §204 (1) no 10 BGB.

169 See thereto *Staudinger, and H Coing*,[11] §206 n 11 et seq.

170 BeckOK-BGB, *Henrich*, §206 n 4; *Staudinger, Peters and Jacoby*, §206 n 16.

171 Ibid.

172 BGHZ 126, 87 (97 et seq.); BGH JZ 1996, 971; *Staudinger, Peters and Jacoby*, §206 n 12.

106 *Closed courts*: A standstill of the administration of justice in the competent courts is another reason for the suspension of the running of the prescription period.[173]

107 *Other*: Further reasons are, for instance, a sudden illness/accident which effectively hinders the creditor to take legal steps before the end of the prescription period;[174] the same effect has a wrong legal opinion provided by the competent authority or official person.[175] If the claimant does not know the law or errs about the law this is as such generally no reason to suspend or prolong the prescription period unless even an experienced lawyer could not have given a secure answer on the legal problem in dispute.[176]

108 As explained *supra*, the creditor's grossly negligent unawareness of his or her cause of action is no true reason to postpone prescription but is used in German law with respect to the starting point of the regular (short) prescription period. As long as the creditor is – without gross negligence – unaware of the identity of the tortfeasor and all circumstances giving rise to the claim, this (subjective) prescription period does not run. However, the subsidiary objective 'long-stop' period still runs and remains unaffected by the creditor's unawareness. Thus, the long-stop maximum period may be – and often is – shortened by the creditor becoming aware (or grossly negligently unaware) of the relevant facts but the long-stop period is never prolonged by the unawareness of the creditor of the claim.

## IX. CEILINGS ON THE EFFECTIVE TIME OF PRESCRIPTION

109 *To which kinds of tort claims the ceiling applies*: As mentioned before, German prescription law combines the regular short subjective prescription period with much longer objective maximum periods. The latter apply to all kinds of claims but vary in length.[177]

110 *Commencement – event or damage*: In contrast to the regular short period the maximum periods do not start when the claim arose, and the victim became aware (or grossly negligently unaware) of all relevant facts required for the respective tort. The maximum prescription periods for damages claims commence when

173 BeckOK-BGB, *Henrich*, §206 n 5; *Staudinger, Peters and Jacoby*, §206 n 6.

174 BGH VersR 1963, 93 (94).

175 BGH NJW 2000, 422 (424).

176 BeckOK-BGB, *Henrich*, §206 n 4.

177 See §199 (2)–(4) BGB.

the tortfeasor set the condition for the damage[178] while for all other claims the period starts when the cause of action accrued.[179]

*Length*: The length of the long-stop periods vary between ten and 30 years. Where the cause of action is a damages claim for an injury to bodily integrity or personal freedom (or certain succession claims) the maximum period is 30 years (irrespective of the victim's knowledge).[180] For other damages claims either a ten-year period from the accrual of the claim applies or a 30-year period 'from the date on which the act, breach of duty or other event that caused the damage occurred' whichever is the earlier date.[181] For all other claims the long-stop period is ten years.[182] However, for product liability cases covered by the ProdHaftG – in compliance with the underlying EU-Directive on product liability – a general ten-year cut-off period applies.[183] 111

*Application of rules of prolongation*: All provisions of the German Civil Code on suspension, suspension of expiry and renewal which in fact lead to a prolongation of the prescription period apply as well to the maximum periods.[184] 112

## X. STATUTE INTERPRETATION, JUDICIAL DISCRETION AND LACHES

### A. INTERPRETATION

In their interpretation of the prescription provisions German courts appear to be principally neutral, neither explicitly pro nor specifically against prescription. However, in certain aspects a modest preference for ways to avoid prescription may become apparent: for instance, the courts interpret the term 'negotiations' which suspend prescription[185] generally in a generous manner.[186] It is already such a negotiation if the debtor communicates that he or she is willing to discuss the justification of the claim.[187] Also the elements that the courts require the creditor to know in order to set the short prescription in motion are rather extensive and thus tend to favour creditors. 113

---

178 See §199 (2) and (3) BGB.
179 §200 BGB.
180 §199 (2) and (3a) BGB.
181 §199 (3) BGB.
182 §199 (4) BGB.
183 §13 ProdHaftG.
184 See, eg *Palandt, Ellenberger*, §203 n 1.
185 See §203 BGB.
186 BGH NJW 1983, 2075; BGH WM 2009, 1597 n 16.
187 BGH WM 2014, 1107 n 2.

114 On the contrary, it is not regarded unethical if a debtor invokes the defence of prescription. The mere raising of the defence is thus no abuse of law.[188] Also, the creditor does not regularly abuse the law who institutes legal proceedings for the mere purpose to suspend prescription.[189]

## B. DISCRETION

115 German law grants the courts no discretion to apply or not to apply the provisions on prescription or to modify the length of the different prescription periods. The prescription provisions contain some – rather limited – interpretative range by using a few open terms which meanwhile the case law of the Federal Court has mainly filled.[190] The lower courts generally strictly follow this lead. Besides the possibilities of interpretation, no further discretion is allowed.

## C. LACHES

116 As indicated above, the principle of good faith may require that the defence of prescription is disregarded because the debtor caused the creditor's reasonable belief that the defence would not be raised.[191]

117 Moreover, German law knows the institute of forfeiture ('*Verwirkung*') which in rare cases also has the effect that a claim can no longer be pursued in court. In contrast to prescription the lapse of a time period alone does not suffice. There must be further circumstances because of which it appears as a violation of good faith if the claim is still raised.[192] It is necessary that the creditor made no use of its right or claim for a relatively long time, that the debtor could infer from that behaviour the right or claim would be no more executed and that the debtor already made dispositions in the expectation that the right or claim would not be enforced.[193] Forfeiture cannot be invoked in cases where the short regular prescription period of three years applies. The creditor must be able to dispose of this full period for pursuing its claim.[194]

---

188 See already Motive I 296; *Palandt, Ellenberger*, Überbl v §194 n 17.

189 BGHZ 123, 347; BGH NJW 2016, 233 (235).

190 Besides the examples in the preceding paragraph, 'grossly negligent unawareness' may be mentioned although there is a standard definition which regards a person as grossly negligent if he or she does something or omits something that evidently no reasonable person would do or omit; see, eg BGH NJW-RR 2009, 544 and 812; *Palandt, Ellenberger*, §199 n 39.

191 See *supra* 70.

192 See *Palandt, Ch Grüneberg*, §242 n 92; *Staudinger, Peters and Jacoby*, Vorbem zu §§194–225 n 18 et seq.

193 See, eg BGHZ 25, 47 (52); BGHZ 105, 290 (298).

194 BGH NJW 2011, 212; BGH NJW 2014, 1230.

# XI. CHANGE OF PARTIES

## A. THE PLAINTIFF IS A TRANSFEREE OF THE VICTIM'S CLAIM

Where the victim's claim against the tortfeasor is subrogated to a third person, for instance an insurer, the prescription period that already ran generally continues to run against the third person in the same way as it would run against the original creditor.[195] A limited exception is made in the case that the claim passes to the heirs after the victim's death. In that case the Civil Code provides that the claim is not statute-barred unless six months have passed after the heirs have accepted their position as heirs.[196] Where prescription starts only after the transfer of the claim, for the subjective element of actual or imputed knowledge the state of mind of the new creditor is decisive. 118

## B. THE DEFENDANT IS A TRANSFEREE OF THE TORTFEASOR'S OBLIGATION

If the defendant is the transferee of the tortfeasor's obligation, he or she can raise the defences which the tortfeasor had. In principle the running of the prescription period remains unaffected by the fact that the tortfeasor's obligation passed to someone else. However, where the tortfeasor died the prescription period lapses only six months after the heir has accepted the heirship or the executor or other representative has taken over.[197] Mental illness of the original tortfeasor or of his or her successor is irrelevant for the lapse of the prescription period. Only if the creditor suffers from such handicap and has no legal representative does the Civil Code provide for an additional six-month period commencing on the date when a representative has been appointed.[198] 119

## C. CONTRIBUTION CLAIMS

Claims which in a sense substitute the original cause of action as contribution claims among joint tortfeasors are regarded as independent claims with their own prescription that is independent of the prescription of the claim of the original victim.[199] Even if the claim of the original victim is prescribed this has no bearing on the prescription of the contribution claim. 120

---

195 See, eg, MünchKommVVG, *H Möller and S Segger* (2nd ed, 2016) §86 VVG n 318.

196 §211 BGB.

197 §211 BGB.

198 §210 BGB.

199 See for contribution claims among joint tortfeasors BGH VersR 2010, 396 n 11; MünchKommVVG, *Möller and Segger* (2nd ed, 2016) §86 VVG n 321.

## D. DEPENDANTS' CLAIMS

121 Claims for lost maintenance are also regarded as independent claims with their own prescription that is independent of the prescription of the claim of the original victim.[200] Even in the unlikely case that the claim of the original victim (the deceased nourisher) should be prescribed this has no bearing on the prescription of the maintenance claim.

# XII. OTHER ASPECTS OF PRESCRIPTION LAW

## A. STIPULATION

122 Under German prescription law the parties have no full freedom to agree on modifications of the statutory rules on prescription. This is true both for contractual and extra-contractual claims although in fact agreements on prescription seem to be rare in tort law already for the factual reason that the parties often had no opportunity to agree before the tort and are unwilling to do so afterwards. However, the restrictions on the parties' freedom to agree are few: Where liability is based on intent, ie where the tortfeasor acted with intent, the parties cannot validly relax the statutory prescription period in advance.[201] On the other hand, by individual agreement they can do so afterwards and they can agree on an extension of the prescription period because the forbidden relaxation means only any reduction of the statutory prescription period or other facilitation that the claim prescribes.[202]

123 On the contrary, the parties cannot prolong the prescription period beyond the 30-year period by agreement.[203] A total exclusion of the defence of prescription would violate this principle. Yet, a defendant is never hindered not to raise the defence of prescription in court and thereby actually to waive the defence.

124 Further restrictions concern modifications of prescription provisions in standard contract terms. They must not unreasonably deviate from 'essential principles of the statutory provision'.[204] Otherwise they are invalid. This is particularly true

---

200 For claims concerning lost maintenance it is more or less self-understanding that they are independent of the claim of the deceased nourisher because they come into existence only after the death of the latter and only in exceptional cases will the latter's claim then already be prescribed; see also *Palandt, Sprau*, §844 n 1a.

201 §202 (1) BGB.

202 See NomosKommentarBGB, *Mansel and Stürner*, §202 n 16 et seq.; *Palandt, Ellenberger*, §202 n 8; *Staudinger, Peters and Jacoby*, §202 n 12 et seq.

203 §202 (2) BGB.

204 §307 (2) no 1 BGB (in the semi-official translation authorised by the Geman Ministry of Justice and for Consumer Protection on <http://www.gesetze-im-internet.de/englisch_bgb>).

for agreements which shorten the statutory prescription period for claims based on the violation of life, body or health as well as for damages claims where the debtor acted with gross negligence or intent.[205] Furthermore, extremely short prescription periods in standard terms would also violate the essential principle that creditors must be granted a fair chance to pursue their claim.[206]

It is disputed whether or not the parties can agree on modifications of the suspension and renewal rules of the Civil Code. The prevailing view admits such agreements.[207] 125

Admissible agreements on prescription require no form.[208] 126

The debtor can at any time validly waive the defence of prescription.[209] Unless the waiver has to be interpreted as an offer which the creditor accepted (within the borders the Civil Code sets for agreements on prescription) the one-sided waiver is considered to be revocable.[210] However, if the debtor first waives the defence and then in a later litigation tries to revoke it whereas the creditor trusts that the defence will not be raised, the court will reject the defence, again as a violation of the principle of good faith (§242 BGB). 127

## B. MEANING OF 'FILING A CLAIM' THAT INTERRUPTS THE RUNNING OF PRESCRIPTION

As indicated above the creditor can stop the running of prescription by several procedural acts.[211] In any event, the institution of legal proceedings suspends prescription.[212] Institution of legal proceedings requires that a valid statement of claim has reached the court and has been served on the debtor.[213] If the document is served soon after it reached the court, the date relevant for prescription is the date when the statement of claim reached the court.[214] 'Soon after' can mean even several months if the party is not responsible for the delay of the service (if and because the court is responsible for the service and its delay).[215] If the party 128

---

205 §309 no 7 (a) and (b) BGB; the provision is the German implementation of the respective provision of the EU Directive on unfair contract terms.

206 See *Palandt, Ellenberger*, §202 n 13.

207 See MünchKommBGB, *Grothe*, §202 n 5; NomosKommentarBGB, *Mansel and Stürner*, §202 n 10; *Palandt, Ellenberger*, §202 n 4; however, contra *Staudinger, Peters and Jacoby*, §202 n 13.

208 *Erman, Schmidt-Ränsch*, §202 n 3; MünchKommBGB, *Grothe*, §202 n 5; Nomos KommentarBGB, *Mansel and Stürner*, §202 n 9.

209 BGH NJW 1973, 1690; BGH ZIP 2007, 2206 n 15.

210 *Staudinger, Peters and Jacoby*, §202 n 5.

211 See the list of the 14 different kinds of procedural activities in §204 (1) BGB.

212 §204 (1) no 1 BGB.

213 See §253 ZPO.

214 See §167 ZPO.

215 See BGHZ 103, 20 (29); MünchKommZPO, *M Häublein* (5th ed, 2016) §167 ZPO n 9.

(or its lawyer) is responsible, 'soon after' means only about two weeks or as a maximum one month.[216]

129 However, the filing of a claim interrupts prescription merely if the person filing the claim is in fact entitled to file it and if the claim in fact exists. The institution of proceedings by a 'wrong' person or for a non-existing claim does not have any interrupting effect. The same is true if the defendant is the 'wrong' defendant who in fact is not obliged.[217]

## C. WHEN SHOULD THE DEFENCE BE RAISED AND DECIDED?

130 The debtor should invoke the defence as early as possible[218] but in fact can raise it at any stage of the court instances that examine the facts, for example even in the second instance. However, the court has discretion to reject the defence if brought so late that the proceedings would be delayed or if the delay is not sufficiently excused.[219]

131 The court will decide on prescription in its final judgment. The German Civil Procedure Code offers the possibility to decide in split judgments first on the existence of the cause of action and then later on the amount.[220] However, it will usually be impracticable to decide separately on the issue of prescription even if this aspect is particularly disputed.

## D. WHO MAY RAISE THE DEFENCE?

132 Prescription must be invoked by the party who profits from it, regularly the debtor. The court cannot recognise it *ex officio*.[221]

133 Regularly, the defence of prescription cannot be raised by third parties. A joint tortfeasor cannot refuse contribution because another joint tortfeasor has satisfied the claim of the victim although that claim was already prescribed. The contribution claim is regarded as a separate and independent cause of action which is not affected by the lapse of the prescription period of the original claim of the victim of the joint tortfeasors.[222]

216 BGHZ 150, 221 (225); BGH NJW-RR 2006, 1436; contra: MünchKommZPO, *Häublein*, §167 ZPO n 10.
217 See to these situations *Staudinger, Peters and Jacoby*, §204 n 6 et seq.
218 §282 ZPO.
219 See §296 ZPO.
220 §304 ZPO.
221 See already *supra* 70.
222 See BGHZ 58, 216 (218); BGH NJW 2010, 62 (63); *Staudinger, Looschelders* (2012) §426 n 14.

## E. BURDEN OF PROOF (OF ELEMENTS AND OF RULES OF PROLONGATION)

The party who invokes the defence of prescription has the burden to prove that the prescription period lapsed.[223] This is usually the debtor of the obligation. The burden comprises the proof of the beginning and fulfillment of prescription and includes, as the case may be, the grossly negligent unawareness of the claimant.[224] The claimant on the other hand has to prove any suspension or renewal of the prescription period on which he or she relies.[225] 134

223 See *Palandt, Ellenberger*, Überbl v §194 n 24 with further references.
224 See BGH NJW 2007, 1584 n. 32; BGH NJW 2008, 2576 n 25.
225 *Palandt, Ellenberger*, Überbl v §194 n 24 with further references.

# PRESCRIPTION IN TORT LAW: GREECE

Eugenia Dacoronia

## I. INTRODUCTION

1 The Greek Civil Code devotes a whole chapter (chapter 10, arts 247–280 GCC) to prescription and peremption.[1] The provisions on prescription apply to all kinds of claims, unless otherwise provided. More particularly, arts 247–278 GCC refer to the prescription of claims and arts 279 and 280 GCC to peremption, to which, as art 279 GCC provides, the provisions on prescription also apply by analogy. In contrast to Roman Law, where prescription was an institution of a more general nature, which had as a consequence the acquisition, loss and deactivation of rights due to their exercise or omission to exercise (*praescriptio acquisitiva* or *praescriptio extinctiva*),[2] the GCC adopts a narrow notion of prescription and, according to it, only the claim, ie the right to seek a performance from another, consisting of an act or omission, is prescribed (art 247 GCC).[3]

## II. DEFINITION OF PRESCRIPTION

2 The definition given by the editors of the book, ie that 'Prescription in tort law is the legal institution that prevents P from enforcing an alleged right against D

1 For a list of relevant bibliography see *Ap Georgiades*, in: Georgiades and Stathopoulos, Civil Code, General Principles (2nd ed, 2016), Vol IB, Introd. Remarks on arts 247–280.

2 See, from the Greek bibliography, *P Ladas*, General Principles of Civil Law, II (2009), §29 no 9; *Stymfaliades*, General Principles of Civil Law (1953), §77, p. 238.

3 *Ap Georgiades*, in: Georgiades and Stathopoulos, Civil Code, General Principles, Introd. Remarks on arts 247–280, nos 4, 5.

because of the running of a specified period of time on the tort claim' also suits the Greek jurisdiction. Accordingly, prescription in tort law, as prescription in general, is the legal institution, according to which a claim can no longer be judicially enforced, because the claimant failed to exercise it within a specific time limit designated by law.[4]

## III. THE NATURE OF PRESCRIPTION AND ITS EFFECTS

According to art 272 §1 GCC, which also applies to tort claims, when the period of prescription has been completed, the obligor may refuse performance. The claim continues to exist, however, as an *imperfect* or *natural* obligation,[5] which means that, as explicitly mentioned in art 272 §2 sent a GCC, whatever was paid without the knowledge of prescription may not be claimed back. 3

The lapse of time does not lead to P's claim becoming extinguished, but the latter remains intact. The effect of the prescription is to provide D with a procedural defence that bars P's ability to litigate the right in court.[6] 4

## IV. CONSIDERATIONS FOR AND AGAINST PRESCRIPTION OF TORT CLAIMS

### A. AGAINST

It has been mentioned that the institution of prescription may lead, in some cases, to 'injustice' against certain creditors, as not only the person who has fulfilled his obligation and just has no means to prove that he does not owe any more can invoke it, but also the debtor who knows that he has never fulfilled his obligation, taking advantage of the inaction of the creditor – inaction which may also be due to the fact that the latter was not aware of the existence of the debt.[7] However, legal doctrine in Greece approves the choice of the legislator to burden the negligent creditor with the negative consequences, when balancing the contrasting interests.[8] 5

---

4 For the prescription in general see, among others, *Ap Georgiades*, General Principles of Civil Law (4th ed. 2012), 331–355 and (in English) *P Agallopoulou*, Basic Concepts of Greek Civil Law (2005), 97–102.

5 *Georgiades*, *supra* fn 4, 353.

6 *Georgiades*, *supra* fn 4, 352.

7 *A Kornilakis*, in: Georgiades and Stathopoulos, Civil Code, IB, art 249 no 3.

8 See, among others, *Ap Georgiades*, in: Georgiades and Stathopoulos, Civil Code, IB, Introd. Remarks on arts 247–280, no 11; *Kornilakis*, *supra* fn 7.

## B. FOR

6 Similar justifications for the institution of prescription with the ones given by the editors for the institution of prescription are given in Greece and apply to Greek Civil Law. The main goal of this legal institution is certainty of law, which would be jeopardised in case of pending forever claims and uncertain legal relations. Prescription is even imposed by the public interest that requires the clearing of legal relations of the past which, in case they remain open for a long time, create uncertainty and insecurity.[9] Social peace is also protected through prescription as well as the feeling of trust of third persons in good faith, who base their confidence in settled situations.[10] Additionally, evidence and witnesses are more difficult to be found for old cases; the task of finding the truth is more difficult with the passing of time. The delay on the plaintiff's part may also be considered as a kind of neglect or an indication of waiver, which weakens his claim to enforce an alleged right.[11]

# V. ELEMENTS OF PRESCRIPTION – AN OVERVIEW

7 In Greek Civil Law, there are also four sets of rules, that together comprise prescription law:

8 (1) *Rules of accrual (or birth)*, which determine the date the prescription period starts to run.[12] According to art 251 GCC prescription starts to run from the time the claim was born, and it can be judicially pursued.

9 (2) *The prescription period*, meaning the statutory period of time that after its running the claim for remedy is prescribed. According to the general rule of art 249 GCC, unless stipulated otherwise, claims are prescribed after 20 years have passed since the claim was born.[13] It is otherwise stipulated in art 937 GCC, which provides in §1 that the claim arising from tort is barred by prescription five years after the time the victim has had knowledge of

---

9 *Ap Georgiades*, in: Georgiades and Stathopoulos, Civil Code, IB, Introd. Remarks on arts 247–280, no 9, with reference to additional relevant bibliography and jurisprudence in fn. 28; *A Kornilakis*, in: Georgiades and Stathopoulos, Civil Code, IB, art 249 no 2.

10 *Georgiades*, *supra* fn 4, p. 332; ibid, in Georgiades and Stathopoulos, Civil Code, Vol IB, Introd. Remarks on arts 247–280 no 9; *Chr. Michailidou*, in: Georgiades, Brief Interpretation of the Civil Code (Syntomi Erminia tou Astikou Kodika/SEAK), 2010, Vol 1, Introd. 247–280, no. 2; *G. Georgiades*, ChrID I (2010), 753.

11 *I Karakostas*, Civil Code: Interpretation, Commentaries, Case Law (Civil Code), Vol 2 (2005), art 247 no 1480, 648.

12 *Georgiades*, *supra* fn 4, 336–339.

13 *Georgiades*, *supra* fn 4, 334–336; *Agallopoulou*, *supra* fn 4, 98; AP 343/2007, published in the Legal Data base of the Athens Bar 'Isokratis'.

the damage[14] and of the person bound to pay damages[15] and without regard to such knowledge, in 20 years from the commission of the act. In order for the certitude of law to be served, a maximum time limit has been enacted (20 years from the commitment of the tort), without regard to whether the person who sustained the damage took knowledge of the damage or of the tortfeasor. The act is considered to be committed at the time of the tortfeasor's behaviour (positive act or omission) and not at the time of the manifestation of the damage. Consequently, the 20-year prescription may begin, by derogation from the rule of art 251 GCC, even before the manifestation of the damage.[16]

Article 937 §2 GCC provides that if the tort is at the same time a punishable act for which criminal law prescribes a longer period of prescription, such 10
longer prescription prevails.[17] According to the Court of Cassation (sitting in full bench),[18] the legislator, referring in para 2 of art 937 GCC to the 'longer prescription period according to criminal law', means the period provided *in abstracto* by art 111 of the Greek Penal Code (GPC) and not the one after taking into account the period of suspension of the prescription of the offence according to art 113 GPC. This period of suspension has no legal effect on the prescription of the claim. The latter is neither interrupted

14 Knowledge of the damage is understood to be the knowledge of the detrimental consequences, even future, of the act [AP (in full bench) 38/1996 Greek Justice (Elliniki Dikaiosini, EllDni) 38 (1997), 41; AP 374/2001 Chronicles of Private Law (Chronika Idiotikou Dikaiou, ChrID) A' (2001), 417; 807/1997 Journal of Greek Jurists (Ephimeris Ellinon Nomikon, EEN) 65, 753], not the knowledge of the exact extent of the detriment or of the amount of damage (AP 1239/2000 ChrID A' (2001), 313, 314).

15 Knowledge of the person bound to pay damages is understood to be the knowledge of such facts that allow the filing of a suit against a certain person with hopes of success; simple suppositions, suspicions or no knowledge of the tortfeasor due to negligence do not suffice; when such knowledge exists is a factual issue, depending on the particular facts of each case (AP 737/2012 Legal Tribune (Nomiko Vima, NoV 2012 (60), 2401; 141/2007 NoV 2007 (55), 1392. See also *A Karampatzos*, The Institution of Prescription in the Common Frame of Reference as *Occasio* for a Reform of the Law of Prescription of the Greek Civil Code, ChrID ID' (2014), fn 11, 574.

16 See AP 951/2008, published in legal data base NOMOS = NoV 57 (2009), 520. For a brief summary of the facts, the judgment of the court and relevant commentary in English see *E Dacoronia*, in: H Koziol and B Steininger, Tort Law Yearbook (2008), 332–338, nos 27, 32 and 40.

17 According to AP 779/2002 ChrID B' (2002), 696, 697, if the act is a misdemeanour, which is prescribed according to arts 111 §3 and 112 of the Greek Penal Code (GPC) in five years from the commission of the act, then this prescription does not prevail, as the prescription of art 937 §1 GCC is longer; it is the prescription of art 937 §1 GCC that prevails. For a brief summary of the facts, the judgment of the court and relevant commentary of AP 779/2002 in English see *E Dacoronia*, in: H Koziol and B Steininger, Tort Law Yearbook (2002), 248–249, nos 66–70.

18 AP 21/2003 (full bench) ChrID C' (2003), 613–614 = Archeio Nomologias (Archive of Jurisprudence, ArchN) 34 (2003), 481–483, followed by a note of *Chr Nikolaides*. For a brief summary of the facts, the judgment of the court and relevant commentary in English see *E Dacoronia*, in: H Koziol and B Steininger, Tort Law Yearbook (2003), 221–222, nos 34–37.

nor suspended with the suspension of the prescription of the offence. The suspension and interruption of the prescription of the claim are governed by the relative provisions of the GCC and not by those of the Penal Code. The rules on penal prescription and the rules on civil prescription constitute two separate systems of rules.[19] Thus, the acts that entail the interruption or suspension of the prescription are judged separately in the Civil Code and in the Penal Code. Consequently, the period of suspension of a misdemeanour (maximum three years during the main penal proceedings and until the sentence becomes irrevocable according to art 113 §3 GPC), is not taken into account when comparing whether the penal prescription is longer than the civil prescription. The penal prescription of art 937 GCC only refers to the general regulation of art 111 GPC, from which it derives whether the penal prescription is longer or not. The view that the three-year period of suspension of the penal prescription is added to the basic (*in abstracto*) five-year penal prescription does not satisfy the principle of certainty of law, which dictates that the duration of the prescription must be determined from the beginning.

11 According to the view of one member of the court, however, if the claim derives from an unlawful act which is also a misdemeanour, the longer prescription can be eight years and starts from the day the offence was committed. According to the view of the minority, the legislator wanted the claim of the state for the punishment of the tortfeasor as well as the claim of the victim against the tortfeasor to be submitted to the same period of prescription; a different solution, where the civil liability is excluded whilst the penal claim of the state continues to exist, is contrary to the principle of proportional measures, as civil claims will be extinguished, whilst the tortfeasor will still run the risk of being deprived of more important rights, such as the right to freedom.[20]

12 (3) *Rules of prolongation:*

13 (a) *Rules of suspension*, that postpone the running of the prescription period (arts 255–259 GCC).[21] The period of suspension does not count for the completion of prescription (art 257 §1 GCC). The prescription continues after the cessation of the suspension but may not be completed before the lapse of six months thereafter (art 257 §2 GCC).

---

19 This view is followed by the majority of legal writers. See *KA Kafkas*, Law of Obligations – Special Part (7th ed, 1975), Vol B', 935; *I Spyridakis*, Tort according to art 914, Theoretical problems and practical applications (1999), 166.

20 This is also the view of *P Filios*, Law of Obligations – Special Part (1998), §191C II, 134.

21 For an analysis of said articles see, from the most recent bibliography, *D Papadopoulou – Klamari*, in: Georgiades and Stathopoulos, Civil Code, $I^B$, arts 255–259; *S Symeonides*, in: K Kerameus and P Kozyris, Introduction to Greek Law (3rd ed, 2008), 98 and 99.

Suspension of the limitation period falls within two kinds: either *absolute* (which is activated no matter in which time during the prescription period its cause arises)[22] or *suspension of completion* (the cause of activation of the suspension arises during the last six months of the prescription period and, thus, prevents its completion).[23] 14

(b) *Rules of interruption*, that cancel the time of prescription that has already passed and renew the running of the prescription period by starting its count from the beginning (arts 260–270 GCC).[24] For instance, these rules apply when D recognises his obligation in any way or when P files an action for the claim.[25] 15

(4) *Ceiling on the effective time of prescription* (rules of 'long-stop' or 'repose') 16

The Greek law of prescription does not employ 'ceiling periods', under which a claim is prescribed after a certain long period expires even if the prescription period has not yet expired because of the prolongation rules of postponement, renewal and extension. The 20-year prescription period from the commission of the act provided in art 937 GCC even if the victim has not had knowledge of the damage and of the person bound to pay damages is considered as a rule of 'long-stop' or 'repose' but even this period is subject to the general prolongation rules of postponement, renewal and extension.[26] It is clear in Greek literature that the provision of art 937 GCC titled 'prescription' does not introduce a 'ceiling period' in the meaning that the general prolongation rules of postponement, renewal and extension do not apply;[27] its meaning is only that if the victim has had knowledge of the damage and of the person bound to pay damages after 20 years from the commission of the act he cannot file an action because his claim will be prescribed but only if there is no prolongation of the prescription period because of postponement, renewal or extension according to the general rules. 17

---

22 *Agallopoulou, supra* fn 4, 99 and 100.

23 *Agallopoulou, supra* fn 4, 100 and 101.

24 For an analysis of said articles see, from the most recent bibliography, *D Papadopoulou-Klamari*, in: Georgiades and Stathopoulos, Civil Code IB, arts 260–270; *Agallopoulou, supra* fn 4, 101 and 102.

25 *Georgiades, supra* fn 4, 343–351.

26 *Georgiades*, in: Georgiades and Stathopoulos, Civil Code, Law of Obligations – Special Part, Vol 4 (1982), art 937 nos 1 and 52; *G Georgiades*, in: Ap Georgiades, SEAK, 937 no 38.

27 There is no article in the GCC equivalent to art III.-7:307 of the Common Frame of Reference according to which 'The period of prescription cannot be extended, by suspension of its running or postponement of its expiry under this Chapter, to more than ten years or, in case of rights to damages for personal injuries, to more than thirty years. This does not apply to suspension under III.-7:302 (Suspension in case of judicial and other proceedings).'

# VI. THE STARTING POINT OF THE PRESCRIPTION PERIOD

## A. THE MEANING OF 'ACTION' AND 'CAUSE OF ACTION'

18 In Greek civil law, a cause of action is a set of facts sufficient to justify a plaintiff's right to file an action against the defendant. Generally, it encompasses the historical facts, on which the action is based, the legal base (the legal wrong the plaintiff claims to have suffered) and the remedy (the relief a court is asked to grant). There are numerous specific causes of action, including: contract-based actions[28] or statutory causes of action, such as torts,[29] unjust enrichment,[30] etc.

## B. BROAD OR NARROW CONCEPTION OF 'CAUSE OF ACTION'?

**Case 1** – *D, a ski instructor, negligently fails to make sure that all skiers in her 'off-piste' group wear helmets. P, a skier in the group, hits a tree. P immediately suffers head injury X, and years later another head injury Y that developed from the same accident.*

19 According to art 937 GCC, P's claim for compensation accrues from the time he becomes aware of the inflicted damage. Knowledge of the exact extent of the damage is not necessary.[31] In case the damaging consequences of D's behaviour make their appearance later or new damages are added to the already existing ones, the following rules apply: If the additional damage could be foreseen by the time P became aware of the damage, then all of them, deriving from the tort, form a cohesive unit and the claim for compensation is subject to one, undivided prescription.[32] Otherwise, if the new damage could not be foreseen, an independent prescription period accrues from the time P came to know its occurrence and its causal link with the tort.[33] The cause of action for injury Y accrues with injury X (one cause of action) as long as it was predicted and anticipated by the time X took place. If injury Y could not be predicted at the time

---

28 *Ap Georgiades*, Law of Obligations, General Part (Law of Obligations) (2nd ed, 2015), 52 and 53.

29 *Georgiades*, Law of Obligations, 71.

30 *Georgiades*, Law of Obligations, 71 and 72.

31 AP 666/2010 Review of Private Insurance Law (Epitheorissi Dikaiou Idiotikis Asfalissis, EpiDikIA) 8, 386; 795/2008, published in NOMOS.

32 AP 953/2012, NoV 61 (2013), 151; 21/2012, NoV 60 (2012), 531; 1730/2010 ChrID IA' (2011), 584.

33 *Ap Georgiades*, Law of Obligations, 717–718; AP 935/2010 published in NOMOS. See also *E Dacoronia*, Issues from the Extension of the Prescription Period in Case of Confirmation of the Claim by a Judgment not Subject to Appeal According to Art. 268 sent. a GCC, ChrID Z' (2007), 106, 107 (Essays in Honour of K D Kerameus) (2010), 173–175.

of injury X, then two causes of actions exist with different accrual prescription periods each. It does not matter whether Y is much more severe than X or vice versa. Injuries X and Y need to be causally connected to the accident (hitting the tree).

**Case 2** – *Physician D treats patient P negligently and performs three mistakes on the day of the treatment: A, B and C. Mistake A causes harm X after a year. Mistake B causes harm Y after two years. Mistakes A and C together cause harm Z after three years.*

As above under Case 1. So, if harms X, Y and Z could be foreseen from the start, they all accrue from the time P finds out about the damage, whereas, if one or some of them could not be foreseen, they form a different cause of action and a new prescription period begins.[34] 20

**Case 3** – *Builder D lays down defective foundations for a building thereby creating the risk of future collapse. As a result, the value to the owner of the building (P) decreases (harm A). Two years later the foundation subsides and requires fixing paid by P (harm B). Three years later cracks appear in the building fixed by P (harm C). Four years later the building collapses (harm D).*

According to Greek Civil Law, every adverse change in legal goods, related to property or not, following an incident, constitutes damage.[35] This change occurs at the time the harm is actually materialised, which is also the time the prescription period starts running, ie the cause of action accrues when D's tortious conduct causes harm to P, as is often the case. As a result, on one hand, the economic loss due to the building's defective foundations occurs at the time those foundations were laid down by builder D and at that time harm A occurred for prescription purposes. 21

However, the situation differs in case of a risk of certain future harm, ie the issue which causes problems is when D's behaviour creates a risk of harm which materialises later. 22

This was the case of the September 1999 Athens earthquake which, as already mentioned, caused the collapse of a factory and the death of 39 employees disclosing that the civil engineer of a factory had not complied with the generally accepted technical rules and standards of building construction, allowing the defective construction of the factory, which lacked stability and resistance, thus endangering the life and health of the employees and leading to their death 23

34 See relatively *Ap Georgiades*, in: Georgiades and Stathopoulos Civil Code (1982), Vol 4, 937 no 19; *P Kornilakis*, Law of Obligations, Special Part (2000), §132, 437, fn 91; ibid., Law of Obligations, Special Part, I (Law of Obligations I) (2002), §107 9, 657.

35 *Ap Georgiades*, Law of Obligations, 141.

because of the collapse of the building which would not have happened if the civil engineer had properly acted.

24 The Greek Court of Cassation[36] ruled that the civil engineer was under a special legal duty to take particular care to protect the goods that had been exposed to danger, by taking preventive measures and by repairing the defective building. The said legal obligation arose in April 1979, when the construction of the building was completed, and lasted until the danger was realised in September 1999 with the collapse of the building because of the earthquake. The engineer's unlawful behaviour consisted of both the act of constructing a defective building and of the omission to repair it, though he had the legal duty to avert the danger, a legal duty which derived from the defective construction of the building. As a consequence, according to the Court, the claim of the victims' relatives was not prescribed, because the 20-year prescription period provided for by art 937 GCC had not elapsed, given that the engineer's omission to repair the building lasted until 1999, when the factory collapsed. The approach of the Greek Court focused on the continuing omission of repairing the defective building and it did not approach the issue of whether the risk of harm to P should be considered a harm or whether harm should actually occur.

25 Following the above-mentioned decisions of the Court of Cassation, D's unlawful behaviour in this case consisted of both the act of constructing a defective building and of the omission to repair it, though he had the legal duty to avert the danger. The certainty of an upcoming damage leads to the characterisation of D's behaviour as harmful and, thus, in the cases of harms B, C and D P's claims will not prescribe as long as the omission to repair the building lasts.

## C. THE STARTING POINT – BREACH OF DUTY OR OCCURRENCE OF DAMAGE?

**Case 4** – *D enters P's premises without P's permission, thereby committing a tort of trespass but without causing damage. P can file a claim against D asking for the remedy of D's eviction but fails to do so. A year later D causes physical harm to P's premises. P files a claim to compensation for the loss.*

26 The narrow conception is followed in the Greek legal system. The difference between the remedy of *enforcing P's right* and the remedy of *compensating P for harm caused by the infringement of the right* is a substantial one that justifies treating claims for these different types of remedies as different causes of action. The claim for compensation will *not* prescribe with the claim for eviction

[36] AP 8/2005 NoV 53 (2005), 1063 = EllDni 2005 (46), 694; 9/2005; 10/2005 ChrID E' (2005), 504; 11/2005 Arch N 56, 456, cmt by *C Nikolaidis*; 12/2005 ChrID ΣΤ' (2006), 40; 13/2005 (full bench).

because the starting point for the latter is the damage while the starting point for the former is the tortious activity.

It has to be mentioned here, however, that according to the Greek legal system trespass is not qualified as a tort. The remedy for the eviction of the trespasser is not a tort claim but an action provided by the Real Property Law provisions of the GCC for the protection of ownership (revendicatory action, art 1094 GCC[37]) or for the protection of possession (art 987 sent a GCC,[38] 997 GCC[39] in combination with 987 GCC), depending on the quality of the person evicted (owner, possessor or holder). 27

## D. WHAT IS CONSIDERED 'HARM' FOR PRESCRIPTION PURPOSES?

**Case 5** – *In an accidental event, D negligently caused an explosion that damaged P's ears. During the first two years P has to raise the volume to enjoy music. During the following three years P needs a hearing device. After a further five years P becomes deaf.*

Same answer as under Case 1. If the additional damage could be foreseen by the time P became aware of the damage, then all of them, deriving from the tort, form a cohesive unit and the claim for compensation is subject to one, undivided prescription. Otherwise, if the new damage could not be foreseen, an independent prescription period accrues from the time P came to know its occurrence and its causal link with the tort. 28

**Case 6** – *Builder D lays down defective foundations for a bridge, thereby creating the risk of future collapse if heavy rain falls. Two years later heavy rain indeed falls, and the collapse becomes only a matter of time, as indeed happens four years after the laying of foundations.*

According to Greek Civil law, every adverse change to legal goods, related to property or not, following an incident, constitutes damage.[40] This change occurs at the time the harm is actually materialised, which is also the time the prescription 29

37 Article 1094 GCC. *Revendicatory action.* The owner of a thing has the right to demand by the possessor (in Greek 'nomeas') or the holder (in Greek 'katohos') the recognition of his ownership and the return of the thing.

38 Article 987 GCC. *Protection in case of eviction.* A possessor evicted unlawfully and without his consent has an action for the recovery of possession from him who possesses defectively against him.

39 Article 997 GCC. *Protection of a holder.* In the case of an unlawful disturbance of the possession of a thing or of a right or in case of eviction from possession, the person who holds property for another in the capacity of a lessee, depositary or some other similar relationship, is granted the same protection as a possessor.

40 *Georgiades*, Law of Obligations, 141.

period starts running. However, the situation differs in case of a risk of certain future harm. Following the above-mentioned decisions of the Court of Cassation, D's unlawful behaviour consisted of both the act of constructing a defective bridge and of the omission to repair it, though he had the legal duty to avert the danger. The certainty of an upcoming damage leads to the characterisation of D's behaviour as harmful and, thus, P's claim will not prescribe as long as the omission to repair the defective foundations of the bridge lasts.

## E. THE STARTING POINT (ACCRUAL) IN CONTINUOUS TORTS

30 Greek Civil Law does not specifically regulate continuous tort in its provisions. However, this notion comes into play when the damaging consequences of a tort have some continuing feature, for instance continuous trespass, continuous environmental nuisance, repetitive discriminatory publications and so on. In order for the ensuing harms to be considered 'continuous' and not distinct, it is necessary that they derive from the same cause of action, they are produced in proximity and through an uninterrupted length of time and, in general, they belong to a cohesive unit of actions. In that case, the cause of action does not accrue each time that similar, continuous harms are produced, but only once, from the moment the tort began to emit damaging consequences.[41] As a result, the prescription time starts running from the time the plaintiff came to know the damage and the defendant's identity (art 937 GCC),[42] while the continuation of the harmful behaviour does not hinder the start and completion of the prescription period.[43] On the contrary, if every continuing repetition of the tort induces new damage, a new independent five-year prescription period starts in regard to each one of them.[44]

31 However, if the repetitive cause of damage is due to a continuous omission of the tortfeasor to remedy a certain unlawful situation that he caused, the prescription of the claim is impeded whilst the omission continues to exist and starts from the moment the tortfeasor undertakes the omitted act and the victim knows the extent of the damage sustained.[45]

41 AP 809/2007, NoV 55 (2007), 2161.

42 *Ap Georgiades*, in: Georgiades and Stathopoulos Civil Code, Vol 4, 937 nos 16–28.

43 *Georgiades*, Law of Obligations, 718; *M Georgiadou*, in: I Karakostas, Civil Code, Vol 6 (2009), art 937, no 20, 1273–1274.

44 AP 674/2013, NoV 61 (2013), 2435; 935/2010, published in 'Isokratis'; 719/1983 NoV 32, 280.

45 *Ap Georgiades*, in: Georgiades and Stathopoulos, Civil Code, Vol 4, 937 nos 23, 24; *Georgiades*, Law of Obligations, 718; *G Georgiades*, SEAK, 937 GCC no 21; *M Georgiadou*, in: I Karakostas, Civil Code, Vol 6, art 937 no 21, 1274; *I Karakostas*, The Law of Tort (2014), 423, where also reference to relevant jurisprudence in fn. 1886; *P Kornilakis*, Law of Obligations I, §107 9, 658.

Accordingly, the Court of Cassation dealing once again[46] with the 1999 earthquake that took place in Athens which revealed omissions of civil engineers and constructors leading to detrimental consequences has repeated once again that in case of omissions the prescription period does not start as long as the person who has to act can still take the appropriate measures in order to avoid the damaging effects of his omission[47] (collapse, as already mentioned, of a factory and the tragic death in its ruins of 39 workers, collapse of a four-floor building resulting in the tragic death of 16 residents and the serious injury of 12 other residents as well as in material damage, ie the total destruction of the apartments of the building as well as of the cars that were parked close by). 32

According to the Court of Cassation, the engineer and constructor had the legal duty to eradicate the consequences of the violation of the generally accepted technical rules and building standards, during the whole period from the construction of the building until its collapse. This was to be either by repairing the defective building or, in case they could not repair the defects, by informing the competent authorities about its non-conformity with the generally accepted technical rules and building standards so that the appropriate measures could have been taken (for example, evacuation of the building, no use of it, etc); thus the 20-year prescription provided for in art 937 GCC had not been completed, though more than 20 years had elapsed from the completion of the construction of the building. 33

It had been commented, however,[48] that this construction of the Court of Cassation is artificial and uncertain, in particular if somebody would try to generalise; and this even more so when previously the Court of Cassation had held[49] that when a tort is committed by a continuing omission, its prescription starts from the moment the omission first occurred, otherwise the prescription provided for in art 937 §1 sent B GCC would be annulled. 34

**Case 7** – *Every week, during a month, D1 publishes a defamatory article on P1, each time in another newspaper and on a different topic. During the same period D2 publishes a defamatory article on P2, every second day, on the same topic and in the same newspaper.*

Each libel by a newspaper article constitutes a separate unlawful behaviour and, thus, creates an independent obligation for compensation. It is not an issue of 35

---

46 See previously AP (in full bench) 8/2005 NoV 53, 1063 = EllDni 46 (2005), 694; 9/2005, published in NOMOS; 10/2005 ChrID E/2005, 504; 11/2005 ArchN 56, 456 cmt by *C Nikolaidis*; 12/2005 ChrID ΣΤ'2006, 40; 13/2005, published in NOMOS. For said decisions (in English) see *E Dacoronia*, Greece, in: H Koziol and B Steininger (eds), ETL 2005 (2006) 306 no 19ff.

47 AP 602/2015 published in NOMOS.

48 *Kl Roussos*, Prescription of the Claim Based on Tort, ChrID ΣΤ/2005, 89.

49 AP 420/2002 Epitheorissi Ergatikou Dikaiou (Review of Labour Law, EErgD) 2003, 1025.

a complete tort inducing its damaging consequences continuously,[50] but of a number of separate unlawful acts by D, each one of which causes additional damage to P and marks a new prescription accrual. Where each repeated tort inflicts a brand new damage, an independent claim for compensation is born, which, in turn, is subject to an independent five-year prescription period.[51] Means of publication and form of defamation are not deemed sufficient to lead to the behaviour's characterisation as a 'continuous tort'.

**Case 8** – *D, a landowner, negligently exposes P, a neighbour, to unreasonable noise for three years. P's hearing is thereby weakened on a daily basis, gradually restricting P's ability to communicate and enjoy music.*

36 In general, following a completed tort that inflicts continuous harmful conditions to P, the latter's right to remedy is born from the time D's misconduct began to produce its damaging consequences.[52] In case of a continuing damage, the claim of damage is not being reborn continuously; the claim for the future damage is also born from the beginning, from the moment the act has started to send out its detrimental consequences, given that, according to the usual course of things, such a future damage could be foreseen. From this moment the five-year prescription period provided by art 937 §1 GCC starts running for the whole damage.[53]

37 However, D's behaviour constitutes a 'continuous tort', as D not only created the harmful situation but also omits to stop it. For this reason, the tort cannot be considered 'completed', meaning that the cause of action accrues from the time P becomes fully aware of the inflicted damage.[54]

**Case 9** – *A waste management company digs bins of toxic content into the soil. Toxic substance leaks into the soil and ground water, causing an apparent damage to crops and expenditure on cleaning on a daily basis. After two years the bins are removed from the soil.*

38 The difference in the damage, ie that there is not bodily injury, but property damage and pure economic loss does not affect the answer which will not differ from the one given to Case 8.

---

50 See *M Georgiadou*, in: I Karakostas, Civil Code, Vol 6, art 937 no 20, 1273.

51 *Ap Georgiades*, in: Georgiades and Stathopoulos, Civil Code, Law of Obligations – Special Part, Vol 4 (1982), art 937 no 21; *G Georgiades*, in: Georgiades, SEAK, 937 no 22; *M Georgiadou*, in: I Karakostas, Civil Code, Vol 6, art 937, 1274; *I Deliyannis and P Kornilakis*, Law of Obligations, Specific Obligations, Vol III (1992), §386, 301 and 302.

52 *Ap Georgiades*, Law of Obligations, 718; AP 347/2010 NoV 58 (2010), 2247-2253; 1024/2008, published in 'Isokratis' and NOMOS.

53 AP 1239/2000 ChrID A' (2001), 313, 314; 53/2002 ChrID B' (2002), 213-214; AP 1024/2008, *supra*.

54 *Ap Georgiades*, Law of Obligations, 718; *G Georgiades*, in: Georgiades, SEAK, 937 no 21; AP 1024/2008; 832/2008 both published in NOMOS; 347/2010, *supra*; 1730/2010, *supra*.

## F. IS THE LATE DISCOVERY RULE A RULE OF THE STARTING POINT (ACCRUAL) OR A RULE OF PROLONGATION?

There is no discussion in Greek literature on whether the late discovery rule is a rule of the starting point or a rule of prolongation. The common approach though is that it is a rule of the starting point. 39

More particularly, a distinction is made in the Greek Civil Code between: 40

(1) Claims which are prescribed after 20 years have passed since the claim was born (art 249 GCC). This is the general rule, the usual prescription; all claims are prescribed after 20 years, unless it is otherwise stipulated by a specific provision of the law, which provides for a shorter prescription.[55] According to art 251 GCC prescription starts to run from the time the claim was born and it can be judicially pursued. 41

(2) Particular claims described in art 250 GCC which are prescribed after five years have passed since the claim was born. According to art 253 GCC, the prescription of those claims starts running from the expiration of the year during which said claims were born and could be judicially pursued or, in case a previous notice was required for the claim of the performance, from the expiration of the year during which the notice was possible. If, except from the notice, the expiration of a certain period of time is required, prescription begins to run as from the time the notice can be given, and the period of time has lapsed.[56] 42

(3) Claims deriving from torts which are time-barred five years after the time the victim has had knowledge of the damage[57] and of the person bound to pay damages[58] and without regard to such knowledge, in 20 years from the commission of the act (art 937§1 GCC). 43

---

55 See, among many others, *Georgiades*, *supra* fn 4, 334.

56 Article 251 GCC. *Commencement of prescription.* Prescription starts from the day the claim was born it could be judicially pursued.
Article 252 GCC. If for the claim of the performance, a previous notice is required, the prescription begins to run as from the time the notice can be given. If except from the notice the expiration of a certain period of time is required, prescription begins to run as from the time the notice can be given and the period of time has lapsed.
Article 253 GCC. The prescription of the claims which are mentioned in art 250 GCC starts running from the expiration of the year during which the prescription mentioned in the two previous articles began.

57 Knowledge of the damage is understood to be the knowledge of the detrimental consequences, even future, of the act [AP (in full bench) 38/1996, EllDni 38 (1997), 41; AP 374/2001 ChrID A' (2001), 417; 807/1997 EEN 65, 753], not the knowledge of the exact extent of the detriment or of the amount of damage (AP 1239/2000 ChrID A' (2001), 313, 314).

58 Knowledge of the person bound to pay damages is understood to be the knowledge of such facts that allow the filing of a suit against a certain person with hopes of success; simple suppositions, suspicions or no knowledge of the tortfeasor due to negligence do not suffice;

44 As can be deduced from the above and it is stated in the Greek doctrine,[59] 'the knowledge or ignorance of the existence of the claim does not, as a rule, affect the starting of the prescription. As an exception, special provisions make *the starting of the prescription* also dependent on other facts, such as the knowledge of the damage and of the person bound to pay damages (art 937 GCC) [...]'.

## VII. PRESCRIPTION PERIODS

45 In Greek Civil Law, there is a general rule regarding the period of prescription which is common to all private claims, including claims deriving from contracts and unjust enrichment,[60] and is set at 20 years (art 249 GCC). However, there are a lot of notable exceptions, where a shorter time of prescription is laid down.[61] To begin with, speed of transactions in the marketplace creates the need for a shorter prescription period in comparison to non-commercial transactions; the dealings must be cleared faster, as their prolongation impedes the progress of national economy and afflicts commerce in general.[62] Accordingly, art 250 GCC provides for a five-year prescription period for 18 categories of claims, enumerated in said article, which are common in everyday transactions and relate to the circulation of goods and the supply of services.[63] Furthermore, shorter prescriptions are provided in art 554 GCC (for material defects or lack of conceded qualities: five years in regard to land, two years in regard to movables), arts 602–603 GCC (claims of the lessor for damages due to modification or deterioration and of the lessee for expenses: six months), art 946 GCC (for the contest of every alienation which was made by the debtor: five years), art 992 GCC (claims on eviction and disturbance: one year) and art 937 GCC concerning torts (five or 20 years, as above-mentioned).[64] The justification behind that different regulation concerning torts lies in the

when such knowledge exists is a factual issue, depending on the particular facts of each case (AP 737/2012 Legal Tribune (Nomiko Vima), NoV 2012 (60), 2401; 141/2007 NoV 2007 (55), 1392). See also *A Karampatzos*, The Institution of Prescription in the Common Frame of Reference as *Occasio* for a Reform of the Law of Prescription of the Greek Civil Code, ChrID ID' (2014), 574, fn 11.

59 See, among many others, *Georgiades*, *supra* fn 4, 338.

60 *Georgiades*, Law of Obligations, General Part, 594.

61 *Chr Michailidou*, in Georgiades, SEAK, 249 nos 2–9; AP 593/2015 and 664/2015, both published in 'Isokratis'.

62 *I Rokas*, Prescription of Stock Broker's Claims Against the Commission Principal for the Return of the Share Purchase Price, Issue of EET (Hellenic Bank Association), 2007, First Trimester, 37.

63 *Georgiades*, *supra* fn 4, 334–336.

64 For an analysis of art 937 GCC see, from the most recent bibliography, *G Georgiades*, in Georgiades, SEAK, 937 nos 10–30 and (in English) *E Dacoronia*, Tort Law in Greece (2017), nos 161 ff.

need for quick resolution of loose threads and for legal certainty, while evidence clearly weakens as time passes by.[65]

If the claim was certified by a final judgment or by an enforceable public document it is prescribed after 20 years (art 268 GCC). 46

No different periods for different tort claims are provided in the Greek Civil Code. Only, as mentioned above, art 937 §2 GCC provides that if the tort is at the same time a punishable act for which criminal law prescribes a longer period of prescription, such longer prescription prevails. 47

Different prescription periods can be provided by special laws.[66] As an example we mention the following: 48

- Law 3950/1911 on Liability for Automobiles,[67] which provides in art 4 that the owner, driver or the possessor of a car are liable to pay damages for any damage caused to third parties from its operation, also provides in art 7 that the action for damages is time-barred two years after the date of the accident. The reason for this short prescription period is because the liability in case of road and traffic is strict, the legislator wants a quick resolution and legal certainty, given that evidence clearly weakens as time passes by. 49
- There is also a short, two-year time-limit of claims of State's employees against the State, including claims for damages from unlawful acts of its organs.[68] The reason for this short time limit, which is provided in art 48 §3 of L.D. 496/1974, in art 90 §3 of L. 2362/1995 and in art 140 §3 of L. 4270/2014,[69] is, according to the Greek Court of Cassation,[70] the power of the legislator to legislate special regulations for the State and for certain categories of persons, when this is imposed by grounds of a more general social or public interest; such grounds exist in the case of the State which from its nature has as a mission and work to serve the citizens.[71] 50
- Also in cases of unfair competition, where whoever undertakes unfair activities leading to breach of contract may be sued for refraining from such acts and for 51

65 *Georgiades*, Law of Obligations, 717.
66 See about said laws *G Georgiades*, in: Georgiades, SEAK, 937 no 4.
67 The force of Law 3950/1911, as amended by subsequent laws, has been extended across the entire Greek State according to art 114 of the Introductory Law of the GCC.
68 Tort claims against the State of persons who are not its employees are time-barred after five years (see art 90 §1 of L. 2362/1995 and art 140 §1 of L. 4270/2014). Article 90 of L. 2362/1995 has been abolished by art 177 of L. 4270/2014.
69 See also *Sp Vlahopoulos*, Prescription of claims in favour of the State and against the State, in: P Papanikolaou (ed), Issues of the law of prescription (2015), 967.
70 AP 3/2006 (in full bench with a minority, however, of eight judges) EllDni 47 (2006), 412; AP 363/2006, published in NOMOS.
71 About the constitutionality of said provisions see *E Dacoronia*, Greece, in: K Oliphant (ed), The Liability of Public Authorities in Comparative Perspective (2015), 202–204.

damages (art 1 of L. 146/1914),[72] the prescription period is 18 months from the moment the claimant has had knowledge of the act and of the person who is liable for damages and, in any case, five years from the act. The prescription does not start before the moment the damage was caused (art 19 of L. 146/1914, as amended by art 29 §2 of L. 3784/2009).

52 It has to be mentioned that, as a rule and because of the special law, which provides for a shorter prescription, said prescription prevails against the prescription of art 937 GCC. However, it is proposed in legal doctrine[73] that this solution should not be adopted without distinction, but that it should be examined in each case on which basis the plaintiff has based his claim; eg if the tortfeasor is strictly liable according to a specific provision of law, such as the above-mentioned art 4 of L. 3950/1911, and in parallel liable according to the provisions of tort that require fault (art 914 GCC) and the plaintiff chooses to sue on the basis of the tortious liability, then not the shorter prescription period but the longer one of art 937 GCC should apply.

53 A claim can be equally based on more than one cause of action with diversified prescription periods.[74] For example, a taxi passenger who gets injured following a negligent behaviour of the taxi driver can claim compensation either on the basis of contractual liability (art 681 GCC) or on the basis of tortious liability (art 914 GCC).[75] In the Greek legal system,[76] the plaintiff is entitled to support his claim on the cause of action that offers him a lesser limitation, meaning that, in this case, he will prefer to choose the second one (five years according to art 937 GCC) over the first one (six months according to art 693 GCC). This conduct of 'period shopping' may give rise to disputes. Nevertheless, it is legal, provided that his claim can be rightfully grounded in the chosen cause of action.[77] Though it may be argued that the specific provisions governing the violation of contractual obligations (arts 330, 335 et seq., 362 et seq., 382 et seq. GCC), as special provisions, prevail over those regarding tortious liability and they do not concur with them (principle of non cumul), the Greek jurisprudence

---

72 See *N Deloukas*, in KD Kerameus and PJ Kozyris (eds), Introduction to Greek Law (in English) (1988), Ch 10, 163 and *N Deloukas* revised by *Ev Perakis*, in: KD Kerameus and PJ Kozyris (eds), Introduction to Greek Law (in English) (3rd rev ed, 2008), Ch 11, 229, Thessaloniki Court of Appeal 1465/2009 and 3000/2005, both published at 'Isokratis'. Articles 914, 919, 281 and 57–59 GCC are complementary to the special provisions of L. 146/1914.

73 See *Ap Georgiades*, in Georgiades and Stathopoulos, Civil Code, Vol 4, 937 no 3; *G Georgiades*, in: Georgiades, SEAK, 937 no 5.

74 *Ap Georgiades*, in: Georgiades and Stathopoulos, Civil Code (1978), Vol 1, 247 nos 26–33; *Chr Michailidou*, in: Georgiades, SEAK, 247 no 28; AP 1173/2015, published in 'Isokratis'.

75 *Georgiades*, *supra* fn 4, 283.

76 See, among others, AP 361/2014, NoV 62 (2014), 1656; 1596/2014, published in 'Isokratis'; 1494/2008, NoV 57 (2009), 429.

77 *Ap Georgiades*, in: Georgiades and Stathopoulos, Civil Code, Vol 4, 937 no 7.

adopts the principle of 'free concurrence of claims'.[78] According to this principle, when the act or omission which constitutes the contractual non-performance is simultaneously and in itself unlawful, the two liabilities, delictual and contractual, concur (principle of cumul);[79] the relevant claims are submitted to different prescription periods depending on the different legal basis. According to Greek law, there is no reason why different legal basis of claims should deprive the plaintiff from the advantages that each one of them provides.[80]

## VIII. RULES OF POSTPONEMENT, SUSPENSION, RENEWAL AND EXTENSION

As mentioned above, the GCC explicitly provides for rules of suspension (arts 255–259 GCC) and rules of interruption (arts 260–270 GCC): 54

(1) The *rules of suspension* postpone the running of the prescription period (arts 255–259 GCC). The period of suspension does not count for the completion of prescription (art 257 §1 GCC). The prescription continues after the cessation of the suspension but may not be completed before the lapse of six months thereafter (art 257 §2 GCC). 55

Suspension of the limitation period falls within two kinds: either *absolute* (which is activated no matter in which time during the prescription period its cause arises)[81] or *suspension of completion* (the cause of activation of the suspension arises during the last six months of the prescription period and, thus, prevents its completion).[82] 56

(2) The *rules of interruption* cancel the time of prescription that has already passed and renew the running of the prescription period by starting its count from the beginning (arts 260–270 GCC).[83] For instance, these rules 57

---

78 For the disadvantages of the free concurrence of claims see, among others, *P Kornilakis*, Law of Obligations I, §79 4 IIβ, 463 ff.

79 See relatively *P Kornilakis*, Law of Obligations I, §79 4, 461 ff, where also (462, fn 3) reference to the abundant relative jurisprudence is made. *M Stathopoulos and A Karampatzos*, Contract Law in Greece (in English) (3rd ed, 2014), §41; *M Stathopoulos*, Law of Obligations, General Part (2004), §15 no 10. See also AP 895/2004 ChrID D' (2004), 1009; 1145/2003, EllDni 45 (2004), 457, 458 = Business and Company Law (Dikaio Epiheiriseon kai Etairion, DEE) 10 (2004), 1179 = Commercial Law Review (Epitheorissi Emporikou Dikaiou, EEmpD) (2004), 819 = ChrID D' (2004), p. 55 followed by comments of *El Kastrissios*; 1538/2002, published in NOMOS; 836/2002 DEE 8 (2002), 1267 = ChrID B' (2002), 599 ff followed by a note of *E Nezeritou*; 587/2002 ChrID B' (2002), 605.

80 *Georgiades*, *supra* fn 4, 287.

81 *Agallopoulou*, *supra* fn 4, 99, 100.

82 *Agallopoulou*, *supra* fn 4, 100, 101.

83 For an analysis of said articles see, from the most recent bibliography, *D Papadopoulou-Klamari*, in: Georgiades and Stathopoulos, Civil Code $I^B$, arts 260–270; *Agallopoulou*, *supra* fn 4, 101, 102.

apply when D recognises his obligation in any way or when P files an action for the claim.[84]

## A. UNAWARENESS – THE LATE DISCOVERY RULE

### 1) *Unawareness of what Elements of Liability?*

58 P's subjective unawareness of the facts constituting the claim can sometimes extend the effective time of prescription, the most notable example being the provision in art 937 GCC, according to which P's right for remedy following a tortious act does not accrue until P becomes aware:

59 (a) *of the damage*. Knowledge of the exact amount of damage is not required. Accordingly, the unawareness of the exact magnitude of the damage does not prevent the prescription period to start running.[85] Prescription starts running for the whole damage from the point the person who sustained the damage has had knowledge of the first detrimental consequences of the tortious act.[86] Awareness to 'significant' harm or awareness to the full scope of harm (its stabilisation) is not required. However, if certain detrimental consequences are born later and were not foreseeable before, a new independent prescription period starts from the point in time the person who sustained the damage has had knowledge of those new detrimental consequences and their causal link to the unlawful conduct.[87]

60 and

(b) *of the person bound to pay damages*, who does not necessarily coincide with the person who acted unlawfully (cf art 922 and art 923 GCC[88]).[89] According

---

84 *Georgiades*, *supra* fn 4, 343–351.

85 *Ap Georgiades*, in: Georgiades and Stathopoulos, Civil Code, art 937 no 16; *G Georgiades*, in: Georgiades, SEAK, 937 no 15.

86 *Ap Georgiades*, in: Georgiades and Stathopoulos, Civil Code, art 937 no 17; *G Georgiades*, in: Georgiades, SEAK, 937 no 17 (where also a number of relevant decisions of the Court of Cassation is, indicatively, listed).

87 See, among others, AP 1581/2008 EllDni 52 (2011), 1048; 233/2007; 1014/2007, both published in NOMOS; *G Georgiades*, in: Georgiades, SEAK, 937 no 19.

88 Article 922 GCC. *Vicarious Liability*. The master or the person who appoints another person to perform a function is liable towards a third party for the damage unlawfully caused to the latter by the servant or this other person in the execution of his task.
Article 923 GCC. *Liability of the person who supervises another person*. Whoever has the supervision of a person under age or of a person of age placed under judicial assistance is liable for damage that such persons unlawfully causes to a third party unless he proves that he has properly exercised the duty of supervision or that the damage could not have been avoided. The person who performs the duty of supervision by virtue of a contract has the same liability. (As amended by art 21 of L. 2447/1996.)

89 *Ap Georgiades*, in: Georgiades and Stathopoulos, Civil Code, art 937 no 25.

to the Court of Cassation,[90] it is considered that P is aware of the person bound to pay damages when he knows those facts that allow him to file an action with hopes of success. Simple suppositions, suspicions or unawareness due to negligence do not suffice. When an action can be filed with hopes of success depends on the total estimation of the particular case. If the name and address of the person bound to pay damages can be verified without a lot of difficulties or costs, then it is considered that P is aware of D.[91] It has been also held,[92] that, in case of a car accident, the awareness of the license plate of the car that caused the accident suffices for the prescription to start running.

61 Full knowledge of all details of the damaging fact is not required. Only the knowledge of the facts on which the claim is based is necessary.[93]

62 The late discovery rule applies to all causes of action and not only to some torts, such as bodily injury nor to some kinds of conducts (intentional, reckless).

63 Apart from the awareness of *D's identity*, *D's conduct* and *P's harm*, as above described, also awareness of *causation*, ie that P's harm was in fact caused by D's conduct, is necessary. So, the late discovery rule applies where there is unawareness of those four elements. Unawareness of the legal norm does not hinder the running of the prescription.

**Case 10** – *Chemical plant D negligently exposes bordering lands to toxic substances. As a result, P, a nearby resident landowner, contracts a lung disease. P failed to sue in time because his former lawyer told him that the exposure was not tortious, and only his new lawyer told him, after the running of time, that it was tortious.*

64 P was aware that his harm was linked to the chemical plant operators' negligence, so P's claim prescribed. The fact the lawyer did not inform P on the tortious character of the exposure does not play a role, as ignorance of law is not allowed, according to the Greek legal system. This fact cannot qualify either as a *force majeure* which would suspend the prescription if it occurred within the last six months of the period of prescription (art 255 sent 1 GCC).

### 2) *Objective or Subjective Unawareness?*

65 The justification in art 937 GCC, according to which P's prescription of the claim based on a tortious act does not accrue until P becomes aware of the damage and D's identity, is subjective.

---

90 AP 141/2007 ChrID Z' (2007), 495.

91 AP 374/2001EllDni 43 (2002), 158; 1385/2007, published in 'Isokratis'.

92 AP 1385/2007, *supra*. See also *Ap Georgiades*, in: Georgiades and Stathopoulos, Civil Code, art 937 no 26; *G Georgiades*, in: Georgiades, SEAK, 937 no 23; *A Kritikos*, Damages from Car Accidents (4th ed, 2008), §23 no 5.

93 *Ap Georgiades*, in: Georgiades and Stathopoulos, Civil code, art 937 no 12.

### 3) *What is Considered Awareness of an Element of Liability?*

66 See above under Section VIII.A.1.

### 4) *How Heavy is the Burden to Acquire Knowledge?*

**Case 11** – *Chemical plant D negligently exposes bordering lands to toxic substances. As a result, P, a nearby resident landowner, contracts a lung disease, but is unaware of the causal link between exposure and disease because his physician fails to detect it. P does not seek a second opinion. After the prescription period runs on the disease P consults his new physician that tells him about the link. Did P's claim against D prescribe?*

67 No, because P was not aware that his harm was linked to the chemical plant operators' negligence (art 937 GCC). P does not in principle incur the burden of seeking a second opinion. The courts, however, depending on the circumstances (eg other employees whom P knows were also exposed and their physician managed to detect the causal link between exposure and disease), might expect that P seeks a second opinion. In such a case, the prescription will start running from the point P should have sought the second opinion.

## B. OTHER RULES OF PROLONGATION

### 1) *D is to Blame for the Delay*

68 The prescription is suspended for all the period in the last six months of the period of prescription the obligor prevented out of intent the obligee from pursuing his claim (art 255 sent 2 GCC).[94] The prescription continues after the cessation of the suspension but may not be completed before at least a further six months from the cessation of the suspension causing event (art 257 §22 GCC).

### 2) *Admission by D of P's Right or Partial Performance of P's Right by D*

69 The prescription is interrupted, if the debtor acknowledges in any way the claim (art 260 GCC).[95] After such an acknowledgement a new prescription period starts.

---

94 See *Chr Michailidou*, in: Georgiades, SEAK, 255 nos 6–9; *D Papadopoulou-Klamari*, in: Georgiades and Stathopoulos, Civil Code $I^{B}$, art 255 nos 19–25; AP 439/2015, published in 'Isokratis'; 830/2015, Armenopoulos (Arm) 69 (2015), 1543.

95 For an analysis of art 260 GCC and an enumeration of cases that illustrate when there is acknowledgement of the debt see, from the most recent bibliography, *Chr Michailidou*, in: Georgiades, SEAK, 260 no 1–8 and in particular nos 6 and 7; *D Papadopoulou-Klamari*, in: Georgiades and Stathopoulos, Civil Code, $I^{B}$, art 260 and, in particular, no 28; AP 148/2006, NoV 54 (2006), 1459; 68/2001, EllDni 42 (2001), 726, 727; 1049/2014, EEmpD 2015, 142.

### 3) *Special Relations between D and P*

*Parents/children*: The prescription of claims is suspended between parents and children during their minority (art 256 §2 GCC).[96] 70

*Spouses*: The prescription of claims is suspended between spouses during marriage, even if the marriage is later declared null, as well as between persons having signed the cohabitation pact for as long as it is in force (art 256 §1 GCC, as replaced by art 12 of L. 3719/2008).[97] 71

*Guardian/ward*: The prescription of claims is suspended between tutors and wards during their tutelage (art 256 §3 GCC). 72

*Attorney/client; Partners in partnership; Legal entity/organs; Employer/employee*: The prescription of claims is suspended between masters and servants during the time of their master-servant relationship but for no more than 15 years (art 256 §4 GCC). According to the Greek legal doctrine and jurisprudence the provision of art 256 §4 GCC should be interpreted narrowly only for certain categories of working people who are in a close personal relationship to the master and not to all employees.[98] 73

*Physician/patient*: No specific provision. 74

**Table 1. Special relations between D and P**

| Relations | Rule of prolongation | Comments |
|---|---|---|
| Parents/children | Suspension | During the children's minority |
| Spouses | Suspension | During marriage |
| Guardian/ward | Suspension | During tutelage |
| Attorney/client | | |
| Partners in partnership | | |
| Legal entity/organs | | |
| Administrator/heirs | Extension | Of six months from when the heir acquired the succession, or an administrator was appointed |

*(continued)*

96 For an analysis of art 256 GCC see *M Chr Kalogera*, in: Georgiades and Stathopoulos, Civil Code (1978), Vol 1, art 256; *Chr Michailidou*, in Georgiades, SEAK, 256; *D Papadopoulou-Klamari*, in: Georgiades and Stathopoulos, Civil Code, $I^B$ (2nd ed, 2016), art 256.

97 AP 43/2015; 1314/2015, both published in 'Isokratis'.

98 *Georgiades*, *supra* fn 4, 340, note 25; *M- Chr Kalogera*, in: Georgiades and Stathopoulos, Civil Code, art 256 no 1; *D Papadopoulou-Klamari*, in: Georgiades and Stathopoulos, Civil Code, art 256 no 23; AP 407/1963 NoV 1964, 95; AP 442/1964 NoV 1964, 1071.

Table 1 *continued*

| Relations | Rule of prolongation | Comments |
|---|---|---|
| Liquidator/debtors | | |
| Employer/employee | | |
| Physician/patient | | |
| Other (master/servant) | Suspension | During the time of the master-servant relationship but for no more than 15 years |

### 4) P's Lack of Legal Capacity

75 *Minor with representative; Minor without representative*: See *infra* 76.

76 *Adult with mental disability with representative; Adult with mental disability with no representative*: Prescription runs against persons with no or limited capacity to enter into juridical acts (art 258 §1 GCC). Articles 128 and 129 GCC define who have no or limited capacity to enter into juridical acts.[99] If these persons do not have a tutor or a judicial guardian, the prescription is not completed before six months from the acquisition of full capacity or the appointment of a tutor or a judicial guardian. This provision is not applied, if the person with no or limited capacity has the capacity to appear in court (art 258 §2 GCC).[100]

77 Thus, if P suffers from mental disability which renders him unable to take care of his business affairs is incapable of entering into juridical acts (art 128 GCC). If P, because of his mental disability, needs a judicial assistant but does not have one, the prescription is not completed before six months from the appointment of such a judicial guardian, unless P has the capacity to appear in court (art 258 §2 GCC).

99 Article 128 GCC. *Incapable of entering into juridical acts.* Incapable of concluding juridical acts are: 1. those who have not yet completed the tenth year of age; 2. those who are placed under total privative judicial guardianship.
Article 129 GCC. *Persons with limited capacity.* The following persons have limited capacity: 1. minors above the age of ten; 2. persons placed under total privative judicial guardianship; 3. persons placed under concurrent judicial guardianship.

100 For an analysis of art 258 GCC see *M- Chr Kalogera*, in: Georgiades and Stathopoulos, Civil Code (1978), Vol 1, 258 nos 1–4; *Chr Michailidou*, in Georgiades, SEAK, 258, nos 1–5; *D Papadopoulou-Klamari*, in: Georgiades and Stathopoulos, Civil Code, $I^B$, art 258.

Table 2. P's lack of legal capacity

| Kind of disability | With representative | Without representative | Kind of prolongation | Comments |
|---|---|---|---|---|
| Minority | No prolongation | Yes (prolongation) | Extension | Six months from the acquisition of full capacity or the appointment of a tutor |
| Adult with unsound mind | No prolongation | Yes (prolongation) | Extension | Six months from the appointment of a judicial guardian |

### 5) *Absence of Parties from the Jurisdiction*

There is no specific provision. No prolongation 78

### 6) *Former Legal and Other Proceedings between the Parties*

*Before a court*: The commencement of legal proceedings interrupts the prescription. 79
The period of prescription that was interrupted in this way begins to run anew from the last act of procedure of the litigants or of the court (art 261 GCC).[101]

Every prescription which was interrupted by the filing of an action, is deemed 80
never to have been interrupted if the plaintiff abandoned the action, or the action was dismissed not on the merits grounds (art 263 §1GCC).

If the plaintiff files the action again within six months, the prescription is deemed 81
to have been interrupted by the previous action (art 263 §2 GCC).

The prescription shall also be interrupted by: (1) the notification of an order of 82
payment under an enforceable judiciary act; (2) the announcement of a claim for its confirmation in bankruptcy proceedings; (3) the announcement of a claim for inclusion in the distribution following a sale by public auction; (4) the raising of a plea of set off of the claim (art 264 GCC).[102]

*ADR*: No relevant provisions yet. 83

*Arbitration*: The submission of the dispute to arbitrators or to an administrative 84
authority or to an administrative court or to another special court mentioned in the claim interrupts the term of prescription (art 269 GCC).[103]

---

101 AP 252/2016, published in 'Isokratis'; 950/2015, NoV 64 (2016), 97; 61/2013, NoV 61 (2013), 949.

102 *Chr Michailidou*, in: Georgiades, SEAK, 264 nos 1–6; *D Papadopoulou-Klamari*, in: Georgiades – Stathopoulos, Civil Code I$^{B}$, art 264.

103 For an analysis of art 269 GCC see, among others, *Chr Michailidou*, in: Georgiades, SEAK, 269 nos 1–6; *D Papadopoulou-Klamari*, in: Georgiades and Stathopoulos, Civil Code, I$^{B}$, art 269; AP 138/2012, NoV 60 (2012), 1484.

85 *Negotiations*: The proposition for an immediate payment of a lesser amount after a settlement constitutes an acknowledgement which interrupts the prescription according to the above-mentioned art 260 GCC.[104] After the acknowledgement a new prescription period starts.

**Table 3. Former legal and other proceedings between the parties**

| Former proceedings | Prolongation | Rule | Comments |
|---|---|---|---|
| Legal | Yes | Renewal | Articles 261 and 263 §§1 and 2 GCC |
| ADR | No | | |
| Arbitration, Administrative | Yes | Renewal | |
| Settlement | Yes | Renewal | |

*7) Victim's Death*

86 The prescription of a claim by or against a succession is not completed before the end of six months from when the heir before six months have elapsed from when the heir acquired the succession or from when the claim can be filed by or against an administrator (art 259 GCC).[105] According to said provision, the prescription period does not start afresh from the victim's death but a six-month extension is given from when P acquired the succession or an administrator was appointed.

*8) Victim's Bankruptcy*

87 As mentioned above, the prescription shall also be interrupted by the announcement of a claim for its confirmation in bankruptcy proceedings (art 264 GCC).

**Table 4. Victim's bankruptcy**

| Contingency | Prolongation | Kind | Comments |
|---|---|---|---|
| V's death – P is an heir | Yes | Extension | Of six months from when P acquired the succession or an administrator was appointed |
| V's bankruptcy | Yes | Renewal | |

*9)* Force Majeure

88 As mentioned above, the prescription is suspended for as long as the obligee is prevented by *force majeure* from pursuing his claim within the last six months

104 *D Papadopoulou-Klamari*, in: Georgiades and Stathopoulos, Civil Code, $I^{B}$, art 260 no 28.
105 *Georgiades*, *supra* fn 4, 340–342.

of the period of prescription (art 255 sent 1 GCC).[106] As *force majeure* is defined as any unforeseeable event, which renders the pursuing of the claim impossible, even though the utmost care and diligence has been demonstrated.[107]

*Natural disaster; Wars*: Natural disaster and wars[108] are included in *force majeure*, so the prescription is suspended for as long as the obligee is prevented from pursuing his claim within the last six months of the period of prescription. 89

*Military service*: According to the Greek jurisprudence, the military service is not included in the notion of *force majeure*.[109] 90

*Imprisonment*: According to the Greek jurisprudence, the sudden arrest and imprisonment constitutes *force majeure*.[110] 91

*Legal inability to file a claim*: There is no specific provision regarding suspension of the prescription. Only art 251 GCC provides that the prescription starts to run from the moment the claim is born and *it can be judicially pursued*. 92

*Closed courts*: Prescription is suspended for as long as the obligee is prevented because of closed courts from pursuing his claim within the last six months of the period of prescription (art 255 sent 1 GCC). 93

**Table 5.** ***Force majeure***

| **Contingency** | **Prolongation** | **Kind** | **Comments** |
|---|---|---|---|
| General clause of *force majeure* | Yes | Suspension for as long as the obligee is prevented from pursuing his claim within the last six months of the period of prescription | |
| Wars | Yes | Suspension as above | Included in *force majeure* |
| Closed court | Yes | Suspension as above | |
| Natural disaster | | Suspension as above (see General clause of *force majeure*) | Included in *force majeure* |
| Legal inability to sue | No | | No specific provision |

*(continued)*

106 See, among others, *Chr Michailidou*, in Georgiades, SEAK, 255 nos 1–6; *D Papadopoulou-Klamari*, in: Georgiades and Stathopoulos, Civil Code $I^B$, art 255 nos 14–18; AP 738/2016, published in 'Isokratis'; 1657/2008, NoV 57 (2009), 1084; 1285/2005, published in 'Isokratis'.

107 *D Papadopoulou-Klamari*, in: Georgiades and Stathopoulos, Civil Code $I^B$, art 255 no 14.

108 See *D Papadopoulou-Klamari*, in: Georgiades and Stathopoulos, Civil Code $I^B$, art 255 no 17.

109 See *D Papadopoulou-Klamari*, in: Georgiades and Stathopoulos, Civil Code $I^B$, art 255 no 18.

110 See Thessaloniki Court of Appeal 3344/1995 EllDni 37 (1996), 192, followed by a note of *G Diamantopoulos*; *D Papadopoulou-Klamari*, *supra*.

Table 5 *continued*

| Contingency | Prolongation | Kind | Comments |
|---|---|---|---|
| Military service | No | | Not included in *force majeure* |
| Imprisonment | No, as a rule | | Not included in *force majeure*, unless sudden arrest and imprisonment |

*10) Other*

94 *Evidential or financial difficulties*: Evidential difficulties of a plaintiff who needs time to gather evidence or financial difficulties of a plaintiff in raising the money required for litigation play no role to the prescription period.

95 *Prolongation by courts on grounds of justice*: According to Greek law, the rules on prescription are mandatory. The courts have no authority to prolong the prescription period on grounds of justice.

## IX. CEILINGS ON THE EFFECTIVE TIME OF PRESCRIPTION

96 As mentioned above, the Greek law of prescription does not employ 'ceiling periods', under which a claim is prescribed after the ceiling period expires even if the prescription period has not yet expired because of the prolongation rules of postponement, renewal and extension. The 20-year prescription period from the commission of the act provided in art 937 GCC[111] even if the victim has not had knowledge of the damage and of the person bound to pay damages is considered as a rule of 'long-stop' or 'repose' but even this period is subject to the general prolongation rules of postponement, renewal and extension (See *supra*, under Section V).

## X. STATUTE INTERPRETATION, JUDICIAL DISCRETION AND LACHES

97 Judges are rather sympathetic towards prescription, though they are not given a wide discretion when interpreting, as the relevant provisions on prescription are mandatory and their wording rather restrictive.

[111] *Ap Georgiades*, Law of Obligations, 719; AP 603/2015, published in 'Isokratis'; 951/2008, NoV 57 (2009), 520.

According to art 249 GGC, unless stated otherwise, the plaintiffs' claims are prescribed 20 years after their birth (five years in case of torts, according to art 937 GCC), a time period deemed as sufficient. Legal experience shows that a pending claim, frequently described as a 'bad claim', undermines the need for legal certainty and safety.[112] Therefore, rejecting a claim on the basis of rules of prescription is not seen as unethical. However, as explicitly provided in art 277 GCC, the court does not take into account *ex officio* the prescription which has not been pleaded. 98

The Greek legal system opts for the statutory regime. The Greek prescription law does not use general, open terms such as 'reasonableness' or 'good faith'. It does not allow judicial discretion (implicit or explicit) on a case-by-case basis, but it sets mandatory rules concerning the prescription period, its accrual, suspension, interruption and legal consequences for the reasons mentioned in the Questionnaire and for the stability of law. Judges do not interpret the rules of prescription differently from other rules within private law. 99

Greek jurisprudence has developed, based on art 281 GCC on abuse of rights, the notion of 'deactivation of rights' which resembles to the legal doctrine of laches. A right may 'lose its force' if the obligee fails to exercise it for an inordinately long (though shorter than the applicable prescription period) time, under conditions that have led the obligor reasonably to believe that the right has been renounced or would not be exercised, and when the enforcement of the right would render severely onerous the condition of the obligor. All private rights, including the ones that are not subject to prescription, are subject to 'deactivation'. 100

However, Greek doctrine and jurisprudence do not relate this institution to the prescription one, as deactivation refers to rights whilst prescription to claims. 101

## XI. CHANGE OF PARTIES

### A. THE PLAINTIFF IS A TRANSFEREE OF THE VICTIM'S CLAIM

The transfer of the contractual claim from the victim to the plaintiff through special succession does not alter the nature of the claim. Thus, the prescription period that started running on the victim's claim continues on plaintiff's claim under the same conditions and does not start afresh, when plaintiff acquires the right of subrogation.[113] 102

[112] *Karakostas*, *supra* fn 11.

[113] *Georgiades*, *supra* fn 4, 351.

## B. THE DEFENDANT IS A TRANSFEREE OF THE TORTFEASOR'S OBLIGATION

103 To the extent that liabilities of tortfeasors may be transferred to others (eg by inheritance law to the estate of the tortfeasor), such a change does not start a new period of prescription but according to art 259 GCC, the prescription of a claim against a succession is not completed before six months have elapsed from when D acquired the succession.

## C. CONTRIBUTION CLAIMS

104 According to art 926 GCC on multiple tortfeasors, if several persons unlawfully and culpably caused damage, or if several persons are responsible for certain damage, they are jointly and severally liable. The next article regulates the recourse among them and stipulates that the tortfeasor who has paid compensation to the injured person according to the previous article has a right of recourse against the other tortfeasors. The court allocates the damage among the tortfeasors according to the degree of the fault of each single tortfeasor. If this degree cannot be ascertained, the damage is divided between all equally (art 927 GCC).

105 The contribution claim provided in art 927 GCC is independent[114] and does not equal a claim arising from tort. Its source is the society of debt between the tortfeasors, who are jointly liable towards the damaged party.[115] It is subject to the standard 20-year prescription period (art 249 GCC) and it is born at the time of payment.[116]

## D. DEPENDANT'S CLAIM

106 Article 928 sent 2 GCC on loss of support obliges the defendant to compensate plaintiffs who are entitled by law to claim maintenance or the performance of services by the victim. The plaintiff's claims are regarded as independent and the cause of action accrues from the moment of the victim's death.

---

114 AP 1229/2013, NoV 62 (2014), 92.

115 *M Georgiadou*, in: I Karakostas, Civil Code, Vol 6, art 927 no 10 1118, 1120; *P Kornilakis*, Law of Obligations I, §98 4, 591.

116 *Ap Georgiades*, Law of Obligations, 740, 742; *M Georgiadou*, in: I Karakostas, Civil Code, Vol 6, art 927 14, p. 1120; *I Karakostas*, The Law of Tort (2014), 379; *P Kornilakis*, Law of Obligations I, §98 4, 592; AP 218/2014, published in 'Isokratis' and NOMOS.

# XII. OTHER ASPECTS OF PRESCRIPTION LAW

## A. STIPULATION

Prescription is a legal institution of public order as it serves the public interest of legal certainty.[117] This is explicitly regulated in art 275 GCC, according to which a contract between parties is null, if it excludes prescription provisions or determines a prescription period shorter or longer than the one regulated by law or renders, in general, the prescription terms harsher or softer, such as by creating more rules of suspension or interruption of prescription.[118] Although the parties cannot validly alter rules of prescription in advance, the waiver of prescription after the prescription period elapses is valid (art 276 GCC). 107

If D informs P before trial, by a unilateral act, that she waives her prescription defence, she can nevertheless raise the defence at court, as waiver of the prescription before the prescription period elapses is not valid. Completion of the prescription period is necessary according to art 276 GCC for a valid waiver.[119] 108

## B. MEANING OF 'FILING A CLAIM' THAT INTERRUPTS THE RUNNING OF PRESCRIPTION

The plaintiff's filing of an action leads to the interruption of the prescription period, according to art 261 GCC.[120] In order for that procedural act to interrupt the prescription period, it is necessary that the action is validly served on the defendant,[121] unless the latter, despite not having received the action's copy, is present at the hearing process and does not invoke the plaintiff's omission.[122] Also counterclaims, interventions, lodging an appeal,[123] etc. are assimilated to the filing of an action regarding their effects on the prescription period.[124] It must 109

---

117 *I Karakostas*, ibid, where there also more references to legal doctrine and jurisprudence; AP 2212/2013, NoV 62 (2014), 1121.

118 See, among others, *Agallopoulou*, *supra* fn 4, 98; *A Karampatzos*, ChrID ID' (2014), 581 and 583, who is of the view that it is high time that the Greek legislator abolishes art 275 GCC or at least amends it preferably towards the direction of either §202 of the German Civil Code (BGB) or of art III.-7.601 of the Draft Common Frame of Reference.

119 See *A Kornilakis*, in: Georgiades and Stathopoulos, Civil Code, I$^{B}$, art 276 no 2; *Chr Michailidou*, in: Georgiades, SEAK, 276 nos 1 and 2.

120 AP 732/2015, published in 'Isokratis'.

121 *I Karakostas*, Civil Code, Vol 2, art 261 no 1628, 727.

122 AP 622/1994, DEE 1 (1995), 305; 1211/1984, EEN 52, 585–586.

123 AP 761/2010, NoV 58 (2010), 2339.

124 *Ap Georgiades*, General Principles, 343–344; *I Karakostas*, Civil Code, Vol 2, art 261, nos 1638–1641, 728, 729; *Chr Michailidou*, in: Georgiades, SEAK, 261 no 6; *D Papadopoulou-Klamari*, in: Georgiades and Stathopoulos, Civil Code I$^{B}$, art 261 no 19.

be noted that, according to art 263 GCC, every prescription that was interrupted due to the filing of an action, is considered as if it was never interrupted, if the plaintiff abandoned the action or the action was dismissed on grounds not on the merits without possibility of appeal.[125] If a new action is filed within six months from the abandonment of the action or from the final decision that dismissed the action on grounds not on the merits, the prescription is deemed to have been interrupted by the previous action.[126]

110 According to art 264 GCC, the prescription shall also be interrupted by: (1) the notification of an order of payment made out in the form of an enforceable judiciary act; (2) the production of a claim for its confirmation in bankruptcy proceedings; (3) the production of a claim for inclusion in the distribution following a sale by public auction; (4) the raising of a plea of set off based on the claim.

111 According to art 277 GCC, the court cannot raise *ex officio*, ie on its own motion, a prescription defence; the defendant needs to plead the prescription defence in court, so that it produces its legal effects.[127] It is possible that the prescription defence is rejected by the court as abusive.[128]

## C. WHEN SHOULD THE DEFENCE BE RAISED AND DECIDED?

112 Means of defence or offence of the defendant are pleaded through statements of defence during the hearing in the first instance court.[129] According to art 237 of the Greek Code of Civil Procedure (GCCP), the parties must file their statements within 100 days by the action's filing. Thus, during this procedural stage, the defendant needs to raise the defence of prescription. Overdue statements are not taken into account by the court (art 237 §2, sent 3 GCCP), thus, failure to raise the objection during that time leads to its rejection as inadmissible. Through an oral statement, the defendant is able to amend his allegations (art 262 GCCP).

113 The prescription issue is decided along with the other pleadings made by the parties through their statements in court hearing.

---

125 *M- Chr Kalogera*, in: Georgiades and Stathopoulos, Civil Code, 1978, Vol 1, 263 nos 1–3; *Chr Michailidou*, in: Georgiades, SEAK, 263 nos 1–3; *D Papadopoulou-Klamari*, in: Georgiades and Stathopoulos, Civil Code, I$^{B}$, art 263 nos 5–10.

126 AP 664/2015; 695/2014; 2155/2014; 43/2015, all of them published in 'Isokratis'.

127 *Agallopoulou*, *supra* fn 4, 97; *A Kornilakis*, in: Georgiades and Stathopoulos, Civil Code, I$^{B}$, art 277 nos 4–7.

128 *Ap Georgiades*, in: Georgiades and Stathopoulos, Civil Code, Vol 1, Introd. 247–280 nos 12–16; *Chr Michailidou*, in: Georgiades, SEAK, Introd. 247–280 nos 9–11; AP 852/2002, EllDni 44 (2003), 1315–1316.

129 *K Makridou*, in: Kerameus, Kondylis and Nikas, Interpretation on Greek Code of Civil Procedure (2000), Vol 1, 269 no 4.

## D. WHO MAY RAISE THE DEFENCE?

According to art 278 GCC, creditors of the defendant[130] or any other person having a legal interest (eg guarantor) are entitled to raise the defence, in case the defendant does not raise it or has waived from his right. As far as creditors are concerned, it does not matter whether they became creditors of the defendant before or after the completion of the prescription period.[131] 114

## E. BURDEN OF PROOF (OF ELEMENTS AND OF RULES OF PROLONGATION)

According to art 338 GCCP, both the plaintiff and the defendant are required to prove the facts needed to support their independent claims or counterclaims. In other words, each litigant incurs the burden of proof regarding facts that constitute prerequisites for the application of rules of law favourable towards him.[132] Therefore, it is the defendant's obligation to prove that the prescription period has passed, whereas the plaintiff must prove that the running of time was or has been suspended or renewed and that, as a result, the prescription period has not elapsed. 115

---

130 AP 251/2013, Arm 68 (2014), 240.

131 *I Karakostas*, Civil Code, Vol 2, art 278 no 1759, 792.

132 *I Tentes*, in: Kerameus, Kondylis and Nikas, Interpretation on Greek Code of Civil Procedure, 338 no 3.

# PRESCRIPTION IN TORT LAW: ITALY

Giovanni COMANDÉ and Elena OCCHIPINTI

## I. INTRODUCTION

1 Prescription is a legal arrangement linking certain legal effects to the passage of time: specifically, in civil law it indicates the phenomenon whereby a subjective right is extinguished if its holder does not exercise that right within a legally-prescribed amount of time. The standard's purpose is to preserve the predictability of legal relations.

2 The roots of prescriptions are found in ancient roman law. Already during the Roman Republic (between 509BC and 27BC) Pretors had imposed time limits for the exercise of the formulae (the '*procedura formulare*'). Yet a general legal framework can be found only in the era of Justinian (527AC– 565AC) when the principle of *longi temporis praescriptio* is upheld.[1] Such a framework was incorporated in Italian law by the civil code of 1865 (CC) – art 2105 –, proposing a unitary definition of the institute of prescription that combines both the so-called acquisition and the extinctive model. The civil code of 1942 in force – arts 2934 ff – adopts this distinction, translating the

[1] *M. Amelotti*, La prescrizione delle azioni in diritto romano (Milano, 1958); *M. Varvaro, Ricerche sulla praescriptio* (Torino, 2008).

acquisition model in the institute of *usucapione* (acquisition of property by prescription) and the extinctive model into the generic institute of prescription. After the entering into force of the Republican constitution of 1948, the constitutionality of the institute of prescription was raised; specifically, it was assumed to be incompatible with existing constitutional rights. However, the constitutional court decision of 10 June 1966, n 63 confirmed its constitutionality as a means to ensure the legal certainty, which involves any right, including constitutionally guaranteed ones.

## II. DEFINITION OF PRESCRIPTION

In Italian law, the limitation period is governed by arts 2934 ff of the civil code. It is defined as an extinction of rights resulting from the failure to exercise them within a period of time prescribed by law. Italian law, privileging the certainty of legal relations, requires rightholders to exercise their rights within a set time frame, and continued disinterest in exercising one's rights justifies the rights' extinction. 3

The civil code regulates the period of prescription: unless the law provides otherwise, the 'ordinary' prescription period is ten years: rights not exercised within ten years will be automatically extinguished (art 2946 CC). There are some exceptions; for instance the rights arising from torts (art 2947, c 1, CC) are prescribed to a shorter period of five years, which period is reduced to two years in the case of compensation due to the circulation of vehicles of all species (art 2947, c 2). Rights relating to the renting of houses; to all monthly fee rentals and interests; to all yearly fees, rentals, and interests; indemnities due upon the end of an employment relationship; and rights deriving from social relationships are prescribed at the end of a five-year period (arts 2948 and 2949 CC). However, rights exercised by the insured in respect of an insurance contract and rights deriving from reinsurance contracts (art 2952, para 2 CC), shall be barred in the shorter term of two years.[2] The rights to payment of insurance premiums (art 2952, para 1 CC) shall be barred at the passing of one year. 4

Under Italian law, judicial interpretation plays a decisive role, often helping to clarify the nature of certain legal relationships and thereby resulting in a significant impact on the regulation of the limitation period: judicial 5

2 Cass. 24 January 2020, n 1575, in: *Giust. civ. Mass.*, 2020: the right to compensation for damages, caused by an insurance 'broker', is prescribed in the ordinary ten-year term and not in the two-year term referred to in art 2952, paragraph 2 of the civil code, being an obligation arising from the law and not deriving from the insurance contract.

interpretation of the involved legal relationship governs the applicable prescription rules.[3]

6 Finally, the Italian legal system provides that certain kinds of rights, such as property rights, inalienable rights, invalidity actions to declare the nullity of legal transactions, and family actions cannot be subject to prescription.

## III. THE NATURE OF PRESCRIPTION AND ITS EFFECTS

7 Although Italian law explicitly allows for the extinction of rights via prescription, actual practice with regard to the doctrine has led to the widely held scholarly view that extinction does not actually extinguish rights, but merely operates to attenuate their efficacy.[4] Such a view is supported, first, by art 2938 CC, according to which a judge cannot apply *ex officio* a prescription that was not raised by parties, and, second, by art 2940 CC, which disallows recovery of amounts already spontaneously paid in fulfilment of a debt for which prescription already occurred. Both rules would seem, in fact, to exclude the actual extinction of the right because such extinction would assume both that prescription could be raised *ex officio* and that recovery of amounts paid in connection with the credit for which prescription has occurred is available.

8 The accruing of prescription extinguishes the right under substantive law. However, if the prescribed right is still actioned, such as in the case of payment of a debt, recovery of amounts already paid cannot be sought.

---

3 Consider, for example, the scope of medical responsibility, the qualification of which has changed over time as a result of the case-law: after being initially treated as non-contractual (Cass. 24 March 1979, n 1716), courts have settled on a contractual nature (Cass. 3 March 1995, n 2466 and Cass. 11 April 1995, n 4152) coining the peculiar case of 'social contact' (Cass. 22 January 1999, n 589 and Cass., sez. a., 11 January 2008, n 577).

4 See in general *A. Auricchio*, Appunti sulla prescrizione (Napoli, 1971); *G. Azzariti and G. Scarpello*, Della prescrizione e della decadenza, in: Comm. S.B., sub arts 2934–2969 (Bologna-Roma, 1977); *L. Bigliazzi-Geri, U. Breccia, F.D. Busnelli and U. Natoli*, Diritto civile e commerciale, I (Torino, 1990); *M. Carnelutti*, Appunti sulla prescrizione, in: Riv. dir. proc. civ., 1933, 32; *R. Ferrucci*, Della prescrizione e della decadenza, in: Comm. cod. civ. (Torino, 1980); *F.G. Azzoni*, Manuale di diritto privato (Napoli, 1996); *L. Iannaccone*, La prescrizione, II, in: Comm. S. (Milano, 1999); *F. Messineo*, Manuale di diritto civile e commerciale, I (Milano, 1957); *F. Messineo*, Variazioni sul concetto di 'rinunzia alla prescrizione', in: Riv. trim. dir. proc. civ. 1957; *G. Panza*, Contributo allo studio della prescrizione (Napoli, 1984); *G. Panza*, Prescrizione, in: Dig. civ., XIV (Torino, 1996); *P. Perlingieri*, Rapporto preliminare e servitù su 'edificio da costruire' (Napoli, 1966); *F. Roselli and P. Vitucci*, La prescrizione e la decadenza, in Tr. Res., 20 (Torino, 1998); *F. Roselli*, La prescrizione e la decadenza, in: Diritto civile, diretto da N. Lipari e P. Rescigno, coordinato da A. Zoppini, IV, Attuazione e tutela dei diritti, 2, L'attuazione dei diritti (Milano, 2009), in particular 492 ss; *C. Ruperto*, Prescrizione e decadenza, in Comm. Utet (Torino, 1985); *B. Troisi*, La prescrizione come procedimento (Napoli, 1980); *P. Vitucci*, Prescrizione, in: Enc. giur., XXIV (Roma, 1991).

Specifically, recovery of amounts already paid cannot be sought in court on the basis of accrued prescription; however, it is possible to argue the merits of the claim – for instance, by asserting that the debt is invalid or has been rendered invalid by subsequent events. Applying such a principle, the Supreme Court upheld a decision of merit granting the request of an insurance company that, in seeking to recover sums paid to the insured, argued that the payments exceeded the amount of the insurance claim that was actually due, rather than arguing that the debt was prescribed at the time of payment.[5]

## IV. CONSIDERATIONS FOR AND AGAINST PRESCRIPTION OF TORT CLAIMS

### A. AGAINST

The operation of prescription creates a discrepancy between the substantive reality and what is established during trial, since in the Italian legal system the effects of prescription are produced only when an exception is raised by the interested party at trial. Thus, if prescription emerges by the documents in the case file but it is not raised as an exception the judge is forced to ignore it and to pronounce a decision on the substance of the matter even if this result might appear unfair. Nevertheless, such discrepancy is accepted because according to rule of law principles the 'justice' of a decision is not measured on the basis of its coincidence with the substantive reality of the matter, but with its correspondence with the formal rules through which facts enter the trial to become the formal 'truth', the only one relevant for the legal system. 9

### B. FOR

Under Italian law, time limits are justified primarily in order to preserve legal relationships by preventing the risk of specious requests based on alleged rights acquired so long ago as to obstruct the capacity for justice by making it difficult for the defendant to uncover evidence and problematic for the judge to construct historical reality. 10

The Italian Constitutional Court, in reviewing a potential conflict between arts 2948, nn 4 and 5, 2955, n 2, 2956, n 1 CC and arts 3, 4 and 36 of the Constitution, has made it clear that the constitutional guarantee of a right does not preclude, in itself, the extinguishing of that right via the passage of 11

5 Cass., sez. III, 18 September 2014 n 19654, in: *Giust. civ. Mass. civ.*, 2014.

time: while constitutional rights are imbued with greater strength, and are thus entitled to heightened protection beyond that conferred by ordinary law, even these rights are not entitled to perpetual potency, outweighing even the need for certainty in legal relations. Prescription, which relies in principle on the importance of such certainty, thus affects, as a rule, any right, including those that are constitutionally guaranteed.[6]

12 Thus, in Italy, the time factor determines the worth of legal protection for those who have a certain right, whatever its rank in the system. The positive effects of prescription are based on the assumption that the establishment of a trial over old facts would make it difficult to reconstruct a truthful picture of reality. Accordingly, those who have a hypothetically justified claim are critically situated to provide the necessary evidence to support it. On the other hand, excluding the judge's ability to raise the defence of prescription satisfies the other foundational quality of the prescription principle – namely, that the sacrifice of substantive protection is justified to the extent that the other party opposes the claim by raising the defence: if a party does not raise the defence of prescription, the judge must examine the dispute on the merits.

## V. ELEMENTS OF PRESCRIPTION – AN OVERVIEW

13 Under Italian law, the prescription period begins to run (the first element: when prescription begins) on the day on which the right may be claimed; namely, from the first moment that there are no legal impediments – such as the presence of any term or condition precedent – hindering the exercise of the right.

14 Setting aside the hypothesis of interruption and suspension, if the right is not exercised within the time provided by law, the right is prescribed, extinguishing itself (second element).

15 Italian law does not recognise factual circumstances that might hinder exercise of a right – such as lack of knowledge of its existence – as impediments to the commencement of the prescription period. Nevertheless, it is important that the right is objectively perceptible.

16 Italian law also regulates instances in which the limitation period may be suspended or interrupted (third element): these are rules of extension that prolong the time for exercising the right prescribed by law.

17 As for suspension, the law outlines the circumstances in which the running of the prescription period may be halted, distinguishing between those deriving

[6] Court Cost. 10 June 1966, n 63, in: *Mass. giur. lav.*, 1966, 133.

from a special relationship between the parties (art 2941 CC) and those deriving from some condition of the rightholder (art 2942 CC). Among the former are relations between spouses, between individuals with parental responsibility and their charges, between curators and their clients, between legal entities (corporations, limited companies, non-profit organisations, etc) and their directors, between debtors who have deliberately concealed their debt and their creditors so long as the debt remains concealed. Suspension may also arise with regard to rightsholders who are unemancipated minors or individuals deemed insane by court decree, persisting while they lack legal representation and for six months after the appointment of such representation, or ceasing when incapacity terminates. Finally, suspension applies to rightsholders who, during times of war, are in active military service or who belong to the State's armed forces or are, for reasons of military service, otherwise embedded with the armed forces for the time indicated by the provisions in the laws of war.[7]

In any of these aforementioned circumstances, the limitation period will cease running; however, it will begin to run again as soon as the legal cause justifying inertia is overcome. When the prescription period resumes, the amount of time that had expired prior to suspension is tacked-on to the end of the statutory limitation period applicable to the particular right in question. For example, consider a rightsholder with a claim falling under the ordinary ten-year limitation period who has to serve three years in the military in a time of war. If his service begins after six years of the ten-year prescription period have already passed, when he returns from his service he will still have four years to make a claim. Thus, including the time period during which the limitation was suspended, the soldier's right remains alive for a total of 13 years, thanks to the suspensive clause. 18

Interruption of prescription occurs when the rightholder accomplishes a task likely to reveal his will to exercise the right: from this moment the clock on the limitation period is renewed – it is set back to zero. Unlike suspension, interruption is not a parenthesis grafted into the limitation period; instead, it restarts the period of limitation entirely, cancelling any time previously elapsed. For example, the owner of a right to compensation for damages has five years to assert her right. If she decides to take legal action in respect of 19

[7] *P. Albanese*, Sospensione della prescrizione per cause unilaterali e responsabilità, in: Resp. civ. (2006), 653; *A. Buldini*, Accettazione dell'eredità devoluta al minore e conflitto d'interessi nell'interpretazione adeguatrice dell'art. 2942, n. 1 c.c., in: Fam. e dir. (2007), 905 ff; *V. Carbone*, Sospensione della prescrizione: conflitto tra minore e rappresentante legale, in: Corr. giur. (2007), 905–910; *F. Valenza*, Chiamato all'eredità incapace e sospensione della prescrizione del diritto di accettare per conflitto di interessi con il legale rappresentante, in: Fam. pers. e succ. (2007), 695–703.

the damaging event, the notification of the summons will interrupt this limitation period and initiate a new prescription period of five years. Article 2943 CC outlines the circumstances under which interruption occurs, including: the beginning of a trial,[8] the proposition of action during a pending case, action constituting formal notification of a debtor's default, action constituting recognition of the rightholder's right by the person against whom the right is exercised, and any material action revealing exercise of the right.

20 In addition, to avoid scenarios in which the length of trial frustrates a rightholder's request for protection by running down the limitation period, art 2945 CC provides that the prescription period does not run until a judgment becomes final and legally binding.[9]

21 To avoid such indeterminate prolongation, Italian law does not set an upper limit (fourth element) – or ceiling period – to the actual time of the prescription, after the running of which the cause of action is prescribed even if the prescription period has not yet expired due to prolongation.

## VI. THE STARTING POINT OF THE PRESCRIPTION PERIOD

### A. THE MEANING OF 'ACTION' AND 'CAUSE OF ACTION'

22 In the Italian system, the prescription period begins to run 'on the day on which the right may be exercised.' Thus, this day marks the moment at which the cause of action comes into being for prescription purposes.

23 Article 2947 CC provides that the right to compensation for damages arising out of tort/delict shall expire five years from the day on which the facts generating the basis of the claim occurred. This provision, in accordance with arts 2043 and 2935 CC, is interpreted to mean that the limitation period begins on the date of the damage. Such an interpretation makes sense in light of the reality of latent damage: if the facts of the occurrence and the materialisation of injury were, for instance, separated by more than five years, injured parties might be deprived of protection for torts that have undoubtedly occurred.[10]

---

8 Lastly, Cass. 8 January 2020, n 124, in: *Diritto & Giustizia*, 2020, 13 February.

9 Cass., sec I, 24 November 1983, n 7023, in: *Il Civilista*, 2010, fasc. 10.

10 Cass., sec III, 29 May 2013, n 13438, in: *Giust. civ.*, 2013, 10, I, 1988; Cass., sec VI, 6 December 2012, n 22002, in: *Riv. arb.*, 2013, 3, 699; Trib. Napoli, sec V, 30 October 2012, in: *Giur. Mer.*, 2013, 2, 330; Cass., sec III, 7 October 2011, n 20609, in: *Il Civilsta*, 2011, 11.

The action can therefore be defined as the right to take legal action in order to obtain judicial protection, on the basis of the bare assertion that a right has been violated. The cause from which the action originates is the fact from which the right that is meant to be invoked has arisen. 24

Similar conduct, for example negligent medical performance against a patient, can raise more causes of action. 25

## B. BROAD OR NARROW CONCEPTION OF 'CAUSE OF ACTION'?

Italian case law is almost unanimous in considering that, in tort, the birth of a right to compensation (and therefore the moment from which the prescription period begins to run) occurs when the damage is 'externally' perceivable and capable of detection. Hence and for instance, the Supreme Court has concluded, in a case in which the injured party's permanent reduction of limb function did not emerge until after the removal of a plastic arm cast, that the prescription period could not have commenced prior to this ascertainment.[11] 26

Similarly, in the case of infections caused by blood transfusions, Italian law specifies, in accordance with arts 2935 and 2947 para 1 CC, that for parties alleging the contraction of infectious diseases as a result of a third party's wilful or negligent actions, the limitation period of five years only begins to run from the day on which the disease was or could have been perceived (using ordinary diligence and taking into account the dissemination of scientific knowledge) as a wrongful damage resulting from a third party's behaviour – not from the day on which the damage was caused or on which the infection or disease appeared.[12] 27

Thus, generally speaking where damages are not immediately apparent the statute of limitations begins to run when the victim, with the use of ordinary diligence, is able to perceive both: (a) the fact of the damage; and (b) its traceability to the tort.[13] 28

Similarly, the prescription period for the right to compensation for damages deriving from professional liability does not run from the moment that the 29

---

11 Cass., III, 24 February 1983, n 1442, in: *Giust. civ. Mass.*, 1983, fasc. 2.

12 Cass., sez. III, 3 May 2016, n 8645, in: *Ridare.it*, 28 September, with comment of *De Matteis*, Per una teoria unitaria sulla decorrenza della prescrizione civile nei diritti nascenti in situazioni lungolatenti. *De Mattesi-Ossicini*, Infortuni e malattie professionali con postumi inferiori al minimo indennizzabile: quale decorrenza per la revisione?, in: Prevention&Resaearch.com (August 2016). For a general description of the institute see: *Messineo*, Manuale di diritto civile e commerciale (Milano, 1957), I, 178. Lastly, Cass., sec. VI, 27 September 2019 n 24164, in: *Giust. civ. Mass.*, 2019.

13 Cass., sec III, 23 October 2014, n 22507, in: *Guida al dir.*, 2015, 3, 39.

practitioner performed the allegedly damage-causing conduct, but instead from the moment that the harmful event actually occurred and became objectively perceivable by any individual with an interest in taking action on it.[14]

30 In Italy, the advent of a right to compensation (and therefore the point at which the prescription term commences) is realised when the damage materialises and actually becomes known. Therefore, the time limit for claiming damages in relation to a second head of injury, caused by the same accident several years earlier, will take effect from the time when it is apparent to the injured party, who can sue the wrongdoer with the burden of showing the causal connection with the ski instructor's negligence (see the example in **Case 1**).

31 The same conclusions for Case 1 apply.

32 Again, in this case one will have to wait for the externalisation of the damage in order to be able to correlate it with the kind of right the claimant intends to assert and the corresponding time limits that the law attaches to it. As long as harm A, B, C are independent their respective clear manifestation sets the beginning of the prescription time attached to them (see **Cases 2, 3** and **5**).

## C. THE STARTING POINT – BREACH OF DUTY OR OCCURRENCE OF DAMAGE?

33 As mentioned above, under Italian law the starting point is the actual manifestation of the occurrence of damage.

34 In the Italian system, the case proposed assumes distinct and independent cause of actions, for which autonomous statutory terms laid down by law apply. One relates to the untitled occupation of the property (see **Case 4**) and the other one relates to compensation for damage to the bridge (see **Case 6**). In the first case prescription begins when physical harm to premises is perceivable while in the second case when P is (can be aware) of the loss due to the defect in the irrigation system.

## D. WHAT IS CONSIDERED 'HARM' FOR PRESCRIPTION PURPOSES?

35 In this case, the harming event is caused by the negligent conduct of the employer who does not provide the appropriate safeguards to protect the health of her workers, causing damage to one of them.

[14] Cass., sec II, 3 May 2016, n 8703, in: *Rivista del Notariato*, 2016, 3, 539.

The disease and its progression originate from the same event (the employer's negligence). Thus, the term of prescription will start from the first outbreak of the disease: subsequent deterioration may be detected for the purpose of awarding compensation. 36

In a case brought to the attention of Italian judges based on the employer's liability arising from the failure to fulfil its obligations imposed by art 2087 CC (omitted cautions by the employer), the judge ruled that the ten-year limitation applicable to the case ran from the moment the damage occurred, becoming objectively perceptible and recognisable, and not from the time of a subsequent aggravation that is not due to an autonomous cause, with its own causal efficiency.[15] 37

Article 2935 CC stipulates that the prescription starts to run from the day on which the right can be invoked. It is therefore necessary that the right is extant and current: case law then specifies that it is not enough for the damage to simply materialise; instead, its externalisation, recognisability, or perceptibility – as well as its legal relevance – is essential. It is only when these requirements are fulfilled that the legal system recognises the birth of the right to compensation and thus the ability to exercise the related powers.[16] 38

## E. THE STARTING POINT (ACCRUAL) IN CONTINUOUS TORTS

Given that the right to compensation for damages resulting from illicit acts shall expire five years from the moment of factual occurrence, that moment must be understood as the time when the damage is externally perceivable. Thus, the determination of the moment at which the limitation period commences is necessarily affected by the manner in which damages appear. For instance, it is easy to set the *dies a quo* when the wrongful event is static (think of the damages caused by a tree falling on a parked car). But the determination is more problematic when the tort precipitates further harmful consequences extending past the date of its initial commission. Accordingly, it is customary to distinguish between instantaneous torts and 'permanent' torts. 39

With instantaneous torts, the tort is characterised by an action that is exhausted in a defined period of time and the prescription of damages begins to run immediately upon the action's occurrence. 40

With non-instantaneous torts, where the initial event precipitates additional adverse consequences, the time limit for such further damages runs from 41

[15] Cass. 30 March 2011, n 7272, in: *Foro it.*, 2011, 9, I, 2353.

[16] Cass. 7 October 2011, n 20609, in: *Foro it.*, 2013, 1, I, 328.

the moment of their occurrence so long as they do not constitute mere development or aggravation of the damages already ensued, in which case they will be governed by the prescription period commencing upon the occurrence of the initial tort. However, where further damages are new and independent of the damage caused by the initial tortious action, they will be governed by an independent prescription period that is tied to their discrete occurrence (see **Case 7**, where each period of limitation shall run for each individual publication).

42 Case law has clarified that instantaneous torts can have permanent effects without thereby becoming permanent torts. This will be the case where there is a mere extension of the adverse effects caused by improper conduct (for instance, an owner's incapacity to make available property that is the subject of a fraudulent contract with a wrongdoer). In such cases, the permanent effects are integrated within the instantaneous tort such that it can be said that the right to recovery arises upon the completion of the fraudulent contract and from thereon recurs 'continuously' throughout the standard, five-year prescriptive period. Because this right arises continuously throughout the prescription period, it must be acted upon within that time, and does not precipitate an independent prescription period or an extension of the prescription period. Thus, instantaneous torts with permanent effects are characterised by an action that *uno actu perficitur* – that runs out in a defined period of time even if it maintains its effects over time. For these torts, the combined provisions of arts 2935 and 2947 CC require that prescription shall run from the date on which damages occurred, ie the date on which prejudicial consequences are caused to a legal interest, as long as the injured party is aware of them and there are no legal impediments to bringing the claim.[17]

43 In the case of permanent torts, the actionable event accrues continuously along with the damages it causes; thus, the prescription period recommences every day following the date on which the damage occurs for the first time, until the end of the damaging conduct. Accordingly, the right to compensation arises continuously and is continuously extinguished if not exercised within five years from the moment it occurs.[18]

44 Both examples in the case are permanent torts being part of the same ordered action: the limitation period starts to run every day after the day in which the damage occurred for the first time, until the cessation of the harmful conduct,

17 This is exactly what the court determined in the referenced case dealing with unavailability of property due to fraud. See Cass., sec III, 28 May 2013, n 13201, in: *Giust. civ. Mass.*, 2013.

18 Cass., SS. UU., 14 November 2011, n 23763, in: *Giust. civ. Mass.*, 2011, 11, 1606; guidance confirmed by Cass., sez. I, 15 March 2016 n 5081, in: *Foro it.*, 2016, 6, I, 2071.

so that the right to compensation arises continuously meanwhile the damage occurs. It is barred continuously if it is not exercised within five years from the moment in which it occurs.

The right to compensation for the continuous loud noise accrues from the moment in which the victim has become aware of the causation of his own pathological state. The aggravation of the disease will then only affect the quantification of the damage (see **Case 8**). 45

Also, in this case, the right to compensation for damages accrues from the moment in which the rightsholders acquire awareness of the damage suffered. The subsequent removal of the containers does not affect the validity of the claim for damages. The time spent in the soil by the bins is irrelevant for prescription purposes as well (see **Case 9**). 46

## F. IS THE LATE DISCOVERY RULE A RULE OF THE STARTING POINT OR A RULE OF PROLONGATION?

In the right to compensation for damages for both contractual and non-contractual liability, the limitation period does not begin to run at the moment when the fact of the third party infringes the rights of others. It begins when the production of the damage is perceivable and recognisable. Thus, the late discovery rule is related to the moment in which the limitation period begins to run.[19] 47

Italian case law favours an interpretation very attentive to due process in those cases hypothetically generating damages (so-called long tail damages). Case law considers that the limitation period should run from the time the tort is complete in all of its elements, and, therefore, from the time when damage occurs. Accordingly, the most frequent cases relate to damages to health arising from conduct committed many years before, as can happen in cases of contagion of a disease that only clearly manifests itself later. 48

In order to ensure that the broadest protection of rights is available to the injured, case law expands the notion of the *dies a quo* with regard to the commencement of the prescription period, not only until the point at which the disease is clearly evident, but also beyond that to the point at which, exercising ordinary diligence and with regard to the dissemination of scientific knowledge, it is possible to perceive the relevant injury as caused by the wilful or negligent misconduct of a third party.[20] Such an interpretation fully 49

---

19 Principle confirmed last by Trib. Milano, 3 February 2020, n 93.

20 Cass., sec III, 21 February 2003, n 2645, in: *Giur. it.*, 2004, 285.

reflects the values of the Italian Constitution and, in particular, those dictated by art 24, according to which everyone should be able to take legal action to protect their rights. From the application of this principle it follows not only that the *dies a quo* must coincide with the moment at which damages arose, but also that the injured party should be put in a position to perceive the wrongfulness of damage, the causal link, and the liability of a third party: only the full awareness of all these elements will allow the injured person to decide whether to take legal action in compliance with art 24 of the Constitution.

## VII. PRESCRIPTION PERIODS

50 Italian law provides for an ordinary general period and a variety of short-term prescription periods.

51 The ordinary periods of limitation/prescription are defined according to the kind of credit; generally, except where the law provides otherwise, claims covered by the ordinary period expire after ten years (art 2946 CC).

52 The course of the prescription of the claim can be aborted with notification to the debtor of an act by which the creditor explicitly manifests an intention to interrupt the course of prescription and place the debtor in default The limitation period begins to run anew from the date on which the debtor received notice of that act.

53 For some rights, a significantly shorter limitation period than the ordinary limitation period of ten years applies.

54 Below is a summary:

**Table 1. Shorter limitation periods**

| **Cause of action or tort** | **Discovery rule** | **Prescription period** |
|---|---|---|
| • perpetual annuities or life annuities;<br>• the nominal capital of government bonds;<br>• instalment payments of pensions;<br>• rents of houses, rents for rustic heritages and every other consideration for leases;<br>• utility bills (electricity, gas, water, telephone, waste);<br>• mortgage payments;<br>• common charges;<br>• renovation expenses;<br>• insurance;<br>• tax returns, VAT and accompanying documentation;<br>• fines | Yes | Five years |

*continued*

Table 1 *continued*

| Cause of action or tort | Discovery rule | Prescription period |
|---|---|---|
| • interest, and in general, all payments that must be made periodically, yearly or in shorter terms;<br>• allowances payable for termination of employment;<br>• rights that derive from social relations, if the company is registered in the commercial register;<br>• liability action of creditors against company administrators;<br>• right to compensation for damages arising from torts. | | |
| • the vehicle circulation tax commonly referred to as 'road tax';<br>• the right of employees for payroll due for periods longer than a month (starting on the date of termination of employment);<br>• the right of professionals for the remuneration of their work and for reimbursement of related expenses;<br>• the right of notaries, for their acts;<br>• the right of teachers, for the remuneration of lessons given in longer than a month. | Yes | Three years |
| • damages caused by the circulation of vehicles | Yes | Two years |
| • intermediaries' right to payment of a commission;<br>• rights deriving from a contract of shipment/transport; but, if the transport operation starts or ends outside of Europe, the prescription period is 18 months;<br>• rights against public service operators;<br>• rights to the payment of instalments of liability insurance, theft, and fire insurance premiums; all other rights under insurance/reinsurance contracts are barred after two years;<br>• the right of teachers, for the remuneration of lessons given in months, days, or hours;<br>• school fees;<br>• subscriptions to gyms, pools, and sports complexes;<br>• the right of employees for payroll expenses for periods not exceeding a month;<br>• the right of those administering boarding school education and/or home education, for the cost of boarding and education;<br>• the right of judicial officers to compensation for acts performed in their offices; the right of traders for the price of goods sold to those who do not do business;<br>• the right of pharmacists for the price of medicines. | Yes | One year |
| • the right of hoteliers and hosts for lodging and meals that they delivered;<br>• the right of all who give accommodation with or without pension. | Yes | Six months |

## VIII. RULES OF POSTPONEMENT, SUSPENSION, RENEWAL AND EXTENSION

Article 2941 CC permits suspension of the limitation period in the following circumstances. 55

56 The prescription is suspended:

(1) between spouses;
(2) between those having parental responsibility or the powers inherent to it and their charges;
(3) between the guardian and the child or the interdict subject to guardianship, until the final bill has been produced and approved, except as provided in art 387 for actions related to guardianship;
(4) between the guardian (*curatore*) and the emancipated minor or the incapacitated;
(5) between the heir and the inheritance accepted under benefit of inventory;
(6) among people whose assets are subject, by law or court decision, to the administration of others and those by whom such administration is exercised until the final bill has been produced and approved;
(7) between legal entities and their administrators so long as those administrators remain in control of the relevant entity, for actions for damages against them;
(8) between the debtor who has maliciously concealed the existence of the debt and the creditor until the malice is discovered.

57 Article 2942 CC provides for situations related to the condition of the rightholder, by providing that the prescription remains suspended:

(1) against children not emancipated and those under interdict for insanity, for as long as they have legal representation and for six months following the appointment thereof or the cessation of incapacity;
(2) in time of war against those in the military and the armed forces of the State and against those who are following the same forces for service reasons, for the time indicated by the provisions of the laws of war.

58 Italian law applies the principle that ignorance of law does not preclude prescription, with the only mitigation resulting from n 8) art 2941 CC, which provides for the suspension of prescription in cases where the debtor has fraudulently concealed the existence of a debt, so long as the debt remains concealed.

59 Thus, ignorance of the law is relevant not in and of itself, but only if it is the result of an intentional act undertaken to conceal the existence of a right.

60 Thus, in relation to a tort committed by a notary for drawing up a void memorandum of mortgage, the Supreme Court stated that the damage had occurred with the writing of the void act. Thus, the prescription period ran

from the day on which the memorandum was written, not from the subsequent determination of invalidity.[21]

Additionally, as previously noted, in the case of disease, the limitation period begins to run only from the moment that the disease is perceived or can be perceived, using ordinary diligence and considering the dissemination of scientific knowledge, as harm caused by the wilful or negligent misconduct of a third party. 61

Similarly, the Supreme Court[22] has recognised the claim of the parents of a boy interdict, despite the fact that they submitted their formal claim ten years after the harm-causing event. The child suffered harm at birth and was permanently impaired – reduced to a vegetative state equal to 90–95% of permanent impairment – in 1983. However, the court determined that the ten-year prescription period did not commence until 1984, at which point the parents had gained unquestionable knowledge of the impairment and of the causal traceability of the infirmity to the particular conduct of the hospital staff during their child's hospitalisation as a baby – and not to any natural event(s). 62

## A. UNAWARENESS – THE LATE DISCOVERY RULE

### 1) *Unawareness of what Elements of Liability?*

For all the above, this case – in Italian law – would be resolved in the sense that the injured party could sue the first attorney for professional liability, resulting from the attorney's conduct (by providing an incorrect statement, exposed his client to the time limit). The late discovery of the negligent attorney's counsel does not affect the running of the prescription time. As mentioned above, the rightholder's ignorance of the facts generating the right or the subjective doubt about the existence of that right or the delay caused by the necessity of his finding are important for the running of the prescription (see **Case 10**).[23] 63

---

21 Cass., sec III, 7 November 2005, n 21495, in: *Giust. civ.*, 2006, 6, I, 1223.

22 Cass. 23 September 2013, n 21715, in: *Rassegna di diritto farmaceutico*, 2014, 2, 289. In this decision the court accepted the compensation claim of the parents of an interdicted boy, even if the formal request for compensation had been filed by them after ten years from the harmful event. The damage suffered by the minor at birth and consisting in an incapacity of 90–95% had taken place in 1983; nonetheless, the Supreme Court decided to start the ten-year prescription period since 1984, when at the occasion of an hospitalisation, parents had acquired a clear knowledge of the pathology from which their child was afflicted. Only upon this occasion, they learned the incapacity was not due to a natural event, but to human behaviour, and in particular to the behaviour of hospital personnel.

23 Cass., civ., sez. III, 6 October 2014, n 21026, in: *Giust. civ. Mass.*, 2014; Cass. civ., sez. VI, 7 March 2012, n 3584, in: *Giust. civ. Mass.*, 2012, 3, 285.

*2) Objective or Subjective Unawareness?*

64 The subjective unawareness of the injured person is relevant.

65 Case law has often decided on the issue,[24] often in cases of long-term illnesses, since they are not immediately perceptible, nor can they be traced back immediately to a medical error. With regard to these pathologies, the prescription does not begin to run neither from the moment in which the cause of the damage occurred, nor from the moment of the simple externalisation of the latent illness. It does run from the moment in which the individual has acquired knowledge – or has been able to acquire knowledge – of the causal connection between the harmful event and the negligent behaviour of a specific subject. Thus, the limitation period begins only when, using ordinary diligence and taking into account available scientific knowledge, the disease is perceived or can be perceived as a wrongful harm resulting from the malicious or negligent behaviour of a third party.

*3) What is Considered Awareness of an Element of Liability?*

66 The victim must be aware of the elements constituting the tort: in other words, of the damaging event and of the causal connection between the conduct of the wrongdoer and the damaging event itself.

*4) How Heavy is the Burden to Acquire Knowledge?*

67 Depending on the case, it can be very difficult to acquire awareness of the damage and in fact in the Italian system the attribution of the burden of

[24] The Supreme Court (Cass., sec III, 3 May 2016, n 8645, cited above) had accepted the claim for compensation submitted after the five-year prescription period, by a person who had been transfused with blood infected in 1991 causing an infection with hepatitis C, the existence of which had been ascertained only in 1994. The corresponding action for compensation for damage in the event of non-contractual liability had instead been brought against the Ministry of Health only in 1999. The filing of the compensation request eight years after the event was not barred by prescription because plaintiff provided proof of having perceived the damage suffered as a result of transfusions with infected blood only as a consequence of an independent communication of 12 July 1994. This communication came, in particular from the hospital structure where he used to go, being affected by thalassemia and therefore in need of periodic transfusions. Only after this communication had the plaintiff been informed of the causal relationship of the disease to the transfusions received previously: for this reason, the prescription period had to start only from that moment. In terms of medical responsibility, the five-year and ten-year prescribed provisions may start to run even after the harmful event, but on the condition that the injured proves to have behaved diligently and to have become aware of the damage and the related medical liability only in a second moment. This solution is perfectly compatible with the provisions of art 2935 CC.

proof is on those who are in a favourable condition to acquire it, according to the so-called criterion of proximity to the proof. To establish knowledge objective data and the subjective situation is taken into account.

In the Italian legal system it is undisputed in case law that the prescription term begins, according to arts 2935 and 2947, para 1 CC, not from the day on which the third party causes the damage or the time when the disease is manifested, but from the moment in which the disease is perceived or can be perceived as wrongful harm ensuing from the behaviour of the third party, using ordinary diligence and taking into account the existing scientific knowledge.[25] In the proposed case, however, the lack of knowledge has depended on a further circumstance, that is, the doctor's expertise, which has not been able to correctly diagnose the causes of the disease: the right to compensation is then prescribed and the injured person can claim damages from the doctor who has not correctly framed the disease, thus preventing him from acting within the prescription period (see **Case 11**). 68

## B. OTHER RULES OF PROLONGATION

When the right holder is an unemancipated minor or under interdict for insanity, art 2942 CC provides that the prescription remains suspended until the rightholder has a legal representative and for six months following the appointment thereof or from termination of incapacity. 69

This rule determines the 'ceiling' of the prescription or the maximum extension of the period of limitation that operates, outside ordinary rules, in the event that there are such strict conditions of the rightholders. 70

### *1) D is to Blame for the Delay*

Pursuant to art 2941 CC no 8, if the debtor has maliciously concealed the existence of the debt to the creditor, prescription begins to run only when the fraud has been discovered. 71

### *2) Admission by D of P's Right or Partial Performance of P's Right by D*

Pursuant to art 2944 CC (interruption due to recognition) prescription is interrupted by the recognition of the right from the one against whom the right itself can be actioned. In this case a new period begins. 72

25 Cass., sez. III, 3 May 2016, n 8645, quoted.

### 3) *Special Relations between D and P*

73 Please refer to the following table:

**Table 2. Special limitations due to special relationships**

| Relations | Rule of prolongation |
|---|---|
| Between spouses; | Suspension of prescription |
| Between those having parental responsibility or the powers inherent to it and their charges; | Suspension of prescription |
| Between the guardian and the child or the interdict subject to guardianship, until the final bill has been produced and approved, except as provided in art 387 for actions related to guardianship; | Suspension of prescription |
| Between the guardian (*curatore*) and the emancipated minor or the incapacitated; | Suspension of prescription |
| Between the heir and the inheritance accepted under benefit of inventory; | Suspension of prescription |
| Among people whose assets are subject, by law or court decision, to the administration of others and those by whom such administration is exercised until the final bill has been produced and approved; | Suspension of prescription |
| Between legal entities and their administrators so long as those administrators remain in control of the relevant entity, for actions for damages against them; | Suspension of prescription |
| Between the debtor who has maliciously concealed the existence of the debt and the creditor until the malice is discovered. | Suspension of prescription |

### 4) *P's Lack of Legal Capacity*

74 Please refer to the following table:

**Table 3. Special limitations due to capacity**

| Kind of disability | With representative | Without representative | Kind of prolongation | Comments |
|---|---|---|---|---|
| Minority | Yes | No | Suspension | The prescription is suspended until they have a legal representative and for the six months following the appointment or termination of the inability. |
| Adult with unsound mind | Yes | No | Suspension | The prescription is suspended until they have a legal representative and for the six months following the appointment or termination of the inability. |

### 5) *Absence of Parties from the Jurisdiction*

Please refer to the following table: 75

**Table 4. Special limitations due to absence**

| Absence | Prolongation | Rule | Comments |
|---|---|---|---|
| In times of war, soldiers in service and members of the State's armed forces and those who are in for service reasons following the forces themselves | Yes | Suspension | For the time indicated by the provisions of the laws of war |

### 6) *Former Legal and Other Proceedings between the Parties*

Please refer to the following table: 76

**Table 5. Special limitations due to other proceedings**

| Former proceedings | Prolongation | Rule | Comments |
|---|---|---|---|
| Legal cognitive, conservative or executive claim | Yes | Interruption and the new prescription period begins to run *ex novo* | From the notification of the claim and until the time when the judgment defining the judgment is final |
| ADR | Yes | Interruption and the new prescription period begins to run *ex novo* | From the notification of the ADR request until reaching the agreement or the minutes of non-agreement |
| Arbitration | Yes | Interruption and the new prescription period begins to run *ex novo* | From the notification of the application until the award is adjourned |
| Recognition of the right by the one against whom the right is claimed | Yes | Interruption and the new prescription period begins to run *ex novo* | |

### 7) *Victim's Death*

Not applicable 77

### 8) *Victim's Bankruptcy*

Pursuant to arts 2941 and 2942 CC bankruptcy does not suspend prescription time. The declaration of bankruptcy does not affect the time for prescription 78 since third parties can exercise their right against the bankruptcy trustee as provided for by arts. 42 and 43 of the bankruptcy statute.[26]

*9)* Force Majeure

79 Please refer to *supra* 75 for the case of war. The general rule applies to cases of natural disaster, military service, imprisonment, legal inability to file a claim and closed courts.

*10) Other Instances*

80 Please refer to the following table:

81 **Table 6. Other instances**

| Scope | Commencement | Length | Prolongation | Comments |
|---|---|---|---|---|
| Defect in goods | From discovery | Eight days | One year to file the claim | |
| Defects in consumption goods | From discovery | Two months | Two years to file the claim | |
| Tender | From discovery | One year | Maximum ten years | Vizi di costruzione |
| Medical liability | From discovery | Five years | No | Law 8 March 2017, n 24 |
| Medical liability | From discovery | Ten years | No | Law 8 March 2017, n 24 |

## IX. CEILINGS ON THE EFFECTIVE TIME OF PRESCRIPTION

82 Does not exist in Italy.

## X. STATUTE INTERPRETATION, JUDICIAL DISCRETION AND LACHES

83 Prescription introduces a limitation to the protection of rights that is justified insofar as it aims to ensure the certainty of legal relations and to offer citizens effective justice – which would be hopelessly compromised by a total lack of time-limit on the presentation of claims.

26 Cass. 19 July 2016, n 1437, in: *Ilfallimentarista.it*, 2016.

84 If it is true, then, that in the abstract prescription amounts to de facto extinguishment of rights, depriving rightsholders of the opportunity to obtain protection in court, any accusation regarding the 'immorality' of such a doctrine cannot overcome the need to reconcile the predictability of legal relations with the positive rules governing their operation.

85 In particular, one must stress that in Italian law the judge does not have the power to raise prescription *ex officio*. Thus, the parties are invested with the power to trigger its application or not.

86 If the plaintiff is acting to protect a right already prescribed, the respondent is responsible for raising the exception regarding extinction: in the absence of exception, the trial will proceed to a determination on the merits of the claim.

87 The rule preventing recovery of amounts spontaneously paid in fulfilment of a prescribed debt derives from the same rationale. Because prescription does not operate automatically, case law treats such a scenario as generating just a normal civil obligation: such payment manifests a tacit waiver of prescription on behalf of the debtor. Thus, the spontaneity of the payment, which prevents repeating payment of the sum in fulfilment of a prescribed debt, prevents those who have paid from denying and seeking to recover the sum in restitution.[27]

88 However, prevailing scholarship[28] considers this as a variety of natural obligation, regulated by art 2034. Accordingly, the payment of a debt already prescribed is considered a moral commitment, not a legal one.

---

27 Cass., 17 April 1996, n 3636, in: *Giust. civ. Mass.*, 1996, 594; Cass., sec III, 18 April 2014, n 19654, in: *Giust. civ. Mass.*, 2014.

28 For further information see *Albanese*, Il pagamento dell'indebito (Padova, 2004); *C.M. Bianca*, Diritto civile, L'obbligazione (Milano, 2011), 785 ss; *F. Caringella and L. Buffoni*, Manuale di diritto civile (Roma, 2016), 532; *P. Gallo*, Ripetizione dell'indebito. L'arricchimento che deriva da una prestazione altrui, in: Dig. civ. (Torino, 1998); *F. Moscati*, voce Indebito (pagamento e ripetizione), in: Enc. dir., XXI (Milano, 1971); *F. Moscati*, voce Obbligazioni naturali, in: Enc. dir., XXXIX (Milano, 1979); *F. Moscati*, Gestione d'affari: pagamento dell'indebito (Bologna, 1981); *E. Navarretta*, La causa e le prestazioni isolate (Milano, 2000); *L. Nivarra*, Obbligazione naturale, in: Dig. civ. (Torino, 1995); *Perlingieri*, Le vicende delle obbligazioni naturali, in: Riv. dir. civ. (1969), I, 357; *P. Rescigno*, Ripetizione dell'indebito, in: Nss. D.I., XV (Torino, 1968); *F. Torrente and P. Schlesinger*, Manuale di diritto privato (Milano, 2015), 386. Please note that recent case law has specified that the payment done in execution of a contractual agreement subsequently declared void can be asked back because it is not possible to qualify it as fulfillment of a natural obligation since there is no spontaneity of payment nor the execution of a moral or social duty: Cass., sez. I, 27 June 2017, n 15954, in: *Giust. civ. Mass.*, 2017.

89 As mentioned, the exception of prescription must be raised by one of the parties, not the court. Whoever raises the prescription has the burden of attaching the facts and evidence on which it is based.

90 The 'discretion' of the judge, then, seems confined to review of the abovementioned evidence.

91 Italian law does not enumerate specific rules governing the formation of judicial opinion on an issue, save for requiring justification in the decision.

92 However, judges might have 'discretion' in interpreting the nature of the right targeted by an exception of prescription, treating it as either contractual or non-contractual, and thereby applying a different prescription period.

93 This has been the case, for instance, in the context of medical liability, where the law, which initially treated such liability as a form of tortious liability, has begun to treat it as contractual in nature.

94 Non-contractual nature. According to an initial construction, the acceptance of a patient in a hospital, as inpatient or outpatient, involves the conclusion of a contract between hospital and patient in which the hospital assumes obligations to the patient to carry out diagnostic work and subsequent therapeutic activity in relation to the patient's specific situation. However, the physician-employee does not participate in this contractual relationship, and his potential liability towards the patient as a result of diagnostic or therapeutic error is considered non-contractual liability. Thus, the right to compensation for damages against the doctor is prescribed in the five-year term established by para 1 of art 2947 CC.

95 Contractual nature. This approach was followed in order to qualify medical liability in contractual terms. Thus, the responsibility of the public health service hospital and of its employees for damages suffered by an individual due to the negligent performance of medical acts is considered to be of a contractual nature. It follows that the responsibility of the institution and of the doctor inserted organically into the organisation of the service, shall be governed mutatis mutandis by the rules governing liability of medical professional performance in execution of a contract for professional services.[29]

96 The consequences in terms of the qualification in terms of prescription. Contractual medical liability has important implications as well in terms of the burden of proof, even on the prescription of the right. Pursuant to art 2946 CC, to contractual liability shall apply the limitation period of ten years, compared with the five-year time limit period provided for by art 2947 CC for damages.

---

[29] Cass. 11 April 1995, n 4152, in: *Riv. it. medicina legale*, 1997, 1073.

Innovations inserted by Law no 189/12 – art 3, c 1. Law no 189/2012 provides that health professionals who, in carrying out their activities, follow guidelines and best practices accredited by the scientific community, cannot be criminally liable for negligence. In such cases the provision laid down in art 2043 CC continues to apply. The judge, in determining damages, shall take due account of the conduct referred to in the first sentence. The wording of this new legal rule was immediately proclaimed to be a reintroduction of tortious liability. In fact, the new formulation inadvertently recalls 'the requirement laid down in article 2043 of the civil code', despite the reality that the full scope of medical liability has been deemed subject to the application of the contractual liability regime. 97

The mentioned provisions of Law no 189/2012 were interpreted by trial courts in divergent ways (while the Supreme Court denied to them any relevance in civil matters). For instance, Trib. Varese[30] interpreted the text as constituting liability in tort for medical malpractice. More precisely, the ensuing line of case law argued that the legislature consciously reallocated medical liability to the interpretation model as designed before 1999 (Cass. 22 January 1999, n 589), in which the patient could request damages in tort. 98

On the other hand, another line of cases opened by Trib. Arezzo 14 February 2013[31] said that the new legislation did not modify the contractual nature of medical liability. These cases argued that the legislative text is designed to restrict (in the first period) the determination of exempting circumstances in criminal proceedings, to restrict (in the second period) the obligation to compensate, and to point out (in the third period) the relevance of the guidelines and good practices in the actual establishment of liability. 99

The Supreme Court has resolved the conflict among trial courts, clarifying that the new statutory rules indicated a particular development in criminal law, with a view to facilitating the useful exercise of the medical arts and reducing the risk of specious claims. The Supreme Court concluded that the statute did not change the rules of civil liability as established by case law,[32] with subsequent confirmation of the application of the ten-year limitation period in order to enforce the right to compensation. 100

The Law of 8 March 2017 n 24 establishes a 'double binary' for civil liability related to healthcare services. It establishes that the civil liability of health professionals is of a non-contractual nature (albeit with the exception of those who act in the execution of a contractual obligation assumed directly 101

---

30 Trib. Varese of 26 November 2012, n 1406, in: *Guida al diritto*, 2013, 17, 23.

31 Trib. Arezzo of 14 February 2013, in: *Redazione Giuffré.*

32 Cass., 19 February 2013 n 4030, in: *Guida al diritto*, 2013, 17, 25 and Cass. 23 January – 12 March 2013, n 6093, in: *Diritto and Giustizia*, 2013, 13 March.

with patients), while healthcare facilities, whether public or private, are always liable under contract law.

102 This distinction influences mainly on the allocation of the burden of proof. However, there are other consequences of creating this 'double binary' that concern the terms of prescription. In fact, the non-contractual liability of the physicians implies, as a direct consequence, that the action for damages brought against them is subject to the five-year prescription term. This is due to the express provision in art 2947 CC, which states that 'the right to compensation for unlawful conduct shall be prescribed within five years of the date on which the facts occurred'.

103 The contractual liability of the public or private health care organisation, on the other hand, involves the imposition of the ten-year ordinary prescription term, provided for in art 2946 CC, under which 'except in cases where the law provides otherwise, the rights expire on prescriptions for ten years'. This last reform, therefore, would have clarified this aspect of the matter, limiting – in matters of medical liability – the discretion of the judge in interpreting the nature of the obligation subject to prescription.

104 A legal doctrine parallel to prescription that calls for judicial discretion is laches. It allows courts to reject P's claim because of the passage of time since its accrual if the delay in filing harmed D because she legitimately relied on P's omission to file during that period. The doctrine of laches can function as a judicial, discretionary, alternative to prescription or as additional defence. As an additional defence it may bar P's claim before the expiration of the prescription period and such an outcome may be considered undesirable as it undermines prescription law (claim may be subjected to laches before it is subjected to prescription).

105 Italian judges are required to apply the rules on prescription and do not have any power to assess the reasons for the delay with which a given right is exercised, rendering irrelevant any subjective reasons (which would be relevant in the doctrine of laches) that would have justified the delay.

## XI. CHANGE OF PARTIES

### A. THE PLAINTIFF IS A TRANSFEREE OF THE VICTIM'S CLAIM

106 Normally if a claim is transferred from one individual to another, the transfer does not affect prescription. Also, if a claim is dependent from another claim (a recourse action of one tortfeasor against the other joint and several tortfeasors) but it is independent, it is not affected by the previous running of time. A prominent example is contribution claim of one tortfeasor (D1) against

another tortfeasor (D2) where D1 and D2 are jointly liable to V. Another example is claims made by the dependants (Ps) of the deceased V, against D who injured V, injury that later caused V's death, for loss of financial support that D would have otherwise provided. Such claim actually substitutes V's claim for loss of earnings (see *supra* 26 ff).

Case law[33] supports the prescriptive nature of the ten-year term envisaged by art 480 CC for the acceptance of inheritance, since the course of time involves the loss of a right, even if it is potentially through the inertia of its holder. The retention of the prescriptive nature of the ten-year term implies the applicability of the grounds of suspension provided for by arts 2941 and 2942 CC. Therefore, in the case of mental illness, the suspension will continue for the period when the subject has no legal representative and for the six months following the appointment of the same or the cessation of inability. 107

When the victim brings a civil action in a criminal proceeding, the prescription of the right to compensation shall run from the judicial declaration preventing continuation of the trial even in the case of the death of the indicted person. 108

Case law,[34] overcoming a previous line of interpretation, has clarified the terms on which the statute of limitations operates in the case of extinction of a criminal trial. The prevailing view now holds that a civil claim in a criminal proceeding interrupts the prescriptive period until the criminal judgment is final and legally binding. Thus, the period does not run again from the death of the indicted, but from the moment that the judgment becomes final and irrevocable. 109

The Supreme Court[35] followed this line of reasoning in a case when it overturned the denial of an action for damages brought by the heirs of a victim of a traffic accident because the trial court had calculated the prescription period from the death of the indicted. It accepted in full the applicant's argument which claimed the permanent interruption effect of the filing of a criminal proceeding until the criminal judgment is made final and irrevocable. 110

When such a judgment becomes final and irrevocable, the interruption of prescription ceases and responsibility to revive the action again in civil proceedings arises. 111

A different interpretation of the course of limitation periods would violate arts 3 and 24 of the Constitution, by treating differently the death of an offender, the extinguishment of a criminal trial, and other similar cases such as the extinction of an offence due to an amnesty. 112

---

33 Cass., sez. II, 27 September 2012, n 16426, in: *Giust. civ. Mass.*, 2012 9, 1147.

34 Cass., SS. UU., 5 April 2013 n 8384, in: *Giust. civ.*, 2013, 10, I, 2031.

35 Cass., SS. UU., 5 April 2013 n 8384, quoted.

113 The victims' death enables their heirs to assert the right to compensation claimed by the deceased. Also, in this case the rule that the limitation period begins to run from the discovery of the damage.

114 Thus, if the injured victim had already discovered the harm the limitation period began to run from that moment and will continue in the hands of the heirs. For instance, this happens when the injured dies a year after sending a letter to the tortfeasors requesting compensation for damages incurred. The heirs will have four years to assert the right to compensation *iure hereditatis* (until the expiration of the five-year period).

115 If the injured party dies without ever having exercised her right to compensation because harm was not discovered, the heirs will be able to fill an action *iure hereditatis* for the first time within the five-year statutory limitation period running from their discovery of the harm suffered by the injured victim. It is worth noticing that the application of the rule may delay prescription for a long time. For instance, if heirs discover after a number of years (say 20) that their relative died for an illicit act the limitation period of five years will begin to run in the moment of discovery because case law considers the harm is happening only in that moment. As explained *supra* 22 ff, pursuant to art 2947 CC, the right to obtain compensation is time limited to five years from the day on which the event occurred. Please remember that, according to case law, harm occurs in the moment of its discovery.[36] Of course, difficulties in proving all the elements of the case make it extremely unlikely such an occurrence of 'long life' of the action, but theoretically it is possible.

## B. THE DEFENDANT IS A TRANSFEREE OF THE TORTFEASOR'S OBLIGATION

116 Article 1310 CC provides that acts with which the creditor interrupts the prescription against one of the joint debtors, or one of the creditors permanently interrupts the prescription against the common debtor, produces effects for the other debtors or creditors. The joint debtor who has paid the entire debt may repeat the portion of each of the other debtors and, with respect to this right of recourse, a new limitation period for the holder begins.

117 In case of inability of discernment, art 428 s 3 CC provides that the limitation period runs from the time the act was committed. As such, it is possible that, in practice, a rightholder might never be capable of bringing an action due to an inability condition that persists throughout the five-year prescription period.

---

[36] Cass., 15 May 2012, n 7553, in: *Giust. civ. Mass.*, 2012, 5, 615.

In fact, however, the rule that the *dies a quo* starts from the end of the condition of impairment is an application of the rule provided in art 2935 CC that applies only to contracts involving legally incompetent subjects, and not to impediments of fact – such as in the case of a so-called natural inability.

Indeed, legal incapacity arises as an impediment in law, as it also results from legal publicity (civil status registers). To the contrary, natural incapacity is not detectable in any way with legal instruments. However, in this case, the last paragraph of art 1442 CC provides that where the contract has not been performed voidability can always be opposed as an exception. 118

## C. CONTRIBUTION CLAIMS

Article 1310 CC provides that the acts by which the creditor interrupts prescription against one of the joint and several debtors, or one of the joint and several creditors interrupts the prescription against the common debtor, shall have effect with respect to the other debtors or creditors. This rule applies to every act of interruption, both to instantaneous effects and to permanent effects.[37] 119

The extension of the interrupting effect to the other joint debtors also operates when the interruption is due to a deed of formal notice, although the direct effects of the formal notice do not extend to the other joint debtors pursuant to art 1308 CC. 120

Similarly, a judicial request interrupts prescription against all the debtors, including those who have not participated in the trial or against whom the action has not continued due to the extinction of the civil trial or the cessation of the effects of civil filings in a criminal trial upon the extinction of the crime due to the accused death.[38] 121

Please note that the interrupting effect acts also in favour of the defendant with regard to her right to act in recourse against her co-debtors, since it is merely a subjective extension of the request made against her.[39] 122

To the contrary, the exception of prescription raised by one of the joint and several debtors does not produce effects for the others, pursuant to the general rules described above.[40] 123

---

37 Cass., sez. I, 7 April 1983 n 2449, in: *Giust. civ. Mass.*, 1983, fasc. 4.

38 Cass., sez. III, 6 December 2000, n 15511, in: *Giust. civ. Mass.*, 2000, 2560.

39 Cass., sez. I, 13 January 1978, n 157, in: *Rass. avv. Stato*, 1978, I, 575

40 Cass., sez. III, 9 April 2001, n 5262, in: *Giust. civ. Mass.*, 2001, 753.

124 The joint and several nature of the obligation to compensate owed by the insurer, the vehicle owner and possibly the driver implies that, for the purpose of prescription, the interruptive acts performed by the injured party against the insurer produces effects also towards the owner and the driver of the damaging vehicle.[41]

125 The limitation period for the right of recourse starts from the payment and not from the day of the harmful even: it is an independent right.[42]

126 Note that this rule applies exclusively to the law of obligations. Thus, it cannot be applied to property rights and, in particular, to the acts of interruption of possession useful for acquisition of property by prescription in favour of the other co-owners.[43]

127 The suspension of the running of prescription of one joint and several debtor/creditors has no effect on the others. However, the debtor who has been forced to pay has recourse action against the joint and several debtors whose debt has been cancelled because of prescription.

128 The same provision on recourse is also applicable to creditors. Thus, the creditor against whom prescription has accrued has recourse action against the other creditors for whom suspension did not apply and obtained fulfilment of their credit. Yet, another scholarly opinion maintains that the debtor can deduct from the payment requested a pro-quota extinction of the debt due to the prescription accrued against one of the joint and several creditors. If this interpretation is accepted, such an exception would preclude a right of recourse for the creditor for whom prescription accrued.[44]

129 Finally, pursuant to the third para of art 1310 CC, the renunciation of prescription made by one of the joint and several debtors has no effect with respect to the others. To the contrary, if it is made to joint and several creditors it enables all creditors to profit from it. The co-debtor who has renounced to the effects of prescription has no right of recourse against the other debtors released because of prescription.

## D. DEPENDANT'S CLAIM

130 There are no specific rules relating to the requirement of the heir's right to make a claim for damages against those who caused the death of the relative.

41 Cass., sez. III, 27 June 2014, n 14636, in: *Arch. giur. circ.*, 11/14.

42 Cass., sez. III, 28 March 2001, n 4507, in: *Giust. civ. Mass.*, 2001, 612.

43 Cass., sez. II, 3 April 2012, n 5338, in: *Giust. civ. Mass.*, 4, 441.

44 See *C.M. Bianca*, Diritto civile, IV, L'obbligazione (Milano, 1997).

The general rules therefore apply, as it is an action that the heirs promote autonomously and not in derivation of the rights deriving from the deceased.

## XII. OTHER ASPECTS OF PRESCRIPTION LAW

### A. STIPULATION

Article 1310 CC provides that acts with which the creditor interrupts the prescription against one of the joint debtors, or one of the creditors permanently interrupts the prescription against the common debtor, produces effects for the other debtors or creditors. The joint debtor who has paid the entire debt may repeat the portion of each of the other debtors and, with respect to this right of recourse, a new limitation period for the holder begins. 131

In case of inability of discernment, art 428, s 3 CC provides that the limitation period runs from the time the act was committed. As such, it is possible that, in practice, a rightholder might never be capable of bringing an action due to an inability condition that persists throughout the five-year prescription period. In fact, however, the rule that the *dies a quo* starts from the end of the condition of impairment is an application of the rule provided in art 2935 CC that applies only to contracts involving legally incompetent subjects, and not to impediments of fact – such as in the case of a so-called natural inability. 132

Indeed, legal incapacity arises as an impediment *in law*, as it also results from legal publicity (civil status registers). To the contrary, natural incapacity is not detectable in any way with legal instruments. However, in this case, the last paragraph of art 1442 CC provides that where the contract has not been performed, voidability can always be opposed as an exception. 133

### B. MEANING OF 'FILING A CLAIM' THAT INTERRUPTS THE RUNNING OF PRESCRIPTION

There are three causes of interruption of prescription. Specifically: 134

(1) where a claim has been filed also in front of an arbiter (art 2943 paras 1, 2, 3 and 4 CC);
(2) when the rightholder has put the debtor in default, ie request or written intimation to fulfil to the debtor in accordance with art 1219 CC (art 2943 subpara 4 CC) or;
(3) when there has been an acknowledgement of debt by the debtor (art 2944 CC).

135 In all these cases the limitation period renews.

136 (1) Article 2943 s 1 CC refers to the number one cause of interruption (claim) in terms of 'service of the document with which a trial is filed'.

137 Pursuant to art 149 Codice di Procedura Civile (CPC), the notification is completed, for the notifier, upon delivery of the notice to the bailiff and, for the recipient, when she has legal knowledge of the document.

138 The permanent interruption of the prescription begins from the summoning of the claim. The summons not only causes the interruption of the limitation period, but also entails the suspension of the same throughout the trial until there is a final judgment. The new limitation period will begin to run again after a final judgment with the force of *res judicata*, concerning the right for which prescription was running, comes into effect.

139 (2) The second cause of interruption are those acts capable of putting the debtor in default by a notice or request made in writing. The creditor, who does not want to suffer prescription but also does not want to submit a claim, can simply ask the debtor to comply with any written document.

140 Case law[45] has clarified the requirements of a valid written notice sufficient to produce interruption. Specifically, the notice must contain (1) a clear indication of the debtor; (2) a clear expression of the specific claim (eg the payment of a certain sum of money) and, finally, (3) the express intimation of performance, capable of manifesting the unequivocal will of the holder of the claim to assert their rights against the party alleged, with the substantial effect of constituting notice to her.

141 Therefore, for the purposes of interruption of prescription, out-of-court requests shall be submitted by the creditor in such a way as to bring out in an absolutely clear and unequivocal manner the intent to exercise one's own right.

142 Therefore, verbal requests to perform or written solicitations lacking proper intimation, as well as the mere production of documents unaccompanied by an intimation of performance and negotiations to settle the dispute amicably will be insufficient to cause interruption – except perhaps where, in amicable negotiations, the debtor's conduct amounts to recognition of the existence of the right of credit within the meaning and for the purposes of art 2944 CC.[46]

143 In the case of out-of-court acts of formal notice, the aforementioned rule of art 149 CPC does not apply. Thus, the creditor who wishes to halt the

---

45 *Ex multis*, Cass. civ., sez. III, 29 May 1987 n 4804, in: *Giust. civ. Mass.*, 1987, fasc. 5.

46 Cass., 5 August 2019, in: *Guida al Diritto*, 2020, 2, 65.

commencement of the period of limitation shall use a communication medium for the intimation capable of attesting to the moment when the notice has been received at the recipient's address.

Case law has made clear that it is not strictly necessary that the interruption is actually known by the recipient. It is sufficient that the request is received at her address in good time, thereby ensuring potential awareness of the legal act interrupting prescription (out of court) before the period of limitation is exhausted.[47] 144

(3) Finally, the recognition of the right by the person against whom the right may be claimed constitutes a cause of interruption. 145

The act of recognition is not subject to any requirement of form and it can come from the debtor or her representative. An essential requirement for it is that the recognition manifest a clear and unambiguous recognition of the rights of others, capable of excluding the possibility that the same action or behaviour could have been performed for other purposes incompatible with the desire to recognise the rights of others. 146

## C. WHEN SHOULD THE DEFENCE BE RAISED AND DECIDED?

The exception of prescription must be raised by the defendant, under penalty of forfeiture, in the reply to the summons. After this date, the grievance will be late and may not be discussed during the trial. That exception, although it does not require a specific formula, must contain an unequivocal manifestation of the will to resist to the claims summoned by the counterpart. 147

The exception of prescription is a preliminary issue of merit, whose positive solution can put an end to the dispute. For this reason, the court must deal with the question prior to turning to the merits of the claim, since it would be completely useless (and expensive) to deal with the merits of the case if prescription applies. 148

## D. WHO MAY RAISE THE DEFENCE?

Normally, the defendant has the burden to raise the exception of prescription. 149

A third party with a legal interest in doing so can raise the exception of prescription even if the rightholder does not do so and even if she has waived 150

47 Cass., sec Lav. 6/27/2008 n 17644, in: *Giust. civ. Mass.*, 2008, 6, 1039.

it. Thus, for instance, the exception of prescription raised by a joint and several debtor has a favourable impact for the other debtors.[48]

151 In general, the burden of proving prescription remains on those who intend to make use of it, who must allege and prove the circumstances that demonstrate the successful expiration of the limitation period. Thus, the defendant opposing prescription to a right claimed by the plaintiff will need to show expiration of the time limit provided for by the law that is applicable to the claimed right.

## E. BURDEN OF PROOF (OF ELEMENTS AND OF RULES OF PROLONGATION)

152 It could happen that the plaintiff reacts to the exception of prescription with the exception of interruption of the limitation period, which, as an exception *lato sensu* can be raised also *ex officio* at any moment during the trial on the basis of allegations and evidence, including documents, officially acquired to the trial.

153 It follows that in a plea of prescription, the one against whom prescription is raised has the burden not to propose a counter-objection of interruption of prescription, but to allege and demonstrate the existence of the interrupting act, if such proof is not already produced, in the procedural period after prescription has been raised.[49]

154 With reference to evidence, the civil code provides for short prescription terms (so-called presumptive prescriptions) in particular cases in which the payment of a debt takes place, usually without the debtor seeking a receipt. In these cases, after a short period, it is assumed that the debt has been satisfied and is therefore extinct. These are not cases of prescription but of 'presumptions of extinction of rights' that the Italian legislature has chosen among less significant instances of patrimonial rights of tenuous value relevant to everyday life, such as – for example – the right of teachers to their remuneration for lessons given in months, days and hours.

155 For the purposes of the limitation of these rights, the law provides for a special system of proof that the rightholder may take advantage of in the case that the debtor contests the extinction of the right. For instance, it may happen that the plaintiff sues the debtor to obtain the payment of a certain sum of money – say for example the fees to the educational institution attended by

48 Cass., sec III, 9 June 2014, n 12911, in: *Guida al diritto*, 2014, 33, 37.

49 Cass., sec Security jobs, 12 October 2009, n 18250, in: *Giust. civ. Mass.*, 2009, 7–8, 1190.

the son of the defendant – and that the latter seeks to rely on the extinction of the right, stating that the school has been paid. At this point, the plaintiff cannot do anything else than asking the judge to admit the probative oath, which means that the defendant is asked to swear of having paid. If the defendant admits under oath that the right was not extinguished, the creditor wins the case. If the debtor under oath confirms the extinction of the right, the plaintiff loses the lawsuit, but has a chance to prove in a criminal judgment that the defendant had actually sworn falsely.

# PRESCRIPTION IN TORT LAW: THE NETHERLANDS

Anne LM Keirse*



* The author thanks Tom Bouwman, a student research assistant at the time, for his enormous work, without whom this contribution would not have seen the light of day.

## I. INTRODUCTION

1 Before the enactment of the new *Burgerlijk Wetboek* (Dutch Civil Code, hereafter 'BW') in 1992, in the Netherlands there was only one prescription period of 30 years for all private law claims. That period accrued the moment the plaintiff was entitled to claim performance of the obligation, which for tort claims was the moment the cause of action occurred.[1] In the current Dutch Civil Code, not only is a distinction made between different claims – contractual, tort, etc – but also between two different prescription periods. For tort claims, there is the, so-called, 'subjective' or 'relative' period of five years whose running is postponed until the day after the plaintiff is aware of both the damage and the thereof responsible person. And there is the, so-called, 'objective' or 'absolute' period of 20 years which starts to run following the moment the cause of the damage occurred.[2] Although in general, this reform of the rules of prescription of tort claims was perceived as an improvement, there was still a lot of criticism on its functioning. Therefore, both the Dutch legislator and the Dutch Supreme Court made some changes to *inter alia* the commencement of the subjective

1 *MWE Koopmann*, Monografieen BW: Bevrijdende verjaring (2010), 3–4.

2 Article 3:310(1) BW; art 3:310(5) BW.

prescription period and the prescription period of damage that is caused by injury or death.[3]

2 In this report it will be explored how – and why – the passage of time on alleged tort claims affects the claim, the parties and third parties through the defence of prescription in the Netherlands. In order to do this, first in Sections II and III, the definition and the nature of prescription in the Netherlands will be introduced. After this, in Section IV the considerations for and against the prescription of tort claims will be discussed. Section V gives an overview of the elements of prescription. Subsequently, the starting point of the prescription period in the Netherlands will be examined in Section VI, and hereafter, in Section VII, the length of the Dutch prescription period for tort claims will be discussed. Furthermore, the rules of postponement, suspension, renewal and extension of the prescription period are studied in Section VIII, and in Section IX the ceiling on the effective time of prescription in the Netherlands is explained. Lastly, Sections X, XI and XII deal with, respectively, the interpretation and application of prescription rules in the Netherlands, the effects of change of parties and other general aspects of Dutch prescription law.

## II. DEFINITION OF PRESCRIPTION

3 In Dutch law, the rules on prescription of tort claims are part of the legal concept extinctive prescription (*bevrijdende verjaring*). The Dutch legislator has not defined extinctive prescription as such, and Dutch legal scholars also use different definitions of the concept.[4] Asser and Sieburgh define extinctive prescription as follows:

> The elapse of a period of time that is determined by law, during which no legally relevant facts occur which shows that the creditor claims his right or the debtor acknowledges his fault, after which the debtor, in case he invokes it, can no longer be forced to perform his obligation.[5]

---

3 This will be discussed in following sections.

4 *Koopmann*, *supra* fn 1, 22; *CJ van Zeben, JW Du Pon and MM Olthof* (eds), Parlementaire geschiedenis van het nieuwe burgerlijk wetboek: Boek 3: vermogensrecht in het algemeen (1981), 917–920.

5 *CH Sieburgh*, MR. C. Assers Handleiding tot de beoefening van het Nederlands Burgerlijk Recht: Verbintenissenrecht: De verbintenis in het algemeen, tweede gedeelte (2017), (hereafter: Asser and Sieburgh 6-II), para 377. Own translation. Original text: 'Het verlopen van een door de wet bepaalde tijdsduur, gedurende welk zich geen door de wet als relevant beschouwde feiten voordoen waaruit blijkt dat de crediteur aanspraak maakt op zijn recht of de debiteur het bestaan van zijn schuld erkent, na welk tijdsverloop de debiteur, zo hij zich daarop beroept, niet meer tot nakoming van zijn verbintenis kan worden aangesproken.'

4 Although the definition of Asser and Sieburgh is criticised by some Dutch legal scholars for not describing all relevant elements of extinctive prescription – for instance, it does not stress that the start of the prescription period is of importance and that it is only the action that ceased to exist[6] – its basic elements seem to reflect the definition of the EGTL quite well.[7] The only difference is that the definition of Asser and Sieburgh does not specify what the meaning of the term 'obligation' is. This is because their definition is a definition of extinctive prescription in general, not specified to the context of tort law. Specified to the context of tort law, 'obligation' here means the obligation to pay compensation for damages caused by tortious conduct.[8]

## III. THE NATURE OF PRESCRIPTION AND ITS EFFECTS

5 In Dutch law, prescription provides the defendant with a substantive defence that prevents the plaintiff from enforcing the right to remedy although it is not extinguished. In the parliamentary history of art 3:306 BW, which sets the ground norm for prescription in Dutch law, it is stressed that 'extinctive prescription extinguishes the legal action, not the legal right.'[9] Therefore, after a defendant successfully invoked prescription, the obligations to pay compensation for damages caused by tortious conduct remains to exist as a, so-called, natural obligation (*natuurlijke verbintenis*).[10] This means that if a defendant successfully invokes prescription but still compensates – for instance by mistake – the damage of the plaintiff, then the defendant does not have the right to restitution under the law of undue payments or unjust enrichment.[11]

6 Prescription in Dutch law can be invoked in and out of court.[12] However, when prescription is invoked out of court, but a judicial proceeding is still commenced, then the defendant has to invoke the prescription defence once again in court. This is because the judge is not allowed to invoke prescription *ex officio*.[13]

---

6 *Koopmann*, *supra* fn 1, 22–23.

7 EGTL defined prescription as follows: 'prescription in tort law is a legal institution that prevents the plaintiff from enforcing an alleged right against the defendant because of the running of a specified period of time on the tort claim.'

8 Article 3:310(1) BW.

9 *Van Zeben, Du Pon and Olthof*, *supra* fn 4, 917. Own translation. Original text: 'de bevrijdende verjaring doet de rechtsvordering, niet ook het recht tenietgaan.'

10 *Asser and Sieburgh 6-II*, *supra* fn 5, para 390.

11 *J Spier and T Hartlief*, Verjaring, in: T Hartlief, ALM Keirse, SD Lindenbergh and RD Vriesendorp (eds), Verbintenissen uit de wet en schadevergoeding (8th ed, 2018), no 334.

12 *Asser and Sieburgh 6-II*, *supra* fn 5, para 389.

13 Article 3:322 (1) BW.

## IV. CONSIDERATIONS FOR AND AGAINST PRESCRIPTION OF TORT CLAIMS

Prescription can deprive a plaintiff of the opportunity to pursue and enforce his alleged right against a defendant. It closes the doors of courts and thus also limits the right to 'open courts'. Despite these negative effects, prescription is – generally – seen as justified because there are interests that counterbalance the negative effects of prescription. Four categories of interests can be distinguished in the discussion about the pros and cons of prescription in the Dutch legal literature and parliamentary history: the interest of the defendant, the interests of third parties, the general interest, and the interest of the plaintiff.[14] Each of them is discussed here. 7

First, the interest of the defendant. According to most Dutch legal scholars, the defendant has two major interests in the existence of rules on prescription. The first interest is that after the passing of time it becomes more difficult for the defendant to defend his case, because, for instance: witnesses are untraceable, memories become blurred, and written documents get lost or are thrown away. Therefore, prescription protects the defendant against unfounded – also referred to as 'bad' – claims.[15] The second interest of the defendant in the existence of rules on prescription that is recognised, is that at a certain point of time a defendant should be able to legitimately expect that his financial position will not be affected by a claim and that he therefore also does not have to preserve evidence on the case. This is especially the case when the defendant does not even know that he has to face a claim.[16] 8

Second, the interests of third parties. Smeehuijzen has argued that third parties also have to be recognised as having an interest in prescription because they should be able – at least after a certain period of time – to have the confidence that their right will not be disturbed by a long-forgotten claim. For instance, in case of a credit agreement.[17] 9

Third, the general interest. Some legal scholars have argued that the general interest also benefits from prescription because prescription keeps peace, makes sure that conflicts come to an end, unburdens the judicial power, and ensures the smooth running of economic transactions.[18] The institute of prescription improves legal certainty and therefore general welfare. It is, however, contested 10

---

14 See also *Smeehuijzen, infra* fn 25, 25 ff.

15 *Asser and Sieburgh 6-II, supra* fn 5, para *382; Koopmann, supra* fn 1, 21 ff; *Smeehuijzen, infra* fn 25, 25 ff.

16 *Asser and Sieburgh 6-II, supra* fn 5, para 382; *Koopmann, supra* fn 1, 21 ff; *Smeehuijzen, infra* fn 25, 29 ff.

17 *Smeehuijzen, infra* fn 25, 43 ff; *Asser and Sieburgh 6-II, supra* fn 5, para 383.

18 *Asser and Sieburgh 6-II, supra* fn 5, para 383.

in the Dutch legal literature whether the institute of prescription is the best instrument to serve these interests.[19] Above all, prescription rules serve legal certainty by providing fixed time limits.

11 Finally, the interest of the plaintiff. It is recognised that it is in the interest of the plaintiff to have a prescription period that is as long as possible because then he has more time to file his claim.[20]

12 In the field of prescription law, *ius strictum* (legal certainty) and *ius aequum* (justice in individual cases) are struggling for supremacy, but the one should not predominate over the other. Neither goal can replace the other.[21] On the one hand it cannot be maintained that the sole purpose of justice is to guarantee the certainty of the law. On the other hand, there is no merit to the assertion that real legal certainty is the certainty that justice will prevail. Quite the contrary, both aspects of the law deserve acknowledgement. It comes down to a balancing act. This balancing act endeavours to strengthen the trust and credibility of the legal system and its fairness.

13 Dutch legal scholars seem to – more or less – agree that the subjective prescription period of five years is justified because if the plaintiff is able to bring a claim for damages – because he is aware of all the relevant information –, the interest of the defendant in knowing after five years whether he could expect a claim weights more than the plaintiff's interest in a longer period in which he can be inactive in filing a claim.[22] The objective prescription period of 20 years is justified because the correctness of a claim can ordinarily not be verified with a reasonable degree of certainty after such a long time.[23] However, it should be acknowledged that in some specific situations, such as asbestos cases, this is not completely true; specific facts on which the claim is based may still be (or become) topical and verifiable (this topic will be returned to in Section X.B).

## V. ELEMENTS OF PRESCRIPTION – AN OVERVIEW

14 Analytically, there are four elements – four sets of rules – that together comprise Dutch prescription law: the starting point of prescription, the prescription period, rules on prolongation – postponement, suspension, renewal and extension –, and rules on the ceiling on the effective time of prescription.

---

19 *Smeehuijzen, infra* fn 25, 32 ff; *Asser and Sieburgh 6-II, supra* fn 5, para 383.

20 *Asser and Sieburgh 6-II, supra* fn 5, para 384.

21 *PE Neuhaus*, Legal Certainty versus Equity in the Conflict of Laws, 28 Law and Contemporary Problems (1963) 795–807; *ALM Keirse and T Bouwman*, The Netherlands, in: E Karner and BC Steininger (eds), European Tort Law 2017 (2018), nos 14 and 23.

22 *Asser and Sieburgh 6-II, supra* fn 5, para 385; *Koopmann, supra* fn 1, 9 ff; *Smeehuijzen, infra* fn 25, 73 ff.

23 *Smeehuijzen, infra* fn 25, 73 ff.

15 Article 3:306 BW states that 'unless otherwise provided for by law, rights of action are prescribed on the expiry of twenty years.'[24] This general rule is de facto the exception because in most cases there is a provision that provides a different rule.[25] The for tort actions most relevant exception to the general rule of art 3:306 BW is art 3:310 BW. Paragraph 1 of this article reads:

> A right of action to compensate for damage or to pay a stipulated penalty is prescribed on the expiry of five years from the beginning of the day following the one on which the prejudiced person becomes aware of both the damage or that the penalty becomes exigible and the identity of the person responsible therefor, and, in any event, on the expiry of twenty years following the event which caused the damage or made the penalty exigible.[26]

16 There are therefore two different starting points in Dutch prescription law that simultaneously also determine the length of the prescription period. There is the, so-called, subjective period of five years whose running is postponed until the day after the plaintiff is aware of both the damage and the thereof responsible person. And there is the, so-called, objective period of 20 years which starts to run following the moment the cause of the damage occurred.[27]

17 Next to the subjective prescription period – a late discovery rule – there are also rules on renewal and extension in Dutch law that prolong the running of prescription periods. Article 6:231 BW contains an exhaustive list of grounds for extension (more on this in Section VIII) and, according to art 6:310(1) BW, a prescription period can be renewed by interruption (*stuiting*).

18 The ceiling on the effective time of prescription is determined by the objective prescription period, which is – in most cases – 20 years. After the running of the objective prescription period a claim prescribes regardless of whether the subjective prescription period started to run or is still running. However, the objective prescription period may be prolonged by extension, interruption or when the principles of reasonableness and fairness require so.

---

24 Translation from *H Warendorf* (ed), Warendorf Dutch Civil and Commercial Law Legislation (2013). Original text: 'Indien de wet niet anders bepaalt, verjaart een rechtsvordering door verloop van twintig jaren.'

25 *JL Smeehuijzen*, De bevrijdende verjaring (2008), 109.

26 Translation from *Warendorf*, *supra* fn 24. Original text: 'Een rechtsvordering tot vergoeding van schade of tot betaling van een bedongen boete verjaart door verloop van vijf jaren na de aanvang van de dag, volgende op die waarop de benadeelde zowel met de schade of de opeisbaarheid van de boete als met de daarvoor aansprakelijke persoon bekend is geworden, en in ieder geval door verloop van twintig jaren na de gebeurtenis waardoor de schade is veroorzaakt of de boete opeisbaar is geworden.'

27 Article 3:310(1) BW.

# VI. THE STARTING POINT OF THE PRESCRIPTION PERIOD

## A. THE OBJECTIVE PRESCRIPTION PERIOD AND SUBJECTIVE PRESCRIPTION PERIOD

19 The first element of prescription is the starting point of the prescription period. As mentioned *supra* 1, in Dutch law there are two starting points.[28] There is an objective prescription period, whose starting point will be discussed first in this section, and there is a subjective prescription period – also referred to as 'the late discovery rule' – whose starting point will be discussed in Section VIII.A as that makes the structure of this report more logical. It should however be mentioned that the Dutch late discovery rule is also a rule of the starting point (accrual). According to Dutch law there are two prescription periods with two independent starting points.

## B. THE STARTING POINT OF THE OBJECTIVE PRESCRIPTION PERIOD

20 In Dutch law, the starting point of the objective prescription period is the occurrence of the tortious act that constituted the damage (hereafter also referred to as the 'cause of action').[29]

## C. THE SCOPE OF 'CAUSE OF ACTION'

21 When an occurrence contains multiplicity of conducts and/or of caused damages which are tortious under tort rules, it may produce a variety of particular tort actions which differ from each other in facts, damages and applicable torts. Yet, when a group of particular actions have a common factual/legal source it is said that all these particular actions belong to the same source, the same cause of action. The cause of action may therefore be the occurrence as a whole or part of it. Take for instance '**Case 2**': a physician treats a patient negligently and performs three mistakes on the treatment's day: A, B and C. Mistake A causes damage X after a year. Mistake B causes damage Y after two years. Mistakes A and C together cause damage Z after three years. The question then raises whether the damages X, Y and Z all have a different cause of action so that the cause of action for each damage may accrue at a different moment in

[28] Article 3:310 (1) BW.
[29] Article 3:310 (1) BW.

time – 'cause of action' in the narrow sense – or whether the different damages belong to the same cause of action so that they are all accrue with harm X – 'cause of action' in the broad sense.

22 It can be inferred from a case of the Dutch Supreme Court about the illegal dumping of industrial waste that 'cause of action' in the Netherlands is interpreted in the narrow sense.[30] In this case, a municipality discovered an illegal dumping in 1988, but waited until 1995 with filing the claim for damages. What the municipality did not know until then was that the company had kept on dumping waste after the initial discovery of the dumping in 1988. This raised the legal question whether each dumping had to be seen as an individual tort – so that the dumping activities after 1990 did not prescribe – or whether the dumpings all accrued together as the company simply did not stop dumping.[31] The Dutch Supreme Court decided that each of the dumping activities had to be seen as an individual tort. Coming back to 'Case 2', this means that the damages X, Y and Z belong to different causes of action as each of the mistakes constitute an individual tort – they are caused by different sets of facts, namely the three different mistakes. However, since the three mistakes were made on the same day, the objective prescription period starts to run that day for all three causes.

23 In case one and the same tortious action constitutes different damages, these different damages in principle all prescribe together. Take for example '**Case 1**' in which a ski instructor negligently fails to make sure that all skiers in her 'off-piste' group wear helmets. Suppose that one skier in the group hits a tree and then suffers immediately from head injury X and years later from another head injury Y – that developed from the same accident. Disregarding the subjective prescription period and disregarding the fact that in the Netherlands there is no objective prescription period for bodily injury,[32] these two harms would prescribe on the same day as their cause of action – the negligent conduct – is the same.[33]

24 That different harms will prescribe together in case these harms are constituted by one and the same tortious action can also be illustrated by '**Case 3**'. Suppose a builder has laid down a defective foundation for a building and thereby created the risk of a collapse when heavy rain falls. Suppose that, as a result, the value of the building decreases, cracks appear three years after the effective foundation was laid down, and after four years the building collapses. Disregarding the subjective prescription period, these different damages all have the same cause

30 HR 02.09.2011, *NJ* 2001/650.
31 At that time, paras 2 and 3 of art 3:310 BW were not yet into function.
32 Article 3:310(5) BW.
33 Article 3:310(1) BW.

of action, namely the tortious conduct of the builder and therefore also the same starting point for the objective prescription period.

25 Another question is whether the breach of duty (the tortious act) or the occurrence of the damage is the starting point. The clear-cut answer to this question is that according to Dutch law, the starting point is the occurrence of the tortious act that constituted the damage. However, the question asks for a more nuanced answer as can be illustrated by means of '**Case 4**'. Suppose, D enters someone's premises without permission and remains there, without causing any damage. The owner of the property can file a tort claim against D asking for the remedy of his eviction but fails to do so. A year later D causes physical harm to the premises. The owner wants to file a claim to compensation for the loss. Because art 3:310(1) BW states that the starting point of the objective prescription period is the occurrence of the tortious act that constituted the damage and it can be inferred from the case about illegal dumping that is discussed *supra* 19 that each time someone trespasses a new tort occurs, it can be concluded that, disregarding the subjective prescription period, the prescription period for the damage suffered by the owner starts the day he suffered the damage as at that day also a new tort action occurred.

## D. THE NOTION OF CONTINUOUS TORT

26 Another question regarding the notion of 'cause of action' is whether and to what extent a notion of 'continuous tort' is recognised. In Dutch law, a notion of continuous tort is only recognised for damage that is the result of the effects of hazardous materials, or of air, water or soil pollution. Article 3:310(3) BW states that within the context of damage that is the result of the effects of hazardous materials, or of air, water or soil pollution, 'cause of action' means 'a suddenly occurring fact, a continuous fact, or a succession of facts with the same cause.'[34] The article continuous to explain that when the cause of action:

> [...] consists of a continuous fact, the period of thirty years referred to in paragraph 2 shall start to run after this fact ceases to exist. Where the event consists of a succession of facts with the same cause, the period shall start to run after the last fact.[35]

Suppose by way of example, that a waste management company digs bins of hazardous materials into soil and thereby toxic substance leaks into the soil and

[34] Translation from *Warendorf*, *supra* fn 24. Original text: 'een plotseling optredend feit, een voortdurend feit of een opeenvolging van feiten met dezelfde oorzaak.'

[35] Translation from *Warendorf*, *supra* fn 24. Original text: '[...] een voortdurend feit, dan begint de termijn van dertig jaren bedoeld in lid 2 te lopen nadat dit feit is opgehouden te bestaan. Bestaat de gebeurtenis uit een opeenvolging van feiten met dezelfde oorzaak, dan begint deze termijn te lopen na dit laatste feit.'

ground water, causing an apparent damage on a daily basis ('**Case 9**'). If the bins are removed from the soil after two years, then, according to art 3:310(3) BW, the prescription period starts to run the moment after the bins have been removed from the soil because then the continuous fact has ceased to exist.

In a case that dates back to 1999, the Dutch Supreme Court decided that the rules of art 3:310(3) BW do not apply analogously to the 'cause of action' of other tort cases than cases where the damage is the result of the effects of hazardous materials, or of air, water or soil pollution.[36] The case in which this was decided was about a boy who sued his father for mentally and physically mistreating him from 1960 till 1976. The father argued that the facts that occurred before 1974 prescribed. The son argued that the mistreatment of his father can – analogously to art 3:310(3) BW – not be divided into separate causes of action, and that therefore the facts that occurred between 1960 and 1976 should be seen as one tort that ended in 1976. The Dutch Supreme Court disagreed with the reasoning of the son, which means that the Dutch notion of 'continuous tort' only applies in a limited type of cases. It does, for instance, not apply in cases about the continuous publishing of defaming articles ('**Case 7**') or continuous unreasonable exposure to noise ('**Case 8**'). However, in 2019 the Dutch Supreme Court provided a nuance to this previous ruling from 1999, where art 3:310(3) BW was ruled to be only applicable for claims based on art 3:310(2) BW. The case concerned a liability claim on the basis of art 6:174 BW. This provision establishes liability of the possessor of a constructed immovable thing which constitutes a danger for people or things because it does not meet the standards which may be set for such a thing, for the damage caused by the materialisation of this danger. In this case, the event that caused the damage, the defective and dangerous condition of the constructed immovable thing, could not be pinpointed to one moment in time. It concerned a wall that had been skewed for years due to a constant pressure that should not have been there. The Dutch Supreme Court ruled that in such a case the objective prescription period only starts to run as soon as the defective and dangerous condition that caused the damage has ceased to exist.[37] 27

It is possible that – in cases that are not about damage that is the result of the effects of hazardous materials, or of air, water or soil pollution – the cause of action is subdivided into two pieces of which one did prescribe and the other did not.[38] This effect of the limited application of the notion of 'continuous tort' of which it is unclear how courts should deal with it, is – amongst others – criticised by Smeehuijzen.[39] 28

36 HR 25.06.1999, *NJ* 2000/16.

37 HR 22.03.2019, ECLI:NL:HR:2019:412.

38 *Smeehuijzen*, *supra* fn 25, 264 ff.

39 *Smeehuijzen*, *supra* fn 25, 264 ff.

# VII. PRESCRIPTION PERIODS

## A. THE PRESCRIPTION PERIOD AND THE EFFECTIVE TIME OF PRESCRIPTION

29 In the old Dutch Civil Code, which was in force until 1992, there was only one prescription period of 30 years for all private law claims.[40] In the current Dutch Civil Code, not only is a distinction made between a subjective prescription period and an objective prescription period, but the general objective prescription period, which is comparable to the old 30-year prescription period, is also shortened to 20 years. The reason for this is that in most cases there was no justified reason for such a long prescription period.[41] Nowadays, the current 20-year objective prescription period is accompanied with on the one hand rules that can prolong the effective time of prescription period and on the other hand the subjective prescription period of five years which can shorten the effective time of prescription.

## B. THE ACTUAL PRESCRIPTION PERIODS

30 In the Netherlands, the general objective prescription period is 20 years, and the general subjective prescription period is five years. In general, there is therefore not much differentiation between the prescription period of different – contractual, tort, etc – private law claims in the Netherlands. There are, however, a few – for tort law relevant – exceptions to these general prescription periods. First to be discussed are the exceptions to the subjective five-year period and the objective 20-year period. Then some, for tort law relevant, situations that have their own prescription period will be reviewed. The section ends with the expiry period of product liability claims. For an overview of the prescription periods, see the table at the end of this section.

31 The first, for tort claims relevant, exception to the general subjective prescription period of five years is art 3:310(4) BW. This article states a rule for damage that is caused by a criminal offence. A claim based on such a cause of action does not prescribe as long as the right to a criminal proceeding has not ceased to exist because of – criminal – prescription or the death of the accused.[42] The second, for tort claims relevant, exception to the subjective prescription period of five years applies when damage is caused by injury or by death and the plaintiff is under age at the moment he or she has become aware of

[40] *Koopmann*, *supra* fn 1, 3–4.
[41] See also *supra* 13.
[42] Note that this can also prolong the objective prescription period.

the damage and the thereof liable person. The subjective prescription period of five years then starts to run the day after he or she becomes of age.[43]

There are also two, for tort law relevant, exceptions to the objective prescription period of 20 years. Article 3:310(2) BW states that damage that is the result of the effects of hazardous materials, or of air, water or soil pollution has an objective prescription period of 30 years. The ratio behind this rule is to give plaintiffs better possibilities for redress in case of pollution.[44] The most important exception to the objective prescription period is art 3:310(5) BW which states that claims which are the result of damage that is caused by injury or death have no objective prescription period. Damage caused by injury or death therefore only has a subjective prescription period of five years. The idea behind this rule is that it is unreasonable if a claim prescribes before the damage consisting of injury or death has occurred, what, for instance, would have happened in asbestos cases if the Dutch Supreme Court had not intervened.[45] The exception of art 3:310(5) BW is criticised by – amongst others – Smeehuijzen for also protecting plaintiffs in situations where there is no need to protect them against the effects of prescription.[46] Moreover, one should be aware of the fact that this exception stipulating that there is no objective prescription period for damage caused by injury or death only came into effect on 1 February 2004 and has no retroactive effect. This means that claims regarding torts that took place before this date still prescribe after 20 (or 30) years. 32

For some – more specific – situations there are arrangements of prescription that are different from the general rule of art 3:310 BW. For instance, if a tort action of a buyer against a seller is in fact based on the non-conformity of the good, then the prescription period is only two years and starts to run following the moment the buyer notified the non-conformity to the seller as provided in art 7:23 BW.[47] Also, actions based on tort in cases that are governed by the Dutch provisions on transport (Book 8 of the Dutch Civil Code) often have a shortened prescription period as well.[48] For instance, in case of collision, art 8:1790 BW states that the prescription period is two years and starts to run following the moment the collision occurred. There is also a special prescription period for claims based on the Civil Liability Insurance (Motor Vehicles) Act (hereafter 'WAM'). Article 10 WAM states that if a claim of the injured party against the insurer ensues from the act, then the claim prescribes three years after the fact occurred that caused the damage. 33

43 Article 3:310(5) BW.

44 *CC van Dam*, De verjaringstermijn terug naar dertig jaar (1992) 29 Nederlands Juristenblad (NJB) 932.

45 *Asser and Sieburgh 6-II*, *supra* fn 5, paras 414, 416.

46 *Smeehuijzen*, *supra* fn 25, 106 ff.

47 HR 21.04.2006, *NJ* 2006/272.

48 Article 8:361 BW; art 8:1700 BW; art 8:1790; art 8:31 BW; art 8:91 BW.

34 In Dutch law, some claims have an expiry period instead of a prescription period. One such, for tort claims relevant, exception is the expiry period of product liability claims based on the arts 6:185 ff BW, that form the implementation of the European Directive 85/374/EEC on product liability. Article 6:191(1) BW states that such a claim expires 'by the expiry of three years from the beginning of the day following that on which the injured person became or should have become aware of the damage, the defect and the identity of the producer',[49] or anyhow after ten years.[50] Because this is an expiry period, it is assumed that it extinguishes the plaintiff's right to remedy and is applied *ex officio*.[51]

35 The following table presents an overview of the various prescription periods:

**Table 1. Overview of prescription periods**

| Action | Subjective prescription period | Accrual | Authority | Objective prescription period | Accrual | Authority | Rules on prolongation |
|---|---|---|---|---|---|---|---|
| Tort in general | 5 years | The day after the plaintiff is aware of the damage and the thereof responsible person | Article 3:310(1) BW | 20 years | The day the event that caused the damage occurred | Article 3:310(1) BW | By interruption (art 3:316 BW ff), by extension (art 3:321 BW), or if the principles of reasonableness and fairness require so (art 6:2 BW) |
| Damage that is the effect of hazardous materials, or of air, water or soil pollution | 5 years | The day after the plaintiff is aware of the damage and the thereof responsible person | Article 3:310(1) BW | 30 years | The day the event that caused the damage occurred. In case of a continuous tort, the moment the event stopped (art 3:310(3) BW) | Article 3:310(2) BW | By interruption (arts 3:316 BW ff), by extension (art 3:321 BW), or if the principles of reasonableness and fairness require so (art 6:2 BW). |

*(continued)*

49 Translation from *Warendorf, supra* fn 24. Original text: '[...] door verloop van drie jaren na de aanvang van de dag, volgende op die waarop de benadeelde met de schade, het gebrek en de identiteit van de producent bekend is geworden of had moeten worden.'

50 Article 6:191(2) BW.

51 *Smeehuijzen, supra* fn 25, 338 ff.

**Table 1** *continued*

| Action | Subjective prescription period | Accrual | Authority | Objective prescription period | Accrual | Authority | Rules on prolongation |
|---|---|---|---|---|---|---|---|
| Damage caused by injury or death | 5 years | The day after the plaintiff is aware of the damage and the thereof responsible person. Or, if the plaintiff is underage, the day he or she becomes full of age and meets the aforementioned criteria (art 3:310(5) BW) | Article 3:310(5) BW | - | - | Article 3:310(5) BW | By interruption (arts 3:316 BW ff), or by extension (art 3:321 BW) |
| Damage that is caused by a criminal offence | - | - | - | - | A claim based on such a cause of action does not prescribe as long as the right to a criminal proceeding has not ceased to exist because of – criminal – prescription or the death of the accused | Article 3:310(4) BW | By interruption (arts 3:316 BW ff), or by extension (art 3:321 BW) |
| Product liability (note: this is an expiry period, not a prescription period) | 3 years | The day after the plaintiff became or should have become aware of the damage, the defect and the identity of the producer | Article 6:190(1) BW | 10 years | The day following that which the producer put the thing which caused the damage into circulation | Article 6:190(2) BW | - |
| Claim based on non-conformity of the good | - | - | - | 2 years | The day the buyer notified the non-conformity to the seller | Article 7:23 BW | - |
| Claim based on the Civil Liability Insurance (Motor Vehicles) Act | - | - | - | 3 years | The day the fact occurred that caused the damage | Article 10 WAM | By interruption (art 10 WAM and arts 3:316 BW ff) |

### C. PERIOD SHOPPING

36 It is possible that problems of classification of claims or of 'period shopping' arise in case a jurisdiction has diversified periods adjusted to different kinds of tort claims, or different periods for tort claims and other claims that concur with tort claims. In the Netherlands, this is not recognised as an issue. This is probably because the prescription period for – almost – all private law claims is either five or 20 years. However, there is one situation in which period shopping is possible, namely in product liability cases. As mentioned before, art 6:191 BW states that product liability claims based on art 6:185 BW have an expiry period of three or ten years – depending on the knowledge of the plaintiff. If a product liability claim that is based on art 6:185 BW has expired, then the plaintiff can 'shop' a longer period by basing his claim on the general tort provision of art 6:162 BW, which has a prescription period of five years (the subjective period) or 20 years (the objective period). It is therefore possible that a product liability claim has expired when it is based on art 6:185 BW, but not yet prescribed when it is based on art 6:162 BW.[52] The prerequisite is of course that all the requirements of art 6:162 BW have to be met, but this is likely to be the case since bringing a defective product on the market is regarded as a tortious act. Judges do allow this form of period shopping.

## VIII. RULES OF POSTPONEMENT, SUSPENSION, RENEWAL AND EXTENSION

### A. THE SUBJECTIVE PRESCRIPTION PERIOD

37 In Dutch prescription law, the most important rule of postponement is the subjective prescription period. The subjective prescription period starts to run the day after the plaintiff is aware of both the damage and the thereof liable person. The subjective prescription period also has its own prescription period, namely five years (see *supra* 34 for the exceptions to this period).

#### *1) Unawareness of what?*

38 As mentioned, the running of the subjective prescription period is postponed until the day after the plaintiff is aware of both the damage and the thereof liable

[52] *ALM Keirse*, Productaansprakelijkheid, in: T Hartlief, ALM Keirse, SD Lindenbergh and RD Vriesendorp (eds), Verbintenissen uit de wet en schadevergoeding (8th ed, 2018), no 149; *ALM Keirse*, The Netherlands, in: P Machnikowski (ed), European Product Liability (2016), 349 ff; *Smeehuijzen*, *supra* fn 25, 285 ff.

person. In the *Saelman* case the Dutch Supreme Court, however, interpreted this as meaning the day after the plaintiff is 'truly able to file a claim for the compensation of the damage',[53] which, applied to the facts of the case meant according to the Dutch Supreme Court that:

> in case someone has suffered an injury during his birth that could have been caused by the natural course of the pregnancy, the short prescription period of art 3:310(1) BW starts to run as soon as the legal representative knows sufficiently certain – which does not have to be absolute certainty – that the injury is (partly) the result of medical treatment that falls short or is erroneous.[54]

39 In a later case about a roofer who had made a mistake, the Dutch Supreme Court decided that:

> [...] different than the plea seems to suppose, this does not mean that for the running of the prescription period the injured party also has to be aware of the cause of the damage.[55]

40 This last ruling has to be interpreted in the light of the *Saelman* case, which would mean that a plaintiff must not only be aware of the damage and the identity of the defendant for the running of the subjective period, but also of the fact that someone made a mistake and that this mistake resulted in damage, which – as the case about the roofer shows – is a less stringent criterion than knowing about the causal link between the damage and the tortious act.[56] This is recently confirmed by the Dutch Supreme Court in a ruling in which the Court gave an overview of *inter alia* the aforementioned case law.[57]

### 2) *Objective or Subjective Unawareness?*

41 A major question about postponement because of unawareness – in Dutch law, the subjective prescription period – is whether this ground is subjective

---

53 HR 31.10.2003, *LJN* AL8168, 3.4. Own translation. Original text: 'daadwerkelijk in staat is een rechtsvordering tot vergoeding van deze schade in te stellen'.

54 HR 31.10.2003, *LJN* AL8168, 3.5. Own translation. Original text: 'indien iemand bij zijn geboorte lichamelijk letsel heeft opgelopen dat door het natuurlijk verloop van de zwangerschap en bevalling zou kunnen zijn veroorzaakt, de korte verjaringstermijn van artikel 3:310 lid 1 BW pas begint the lopen zodra hij of diens wettelijke vertegenwoordiger, voldoende zekerheid – die niet een absolute zekerheid hoeft te zijn – heeft gekregen dat het letsel (mede) is veroorzaakt door tekortschietend of foutief medisch handelen.'

55 HR 20.01.2004, *RVDW* 2004/37, 3.9. Own translation. Original text: 'anders dan waarvan het middel kennelijk uitgaat, betekent zulks niet dat de benadeelde steeds ook met de oorzaak van de schade bekend dient te zijn, wil de verjaringstermijn een aanvang nemen.'

56 *Smeehuijzen*, *supra* fn 25, 217.

57 HR 31.03.2017, *NJ* 2017/165 (Mispelhoef/Staat).

or objective. In case it is subjective the running of time is postponed until the plaintiff actually – subjectively – becomes aware of the facts constituting the claim, and in case it is objective, the running is postponed or suspended only until a reasonable person would have discovered the relevant facts, even if the plaintiff did not.

42 In Dutch law, the plaintiff has to actually – subjectively – become aware of the facts that constitute the claim for the running of the subjective prescription period. This was decided by the Dutch Supreme Court in the case *Vellekoop/ Wilton Fijenoord.*[58] This case was about a pipefitter that worked between 1951 and 1972 for the firm Wilton Fijenoord. In 1987, the pipefitter was diagnosed with cancer (mesothelioma) of which he died in 1988. In 1994, his widow sued Wilton Fijenoord because only by that time had she heard from a third party that her husband's disease was caused by his work as a pipefitter for the firm Wilton Fijenoord. Wilton Fijenoord claimed that the action prescribed because a reasonable person would have known this. The Dutch Supreme Court disagreed and decided that the actual knowledge of the widow – so her subjective knowledge – was decisive for the running of the subjective prescription period.[59]

43 Although in Dutch law the subjective prescription period is truly subjective, unawareness of the fact that tort law provides the plaintiff a remedy for his damage (*rechtsdwaling*) is, according to the Dutch Supreme Court, not a justification for postponement of the subjective prescription period because:

> Requiring this would not concur with the, for a reasonable course of legal matters acknowledged, starting principle that reliance on unawareness of the fact that the law provides a remedy cannot be accepted as justification, and, moreover, it would lead to legal inequality because not everyone has the same legal knowledge. It would also be contrary to the principle of legal certainty in case the start of a prescription period depends on when the injured party seeks legal advice. Also, the principles of reasonableness and fairness, that according to the last mentioned case are, next to the principle of legal certainty, also applicable to the short prescription period, does preclude the claim. Otherwise, the injured party could, for example, without nuisance of the prescription period profit from a later announced insight of the legal situation, while the liable person has guided his behaviour by the earlier insight.[60]

---

58 HR 06.04.2001, *NJ* 2002/383.

59 HR 06.04.2001, *NJ* 2002/383, 3.4.1–3.4.2.

60 HR 26.11.2004, *RvdW* 2004/134, 3.4. Own translation. Original text 'Het stellen van die eis zou niet in overeenstemming zijn met het voor een behoorlijk verloop van het rechtsverkeer te aanvaarden uitgangspunt dat een beroep op rechtsdwaling in het algemeen niet kan worden aanvaard, en zou tot rechtsongelijkheid aanleiding geven waar juridische kennis niet in gelijke mate bij eenieder aanwezig is. Het zou ook in strijd zijn met de rechtszekerheid wanneer de aanvang van de verjaring afhankelijk zou zijn van het tijdstip waarop de benadeelde juridisch

Applied to '**Case 10**' this means that if a defendant failed to sue in time because his former lawyer told him that a certain act was not tortious, and his new lawyer only told him this after the running of the prescription period, that in such a situation, the subjective prescription period has started to run because unawareness of the fact that tort law provides a remedy is not a justification for postponement in Dutch law.[61] However, it would be possible for the defendant to sue his former lawyer for the damages that his failure has caused him. 44

*3) The Degree of Awareness Needed about the Damage*

For the running of the subjective prescription period, the materialisation of damage is – generally – considered as 'harm'. This will be illustrated using two cases. The first case ('**Case 6**') is about a builder that has laid down a defective foundation for a bridge and thereby created the risk of a collapse when heavy rain falls. Two years later heavy rains indeed fall and two years after that the building collapses. The second case ('**Case 5**') is about a plaintiff whose ears are damaged due an explosion for which D is liable. As an immediate result the plaintiff has to raise the volume to enjoy music, after two years he needs a hearing device, and after five years he becomes deaf. 45

In both cases the question raises at which moment the 'harm' occurs for prescription purposes. As said, in Dutch law it is the actual materialisation of harm that is considered as harm. This can be inferred from a case of the Dutch Supreme Court about a tax consultant who had made a mistake of which his client knew well in advance that it was going to cause him damage.[62] This raised the legal question whether the subjective prescription period started to run the day after the client knew that he was going to suffer damage or the day after the moment he actually suffered the damage. The Supreme Court decided the latter: 46

> For the accrual of the five-year prescription period it is [...] in any event required that the damage did actually arise.[63]

Applied to the two cases, this means that for prescription purposes the damage occurs from the moment it materialises. In 'Case 6' this is the moment the

---

advies inwint. Ook de billijkheid, die naar in het laats vermelde arrest is overwogen bij de korte verjaringstermijn naast de rechtszekerheid van betekenis is, staat aan het stellen van die eis in de weg. De benadeelde zou immers zonder hinder van verjaringstermijn kunnen profiteren van een eerst veel later bekend geworden inzicht met betrekking tot de juridische situatie ten tijde van het ontstaan van de schade, terwijl de aansprakelijke persoon zijn gedrag heeft gericht naar de toen geldende inzichten.'

61 HR 26.11.2004, *RvdW* 2004/37, 3.4.

62 HR 10.10.2003, *NJ* 2003/680.

63 HR 10.10.2003, *NJ* 2003/680, 3.4.1. Own translation. Original text: 'Voor de aanvang van de vijfjarige verjaringstermijn is [...] in elk geval vereist dat daadwerkelijk schade is ontstaan.'

defective foundation subsided and in 'Case 5' this is each time a new damage has occurred.

47 However, there is a decision from the Dutch Supreme Court from which it can be inferred that when one event causes separate damages, and a later occurring damage was not unexpected at the time the first damage that was caused by the damaging event occurred, then the later occurring harm should be considered as part of the harm that occurred first:

> [the plea] complains that the Court of Appeal did not pay attention to the statement of [the plaintiff] that his damage did not occur at once, but that it is continuous of nature, which means that the claim of [the plaintiff] did not prescribe for as far it relates to the damage that is suffered within five years before the claim for liability. [...] this limb cannot lead to appeal in cassation. This case is about separate elements of the entire, by the wrongful act caused, – continuous – damage. It is not argued during the proceedings of the fact-finding instances that one or more – earlier unexpected – loss items have occurred.[64]

For 'Case 5' and 'Case 6' this means that if the latter occurring harms were not unexpected during the occurrence of the first harms, the claims for the latter occurring harms prescribe together with the claim for first occurring harms.

### 4) *The Degree of Awareness Needed about the Causal Link*

48 As mentioned before for the running of the subjective prescription period the plaintiff must know that the tortious conduct resulted in the damage, which is a less stringent criterion than knowing about the causal link between the damage and the tortious act.[65]

49 In case of physical complaints, the Dutch Supreme Court decided that

> [...] one is truly aware of the damage in case it can be said with a sufficient degree of certainty what the origins of the complaints are. Generally, this degree of certainty – that does not have to be absolute certainty – exists when the cause is diagnosed by a, in this matter, specialist doctor.[66]

---

64 HR 24.05.2002, *NJ* 2003/268, 3.8. Own translation. Original text: '[Het middel] klaagt dat het Hof geen aandacht heeft besteed aan de stelling van [eiser] dat zijn schade niet ineens is geleden, maar voortdurend van aard is, zodat de vordering van [eiser] niet is verjaard voor zover deze betrekking heeft op schade geleden binnen 5 jaar voor de aansprakelijkheidstelling. [...] dit onderdeel niet tot cassatie leiden. Het gaat hier om afzonderlijke elementen van de gehele door de onrechtmatige daad veroorzaakte – doorlopende – schade. In de feitelijke instanties is niet aangevoerd dat zich daarbij een of meer nieuwe – eerder niet voorziene – schadeposten voordoen.'

65 *Smeehuijzen*, *supra* fn 25, 217.

66 HR 24.01.2003, *NJ* 2003/300, 3.4.2. Own translation. Original text: '[...] kan van daadwerkelijke bekendheid met de schade pas sprake zijn wanneer met voldoende mate

If the identity of the liable person is very easy to find out with a simple act of research, the plaintiff may not sit still and cannot call on his subjective not knowing. Some sort of effort to find out who is responsible for the harm can be expected.[67] Having said this, in the circumstances of '**Case 11**' the fact that the plaintiff did not seek a second opinion would not preclude the application of the late discovery rule. In this case a landowner contracts a long disease but is unaware of the causal link between a tortious exposure and his disease because his physician fails to detect it. Only when another physician tells him about the link, possibly many years later, will the subjective prescription period start to run. After all there is no subjective awareness and that is the test to be applied according to Dutch law. 50

## B. OTHER RULES OF PROLONGATION

### 1) *The Defendant is to Blame for the Delay*

First of all, it should be mentioned that circumstances that mislead or threaten the plaintiff could influence the starting point of the subjective prescription period. After all, the plaintiff has to be truly able to file a claim for the compensation of the damage, before the period starts to run. This should be interpreted in light of the principles of reasonableness and fairness. In case of sexual abuse, for example, the plaintiff may only be able to file a claim after a long time, given the circumstances and in light of the difficulties that victims of sexual abuse encounter. So even though the plaintiff may know the victim and harm from day one, it can take a much longer time before the plaintiff is supposed to be able to file a claim and thus before the subjective prescription period starts to run. The subjective prescription period will only start to run when there are no longer such circumstances preventing the plaintiff to come forward and file a claim.[68] 51

Furthermore, art 3:321(1)f BW states that a ground for extension exists if – in the relationship between a debtor and a creditor – the debtor deliberately conceals the existence of a debt or the fact that it has become due and demandable. Article 3:320 BW states that when a prescription period expires during the existence of this ground or within six months after the ground has ceased to 52

van zekerheid is vastgesteld waardoor de klachten zijn ontstaan. In het algemeen zal deze vereiste mate van zekerheid – die niet een absolute zekerheid hoeft te zijn – pas aanwezig zijn wanneer de oorzaak door te dier zake deskundige arts is gediagnostiseerd.'

67 HR 03.12.2010, *NJ* 2012/196 (Bemoti); *J Spier and T Hartlief*, Verjaring, in: T Hartlief, ALM Keirse, SD Lindenbergh and RD Vriesendorp (eds), Verbintenissen uit de wet en schadevergoeding (8th ed, 2018) no 335a.

68 See HR 23.10.1998, *NJ* 2000/15; HR 25.06.1999, NJ 2000/16; HR 11.10.2002, NJ 2002/558.

exist, that then the prescription period continues to run until six months have passed since the ending of the ground for extension.

*2) Admission by the Defendant of the Plaintiff's Right or Partial Performance of the Plaintiff's Right by the Defendant*

53 Article 3:318 BW states that 'acknowledgment of the right which a right of action serves to protect shall interrupt the prescription of the right of action as against the person who acknowledges the right.'[69] Acknowledgement (*erkenning*) can be given explicitly and implicitly. For instance, by paying part of the debt. If the prescription period interrupts because of acknowledgement, a new prescription period starts to run as of the day following the day of interruption. The new prescription period has the same duration as the original, yet no longer than five years.[70]

*3) Special Relations between the Defendant and the Plaintiff*

54 According to art 3:321(1) BW, a ground for extension exists between: spouses not separated from bed and board; registered partners; a legal representative and the represented person who misses (full) legal capacity; a legal administrator of property under (fiduciary) administration and the person entitled to that property; a legal person and his directors; and an heir and the estate of a deceased that is accepted by this heir under the condition that the value of the assets of the estate will exceed its debts. Article 3:320 BW states that when a prescription period expires during the existence of such a ground or within six months after such a ground has ceased to exist, that then the prescription period continues to run until six months have passed since the ending of the ground for extension.

*4) The Plaintiff's Minority or Mental Disability – Does it Matter whether the Plaintiff has a Representative?*

55 The minority of the plaintiff plays a role in case the damage is caused by injury or death. If a plaintiff is underage at the time he or she becomes aware of both the damage – that is caused by injury or death – and the thereof responsible person, then the running of the subjective prescription period of five years is postponed until the day after he or she becomes of age.[71] This rule does also apply in case

---

69 Translation from *Warendorf, supra* fn 24. Original text: 'erkenning van het recht tot welks bescherming een rechtsvordering dient, stuit de verjaring van de rechtsvordering tegen hem die het recht erkent.'

70 Article 3:319 BW.

71 See art 3:310 sub 5 BW,

the plaintiff has a representative because this rule is aimed at protecting children against – legal – negligence of their representatives.[72]

In Dutch law, the plaintiff's mental disability is as such not a ground for postponement, suspension, renewal, or extension. In order to give the full picture, however, it should be mentioned, that according to art 3:321(1) BW, a ground for extension exists between a legal representative and the represented person who misses (full) legal capacity. Article 3:320 BW states that when a prescription period expires during the existence of this ground or within six months after such a ground has ceased to exist, that then the prescription period continues to run until six months have passed since the ending of the ground for extension. 56

*5) Absence of Parties from the Jurisdiction*

In Dutch law, the plaintiff's and/or the defendant's physical absence from the jurisdiction is not recognised as a ground for postponement, suspension, renewal, or extension. 57

*6) Former Legal and Other Proceedings between the Parties*

According to art 3:316(2) BW, former litigation between parties that ends without final ruling or ongoing litigation is not a ground for postponement, suspension, renewal, or extension in Dutch law. Prescription of a right of action is interrupted by the institution of an action or by any other act of judicial recourse instituted in the required form by the person entitled to do so. However, where an action which has been instituted is not allowed, prescription shall not be interrupted, unless, within six months after the final decision or other termination of the suit, a new action is instituted and is later allowed. The institution of an action that is not allowed, because the judge or arbitrator declines jurisdiction in light of an arbitration clause, also interrupts prescription of a right of action. Where an act of judicial recourse is withdrawn, prescription is not interrupted. 58

ADR and settlements proceedings are generally not a ground for postponement, suspension, renewal, or extension in Dutch law.[73] However, there are two exceptions to this rule. First, when a claim is based on the Civil Liability Insurance (Motor Vehicles) Act (WAM), the claim is interrupted – and thus renewed – by any form of negotiations between the insurer and the injured party.[74] And second, art 3:316(3) BW states that prescription of a right of action 59

72 *Kammerstukken II* 2000/01, 26824, 8.

73 HR 01.02.2002, *NJ* 2002/195.

74 Article 10(5) WAM.

shall also be interrupted by an act to obtain a binding opinion, provided that the other party is expeditiously notified of it and that a binding opinion actually results.[75] Where this is not the case prescription shall not be interrupted.

### *7) Victim's Death or Bankruptcy*

60 In Dutch law, the victim's death or bankruptcy is not recognised as a ground for postponement, suspension, renewal, or extension. According to art 3:315 BW the prescription period of a right of action to claim a succession starts to run at the beginning of the day following the one of the death of the deceased.

### *8) Other Recognised Justifications*

61 Under certain circumstances it can be considered contrary to the principles of reasonableness and fairness to invoke the subjective prescription period of five years. This follows from case law from the Dutch Supreme Court.[76] Furthermore, an important ground for renewal is interruption (*stuiting*). According to arts 3:316 BW and 3:317 BW, a prescription period is interrupted *inter alia*: when a legal claim is brought to court by the person entitled to do so; by a letter of formal notice in which performance is demanded; or by a written announcement in which the creditor unambiguously reserves his right to claim performance. If the prescription period is interrupted, a new prescription period starts according to art 3:319 BW as of the day following the day of interruption. The new prescription period has the same duration as the original, yet no longer than five years.

## IX. CEILINGS ON THE EFFECTIVE TIME OF PRESCRIPTION

62 In Dutch law, the objective prescription period functions as a 'ceiling period'. The objective prescription period applies to all tort claims, except for claims that are the result of injury or death.[77] The objective prescription period is generally 20 years and 30 years in case the damage is the result of the effects of hazardous materials, or of air, water or soil pollution. The objective prescription period

---

75 Translation from *Warendorf*, *supra* fn 24. Original text: 'De verjaring van een rechtsvordering wordt ook gestuit door een handeling, strekkende tot verkrijging van een bindend advies, mits van die handeling met bekwame spoed mededeling wordt gedaan aan de wederpartij en zij tot verkrijging van een bindend advies leidt. [...]'

76 HR 23.10.1998, *NJ* 2000/15; HR 23.11.2018, ECLI:NL:HR:2018:2047. See also *supra* fn 90 hereafter.

77 Article 3:310(5) BW.

starts to run from the moment the event that caused the damage took place. If 20 – or 30 – years have passed from this moment, then the claim prescribed regardless of whether the subjective prescription period started to run or did not finish running.[78] However, the objective prescription period may be prolonged by the rules on interruption, renewal and extension, and in case reasonableness and fairness require so (more about this last point in Section X.B).

# X. STATUTE INTERPRETATION, JUDICIAL DISCRETION AND LACHES

## A. STATUTE INTERPRETATION

Given the pros and cons of prescription, both the legislature and the courts are required to seek for what they view as the right balance between the diversified and often conflicting considerations. In balancing the pros and cons of prescription and balancing legal certainty with justice judges may differ as to where the right balance lies. This raises the question whether judges in the Netherlands are hostile, neutral or sympathetic to prescription, or differ in their approach, and whether it is in any way regarded unethical to reject a claim on the basis of rules of prescription. Answering these questions is, however, quite hard because of a few reasons. One important reason is that – at least originally – the task of the judge in the Netherlands is seen as solely entailing applying the law to the facts of the case. Nowadays, it is recognised that judges also have to interpret the law, but their freedom in doing so is limited because of the *trias politica*. Strictly speaking there is therefore no room for the Dutch judge to be hostile, neutral, or sympathetic towards prescription. Moreover, there are no concrete indications that Dutch judges are in practice either hostile, neutral, or sympathetic towards prescription. Another problem is that in the Netherlands the, so-called, '*geheim van de raadkamer*' exists, which means that possible disagreement amongst judges during their deliberations is not revealed in the judgment. This makes it hard to say whether judges differ a lot in their approach towards prescription. Instead of giving a concrete answer to the questions, this report will therefore describe the changes the prescription rules in the Netherlands have undergone in the last two decades. Hopefully this will give some indications of how prescription is perceived in the Netherlands (by judges). 63

Before the introduction of the current Dutch Civil Code in 1992, there was only one prescription period of 30 years for all private law claims.[79] With the introduction of the current Dutch Civil Code in 1992, the Dutch legislator 64

[78] Article 3:310 BW.

[79] *Koopmann*, *supra* fn 1, 3 ff.

replaced the single period of 30 years with a subjective prescription period of five years and an objective prescription period of 20 years. The shortened periods were received positively because everyone agreed that 30 years was too long.[80] Some legal scholars even argued that a subjective prescription period of three years would have been more appropriate.[81] Far more controversial was the accrual of the subjective prescription period and the rigidness of the objective prescription period. For example, this controversy caused the front page of the Netherlands Law Journal (NJB) to state: 'Extinctive prescription: failed part of the Civil Code?'[82] Article 3:310 BW especially, which provides the prescription of tort claims, was highly contested because its single paragraph seemed to lead to unfavourable outcomes.[83]

65 Because of this criticism, both the legislator and the Dutch Supreme Court tried to 'repair' the Dutch provision on the prescription of tort claims. Only 12 months after the introduction of the new Dutch Civil Code, the legislator already introduced paras 2 and 3 of art 3:310 BW, which replaced the 20-year objective prescription period for a 30-year period in case of damage that is the result of the effects of hazardous materials, or of air, water or soil pollution.[84] In 1994, para 4 was added to art 3:310 BW, which states that a claim for damages that is caused by a criminal offence does not prescribe as long as the right to a criminal proceeding has not ceased to exist because of – criminal – prescription or the death of the accused.[85] Finally, in 2003 the most important addition was added, namely para 5 which states that damage caused by injury or death has no objective prescription period, and that in case the plaintiff is underage at the time he or she becomes aware of the damage and the thereof responsible person the subjective prescription period starts to run following the day after he or she becomes of age.[86] This means that there is no longer a prescription period for undiscovered damage that is the result of injury or death. It should be noted, however, that this new exception stipulating that there is no objective prescription period for damage caused by injury or death does not apply to damaging events that occurred before 1 February 2004, the day when this amendment entered into force. After all, according to the transitional Act, this rule has no retroactive effect. This means that claims regarding torts that took

80 *Van Zeben, Du Pon and Olthof, supra* fn 4, 917.

81 See for an overview *Smeehuijzen, supra* fn 25, 137–142.

82 Own translation. Original text: 'Bevrijdende verjaring: mislukt onderdeel van het BW?' The reason for this was the critical article of Van Dijk. See *H van Dijk*, Bevrijdende verjaring: een mislukt onderdeel (2007) 17 Nederlands Juristenblad (NJB) 1044–1050.

83 *Smeehuijzen, supra* fn 25, 2.

84 Wet van 24 december 1992, Stb. 1992, 691.

85 Wet van 7 juli 1994, Stb. 1994, 529.

86 Wet van 27 november 2003 tot wijziging van de regeling van de bevrijdende verjaring in het Burgerlijk Wetboek voor gevallen van verborgen schade door letsel of overlijden, Stb. 2003, 495.

place before this date still prescribe in any case after 20 years or, if the damage is the result of the effects of hazardous materials or pollution, after 30 years – even when the injured party did not know that he had a claim.

Simultaneously, the Dutch Supreme Court interpreted art 3:310 BW in such a way that it caused some important changes to the working of the subjective and objective prescription periods as well. In 2000 the Dutch Supreme Court decided that under certain circumstances it is contrary to the principles of reasonableness and fairness to invoke the objective prescription period of 20 or 30 years, in 2003 the Dutch Supreme Court ruled that the criterion 'aware of both the damage and the thereof responsible person'[87] had to be interpreted as meaning 'truly able to file a claim for the compensation of the damage'[88] and in 2018 case law learned that the principles of reasonableness and fairness can also stand in the way of successfully invoking the subjective prescription period of five years.[89] 66

## B. JUDICIAL DISCRETION

According to art 6:2(2) BW, the principles of reasonableness and fairness apply to the Dutch prescription rules. As mentioned before the Dutch Supreme Court interprets the prescription periods in light of the principles of reasonableness and fairness. First of all, it ruled that the subjective prescription period only starts running after the plaintiff, being aware of the damage and the liable person, is truly able to file a claim for the compensation of the damage. Furthermore, the most important feature of the principles of reasonableness and fairness within the context of prescription is that they can set aside the (objective and subjective) prescription period.[90] As regards the objective prescription period, this was decided by the Dutch Supreme Court in the *Van Hese/De Schelde* case.[91] This case was about Van Hese, a man who was diagnosed with mesothelioma, which is 67

87 Article 3:310 sub. 1 BW.

88 Article 3:310 sub. 1 BW.

89 HR 23.11.2018, ECLI:NL:HR:2018:2047.

90 In HR 23.10.1998, *NJ* 2000/15 it was decided that art 6:2 BW can also set aside the subjective prescription period, but this decision became less important from the moment the Dutch Supreme Court decided in the *Sealmaen* case that the subjective prescription period accrued the day after the plaintiff is 'truly able to file a claim for the compensation of the damage' instead of the former 'aware of the damage and thereof liable person'. See also *JHM van Swaaij*, Verjaring van rechtsvorderingen tot vergoeding van schade: (waar) ruimte voor derogerende werking van redelijkheid en billikheid? (2017) 3 Overheid & Aansprakelijkheid 18. Nevertheless, in 2018 the Dutch Supreme Court ruled again that the principles of reasonableness and fairness can – under certain circumstances and on a case by case basis – set aside the subjective prescription period, *supra* fn 89.

91 HR 28042000, *NJ* 2000/430.

a type of cancer that can only have one cause, namely breathing in asbestos dust, and has an incubation period of 20 to 40 years. Van Hese breathed in asbestos dust during his work for De Schelde between 1959 and 1963, after which he became ill in 1996. Because the objective prescription period had already passed before he could even have known that he had a claim, the Dutch Supreme Court had to answer the legal question whether the principles of reasonableness and fairness could set aside the objective prescription period.[92] The Dutch Supreme Court answered this question in the affirmative. If there is uncertainty over a long period of time as to whether an event that can cause damage will actually do so and therefore the damage has remained hidden until after the expiry of the prescription period, the principles of reasonableness and fairness can lead to an extension of the 30-year prescription period. In order to decide whether, in view of all circumstances of the case, the prescription period should be prolonged, a court must at least consider the following seven aspects:

> (a) whether the case concerns the compensation of material damage or non-material damage and – in connection therewith – whether the claimed compensation is for the benefit of the victim himself/herself, his/her heirs or a third party; (b) to what extent the victim, or his/her heirs are eligible for compensation on any other basis; (c) to what extent the occurrence of the harm can be blamed on the defendant; (d) to what extent the defendant took into account or should have taken into account before the expiry of the prescription period that there was the possibility that he/she would be liable for the damage; (e) whether the defendant reasonably has the possibility to defend himself/herself against the claim; (f) whether the liability is (still) covered by an insurance; (g) whether the liability claim and claim for damages was filed within a reasonable period of time after the discovery of the damage.[93]

---

92 Article 3:310(5) BW which stipulates that there is no objective prescription period for damage caused by injury or death did not apply to this case because that rule came into effect on 1 February 2004 and has no retroactive effect. See about the question whether art 6:2 could require that the objective prescription period should be set aside in other cases then where the objective prescription period already ended before the damage did occur *Van Swaaij*, *supra* fn 90, 15–26.

93 HR 28.04.2000, *NJ* 2000/430, 3.3.3. Own translation. Original text: '(a) of het gaat om vergoeding van vermogensschade dan wel van nadeel dat niet in vermogensschade bestaat, en – mede in verband daarmede – of de gevorderde schadevergoeding ten goede komt aan het slachtoffer zelf, diens nabestaanden dan wel een derde; (b) in hoeverre voor het slachtoffer respectievelijk zijn nabestaanden ter zake van de schade een aanspraak op een uitkering uit anderen hoofde bestaat; (c) de mate waarin de gebeurtenis de aangesprokene kan worden verweten; (d) in hoeverre de aangesprokene reeds vóór het verstrijken van de verjaringstermijn rekening heeft gehouden of had behoren te houden met de mogelijkheid dat hij voor de schade aansprakelijk zou zijn; (e) of de aangesprokene naar redelijkheid nog de mogelijkheid heeft zich tegen de vordering te verweren; (f) of de aansprakelijkheid (nog) door verzekering is gedekt; (g) of na het aan het licht komen van de schade binnen redelijke termijn een aansprakelijkstelling heeft plaatsgevonden en een vordering tot schadevergoeding is ingesteld.'

Although there has been some criticism on these seven subjects and their functioning,[94] the Dutch Supreme Court recently confirmed and clarified this formerly established case law.[95] This recent case also concerned an asbestos claim for damages, which was prescribed before the injured party knew he had a claim. In fact, more than 40 years had passed between the event that caused the damage – the exposure to asbestos – and the discovery of the damage – the diagnosis with mesothelioma. The Dutch Supreme Court repeated that, under these circumstances, the Dutch prescription period of 30 years is applicable, but the principles of reasonableness and fairness can, in exceptional circumstances, prolong this prescription period. After giving due weight to the specific circumstances of the case, the Dutch Supreme Court decided that in this case the claim was prescribed. The Dutch rules on the prescription of tort claims were found to be *ex aequo et bono* and not in breach of fundamental rights, such as art 6 ECHR, since they allow for a balancing act and a prolonging of the prescription period based on a weighing of the circumstances of the case and interests involved. 68

## C. LACHES

A legal doctrine parallel to prescription that calls for judicial discretion is laches. 69
It allows courts to reject the plaintiff's claim because of the passage of time since its accrual if the delay in filing harmed the defendant because he legitimately relied on the plaintiff's omission to file during that period. In Dutch law, courts can reject a claim on the ground of a similar doctrine, namely the forfeiture of rights (*rechtsverwerking*).[96] The legal basis of the tenet of forfeiture of rights is the restrictive effect of reasonableness and fairness of art 6:2(2) BW.[97] According to the Dutch Supreme Court, reliance on the tenet of forfeiture of rights can 'only in exceptional circumstances be considered well-founded'.[98] It is established case law of the Dutch Supreme Court that only the passage of time is not enough for forfeiture of rights.[99] For successful reliance on the tenet of forfeiture

---

94 See for instance: *WH van Boom*, Verjaring mesothelioomclaims doorbroken (2000) Aansprakelijkheid & Verzekering 65–67; *EH Hulst*, De verjaring van mesothelioom: asbest op zijn slechtst? (2012) Tijdschrift voor Gezondheisschade, Milieuschade en Aansprakelijkheidsrecht 21; *Smeehuijzen*, *supra* fn 25, 251–263.

95 HR 24.03.2017, ECLI:NL:HR:2017:494, *JAR* 2017/112. See also *ALM Keirse and T Bouwman*, The Netherlands, in: E Karner and BC Steininger (eds), European Tort Law 2017 (2018), nos 17–23.

96 *RPJL Tjittes*, Monografien BW: Rechtsverwerking en klachtplichten (2013) 9.

97 *Tjittes*, *supra* fn 96, 9.

98 HR 20.05.2005, *RvdW* 2005/75. Own translation. Original text: 'slechts in uitzonderlijke omstandigheden gegrond worden geoordeeld.'

99 See eg HR 07.06.1991, *NJ* 1991/708; HR 18.11.1992, *NJ* 1993/152.

of right there have to be special circumstances – other than the passage of time – that in all fairness and reasonableness cannot be reconciled with filing a claim at this late stage. These special circumstances may have created the legitimate expectation of the defendant that the plaintiff is not going to enforce his claim. An example of such a situation is a case of the Dutch Supreme Court wherein a lawyer made a professional error and in which the lawyer's client threated to sue him six times in a period of nine years. The Dutch Supreme Court concluded that the client forfeited her rights because during these nine years she did not suit the action to the word.[100] Another ground for forfeiture of rights – next to the legitimate expectations – could exist in case the situation of the defendant becomes unreasonably prejudiced when the plaintiff enforces his claim.[101] This can, for instance, be the case if the defendant is unreasonably prejudiced in proving his case. An illustration of such a case is a case of the Dutch Supreme Court wherein the victim of a car crash filed his claim more than 14 years after the crash.[102]

70 In case of forfeiture of rights, a plaintiff can no longer enforce his right.[103] Note that the tenet of forfeiture of rights has become less relevant in practice since the prescription period of 30 years is replaced in 1992 with the current subjective prescription period of five years and the objective prescription period of – generally – 20 years.[104]

## XI. CHANGE OF PARTIES

### A. TRANSFER OF THE ORIGINAL CLAIM

71 Sometimes, the claim of the victim of a tort against the tortfeasor is either transmitted (by law) or transferred by agreement (if the law allows) to another person, for example to heirs or insurers. The question is then whether and how such change affects prescription. If, for instance, the victim's right against the defendant is subrogated to an insurer that compensated the victim under the insurance policy for harm caused by the defendant, does the running of time on the claim then start afresh when the insurer acquires the right of subrogation? Or does the running on the victim's claim continue on the claim of the insurer? In Dutch law, a change of tortfeasor does not start a new period of prescription because art 6:145 BW states that 'the transmission of a claim does not affect

---

100 HR 28.11.2003, *NJ* 2004/328.

101 *Tjittes*, fn 96, 37 ff.

102 HR 30.05.1997, *NJ* 1997/544.

103 *Tjittes*, *supra* fn 96, 40 ff.

104 *Smeehuijzen*, *supra* fn 25, 313 ff.

the obligor's defences.'[105] Although this is not – yet – confirmed by the Dutch Supreme Court, it seems logical to say that this also means that if the new tortfeasor is eligible for a ground for suspension on the basis of art 3:319 BW, this cannot be evoked against the new defendant. This means, coming back to the example, that the running of time of the insurer's claim therefore does not start afresh when he acquires the right of subrogation, but continues to run either from the moment the cause of action occurred (the objective prescription period), or the day after either the victim or the insurer had become truly able to file a claim for the compensation of the damage (the subjective prescription period).

## B. CONTRIBUTION CLAIMS BETWEEN TORTFEASORS

Another situation that can give rise to difficulties occurs if, for instance, X and Y are jointly liable against a victim, and a month before the prescription period on the victim's claim against X and Y expires, X compensates the victim. The question then arises, whether – also after the prescription of the victim's claim – X can sue Y for contribution. In Dutch law, X's claim on Y has its own prescription period, because X's right to recourse is an independent right. However, what is unclear in Dutch law is when the subjective prescription period starts to run in such a situation.[106] 72

The answer to this example, however, would be different if X had compensated the victim after the running of the prescription period. In Dutch law, this situation is governed by art 6:11(3) BW which states: 73

> The person who has been called upon to contribute may not invoke the prescription of the right of action of the obligee, unless both he and the person who demands the contribution could have invoked the expiry of the prescription period against the obligee at the time when the obligation to contribute arose.[107]

Therefore, if X had compensated the victim after the running of the prescription period, then Y could have relied on his prescription defence against X.

---

105 Translation from *Warendorf*, *supra* fn 24. Original text: 'overgang van een vordering laat de verweermiddelen van de schuldenaar onverlet.'

106 *Smeehuijzen*, *supra* fn 25, 241 ff.

107 Translation from *Warendorf*, *supra* fn 24. Original text: 'Een beroep op verjaring van de rechtsvordering van de schuldeiser komt de tot bijdragen aangesprokene slechts toe, indien op het tijdstip van het ontstaan van de verplichting tot bijdragen zowel hijzelf als degene die de bijdrage verlangt, jegens de schuldeiser de voltooiing van de verjaring had kunnen inroepen.'

### C. DEPENDANTS

74 Where the victim of a tort dies due to the injury caused by the defendant, and the law provides that the victim's dependants are entitled to compensation from the defendant for loss of financial support that the victim would have otherwise provided, the question is whether there are special rules of prescription that apply to the victim's dependants' claim. In the Netherlands, because the victim's dependants have an independent claim, the running of their prescription period has to be determined by the rules of art 3:310 BW independently of the prescription period of the victim.

## XII. OTHER ASPECTS OF PRESCRIPTION LAW

### A. STIPULATION

75 Another question is whether parties can agree on rules of prescription different from the statutory rules. Article 3:322(2) BW states that 'prescription may be renounced by a declaration of the person who can invoke it',[108] and art 3:322(3) BW states that: 'there can be no renunciation of prescription until its completion.'[109] A defendant can thus only waive his entitlement to prescription after the running of the prescription period. Such a waiver can be done by unilateral notice and has no prescribed form. The notice has effect from the moment it has reached the plaintiff.[110] Once a defendant has waived his entitlement to prescription, a new prescription period starts to run, which means that after the running of that new prescription period the defendant is allowed to raise the prescription defence again. The new prescription period has the same duration as the original period, yet no longer than five years. A waiver commences a new prescription period instead of truly waiving the prescription defence because it is perceived as undesirable that – even after a waiver – a plaintiff can file his claim indefinitely.[111]

76 Shortening the prescription period by means of a contractual clause is allowed as long as the stipulation is, for instance, not unreasonably onerous.[112]

[108] Translation form *Warendorf*, *supra* fn 24. Original text: 'afstand van verjaring geschiedt door een verklaring van hem die de verjaring kan inroepen.'

[109] Translation form *Warendorf*, *supra* fn 24. Original text: 'voordat de verjaring voltooid is, kan geen afstand van verjaring worden gedaan.'

[110] Article 3:37(3) BW.

[111] *Koopmann*, *supra* fn 1, 63.

[112] *Koopmann*, *supra* fn 1, 64.

## B. MEANING OF 'FILING A CLAIM' THAT INTERRUPTS THE RUNNING OF PRESCRIPTION

In Dutch law, there is not one particular procedural act that has to be performed by the plaintiff to stop the running of the prescription period. Instead, the prescription period is interrupted 'by the institution of an action or by any other act of judicial recourse instituted in the required form by the person entitled to do so.'[113] The prescription period is – retroactively – not interrupted – and thus maybe expired – when the plaintiff withdraws the legal action.[114] 77

## C. WHEN SHOULD THE DEFENCE BE RAISED AND DECIDED?

Article 1988 of the Old Dutch Civil Code stated that 'one can rely on prescription in every phase of the proceedings, even in appeal.'[115] This rule is, although not codified in the new Dutch Civil Code, seen as still applicable.[116] In case the plaintiff raises the defence in appeal during the defence on appeal, then the defendant should be given the opportunity to react to the defence.[117] And, when the defence is raised at such a stage of the proceeding that the defendant cannot respond to the defence, then the defence can be contrary to due process of law.[118] 78

## D. WHO MAY RAISE THE DEFENCE?

The prescription defence can only be raised by the defendant. According to art 3:322(1) BW, courts may not raise prescription as a defence *ex officio*. 79

## E. BURDEN OF PROOF

In Dutch law, the defendant who relies on prescription has to furnish the facts that form the basis of the prescription defence. The defendant has the burden of proof in case the plaintiff reasonably challenges the facts.[119] 80

---

113 Article 6:316(1) BW. Translation from *Warendorf*, *supra* fn 24. Original text: 'het instellen van een eis, alsmede door iedere andere daad van rechtsvervolging van de zijde van de gerechtigde, die in de vereiste vorm geschiedt.'

114 Article 6:316(2) BW.

115 Own translation. Original text: 'In elken staat van het geding kan men zich op verjaring beroepen, zelfs in hooger beroep.'

116 *Koopmann*, *supra* fn 1, 24; *Asser and Sieburgh 6-II*, *supra* fn 5, 389.

117 HR 04.09.2009, *NJ* 2009/397.

118 *Koopmann*, *supra* fn 1, 24; Hof Amsterdam 13.09.2001, *NJ* 2004/88.

119 *Koopmann*, *supra* fn 1, 25.

# PRESCRIPTION IN TORT LAW: NORWAY

Bjarte Askeland

## I. INTRODUCTION

1 The law of prescription regarding tort claims in Norwegian law is regulated in the general act on prescription of claims.[1] The origin of the provision is the former act on prescription of claims of 1896. The subject of prescription has not generated much discussion over the years. The major literature on the field is primarily one comment to the statutory law and a doctoral thesis on the starting point of the prescription period, apart from a few other contributions.[2] A few minor doctrinal works analyse the special problems of prescription regarding tort claims.[3]

## II. DEFINITION OF PRESCRIPTION

2 The definition of prescription under Norwegian tort law is very much in accordance with the definition 'a legal institution that prevents P from enforcing an alleged right against D because of the running of a specified period of time on the tort claim'.

---

1 See *Foreldelsesloven*, Lov om foreldelse av fordringer 18 May 1979 no 18 (hereinafter, fel.)

2 See *Anne Cathrine Røed*, Foreldelse av fordringer (4th ed, Oslo 2019); *Miriam Skag*, Startpunktet for foreldelsesfrister (Oslo 2012). See also *Trygve Bergsåker*, Hva er foreldelse?, Tidsskrift for Rettsvitenskap (2011), 353–440.

3 See *Magnus Matningsdal*, Foreldelse av erstatningskrav krav ved personskade, TfR (1980), 472–511; *Steinar Tjomsland*, Foreldelse av erstatningskrav (Jussens venner 1987), 333–343.

The claim is a right to damages for harm caused that comes into being once the defendant has committed the tortious act. This is the general starting point, but there are some modifications, see *infra* 27–30. 3

## III. THE NATURE OF PRESCRIPTION AND ITS EFFECTS

The Norwegian concept of prescription only affects the claimant's right to compensation when not suing within the time period. Hence, the material obligation for the defendant exists after the prescription period in the sense that a debtor who mistakenly has paid a claim after the prescription period has expired, cannot claim restitution based on unjust enrichment. The effect of barring the claim is considered to be material, having effect both within and outside courts. It is not merely a procedural defence for the defendant. In fact, one may on principle file a claim after the prescription period has expired, because the civil litigation rules accept the plaintiff's *pretention* of having a valid claim. In the doctrinal literature the prescription claim is in general perceived as a material, not a procedural matter.[4] 4

The choice of prescription as a substantive defence seems to function very well in Norway. To look upon prescription as merely a procedural bar would contradict the tradition and general understanding of the line between material and procedural law. A merely procedural approach would not fulfil the purpose of the rule as it has developed in Norwegian and Scandinavian private law. 5

## IV. CONSIDERATIONS FOR AND AGAINST PRESCRIPTION OF TORT CLAIMS

The major consideration behind the prescription act is that the defendant should not face the possibility of a lawsuit for torts many years after his alleged harmdoing has taken place. Thus, an important argument for the prescription rules has been the idea that the defendant should be protected against surprising, old claims. His adaptation to status quo with no claim should be protected. In addition, the general part of the preparatory works mentions the following arguments.[5] 6

In general, it is a societal benefit that claims are paid and that the claim relation between creditor and debtor is ended. The rules of prescription give the creditor 7

4 See *Bergsåker* with references 367–369, however also suggesting that it is possible to perceive the rules as procedural, 417–418.

5 The following is based on the presentation of considerations given in *C Røed*, Foreldelse av fordringer, secs 50–53.

an incentive to file his or her claim.[6] The fact that the claimant is urged to claim, increases the probability that it is possible to prove the facts on which the claim rests.[7] The debtor will otherwise adapt to a situation where he is not obliged to pay. The longer the period of no claim is, the more the debtor will adapt to the situation and the more likely he will be to spend his money elsewhere. There are also practical and technical advantages to a system that urges a claimant to come forward with his claim rather sooner than later.

8 There is safety for the citizen connected to the fact that he or she does not risk being confronted with old claims. Rules of prescription enhance values like foreseeability and trust in the legal system.[8]

9 There are few arguments put forward *against* the prescription rules. It is, however, pointed to the fact that a claimant should be granted the right to have his claim paid, regardless of the time periods, because this is the profound principle of private law, cf pacta sunt servanda. The prescription rules may thus be seen as a sort of infringement of profound rights on the part of the claimant.[9] A theorist, Skag, has however, evaluated critically the arguments presented in *supra* 6–8, and found several reasons for nuancing the historically accepted considerations.[10] She maintains for example that the rules may be too generous in favour of a defendant who knows about his obligations but is unwilling to pay.[11]

10 In favour of the special prescription rule of tort claims, it is especially mentioned in the preparatory works that the tortfeasor should not be compelled to preserve documents and other kinds of evidence for too long a time.[12] It is also mentioned that the limitation periods are chosen to balance the interests of the claimant and the tortfeasor. It is suggested that the prescription periods are lengthy enough to take sufficient care of the interests of the claimant. These considerations concern the special provision on delictual claims, §9, whereas there are several considerations valid also for the general question of prescription.

11 One may infer that the policy considerations are very much tied to practical and pragmatic approaches meant to produce incentives for smoothness in commercial matters and other areas of life where claims of money occur. The ideas behind the rules also apply to the tort claims, but maybe not to the full extent that it does for the contractual claims, which, of course, are more closely connected to commercial life.

---

6 *Skag*, *supra* fn 2, 42–43.
7 *Skag*, *supra* fn 2, 43–46.
8 *Skag*, *supra* fn 2, 50–51.
9 See *Røed*, *supra* fn 2, 52.
10 *Skag*, *supra* fn 2, 37–56.
11 *Skag*, *supra* fn 2, 49–51.
12 See Ot. prp. no 38 (1977–78).

## V. ELEMENTS OF PRESCRIPTION – AN OVERVIEW

The suggested four elements, (rules of accrual of cause of action, prescription period, rules of prolongation, renewal, etc, and a long-stop rule) are all present in the Norwegian system. A brief survey may be thus: The accrual of the cause of action is based on the damaging event. There is a rule on commencement of the prescription period based on the existence of a claim. The important point in time in practice is the when the claimant factually discovers all the facts constituting the claim. If the situation is such that the claimant has not in fact discovered these facts, but on the other hand ought to have discovered them, the period also commences. Hence for example mental or physical illness may postpone the commencement of the prescription period. 12

The prescription period running from the said point in time is three years. The period may be postponed for example because of the plaintiff's lack of knowledge of the defendant and the other factual and legal elements constituting a claim. Such postponement lies within the rule. 13

After the prescription period has started running, it may be suspended by several possible factors, for example the fact that the defendant has disappeared. The rules of suspension are, however, designed in a special manner: They constitute additional time periods with their own starting point and their own length. When such an additional time period supersedes the general prescription period, the practical effect is the same as by mere suspension as defined in the general report. One may, however, to be accurate, note that this is a special 'breed' of suspension, based on a parallel time period (see *infra* 79–80). 14

There is a rule of a 'ceiling' or 'long-stop', which bars the claim even if there have been reasons for postponements or prolongations. The ceiling is 20 years. This limit does, however, not apply to certain kinds of personal claims which have no limits cf *infra* Section IX. 15

## VI. THE STARTING POINT OF THE PRESCRIPTION PERIOD

### A. THE MEANING OF 'ACTION' AND 'CAUSE OF ACTION'

The Norwegian private law system and doctrine builds upon a notion of 'a claim'. The concept of a claim is essential for civil procedural law.[13] It is probably the most equivalent concept to the common law concept 'cause of action'. The claim 16

[13] See the Norwegian Act on Civil Litigation, Tvisteloven 2005 §§1–3.

has for practical purposes its departure in the point in time of the occurring damage, regardless of whether the damage produces pecuniary or non-pecuniary loss. However, there are some complications as to the starting point, see *infra*.

## B. BROAD OR NARROW CONCEPTION OF 'CAUSE OF ACTION'

17 An event that leads to a harm that is recognised within the tort law catalogue of inflictions or interests (that qualifies for compensatory damages), will constitute a claim, hence a cause of action. One event may cause infringement of several protected interests. This means that one event may create several claims, with respectively starting points of the prescription period in the same event. Adhering to the concepts and distinctions made in the general report, the Norwegian system definitely operates with a *narrow* conception of a claim.

18 Hence in the example of the physician's mistakes and harms (Case 2, *infra*), each mistake and each harm taken together constitute separate, different claims. However, if one mistake leads to several types of harm, for example brain damage and paralysation, this is regarded as part of the same claim. This has to do with procedural frames of what is considered a claim for procedural purposes within the law of civil litigation.[14]

19 The system featuring a narrow conception of a claims functions well and safeguards the plaintiff in the sense that he may have claims according to the actual inflictions of his rights.

**Case 1** – *D, a ski instructor, negligently fails to make sure that all skiers in her 'off-piste' group wear helmets. P, a skier in the group, hits a tree. P immediately suffers head injury X, and years later another head injury Y that developed from the same accident.*

20 The cause of action accrues at the point in time when the damaging event occurs. Hence the claim for the damage Y on principle emerged already at the time of the accident. This rather theoretical construction is of course not material to the question of prescription, which is governed by the rules mentioned below.

21 As for the case illustrated above, it seems clear that the Norwegian solution is to treat the separate incidents and corresponding harms individually. Hence the mistake A and harm X together constitute a claim.

22 The existence of a claim presupposes (regardless of the complications mentioned *infra* 27–30) that there has occurred harm, that the physical, psychic or economic

[14] See *Jens Edvin Skoghøy*, Tvisteløsning, (3rd ed, Oslo 2017) 367 ff.

sphere of the plaintiff is in any way inflicted. The facts of Case 1 will produce two separate claims, with their corresponding commencement of prescription periods, see the system described *supra* 17–19. It does not on principle matter whether one of the damages is more severe than the other.

As mentioned above, it has for a long time been a broad perception that the claim arises at the point in time when the harming action is performed or when the harming event occurs.[15] This means for example that a claim against a bankruptcy estate is established even before the harm has occurred, and it is held that the same solution is valid generally. 23

**Case 2** – *Physician D treats patient P negligently and performs three mistakes on the day of the treatment: A, B and C. Mistake A causes harm X after a year. Mistake B causes harm Y after two years. Mistakes A and C together cause harm Z after three years.*

According to the presuppositions mentioned above, the three mistakes and corresponding occurrences of damage each constitute a claim for damages. The fact that the act causing three kinds of damage happened on the same day is not decisive for the question of when the cause of action occurs. The cause of action comes into being on the day of the mistakes. But here are still, on principle, three claims and three accruals of prescription periods. This follows from the concept of a cause of action, a claim within Norwegian civil procedural law. 24

**Case 3** – *Builder D lays down defective foundations for a building thereby creating the risk of future collapse. As a result, the value to the owner of the building (P) decreases (harm A). Two years later the foundation subsides and requires fixing paid by P (harm B). Three year later cracks appear in the building fixed by P (harm C). Four years later the building collapses (harm D).*

The question of whether the four harms each constitute a separate cause of action must be answered in the affirmative. This is because the factual grounds of the claims are different, something that according to Norwegian civil litigation law is interpreted narrowly.[16] 25

Each harm occurred on principle at the respective point in time that the harm materialised. This is a necessary implication of the system of prescription, which presupposes all along that the claimant is able to be aware of the harm. Hence one must wait until the harm actually occurs to be able to state that there is a harm that potentially may be an object for the claimant's awareness (the third element). Only at this point in time may one conclude that there is a claim. As for the point in time of which the claim came into being, one may in retrospect 26

[15] See for example *Nils Nygaard*, Skade og ansvar (6th ed, Bergen 2007), 423.

[16] See *JE Skoghøy*, Tvisteløsning (3rd ed, Oslo 2017), 1087–1088.

infer that it accrued at the point in time of the tortious act, here the laying down of the defective foundation.

## C. THE STARTING POINT – BREACH OF DUTY OR OCCURRENCE OF DAMAGE?

27 The cause of action arises on principle on the day of the damaging act.[17] This point in time is for example the valid one with regard to the right to submit a claim for bankruptcy.[18] A special work on this subject elaborates the problem thoroughly and concludes that the claim generally arises at the point in time when the damaging act is done.[19] Hence, on principle the cause of action under Norwegian law emerges with the damaging act also for purposes of prescription.

28 The main reason for the mentioned conclusion is that the defendant at this point in time has done all that is necessary for the damage to occur. Furthermore it is referred to the fact that such a point in time is useful for practical purposes connected to 'legal technique'.[20] The existence of a claim can, however, only be verified in *retrospect*, after the act or event has led to some kind of 'negative effect', what is regarded as the damage.[21] Hence the idea of the cause of action arising with the damaging act is logically problematic.[22]

29 However, independent of the critique based on logic, there may be exceptions from the rule, especially in cases where it is unknown who will be the victim of the damaging act. An important consideration is that there must be some evidence of who will be the plaintiff and some kind of connection between the defendant and the plaintiff, before one can conclude that a claim, a cause of action has come into being. Where there is no identified plaintiff, the profound requirements of a cause of action, a claim, is not met.[23] An example is where someone has poisoned a bottle of wine in the liquor store, and it is yet unknown who will be the unlucky buyer and victim. These problems may arise in connection with omissions, continuous harming activity and variations of

---

17 See *Nygaard, supra* fn 15, 423; *Viggo Hagstrøm and Are Stenvik*, Erstatningsrett (2nd ed, Oslo 2019) 592; *Silje Nordtveit*, Når oppstår en fordring (Oslo 2017), 149.

18 See *Mats Andenæs*, Konkursrett (Oslo 2009), 392 and *T Sandvik*, Lærebok i materiell konkursrett (Oslo 1985), 114.

19 See *Nordtveit, supra* fn 17 135–149.

20 Cf The Norwegian term 'rettstekniske hensyn', *Nordtveit, supra*, fn 17 138.

21 Cf the idea of 'realskade', which may be translated as 'real, physical damage', see *Nygaard, supra* fn 15, 59.

22 See an elaboration of this pint in *Askeland*, Om tidsforståelse i erstatningsretten, TfR (2014), 231–274, 340–343.

23 *Nordtveit, supra* fn 17, 149.

strict liability.[24] A possible solution to the problem is to establish an additional requisite in these situations, a requirement of connection between the defendant and the special victim/potential plaintiff.[25]

For the purpose of prescription, one must take the consequence of the mentioned theoretical stance, which is very well embedded in the doctrine. This means that many questions regarding the first element must be answered by pointing to the damaging event or the tortious act. However, for practical purposes, many of the problems will 'vanish' due to the fact that the questions are approached in retrospect.[26] At the point in time when legal decision-making is due, it is known that the tortious act inflicted upon a special victim in a certain way, causes a certain damage. One may at this point operate with the point in time of the tortious act as the starting point of the prescription period in the sense of the first element. All legal problems connected to the uncertainty in the period after the accrual of a cause of action will be solved by the retrospective approach and of course, by other rules of prescription, such as the late discovery rule, which belongs to the third element. 30

**Case 4** – *D enters P's premises without P's permission, thereby committing a tort of trespass, but without causing any damage. P can file a claim against D asking for the remedy of D's eviction but fails to do so. A year later D causes physical harm to P's premises. P files a claim to compensation for the loss.*

A cause of action arises on principle already on the point in time when D enters the premises, because P's right to his own property is infringed, see the principle of accrual of cause of action by the tortious act. P can, however, only file a tort claim in so far that he can prove that he has had an economic loss. Therefore, there is no claim existing. 31

Even though the actual cause of the loss is the situation connected to the defect in the irrigations system, the tortious conduct could be regarded to commence by the first entering of the premises. This will be the logical consequence of the system of claims arising with the tortious acts, explained above.[27] The fact that a tortious conduct leads to damage only at a later point in time is a common phenomenon. 32

This line of reasoning may however be refuted by referring to the recurrence model, which is applied in Norwegian law. The tortious act of D happens every day. Only the day of the incident with the irrigation system did the tortious act result in damage, a cause of action. It was the presence this day that resulted 33

24 *Nordtveit, supra* fn 17, 140–145.

25 *Nordtveit, supra* fn 17, 146–149.

26 See the importance of the retrospective angle, especially *Askeland, supra* fn 22, 337–340.

27 See also especially, *S Nordtveit, supra*, fn 17, 135–140.

in damage, not the days before. Hence, the best way to conceive the problem in accordance with Norwegian law, would be to say that the cause of action commenced the day of the prevention. Since there is no concept of continuous tort, this will probably be the solution. This is more a consequence of the recurrence model than an opinion embracing that the time of the occurring harm should be the starting point of the cause of action.

## D. WHAT IS CONSIDERED 'HARM' FOR PRESCRIPTION PURPOSES?

34 The question has been discussed under Norwegian law both in theory and in court practice with an eye to whether the plaintiff had enough information to go to court in the context of fel. §3 (the late discovery rule, the third element). Still, the focus in these cases is placed on whether the *harm has developed sufficiently* that there is an actual claim. So, in the context of developing damage, the first and the third element in practice overlap. This is a necessary implication of the system of prescription which presupposes all along that the claimant is able to be aware of the harm. Hence one must wait until the harm actually occurs to be able to state that there is a harm that may be an object for the claimant's awareness.

35 The general attitude is that the question is whether there is a such a degree of development that one has sufficient information for stating that there is a claim.[28] As for personal injuries, the crucial point is when there is sufficient grounds for inferring that the injury is permanent.[29] A quite similar approach is taken for damage to things.[30]

**Case 5** – *In an accidental event, D negligently caused an explosion that damaged P's ears. During the first two years P has to raise the volume to enjoy music. During the following three years P needs a hearing device. After a further five years P becomes deaf.*

36 With the theory of accrual of cause of action by the tortious act in mind (see *supra*), one still needs a connection to a certain victim to conclude that there is a claim. Hence, for practical purposes the question of occurrence is transformed to the point in time when a harm has materialised. When a damage is increasing, one must look at the point in time when it was more probable than not that qualified damage (in the eyes of the law) would occur. As for the plaintiff's case,

28 See *Skag, supra* fn 2, 439–447 with references to important cases.
29 See Rt. 1952, 74 and *Skag, supra* fn 2, 440 ff.
30 Rt. 1982, 588 and *Skag, supra* fn 2, 445–448.

at one certain point during the period it became more probable than not that the exposure would lead to a personal injury. Judging from the facts it seems to be after two years, since at this point the plaintiff is in need of a hearing aid.

On principle the cause of action accrues only at the point in time when it is possible to prove that a tortious act has taken place. The Norwegian solution thus fits very well with the intermediate developed harm approach. 37

**Case 6** – *Builder D lays down defective foundations for a bridge, thereby creating the risk of future collapse if heavy rain falls. Two years later heavy rain indeed falls and the collapse becomes only a matter of time, as indeed happens four years after the laying of foundations.*

Based on these general principles, the case should be solved by concluding that the cause of action accrues at the point in time when the heavy rains fall. It is only at this point in time that one knows with sufficient probability that a damage will indeed occur. Even though the theoretical stance under Norwegian law is that the claim arises with the tortious act, it is not possible to say that there existed a claim even before the materialisation, to the degree mentioned above. A different solution would contradict the idea that danger is not enough to constitute a cause of action, only the damage itself. Hence, for all practical purposes, the description above is valid. 38

## E. THE STARTING POINT (ACCRUAL) IN CONTINUOUS TORTS

There is no concept or notion of continuous torts within the Norwegian law. The doctrinal literature has, however, in some connections referred to 'suksessive tap', which may be translated as 'successive losses'.[31] The meaning of the term is not quite equivalent to what is referred to as continuous damage in the Questionnaire. The term 'continuous tort' refers to a continuous infliction of the claimant's sphere of interests, whereas successive losses rather depict a continuous loss stemming from a past infliction of the sphere, typically a personal injury. 39

As for the question of the starting point of the prescription period, the material point seems to be whether the loss is so foreseeable day by day that a lump sum award is possible to estimate. If one must assume that the loss will differ through futural time intervals, the prescription period starts running day by day.[32] Otherwise, one will reach a point in time when it is possible 40

31 See *Skag*, *supra* fn 2, 447–451.
32 See *Skag*, *supra* fn 2, 447–451 with reference to case law.

to foresee a future loss that may be awarded as a lump sum. On principle, a prescription period starts for all of the loss at this point in time.[33] The solution is debatable due to the fact that it allows for prescription of loss that has not yet materialised.

41 A number of provisions and doctrine presuppose, however, that a claim can be based on a damage that materialises successively, day by day.[34] Important in this respect is of course omissions which, given the right circumstances, constitute a claim day by day. One may therefore hold that the principal stance on continuous torts in Norway is that the prescription period starts day by day (the recurrence model).

**Case 7** – *Every week, during a month, D1 publishes a defamatory article on P1, each time in another newspaper and on a different topic. During the same period D2 publishes a defamatory article on P2, every second day, on the same topic and in the same newspaper.*

42 As long as the respective single publications are regarded as inflictions of the rights of the infringed person, they are considered to be separate, individual harms, which on principle constitute separate claims, cf the recurrence model. This applies to both D1 and D2.

43 However, the defamation will, by the claimant, be perceived as successively occurring non-pecuniary loss. There are good reasons for cumulating the losses day by day to a lump sum, and this is how such cases have been treated in court practice. The solution therefore would probably be equivalent to what is described above as successive loss. Hence the different claims will be transformed into one claim. This follows from the tradition of what is considered separate claims in civil litigation.

44 For the purpose of prescription, it is, however, conceivable that the claims based on the first days are cut off by the late discovery rule, for example because the plaintiff uses more time than needed to file a lawsuit.

**Case 8** – *D, a landowner, negligently exposes P, a neighbour, to unreasonable noise for three years. P's hearing is thereby weakened on a daily basis, gradually restricting P's ability to communicate and enjoy music.*

45 The exposure would be considered to be a damage constituting a claim at the first point in time when the noise caused a pathological weakening of the hearing. The material point would be when the exposure caused a medical invalidity of 15%, which is necessary to be able to claim compensation for

---

[33] See for example *Skag*, *supra* fn 2, 448 and *Matningsdal*, *supra* fn 3, 491–493.

[34] See importantly the rule in §9 second para; *Nygaard*, *supra* fn 15, 430; *Bugge*, Forurensningansvar (Oslo 1999), 460–462.

non-pecuniary loss.[35] Hence the claim arises at this point, and the subsequent prescription period commences at the point in time when the claimant was aware or ought to be aware of the fact that the injury had reached the said level.

Of the four models in the analysis, the recurrence model is the closest to the Norwegian solution. As the point in time is fixed to a date in between the start and the end of the exposure, the Norwegian solution also resembles the interim model. However, it is not any question of an 'average date', rather a question of when the infliction is serious enough to pass the threshold of damage for tort law purposes. 46

The exposure to noise would, however, be considered a continuous tort with regard to the long-stop period. 47

**Case 9** – *A waste management company digs bins of toxic content into the soil. Toxic substance leaks into the soil and ground water, causing an apparent damage to crops and expenditure on cleaning on a daily basis. After two years the bins are removed from the soil.*

As Norwegian law subscribes to the recurrence model, the claim for damages arises day by day, on principle so that the there is a multiplicity of dates of accrual. 48

## F. IS THE LATE DISCOVERY RULE A RULE OF THE STARTING POINT (ACCRUAL) OR A RULE OF PROLONGATION?

Based on the general analysis it seems clear that the late discovery rule belongs to the third element of prescription. It is a rule of prolongation. This follows from the fact that the 'P's knowledge is not part of the substantive requirements, the essentials, that constitute P's cause of action against D'. This characterisation fits very well with Norwegian law and thinking, with regard to existing claims. The claims (causes of actions) may on principle be present and valid even though no one has yet discovered them. Hence it would be the most adequate way to describe the late discovery rule as a rule of postponement: The start of the prescription period is postponed until the claimant has sufficient knowledge about the already existing claim. 49

In the special case where A has obtained the sufficient knowledge and afterwards dies, the commencement of the period is suspended until the heir B obtains sufficient knowledge. However, the prescription period will start again with three years for B. Hence one may –most accurately – say that the prescription period 50

35 This threshold follows from an interpretation of skl. §3-2 in light of the preparatory works and Supreme Court practice.

in such a case is postponed until the day the successor of the claim has obtained sufficient knowledge. Where the prescription period has started running, and afterwards stops, one may not actually speak of suspension. The transferee will enjoy the benefit that the prescription period starts from the beginning. Therefore, it is most precise to refer to the effect of 'renewal'.

## VII. PRESCRIPTION PERIODS

51 For tort claims the prescription period commences by the point in time when the claimant discovered or ought to discover that the factual and legal essentials constituting a claim is present. The prescription period is three years.[36]

52 The effective time of prescription may under Norwegian law very well be ten or 20 years. Since the cause of action accrues by the damaging event, there may be a period of time when the damage is unfolding, and another period of time before the plaintiff discovers or ought to discover the rule, so that the prescription period of three years is activated. The effective time period may also be affected by other rules of postponement and other forms of prolongation, see the special rules on prolongation below. In most cases the effective time period is five to six years. This is a short enough period to secure that evidence is not too old, and also in other ways such a period safeguards that the process all in all is fulfilled within a reasonable period of time.

53 Hence the technical solution is a rather short period (three years), combined with a major rule of postponement (the late discovery rule), and a few rules of prolongation. There has been no debate on substituting the three-year period for a longer period.

54 In the Norwegian system there is one major rule governing questions of prescription both in contracts and for extra-contractual relations, cf the general act on prescription §3. This rule is that a claim is prescribed after three years both within contract and in extra-contractual contexts (delict), see also §9 in this respect.

55 For a number of special kinds of private law claims there are established specific prescription periods, for example periodical payments like money obligations tied to documents (ten years, see §5) and pensions (ten years, see §6).

56 Many acts on societal areas of contract law or for example insurance law refers to the general clause in fel. §3, sometimes with minor modifications dependent on the special area of life. One example is the point of commencement as adapted

36 See fel. §9 first para.

to the Industrial Accidents Act (Ysfl).[37] Pursuant to a special regulation the commencement of the prescription period is moved to the end of the year of which the personal injury was discovered.

The prescription periods do not differ with the degree of fault. The ordinary prescription period is the same regardless of which kind of damage the case is about. 57

In general, the plaintiff may choose to claim in tort or contract or both. Hence the plaintiff will choose the regime most advantageous for his purpose. If he succeeds in showing that the requisites are met, it does not matter whether the result would have been otherwise if he had sued on a different legal basis. There is no rule of 'non-cumul' in Norwegian private law. Period shopping may thus occur, but it does not in practice cause any problems worthy of mentioning. 58

It occurs sometimes that a claim is filed both on the basis of contract and additionally on the basis of delictual tort. In such cases the starting point of the prescription period may differ between the two approaches to the facts of the case. In general it will, with regard to prescription, be the most advantageous to the claimant to sue in torts, because the period commences only after *discovery of the basis of a claim*, whereas the prescription period for the contract claim commences already by the objective breach of duty, regardless of the subjective knowledge of the claimant (contractual creditor).[38] In cases where the actual breach of contract may be hard to discover, the claim may be prescribed in a 'hidden manner', something that theorists have questioned.[39] 59

The three-year period is applied to most areas, see the table below: 60

**Table 1. Types of damage**

| Cause of action or tort | Discovery rule | Prescription period | Notes |
|---|---|---|---|
| Bodily injury | Yes | 3 | |
| Property damage | Yes | 3 | |
| Defamation | Yes | 3 | |
| Intentional torts | Yes | 3 | |
| Contractual claims | No, see the note column | 3 | Commencement by breach of contract, plus rules of prolongation. |

37 Yrkesskadeforsikringsloven June 16 1989 no 65.

38 See *Foreldelsesloven* §3.

39 See *Kai Krüger*, Foreldelse av erstatningskrav i kontraktsforhold (særlig om den 'skjulte' foreldelse), in: Kai Krüger, Kåre Lilleholt and Gudrun Holgersen (eds), Nybrott og odling (Bergen 2002), 135–149.

# VIII. RULES OF POSTPONEMENT, SUSPENSION, RENEWAL AND EXTENSION

## A. P'S UNAWARENESS – THE LATE DISCOVERY RULE

### 1) *Introduction*

61 Unawareness is by far the most practical and important reason for postponement of the commencement of the time period. This follows directly form the wording in fel. §9. The key requisite for the commencement of the prescription period is that the plaintiff knew or ought to have known about the claim and the person responsible for the claim. This requisite of knowledge has been developed through many cases.[40]

62 On principle the justification is objective. In court practice one has developed certain standards for the reasonable behaviour of a potential plaintiff. It has in the legal doctrine been maintained that the fact that the plaintiff innocently and unwillingly has been put in a position as a claimant/plaintiff, speaks for a rather lenient standard of expectations, especially when the damage is personal injury.[41]

### 2) *Unawareness of what Elements of Liability?*

63 P must according to the wording of §9 be unaware of the damage ('skaden'; the damage) and the responsible subject ('den ansvarlige'). In legal doctrine and court practice this wording has been interpreted widely, namely so that it comprises also *the facts* that constitutes a basis of liability, and *a causal link* between the two mentioned factual circumstances. As for the question of a causal link, the problem may be that it is uncertain whether various symptoms are caused by a disease for which the defendant is responsible, see for example Rt. 1997, 1070: The uncertainty whether nausea and lack of concentration were caused by toxic substances that the plaintiff had been exposed to in his working place, constituted sufficient grounds for postponement of the starting point of the prescription period.

64 Various writers differ in the perception of whether there are two or three elements of fact of which the plaintiff must be aware of. In legal doctrine it has been criticised that the wording is somewhat unclear at this point, but the mentioned interpretation is regarded 'safe'.[42]

40 See for example Rt. 1992, 603, Rt. 1996, 1134 and Rt. 1997, 1070.
41 *Skag, supra* fn 2, 455.
42 *Skag, supra* fn 2, 452.

Some theorists adhere to the opinion that the provision contains three requirements: The plaintiff must have known or ought to know about (1) the occurrence of the damage, (2) the identity of the responsible party and (3) that the acts of the alleged tortfeasor qualified for rendering him liable.[43] 65

The knowledge of the responsible party may regard the identity of the defendant.[44] The knowledge also regards the question of the whereabouts of the alleged tortfeasor.[45] 66

The question of whether the plaintiff ought to be aware of the relevant facts often boils down to the question of whether the plaintiff has sufficiently investigated the facts. The question of when the plaintiff ought to have known a sufficient amount of facts, must be seen in the light of *res judicata*.[46] It has been held in theory and practice that the fact that the plaintiff faces the possibility of a decision deciding the case once and for all, speaks for a leniency regarding how soon the plaintiff may be expected to file a lawsuit.[47] 67

On principle unawareness of rules within the law does not lead to postponement. The general maxim of *error juris semper nocet applies*.[48] Postponement will only be the case where the unawareness is excusable. The tradition tends in general to operate with quite a high threshold for excusable ignorance. 68

However, there are some examples of cases where the lack of subjective knowledge of the plaintiff has led to postponement of the starting point of the prescription period. Thus, in Rt. 1959, 425, the plaintiff did not know about the possibility to sue a union of traffic insurers for compensations for damage caused by an unidentified vehicle. There are also examples of postponement due to ignorance of law in combination with special individual handicaps on the part of the plaintiff.[49] 69

**Case 10** – *Chemical plant D negligently exposes bordering lands to toxic substances. As a result P, a nearby resident landowner, contracts a lung disease. P failed to sue in time because his former lawyer told him that the exposure was not tortious, and only his new lawyer told him, after the running of time, that it was tortious.*

In this case the main rule of '*error juris semper nocet*' applies. The error of the lawyer is attributed to the plaintiff, and he must seek compensation from his lawyer, which has a mandatory insurance coverage, probably covering the case. 70

---

43 *Nygaard, supra* fn 15, 428.

44 See *Skag, supra* fn 2, 452, with references.

45 See the preparatory works, Ot. prp no 38 (1977–78), 64.

46 Nygaard, *supra* fn 15, 428.

47 See *Nygaard, supra* fn 15, 428. *Matningsdal, supra* fn 3, 481–83 and Rt. 1998, 587, 592.

48 See for example *Røed, supra* fn 5, 442.

49 Rt. 1979, 492 (ethnic minority group), Rt. 1992, 64 (the medical situation of the plaintiff).

### 3) *Objective or Subjective Unawareness?*

71 On principle the qualification of 'prudent unawareness' is objective. In court practice one has developed certain standards for the reasonable behaviour of a potential plaintiff. There must objectively be sufficient reasons for suing.[50] It has in the legal doctrine been maintained that the fact that the plaintiff innocently and unwillingly has been put in a position as a claimant/plaintiff, speaks for a rather lenient standard of expectations, especially when the damage is personal injury.[51]

72 As for the degree of awareness the Supreme Court has taken the stance that the plaintiff must have had evidence in such a degree that he could have taken the case to the court. Hence the damage must have developed to such a degree that it is more likely than not that all the elements of liability may be proved. This means for example that a personal injury must have stabilised or be an object of a clear prognosis, satisfying the demands of proof mentioned.

73 The late discovery rule applies to all kinds of tort claims.

### 4) *What is Considered Awareness of an Element of Liability?*

74 The Supreme Court holds that a damage must have been manifesting itself in such a manner that there are objectively sufficient grounds for filing a lawsuit.[52] This will be the case when there are clear symptoms of damage that can be observed by medical personnel. In the doctrine it is suggested that there may not necessarily occur clear symptoms, seemingly suggesting that the late discovery rule applies even when such manifestations have not occurred.[53] Another theorist suggests that the material point is that a prudent victim ought to have seen that there would occur concrete economic damage. It is maintained that such knowledge is only possible where the damage in any way has manifested itself objectively.[54]

### 5) *How Heavy is the Burden to Acquire Knowledge?*

75 In general, the plaintiff must show prudent behaviour in this area of life as well as in other areas. This means that he needs to investigate adequately whether he has a claim or not. This duty in fact follows from the wording

50 See for example Rt. 1994, 190 and Rt. 1998, 587.
51 *Skag*, *supra* fn 2, 455, *Røed*, *supra* fn 2, 265, also 268.
52 See Rt. 1994, 190 and Rt. 1998, 587.
53 *Skag*, *supra* fn 2, 435.
54 *Røed*, *supra* fn 2, 413.

'burde' in fel. §9, which means 'ought to'. The question is whether he or she ought to understand that the factual and legal requirement for a lawsuit was present.

It seems that the preparatory works did not presuppose any heavy duty for the victim to investigate whether he or she has a claim. The general formulation is that there must occur such circumstances that make it 'natural' for the victim to try to find out whether or not she has a claim.[55] It is, however, presupposed that this may be done with a 'reasonable effort'.[56] If a plaintiff has somewhat lasting pains or other symptoms of illness, she must be expected to visit a doctor.[57] On the other hand, if a doctor, who is not a specialist, concludes that there is nothing wrong with the patient, she is not obliged to seek a second opinion from a specialist.[58] Commentators have, based on the practice of the Supreme Court, suggested that the duty to investigate with regard to personal injuries is rather modest.[59] There is support for such a stance also in preparatory works regarding amendments of the prescription act.[60] This tendency has been criticised for undermining the rules on prescription.[61] 76

**Case 11** – *Chemical plant D negligently exposes bordering lands to toxic substances. As a result P, a nearby resident landowner, contracts a lung disease, but is unaware of the causal link between exposure and disease because his physician fails to detect it. P does not seek a second opinion. After the prescription period runs on the disease P consults his new physician that tells him about the link.*

The opinion of the Supreme Court is that the question is whether a standard medical professional would have discovered the illness or disease. If not, the prescription period will not start running. It is not expected that the plaintiff ought to have consulted a specialist. This is quite distinctively articulated in Rt. 1998, 587 at pp 593–594. Hence P's claim against D did not prescribe. 77

## B. OTHER RULES OF PROLONGATION

In general, the technique is that certain named circumstances have the effect that the commencement of the period is postponed or that the period is suspended. In some of the circumstances mentioned a *new prescription* period 78

55 *Røed, supra* fn 2, 434.
56 Rt. 1994, 190.
57 NOU 2000, 16, 339.
58 Rt. 1998, 587.
59 See *Røed, supra* fn 2, 434–436, based on Rt. 1967 s. 1182, Rt. 1992 s. 603 and Rt. 1994 s. 190.
60 See Innst. O. no 35 (1993–94), 2.
61 See *Røed, supra* fn 2, 439–440.

commences, independently of the previous one. Hence, also renewal occurs. An example is cases where a board of complaints for insurance holders has passed an 'advisory' decision without deciding the case. A special provision reads that the prescription period in such cases starts anew, see fel. §21 no 2.[62]

79 The Norwegian system comprises additionally a number of rules granting the claimant *additional* periods of prescription. These additional periods are mainly designed for claims in contract, but some of them apply also to delictual tort claims. These additional periods run parallel to the ordinary period. This means that they are not suspending the general period, and they will only have an effect if they commence towards the end of the general period activated by the late discovery requisites. For example: If the defendant has moved abroad two months before the expiry of the general three-year period, there are ten months of effective time left for the plaintiff. This follows from the fact that the additional period is 12 months (one year).[63]

80 Summing up, the consequence of occurring circumstances affecting the prescription period may be postponement, suspension, renewal and extension. The extension comes in the form of the parallel period explained above. All four instruments are at play depending on which circumstances are coming into being.

*1) D is to Blame for the Delay*

81 In case of D's concealment or misleading of P, there can only be suspension by the use of the late discovery rule, which quite naturally will apply in such cases. There are no other special statutory provisions or established case law that regulates the described situation.

*2) Admission by D of P's Right or Partial Performance of P's Right by D*

82 If D Acknowledges P's claim, a new prescription period commences, see fel. §20. This provision reads also that a promise to pay a debt or payment of interest qualifies as admissions in the eyes of the law. Also, partial payment of claim qualifies for acknowledgement according to the rule in §14. The prescription period starts independently of the running of the earlier period. The most correct description is therefore renewal of the prescription period.

---

62 See Ot. prp. no 44 (1997–98) 15–17 and *Røed, supra* fn 2, 843–844.

63 See *Røed, supra* fn 2, 467–469.

### 3) *Special Relations between D and P*

As for relations between the parties, there are special rules regarding certain kinds of close relationships. Thus, a *child* is granted a minimum one-year suspension of the prescription period after having passed the age of 18 years. However, no such rules apply to the relationship between *spouses*. In the preparatory works of fel. (enacted 1979) it was pointed to the need for spouses to finish off claims between them successively, and also to the fact that it would be inconsistent to have such a rule as long as two partners living together may have just as close a relationship.[64] 83

A child's claim against a *guardian* or the public administration of guardianship will enjoy an additional period of one year at the least after the age of 18, see fel. §12 no 1. A). 84

A similar system applies to an 'unpersonal holder of a right', such as limited or unlimited companies. These are granted an additional period of one year commencing after the relationship has ended.[65] This rule applies to claims against other owners or members of *organs* of a *legal entity*, typically a company's board members. Hence there is a special regulation for the relationship between legal entities and their organs. 85

There are, however, no such rules regarding *partners* in *partnerships*. 86

The same goes for contractual-based relationships such as employee and employer, attorneys and clients, and physician and patient, no special rules apply. A patient may thus be forced to file a claim against his doctor while still being his patient. 87

The relations mentioned may most conveniently be treated under *the awareness rule*. It is somewhat inconsistent that the need for a special rule because of the inconvenience attached to relations is recognised for some relations, and not for others. 88

### 4) *P's Lack of Legal Capability*

All minors will have appointed a designated guardian who represents them in legal matters, most practically biological parents, however also appointed guardians. If no physical person is appointed, 'overformynderiet', a public entity responsible for all minors will be held accountable. Thus, there is no occurrence of minors 'without representatives' under Norwegian law. 89

---

64 See Ot. prp. no 38 (1977–78), 67.

65 See *Foreldelsesloven* §12 no 1.

90 Minors will be 'identified with' his or her representative in legal matters, most practically the parents.[66] This means that if a period expires due to negligence on the part of the parent (or other legal representative), the minority will lose the claim. In court practice there is an example where the Supreme Court solved a question of prescription by referring to the fact that the representatives of the child had the sufficient knowledge to file a lawsuit, see Rt. 1959, 525. In this case the claim was, however, accepted due to the fact that the representatives ought not to be aware of who to sue, cf the awareness rule. The question has, however, not been a subject to trial by the courts.

91 Whenever P has a mental disability, the prescription period will not start to run due to the requisite 'ought to be aware' which is interpreted so that the mental disability precludes awareness in the eyes of the law. If the mentally disabled is represented by a legal representative the question of ought to may depend on the latter person's awareness. The negligence of the representative may in such cases be attributed to the mentally disabled. If the case regards personal injury, the court may tend to allow the claim, ie deem it not to be prescribed.[67]

92 The doctrinal point of view is that physical obstruction due to illness may postpone the point in time when it is reasonable to file a lawsuit. Where a plaintiff in a personal injury case has lost consciousness due to the injury, the prescription period will not commence until the plaintiff has regained consciousness.[68] A similar point of view is held regarding patients in hospital, something that is supported by a Supreme Court case Rt. 1956, 365. In another case, Rt. 1992, 64, the plaintiff had communication problems due to the personal injury caused by the tortfeasor. Because of the huge disablement caused by a defective pill, the plaintiff was unable to take care of her interests for six-and-a-half years, ie at least a three-and-a-half-year suspension of the commencement of the prescription period was accepted.[69]

### 5) *Absence of Parties from the Jurisdiction*

93 The provision in §23 prescribes a procedure for claiming abroad. Hence the provision presupposes that a lawsuit abroad is necessary in order to interrupt the prescription period timely.[70] In fel. §10 no 3 there is, however, granted to the plaintiff an additional prescription period of one year after the point in time

66 'Identification' means that the acts or omissions of the representatives are attributed to the minor and her legal position.

67 *Røed, supra* fn 2, 436–439.

68 *Matningsdal, supra* fn 3, 504.

69 Further on the subject, *Røed, supra* fn 5, 436–438.

70 *Røed, supra* fn 2, 893–896.

when the plaintiff obtained knowledge or ought to have obtained knowledge of the fact that it is possible for the defendant to sue in Norway due to homecoming.

The provision may be applicable in cases where the defendant leaves the country so that the claimant no longer has the knowledge of the defendant's whereabouts, hence is unable to sue.[71] 94

### 6) *Former Litigation between the Parties*

If litigation ends without final ruling the running of the prescription period is suspended for one year after the closure of the case, see fel. §22 no 1 first sentence. If the claimant has not been informed of the closure of the case, the period of one year starts running when he gets the information. The postponement of the prescription period can, however, not last longer than three years from the closure of the case, hence this is a sort of additional, parallel time limit. In other words, this prescription period works the same way as a long-stop, however designed only for these special kinds of circumstances. 95

When a claim is subject to ADR, the running of the prescription period is postponed, see fel. §15. If ADR instruments are agreed between the parties beforehand, the claimant has to file a lawsuit for the ADR court. More relevant to tort claims are cases where the claimant claims that the case should be solved by ADR. Prescription is in such a case postponed only when the party has claimed ADR and suggested a judge.[72] 96

Norwegian law has in many areas established administrative boards with the competence to solve disputes between parties to tort claims, for example 'Finansklagenemnda', a board solving disputes between insurance holders and insurance companies, and 'Norsk Pasientskadeerstatning', an administrative unit deciding personal injury cases stemming from medical treatment. If a case is brought to such an administrative board, the prescription period is interrupted, hence suspended, see fel. §16 and §21 no 1. If such a case ends with no decision and is granted a period of one year after the plaintiff has been notified that the case is ended, see fel. §22 no 1. The suspension of prescription may, however, not occur in any case any later than three years after the ending of the case before the administrative board, see fel. §22 no 1. 97

Out-of-court settlement proceedings or other forms of *negotiation* does not lead to suspension or extension of any kind. In the preparatory works of the new act on civil litigation the question of suspension was raised but rejected by 98

---

71 See *Asbjørn Kjønstad and Steinar Tjomsland*, Foreldelsesloven (Oslo 1983), 118, tacitly supported by *Røed, supra* fn 2, 894.

72 See Ot. prp. no 28 (1977–78) s 68 and *Røed, supra* fn 2, 387.

the law committee. The reason for this choice was that one wanted to avoid the need to distinguish between qualified and not qualified settlement proceedings. Moreover, it was referred to the fact that the parties have the opportunity to lengthen the prescription period by contract, cf fel. §28 or file a lawsuit in order to achieve renewal of the period, cf fel. §15.

99 If the claim is acknowledged by a judicial decision, a new prescription period of ten years commences from the day of acknowledgement, see fel. §21 no 2.

100 There are no special rules on P's right to prolongation in order to gather evidence. On the other hand the plaintiff's need to gather evidence may very well be a legitimate reason for his subjective ignorance of the claim and of the identity of the claimant, see *supra* 65–67.

101 The lack of financial resources will not bring the claimant any postponement of the prescription period. The general rule under Norwegian private law is that the citizen himself carries the risk of lack of money.

102 The courts do not in general have any possibility of prolonging the period. There is no legal basis for such decisions. There are no other recognised justifications for prolongation within Norwegian private law.

### *7) Victim's Death*

103 Under Norwegian law the ceiling period runs regardless of V's death. As for the question of knowledge it seems probable that the P may claim that he did not know and that he did not ought to have known either. Hence P's lack of knowledge will postpone the prescription period.

### *8) Tortfeasor's Bankruptcy*

104 When the tortfeasor goes bankrupt, this will not have an effect on the claims against him. The victim must as a creditor notify the estate that he or she has a claim, just as any other creditor.[73]

### *9)* Force Majeure

105 There is a special provision in fel. §10 no 2 which prescribes an additional prescription period of one year in the case 'uovervinnelig hindring', something that may be translated to 'undefeatable hindrance'. The wording is meant to cover

[73] See the Norwegian Act on Bankruptcy, Konkursloven 8 June 1984 no 58 §109.

the typical *force majeure* situation.[74] This means that such incidents as *natural disasters* and *war* are included in the provision.[75]

The claimant's duty to do his or her *military service* is not regarded as any *force majeure* situation. 106

The fact that the claimant is prosecuted by the criminal authorities or *imprisoned* does not amount to *force majeure* in the eyes of the law.[76] In case of any legal inability to sue, this problem is probably governed by the late discovery rule. 107

There are no special rules governing *closed courts*, apart from the procedural rules on what is known as dismissal of the case. In case the court in fact is closed, for example due to an epidemic incident, the general rule on *force majeure* probably applies. There are no other special rules that have the same effects as the *force majeure* rule. It may be assumed that the late discovery rule is applicable to many factual hindrances of filing a lawsuit. 108

## IX. CEILINGS ON THE EFFECTIVE TIME OF PRESCRIPTION

There is a general ceiling period of 20 years prescribed in fel. §9 second para. Most claims, whether they are based on personal injuries or other kinds of damage, expire at the latest 20 years after the damaging event, see fel. §9 second para. 109

The period commences at the point in time when the damaging act or event ends. For example, the starting point of the ceiling period may be the point in time when a toxic bin in removed from the soil it is buried in, not the point in timed when it was buried. The period is absolute in the sense that it will not be prolonged in any circumstances. 110

The general ceiling period is absolute in the sense that it will *not be prolonged* in any circumstances. 111

As for the long-stop period there is, however, a difference between certain personal injury claims and other claims. Certain personal injury claims do not expire at all, see fel. §9, second para, second sentence. Pursuant to this provision claims based on personal injuries caused by commercial business or to a person younger than 18 years are, on certain conditions, excluded from the scope of the long-stop rule. 112

74 *Røed, supra* fn 2, 523–525.
75 Regarding war, see *Røed, supra* fn 2, 525.
76 See *Røed, supra* fn 2, 525.1.

113 The first exception aims at late development of personal injuries such as illness caused by asbestos. The exception applies where three requirements are met: Firstly, the injury must have been caused by commercial activity or comparable activity. The last-mentioned alternative means that public activity and activity with ideal goals are included in the rule.[77] Secondly, the rule requires that the responsible party or someone that the responsible party is accounted for, has known or ought to have known that there was a danger to life or a risk for severe personal injury. It is held by commentators that the knowledge of an employee is enough for activating the exception from the long-stop rule.[78] Thirdly, the danger must be concrete, and the knowledge or possible knowledge must occur before the injury actually takes place. It is not required that the actual damage is severe, it is sufficient that the danger is of such a character.[79]

114 The second exception regards young victims, first and foremost of sexual abuse but also of violence and bullying. For such personal injuries it is typical that many victims live through their twenties without having the capability of filing their claims based on severe episodes during childhood. The reason for the exception is thus a wish to make it possible for young victims of sexual abuse to claim damages after having become adults, even though for many years they have lacked the knowledge or capacity to state their claim.

115 Also, for this exception there is a requirement regarding the knowledge of the responsible party, or someone attributed to him. In the preparatory works it is mentioned as an example that a teacher must have known or ought to know that a pupil was subject to bullying.[80] If no such possibility of knowing may be proved, the exception does not apply and hence the claim may expire based on the general ceiling applying to other claims.

Table 2. **Long-stop rules**

| Scope | Commencement | Length | Prolongation | Comments |
|---|---|---|---|---|
| Product liability | D's conduct – marketing | 10 | No | |
| Damage to property | D's tortious conduct ends | 20 | No | |
| Personal injury to persons under 18 years or to persons in work | | No limit | | Additional requisite that the tortfeasor knew or ought to know |

77 See Ot. prp. no 48 (1987–88), 17 and *Røed, supra* fn 5, secs 338–339.
78 *Røed, supra* fn 5, 459.
79 See Ot. prp no 48 (1987–88), 13.
80 See Ot. prp. no 38 (2003–2004), point 9.1.

# X. STATUTE INTERPRETATION, JUDICIAL DISCRETION AND LACHES

## A. STATUTE INTERPRETATION

Judges are neutral to prescription, applying the rules according to law in the normal manner. Because of a widespread social attitude towards personal injury cases there may be a certain tendency to interpret the rules so that prescription does not apply in cases where it would deprive a plaintiff of damages for personal injury.[81] 116

It has been debated among theorists whether morally one should be allowed to reject a claim on the basis of prescription. Especially, it been held that the State or other public authority should not make use of this defence. 117

## B. DISCRETION

There are no general clauses of 'reasonableness' or 'good faith' used in the statutory provisions dealing with prescription issues. The most important interval of discretion allowed by the statutes is found with the 'ought to' alternative regarding knowledge. One may hold that the Supreme Court in some cases has shown elements of discretion when deciding whether 'weaker' parties have a claim, typically the victims of personal injury. The Norwegian law does not mandate any judicial discretion apart from the 'ought to' criterion mentioned above. 118

In general, the rules of prescription are interpreted the same way as other private law rules. It is mostly a question of modifying the wording in the light of preparatory works and case law as well as the concrete merits of the case. In accordance with other private law regulations there is a tendency to respect the lawmaker's choice. The spirit of and the purpose behind the act on prescription do not invite the judge to make free considerations of prescription effects. 119

One may detect a slight tendency to interpret the rules in favour of the plaintiff, in order to meet social needs, especially in personal injury cases. 120

---

81 See Tvisteloven 17 June 2005 no 90 §§9–16.

### C. LACHES

121 There is legal basis for rejecting a claim on the ground of laches.[82] There is such a principle which is uncodified and general, based on a set of considerations applied to conduct of the parties in the concrete case. In general the opinion is that there is quite a considerate threshold for applying the principle.[83] It seems hard to imagine a situation where the passive attitude of a claimant is sufficiently grave that he loses his claim within the short period of time for tort claims, three years. Not surprisingly, this general principle has never been applied to cases of tort claim.

## XI. CHANGE OF PARTIES

### A. THE PLAINTIFF IS A TRANSFEREE OF THE VICTIM'S CLAIM

122 When a claim is transferred from P1 to P2 for example by the death of P1, it is not considered a new claim. The late discovery rule may, however, still be applied for some parties in P's position.

123 When a claim is overtaken by *an insurer*, it is subrogated with all its accessories. The general rule is then that the claim with all its accessories is subrogated to the insurer. Hence the running of time in V's claim continues.

124 However, if a claim is taken over by *an estate* because of V's death, the estate probably gains the benefit of the late discovery rule. Hence the prescription is postponed until P2 gains the sufficient knowledge of the claim. Only then will the prescription period commence. The solution at this point is, however, disputed, see *infra* 125.

125 Where P1 dies after having activated the late discovery rule and the period has begun, the theorists disagree on the question whether the prescription period is suspended or not. One view is that the successor P2 (the heir) cannot gain a better position than P1, based on a general private law principle embedded in civil law elsewhere.[84] This view is supported by systematical considerations – of which solution fits the best in a coherent set of prescription rules.[85]

---

82 See *Miriam Skag*, Adgangen til å supplere foreldelsesloven med ulovfestede passivitetsregler, TfR 2010, 523–564.

83 See *Skag*, *supra* fn 82, 563–564.

84 See Gjeldsbrevloven 17 February 1939 no 1 §25, *Røed*, *supra* fn 5, 519.

85 See *Miriam Skag*, Tilleggsfrist etter foreldelsesloven §10 nr. 1 ved kreditorskifte, Tidsskrift for forretningsjus (2019), 15–37, 30.

Hence the claim may prescribe even if P2 is ignorant of the fact that the claim exists. Another view is that the late discovery rule applies to the heir. This view is, however, based on a weak authority, only by antithetical interpretation of a lower court decision.[86] In the author's opinion the latter view still seems the most sensible in light of the fact that P1 actually is dead, and accordingly the knowledge of the existence of the claim may be hard to obtain in a short period of time after his death. Actually, one may hold that there is a physical need for rules that allows for some time to discover the claim. Otherwise the debtor may have a coincidental advantage because of his creditor's death, something that is not an appealing solution. If P1's heirs are not granted the benefit of the late discovery rule, they may be deprived of large sums of money that actually belong to the estate. This becomes clear if P1 dies a short period before his period expires. Skag suggests a middle solution, offering the new creditor an additional time limit of one year from discovery, based on fel §10 no. 1.[87]

If the claim is transferred from one debtor to another, this has no effect on the prescription rules governing the plaintiff's legal position. This follows from a general civil law principle saying that the successor may not gain a better position than his predecessor.[88] 126

The mental illness of a tortfeasor does not affect his liability at all, provided of course that a claim has arisen according to the tort law rules on bases of liability (which make excuses for mental illness). The tortfeasor, who has become liable, will still be liable no matter what his condition is. If the transferee is mentally ill, he will be just as liable as the first one, with no regard to the mental illness of the transferee. There are no other rules of postponement or suspension applying in this situation either. The overall picture is that the fact that a liability is transferred does not affect the content of the liability, and that the legal position of the defendant in view of the prescription rules are not altered. 127

## B. THE DEFENDANT IS A TRANSFEREE OF THE TORTFEASOR'S OBLIGATION

The overall picture is that the fact that a liability is transferred does not affect the content of the liability, and that the legal position of the defendant in view of the prescription rules are not altered. For example, if D's position as a defendant is taken over by his estate, the estate is liable on the same terms in every way, also 128

---

86 *Trygve Bergsåker*, Foreldelse – noen praktiske spørsmål, Juriskontakt no 1 1998.

87 *Skag, supra* fn 85, 30–31.

88 This principle is often based on a general act on money claims in Norwegian civil law, Gjeldsbrevloven 17 February 1939 §25.

with regard to the prescription rules. There are no other rules of postponement or suspension applying in this situation either.

### C. CONTRIBUTION CLAIMS

129 When a joint tortfeasor D1 claims contribution from D2 after having paid the victim, his claim is considered *derivative* from P's original claim against D2. The claim is a subrogation of the claim that P had against D2.

130 A special statutory provision regulates the rights of the parties: Under Norwegian law a joint tortfeasor who has paid the claimant V before the prescription period has expired will be granted a one-year period of claiming other tortfeasors responsible for the same claim, see fel. §8. If P pays V after the prescription period has expired, he may only sue D if D has been notified of the payment within a reasonable time, see §8 fourth sentence.

### D. DEPENDANTS' CLAIMS

131 The dependant's claim is independent of a victim's claim before his death. Dependants sue for their personal loss of support. This means that the starting point of the dependant's claim (date of accrual) is V's death and not V's injury. Even though from the perspective of the dependant it is the same money that has to be paid, it is considered a different claim in most ways, and definitely in respect of prescription. It is confirmed by the Supreme Court that the dependants do not have a claim for support in case a victim has already claimed and received compensation for loss of earnings.[89]

132 The fact that the defendant can be confronted with a claim a rather long time after his tortious act has not been addressed as a problem in the doctrinal literature.

## XII. OTHER ASPECTS OF PRESCRIPTION LAW

### A. STIPULATION

133 The freedom of contract allows for prolonging the prescription periods. A special provision allows also for suspension of the time period for three years, see fel. §28 first para As for Norwegian law all the questions of agreements on prescription matters are governed by the principle of freedom of contract.

---

[89] See Rt. 2012, 1515.

Hence shortening of the prescription period may be agreed upon, by an antithesis of the wording in fel. §28. If the potential plaintiff is the party with the weaker resources, the agreement on shorter prescription period may, however, be considered void according to the general act on contracts.[90] The defendant may not by agreement eliminate the effect of the prescription, cf fel. §28. 134

## B. MEANING OF 'FILING' A CLAIM THAT INTERRUPTS THE RUNNING OF PRESCRIPTION

The procedural act that stops the running of the prescription period is filing a lawsuit against D, see fel. §15. Filing a lawsuit must be done within the frames and procedures governed by the Civil Litigation Act.[91] He may also rely on a statement from the defendant that he actually is the debtor to the tort claim, see fel. §14. 135

## C. WHEN SHOULD THE DEFENCE BE RAISED AND DECIDED?

The defence should be pleaded by the beginning of the proceedings, otherwise the defendant risks that the defence is precluded by the rules of preclusion within the law of civil litigation.[92] 136

## D. WHO MAY RAISE THE DEFENCE?

The defence has to be pleaded by D. The general opinion is that the rules cannot be applied *ex officio*. The question has been debated by theorists, and the preferred view seems to have prevailed.[93] However, the judge may, in accordance with the ordinary practice of leading the court pleadings, ask the defendant whether he pleads that the prescription period has expired. 137

As long as there is a real and factual interest on the part of T, he may join the case and claim that the prescription period has expired. T has, however, to join the case according to ordinary civil litigation rules. 138

---

90 See Avtaleloven 15 May 1918 §36.

91 See Tvisteloven 17 June 2005 no 90, chapter 12 cf also §6-3 and §9-2.

92 Tvisteloven 17 June 2005 §9-16.

93 See *Kai Krüger*, Pengekrav (1984), 434–435.

139 The defence should be pleaded by the beginning of the proceedings, otherwise the defendant risks that the defence is precluded by the rules of preclusion within the law of civil litigation.

## E. BURDEN OF PROOF (OF ELEMENTS AND OF RULES OF PROLONGATION)

140 P has the burden of proof with respect to the existence of his claim. The burden of proof with respect to the fact that the prescription period has expired lies, at the outset, on the part of the defendant. Once the question of prescription has arisen, the burden of proof for practical purposes is shifted to the plaintiff, especially because the question often turns to what the plaintiff ought to have known.

# PRESCRIPTION IN TORT LAW: POLAND

Ewa Bagińska

## I. INTRODUCTION

1 Polish law knows two types of limitation of claims or rights linked to the lapse of time: 'absolute time/preclusion limits' (*terminy zawite*) and prescription (*terminy przedawnienia*). The so-called extinctive prescription (as it is understood in the French legal doctrine) is thus dichotomous. The origins of the dichotomy are found in the history of Polish private law. There is, however, a terminological chaos which has influenced theoretical analyses until today.

2 The group of preclusion periods, lacks a general regulation or even systematisation. They are scattered all over civil law, except for tort law, and are imposed by the law on various claims or actions, whether patrimonial or non-patrimonial, to seek court remedy or to seek remedy outside the court system, including a right of withdrawal or cancellation of contract concluded under error, a right to self-help in order to protect possession of a thing, some of the warranty claims or claims, pleas and objections as to the civil proceedings. The rights or entitlements extinct after the lapse of time (typically very short). If despite the time lapse, the creditor demands the performance or files an action, the court will *ex officio* reject the demand or action. Hence, this type of extinctive period which results in extinguishing a substantive claim/right recalls a limitation of action as it is understood in common law. It is more procedural in nature; at the same time, it should not be confused with purely procedural time limits imposed by the law or by a court in a civil process.

3 The second type of limitations of claims is prescription (*przedawnienie*), which leads to the non-enforcement of a right. Historically speaking,

the true prescription was confused with time-limits leading to complete extinction of claims. Accordingly, under the Code of Obligations of 1933 [*kodeks zobowiązań*, KZ], the lapse of a period of time stipulated by the law could bring about one of two consequences: the termination of the right or the barring of a remedy, depending on the exact wording of a rule.

Under the binding Civil Code [*kodeks cywilny*, KC] the two types of limitations are clearly separated. Under the influence of German law, the general regulation of prescription is contained in the General Part of the Civil Code (arts 117–125 KC). Specific regulations exist for some types of claims in (a) nominate contracts, (b) torts – in the Civil Code Titles VI and VI prim (for products liability), and also (c) in special laws. The rules on prescription of tort claims are placed in the Title on Torts (former art 442, present art $442^1$). They originate in the Code of Obligations. They were not reformed until 1990, with the exception of the shortening of the long-stop period from 20 to ten years in 1950.[1] A major reform took place in 2007[2] and was slightly corrected in 2017, on the occasion of introducing special rules on claims for compensation for harm caused by an infringement of competition law.[3] 4

## II. DEFINITION OF PRESCRIPTION

Prescription is a legal institution that prevents the creditor (the injured) from enforcing his rights against the debtor (a person liable in tort) because of the running of a specified period of time on the (tort) claim. Prescription is confined solely to pecuniary (financial) claims, regardless of their bases (cause of action).[4] Where the language of the law is not entirely clear, but the nature of the claim is patrimonial, the unclear legal rule will be considered to impose a period of prescription and not an absolute time-limit. 5

There are a few exceptions to the rule that pecuniary claims prescribe with time, most importantly claims related to protection of immovable property and the right to dissolve co-ownership. Also among tort claims certain claims stemming from the violation of personal interests are not subject to prescription, in particular the claim against a person who committed the violation of a personality right to perform acts necessary to remove the negative effects and in particular 6

1 Ie before the Civil Code was enacted in 1964.

2 The Act of 16 February 2007 on the Revision of the Civil Code. Dz. U. 2007, no 80, item 538 in force as of 24 May 2007.

3 The Act of 21 April 2017, rules on claims for compensation for harm caused by an infringement of competition law, in force as of 27 June 2017.

4 Article 117 KC: Subject to exceptions provided for by statute, pecuniary claims shall be subject to limitation.

to make an apologetic statement. The mentioned type of claims is not subject to prescription because of their non-financial nature. If the victim demanded pecuniary compensation for their non-pecuniary loss, the latter claim would be subjected to prescription according to tort rules.

## III. THE NATURE OF PRESCRIPTION AND ITS EFFECTS

7 The nature and effects of prescription are subjects of intense theoretical discussions in the Polish legal academic writings.[5] Particular attention is drawn to the questions of prescription in personal injury cases.

8 It is agreed that prescription does not extinguish a pecuniary claim. The duty to perform on the part of the debtor becomes a natural obligation, principally once the latter raises the plea of prescription (see *infra* 10). Whatever has been performed in order to discharge the claim may not be reclaimed merely because the period of prescription had expired; thus, no restitution is possible.[6]

9 If the debtor, when sued, chooses to raise a *substantive defence* of prescription, the court will generally dismiss the claim. Should the debtor not raise the defence, the court will enforce a valid claim, because it has no competence to apply prescription *ex officio*. Prior to the major revision of the Civil Code in 1990 the Code provided that a court took account *ex officio* of the lapse of the period of prescription. At the same time the lapse of time could be disregarded if the period of prescription did not exceed three years and the delay in bringing that claim was justified by exceptional circumstances and was not excessive. This exception thus operated under the rule that prescription was not a plea of defence. The change of the law in 1990 was justified by the need to reinforce the will of the parties, to reduce the competence of the court to interfere in the civil law relations and by the simultaneous changes in the civil procedure, which brought about an adversarial and contradictory model of a civil process. Presently, the Civil Code explicitly provides that: 'Following the lapse of the period of prescription, the one against whom a claim is to be pursued may avoid the duty to satisfy it unless he waives his right to use the defence of limitation. However, waiving the defence of limitation before the lapse of the period of limitation shall be invalid' (art 117 §2 KC).

---

5 See *J Kuźmicka-Sulikowska*, Idea przedawnienia i jej realizacja w polskim kodeksie cywilnym (2015).

6 Article 411 point 3 KC.

Nevertheless, the latest revision of the Civil Code (2018) reintroduced the *ex officio* operation of prescription rules for claims against consumers.[7] The legislator has also shortened the general prescription period of ten years to six years.[8] According to the new rule 'After the lapse of prescription period the creditor cannot demand payment of the claim against a consumer.'[9] With a view to enhance the protection of consumers the nature of the prescription which runs in favour of the consumer has been changed in the way that the obligation turns into a natural obligation by operation of law as soon as the prescription time lapses and regardless of whether the consumer has raised the plea of prescription. This strict rule has been mitigated by the new competence of a court not to take the prescription into account when justice so requires. 10

In Polish law only court litigation and court enforcement are barred. This means that the creditor has no competence to demand from a court or an executor to use compulsory measures in order to induce the debtor to effect performance.[10] The plaintiff can still enforce his/her right outside the court under certain conditions of set-off. According to the Civil Code a time-barred claim may be set-off provided the limitation had not yet occurred at the moment the set-off could first have been effective.[11] Hence, the lapse of a period of prescription creates a legal situation in which the debtor has a subjective right to refuse performance, and he can raise a defence of prescription, although he has no duty to use this right or defence.[12] 11

## IV. CONSIDERATIONS FOR AND AGAINST PRESCRIPTION OF TORT CLAIMS

### A. AGAINST

Traditional arguments for and against prescription, which are recognised in other legal systems, are also raised and developed in the Polish jurisprudence. The discussion related to the justification of prescription does not aim at abolishing it, but rather to explain and shape some of its elements. 12

7 The Act of 13 April 2018 on the revision of the civil code, Dz. U. 2018 item 1104. In force as of 9 July 2018.

8 It is nowhere explained why six years and not another time limit.

9 Article 117 §2[1] KC.

10 See *P Machnikowski*, in: E Gniewek and P Machnikowski (eds), Kodeks cywilny. Komentarz, (2016), 276.

11 Article 502 KC.

12 See *M Pyziak-Szafnicka*, in: M Pyziak-Szafnicka (ed), Kodeks cywilny – część ogólna Komentarz (2009), 1026, similarly *A Brzozowski*, in: K Pietrzykowski (ed), Kodeks cywilny Komentarz, Vol 1 (2011), comment to art 117.

13 It is rather obvious that the expiration of claims with the lapse of time is against the inherent logic of the system of the protection of subjective rights and collides with justice and constitutional protection of rights, including the right to court. One (a creditor) is not obliged to exercise their right yet choosing to do so for a certain period causes the right to become unenforceable by State institutions. Polish courts underline that the prescription of claims mainly protects the interest of the tortfeasor.

14 Personal injury triggers a particularly intense protection in the legal system and hence there are more cons than pros when justifying prescription of claims arising from personal injury. Sometimes prescription can be excluded in those cases; for example, under Polish Atomic Law[13] personal injury claims are not subject to prescription. The State Treasury guarantees payment of those claims if they could not be covered by the financial indemnity of a nuclear operator. Furthermore, prescription of claims may not be dealt with differently on the grounds of class of defendants, because this would contradict the requirements of justice and equal treatment.[14] The only permissible distinction may be made between damage to persons and damage to property, with better protection granted to the former. This view is justified by the constitutional values (higher protection of life and dignity).

15 Furthermore, in the light of constitutional values the mechanism of prescription should be constructed in the way it would not make pecuniary rights become illusory. Before 2007 the Polish regulation of the prescription of personal injury claims was flawed primarily due to the ten-year long-stop period, which caused many claims to have become prescribed before the occurrence of the damage. In 2006 the Constitutional Tribunal repealed the ten-year long-stop rule because of its unconstitutionality.[15] The Tribunal ruled that the whole structure of prescription of tort claims in the Civil Code, in particular that the situation where some claims may be limited in time before the victim is even aware of the damage, violated constitutional values. The Tribunal suggested that the problem should not be solved by extending the period of limitation, but by identifying a proper moment of its commencement.

16 In the discussion of the functions of prescription one should also highlight the advantages of the institution of declaratory judgments, which can surmount evidentiary burdens as regards damage extended in time. A declaratory judgment enables the injured person to claim compensation for distant consequences of

---

13 Act of 29 November 2000, Dz. U. 2001, no 2 at 18 – art 105.

14 The Constitutional Tribunal in the judgment of 1 September 2006 (SK 14/05), OTK, A- 2006, no 8, item 97.

15 The judgment of 1 September 2006, SK 14/05. See *E Bagińska*, in: H Koziol and BC Steininger (eds), European Tort Law 2006 (2008), nos 83–90.

a tort and it facilitates the burden of proving all conditions of liability for those consequences. Therefore, an injured person has, in principle, legal standing to ask for a declaratory judgment if she pursues her interest simultaneously with a claim for actual damages.[16] The first mentioned purpose of declaratory judgments can also be fulfilled by the rules of extension of prescription period in personal injury cases but the second aim cannot. Assessing tort claims may turn out to be quite a complex task in terms of evidence if a substantial period of time has passed since the initial event, hence there may still exist a legal interest in obtaining a declaratory judgment.

## B. FOR

Public policy and legal certainty require that liability claims are raised and resolved within a reasonable time. Not only does the debtor have an interest in ensuring that the uncertainty as to the existence of an obligation was limited in time and that the ending of this uncertainty could be determined on the basis of clear, objective measures. Society is also interested in this stability and certainty of social relations, which is the primary purpose of the institution of claims prescription. The Supreme Court has opined that a fixed restriction, in the form of long-stop, best serves the stability function.[17] The public policy functions of the prescription, especially when reference to the certainty of law and societal interests is made, are also underlined by the majority of the Polish legal scholars.[18] The argument of the stabilisation of long-term factual situations was also raised as a rationale for shortening the general period of prescription of civil law claims from ten to six years in 2018; and similarly for claims established by final judgments and awards.[19] Shorter periods mean less evidentiary problems and theoretically better management of the justice system. 17

The law should not protect a person who has shown a lack of care in handling her affairs and neglecting her interest (a motivating and punishing function of prescription). The creditor's approach resulting in non-enforcement of claims seems to confirm that she tolerates the existing legal situation (ie that the debtor has not paid while objecting to the demand). Moreover, the debtor cannot be held in suspense indefinitely as to whether he will be made to perform. This is 18

16 SN of 24 February 2009, III CZP 2/09, OSNC 12/2009, item 168, reported in *E Bagińska*, in: H Koziol and BC Steininger (eds), European Tort Law 2009 (2010), nos 34–41.

17 SN Resolution of the Full Civil Chamber, 17 February 2006, III CZP 84/05, OSN 7–8/2006, item 114.

18 See *B Kordasiewicz*, in: Z Radwański (ed), System Prawa Prywatnego. Prawo cywilne – część ogólna, Vol 2 (2008), 578.

19 Articles 118 and 125 KC.

sometimes called the stabilisation function of prescription.[20] The protection of future financial reserves of the debtor is a legitimate interest pursued indirectly by the institution of prescription. This argument is also supported by the need to secure the insurance coverage of (civil liability) claims.

19 An important goal of prescription relates to the elimination of evidentiary problems and uncertainty of the result of the civil process after many years since the event triggering a legal obligation. It has been asserted that factual situations that persevere for a long time are usually compliant with the law or should be legalised. Thus, although expiration of claims with the lapse of time collides with justice, it is nevertheless indispensable in the system of law.[21]

20 Finally, in the light of modern court practice the constant expansion of civil liability based on the protection of personality rights calls for setting time limits to the pecuniary protection of such rights, in particular when the courts are willing to create new claims based on the protection of personality rights to circumvent the traditional inherent limitations of tort rules.[22] The application of the new interpretation of old rules to the closed, past factual situations raises serious concerns (*inter alia* additional costs, no insurance coverage).

## V. ELEMENTS OF PRESCRIPTION – AN OVERVIEW

21 There are four elements of prescription present in Polish law: (a) the starting point, (b) the prescription period, (c) the rules of prolongation: postponement, renewal and extension, and (d) the ceiling on the effective time of prescription.

22 As concerns the starting point, one should observe that the general rule of art 120 §1 KC, which stipulates that the period of limitation begins to run on the day the claim accrues, contains no definition of accrual. For tort claims this is, however, not so important, as the rules on tort claims prescription provide for their own starting points. Since 1933 the general rule has provided that a claim for redress of damage caused by a tort is subject to limitation on the expiration of three years from the day on which the injured person learned of the damage and of the person obliged to redress it. No rules on postponement or extension relating to long-tail personal injuries were in place until 2007, so the negative

---

20 See *T Pałdyna*, Przedawnienie w polskim prawie cywilnym (2012), 38 ff; *J Kuźmicka-Sulikowska*, Idea przedawnienia i jej realizacji w polskim kodeksie cywilnym (2015), chapter II, passim.

21 See *Kordasiewicz*, *supra* fn 18, 575 ff.

22 For example when a claim for bereavement for the next of kin was introduced in 2008, the Polish Supreme Court held that such a claim was possible with respect to earlier events (deaths) based on the violation of a right to family ties. See: *E Bagińska*, Poland: Developments in Personal Injury Law in Poland: Shaping the Compensatory Function of Tort Law, 8 J. Civ. L. Stud. [Journal of Civil Law Studies] (2015), 340 ff.

result for the victims could not be accepted in many cases. The revision in 2007 substantially modified the other element of prescription (see *infra*).[23] However, the Code was revised again by the Act on of 21 April 2017 with respect to the starting point.[24]

The present wording of art $442^1$ §1 reads: 23

'a claim for redress of damage caused by a tort shall be barred after a period of three years from the date on which the injured person learned *or should have learnt* about it and about the person obliged to redress it'.[25] 24

The words 'or should have learnt' have in fact incorporated the existing case law which implemented a more objective test of discovery. 25

The second starting point applies to a situation where damage resulted from a crime or offence. The period of prescription is 20 years and it begins on *the day when the crime or offence was committed*, regardless of when the victim learned about the damage and about the person obliged to redress it (art $442^1$ §2 KC). It should be emphasised that a civil court can decide about the criminal nature of the actor's conduct. 26

Generally, for pecuniary claims rooted in private law the period of limitation shall be six years, and for claims pertaining to periodical performances and claims resulting from an economic activity, three years. The rules are subject to statutory exceptions. Shorter and longer terms are provided in specific provisions in the Civil Code.[26] 27

In Polish tort law there are three 'prescription periods': three, ten and 20 years. 28

The basic three-year period (*a tempore scientiae*), mentioned above, stops running after ten years from the day of the tort (*a tempore facti*). The ten-year period must always be counted from the day of the tort (*a tempore facti*).[27] It is hence without doubt that ten-year period is a long-stop. 29

The 20-year period for claims arising from criminal conduct can be seen as a different starting point or as an 'absolute' time limit for claims specified therein. 30

---

23 They did not modify the interpretation of art $449^8$ KC – the special rule on prescription in the product liability regime which must be construed in conformity with Product Liability Directive 85/374/EEC.

24 Dz. U. 2017, no 113.

25 The wording of art $442^1$ §2 (prescription in criminal cases) and §3 (rule of extension) has not been changed accordingly.

26 They appear typically in nominate contracts and in general law on obligations (eg art 390 §3 KC on preliminary contracts), as well as in property law. Unjust enrichment claims are governed by the general rules of arts 117 ff. Hence, a restitution claim will be time-barred after ten years, unless it is linked with the economic activity of the plaintiff, in which case, the period of three years will apply.

27 SN of 17 February 1982, OSNC 1983 item 8.

It is not a long-stop in the meaning of this project, although part of Polish doctrine would consider it as an absolute period (repose).

31 A further point to note is that a claim confirmed by a final ruling of a judicial body as well as a claim confirmed by a settlement concluded before a mediator and confirmed by a court of law are subject to the prescription period of six years, although the period of prescription of such claims is shorter.[28] As regards periodic payments, the claim for periodic payments to be due in the future is subject to a three-year prescription.

32 The rules of prolongation are contained partly in the general provisions of claims prescription and partly in the tort prescription regime, where they were introduced only in 2007. Hence, the prescription period for tort claims may be suspended on the general grounds for suspension contained in art 121 KC or interrupted (renewed) – based on grounds listed in art 124 KC. Suspension extends a given period of prescription because the interval during which prescription is suspended is not counted towards the given period of prescription, or it postpones the start of the period. After interruption the period runs anew once the ground for interruption ceases.

33 Polish law follows German law in respect of the effects of postponement or suspension, and the situations of postponement have gained importance with the latest reform of prescription of tort claims.

34 Two new cases of extension were added in 2007:

1) prescription of a personal injury claim *may not end* before the lapse of three years from the day on which the injured person learned about the injury and about the person obliged to redress it (art $442^1$ §3 KC).
2) the claims of *minors* for redress of *personal injury* may not expire earlier than two years from the day when they reached maturity.

35 The relations between principles and exceptions are not entirely clear and lacking sufficient court practice, the present system of prescription of tort claims is considered at least as complicated.[29]

36 In 2018 a completely new rule was added to the general provision of art 118 KC setting two general periods of prescription (six and three years). The rule states that a prescription period longer than two years ends on the last day of a calendar year. Hence, the legislator introduced a new type of extension of the

[28] See art 125 KC.
[29] See *A Śmieja*, in: A Olejniczak (ed), System prawa prywatnego. Prawo zobowiązań – część ogólna, t. 6 (2nd ed, 2014), 699.

periods, but it remains unclear whether this general rule should be applied to tort claims (which are *legis specialis*). A functional interpretation speaks against such a possibility; otherwise the extension rules concerning personal injury claims would become partially meaningless.

There is a ceiling period (long-stop) of ten years applicable to torts of a non-criminal nature.[30] It was envisaged in the Code of Obligations of 1933 as a 20-year limit,[31] then was shortened in 1950 to ten years. Courts and doctrine criticised that the long-stop was too short and put at a disadvantage all victims who suffered long-tail personal injury. 37

Product liability claims 'prescribe upon ten years from putting the product into circulation.'[32] Hence, *prima facie* the long-stop period is not a clear extinctive prescription as stipulated by art 10(2) of Directive 375/85.[33] The Directive thus interferes with the classical understanding of the nature of claims prescription. Furthermore, although the mechanism of prescription in the Civil Code and the Directive is similar in the sense that the victim can interrupt the running of the prescription by taking a court action, the Civil Code is not in clear conformity with the Directive as it lists more causes of interruption of the running prescription period than just instituting proceedings against the producer.[34] 38

Another exception relates to nuclear damage. All claims for compensation of damage to property or to environment will extinguish after the passage of ten years since the nuclear accident.[35] 39

## VI. THE STARTING POINT OF THE PRESCRIPTION PERIOD

### A. THE MEANING OF 'ACTION' AND 'CAUSE OF ACTION'

If by a pecuniary claim subject to prescription one understands a right to the redress of damage arising from a tort, then the Polish approach to the notion 40

---

30 Literally: 'However, this term [ie of prescription] cannot be longer than ten years from the date on which the event which caused the damage occurred'.

31 Article 283 §3 and §4 Kodeks zobowiązań.

32 Article 449[8] sentence 2 CC.

33 Under the Directive the rights 'shall be extinguished upon the expiry of a period of 10 years from the date on which the producer put into circulation the actual product which caused the damage, unless the injured person has in the meantime instituted proceedings against the producer'.

34 Article 123 §1 KC.

35 Atomic Law – Act of 29 November 2000, Dz. U. 2018, item 792 consolidated text – art 105 §2.

of 'action in tort' should be seen as broad. The concept of unity of damage (necessarily consisting of different elements and of dynamic nature) speaks for a broader approach to the cause of action as well.[36]

41 In 2006 the Full Chamber of the Supreme Court[37] held that the notions 'an event bringing about the damage' (occurrence) and 'tort' (which includes all elements: the event, damage and causation – E.B.) are not identical. The day of the *event* marks the beginning of the limitation period even if damage – the last element of a tort[38] – has not yet occurred. There are more provisions in the Civil Code that determine a special date marking the starting point for prescription of claims; these rules take account of the nature and contents of a particular claim. According to the Court, before 2007 the general rule of three years' prescription of tort claims did not differentiate between kinds of damage. Therefore, no reference should be made to the notion of 'accrual of claims'.[39]

42 However, in the Polish system in cases of personal injury and death available claims are listed in the Civil Code. The question is whether each claim arising from those injuries can be subject to its own course of prescription. From this point of view one could come closer to the narrow approach to 'action'. In 2015 the Supreme Court held that art $442^1$ KC did not differentiate between the kinds of claims stemming from wrongful death of the injured and hence the prescription periods applied equally to all claims listed in the relevant rule.[40] This statement supports the conclusion that the subject of prescription is not *a particular* action *or particular* claim, but rather its source (cause).

43 Nevertheless, in most recent writings, A Śmieja has noticed that in the context of prescription a claim for redress of pecuniary damage should be seen as independent from a claim for non-pecuniary loss for two reasons. Firstly, because both kinds of losses can sometimes occur at different times; secondly, the losses have different characteristics and legal bases, in particular a claim for redress of non-pecuniary loss needs to be based on an explicit legal rule. The two arguments lead the author to the conclusion that if one event first triggered non-pecuniary loss and later caused pecuniary loss, then the beginning of the prescription period should be counted separately for each of the losses,

---

36 Whilst the victim has a choice of a form of remedy, damage can be redressed only once. The remedy can, however, combine restitution and monetary compensation, or claims provided in personal injury section in the chapter on torts (arts 444–449 KC).

37 III CZP 84/05, OSN 7–8/2006, item 114.

38 In addition, there is a distinction as regards reparation of pecuniary and non-pecuniary losses, even if they both resulted from the same tortious conduct.

39 Article 120 §1 KC.

40 See art 446 KC. See SN of 19 February 2015, III CSK 167/14.

regardless of the link between them.[41] No case law can be cited to support this general interpretative directive.

The concept of concurrence of liability regimes should also be mentioned. Polish courts have established that inflicting bodily injury upon a person always constitutes a tort. If it is caused by a failure to perform or an improper performance of an existing obligation, the victim may choose to base its action on either contract or tort. However, a court is only bound by the factual basis of the claim. Since a claim for non-pecuniary loss is available in the tort regime, a court should take into consideration *ex officio* the possibility of application of the tort regime to such a claim. The court must apply the whole set of rules of a given regime of liability to the claim based on this regime, including prescription rules.[42] In the context of concurrence of claims, the cause of action is thus considered narrowly. 44

## B. BROAD OR NARROW CONCEPTION OF 'CAUSE OF ACTION'?

The starting point of any debate is always the problem of accrual of claims, generally regulated in the civil code.[43] Until damage has occurred there is no claim for its compensation, hence logically one cannot speak of its accrual. However, this general rule is considered by some scholars[44] and after many years also by the Supreme Court (see *supra* 29) – as not applicable to tort claims. Hence, harm has become a part of the cause of action for prescription purposes. 45

The general tort claims prescription rule refers to the moment when two conditions have been met: the injured learned or should have learned about the damage and about the person liable to redress it. The first element of knowledge is explained as the moment when the injured person perceives the negative consequences of an event, the consequences of which indicate the fact of damage and when she has awareness of incurred damage.[45] The extent of the damaging consequences is not relevant in the context of prescription. As to the second element, it is sufficient to identify the person liable for damage so that she/he can be sued. The knowledge of such a person, objectively speaking, confirms 46

41 See *Śmieja, supra* fn 29, 707.

42 See *A Ohanowicz*, Zbieg norm w polskim prawie cywilnym (1963), 118; *M Nesterowicz*, Comment to SN 17 December 2004, II CK 300/04, OSP 2/2006, item 20, at 95.

43 Article 120 §1 KC

44 See *M Nesterowicz*, in: J Winiarz (ed), Kodeks cywilny z komentarzem, Vol I [The Civil Code with a commentary], Vol 1 (2nd ed, 1989), 439.

45 SN of 18 September 2002 III CKN 597/2000, unpublished.

sufficient probability that the person's conduct is causally connected with the alleged damage. It is stressed that the victim should be diligent in their own matters and try to find out reliable information about facts essential to the liability for her damage.[46]

47 The question of a broad or narrow cause of action in Polish law can be illustrated by cases of vicarious liability for a criminal act of an employee. Diverse interpretations are to be found in case law. The first approach recognises the application of a 20-year period to a legal person whose employee committed a criminal act. The goal is the protection of the victims. As long as the damage arises from an offence, it is irrelevant whether the claimant directs his claims against the perpetrator himself or (also) against other persons answerable in tort for that damage.[47] The source of the damage – a criminal act – is a decisive factor. Similarly, the same damaging event should not be evaluated differently for prescription purposes with regard to different persons who are jointly liable to repair the same damage.[48]

48 On some occasions the Supreme Court held to the contrary, ie *that different limitation periods may apply to the same claim* brought against *different* wrongdoers liable for the *same* damage.[49] In a case of the liability of a bank for a criminal act of its employee, the Court concluded that the occurrence of damage might be the result of several separate events (torts) imputable to several persons.[50] Concurrent tortfeasors need not act in the same manner; one may commit a criminal act and the other just a 'regular' tort. Hence, infliction of harm through a criminal act does not necessarily imply that the act created one and the same *tort* by various tortfeasors. A bank can be held liable for its own tort; the damage arising therefrom cannot be regarded as arising from a criminal offence. In consequence, a three-year prescription period applies. The 20-year period applies to a claim against a person vicariously liable for an offence of its servant. In vicarious liability *the sameness of the event triggering* liability of both the servant and its master permits and requires the application of the same prescription period to all claims for redress of the damage caused. In such a situation it may be said that the damage was the result of a criminal act in the meaning of the prescription rule.

---

46 SN of 10 April 2013, IV CSK 611/12.

47 See SN 29 October 1962, 2 CR 1064/61, OSNC 9/1963, item 211; SN 16 January 2008, IV CSK 380/07, OSNC-ZD, D/2008, item 102.

48 See *Nesterowicz*, *supra* fn 44, 440.

49 SN of 11 February 2003, V CKN 1664/00, OSNC 5/2004, item 75, approved by M Nesterowicz, Comment to the judgment, [2004] OSP 55, 237; SN 18 May 2004, IV CK 340/03, Biuletyn Prawa Karnego 1/2005.

50 SN of 19 November 2009, IV CSK 257/09, OSNC 5/2010, item 81, reported in *Bagińska*, *supra* fn 16, nos 66–75.

**Case 1** – *(Failure to ensure the wearing of a ski helmet)*: The ski accident is the occurrence, a tort, which in principle should be treated as one cause of action for all ensuing harms. Should injury Y be qualified by a court as a new, separate injury, the prescription would run independently for the new injury, although it is causally linked to the same tort. The Supreme Court speaks of a 'new injury' which has its own existence and its own beginning of the prescription period.[51] It does not matter whether Y is causally connected to X or rather causally independent of X, or which harm is much more severe. 49

**Case 2** – *(Three mistakes during one treatment)*: The case law and legal scholarship commands that the court should establish whether this is a situation of one tort as all harms originate in a negligent medical treatment by the same person on a single day. The sum of mistakes constitutes fault of the doctor. Personal injury is typically an indivisible harm, which can be dynamic. Harm Z could still be assessed as the enlargement of harm X and Y. Hence, a broad approach is more likely in the Polish system. 50

**Case 3** – *(Consecutive harms from one injury)*: If the action is filed after all the consequences have materialised a court will likely decide that all four harms belong to the same cause of action. Harm A occurs when the value has been reduced; harm B occurs when the foundation has subsided. Harm C appears with the occurrence of the cracks and the collapse is a new harm. All harms are attributed to the same cause. 51

## C. THE STARTING POINT – BREACH OF DUTY OR OCCURRENCE OF DAMAGE?

Polish law does not know torts *actionable per se.* 52

**Case 4** – *(Trespass case)*: In the Polish jurisdiction the starting point of P's claim for compensation for the loss caused is the date of discovery of the damage. The decisive factor is actual or constructive knowledge of the damage. 53

## D. WHAT IS CONSIDERED 'HARM' FOR PRESCRIPTION PURPOSES?

The meaning of 'harm' for prescription purposes is linked to the materialisation of harm. A mere creation of a yet unrealised risk is not considered as 'harm occurrence'. When primary harm occurs, then the claim for its redress will 54

51 SN of 24 November 1971, I CR 491/71, OSNC 1972, item 95. SN 21 May 2003, IV CKN 378/01 Orzecznictwo Sadow Polskich, (OSP) 4/2004, at 55.

embrace all actual and future (certain or highly probable or even foreseeable) effects.

55 The risk of claims being prescribed has always been a significant argument in favour of the inclusion of future losses in judicial awards concerning personal injuries, of which consequences may be unknown or have not yet materialised at the time of adjudication.[52] In particular, compensation for non-pecuniary loss should cover actual harm, the future harm which is certain to occur and the harm which can be foreseen at the moment of adjudication. In a case of a further decline in the victim's health no additional award is allowed unless there appears a new injury that could not have been foreseen based on the facts of the adjudicated case.[53]

56 Moreover, if at the time of adjudication the damage cannot be assessed precisely, then the court may, subject to the particular circumstances of a case, issue a declaratory judgment that would proclaim the defendant's liability for future damage.[54] Then, the limitation period for the new claims would begin to run on the day when the injured person learned of the new damage.[55] This solution has one flaw: it cannot be used whenever the *first* damage did not occur until after ten years since the tort. The late discovery rule does not preclude obtaining a declaratory judgment that the defendant is liable for any future damage originating from the same event (tort).

57 The Polish system deals with the risk of development of harmful consequences by employing the concept of annuity. An annuity is the most important method of redress of actual and foreseeable pecuniary losses stemming from personal injury.[56] Only the right to annuity is subject to prescription rules based on art $442^1$ KC. Any outstanding annuity is subject to prescription of three years as a periodical payment, calculated since the time of accrual of the rent.[57] Moreover, either party may ask the court to adjust the amount or duration of the annuity or to discontinue it completely if circumstances change (eg when the victim's earning capacity increases).[58] Hence, if the scope of pecuniary damage increases,

---

52 The Supreme Court issued a legal principle to this effect on 17 April 1970, III PZP 34/69, OSNICP 1970, no 12, item 217. *E Baginska and M Tulibacka*, Tort law. Poland (2011), no 298.

53 SN (Panel of 7 judges) of 27 November 1967, III PZP 37/67, OSN 7/1968, item 113.

54 SN of 7 August 1969, OSN 1970, item 217, SN 17 February 1972, OSN 1972, item 149.

55 SN of 17 February 1972, OSN 1972, 149.

56 If a victim loses his ability to work completely or partially, or if his needs have increased (eg permanent expenses for treatment or care and assistance by third persons), or his future prospects have diminished (eg inability to carry out a profession), he may demand an appropriate annuity from the person obliged to redress the damage (art 444 §2 KC).

57 Under art 118 KC. See SN (panel of 7 judges) 19 November 1965 III PO 32/64 OSNC 1966, no 6, item 9; SN 7 January 2011 I PK 142/10, OSNP 2012 nos 5–6, item 61.

58 Based on art 907 KC.

the starting point of prescription is dependent on the time of the occurrence of the new elements of the damage. This way the legislator has solved the problem of seeking compensation for losses causally linked to the same tort, but which have been discovered later or come into being over an extended period of time, in particular after the lapse of three years since the injured learned about the damage and the person liable.

**Case 5** – *(Developing ear damage)*: The Polish approach could be described as hybrid. If P discovered the first signs of harm and sued, then the starting point would have been the moment when both discovery of damage and the knowledge of the person liable existed. If P sued after he had become deaf, then a Polish court would use 'the stabilisation approach', and the starting point would be the day a reliable information on the deafness and the person liable for it was acquired. The causal link between the negligence of the employer and the deafness must be adequate. 58

**Case 6** – *(Defective foundations of bridge)*: In Poland the actual materialisation of material harm will determine the first necessary element of the starting point. The risk of collapse can be remedied by the rule on prevention of imminent damage.[59] 59

## E. THE STARTING POINT (ACCRUAL) IN CONTINUOUS TORTS

There is no definition of continuous tort in Poland. A continuous activity usually presupposes that its result is one harm. The long-established jurisprudence states that in continuous activity cases the starting point of prescription is marked by the moment the activity ceases.[60] It thus suggests the approach of a single cause with one starting point. However, the Supreme Court has recently explained that the last day of the continuous conduct is only relevant for the beginning of the long-stop of ten years, calculated from the event triggering the damage, and 60

[59] The rule of art 439 KC stipulated that a person who is directly exposed to the risk of damage resulting from the behaviour of another person, in particular due to lack of proper supervision [...] of the condition of a building or any other installation possessed by him, may demand that that person undertake any measures necessary to avert the immediate danger, and, if necessary, also to give adequate security (eg to place a sum of money in the court deposit). The claim of the person who is endangered is dependent on the proof of concrete danger (eg a disintegrated house on the edge of collapse). Article 439 KC has rarely been used in the court practice.

[60] The Supreme Court issued a legal principle to this effect on 12 February 1969, III PZP 43/68, OSNCP 1969, no 9, item 150; see also SN of 29 November 1996, II PZP 3/96, OSNCP 1997, no 14, item, 269, SN of 10 November 2006, I CSK 222/06, SN of 9 August 2012, V CSK 153/11. See *Nesterowicz*, *supra* fn 44, 440.

not for the general period of three years calculated from the moment when the plaintiff learned or should have learned about the damage.[61]

61 Other views can also be found. In a case regarding the violations of personal rights, filed by an inmate who challenged the conditions in the cell, the Court of Appeal in Warsaw held in the context of prescription that the plaintiff knew about the moral injury and about the person responsible for it at the moment of its existence, ie 'every day of being imprisoned in the conditions which allegedly violate his personal interests'.[62] The plaintiff failed in its argument that he did not know about the illegality of the infringement of his rights, about the grounds for liability of the State and about types of available claims.[63] Thus, this decision reflects the concept of recurrence. However, the cited case may not be regarded as representative for the Polish jurisdiction, and special circumstances lie at its basis (liability of the State, inmates' claims are often considered as 'bad' claims).

62 **Case 7** – *(Continuing defamation)*: In Poland the first situation would likely be considered a series of separate torts, unless the plaintiff was able to establish the continued, same intent to do harm. The second scenario could be treated easier as a continuous tort due to the frequency and similarity of wrongful conduct. The degree of *resemblance* between the successive defamatory acts is a matter for the court to determine. What matters is that defamation is carried out by the same tortfeasor, and less important is whether the same or different newspapers have been used.

63 **Case 8** – *(Noise from the neighbour)*: The employer's negligence which has lasted for three years is a classic example of a continuous tort (a forward condensed single cause). The start of prescription would be the end of exposure; a court is likely to favour P in this respect.

64 **Case 9** – *(Toxic bins)*: A Polish court will likely admit a single tort (digging bins of toxic content into the soil). Regardless of whether the plaintiff discovers the damage and the person liable before or after the bins are removed, the moment will be considered as the moment of accrual for all claims.

## F. IS THE LATE DISCOVERY RULE A RULE OF THE STARTING POINT OR A RULE OF PROLONGATION?

65 In Poland one can say that a discovery rule is the starting point and a rule of extension, because in the absence of the required discovery, the running of the

[61] SN in the judgment of 8 May 2014, V CSK 370/13, unpublished.

[62] Court of Appeals in Warsaw of 16 October 2015, I ACa 148/15, unpublished.

[63] Similarly, Court of Appeals in Łodź of 5 December 2018, I Aca 169/18.

three-year prescription period may not end. This extension applies to personal injury claims only.[64] There are serious doctrinal doubts regarding the relation between the rule of prolongation, two prescription periods, and the ceiling of ten years. It appears that in the absence of the required discovery the running of the prescription period is delayed by a rule of prolongation that suspends its ending. Hence, the long-stop period of ten years and the period of prescription of 20 years (*a tempore facti*) are inoperative in personal injury cases. Z Radwański explains that both 'ceilings' (ten and 20 years) must be disregarded when the claim concerns personal injury.[65] Claims stemming from personal injury will *always* be subject to the prescription of three years since the moment of the required discovery. The ceilings are thus always prolonged or, as Radwański put it, 'there is no long stop period for personal injury claims' in Polish law'.[66] On the other hand, Śmieja comes to almost the same conclusion though with a different justification. He underlines that the 20-year period is generally subject to prolongation under arts 121–123 KC, but the rule of art 442 §3 is not really a prolongation but *a separate rule of prescription of all personal injury claims*. The claims will always prescribe after three years *a tempore scientiae*, even if the injured learned about the damage and the liable person after the ten- or the 20-year period has run. This means that the longer prescription period and the long-stop only apply to damage to property. Hence, the basic discovery rule of art 442[1] §1 KC has in fact lost its feature of generality.

A different interpretation prevailed in earlier case law. The ten-year period was initially considered as a true ceiling, which could not be prolonged for any reasons,[67] and applied equally to future losses and to losses the victim was unaware of. This approach was eventually confirmed by case law.[68] The Supreme Court reacted to the opposite line of case law,[69] which – under the 66

[64] Please, note that art 442[1] §3 KC was not modified in 2017 to incorporate the objective yardstick 'or should have known'. It is unclear whether this was intended.

[65] *Z Radwański*, Przedawnienie roszczeń z czynów niedozwolonych w świetle znowelizowanego art 442 k.c., MoP 2007, nr 11, 594.

[66] See *Z Radwański and A Olejniczak*, Prawo Zobowiązań – część ogolna (2014), 287–288, many other writers agreed: *M Pyziak-Szafnicka*, Commentary (2009), 1061, *M Balwicka-Szczyrba*, W sprawie zasad przedawnienia roszczeń o naprawienie szkody na mieniu w oparciu o art 4421 §1 k.c., Wiadomosci Ubezpieczeniowe 3/2015, 86, *Śmieja*, *supra* fn 29, 701, *A Józefiak*, Przedawnienie roszczen deliktowych w świetle art 442[1] k.c., Przeglad Sądowy 4/2008, 76.

[67] See also *MK Chmielewska*, Przedawnienie roszczen deliktowych o naprawienie tzw. szkody przyszlej, Rejent 3/2006, 120–137, *R Klimek*, Dyskusyjne problemy przedawnienia roszczen, Kwartalnik Prawa Prywatnego (KPP) 3/2006, 633–667.

[68] The Full Civil Chamber of the Supreme Court in the judgment of 17 February 2006, III CZP 84/05, OSN 7–8/2006, item 114, Resolution of the Full Civil Chamber of SN was the response to the preliminary question asked by the Civic Rights Ombudsman.

[69] See SN judgment of 21 May 2003, Supported by T Dybowski and M Nesterowicz in comments to this judgment, in: Przeglad Sadowy 6/2005, 132, OSP 4/2004, 257 respectively, see also

general rule of accrual – required the occurrence of damage as a starting point. The reported judgment from 2006 preceded the mentioned ruling of the Constitutional Tribunal, and eventually led to the legislative change in 2007. The Tribunal suggested that the prescription of pecuniary claims should rather be coupled with the moment when the claim has already arisen and could actually be settled.

67 Effectively, a period of three years from the required discovery is always applicable for personal injury claims.[70] Nevertheless, the Supreme Court still seems to maintain its position even after 2007.[71]

## VII. PRESCRIPTION PERIODS

68 Polish law does not recognise different periods for different tort claims (remedies) or different kinds of damage.[72] The major differentiation has always related to criminal or non-criminal type of a tort.

69 Presently, the 20-year period is the sole longest period of prescription in Polish civil law. In the context of burden of proof it means that it suffices to prove that the criminal act was committed, which led to the damage. However, personal injury cases are subject to the late discovery rule (see *supra* Section VI).

70 The existence of two general periods, three and 20 years, promotes a secondary goal of tort law – deterrence. A functional interpretation of the 20-year rule prevails in case law, which underlies its protective purpose.[73] Most importantly, a civil court decides by itself about the criminal nature of the actor's conduct, given that no criminal verdict was rendered. This functional approach has had a great impact on compensation claims against the Insurance Guarantee

*Z Policzkiewicz-Zawadzka*, Powstanie szkody a bieg 10-letniego terminu przedawnienia z art 442 k.c., Nowe Prawo (1966), nos 7–8; *MS Tofel*, Comment to the Resolution 17 February 2006, III CZP 84/05, Przeglad Sadowy 11–12/2006, 227.

70 See *A Olejniczak*, in: A Kidyba (gen ed), Z Gawlik, A Janiak, G Kozieł, A Olejniczak, A Pyrzyńska, T Sokołowski, Komentarz Kodeks cywilny. Komentarz, t. III, Zobowiązania – część ogólna (2010), 468, who seems to consider it as a special rule rather than an extension of a long period.

71 In a judgment of SN of 19 February 2015, III CSK 167/14, the Court held that the right to annuity prescribes at the latest 20 years since a criminal offence.

72 However, in the Geological and Mining Law of 9 June 2011 (Cons. text Dz. U. 2016, item 1131), claims to redress damage governed by the law prescribed after the lapse of five years since the injured person learnt of the damage.

73 Thus, a juvenile punishable act, for which minor offenders are held responsible in special, juvenile proceedings, is included in the scope of the rule. See SN 18 January 2012, I CSK 157/11, OSNC ZD B/2013, item 30, reported in *E Bagińska and I Adrych-Brzezinska*, in: K Oliphant and BC Steininger (eds), European Tort Law 2012 (2013), nos 37–47.

Fund (hereinafter IGF) in one category of traffic accidents cases. Where the circumstances of a traffic accident clearly show that it was a criminal offence (eg a person has been killed in the accident), but the owner or driver of a motor vehicle was not identified, then the Fund will be liable to pay compensation when the accident would have led to civil liability of the owner or driver had their identity been established.[74] IGF is not a perpetrator, hence the key problem relates to which prescription period should apply to its guarantee-type liability. The Supreme Court has decided[75] that an offence being the source of damage needs to be established in compliance with the rules of criminal law (an objective and subjective element of the offence). If an objective element of an offence is established before a civil court, the court may find, by using objective criteria, that the unidentified person was at fault and committed an offence. Consequently, compensatory claims against the IGF will be time-barred upon the lapse of 20 years from the commencement of an offence. In 2018 the Supreme Court confirmed that a 20-year prescription period should also apply to a person who is strictly liable for a traffic accident, albeit in the circumstances set out in art 31 §1 of the Penal Code, which constitutes a basis for the discontinuation of criminal proceedings for the reason that, under the law, the tortfeasor did not commit the offence (mainly due to mental incapacity). It was emphasised that a longer prescription period does not aim to penalise the tortfeasor, but rather to protect the victim.[76]

The 20-year period also allows an injured party to forestall the negative consequences of the lapse of the three-year limitation period when the victim has become permanently disabled or when she is ignorant of available remedies (the existence of the special Fund and its duty to pay for losses caused by unidentified tortfeasors). Moreover, all injured parties should have a fair chance to bring their claims in the 20-year limitation period. The argument refers to equal treatment of all victims of traffic accidents, whether caused by identified or unidentified vehicles (owners). 71

---

74 In Poland, the IFG is a legal person obliged to compensate for personal injury and property damage in the case of a traffic accident when the identity of the possessor of the motor vehicle or of the driver has not been identified. Article 109a of the Compulsory Insurance Act prescribes that the general rules on limitation periods in torts in the Civil Code (art 442[1] KC) apply. Articles 98 (1) 1 and 2 of the Act on Compulsory Insurance, the Insurance Guarantee Fund and the Polish Motor Insurers' Bureau (Compulsory Insurance Act) of 22 May 2003, Dz U 2003, no 124, item 1152.

75 In the judgment of 29 October 2013, III CZP 50/13, OSN IC 4/2014, item 35, reported in *E Bagińska and K Krupa-Lipinska*, in: E Karner and BC Steininger (eds), European Tort Law 2013 (2014), nos 58–64.

76 SN (panel of 7 judges) of 25 May 2018, III CZP 116/17, OSNC 2018/12, item 112 and III CZP 108/17, OSNC 2018/12, item 111.

72 As mentioned above, concurrence of torts and contractual claims is permitted and most of the prescription periods for contracts are shorter than for torts. This is the reason for 'period shopping' in the Polish practice. Courts have played a primary role in 'dressing' contractual breaches for torts especially in order to award compensation of non-pecuniary loss.[77]

73 **Table 1. Actual prescription periods in tort claims**

| Cause of action or tort | Discovery rule | Prescription period | Notes |
|---|---|---|---|
| Bodily injury | Yes | 3 | |
| Property damage | Yes | 3 | |
| Defamation | Yes | 3 | |
| Intentional torts | No | 20/3 | Only if criminal/if non-criminal |
| Contractual claims | Yes | 10 or 3 | Accrual rule |

# VIII. RULES OF POSTPONEMENT, SUSPENSION, RENEWAL AND EXTENSION

## A. UNAWARENESS – THE LATE DISCOVERY RULE

### *1) Unawareness of what Elements of Liability?*

74 The Polish prescription rule indicates two elements of awareness: D's identity and effects of conduct (harm). It is obvious that all elements of an action in tort must be present. The two elements of awareness are indicated for the calculation of prescription starting point and for the late discovery rule.

75 According to established case law relating to the element of discovery as a starting point the first moment when the injured 'learns about the damage' is the moment she perceives the negative consequences of an event indicative of damage *and* becomes aware of the *occurrence* of damage.[78] For example, in a hospital infection case the starting point is the day on which the patient was informed about the consequences of the infection, and not on the day when he/she was informed about the infection itself. The extent of the damaging consequences is irrelevant for the determination of the starting point. In light

[77] SN of 19 November 2009, IV CSK 257/09, OSP 7–8/2010, item 79 = OSNC 5/2010, item 81.
[78] SN of 18 September 2002 III CKN 597/2000, SN of 21 December 2011, IV CSK 46/11, SN of 24 June 2015, II CSK 544/14, OSNC no 6, item 76.

of the above one may speak of a judicial postponement of the beginning of the period via interpretation of the notion 'learnt or should have learnt about the damage'.

The second important factor is the awareness of the liable person. It is sufficient to identify D in the way that she/he can be sued. Actual or constructive knowledge of the person to whom the damage could be attributed is naturally not only linked with D's identity, but also with a causal relation. 76

**Case 10** – *(Lung disease I)*: – The knowledge of the legal situation is not taken into account by a court in Poland. Neither is the unawareness of remedies considered a justification for postponement (see however an exception *supra* 63). 77

*2) Objective or Subjective Unawareness?*

In doctrine it has been emphasised that the awareness should be established *ad casum*, hence subjectively,[79] but there are also supporters of more objectivised assessment.[80] The case law has leaned towards the objective evaluation.[81] The legislative modification of the starting point rule of 2017 employs the objective yardstick – 'knew or should have known' for all non-personal injury claims – which works in favour of the defendant. 78

*3) What is Considered Awareness of an Element of Liability?*

The scope of the late discovery rule is limited to personal injury originating in a tort. 79

There must be sufficient probability, objectively speaking, that the person's conduct is causally connected with the alleged damage, but eventually it will be established by a court according to the standard of proof. 80

*4) How Heavy is the Burden to Acquire Knowledge?*

The information about P's harm must come from competent and reliable sources.[82] Moreover, P should be diligent in their own matters and try *to find out* reliable information about facts essential to the liability for her damage.[83] 81

---

79 *M Nesterowicz*, Comment to SN judgment of 12 May 2011, III CSK 236/10 OSP 2012, no 11, item 107.

80 *Śmieja*, *supra* fn 29, sec 706.

81 SN of 6 October 2017, V CSK 36/17.

82 SN of 18 September 2002, III CKN 597/00, unpublished, SN of 12 May 2011, III CSK 236/10 OSP 2012, no 11, item 107 with comment by M Nesterowicz.

83 SN of 10 April 2013, IV CSK 611/12.

Miscomprehension of properly given information does not influence the running of a prescription period.

82 **Case 11** – *(Lung disease II)*: – In Poland, it is the probability not the certainty of causation that is sufficient to establish that P was able to sue a given D.[84] There is no clear-cut rule on the need to seek second opinion. The information must come from competent and reliable sources.

83 It is a rule of extension, because in the absence of the required discovery, the running of the prescription period cannot end (the ending is suspended).

## B. OTHER RULES OF PROLONGATION

### 1) *D is to Blame for the Delay*

84 The blame for the delay can be recognised as the ground for application of abuse of rights against the defence of prescription (art 5 KC). The judicial technique is the *rejection of the plea of prescription.*

### 2) *Admission by D of P's Right or Partial Performance of P's Right by D*

85 Recognition of a claim by the person against whom the claim is made (such as eg confirmation of invoice or a request for extension of time for payment) will normally interrupt prescription.

### 3) *Special Relations between D and P*

85a **Table 2. Special relations between D and P**

| Relations | Rule of prolongation | Comments |
|---|---|---|
| Parents/children | Postponement/suspension | Children against parents |
| Spouses | Postponement/suspension | |
| Guardian/ward | Postponement/suspension | Extension if no representative appointed |
| Attorney/client | No | |
| Partners in partnership | No | |

*(continued)*

84 SN of 10 October 2012, III BP 4/11, OSNAPiUS 2013, nos 15–16, item 181 (damage to hearing over years of work).

Table 2 *continued*

| **Relations** | **Rule of prolongation** | **Comments** |
|---|---|---|
| Legal entity/organs | No | |
| Employer/employee | No | |
| Physician/patient | No | |

### 4) *P's Lack of Legal Capacity*

**Table 3. P's lack of legal capacity** 85b

| **Kind of disability** | **With representative** | **Without representative** | **Kind of prolongation** | **Comments** |
|---|---|---|---|---|
| Minority | Yes | | Extension – 2 yrs | Only in cases of personal injury |
| Minority | No | Yes | Extension 2 yrs | |
| Adult with mental disability | No | Yes | Extension 2 yrs | |

### 5) *Absence of Parties from the Jurisdiction*

No special rules exist. 86

### 6) *Former Legal and Other Proceedings between the Parties*

**Table 4. Former legal and other proceedings between the parties** 86a

| **Former proceedings** | **Prolongation** | **Rule** | **Comments** |
|---|---|---|---|
| Before a court | Yes | Renewal | |
| ADR | Yes/renewal | Renewal | As to mediation – only if mandatory |
| Arbitration | Yes | Renewal | |
| Negotiations | No | | |

### 7) *Victim's Death*

No special rules exist. 87

### 8) *Tortfeasor's Bankruptcy*

No special rules exist. 88

### 9) Force Majeure

88a **Table 5.** ***Force majeure***

| Contingency | Prolongation | Kind | Comments |
|---|---|---|---|
| General clause of *force majeure* | Yes | Suspension | Interpreted broadly, includes socialist political regime when the State could not be sued |
| Wars | Yes | Suspension | Included in *force majeure* |
| Closed court | Yes | Suspension | If due of *force majeure* |
| Natural disaster | Yes | Suspension | Included in *force majeure* |
| Legal inability to file a claim | Yes | Extension | |
| Military service | No | | |
| Imprisonment | No | | |

## IX. CEILINGS ON THE EFFECTIVE TIME OF PRESCRIPTION

89 Rules on long-stop effectively apply to all non-personal injury claims based on torts (see *supra* 65).

90 Although the discovery rule as a general starting point is quite flexible, the day of an event triggering damage is the objective moment that best serves as a starting day of the ten-year period (long-stop).[85] The ten-year period concerns torts of a non-criminal nature. The 20-year period applies to criminal acts.

91 **Table 6. Rules on effective time of prescription**

| Scope | Commencement | Length | Prolongation | Comments |
|---|---|---|---|---|
| Product liability | D's conduct – marketing | 10 | No | Extinctive prescription |
| Bodily injury | D's tortious conduct | No long-stop | Yes | |
| Medical malpractice | Treatment | As above | Yes | |

[85] SN – Full Civil Chamber, 17 February 2006, III CZP 84/05, OSN 7–8/2006, item 114.

# X. STATUTE INTERPRETATION, JUDICIAL DISCRETION AND LACHES

In Polish jurisprudence prescription rules are considered strict and neutral. Judges are not hostile to prescription. Nevertheless, their approach can differ between cases of damaged property and personal injury. Polish courts have invented different techniques of interpretation of the long-stop and the general rule on accrual to assist the victim.[86] The Constitutional Tribunal was even more sympathetic towards the injured and less sympathetic to the idea of prescription of personal injury claims than the Supreme Court.[87] The Tribunal ruled that even though the Constitution did not regulate the limitation of claims, the latter institution might have some impact on the protection of subjective rights, including the constitutional subjective rights. 92

In general, strict prescription rules should be interpreted strictly. However, courts have accepted a broad interpretation of '*force majeure*', which effectively led to a judicial postponement of the prescription period and permitted the adjudication of claims.[88] 93

Courts clearly see it as unethical to reject the claim of a minor, who was seriously injured, on the basis of rules of the prescription. In such cases the courts often overruled the plea of limitation of action on the ground of art 5 KC. 94

Until recently, judicial discretion has not been explicit in the context of prescription, mainly because the rules on prescription have always been considered as *iuris cogentis*. In 2018 the general rules on prescription were changed with a view to enhance the protection of consumers. The effects of prescription of claims against consumers will happen automatically, and this strict rule has been mitigated by the new competence of a court not to take the prescription into account when interests of the parties and considerations of justice so require. Listed are the following factors to be considered by the court: (1) the length of the prescription period, (2) the length of the delay in filing the action, (3) the nature of events which caused the failure to enforce the claim, including the impact of the debtor's conduct on the running of the prescription period.[89] 95

Except for the new instance reported above, Polish prescription law does not use general, open terms such as 'reasonableness' or 'good faith' in the context 96

---

86 See SN of 21 May 2003, IV CKN 378/01, OSP 4/2004, item 55, with a note by M Nesterowicz, at 237, reported in ETL 2004, nos 12–18.

87 III CZP 84/05, OSN 7–8/2006, item 114.

88 SN of 29 November 2001, V CKN 1725/88.

89 See new art $117^1$ KC (2018).

of prescription. However, a Polish court uses implicit discretion through the institution of the abuse of rights in order to reject the prescription defence in most private law cases, and in particular in tort law cases.[90] The application of art 5 KC to personal injury cases has been recognised in case law dealing with work accidents[91] and in medical accidents, in order to overcome the problems of long-tail injuries (hospital infection of minor patients, birth-related injuries).[92]

97 Abuse of right may be pleaded in the context of prescription even though the debtor's conduct had no impact on the running of the prescription time. The courts have often overruled the plea of limitation of action on the grounds that the plaintiff should not bear the consequences of being infected with an unknown and incurable virus[93] or when the defendant maintained for years that there was no causation between its maltreatment and the plaintiff's harm.[94] Current practice also takes into account circumstances in the victim's sphere, eg miscomprehension of information, erroneous assessment of health condition,[95] a serious disability that would not have happened if not for the culpable conduct.

98 However, the plea of the abuse of rights can be denied when the main goals of prescription would have been ignored. For example, when the delay is not very long and the evidential uncertainty is of the degree that it does not create greater risk of failure to prove the prerequisites of the defendant's liability and hence of a judgment being issued to the detriment of the plaintiff.[96] For example, the parents' delay in filing the lawsuit and seeking damages may not have a negative influence on the rights of the minor to compensation.[97]

99 Courts are not authorised to reject a claim on the ground of laches or of a similar doctrine.

---

90 By virtue of art 5 KC, the use of one's right may be denied legal protection because of the consideration about the principles of community life (which can be called here 'principles of justice').

91 SN of 11 September 1997, UKN II/1997, 250, OSNAP 13/1998, 406.

92 In earlier case law, for the application of art 5 the courts required proof of a reprehensible conduct of the doctors or of the vicariously liable persons, such as, eg persuading a patient that there would be no adverse effects of the treatment, concealing information on the actual causes and scope of the damage, denying access to medical records, etc. See RC in Wroclaw 20 September 1999 IC 708/96, aff'd CA 1 June 2000 I A Ca 323/00, Prawo I Medycyna 9/2001, 115, reported in Yearbook 2001, no 8.

93 SN of 16 November 2005, V CK 349/05, Prawo i Medycyna 1/2007, 133.

94 RC in Wroclaw of 20 September 1999 IC 708/96, affd CA 1 June 2000 I A Ca 323/00, [2001] Prawo i Medycyna 9, 115, reported in ETL 2001, nos 46–51.

95 SN of 10 April 2013, IV CSK 611/12.

96 See SN of 8 May 2014, V CSK 370/13, the case did not concern personal injury, but geological damage to the ground under the house due to the operation of a mine.

97 SN of 16 November 2005, V CK 349/05, Prawo i Medycyna 1/2007, 133.

# XI. CHANGE OF PARTIES

## A. THE PLAINTIFF IS A TRANSFEREE OF THE VICTIM'S CLAIM

If the victim's claim is transferred to others, it does not cause a new prescription period to start because the claim is transferred in the same shape, as it existed before the transfer.[98] Heirs step into the shoes of the victim with regard to the running on the prescription period. However, limitations as to the inheritance of claims should accounted for.[99] 100

No rule of prolongation applies. Also, in the context of inheritance, the prescription continues to run and the unawareness of the claim by an heir is not considered to be a reason for prolongation. 101

In property insurance (first-party and third-party insurance) subrogation claims of the insurer[100] are subject of prescription defence by the debtor under the same conditions and the same lapse of time is required, as for the original claim. The right of subrogation does not change the running of the period.[101] This holds true also for insurers' recourse in civil liability insurance when the insurer seeks contribution from a co-tortfeasor (not covered by the insurance). 102

## B. THE DEFENDANT IS A TRANSFEREE OF THE TORTFEASOR'S OBLIGATION

If the tortfeasor's liability is transferred to others, it does not influence the period of prescription.[102] It is the claim and not liability that is subject to prescription. 103

However, as regards civil liability insurers, *actio directa* prescribes in the same way as the claim for compensation (art 819 §3 KC). 104

98 See *M Pyziak-Szafnicka*, Commentary, 1049, SN of 17 July 2003, III CZP 43/03, OSNC 2004, no 10, item 15, *B Kordasiewicz*, in: System Prawa Prywatnego (2008), 669.

99 Under art 922 KC the inheritance shall not involve the rights and obligations of the deceased which are closely connected with him as well as the rights which, upon his death, devolve onto designated persons regardless of whether they are his heirs. According to §3, the estate debts shall also involve the expenses of the decedent's funeral to the extent that the customs accepted within a given environment so require.

100 Under art 828 KC §1. Unless it has been agreed otherwise, the claim of the insuring party against a third party liable for the damage shall pass to the insurer by operation of law, up to the amount of damages paid out on the damages' payment day. If the insurer has covered only a part of the damage, the insuring party shall be entitled to priority in satisfaction as to the remaining part of it before the insurer's claim.

101 See SN of 31 May 1985, III CRN, 148/85, OSN No 3 (1986), item 34.

102 See *Kordasiewicz, supra* fn 98, 669.

## C. CONTRIBUTION CLAIMS

105 Polish law does not provide for any special rules concerning the limitation (prescription) of contribution claims. A contribution claim is independent and is not considered to be based on the tort which was the source of the joint and several obligation. Thus, the general rules on prescription apply. The prescription period begins to run on the day when a co-debtor who seeks contribution repaired the damage (paid compensation or restored the property to the previous condition).[103]

106 Special recourse claims of the compulsory traffic liability insurer[104] towards the tortfeasor (driver), hence the insured, are the subject of prescription defence by the debtor based on the general provision on prescription (art 118). The insurer's 'atypical' recourse is considered as an autonomous claim.

107 Recourse towards a vehicle owner or driver by the IGF in traffic liability cases is a controversial issue. The victim's claim towards the Fund will be time-barred based on tort rules, but the recourse claim of the Fund who paid compensation is based on statute and is said to prescribe either under the general provision on prescription (art 118 – three years),[105] but not sooner than three years from payment by the IFG,[106] or on the same tort provisions as the original claim.[107] According to the latter view it is a case of subrogation, which does not change the running of the period.[108]

## D. DEPENDANT'S CLAIM

108 The claims of dependants that arise after death of the directly injured are independent, *sui generis* and they follow their own prescription course.

109 The limitation period for claims of victims par ricochet starts on the day on which those persons learned about the loss of the deceased to whom they were related (art 446 §2 KC) or about a considerable worsening of their material situation (art 446 §3 KC) and about the person liable.[109]

110 If V's death comes later than his injury and there is a possibility that his claims were inherited (art 445 §3 KC) the dependants will be entitled both to their

[103] SN of 16 September 1997, PKN 261/97.
[104] Based on art 43 of the Compulsory Insurance Act.
[105] See SN of 6 November 2013, IV CSK 120/13 OSN No 3 (1986), item 34.
[106] See art 110.4 of the Compulsory Insurance Act.
[107] See *Z Gawlik and A Kidyba* (eds), Commentary to the civil code Vol III (2010), 909.
[108] See SN of 31 May 1985, III CRN, 148/85, OSN 3/1986, item 34.
[109] See *M Nesterowicz*, in: J Winiarz (ed), Kodeks cywilny z komentarzem (1989), 440.

own claims and to the inherited claims of V. Only the latter claims will be transferred in the same shape as they were on the day V died, including the relevant reduction of the prescription period.

The beginning of the period of prescription is marked by the knowledge of the injury, which is typically simultaneous with V's death, but does not have to be. 111

# XII. OTHER ASPECTS OF PRESCRIPTION LAW

## A. STIPULATION

The parties may not shorten or lengthen statutory periods of prescription. Neither can they manipulate the beginning of the period of prescription. Some commentators agree, however, that there is a possibility to move the point of the running of the prescription by determining the accrual of a claim arising from a contract. For example, contractual parties can agree that the performance will be effectuated at a certain point in time after the creditor has called on the debtor to perform. 112

The person against whom a claim is to be pursued may avoid the duty to satisfy it unless he waives his right to use the defence of limitation. However, waiving the defence of limitation before the lapse of the period of limitation is invalid. Waiver after the lapse of time is fully effective. As a legal act the waiver cannot be withheld, so the defence cannot be raised in court after the waiver, regardless of whether it was done outside the court or during the proceedings. The waiver is valid after the claim has already prescribed, so the defence is ineffective anyway. 113

## B. MEANING OF 'FILING A CLAIM' THAT INTERRUPTS THE RUNNING OF PRESCRIPTION

The following procedural acts by P stop the running of prescription: 114

- filing an action for enforcement of the claim or an action for a declaratory judgment or for security measures before a court or other authority appointed to hear cases or enforce claims of a given type or before an arbitration tribunal – provided that the action is taken *directly* to either assert or establish, or satisfy or secure a claim; 115
- initiation of mediation.[110] 116

[110] Article 123 KC.

117 Giving notice or demand does not interrupt the running of the prescription. However, the recognition of a claim by the debtor does.[111]

## C. WHEN SHOULD THE DEFENCE BE RAISED AND DECIDED?

118 The defence should be pleaded at the beginning of the proceedings. It can be pleaded later unless one has a case before a commercial court, where restrictions in the production of evidence and pleadings are in place, or on special short procedure, where forms are used in which the defendant has to raise all defences. It can also be pleaded in the appeal or at the second instance proceeding, provided the defence is based on the facts alleged in the first instance.[112] It cannot be pleaded in the cassation to the Supreme Court.

119 The Court decides a prescription issue when it rules on the case. It is not a preliminary issue, which needs a preliminary decision. In fact, it is decided with the other pleadings, as the case may be that the plaintiff counter pleads abuse of right against the plea of prescription.

## D. WHO MAY RAISE THE DEFENCE?

120 In Polish law prescription is a defence that has to be pleaded by D and the Court cannot raise it on its own. However, there was a time in Polish law that the Court could raise prescription *ex officio*. In 2018 the old scheme was reintroduced for consumer claims.

121 The defence of prescription is a subjective right, which 'belongs' to a person who is obliged to perform. Hence, a third party cannot raise it.[113] If D paid P after the prescription, but had a possibility to raise the defence, this will be

111 See art 123 p 2 KC.

112 SN of 19 July 2001 II UKN 475/00, OSNP, no 8, item 210, *M Pyziak-Szafnicka*, Commentary (2009), 1029. *T Erecinski*, Komentarz do kodeksu postępowania cywilnego part 1, Vol 1, Postepowanie rozpoznawcze (2002), 713 [Commentary to art 381 KPC].

113 However, if P chooses not to sue more joint tortfeasors, but just D, the defendant D may notify the others of the proceedings and call on them to join the case as interveners (art 84 civil procedure code, KPC). The latter, however, are not obliged to join D in the proceedings. A refusal to join will not militate against them.

interpreted as a waiver of the defence of prescription.[114] T can refuse to pay a contribution to D.[115]

## E. BURDEN OF PROOF (OF ELEMENTS AND OF RULES OF PROLONGATION)

As in other European countries the bedrock principle on burden of proof states that one who makes a claim incurs the burden of proof regarding that claim, hence it is the defendant who has to establish that the prescription period passed since the accrual of the plaintiff's right to remedy or that the running of time was or has been postponed, renewed or extended.[116] 122

114 See *A Pyrzyńska*, in: Komentarz do kodeksu cywilnego (2010), 173; *W Dubis*, in: E Gniewek and P Machnikowski (eds), Kodeks cywilny. Komentarz (7th ed, 2016), 685. According to art 371 KC actions and omissions of one of the joint tortfeasors may not be of prejudice to the co-debtors.

115 Only under art 372 KC would T have to pay the contribution to D even though he would have been able to raise the defence of prescription against P. The said provisions state that interruption or suspension of the course of prescription period towards one of the joint debtors is not effective towards the co-debtors. This situation refers to the relations between the creditor and co-debtors. If the first debtor paid because of interruption (suspension), then he will have a contribution claim towards the others.

116 See SN of 6 October 2017, V CSK 36/17.

# PRESCRIPTION IN TORT LAW: SOUTH AFRICA

Johann Neethling

## I. INTRODUCTION

1 The aim of this report is to explore how (and why) the passage of time on an alleged tort law claim affects (and should affect) the claim, the parties (P the plaintiff and D the defendant) and other parties through the defence of *prescription*. Extinctive prescription in South African tort law is presently regulated by the Prescription Act 68 of 1969. The purpose of the Act was to consolidate and amend the laws relating to prescription, and to replace its predecessor, the Prescription Act 18 of 1943. However, the new Act applies only to debts arising after the commencement of the Act (that is, 1 December 1970); debts that arose before that date continue to be regulated by old law. When the Act does not make provision on a point, reference must be made to our

Roman-Dutch common law.[1] The major literature on prescription is stated *infra* fn 1 and 2.

## II. DEFINITION OF PRESCRIPTION

Prescription in tort law is a legal institution that prevents P from enforcing an alleged right against D because of the running of a specified period of time on the tort claim. This definition is acceptable for South African law except for the fact that the Prescription Act 68 of 1969, on which South African law of extinctive prescription is generally based,[2] uses the term *debt*[3] instead of *right*.[4] In the context of the law of delict (tort) the concept of debt refers to the obligation to pay damages for the damage caused by a delict.[5] If the debt cannot be enforced or is extinguished as a result of prescription, naturally the fate of the right or remedy to claim the damages will also be sealed.[6] 2

## III. THE NATURE OF PRESCRIPTION AND ITS EFFECTS

There are different ways by which prescription prevents P from enforcing an alleged right of remedy or debt against D. Its effect may be: (a) to extinguish P's right to remedy; (b) to provide D with a *substantive* defence that prevents P from enforcing the right to remedy although it is not extinguished; (c) to provide D with a *procedural* defence that bars P's ability to litigate the right in courts. 3

1 See sec 16 of the Act; *D Hutchison* (ed), Wille's Principles of South African Law (1991), 500.

2 See generally *MM Loubser*, Extinctive Prescription (1996) *passim*; *M Loubser and R Midgley* (eds), The Law of Delict in South Africa (2nd ed, 2012), 266 ff; *NJ van der Merwe and PJJ Olivier*, Die Onregmatige Daad in die Suid-Afrikaanse Reg (6th ed, 1989), 283 ff; *MM Loubser and E Reid*, Product Liability in South Africa (2012), 138 ff; *J Neethling and JM Potgieter*, Neethling-Potgieter-Visser Law of Delict (7th ed, 2015), 278; *JS Saner*, 'Prescription' 21 (2010) *LAWSA* para 123 ff; *J Neethling*, 'Extinctive prescription of a delictual cause of action' 1 (2020) *TSAR* 182 ff (discussion of *De Lange v Minister of Water and Environmental Affairs* 2019 4 SA 445 (SCA)).

3 The concept of debt is not defined in the Act, but the courts interpret it in 'a wide and general' sense to include any liability in terms of an obligation (see *CJU Insurance Ltd v Rumdel Constrution (Pty) Ltd* 2004 2 SA 622 (SCA) 627–628; *Loubser*, *supra* fn 2, 26–34; *Loubser and Midgley*, *supra* fn 2, 206–207).

4 Section 10(2) states that 'a debt shall be extinguished by prescription after the lapse of the [relevant] period'.

5 See *Loubser and Midgley*, *supra* fn 2, 201.

6 See *Van der Merwe and Olivier*, fn 2, 283–284; *Saner*, *supra* fn 2, para 123; *Evins v Shield Insurance Co Ltd* 1980 2 SA 814 (A) 842.

The nature and effect of extinctive prescription in South African law can be stated as follows:

4 As to (a), sec 10(1) of the Act provides that a debt is extinguished by prescription, but this creates anomalies. Firstly, because sec 10(3) provides that, notwithstanding the provision in sec 10(1), payment by the debtor of a debt after it has been extinguished by prescription shall be regarded as payment of the debt.[7] So, prescription clearly does not extinguish P's right to remedy or debt. A consequence is that D would have no right to restitution under the law of unjust enrichment (*condictio indebiti*) because P's right to compensation still exists before payment.[8] Secondly, sec 10(1) is anomalous as, notwithstanding the fact that prescription is present, it does not take effect by operation of law since sec 17(1) provides that a court may not of its own motion take notice of prescription but it must be invoked by a party to litigation.[9] Be that as it may, South African courts seem to accept the clearly expressed wording or literal meaning of sec 10(1) without further ado.[10]

5 As to (b), to overcome the anomalies created by sec 10(1), the nature and effect of extinctive prescription should be that it confers on D a substantive right or defence that prevents P from enforcing the right to remedy or debt although it is not extinguished.[11] According to Loubser[12] D acquires a right to refuse performance, which he may invoke as a substantive defence (and not merely a procedural denial of action), while the obligation (debt) subsists intact and can still be complied with. This construction appears to him to be logically unassailable and useful for analysis of the positive law position in South Africa.

6 As to (c), the nature and effect of extinctive prescription is not to provide D merely with a procedural defence or denial of P's right of action. Since extinctive prescription prevents P from enforcing a substantive right, D's defence in this regard is also of a substantive nature rather than how the defence must procedurally be implemented. The effect of extinctive prescription is therefore of a substantive rather than a procedural nature.[13]

---

7 See *Loubser, supra* fn 2, 15–16; cf *Van der Merwe and Olivier, supra* fn 2, 284.

8 See *Van der Merwe and Olivier, supra* fn 2, 284; *Loubser, supra* fn 2, 16.

9 See *Loubser, supra* fn 2, 16; see however *Lipschitz v Dechamps Textiles GmbH* 1978 4 SA 427 (C) 430.

10 See, eg *Standard General Insurance Co Ltd v Verdun Estates (Pty) Ltd* 1990 2 SA 693 (A) 669 where the court referred to the 'clear words' of sec 10(1); *Volkskas Spaarbank Bpk v Van Aswegen* 1990 3 SA 978 (A) 986; *Lipschitz v Dechamps Textiles GmbH* 1978 4 SA 427 (C) 430; see also *Loubser, supra* fn 2, 18.

11 In *Kuhne & Nagel AG Zürich v APA Distributors (Pty) Ltd* 1981 3 SA 536 (W) 538 the court stated: 'The extinction […] of a right by prescription is a matter of substantive law.'

12 *Loubser, supra* fn 2, 15.

13 See *Loubser, supra* fn 2, 11–14, 15 for detailed discussion.

With regard to the observations, the concept of prescription as a substantive defence (b) is, as indicated by Loubser, for good reason indeed the proper middle ground for South Africa between the alternatives (a) and (c). There is no indication that different concepts (a, b, c, or others[14]) apply to different areas of tort law. 7

## IV. CONSIDERATIONS FOR AND AGAINST PRESCRIPTION OF TORT CLAIMS

The major pros and cons of extinctive prescription in South Africa are as follows. According to Loubser[15] the major object of extinctive prescription is to create legal certainty and finality in the relationship between the creditor and the debtor after the lapse of a period of time.[16] The emphasis is on the protection of the debtor against a stale claim that has existed for such a long time that it becomes unfair to require the debtor to defend himself against it. The primary consideration is therefore one of fairness to the debtor. With the passage of time the debtor ought to become secure in his reasonable expectation that the slate has been wiped clean of debts owed to his creditor. The creditor is responsible for enforcing his right timeously and must suffer the consequences in this regard.[17] In *Oliff v Minnie*[18] the court stated the considerations for extinctive prescription in Roman and Roman-Dutch law as follows: '[T]he supinity (*desidia*) of a plaintiff who does not enforce his rights, who should therefore blame himself, and the difficulty felt by defendants who have to repel ancient claims.'[19] In the latter regard Loubser[20] explains that delayed enforcement of 8

[14] *Loubser, supra* fn 2, 8–10 also refers to the concepts of extinctive prescription as 'a protection of reasonable reliance' or as 'an irrebuttable presumption of law' but they did not get any recognition in South African law.

[15] *Loubser, supra* fn 2, 22; see also *Myathaza v Johannesburg Metropolitan Bus Service (SOC) Ltd; Mazibuko v Concor lant; Cellucity (Pty) Ltd v Communication Workers Union on behalf of Peters* 2016 37 ILJ 413 (LAC) 29; *DW de Villiers*, Die nuwe artikel 145(9) van die Wet op Arbeidsverhoudinge – uniek, maar welkom 2016 (3) *LitNet Akademies* 733 ff.

[16] The Roman-Dutch law author Voet once remarked that controversies are limited for a fixed period of time lest they should be immortal while men are mortal: *Ne autem lites immortales essent, dum litigantes mortales sunt* (taken from *Loubser*'s, *supra* fn 2, 23 quotation from Story).

[17] See *Loubser, supra* fn 2, 23.

[18] *Oliff v Minnie* 1953 1 SA 1 (A) 4, to which *Loubser, supra* fn 2, 23 fn 135 referred.

[19] In the latter regard the court (4) also referred to *Rhodes v Smethurst* LR 151, 449, where it was said that the underlying principle was 'for the benefit of defendants, to exempt them from being called to account in respect of transactions long gone by, which it might not be easy to explain at a distance of time'.

[20] *Loubser, supra* fn 2, 23. See also *Mohlomi v Minister of Defence* 1997 1 SA 124 (CC) 11 where the court remarked: 'Rules that limit the time during which litigation may be launched are common in our legal system as well as many others. Inordinate delays in litigating damage

a debt causes evidence to disappear (records may be lost or destroyed) and witnesses to forget or be unavailable. According to him the 'judicial economy and smooth functioning of the legal system is best served when parties are obliged to bring their disputes to the courts promptly, so that they can be swiftly resolved while the evidence is available and fresh in the memory of witnesses'.

## V. ELEMENTS OF PRESCRIPTION – AN OVERVIEW

9 Although analytically, there are four elements – four sets of rules – that together comprise prescription law, namely the starting point, the prescription period, rules of prolongation and rules of upper limit, the latter is not applicable to South African law.

### A. THE STARTING POINT (RULES OF ACCRUAL)

10 The prescription period commences to run (unless postponed) as soon as the debt is due[21] and therefore enforceable,[22] and this occurs the moment all the elements of a delict (constituting a cause of action), namely conduct, wrongfulness, fault, causation and harm, are present,[23] provided also that the creditor has knowledge (or ought reasonably to know) of the identity of the debtor (wrongdoer) and the facts from which the debt arises.[24] But a creditor shall be deemed to have such knowledge if he could have acquired it by reasonable care.[25] If the debtor wilfully prevents the creditor from coming to know of

---

the interests of justice. They protract the disputes over the rights and obligations sought to be enforced, prolonging the uncertainty of all concerned about their affairs. Nor, in the end is it always possible to adjudicate satisfactorily on cases that have gone stale. By then witnesses may no longer be available to testify. The memories of ones whose testimony can still be obtained may have faded and become unreliable. Documentary evidence may have disappeared. Such rules prevent procrastination and those harmful consequences of it. They thus serve a purpose to which no exception in principle can cogently be taken.' Cf *Myathaza v Johannesburg Metropolitan Bus Service (SOC) Ltd; Mazibuko v Concor lant; Cellucity (Pty) Ltd v Communication Workers Union on behalf of Peters* 2016 37 ILJ 413 (LAC) 33.

21 Section 12(1) of the Act; *Saner*, *supra* fn 2, para 125. According to *Makhwelo v Minister of Safety and Security* 2017 1 SA 274 (GJ) the due date of a debt in claims for unlawful arrest and detention is the date of release of the plaintiff and not the date of his arrest.

22 In *Truter v Deysel* 2006 4 SA 168 (SCA) 174 the court held that a '"debt due", means a debt, including a delictual debt, which is owing and payable'; see also *Loubser*, *supra* fn 2, 51–52.

23 See *Neethling and Potgieter*, *supra* fn 2, 278; *Loubser and Midgley*, *supra* fn 2, 207–208; *Loubser*, *supra* fn 2, 80, cited in *Truter v Deysel* 2006 4 SA 168 (SCA) 174.

24 See, eg *Truter v Deysel* 2006 4 SA 168 (SCA) 173; cf also *Van Zijl v Hoogenhout* 2005 2 SA 93 (SCA) 102–103.

25 Section 12(3) of the Act; see also *Van der Merwe and Olivier*, *supra* fn 2, 286–287; *Loubser and Midgley*, *supra* fn 2, 208–209; *Loubser*, *supra* fn 2, 79–80.

the existence of the debt, prescription shall not commence to run until the creditor becomes aware of the existence of the debt.[26]

## B. PRESCRIPTION PERIOD

The Act[27] provides for differential periods of extinctive prescription for various kinds of debt. Section 11(d) provides that, excluding the periods for debts catered for in subsections (a)–(c), the period is three years in respect of any other debt save where an Act of Parliament provides otherwise.[28] A delictual debt therefore prescribes three years after it originated.[29] 11

## C. RULES OF PROLONGATION – POSTPONEMENT, RENEWAL AND EXTENSION

### 1) *Postponement, Suspension, Extension, Delay*

The term for the postponement, suspension or extension of extinctive prescription in South African law is the *delay* of prescription. The completion of prescription will be delayed (postponed, suspended or extended) in certain circumstances where any of the impediments listed in the Act[30] are present.[31] Such a delay takes place if, for example, the delictual three-year period of prescription would have been completed, but for the relevant impediment, before, or on, or within one year after the day on which the impediment has ceased to exist. Furthermore, the period of prescription will not be completed before a year has elapsed after the day on which the impediment has ceased to exist.[32] 12

---

26 Section 12(2) of the Act.

27 Section 11; see generally *Loubser, supra* fn 2, 35 ff; *Loubser and Midgley, supra* fn 2, 207; *Saner, supra* fn 2, para 124; *JM Potgieter, L Steynberg and TB Floyd,* Visser & Potgieter Law of Damages (3rd ed, 2012), 346–348.

28 See *infra* 35–38 as to these periods for delictual claims.

29 See *Loubser and Midgley, supra* fn 2, 207; *Van der Merwe and Olivier, supra* fn 2, 285–286; *Neethling and Potgieter, supra* fn 2, 284.

30 In terms of sec 13(1); see *Loubser, supra* fn 2, 117 ff; *Loubser and Midgley,* fn 2, 210–211; *Van der Merwe and Olivier, supra* fn 2, 287–288.

31 See *infra* 40–41 for a discussion of these impediments.

32 See sec 13(1)(i); *Loubser, supra* fn 2, 117; *Loubser and Midgley, supra* fn 2, 210; *Saner, supra* fn 2, para 126. For an interpretation with examples of how this section should be understood and applied, see *ABP 4x4 Motor Dealers (Pty) Ltd v IGI Insurance Co Ltd* 1999 3 SA 924 (SCA) 930 (see also *Loubser and Midgley, supra* fn 2, 210; *Saner, supra* fn 2, para 126). According to the court in some circumstances the impediment will have no effect whatsoever on the running of prescription; in others it will only suspend the running of prescription for a time but also provide what amounts to a virtually new period of prescription (one year), the commencement of which is the date when the impediment ceases to exist.

Saner[33] summarises the position as follows: '[T]he effect which a nominated "impediment" will have depends upon how much time remains available to the creditor to take action when the circumstances cease to exist. If no time, or less than a year remains available, the period of prescription is extended so as to make a full year available. If more than a year remains available, the existence of the circumstances postulated will have no effect at all on the running of prescription or its completion.'

*2) Renewal, Interruption*

13 Interruption of prescription has the effect that the count of the prescription period starts afresh. The Act[34] makes provision for two types of interruption:[35] Firstly, by an express or tacit acknowledgement of liability by the debtor,[36] and secondly, by the service of any process on the debtor whereby the creditor claims payment of the debt (judicial interruption).[37]

### D. THE UPPER TIME LIMIT

14 As far as could be ascertained, South African law does not have rules of a 'long-stop', 'repose' or an upper time limit or ceiling on the effective time of prescription.[38]

## VI. THE STARTING POINT OF THE PRESCRIPTION PERIOD

### A. INTRODUCTION

15 As said, the starting point (the date of the 'accrual of the cause of action') is the date on which P's cause of action against D, which is the subject matter

33 Paragraph 126.

34 Sections 14, 15. See generally *Loubser, supra* fn 2, 123 ff; *Van der Merwe and Olivier, supra* fn 2, 289–291; *Loubser and Midgley, supra* fn 2, 211–213; *Saner, supra* fn 2, paras 129–131.

35 See *infra* 40 for details.

36 Section 14(1). A tacit acknowledgement will for example be where the debtor makes a payment (even partial) into the bank account of the creditor (see *Eerste Nasionale Bank van Suidelike Afrika Bpk v Vermeulen* 1997 1 SA 498 (O) 503). The debtor must make the acknowledgement of liability for the debt in person (or through an agent) and it must be made to the creditor in person (or his agent) (see *Pentz v Government of the RSA* 1983 3 SA 584 (A) 594; cf *Markham v South African Finance & Industrial Co Ltd* 1962 3 SA 669 (A) 676; *Loubser and Midgley, supra* fn 2, 213).

37 Section 15(1) of the Act; see *infra* 55.

38 See *Loubser, supra* fn 2, 36–37.

of prescription, matures so that the prescription period may potentially start to run.

## B. MEANING OF 'ACTION'

An action in tort or delict is the entitlement or remedy to claim damages for damage caused by a delict provided that the requirements for the action have been met. In our law there are basically three delictual actions: the *actio legis Aquiliae*, in terms of which damages for the wrongful and culpable (intentional or negligent) causing of patrimonial damage are claimed; the *actio iniuriarum*, which is directed at *solatium* for the wrongful and *intentional* injury to personality; and the *action for pain and suffering* by which compensation for injury to personality as a result of the wrongful and negligent (or intentional) impairment of bodily integrity is claimed.[39] 16

## C. MEANING AND BROADNESS OF 'CAUSE OF ACTION' FOR PRESCRIPTION PURPOSES

### 1) *Analysis*

In South African law there are two approaches to the concept of a cause of action.[40] Firstly, in terms of the 'single cause' theory, every damage-causing event constitutes only one cause of action.[41] Here the emphasis falls on the conduct which causes damage and not on the damage itself.[42] According to the second approach, a cause of action exists if all its requirements (*facta probanda*) are present. These requirements are the elements necessary before there can 17

---

39 See *Neethling and Potgieter, supra* fn 2, 5.

40 See *Potgieter, Steynberg and Floyd, supra* fn 27, 159–160; *Neethling and Potgieter, supra* fn 2, 236–237; *Loubser, supra* fn 2, 85–86.

41 See, eg *Oslo Land Co Ltd v Union Government* 1938 AD 584, 589; *Casely v Minister of Defence* 1973 1 SA 630 (A) 642; cf *Mntambo v Road Accident Fund* 2008 1 SA 313 (W) 318–319.

42 Here it is accepted that all the different claims consequent upon an unlawful act fall within one cause of action (see, eg *Schnellen v Rondalia Assurance Corp of SA Ltd* 1969 1 SA 517 (W) 521). In *Mntambo v Road Accident Fund* 2008 1 SA 313 (W) 318–319 the court held: 'Here, the plaintiff's cause of action was completed as soon as she suffered damage as a result of the negligence of the insured driver [...] The single wrongful act of the insured driver vested in the plaintiff one single right or claim to compensation, to sue for all loss or damage caused to her by such wrongful act, whether such loss or damage resulted from her claim related to past medical expenses, future medical expenses, general damages or past loss of earnings and future loss of earnings.'

be delictual liability.[43] While the single cause approach is well entrenched in certain typical situations, the most recent cases accept the *facta probanda* theory which is also supported by the majority of authors.[44]

18 In terms of the single cause theory, it is accepted that all the different claims consequent upon an unlawful act fall within one cause of action.[45] In accordance with the *facta probanda* approach, the requisites of two or more claims are compared to establish whether there is a substantial difference despite possible overlapping. If there is no substantial difference, the two claims are regarded as falling within a single cause of action.[46]

19 A cause of action arises at the earliest date when all the requirements for delictual liability are present.[47] Although a cause of action does not arise before damage has been caused, this does not imply that all the damage should have occurred. If all the other elements are present, a cause of action accrues at the earliest stage when the first damage is caused.[48] As said,[49] the prescription period also commences to run when a cause of action arises, that is when the debt in respect of payment of damages is due or claimable, provided also that the creditor has knowledge (or ought reasonably to know) of the identity of the debtor (wrongdoer) and the facts from which the debt arises.

20 In claims for damages *ex delicto* the plaintiff must claim damages for all damage already sustained or expected in future insofar as it is based on a single cause of action – the so-called once and for all rule.[50] A plaintiff who has sued with or without success for a part of his damage may not thereafter sue for another

---

43 Conduct, wrongfulness, fault, causation and damage, or the particular requirements in the case of liability based on risk. See on the *facta probanda* approach *Evins v Shield Insurance Co Ltd* 1980 2 SA 814 (A) 838–839; *Truter v Deysel* 2006 4 SA 168 (SCA) 174; *Mckenzie v Farmer's Cooperative Industries Ltd* 1922 AD 16, 23; *Potgieter, Steynberg and Floyd, supra* fn 27, 162–164; *Loubser, supra* fn 2, 80–81. In accordance with this approach, the requisites of two or more claims are compared to establish whether there is a substantial difference despite possible overlapping. If there is no substantial difference, the two claims are regarded as falling within a single cause of action (see *Evins v Shield Insurance Co Ltd* 1980 2 SA 814 (A) 839; *Potgieter, Steynberg and Floyd, supra* fn 27, 163).

44 See *Potgieter, Steynberg and Floyd, supra* fn 27, 161; *Neethling and Potgieter, supra* fn 2, 236.

45 See, eg *Schnellen v Rondalia Assurance Corp of SA Ltd* 1969 1 SA 517 (W) 521.

46 See *Evins v Shield Insurance Co Ltd* 1980 2 SA 814 (A) 839.

47 *Neethling and Potgieter, supra* fn 2, 233, 237.

48 See also *Loubser, supra* fn 2, 80.

49 *Supra* 10.

50 See generally *Potgieter, Steynberg and Floyd, supra* fn 27, 153 ff; *Loubser and Midgley, supra* fn 2, 404 ff; *Neethling and Potgieter, supra* fn 2, 235–236; see also, eg *Oslo Land Co Ltd v Union Government* 1938 AD 584, 591; *Slomowitz v Vereeniging Town Council* 1966 3 SA 317 (A); *Horwowitz v Brock* 1988 2 SA 160 (A); *Evins v Shield Insurance Co Ltd* 1980 2 SA 814 (A); cf also on this rule *Premier, Western Cape v Kiewitz* 2017 4 SA 202 (SCA); *Member of the Executive Council for Health and Social Development, Gauteng v DZ obo WZ (Member of the Executive Council for Health, Eastern Cape)* 2017 (12) BCLR 1528 (CC).

part if both claims are based on a single cause of action. As far as prescription is concerned, when a cause of action has arisen because some damage has already occurred, the plaintiff must, generally within three years before the prescription is concluded, institute an action in which he claims damages for all damage already sustained as well as that expected in future.[51]

21 Loubser[52] submits that problems concerning the existence of a single or multiple causes of action in the context of prescription should be approached with the overriding policy objective of affording the creditor as wide as possible an opportunity to recover all the damage resulting from a single act or event, *inter alia* by instituting a further action in respect of damage that manifested itself at a later stage: 'Extinctive prescription should not be a blunt instrument for the rigid enforcement of a time bar.'[53]

*2) Cases*

22 **Case 1** – *D, a ski instructor, negligently fails to make sure that all skiers in her 'off-piste' group wear helmets. P, a skier in the group, hits a tree. P immediately suffers head injury X, and years later another head injury Y that developed from the same accident.* The answer is similar to that in Case 2. There is a single occurrence or event that causes X and Y, thus giving rise to a single cause of action. Even if the *facta probanda* approach is followed, there does not seem to be a substantial difference between the two possible claims, and they should therefore be regarded as falling within a single cause of action. The cause of action arises with X (first harm) and P must then within three years before the prescription is concluded, institute an action in which she claims damages for X as well as for harm expected in future (once and for all rule). It is not certain whether Y occurred within or after the three-year prescription period; if the latter, P will not be able to claim damages for Y in spite of the fact that she could not have anticipated Y. It does not seem to matter whether one injury is much more severe than the other. It also does not seem to matter whether Y is causally connected to X or causally independent of X, since both arose from the same negligent act of D.

23 **Case 2** – *Physician D treats patient P negligently and performs three mistakes on the day of the treatment: A, B and C. Mistake A causes harm X after a year. Mistake B causes harm Y after two years. Mistakes A and C together cause harm*

51 See *Potgieter, Steynberg and Floyd, supra* fn 27, 155–157; *Loubser, supra* fn 2, 81 ff; *Oslo Land Co Ltd v Union Government* 1938 AD 584.

52 *Loubser, supra* fn 2, 92, 96.

53 *Loubser, supra* fn 2, 92, 96 suggests that the following factors should be taken into account in deciding whether a single or multiple causes of action should apply: the nature of the various items of damage; whether damage occurred at different stages over a period of time; the duration of the conduct that caused the damage; and whether the damage stemmed from a single event.

*Z after three years.* In this case D's negligent treatment of P by making three mistakes (A, B and C) on the same day causing different kinds of harm after different periods (X, Y, and Z), will probably, because of the closeness of D's medical malpractice, be regarded as a single occurrence or event giving rise to a single cause of action.[54] As stated above, this cause of action will arise when X occurred (the first harm) after one year (provided P knows of the harm). P must then within three years before the prescription is concluded, institute an action in which he claims damages for harm (X and Y) already sustained as well as that expected in future (once and for all rule). Since Z only occurred after three years, P will not be able to claim damages for Z in spite of the fact that he could not have anticipated Z.[55]

On the other hand, as submitted by Loubser,[56] P should be afforded as wide as possible an opportunity to recover damages for all harm resulting from a single event by instituting a further action in respect of harm that manifested itself at a later stage, especially in medical malpractice cases where it is often virtually impossible to ascertain the harm at the time of the negligent act because the treatment causes later complications.[57] If applied, this approach will enable P to also claim damages in respect of Z.

24 **Case 3** – *Builder D lays down defective foundations for a building thereby creating the risk of future collapse. As a result, the value to the owner of the building (P) decreases (harm A). Two years later the foundation subsides and requires fixing paid by P (harm B). Three years later cracks appear in the building fixed by P (harm C). Four years later the building collapses (harm D).* As indicated, in claims for damages *ex delicto* the plaintiff must claim damages for all damage already sustained or expected in the future insofar as it is based on a single cause of action (the so-called once and for all rule).[58] A plaintiff who has sued with or without success for a part of his damage may not thereafter sue for another part if both claims are based on a single cause of action. In our law the tortious activity of laying down defective foundations is a common

---

54 Even if the *facta probanda* approach is followed, there does not seem to be a substantial difference between the three possible claims and they should therefore be regarded as falling within a single cause of action (cf *Neethling and Potgieter, supra* fn 2, 237).

55 For examples of cases dealing with different kinds of harm caused by the same event, see *Green v Coetzer* 1958 2 SA 697 (W); *Schnellen v Rondalia Assurance Corp of SA Ltd* 1969 1 SA 517 (W); *Evins v Shield Insurance Co Ltd* 1980 2 SA 814 (A); *Oslo Land Co Ltd v Union Government* 1938 AD 584. Cf further *Loubser, supra* fn 1, 86 ff; *Neethling and Potgieter, supra* fn 2, 237 ff; *Potgieter, Steynberg and Floyd, supra* fn 27, 167 ff.

56 *Loubser, supra* fn 2, 92, 96.

57 See *Loubser, supra* fn 2, 98.

58 See generally *Potgieter, Steynberg and Floyd, supra* fn 27, 153 ff.; *Loubser and Midgley, supra* fn 2, 404 ff.; *Neethling and Potgieter, supra* fn 2, 235–236; see also, eg *Oslo Land Co Ltd v Union Government* 1938 AD 584, 591; *Slomowitz v Vereeniging Town Council* 1966 3 SA 317 (A); *Horwowitz v Brock* 1988 2 SA 160 (A); *Evins v Shield Insurance Co Ltd* 1980 2 SA 814 (A).

factual/legal basis for all the four harms and ensuing claims, therefore belonging to the same cause of action. If so, then harms B, C and D would prescribe with harm A. P must therefore claim damages for all damage already sustained (harm A: pure economic loss) as well as damage expected in future (harms B, C and D). As proof of the future harms may be very difficult, if not impossible, following the proposal by Loubser,[59] P should be afforded as wide as possible an opportunity to recover damages for all harm resulting from a single event by instituting a further action in respect of harms that manifested itself at a later stage, especially in cases such as the present one, where it will be virtually impossible to ascertain for example the collapse of the building at the time of the laying of the defective foundations. If applied, this approach will enable P to also claim damages in respect of harms B, C and D.

## D. THE STARTING POINT – OCCURRENCE OF HARM OR D's TORTIOUS CONDUCT?

**Case 4** – *D enters P's premises without P's permission, thereby committing a tort of trespass, but without causing damage. P can file a claim against D asking for the remedy of D's eviction but fails to do so. A year later D causes physical harm to P's premise. P files a claim to compensation for the loss.* In South African law concerning trespass the position is that an owner of land who can show patrimonial loss, either through physical damage or merely through deprivation of his use and enjoyment of the land, has an action against the trespasser who caused the loss even if the owner was not in possession of the land.[60] It seems to be accepted by academic writers that trespass *eo nomine* (without loss), and thus D's 'tortious' conduct per se does not constitute a delictual cause of action. Therefore the starting point for prescription of P's claim is the occurrence of the harm which may be the date of trespass if deprivation of his use and enjoyment of the land caused him loss; if not, the starting point will be the date of the physical harm to P's premise. 25

## E. CONCEPT OF OCCURRENCE OF HARM

### 1) *Concept of Harm*

In South African law harm for the purposes of a cause of action means actual harm and not merely the risk of harm to P. A claim cannot be instituted 26

59 *Loubser, supra* fn 2, 92, 96.

60 See *Hefer v Van Greuning* 1979 4 SA952 (A) 957 ff; *PQR Boberg*, The Law of Delict Volume One Aquilian Liability (1984), 170–171.

merely to recover damages for the risk of loss (prospective loss), since a cause of action only exists (and therefore the running of the prescription period commences) if some damage has already been caused.[61] In such a case, damages are awarded for damage already sustained, as well as loss that is expected to occur in future. Although this principle has been criticised, it is certain that an action for damages will not be available in the following situation: X is exposed to radiation through Y's negligent conduct. X does not suffer any immediate harm but there is a 30% risk/chance that he may become seriously ill within four years. X only has an action once the illness (and damage) manifests itself.[62]

27 **Case 5** – *In an accidental event, D negligently caused an explosion that damaged P's ears. During the first two years P has to raise the volume to enjoy music. During the following three years P needs a hearing device. After a further five years P becomes deaf.* As indicated, in delictual claims for damages the plaintiff must claim damages for all damage already sustained or expected in the future insofar as it is based on a single cause of action (the so-called once and for all rule).[63] In this case there is no doubt that as a result of the negligent accident P's claim will be based on a single cause of action (the occurrence of harm by the weakening of his hearing) and he must therefore claim for the initial harm to his ears as well as any harm expected in future which may be difficult to prove. However, as indicated, P should be afforded an opportunity to recover damages for all harm resulting from a single event by instituting further actions in respect of harm that manifested itself at a later stage, especially in medical cases where it is often virtually impossible to ascertain the future harm at the time of the negligent act.[64] If applied, this approach will enable P to also claim damages in respect of the harm that manifested after three years (hearing aid) and even after five years (complete deafness).

---

61 See *Coetzee v SAR & H* 1933 CPD 565: 'I know of no case which goes so far as to say that a person, who has as yet sustained no damage, can sue for damages which may possibly be sustained in the future [...] Prospective damages may be awarded as ancillary to accrued damages, but they have no separate, independent force as ground of action.' See also *Millward v Glaser* 1949 4 SA 931 (A) 942; *Jowell v Bramwell-Jones* 1998 1 SA 836 (W); *Neethling and Potgieter*, *supra* fn 2, 235; *J Neethling*, Causal uncertainty and proportional liability in South Africa, in: I Gilead, MD Green and BA Koch (eds), Proportional Liability: Analytical and Comparative Perspectives (2013), 288, 292.

62 *Neethling and Potgieter*, *supra* fn 2, 235.

63 See generally *Potgieter, Steynberg and Floyd*, *supra* fn 27, 153 ff.; *Loubser and Midgley*, *supra* fn 2, 404 ff.; *Neethling and Potgieter*, *supra* fn 2, 235–236; see also, eg *Oslo Land Co Ltd v Union Government* 1938 AD 584, 591; *Slomowitz v Vereeniging Town Council* 1966 3 SA 317 (A); *Horwowitz v Brock* 1988 2 SA 160 (A); *Evins v Shield Insurance Co Ltd* 1980 2 SA 814 (A).

64 See *Loubser*, *supra* fn 2, 98.

### 2) When does a Given Harm Occur?

As stated, in South African law harm for the purposes of a cause of action means actual harm and not merely the risk of harm to P. Actual materialisation of the risk to P therefore satisfies the requirement of occurrence, but not the mere creation of a yet unrealised risk. 28

**Case 6** – *Builder D lays down defective foundations for a bridge thereby creating the risk of future collapse if heavy rain falls. Two years later heavy rain indeed falls and the collapse becomes only a matter of time, as indeed happens four years after the laying of foundations.* In South African law a claim cannot be instituted merely to recover damages for the risk of loss as a cause of action only exists if some damage has already been caused.[65] Although this principle has been criticised, it is certain that an action for damages will not be available in the present situation: As a result of the defective foundations the risk of future collapse if heavy rain falls has been created. P does not suffer any immediate harm but there is an almost certain chance that the building will collapse when heavy rains fall. P only has an action once the collapse happens and damage occurred.[66]

## F. CONTINUOUS TORT/DELICT

As an exception to the once and for all rule, South African courts have held that in the case of a continuing wrong causing continuing harm, there is a series of rights of action as harm manifests itself constituting separate causes of action in respect of each distinct loss.[67] The harm pertaining to each cause of action is independently subject to extinctive prescription. The prescription period accrues on the date when the loss occurs,[68] therefore in the beginning of each of the series of tortious acts. 29

Two instances of continuous wrongs have been identified but of course they do not constitute a *numerous clausus*. First, where an act causes nuisance, a claim may be instituted each time such nuisance causes damage. The fact that a plaintiff has claimed before does not bar a subsequent action. A plaintiff can obviously not be expected to claim in advance for future damage caused by the repetition or continuation of the original nuisance.[69] Second, in subsidence cases where a 30

65 See *supra* fn 61.

66 *Neethling and Potgieter, supra* fn 2, 235.

67 See *Loubser, supra* fn 2, 92 ff; *Neethling and Potgieter, supra* fn 2, 236; *Potgieter, Steynberg and Floyd, supra* fn 27, 164 ff. See, eg *Symmonds v Rhodesia Railways Ltd* 1917 AD 582, 588; see further *Slomowitz v Vereeniging Town Council* 1966 3 SA 317 (A).

68 See *Loubser, supra* fn 2, 93.

69 See, eg *De Charmay v Day Star Hatchery (Pty) Ltd* 1967 4 SA188 (D); *Loubser and Midgley, supra* fn 2, 407; *Neethling and Potgieter, supra* fn 2, 236.

person causes damage through unlawful excavation, there is a cause of action every time that damage occurs and a plaintiff is not expected to claim once and for all in respect of all such damage.[70]

31 According to *Ngcobo v Minister of Police*[71] it is unclear what duration is necessary for an act to qualify as a 'continuing injury' since every wrongful act has some duration in time. But the court had no conceptual difficulty about a series of repeated acts, each of which would give rise to a fresh cause of action. Loubser[72] suggests that the notion of a continuing delict causing continuing loss seems to be no more than a practically convenient manner of describing an accumulation of delictual causes of action involving repeated acts causing a similar kind of damage or loss. For the purposes of prescription this means that each new manifestation of such harm marks the beginning of the prescription period for the debt arising from this cause of action.

32 **Case 7** – *Every week, during a month, D1 publishes a defamatory article on P1, each time in another newspaper and on a different topic. During the same period D2 publishes a defamatory article on P2, every second day, on the same topic and in the same newspaper.* The repetition of a defaming article on P each time in another newspaper can be regarded as a continuous tort because it involves a series of repeated acts causing a similar kind of harm (infringement of P's fama or reputation) and giving rise to a fresh cause of action with each publication. It would probably not matter if D publishes the same defamation every week in the same newspaper owned by him or defames P differently in different newspapers each time in the same jurisdiction.

33 **Case 8** – *D, a landowner, negligently exposes P, a neighbour, to unreasonable noise for three years. P's hearing is thereby weakened on a daily basis, gradually restricting P's ability to communicate and enjoy music.* This case is analogous to nuisance as an instance of a continuous wrong. Here the harm-causing event (unreasonable noise) at the neighbour's place was continuous but there were a series of successive causes of action until the cause of the harm had been abated. P could therefore have claimed damages whenever there was so-called 'complete' harm which could be ascertained, and he could have instituted a fresh action for any further harm.

---

70 See, eg *Gijzen v Verrinder* 1965 1 SA 806 (D) 811; *D & D Deliveries (Pty) Ltd v Pinetown Borough* 1991 3 SA 250 (D); see generally *Potgieter, Steynberg and Floyd, supra* fn 27, 166–167; *Loubser and Midgley, supra* fn 2, 407; *Neethling and Potgieter, supra* fn 2, 236; *Loubser, supra* fn 2, 96–98.

71 *Ngcobo v Minister of Police* 1978 4 SA 930 (D) 934; cf also *Slomowitz v Vereeniging Town Council* 1966 3 SA 317 (A) 331.

72 *Loubser, supra* fn 2, 94–95. Cf *Slomowitz v Vereeniging Town Council* 1966 3 SA 317 (A); *Ngcobo v Minister of Police* 1978 4 SA 930 (D) for examples.

**Case 9** – *A waste management company digs bins of toxic content into the soil. Toxic substance leaks into the soil and ground water, causing an apparent damage to crops and expenditure on cleaning on a daily basis. After two years the bins are removed from the soil.* The continuous failure of the company to remove the leaking bins that cause harm to the land owner can be regarded as a continuous tort. South African law recognises that the continuance of a wrongful act causing fresh damage from day to day, may give rise to a series of rights of action arising from moment to moment.[73] 34

## G. THE LATE DISCOVERY RULE – A RULE OF THE STARTING POINT (ACCRUAL) OR A RULE OF PROLONGATION?

The date of accrual is, as said, dependent on the fact whether P has knowledge (or ought reasonably to know) of the identity of D and the facts from which the damage arises.[74] The late discovery rule is thus a rule of the starting point but much can be said in favour of considering it as a rule of prolongation. 35

# VII. PRESCRIPTION PERIODS

In South African law the Prescription Act[75] provides that the period of prescription for judgment debts is 30 years[76] while the general period of prescription common to all private law claims, including claims *ex delicto*,[77] is three years save where an Act of Parliament provides otherwise.[78] There are therefore no other general periods for different fields of private law, such as for torts, contracts or unjust enrichment. 36

The Act[79] also makes provision for a diversity of prescription periods for the following different kinds of debts: Thirty years in respect of – a debt secured 37

---

73 See *Potgieter, Steynberg and Floyd, supra* fn 27, 164–166; see for examples *Symmonds v Rhodesia Railways Ltd* 1917 AD 582 (continuing refusal to take back wrongly delivered sheep); *Slomowitz v Vereeniging Town Council* 1966 3 SA 317 (A) (continuous obstruction of supply road to P's shops); *Mbuyisa v Minister of Police, Transkei* 1995 2 SA 362 (Tk) (continuous wrongful seizure and detention of vehicle).

74 See sec 12(2), (3) of the Prescription Act; *Loubser, supra* fn 2, 80; *supra* 10.

75 Section 11 of the Act; see generally *Loubser, supra* fn 2, 35 ff; *Potgieter, Steynberg and Floyd, supra* fn 27, 346–348.

76 Section 11(a)(ii) of the Act; *Loubser, supra* fn 2, 39–41.

77 See *Loubser and Midgley, supra* fn 2, 207; *Van der Merwe and Olivier, supra* fn 2, 285–286; *Neethling and Potgieter, supra* fn 2, 284.

78 Section 11(d) of the Act; *Loubser, supra* fn 2, 43.

79 Section 11(a)-(c); *Loubser, supra* fn 2, 37 ff.

by mortgage bond; a debt in respect of any taxation imposed or levied by or under any law; and a debt owed to the State in respect of any share of the profits, royalties or any similar consideration payable in respect of the right to mine minerals or other substances. Fifteen years in respect of any debt owed to the State and arising out of an advance or loan of money or a sale or lease of land by the State to the debtor. Six years in respect of a debt arising from a bill of exchange or other negotiable instrument or from a notarial contract.

38 There are different periods for some tort claims, for example with regard to 'third-party' claims under the Road Accident Fund Act 56 of 1996[80] the period is three (or five) years; that for claims regarding joint wrongdoers under the Apportionment of Damages Act 34 of 1956 12 months, as well as that for claims under the Compensation for Occupational Injuries and Diseases Act 130 of 1993.[81] With regard to the recovery of debts from organs of state, the Institution of Legal Proceedings against Certain Organs of State Act 40 of 2002 has been brought in line with the provisions of the Prescription Act by repealing the prior prescription periods. As to product liability, the Consumer Protection Act (CPA) 68 of 2008[82] provides that liability does not arise if a claim for damages for death, injury, illness, loss of or damage to property or resultant economic loss caused by a defective product was brought more than three years after the death or injury of a person, or more than three years after the earliest time at which a person had knowledge of the material facts about an illness or the loss of or damage to property; or more than three years after the latest date on which a person suffered any resultant economic loss. Since established terminology of the Prescription Act is not used, it is uncertain whether this Act is also applicable to prescription under the CPA. However, the Prescription Act would probably be applicable for matters which the CPA does not cover, such as the interruption or suspension of prescription.[83] According to Loubser[84] there is an arbitrary element in the selection of a prescription period but nevertheless the practical advantage to particular classes of litigant of having tailor-made periods suitable to particular causes of action. The reasons for the differential periods have not attracted much comments in the courts or legal writing.

---

80 Section 23.

81 Section 43; see further *Potgieter, Steynberg and Floyd, supra* fn 27, 346-348; *Loubser and Midgley, supra* fn 2, 215-216.

82 Section 61(4).

83 See *M Loubser and E Reid,* Product Liability in South Africa (2012), 138 ff for an in-depth discussion of this topic; see also *Loubser and Midgley, supra* fn 2, 257–258; *Neethling and Potgieter, supra* fn 2, 278.

84 *Loubser, supra* fn 2, 35 ff.

There does not seem to be problems of classification of claims or of 'period shopping' because contractual and delictual claims have the same period of extinctive prescription, namely three years. 39

**Table 1. Prescription periods**

| Cause of action or tort | Discovery rule | Prescription period | Notes |
|---|---|---|---|
| Bodily injury | Yes | 3 | Exceptions[85] |
| Property damage | Yes | 3 | |
| Defamation | Yes | 3 | |
| Intentional torts | Yes | 3 | |
| Contractual claims | Yes | 3 | |

## VIII. RULES OF POSTPONEMENT, SUSPENSION, RENEWAL AND EXTENSION

(1) The prescription period will not commence (or will be postponed) unless P has knowledge (or ought reasonably to know) of the identity of the D and the facts from which the debt arises.[86] 40

(2) If D wilfully prevents the creditor from coming to know of the existence of the debt, prescription will not commence (be postponed) to run until P becomes aware of the existence of the debt.[87]

(3) The running of prescription will be interrupted by an express or tacit acknowledgement of liability by D.[88]

(4) Legal relations between D and P will delay (postpone) the completion of prescription in the following circumstances: P is a person under curatorship;[89] P and D are partners and the debt is a debt which arose out of the partnership relationship;[90] P is a juristic person and D is a member of the governing body of such juristic person.[91]

---

85 See above fn 81–82.

86 Section 12(3) of the Act.

87 Section 12(2) of the Act; see *Loubser, supra* fn 2, 101–102. According to the courts 'willfully' does not mean 'fraudulently' (*Jacobs v Adonis* 1996 4 SA 246 (C) 250–251; *Loubser and Midgley, supra* fn 2, 208).

88 Section 14(1) of the Act. The prescription will then commence to run afresh from the day on which acknowledgement takes place or, if at the time of the acknowledgement or at any time thereafter the parties postpone the due date of the debt, from the date upon which the debt again becomes due.

89 Section 13(1)(a) of the Act.

90 Section 13(1)(d) of the Act.

91 Section 13(1)(e) of the Act.

(5) Medical treatment relations – not recognised.
(6) With regard to employment relations an application to set aside an arbitration award in terms of the Labour Relations Act 66 of 1995[92] interrupts the running of prescription in respect of that award.
(7) If P and D are married to each other the completion of prescription will be delayed (postponed).[93] Our law is silent as far as parents and children are concerned.
(8) If P is a minor the completion of prescription will be delayed.[94]
(9) If P is insane the completion of prescription will be delayed.[95]
(10) P's physical disability – not recognised.
(11) If D is outside the country the completion of prescription will be delayed.[96]
(12) If P is prevented by superior force (*force majeure*) from interrupting the running of prescription,[97] the completion of prescription will be delayed (postponed).[98]
(13) The running of prescription will be interrupted by the service on D of any process whereby P claims payment of the debt.[99]
(14) If the debt is the object of a dispute subjected to arbitration the completion of prescription will be delayed (postponed).[100]
(15) If P is prevented by any law or any order of court from interrupting the running of prescription,[101] the completion of prescription will be delayed (postponed).[102]

---

92 Section 145(9); *Myathaza v Johannesburg Metropolitan Bus Service (SOC) Ltd; Mazibuko v Concor lant; Cellucity (Pty) Ltd v Communication Workers Union on behalf of Peters* 2016 37 ILJ 413 (LAC).

93 Section 13(1)(c) of the Act.

94 Section 13(1)(a) of the Act.

95 Section 13(1)(a) of the Act.

96 Section 13(1)(b) of the Act.

97 In terms of sec 15(1) of the Act.

98 Section 13(1)(a) of the Act.

99 However, unless the debtor acknowledges liability, the interruption of prescription will lapse, and the running of prescription will be not be deemed to have been interrupted if the creditor does not successfully prosecute his claim under the process in question to final judgment or if he does so prosecute his claim but abandons the judgment or the judgment is set aside (sec 15(2) of the Act). But where the debtor acknowledges liability, and the creditor does not prosecute his claim to final judgment, prescription will commence to run afresh from the day on which the debtor acknowledges liability or, if at the time when the debtor acknowledges liability or at any time thereafter the parties postpone the due date of the debt, from the day upon which the debt again becomes due (sec 15(3) of the Act). If the running of prescription is interrupted by the service of a process and the creditor successfully prosecutes his claim to final judgment, and does not abandon the judgment or the judgment is not set aside, prescription will commence to run afresh on the day on which the judgment of the court becomes executable (sec 15(4) of the Act).

100 Section 13(1)(f) of the Act.

101 In terms of sec 15(1) of the Act.

102 Section 13(1)(a) of the Act.

(16) Evidential difficulties of P who needs time to gather evidence – not recognised.
(17) Financial difficulties of P in raising the money required for litigation – not recognised.
(18) Closed courts – not recognised.
(19) Prolongation by courts on grounds of justice – not recognised.
(20) Other recognised justifications: If the debt is the object of a claim filed against the estate of D who is deceased or against the insolvent estate of D or against a company in liquidation or against an applicant under the Agricultural Credit Act 28 of 1966;[103] or P or D is deceased and an executor of the estate in question has not yet been appointed,[104] the completion of prescription will be delayed (postponed).

## A. UNAWARENESS (LATE DISCOVERY)

The Prescription Act[105] provides as follows: 'A debt shall not be deemed to be due until the creditor has knowledge of the identity of the debtor and of the facts from which the debt arises: Provided that a creditor shall be deemed to have such knowledge if he could have acquired it by exercising reasonable care.' From this it is clear that the prescription period will not commence unless (or will be *postponed* until) P has knowledge (or ought reasonably to know) of the identity of the D and the facts from which the debt arises.[106] It is also clear that the test is both subjective and objective. 41

Knowledge of D's identity means sufficient information to be able to identify D by name and address.[107] Knowledge of the facts means knowledge of the material facts constituting the cause of action.[108] Until P had knowledge of facts that would have led him to think that possibly (on reasonable grounds) there had been negligence and that this had caused his disability, he lacked knowledge of the necessary facts contemplated in sec 12(3) of the Act.[109] The knowledge which is required is the minimum necessary to enable P to institute action.[110] 42

---

103 Section 13(1)(g) of the Act.
104 Section 13(1)(h) of the Act.
105 Section 12(3).
106 Section 12(3) of the Act.
107 See *Gericke v Sack* 1978 1 SA 821 (A) 830; *Loubser*, *supra* fn 2, 103; *Loubser and Midgley*, *supra* fn 2, 208–209.
108 See *Truter v Deysel* 2006 4 SA 168 (SCA) 175; *Links v Department of Health, Northern Province* 2016 4 SA 414 (CC) 429; *Makhwelo v Minister of Safety and Security* 2017 1 SA 274 (GJ) para 43; *Loubser*, *supra* fn 2, 103–104.
109 *Links v Department of Health, Northern Province* 2016 4 SA 414 (CC) 429.
110 See *Van Zijl v Hoogenhout* 2005 2 SA 93 (SCA) 102–103; *Nedcor Bank Bpk v Regering van die Republiek van Suid-Africa* 2001 1 SA 987 (SCA) 996–997.

This will therefore include P's knowledge (and appreciation) of D's tortious conduct, P's harm and the causal link between the two.[111] P's ability to acquire the requisite knowledge, especially in medical cases, can be hampered by the fact that he can only consult with independent medical professionals at a much later stage.[112]

43 However, knowledge does not require knowledge of the legal conclusions drawn from the facts, as is the case with the delictual requirements of wrongfulness and negligence.[113] In a similar vein, because the Act requires knowledge of facts and not of the legal implications of such facts, according to Loubser[114] this provision should be interpreted to mean that prescription will begin to run even if P is unaware that the facts afford him a legal remedy.

44 As far as the burden or onus of proof is concerned, according to the Constitutional Court[115] the defendant, relying on prescription, bore the onus of showing: (a) what facts P was required to know before prescription would commence; and (b) that P had knowledge of those facts on a certain date. In cases involving professional negligence, a defendant had to show that the plaintiff was in possession of sufficient facts to cause him or her to think, on reasonable grounds, that the injuries were due to the fault of the medical staff.

45 **Case 10** – *Chemical plant D negligently exposes bordering lands to toxic substances. As a result P, a nearby resident landowner, contracts a lung disease. P failed to sue in time because his former lawyer told him that the exposure was not tortious, and only his new lawyer told him, after the running of time, that it was tortious.* Where P was aware of the causal link and therefore of the facts of the cause of action, but because of his former lawyer's wrong advice he was unaware that the facts afford him a legal remedy, his claim against D prescribed.[116]

46 **Case 11** – *Chemical plant D negligently exposes bordering lands to toxic substances. As a result P, a nearby resident landowner, contracts a lung disease but is unaware of the causal link between exposure and disease because his physician fails to detect it. P does not seek a second opinion. After the prescription period runs on the disease P consults his new physician that tells him about the link. Did P's claim against D prescribe?* As said, as long as P remains unaware of

111 *Links v Department of Health, Northern Province* 2016 4 SA 414 (CC) 429.

112 *Links v Department of Health, Northern Province* 2016 4 SA 414 (CC) 29, 46–49.

113 See *Truter v Deysel* 2006 4 SA 168 (SCA) 174–175; *Loubser, supra* fn 2, 80; *Loubser and Midgley, supra* fn 1, 209. But see *Van Zijl v Hoogenhout* 2005 2 SA 93 (SCA) 102–103 where the court also seemed to require knowledge of the ascribing of blame to D where this is a necessary element of the delictual claim.

114 *Loubser, supra* fn 2, 104.

115 *Links v Department of Health, Northern Province* 2016 4 SA 414 (CC) 24.

116 See *supra* 10.

D's tortious conduct, his harm (lung disease) and the causal link between the two,[117] the start of the prescription period will be postponed until P acquires such knowledge through his new physician. However, if P could have acquired the knowledge by exercising reasonable care (in seeking a second opinion which could have detected it) he will be deemed to have such knowledge. Because P failed to do what a reasonable person[118] would have done in the circumstances, his claim against D prescribed.[119]

## B. OTHER RULES OF PROLONGATION

### 1) *D is to Blame for the Delay*

47 If D wilfully prevents the creditor from coming to know of the existence of the debt, prescription will not commence to run (or be postponed) until P becomes aware of the existence of the debt.[120]

### 2) *Admission by D of P's Right or Partial Performance of P's Right by D*

48 The running of prescription will be interrupted or renewed by an express or tacit acknowledgement of liability by D.[121]

### 3) *Special Relations between D and P*

49 **Table 2. Rules of prolongation**

| **Relations** | **Rule of prolongation** | **Comments** |
|---|---|---|
| Parents/children | No | |
| Spouses | Yes | Delayed (postponed)[122] |
| Curatorship | Yes | Delayed (postponed)[123] |

*(continued)*

117 *Links v Department of Health, Northern Province* 2016 4 SA 414 (CC) 429.

118 The test is not purely objective but will take account of P's personal characteristics (see *Brand v Williams* 1988 3 SA 908 (C) 913–916).

119 See *Loubser, supra* fn 2, 105 ff for a detailed discussion.

120 Section 12(2) of the Act; see *Loubser, supra* fn 2, 101–102. According to the courts 'willfully' does not mean 'fraudulently' (*Jacobs v Adonis* 1996 4 SA 246 (C) 250–251; *Loubser and Midgley, supra* fn 2, 208).

121 Section 14(1) of the Act. The prescription will then commence to run afresh from the day on which acknowledgement takes place or, if at the time of the acknowledgement or at any time thereafter the parties postpone the due date of the debt, from the date upon which the debt again becomes due.

122 Section 13(1)(c) of the Act.

123 Section 13(1)(a) of the Act.

Table 2 *continued*

| Relations | Rule of prolongation | Comments |
|---|---|---|
| Attorney/client | No | |
| Partners in partnership | Yes | Delayed (postponed)[124] |
| Legal entity/organs | Yes | Delayed (postponed)[125] |
| Debtors (heirs)/deceased or insolvent estate | Yes | Delayed (postponed)[126] |
| Liquidator/debtors | Yes | Delayed (postponed)[127] |
| Employer/employee | Yes | Extension (interruption)[128] |
| Physician/patient | No | |
| Executor/deceased estate | Yes | Delayed (postponed)[129] |

### *4) P's Disabilities*

50 **Table 3. Disabilities**

| Kind of disability | With representative | Without representative | Kind of prolongation |
|---|---|---|---|
| Minority | Yes | Yes | Delayed (postponed)[130] |
| Adult with unsound mind | Yes | Yes | Delayed (postponed)[131] |

### *5) P's and/or D's Physical Absence from the Jurisdiction*

51 **Table 4. Physical absence**

| Absence | Prolongation | Rule |
|---|---|---|
| D | Yes | Delayed (postponed)[132] |
| P | No | |

124 Section 13(1)(d) of the Act.
125 Section 13(1)(e) of the Act.
126 Section 13(1)(g) of the Act.
127 Section 13(1)(g) of the Act.
128 Labour Relations Act 66 of 1995 sec 145(9); *Myathaza v Johannesburg Metropolitan Bus Service (SOC) Ltd; Mazibuko v Concor lant; Cellucity (Pty) Ltd v Communication Workers Union on behalf of Peters* 2016 37 ILJ 413 (LAC).
129 Section 13(1)(g) of the Act.
130 Section 13(1)(a) of the Act.
131 Section 13(1)(a) of the Act.
132 Section 13(1)(b) of the Act.

### 6) *Former Proceedings between the Parties – Legal and Other*

**Table 5. Proceedings between parties** 52

| Former proceedings | Prolongation | Rule | Comments |
|---|---|---|---|
| Legal | Not applicable | | Act is silent on the topic |
| ADR | Yes | Delayed (postponed)[133] | Arbitration |
| Administrative | No | | |
| Settlement | No | | |

### 7) *Victim's Death and Bankruptcy*

**Table 6. Death and bankruptcy** 53

| Contingency | Prolongation | Kind | Comments |
|---|---|---|---|
| V's death – P is an heir | Yes | Delayed (postponed)[134] | Till one year after appointment of executor[135] |
| V's bankruptcy | No | | |

### 8) *Other Contingencies*

**Table 7. Other contingencies** 54

| Contingency | Prolongation | Kind | Comments |
|---|---|---|---|
| General clause of *force majeure* | Yes | Delayed (postponed)[136] | Specify what is included[137] |
| Wars | | | Included in *force majeure* |
| Closed court | No | | |
| Natural disaster | Yes | | Included in *force majeure* |
| Legal inability to sue | Yes | Delayed (postponed)[138] | Prevented by any law or court order |
| Military service | yes | Delayed (postponed) | Included under previous contingency |
| Imprisonment | Yes | Delayed (postponed) | Ditto |

133 Section 13(1)(f) of the Act.
134 Section 13(1)(g) of the Act.
135 See sec. 13(1)(i) of the Act.
136 Section 13(1)(a) of the Act.
137 The concept of necessity as ground of justification in our law of delict, can probably provide a guideline as to what is included as *force majeure*, superior force or *vis major* (see *Neethling and Potgieter, supra* fn 2, 97–105).
138 Section 13(1)(a) of the Act.

### 9) *Judicial Interruption*

55 The service of any process[139] on the debtor whereby the creditor claims payment of the debt[140] interrupt (renew) the period of prescription with the effect that the count of the prescription period starts afresh.

## IX. CEILINGS ON THE EFFECTIVE TIME OF PRESCRIPTION

56 As stated[141] South African law does not have rules of a 'long-stop', 'repose' or a ceiling on the effective time of prescription.

## X. STATUTE INTERPRETATION, JUDICIAL DISCRETION AND LACHES

### A. INTERPRETATION AND IMPLICIT DISCRETION IN PRESCRIPTION LAW

57 No indication could be found that the judges in the South African jurisdiction are hostile towards prescription. They tend to interpret the provisions of the Prescription Act (as well as that of other relevant acts) in a neutral manner. No evidence could be found either that the courts in any way regard it as unethical to reject a claim on the basis of the rules of prescription.

### B. EXPLICIT DISCRETION TO DISAPPLY THE PRESCRIPTION DEFENCE

58 South African law does not explicitly allow or even mandate judicial discretion on a case-by-case basis to accept or reject the prescription defence in tort claims.

---

139 In terms of sec 15(6) 'process' includes a petition, a notice of motion, a rule *nisi*, a pleading in reconvention, a third-party notice referred to in any rule of court, and any document whereby legal proceedings are commenced. The process must be legally effective (see *Loubser and Midgley, supra* fn 2, 211). It is not necessary that the process should disclose a cause of action (*Sentrachem Ltd v Prinsloo* 1997 2 SA 1(A) 15) or that the cause of action has been amended in a later process as long as the process concerns the same debt. In *Mazubuko v Singer* 1979 3 SA 258 (W) 266 the court said that 'it is inaction, not legal ineptitude, which the Prescription Ac is designed to penalise' (see also *Van der Merwe and Olivier, supra* fn 2, 290; cf *Evins v Shield Insurance Co Ltd* 1980 2 SA 814 (A) 842).

140 Section 15(1) of the Act.

141 *Supra* 4.

Therefore the Act does not set parameters and guidelines for the exertion of this discretion. Judges do not interpret the rules of prescription differently from other rules within private law but interpret the rules neutrally. Judges would have the implicit discretion to employ 'exogenous' concepts such as 'bad faith' and 'abuse of right' to dismiss the defence of prescription using their implicit discretion.

As far as discretion is concerned, South African prescription law does not use general, open terms such as 'reasonableness' or 'good faith'; but the following concepts may be regarded as open: 'debt' which should be interpreted in a wide and general sense;[142] 'cause of action';[143] and knowledge of identity of D acquired by exercising 'reasonable care'.[144] 59

### C. LACHES

As far as could be ascertained, the law in our jurisdiction does not authorise courts to reject a claim, including a tort claim, on the ground of laches or of a similar doctrine. 60

## XI. CHANGE OF PARTIES

### A. WHERE P OR D ARE TRANSFEREES OF THE ORIGINAL CLAIM OR OBLIGATION

Where the claim by V against D is either transmitted by law or transferred by agreement to P, in the absence of direct authority in our law as to extinctive prescription, it is assumed that P will step into the shoes of V with all the associated rights and duties as far as prescription is concerned, and that the rules of prescription will in principle apply to P in the same way that they apply to V. 61

Since insurer P by subrogation effectively steps into the shoes of V as far as V's right against D is concerned,[145] the running of time on P's subrogation claim will not start afresh when P acquires the right of subrogation but the running on V's claim will continue on P's claim.[146] 62

---

142 *Supra* 17.

143 *Supra* 10.

144 Section 12(3) of the Act; see also *Van der Merwe and Olivier, supra* fn 2, 286–287; *Loubser and Midgley, supra* fn 2, 208–209; *Loubser, supra* fn 2, 79–80.

145 *Commercial Union Insurance Co of SA Ltd v Lotter* 1999 2 SA 147 (SCA) 154; *Smith v Banjo* 2011 2 SA 518 (KZP) 521.

146 Cf *Smith v Banjo* 2011 2 SA 518 (KZP) 519, 521.

63 Under our jurisdiction when V dies his estate vests in an executor who subsequently administers it. This he does by first of all collecting all the assets of the estate, *inter alia* debts (such as that owed by D to V).[147] In this process the executor will carry on with the claim against D.[148] If an executor has not yet been appointed, the completion of the prescription of P's claim will be delayed for one year after the executor has been appointed.[149] So as long as the executor institutes the claim within this period, P's debt will not prescribe. Otherwise it does not seem that the running of the prescription will be affected by V's death or by P's knowledge of the claim or his mental disability.[150]

## B. CONTRIBUTION CLAIMS BETWEEN TORTFEASORS

64 The Apportionment of Damages Act 34 of 1956[151] confers upon P (joint wrongdoer) who has satisfied the claim of V a right to recover within 12 months from D (second joint wrongdoer) a contribution even if at that time the prescription in respect of V's claim would have taken effect. P will therefore succeed with his contribution action against D.

## C. DEPENDANTS

65 Under our law the running of the dependant's (P) action for loss of support starts at the death of the breadwinner (V) as this constitutes an independent cause of action, which has different *facta probanda* from V's claim for injuries.[152]

---

147 See in general *Hutchison*, *supra* fn 1, 353, 380.

148 Cf *Neethling and Potgieter*, *supra* fn 2, 267 as to the transmissibility of delictual actions.

149 See *supra* 41.

150 Cf *Armien v Armien* (6943/2008) [2012] ZAWCHC 98 (25 January 2012) [11–14] as to the applicability of extinctive prescription in the context of succession.

151 Section 2(6)(b) of the Act; see on this *Loubser*, *supra* fn 2, 185–186.

152 See *Evins v Shield Insurance Co Ltd* 1980 2 SA 814 (A) 839: 'It is evident that although there is a measure of overlapping, the *facta probanda* in a bodily injury claim differ substantially from the *facta probanda* in a claim for loss of support. Proof of bodily injury to the plaintiff is basic to the one; proof of death of the breadwinner is basic to the other [...] It is evident too that even where both claims flow from the same accident the cause of action in each case may arise at a different time. As I have said, the cause of action in respect of bodily injury will normally arise at the time of the accident [...] [I]n the case of the cause of action for loss of support, this will arise only upon the death of the deceased, which may occur some considerable time after the accident. Until such death there is, of course, no wrongful act *qua* the plaintiff; only a wrongful act *qua* the person who is later to become the deceased.'

# XII. OTHER ASPECTS OF PRESCRIPTION LAW

## A. STIPULATION AND WAIVER

66 In South African law waiver by D to rely on prescription may occur after the prescription period has expired, or in anticipation of prescription taking effect.[153] The courts have recognised the validity of the waiver with regard to claims *ex delicto* in both situations. As to waiver after the prescription period for the debt has expired,[154] such a waiver often occurs after bargaining with regard to certain delictual claims, for example for personal injuries in third-party legislation. The waiver may be effective only for an agreed time and for the purpose of negotiating settlement between P and D.[155] However, as to anticipatory waivers the courts seem reluctant to give effect to a standard form contract whereby D renounces the right to rely on prescription in advance. This may on public policy grounds be considered to be invalid.[156] But where the parties specifically negotiate the waiver, on the basis of particular circumstances or commercial considerations, the waiver could be valid.[157]

67 There does not seem to be a difference in this regard between tort law and other fields of law or between different kinds of torts. Whether the parties can agree to shorten the period or to extend it, or even to change rules of prolongation, are matters of public policy which should be handled with circumspection. There does not appear to be formal requirements for a waiver agreement as the waiver can be express or implied as long P can prove it on a balance of probability.[158]

## B. SOME PROCEDURAL ASPECTS

### 1) *Meaning of 'Filing a Claim'*

68 The running of the prescription period will be stopped by the service of any legally effective process on the debtor whereby the creditor claims payment of the debt. 'Process' includes a petition, a notice of motion, a rule nisi, a pleading in reconvention, a third-party notice referred to in any rule of court, and any

---

153 See generally *Loubser, supra* fn 2, 150 ff.

154 See *Orton v Barhouch* 1973 2 SA 565 (D).

155 See *Loubser, supra* fn 2, 156 ff, 158.

156 See *Ryland v Edros* 1997 2 SA 690 (C) 713; *ABSA Bank h/a Bankfin v Louw* 1997 3 SA 1085 (C) 1088–1089; see however *Nedfin Bank Bpk Meisenheimer* 1989 4 SA 701 (T); *Friederich Kling CMBH v Continental Jewellery Manufacturers* 1995 4 SA 966 (C); see also *Loubser and Midgley, supra* fn 2, 213; *Loubser, supra* fn 2, 150–155, 158.

157 See *Loubser, supra* fn 2, 158.

158 See *Orton v Barhouch* 1973 2 SA 565 (D).

document whereby legal proceedings are commenced. The mere issue of such a process out of court is not sufficient.[159]

*2) Who Else may Raise the Defence?*

69 According to the Act[160] a court may not of its own motion take notice of prescription. It has been held[161] that the pleading of prescription should not only be open for the defendant. The words 'party to litigation'[162] are wide enough to include any party to a litigation who, for some reason, wants to invoke prescription, but must do so in the relevant document filed of record in the proceedings.

*3) When should the Defence be Raised and Decided?*

70 In terms of the Act[163] a court may allow prescription to be raised at any stage of the proceedings.

*4) Burden of Proof*

71 The onus of proof is on the party (usually D) who invokes prescription to establish that prescription has taken effect; this includes *inter alia* the date of the inception of the prescription period.[164] On the other hand, the onus is on P to establish that the running of time of prescription was or has been delayed or interrupted.[165]

---

159 See *supra* 55; *Loubser, supra* fn 2, 127.

160 Section 17 of the Act; see *Loubser, supra* fn 2, 24–25.

161 See *Lipschitz v Dechamps Textiles GmbH* 1978 4 SA 427 (C) 431; *Loubser, supra* fn 2, 25.

162 In terms of sec 17(2) of the Act.

163 Section 17(1) of the Act.

164 See, eg *Gericke v Sack* 1978 1 SA 821 (A) 827–828; *Van Staden v Fourie* 1989 3 SA 200 (A) 216; *Santam Ltd v Ethwar* 1999 2 SA 244 (SCA) 256; see also *Loubser and Midgley, supra* fn 2, 214; *Saner, supra* fn 2, para 137.

165 See, eg *Regering van die Republiek van Suid-Afrika SA v South African Eagle Versekeringsmaatskappy Bpk* 1985 2 SA 42 (O) 47; see also *Loubser and Midgley, supra* fn 2, 214.

# PRESCRIPTION IN TORT LAW: SPAIN

Miquel MARTÍN-CASALS and Albert RUDA*



* This report has been written in the framework of the research project DER2016-77229-R (Spanish Ministry of Economy and Competitiveness) of which the authors are co-directors.

## I. INTRODUCTION

1 Under Spanish law, prescription (*prescripción*) is an institution provided for by statutory law. As regards tort law, its legal regime is laid down mostly by the Spanish Civil Code (hereinafter, CC), but its rules are generally considered confusing, incomplete and outdated. For this reason, it is commonly contended that an in-depth reform is strongly needed.[1] In its present state, Spanish law on prescription is depicted as departing both from comparative law models and its own historical roots, something which is deemed to increase confusion.[2] Some regions have their own statutory regimes, which are to a certain extent more advanced in several respects. Apart from the Navarra 'Foral' regime, the Civil Code of Catalonia[3] is more in line with the latest developments in other jurisdictions, as will be partly shown below. However, this report will mostly focus on Spanish law only.

---

1 Instead of many, see *F Rivero Hernández*, La suspensión de la prescripción en el Código civil español. Estudio crítico de la legalidad vigente (2002), 20 and *MJ Marín López*, El *dies a quo* del plazo de prescripción extintiva: el artículo 1969 del Código Civil, in: MJ Marín López et al (eds), La prescripción extintiva. XVII Jornadas de la Asociación de Profesores de Derecho Civil (2014), 15-234, 28.

2 See *L Díez-Picazo y Ponce de León*, La prescripción extintiva. En el Código Civil y en la jurisprudencia del Tribunal Supremo (2nd ed, 2007), 30.

3 See Act 29/2002, of 30 December, *primera Ley del Código Civil de Cataluña* (Catalan Official Gazette [*Diari Oficial de la Generalitat de Catalunya*] no 3798, 13.10.2003; Spanish Official Gazette [*Boletín Oficial del Estado*, BOE] no 32, 6.2.2003).

The foundation of prescription is the convenience of putting an end to the exercise of rights in an 'out of time' way. That guarantees everyone a state of peace and tranquillity in which the person at stake can feel free of the possibility of being claimed against by another. The benefits of such a purge of claims is very variegated: the potential defendant does not need to keep the memories and the evidence of payment for an indefinite period of time; one does not need to take the risk of being sued in tort when adopting decisions or making 'balances' all lifelong into account. Otherwise, all hereditary transmissions would have to be accepted under the benefice of inventory and the management of risk by tort liability insurers would be hindered to an unaffordable degree. Prescription also makes it unnecessary to have to file a suit in order to eliminate a situation of uncertainty, which would otherwise remain perpetually open, among other advantages.[4] 2

In present legal scholarship, the idea prevails that prescription has an objective foundation, namely that of providing legal certainty to social order, by giving legal force to situations which result after a certain period of time. Therefore the theory that prescription has a subjective grounding – and thus that it is based on a presumed abandonment or carelessness of the holder of the claim affected by prescription – is nowadays rejected by most authors.[5] Accordingly, an objective solution is advanced as regard the suppression of the rule *contra non valentem non currit praescriptio* (arts 1932 and 1934 CC) – as will be seen below.[6] It must be pointed out however that case law is usually confusing in this regard since it usually mixes the objective and subjective approaches. So, for instance, the Spanish Supreme Court (*Tribunal Supremo*) has repeatedly stated that prescription is not strictly based on principles of justice but on the idea of abandonment or carelessness on the side of the right holder as well as legal certainty.[7] On some occasions, it has pointed out that an objective foundation does not exclude that prescription can also be grounded on a subjective basis (STS 17 March 1986 [RJ 1986\1474]). By contrast, the Spanish Constitutional Court comes closer to the objective theory when it states that prescription achieves a balance between the requirements of legal certainty and material justice, whereby the latter may be sacrificed to obtain the former and therefore making an adequate development of legal traffic possible 3

4 See *S Cavanillas Sánchez*, Artículo 1963 et seq, in: R Bercovitz Rodríguez-Cano (ed), Comentario del Código Civil (2013), 13272.

5 Among others see *M Albaladejo García*, La prescripción extintiva (2004), 20.

6 Again, *Cavanillas*, *supra* fn 4, 13272.

7 See, among many others, Sentencia del Tribunal Supremo [Decision of the Spanish Supreme Court, STS] 19 January 2015 [RJ 2015\2325], 4 February 2015 [RJ 2015\506] and 12 February 2016 [RJ 2016\575]).

(Decision of the Constitutional Court [*Sentencia del Tribunal Constitucional*, STC] 147/1986, of 25 November 1986).[8]

4 From a broader perspective, legal scholarship usually distinguishes between two species of prescription: acquisitive prescription (adverse possession, *usucapión*) and extinctive prescription (limitation of actions or simply prescription, *prescripción*). The Spanish Civil Code dealt with both as if they were two manifestations of a single idea. However, it is nowadays clear that they are two different legal institutions and that the conditions or requirements that have to be met for them to have legal effects are also different. In particular, in the case of extinctive prescription the good or bad faith of the beneficiary is irrelevant, whereas it is relevant with regard to adverse possession.[9]

5 Legal scholarship and case law usually draw a distinction between prescription, on the one hand, and so-called 'caducity' (*caducidad*), on the other. Caducity is similar to prescription inasmuch as both have an extinctive or impeditive effect which depends on the passing of a given period of time. However, caducity – in contrast to prescription – affects rights which a statute provides with a life limited beforehand, so such rights will extinguish themselves at any rate when the established period of time arrives. Caducity – unlike prescription – cannot be interrupted and therefore operates 'automatically and *ipso iure*' (as STS 30 March 1983 [RJ 1983\1653] puts it), so any observer may foresee its end if she knows what the initial moment at stake is.[10] From this perspective, caducity – or 'decadence' (*decadencia*), as some ancient authors originally called it[11] – does not require that a situation of 'silence of the legal relationship' has existed, unlike prescription.[12] Therefore it is said that the caducity time period starts counting from the very moment in which the conditions for the birth of the right at stake are met, irrespective of whether the exercise of the right is possible or could actually be requested.[13] This is so because prescription is said to protect the private interest of the passive subject of a right or claim, consisting in not being exposed to old claims, whereas in the case of caducity it is general interests which are protected, namely, those related to providing a prompt certitude to certain legal situations.[14]

---

8 Unless stated otherwise, the Constitutional Court (TC) decisions can be found under <http://www.tribunalconstitucional.es>.

9 Instead of many, see *J Puig Brutau*, Caducidad, prescripción extintiva y usucapión (3rd ed, 1996), 9.

10 *Puig*, *supra* fn 9, 35; *B Gómez Corraliza*, La caducidad (1990), 152; *Cavanillas*, *supra* fn 4, 13287; *Albaladejo*, *supra* fn 5, 30; *Díez-Picazo*, *supra* fn 2, 70.

11 The name 'caducity' was introduced by the translators and commentators of a well-known German treatise, *L Ennecerus and H Nipperdey*, Tratado de Derecho civil, in mid XX century, in particular from the 2nd ed by J Puig Brutau (1950).

12 See the seminal work by *L Alas, D De Buen and E Ramos*, De la prescripción extintiva (1918).

13 See *Díez-Picazo*, *supra* fn 2, 69 and 70.

14 See *Díez-Picazo*, *supra* fn 2, 79.

Therefore, the question usually arises as to whether a particular statutorily established period of time is a prescription or a caducity period. So, for instance, the Act on the protection of the rights of honour, privacy, and own image (LOPCHIPI)[15] provides that there is a period of four years in order to exercise these rights in case of statutory violation, after which 'caducity' takes place (art 9.5). Case law has stated that such a limitation period is one of caducity, not prescription.[16] Such an interpretation is supported at first sight by the language used by the statutory provision under comment. However, it has to be noticed that the Spanish legislature has not always used the legal terminology in a technical manner, and therefore the fact that the word 'caducity' is used in a given case cannot be deemed conclusive as to the true nature of the statutory deadline – which, in the very case of the LOPCHIPI, is in essence similar to every other limitation period in a tort law regime. Therefore, the case law interpretation mentioned above seems at least dubious.[17] Apart from that, the three-month time period laid down in a different statute as regards liability for judicial error (art 293.2 Organic Act of the Judicial Power)[18] is also considered to be one of caducity, not prescription.[19] 6

From a general perspective, it has been maintained that caducity takes place in the case of so-called 'rights or powers of legal configuration' (*facultades de configuración jurídica*), traditionally also called 'potestative rights' (*derechos potestativos*).[20] As examples of such kinds of rights one may make reference to the right to acquire a good with preference to any other person (*derechos de adquisición preferente*) or the possibility to claim a judicial declaration of nullity or rescission. However, it has been pointed out by a scholarly opinion that such a view ignores that there are cases of caducity which do not fit within such a model. So, for instance, in the case where someone breached a promise to get married without any justified ground the claim to damages (pursuant to art 43 CC) is subject to a caducity period, but one may hardly speak of a power of legal configuration in such a setting.[21] 7

---

15 Organic Act 1/1982, of 5 May, *de protección civil del derecho al honor, a la intimidad personal y familiar y a la propia imagen* (BOE no 115, 14.5.1982).

16 Among others, see STS 22 November 2002 [RJ 2002\10364], 21 November 2008 [RJ 2009\9], 25 February 2013 [RJ 2013\2153] and 16 July 2015 [RJ 2015\2781]). In legal scholarship, instead of many, see also *Díez-Picazo*, *supra* fn 2, 246.

17 Similarly, *Cavanillas*, *supra* fn 4, 13292.

18 Organic Act 6/1985, of 1 July, *del Poder Judicial* (BOE no 157, 2.7.1985).

19 In this sense, STS 23 December 1988 [RJ 1988\9810], 10 April 2000 [RJ 2000\2476] and 9 December 2010 [RJ 2011\1403].

20 See *Puig*, *supra* fn 9, 40.

21 See *Díez-Picazo*, fn 2, 80.

## II. DEFINITION OF PRESCRIPTION

8 Despite its statutory nature, as mentioned above, there is actually no statutory definition of prescription but it is commonly considered a defence by which one person bars the exercise of a right or an action by another on the basis that the period of time statutorily laid down has elapsed. Therefore, prescription works as a sort of shield by which the person benefitted by it protects herself as regard the person who tries to put a right or action into exercise. As case law has stated, prescription is 'a limitation to the tardive exercise of the rights, to the benefit of legal certainty'.[22] According to most Spanish legal scholarship, it is the actions, not the rights, which are the object of prescription, as will be explained in the next Section.

## III. THE NATURE OF PRESCRIPTION AND ITS EFFECTS

9 The question as to what the object of prescription is, is a much debated one. From a statutory point of view, the terminology adopted by the Spanish Civil Code is rather unclear – as already noted. Some provisions speak of 'prescription of actions' (art 1961 CC), whereas others speak of 'prescription of rights and actions' (art 1930 CC). It is also worth noting that art 1156 CC, on the causes of extinction of obligations, does not include prescription among them.

10 As pointed out above, the prevailing opinion is that actions, not rights, are the object of prescription, irrespective of whether the extinction of the right also takes place after the extinction of the action. Actions (*acciones*) must be understood in a material, not procedural, sense.[23] Therefore it is the action (*acción*) in the sense of a power to request – or as the German authors call it, the *Anspruch* (*pretensión*, as some Spanish authors translate it) – which is affected by prescription. From this perspective, prescription has a substantive nature and thus provides the defendant (D) with a substantive defence that prevents the plaintiff (P) from enforcing his right to remedy, although the right is not extinguished. Thus, the holder of the right will indeed still have such a right, but no action to claim it. If payment takes place after prescription, the one who paid will not be entitled to restitution, since such a payment is seen as the performance of a 'natural obligation' (*obligación natural*) – ie a non-enforceable debt – even if such a point of view is not free from difficulties.[24] On this ground, some legal scholars point out that prescription lacks extinctive effect. Its effect consists in weakening the right at stake, the satisfaction of

---

22 Among many others, STS 10 March 1989 [RJ 1989\2034] and 5 June 2003 [RJ RJ 2003\4124].

23 See *Díez-Picazo, supra* fn 2, 80.

24 In particular as regards the disagreement on the definition of such obligations. See *Díez-Picazo, supra* fn 2, 97.

which is left to the will of the obliged party, who may – after the passing of the statutorily provided lapse of time – refuse to perform the obligation. According to this perspective, what prescribes is thus the possibility of requesting the performance of the obligation.[25] Yet another opinion holds that the action or claim is not affected by prescription, since the judge will not be able to consider the action time barred unless the defendant raises such a defence. Therefore, it is suggested that prescription merely provides the defendant with a counter-right (ie a material exception proper) which the defendant may exercise or not.[26] However this is mostly a discussion about terminology, which does not really affect the legal effects of the statutory rules on prescription but aims at providing a better theoretical explanation of their meaning.[27]

## IV. CONSIDERATIONS FOR AND AGAINST PRESCRIPTION OF TORT CLAIMS

As already noted, one of the main reasons for prescription is legal certainty, as 11
repeatedly pointed out by case law (eg STS 19 October 1990 [RJ 1990\7984], 14 December 2015 [RJ 2015\5870] and 12 February 2016 [RJ 2016\575]). It may be assumed that such certainty is primarily beneficial to the defendant who would have to pay compensation but for prescription. The defendant may rely on the prescription rules and these cannot be skipped even if that means having to sacrifice justice from the victim's perspective.[28]

On the negative side, the party affected by prescription may allege that it has 12
prevented her from exercising her constitutional right to access to justice (enshrined in art 24 of the Constitution). The Spanish Constitutional Court has not been entirely clear as to whether and under which conditions such restriction may take place. According to one strand of its case law, there is no constitutional violation whenever the Court of Justice dismisses the claim after a full legal proceeding has taken place and therefore there is a decision on the substance matter of the case. By contrast, the right to justice would be infringed if the court merely applied prescription at the very beginning of the trial (*a limine litis*) and thus without examining the merits of the claim – something which in principle might not happen, since prescription has to be alleged by the party benefited by it and accepted or rejected by the court in the final decision of

[25] See *Albaladejo*, *supra* fn 5, 12, 16 and 17.

[26] See *F Cordón Moreno*, Las excepciones de prescripción y caducidad (Leyes 26 y 27 del Fuero Nuevo) (2008) 45 Revista Jurídica de Navarra 77, 80.

[27] See *Cavanillas*, *supra* fn 4, 13280.

[28] See *MP Dominguez Martinez*, La seguridad jurídica fundamento de la prescripción de la acción de responsabilidad civil y la inseguridad en la determinación del día inicial del cómputo (2015) 16 Revista CESCO de Derecho de Consumo 163, 164 <https://www.revista.uclm.es/index.php/cesco/article/view/994>.

the procedure, as will be seen below.[29] That entails that the Constitutional Court adopts a *pro actione* criterion. Therefore, the right to justice is observed even though the tort claim is dismissed on the ground of prescription, after a criminal trial has taken place, even though the victim has not been notified (STC 125/2004). However, a different strand of case law makes the decision depend on whether the claimant has had the possibility of filing the claim without impediments alien to his will and therefore grants the claimant constitutional protection in a substantially identical case (STC 12/2005). Legal scholarship has criticised the hesitating and contradictory position of the Constitutional Court.[30] Moreover, a decision which dismisses a claim on the basis of prescription does not violate the constitutional right to justice, since the decision in that case is based on the elements of the right at stake, as is its time duration.[31] At any rate, it seems that whenever the lower court has examined the substance of the claim and dismissed it on the basis of prescription, there is very little room for granting the claimant constitutional protection, unless the claim has been dismissed in an irrational or arbitrary way (STC 194/2009).

## V. ELEMENTS OF PRESCRIPTION – AN OVERVIEW

13 First of all, it must be noticed that prescription is usually not analysed under Spanish law as consisting in a series of elements and that such an approach is therefore foreign to the same. Having said that, under Spanish law prescription has several of the elements into which one could in theory decompose prescription, in particular a starting point (rules of accrual or *dies a quo*), a prescription period, and some rules on renewal or interruption (which could be seen as 'prolongation' of prescription, although this is also an unusual concept from a Spanish perspective). However, as will be shown below, a fourth element consisting in an upper time limit is generally lacking.

## VI. THE STARTING POINT OF THE PRESCRIPTION PERIOD

### A. THE MEANING OF 'ACTION' AND 'CAUSE OF ACTION'

14 Concerning the starting point in prescription, in general the criterion adopted by the Spanish Civil Code is that the prescription period starts running from

29 See *Cordón*, *supra* fn 26, 100. See *infra* 96 ff.
30 See *Cavanillas*, *supra* fn 4, 13277.
31 See *Cavanillas*, *supra* fn 4, 13278.

the moment in which the right could be exercised (art 1969 CC). This is therefore an objective approach, which makes the accrual of the time period dependent on the possibility or not of the exercise of the right. The possibility which matters to this regard is a legal, not a material one.[32] So, for instance, the prescription period applicable to the action of recovery in the case of liability for the others (pursuant to art 1904 CC) starts running from the moment in which the claimant could have claimed the return of what she paid – ie from the moment when she actually paid.[33]

However, an exception to that approach can be found with regard to tort law, since in that case the time period starts running from the moment in which the victim knew the fact from which the action is born (art 1968.2 CC). If the victim does not know that the exercise of her right is possible, this is a subjective circumstance which prevents prescription from starting.[34] In spite of the fact that two different approaches do coexist in the Civil Code, in practice courts tend to generalise the subjective approach. Thus, accrual generally depends on whether the fact from which the action derives could be known by the person at stake.[35] 15

At any rate, the starting point for the prescription with regard to tort law actions depends on knowledge by the potential claimant. Knowledge must refer to the damaging event. Therefore, it is not required that the claimant is aware or knows that such an event entitles her to file a claim in compensation.[36] Literally, the Spanish Civil Code provides that the prescription period starts counting since 'the victim knew it' (art 1968.2 CC). However, it does not specify to what the pronoun 'it' exactly refers, and thus it remains unclear what the victim is required to know for the prescription period to be triggered. It may be assumed that the legislature was referring to the cause of action, but it remains unclear, and that may be why there is usually no discussion of the concept of cause of action as such within this context. According to legal scholarship, besides knowledge of the damaging event the victim must also know who the tortfeasor was or could be. Otherwise, the prescription period would start running even though the victim did not know against whom to file the claim and such a period could not be interrupted.[37] It is not required, though, that the victim knows the precise amount of damage. 16

Modern case law states that prescription starts provided that the whole damage has taken place according to the stabilisation approach (so-called 17

32 See *Díez-Picazo*, *supra* fn 2, 132.
33 See *Albaladejo*, *supra* fn 5, 206.
34 See *Albaladejo*, *supra* fn 5, 48.
35 As *Albaladejo*, *supra* fn 5, 50 has shown.
36 See *Albaladejo*, *supra* fn 5, 208.
37 See *Albaladejo*, *supra* fn 5, 210.

*consolidación de las secuelas*) and, in the case of personal injury, the victim has obtained medical discharge (*alta médica*, STS 25 February 2009 [RJ 2009\1513]). Accrual may take place in the case of the victim's birth, at her reaching majority, or at her being declared handicapped by the Public Administration, as in the case of damage due to the exposure to Thalidomide in utero – case in which the Supreme Court rejected the claimants' argument that prescription started after they received some later public aid (STS 20 October 2015 [RJ 2015\4226]).[38] When the victim has already obtained such a discharge but some sequelae remain, the prescription period starts running when the latter are known and established (STS 30 July 1991 [RJ 1991\5435], 19 January 2011 [RJ 2011\298] and 2 February 2015 [RJ 2015\488]). This may happen, for instance, by the official recognition by the Public Administration that the victim is 'severely handicapped' (STS 3 September 1996 [RJ 1996\6500]). So, for instance, if the victim has to go on a second leave after she starts suffering from pains related to the original harm inflicted by the defendant, prescription does not accrue until the extent of such sequelae are established (STS 26 June 2001 [RJ 2001\5082]). However, the court may declare that whole damage has taken place at a certain point in time even though the victim has had to undergo some surgical procedure afterwards. For instance, it is possible that the judge states that stabilisation takes place when the criminal procedure ends, although the victim actually had to get ostheosynthesis material withdrawn at a later time (STS 18 July 2011 [RJ 2011\6123]). Leaving this aside, the general criterion is in line with the rules on aid paid by the State to victims of crimes by armed groups, according to which the one-year prescription period starts counting when the victim has fully recovered.[39]

18 The burden of proving that the victim knew of the damage lies on the tortfeasor, according to the general principle that it is the one who states something before the court who bears the burden of proving it (formerly art 1214 CC, now art 214 LEC).[40] However, it may be presumed that the victim knows of the damage instantaneously, so knowledge may be presumed

38 On this case, see *Ruda*, YB 2015, 600 ff.

39 See art 49 of the Royal Decree 671/2013, of 6 September, *por el que se aprueba el Reglamento de la Ley 29/2011, de 22 de septiembre, de Reconocimiento y Protección Integral a las Víctimas del Terrorismo* (BOE no 224, 18.9.2013). A similar rule had already been adopted by previous regulations (each of which supersedes the previous one). See art 5 of the Royal Decree 288/2003, of 7 March, *por el que se aprueba el Reglamento de ayudas y resarcimientos a las víctimas de delitos de terrorismo* (BOE no 65, 17.3.2003); art 5 of the Royal Decree 1211/1997, of 18 July, *por el que se aprueba el Reglamento de ayudas y resarcimientos a las víctimas de delitos de terrorismo* (BOE no 182, 31.7.1997), and art 8 of the Royal Decree 673/1992, of 19 June, *sobre el resarcimiento por el Estado de daños y perjuicios corporales causados como consecuencia de los delitos cometidos por los integrantes de bandas armadas* (BOE no 156, 30.6.1992).

40 In case law, see STS 5 December 1960 [RJ 1960\3787] and 21 May 1992 [RJ 1992\4274].

in many cases. If the victim has been careless or negligent as regards her lack of knowledge, one may equate such ignorance to knowledge to the effect of making the prescription period start running.[41] This seems to be the criterion adopted by case law. Thus, for instance, in the case of a libel, prescription accrues when the libellous publication takes place, since publication is equated with knowledge of the same by the victim (STS 17 July 2008 [RJ 2008\4382]). However, such an approach is not accepted by all authors.[42]

19 Traditionally there has been some controversy regarding continuous torts. At least there are two strands in case law. According to the first, the prescription period must be counted from the moment in which damage starts to be caused, since it is at that point that the victim 'knows' and may thus file a claim. According to the second, one must wait until causation of damage ceases.[43] So, for instance, in the case of defamation because of the inclusion of the claimant's name in a solvency file, the prescription period accrues from the date in which her data were removed from the same (STS 29 January 2014 [RJ 2014\796]). It seems that this is the prevailing view in modern case law. To this regard, the Supreme Court has stated that the statutory rules on accrual lack a mandatory nature, so the court may declare that accrual starts 'when the court itself finds adequate according to the rules of rational critique' (STS 30 July 1991 [RJ 1991\5435]). The decision to this regard cannot be challenged on appeal before the Supreme Court, since it refers to a factual, not legal issue (STS 19 January 2011 [RJ 2011\298]).

## B. BROAD OR NARROW CONCEPTION OF 'CAUSE OF ACTION'?

**Case 1** – *D, a ski instructor, negligently fails to make sure that all skiers in her 'off-piste' group wear helmets. P, a skier in the group, hits a tree. P immediately suffers head injury X, and years later another head injury Y that developed from the same accident.*

20 From a Spanish perspective and according to what has been said above, in the ski instructor case the victim has suffered two independent harms and can therefore file a second, separate claim in compensation years after she filed the first one. Spanish law thus adopts what may be called a narrow approach. At any rate, stabilisation does not apply in these cases. Foreseeability is not relevant in this setting either, since the second injury shows up at a later stage. Seriousness can also be deemed irrelevant.

---

41 See *Albaladejo*, *supra* fn 5, 217.

42 See a different opinion by *Díez-Picazo*, *supra* fn 2, 248.

43 See *Puig*, *supra* fn 9, 77.

**Case 2** – *Physician D treats patient P negligently and performs three mistakes on the day of the treatment: A, B and C. Mistake A causes harm X after a year. Mistake B causes harm Y after two years. Mistakes A and C together cause harm Z after three years.*

21 In the physician case, again, each harm gives rise to an independent cause of action, according to the narrow conception mentioned above.

**Case 3** – *Builder D lays down defective foundations for a building thereby creating the risk of future collapse. As a result, the value to the owner of the building (P) decreases (harm A). Two years later the foundation subsides and requires fixing paid by P (harm B). Three year later cracks appear in the building fixed by P (harm C). Four years later the building collapses (harm D).*

22 In the defective foundations case, it must be noted that liability derived from edification defects is governed by special rules, namely art 1591 CC and the Edification Act [LOE].[44] The first lays down a liability rule for damage caused by building collapse (art 1591 CC), in which case the Code lays down a ten-year period, within which damage must occur for liability to be triggered. Properly speaking this is not a prescription period but a period of guarantee (*período de garantía*). A more modern regime, which actually coexists with that rule, provides that guarantee periods for liability for damage caused by an edification agent – eg a developer, a builder, etc – range from one year to ten years, depending on the kind of damage (the more serious the damage is, the longer the prescription period, art 17 LOE). Therefore, again damage has to show up within that time period. However, the prescription period applicable in those cases will be two years from the moment in which damage is caused (art 18 LOE). The fact that the guarantee periods differ suggests that every damage is considered to give rise to an independent cause of action, according to the narrow conception aforementioned. It may be noticed, though, that the LOE provides for liability for 'material damage caused to the building' (art 17.1). Therefore, the mere building depreciation – consisting in a pure economic loss – does not trigger liability under that Act but, at any rate, under the general rules of the Civil Code.

## C. THE STARTING POINT – BREACH OF DUTY OR OCCURRENCE OF DAMAGE?

**Case 4** – *D enters P's premises without P's permission, thereby committing a tort of trespass, but without causing any damage. P can file a claim against D asking*

[44] Act 38/1999, of 5 November, *de ordenación de la edificación* (BOE no 266, 6.11.1999).

*for the remedy of D's eviction but fails to do so. A year later D causes physical harm to P's premises. P files a claim to compensation for the loss.*

In the case of the person who entered another's premises, unlike other jurisdictions, it has to be made clear that Spanish law lacks a specific tort of trespass. As a rule, eviction of the trespasser may be requested by way of a possessory action (art 250.1.4 of the Civil Procedure Act, *Ley de Enjuiciamiento Civil* [LEC]),[45] whose prescription period is one year since the interference with the claimant's possession (art 439.1 LEC).[46] Despite the fact that in the hypothetical the claimant failed to timely file such a claim, she will still be allowed to claim in tort under the general regime (art 1902 CC), since the unlawful occupation causes a continuous damage to the victim. Therefore, as long as such occupation takes place, the victim may file the claim in compensation and the prescription period will be the one-year general one (art 1968.2 CC). However, it must be made clear that the starting point of prescription is not trespass as such but damage. 23

## D. WHAT IS CONSIDERED 'HARM' FOR PRESCRIPTION PURPOSES?

**Case 5** – *In an accidental event, D negligently caused an explosion that damaged P's ears. During the first two years P has to raise the volume to enjoy music. During the following three years P needs a hearing device. After a further five years P becomes deaf.*

As regards the workplace accident case, as has been mentioned above, Spanish law generally adopts the stabilisation approach.[47] Therefore prescription will not start running until the whole extent of damage – deafness, in the hypothetical – can be determined. 24

**Case 6** – *Builder D lays down defective foundations for a bridge, thereby creating the risk of future collapse if heavy rain falls. Two years later heavy rain indeed falls and the collapse becomes only a matter of time, as indeed happens four years after the laying of foundations.*

As regards the other defective foundations case, from a general perspective under Spanish law, before any damage occurs, there will be no tortious liability, because risk as such is insufficient to trigger it. Therefore, prescription will 25

---

45 Act 1/2000, of 7 January, *de enjuiciamiento civil* (BOE no 7, 8.1.2000).

46 After that, a slower judicial procedure, based on the right of property, may be needed for eviction.

47 See *supra* 17.

start running upon collapse, provided that the victim knew it. Attention must however be paid to the distinction between the guarantee period and the prescription period, as explained above.[48] However, it may be noted that what is important under Spanish law is not collapse as such, but the fact that the building suffers from some sort of defect or vice and it is detected by the claimant. Assuming that the claimant knows about it when it takes place, the relevant moment is the one in which the building was actually built. In the case of a sub-acquirer, if the latter knew when she bought the building, that should have been reflected in the sales price. If she did not know, she may file a claim on contract or under the LOE provisions mentioned above.

## E. THE STARTING POINT (ACCRUAL) IN CONTINUOUS TORTS

**Case 7** – *Every week, during a month, D1 publishes a defamatory article on P1, each time in another newspaper and on a different topic. During the same period D2 publishes a defamatory article on P2, every second day, on the same topic and in the same newspaper.*

26 As to the defamation case: according to case law, for a continuous tort to exist, it must not be possible to divide the damaging activity in single parts or events.[49] Therefore, if it is possible to establish that the activity at stake has already caused some partial damage, one need not to wait until the damaging activity ends or the whole damage has been caused, and can claim compensation for the part of damage which has already been caused.[50] If the victim has already claimed compensation for certain damage and afterwards the same damaging event causes further damage or new damage shows up, or previous damage worsens, the victim may claim further compensation.[51] The prescription period for such late or new damage starts running from the moment in which such damage is discovered by the victim.[52] Therefore, in the hypothetical at stake, every act of defamation may be isolated from the others and give rise to separate causes of action.

---

48 See *supra* 22.

49 Among others, see STS 24 May 1993 [RJ 1993\3727] and 4 July 2016 [RJ 2016\2897]. See *E Llamas Pombo*, La reparación del daño continuado, in: Asociación Española de Abogados Especializados en Responsabilidad Civil y Seguro, Ponencias XVI Congreso Nacional-Málaga 2016 (2016), 93–126.

50 See *Albaladejo*, *supra* fn 5, 214.

51 See STS 16 November 2009 [RJ 2010\105] and 19 January 2011 [RJ 2011\298]. In legal scholarship, see *A Ruda* and *J Solé Feliu*, Spain, in: K Oliphant (ed), Aggregation and Divisibility of Damage (2009) 340 no 18.

52 See *Albaladejo*, *supra* fn 5, 215.

**Case 8** – *D, a landowner, negligently exposes P, a neighbour, to unreasonable noise for three years. P's hearing is thereby weakened on a daily basis, gradually restricting P's ability to communicate and enjoy music.*

The case of the unreasonable noise at the workplace is one of continuous damage and therefore prescription does not start running until exposure to the noise finishes and thus damage ceases being caused, and the victim knows it. Therefore, the so-called forward condensing model is adopted, although such terminology is not normally used under Spanish law. 27

**Case 9** – *A waste management company digs bins of toxic content into the soil. Toxic substance leaks into the soil and ground water, causing an apparent damage to crops and expenditure on cleaning on a daily basis. After two years the bins are removed from the soil.*

As to the waste management company case: From a Spanish perspective, the mere fact that damage consists in property damage instead of personal injury would not be relevant *per se* as regards prescription. However, there are several statutory regimes of liability applicable to the present case due to the fact that there are several kinds of damage arising from soil pollution. First, there is damage to property, which may give rise to a tort claim upon the general rules of liability (arts 1902 ff CC), whose prescription period is one year (art 1968.2 CC). Second, there is damage caused by waste, and therefore the Waste Act (LR)[53] is applicable as well, but the latter does not lay down any specific prescription period as regards liability for damage caused (except for the sanctions which may be established, art 51). Given that damage has been caused to the environment as such, since both the soil and ground water have been polluted, and the Waste Act refers to the Environmental Liability Act [LRM]),[54] a public authority may request restoration of the environmental resources independently from the owner of the resources, if there is any. This other prescription period is five years since the restoration measures ended or the liable person was identified, whatever happens later (art 48.2 LRM). At any rate, the case would not be considered one of pure economic loss under Spanish law, since there *is* pollution to the soil. 28

## F. IS THE LATE DISCOVERY RULE A RULE OF THE STARTING POINT OR A RULE OF PROLONGATION?

As noted above, there is no late discovery rule as such under Spanish law.[55] 29

---

53 Act 22/2011, of 28 July, *de residuos y suelos contaminados* (BOE no 181, 29.7.2011).

54 Act 26/2007, of 23 October, *de Responsabilidad Medioambiental* (BOE no 255, 24.10.2007). See also *infra* 78.

55 See *supra* 45.

## VII. PRESCRIPTION PERIODS

30 The general prescription period for claims based on tort is one year (pursuant to art 1968 2nd para CC). This includes not only damages falling under the general clause of liability for fault (art 1902 CC), but also all the other liability rules which develop or supplement it (thus liability for others, liability for animals, etc; arts 1903 ff CC). Such a period – which is based on historical Castilian law[56] – is almost unanimously found too short.[57] The reason for this is unclear. One may assume that the legislature did not want the potential defendant to wait too much to know what the victim may do, given that there was no previous relationship between them before the accident. However, there are many other tortious situations where such previous contact is lacking. Even in contract, there may be situations where the previous relationship between the parties is minimal – as in the case of a transport contract or an accident while practicing skiing at a mountain resort.[58]

31 In the case of liability of principals for their auxiliaries, the person who paid compensation to the victim has a right of recourse, the prescription period of which is four years (art 1904 CC). This is not an action in tort but an action of recovery of what was paid by the claimant against the person who should have paid it instead.[59]

32 Liability rules outside the Civil Code usually have their own prescription periods, usually longer than the general one. As has been mentioned, this is the case of liability for damage to privacy, the right to honour or the own image (four years pursuant to art 9.5 LOPCHIPI). Some special statutes do not provide anything on prescription, or they merely refer to the general rules (as in the case of art 33.2 Hunting Act).[60]

33 Traditionally there has been a major difference concerning prescription in tort and in contract. The prescription period applicable to actions different than those based on tort was 15 years (pursuant to art 1964 CC). This is the general period of prescription applicable 'to all personal actions lacking another period', as the provision reads. Therefore, claims for breach of contract, unjust enrichment, *negotiorum gestio*, etc, all had a much longer prescription period than those in tort. Criticism that the gap between both periods was too big

---

[56] See *Las Siete Partidas del Rey Don Alfonso el Sabio* [hereinafter, *Partidas*] 7, 9, 22. Available from <http://www.cervantesvirtual.com/obra-visor/las-siete-partidas-del-rey-don-alfonso-el-sabio-cotejadas-con-varios-codices-antiguos-por-la-real-academia-de-la-historia-tomo-3-partida-quarta-quinta-sexta-y-septima--0/html/>.

[57] See *Albaladejo*, *supra* fn 5, 202.

[58] See *Díez-Picazo*, *supra* fn 2, 247.

[59] See *Puig*, *supra* fn 9, 179; *Albaladejo*, *supra* fn 5, 204 and *Díez-Picazo*, *supra* fn 2, 246.

[60] Act 1/1970, of 4 April, *de caza* (BOE no 82, 6.4.1970).

was commonplace.[61] In 2015, the legislature passed a reform of several statutes including the Civil Code,[62] which shortened the general period of prescription sensibly, as a result of which the general prescription period for personal actions is now five years.

It has been a matter of some discussion what the prescription period applicable to liability for damage derived from crime actually is. As is well known, Spanish law is peculiar in that there is a separate statutory regime for tort liability depending on whether the tortious behaviour amounts to crime – so-called 'tort liability *ex delicto*', in which case the Criminal Code[63] applies – or not – in which the other rules apply. Since the Criminal Code does not lay down any prescription period for tort liability *ex delicto*,[64] some court decisions – backed by some scholarly opinions[65] – have applied the longer, 15-year period. However, legal scholarship has criticised that such a duality of statutory regimes is an anomaly and that tort is tort irrespective of whether it is the Criminal Code or another statute which provides its legal regime. Therefore, prescription applicable to tort liability *ex delicto* is one year (as some more recent decisions acknowledge, see eg STS 27 March 2015 [RJ 2015\2688]).[66] 34

As regards court judgments, the Civil Procedure Act provides that there is a time period of five years to implement them. The time starts from the moment in which the decision is final, ie it cannot be challenged before another court (art 518 LEC). This is not a period of prescription but of caducity (*la acción* [...] *caducará*). Therefore, the person who wants to enforce a judgment has to request it within five years. During the parliamentary discussion of the rule, the legislature refused prescription and clearly chose caducity as the preferred option, in spite of the fact that such a caducity cannot be decided upon *ex officio* (art 556.1 LEC). According to legal scholarship, there is no problem from a theoretical perspective in accepting a caducity period which has to be alleged by the party benefited by it.[67] The reasons for such a statutory choice remain unclear, although it seems that the legislature probably wanted to avoid a situation in which a judgment can remain without being executed for an 35

61 Instead of many, see *Díez-Picazo*, *supra* fn 2, 22–23.

62 Act 42/2015, of 5 October, *de reforma de la Ley 1/2000, de 7 de enero, de Enjuiciamiento Civil* (BOE no 239, 6.10.2015).

63 Organic Act 10/1995, of 23 November, *del Código Penal* (BOE no 281, 24.11.1995).

64 Criminal liability has its own prescription periods though (arts 130 ff CP), which range from five to 20 years (art 131).

65 See *Puig*, *supra* fn 9, 141.

66 In legal scholarship see *Albaladejo*, *supra* fn 5, 219 and 220 and *Díez-Picazo*, *supra* fn 2, 255–256.

67 See *A Domínguez Luelmo*, La caducidad de la acción ejecutiva fundada en títulos procesales o asimilados, in: MJ Marín López et al (eds), La prescripción extintiva. XVII Jornadas de la Asociación de Profesores de Derecho Civil (2014), 439–472.

indefinite period of time, merely by interrupting prescription through out-of-court claims.[68] If the party who won the case requests the enforcement of the judgment but it is not effective – eg because the debtor is insolvent – the possibility of execution will thus not remain open for an indefinite period of time, but will be barred by prescription pursuant to the general rule of art 1964 CC (five years).

**Table 1. Prescription periods**

| Cause of action or tort | Discovery rule | Prescription period | Notes |
|---|---|---|---|
| General | Since the victim knew | One year | Applies to all claims unless otherwise provided |
| Defamation | Since the victim 'could file the claim' (art 9.5 LOPCHIPI) | Four years | Caducity period |
| Contractual claims | Breach | Five years | |

## VIII. RULES OF POSTPONEMENT, SUSPENSION, RENEWAL AND EXTENSION

36 As has been pointed out, Spanish law distinguishes between prescription, which may be interrupted, on the one hand, and caducity, which may not, on the other. Indeed, the exclusion of interruption is seen as the very essence of caducity periods.[69]

37 Moreover, Spanish legal scholarship also distinguished between interruption (the Spanish equivalent to 'renewal') and suspension of the time period. In the first case, the period starts anew after interruption has occurred (STS 31 January 1986 [RJ 1986, 444] and 10 January 1990 [RJ 1990\32]). Therefore, interruption sets the clock at a zero position again. In the second case, the time period is merely suspended or frozen while the cause of suspension takes effect. After that, the counter will carry on from where it stopped.

38 To this regard, a further difference between prescription and caducity is that only the latter may be suspended. So, for instance, there is one instance of suspension of caducity in the law of Navarre (art 449 Fuero Nuevo,[70] regarding a right of first refusal [*retracto*]). However, such a difference may become

---

68 Again, see *Domínguez*, *supra* fn 67, 7, with further references.

69 See *Gómez Corraliza*, *supra* fn 10, 256; *Cavanillas*, *supra* fn 4, 13293.

70 Act 1/1973, of 1 March, *por la que se aprueba la Compilación del Derecho Civil Foral de Navarra* (BOE no 57, 7.3.1973).

blurred in practice. An example of that is of the Act on mediation in civil and commercial matters,[71] according to which both prescription and caducity may be suspended by the application to start a mediation procedure (art 4 para 1). But this is a special situation under Spanish law and does not reflect the general statutory regime on prescription.

39 Legal scholarship has remarked that prescription cannot be suspended since the impediments or obstacles to the exercise of a right are taken into account in an abstract or general manner. Therefore, it is irrelevant whether such an exercise is not possible because of the absence of the right holder, or because she ignored that the right at stake existed or that the triggering fact had taken place, etc, in the individual case.[72] It has indeed been argued that such an approach is flawed and that Spanish law should be amended so as to include suspension of prescription in those cases in which the right holder is not in a situation to exercise her right.[73] Such a proposal is consistent with the view that prescription is based on a presumption of abandonment of a right[74] – an idea which has been long abandoned under Spanish law, as has been pointed out above.[75] The current statutory rules do not allow such an interpretation.[76] Moreover, such a reform proposal has been contested by a different opinion, which favours the existing approach of the Civil Code on the basis of policy reasons. According to this latter approach, it remains unclear why the person potentially benefitted by prescription should be borne to know that the other party was affected by a disability, for instance.[77]

40 Prescription may be interrupted on several grounds, namely the judicial exercise of the right, a claim out of court, or the recognition of the debt (art 1973 CC). Interruption is different to a mere postponement in the start of the prescription period.[78] For a judicial interruption to occur, it is sufficient that the party at stake has filed a claim related to the liability in tort. So, for instance, filing a criminal claim interrupts prescription of the claim in tort (pursuant to art 114 Criminal Procedure Act [*LECrim*]).[79] The date in which judicial interruption

71 Act 5/2012, of 6 July, *de mediación en asuntos civiles y mercantiles* (BOE no 162, 7.7.2012).

72 See *Albaladejo*, *supra* fn 5, 45. The Spanish Civil Code does not completely disregard absence. In fact, it is relevant with regard to adverse possession. In the case of an absent right holder, the time period for the right acquisition by a third possessor is longer (art 1958).

73 See *Rivero*, fn 1, 125 ff.

74 See *Puig*, *supra* fn 9, 69.

75 See *supra* fn 5 and accompanying text.

76 See *Albaladejo*, *supra* fn 5, 48.

77 See *Díez-Picazo*, *supra* fn 2, 139.

78 See *Díez-Picazo*, *supra* fn 2, 179.

79 Royal Decree of 14 September 1882, *por el que se aprueba la Ley de Enjuiciamiento Criminal* (BOE no 260, 17.9.1882). However, if a criminal claim was dismissed and the one-year period in tort has already elapsed, it is not possible to file a second criminal claim just in order to renew the tort prescription period once again (STS 10 May 1994 [RJ 1994\4015]).

takes place is the one in which the claim was filed, not the date in which the defendant was notified of such a filing (STS 8 June 2012 [RJ 2012\9317]). In any of the cases mentioned, interruption takes place by those acts which aim at preserving and defending the right at stake. Therefore, a mere will to interrupt is not sufficient unlike the party at stake proves which acts in particular did interrupt prescription.[80] It is well-established case law that the interruptive act must be valid in order to actually interrupt prescription (STS 30 June 1941 [RJ 1941\763] and 19 February 1945 [RJ 1945\259]). Therefore, for instance, there is no interruptive effect if the previous legal proceedings against the defendant were declared void on the basis of a fraud (STS 4 March 1983 [RJ 1983\1422]). A scholarly opinion rejects such an approach by arguing that an invalid act may interrupt prescription provided that it carries a sufficient will of filing a claim or acknowledging the right. So, for instance, if the claim has a defect as a result of which it is invalid, for want of fulfilment of the statutory conditions, it may nevertheless interrupt prescription, if it is clear that the claimant is actually claiming the right at stake.[81] This is also the criterion adopted by case law, if the invalid claim was clear as to the will of claiming the debt and had been notified to the defendant before being withdrawn by the claimant (STS 30 September 2009 [RJ 2009\4599]). Therefore, a claim may interrupt prescription even though it is dismissed on merely procedural grounds if it was known by the other party.[82] Interruption takes place even though the claim has been filed against an indeterminate person, for instance in the case of damage caused by an indeterminate member of a group.[83] Interruption also takes place even though the criminal action has been filed against persons other than those against whom the later civil claim is brought (STS 30 September 1993 [RJ 1993\6665]).[84] However, an application to conciliate out of court on the liability does not interrupt prescription if it referred to contractual, not tortious liability, of the same defendants which later were brought to court in tort (STS 21 May 1992 [RJ 1992\4274]).

41 To this regard, Spanish law is quite innovative, since it accepts interruption both through a judicial and an out-of-court claim (also called 'extrajudicial claim', *reclamación extrajudicial*). Such an approach differs from the one followed by the Spanish Commercial Code, according to which prescription can only be interrupted by a court claim (art 944 CCom). However, case law has drawn both statutory regimes closer by accepting extrajudicial interruption

80 See *Díez-Picazo*, *supra* fn 2, 138.

81 See *Albaladejo*, *supra* fn 5, 227 and 237. According to this author, interruption takes place even though the claim is filed before the wrong judge.

82 See *Díez-Picazo*, *supra* fn 2, 166.

83 In legal scholarship, see *Albaladejo*, *supra* fn 5, 230.

84 In legal scholarship see *Díez-Picazo*, *supra* fn 2, 179.

of prescription also with regard to commercial law claims.[85] Such a criterion conforms to historical tradition, if one takes into account that extrajudicial interruption was already accepted by Medieval Castilian law (although with regard to adverse prescription)[86] and was adopted by the Civil Code as a way of avoiding excessive formalism – such an excessive formalism would render evidence of a will contrary to abandonment of the right too difficult.[87] A scholarly opinion has suggested that the introduction of caducity periods in Spanish legislation aims at avoiding extrajudicial interruptions.[88]

As has been said, for an extrajudicial interruption to occur there must be an 42
out-of-court 'claim' (*reclamación*). However, the technical meaning of the latter word is not very well defined. According to case law, it must be clear that the party at stake wanted to interrupt prescription. The courts have thus repeatedly insisted that a 'will of the creditor' or 'willing acts of claiming' are required to that end (STS 6 December 1968 [RJ 1968\5746] and 10 March 1983 [RJ 1983\1469]). The claim does not need to adopt any particular form and a merely verbal claim is sufficient to that regard.[89] The most clear case is a request to pay sent by way of a Notary, but also another kind of communication may suffice if they are safe enough, as a telegram (eg STS 15 October 2009 [RJ 2009\5576]), a fax (STS 29 February 2012 [RJ 2012\5268])[90] or a registered fax (*burofax*), which is sent through the Spanish Post Office – actually, the latter is the most commonly used to this regard.[91] There is some controversy as to whether the interruptive claim is a so-called 'receptitious' act – ie it has to reach its addressee – or not.[92] Whether prescription has been interrupted or not is a factual issue, which can be decided by the lower courts only. Therefore, the Supreme Court is not allowed to revise such an issue on appeal.[93]

As regards caducity, there is no doubt that it cannot be interrupted by an 43
out-of-court claim, since this is exactly the one possibility that the legislature wants to exclude when providing for a time period of that nature. The same happens if the claim is brought to court, unless the acts done by the claimant

85 See *Díez-Picazo*, *supra* fn 2, 33–34.

86 See *Partidas* 3, 29, available at <https://www.wdl.org/es/item/10642/> and <http://www.cervantesvirtual.com/obra-visor/las-siete-partidas-del-rey-don-alfonso-el-sabio-cotejadas-con-varios-codices-antiguos-por-la-real-academia-de-la-historia-tomo-2-partida-segunda-y-tercera--0/html/>.

87 Again, see *Díez-Picazo*, *supra* fn 2, 34 and 184.

88 See *Díez-Picazo*, *supra* fn 2, 71.

89 See *Díez-Picazo*, *supra* fn 2, 185.

90 The court points out that the fax was the usual way of communication between the parties.

91 However, a mere conversation between the lawyers of the two parties, in which they aim at reaching an agreement, may also be sufficient (STS 6 December 1968, mentioned above).

92 In the affirmative, see *Díez-Picazo,supra* fn 2, 97 and *Puig*, *supra* fn 9, 93; in the negative, see *Albaladejo*, *supra* fn 5, 252 and 257.

93 See *Albaladejo*, *supra* fn 5, 225.

amount to the proper exercise of her right in time.[94] Admission by the defendant of the claimant's right may be considered a waiver, provided that caducity has taken place, and therefore be admissible.[95]

44 Caducity may be suspended if a statutory rule so provides. Legal scholarship has argued *de lege ferenda* in favour of the introduction of general causes of suspension, namely the legal impossibility of preventing caducity from taking place, impossibility as a result of the existence of a criminal procedure and, in some cases, impossibility derived from the lack of capacity to govern oneself.[96] But this is not current practice, as will be shown below.

## A. UNAWARENESS – THE LATE DISCOVERY RULE

### 1) *Unawareness of what Elements of Liability?*

45 As has been said before, the prescription period starts running since the victim 'knew'. Therefore, awareness is essential to prescription accrual, even though what has to be known by the victim is far from clear.[97] At any rate, under Spanish law there is no '*late* discovery rule' as such, since prescription starts upon discovery only. The fact that the victim realises that she can file a claim against the tortfeasor (ie the latter is identified) after all the conditions of liability are actually met is thus not considered a case of 'prolongation', since nothing is prolonged, properly speaking, in that case. Also, knowledge of the legal norm which serves as the basis for the claim is not required, as pointed out above.[98] In sum, in the hypothetical at stake there is no suspension or interruption, but merely a situation in which the right to claim has still not started to count as regards prescription.

**Case 10** – *Chemical plant D negligently exposes bordering lands to toxic substances. As a result P, a nearby resident landowner, contracts a lung disease. P failed to sue in time because his former lawyer told him that the exposure was not tortious, and only his new lawyer told him, after the running of time, that it was tortious.*

46 The solution to the case of the exposure to the toxic substance is unclear, due to the fact that the Spanish Civil Code does not specify what the claimant is precisely required to know for prescription to accrue. On the one hand, the mere fact that a third person behaves in a negligent way does not affect the prescription

---

94 See *Cavanillas*, *supra* fn 4, 13293.
95 See *Cavanillas*, *supra* fn 4, 13293.
96 See *Gómez Corraliza*, *supra* fn 10, 284.
97 See *supra* 16.
98 Again, see *supra* 16.

of the victim's claim. Prescription does not depend on any subjective element on the side of the person affected by it. Therefore, it is independent of the will of the right holder and it is thus not affected by any mistakes or factual obstacles which may have prevented her from exercising her right.[99] On the other, the victim actually did not know that she had suffered a wrong and therefore the prescription period did not start running. If it was concluded that the claim was time barred, the lawyer would be liable for damage (loss of a chance) derived from such prescription, provided that she behaved negligently.

### 2) *Objective or Subjective Unawareness?*

Spanish law seems to leave this question in the open, although it may be guessed that a court would probably apply an objective standard. Therefore, if a reasonable victim should have known the particular victim may be deemed to have known as well and therefore prescription would be triggered. 47

### 3) *What is Considered Awareness of an Element of Liability?*

Again, there are no clear rules on this issue. The Civil Code merely provides that the victim must 'know'. According to case law, knowledge in this context means acquaintance (*saber*, in Spanish), which is gained through direct notice about the facts from which the claim derives (STS 14 October 1991 [RJ 1991\6919]). If the victim knew the total amount of damage in a clear and certain way, prescription accrues (STS 2 April 2014 [RJ 2014\2162]). There is no need to wait for a court decision which precisely establishes the damage in monetary terms if the victim already knows it (STS 8 June 2015 [RJ 2015\2284]). 48

### 4) *How Heavy is the Burden to Acquire Knowledge?*

**Case 11** – *Chemical plant D negligently exposes bordering lands to toxic substances. As a result P, a nearby resident landowner, contracts a lung disease, but is unaware of the causal link between exposure and disease because his physician fails to detect it. P does not seek a second opinion. After the prescription period runs on the disease P consults his new physician that tells him about the link.*

As in the previous case, in the second toxic exposure case it may be argued that the victim did not know that a wrong had taken place for want of causal link and therefore that she could file a claim in tort.[100] Therefore prescription has not 49

[99] See *Díez-Picazo, supra* fn 2, 126.

[100] See *supra* 15 and 16.

started running. As to whether the victim has a burden to ask a second medical opinion, that depends on the circumstances. If for instance an average person would realise that the physician was acting negligently – eg she failed to examine the victim or have any tests done – the victim could be deemed to 'know', but this is speculative.

## B. OTHER RULES OF PROLONGATION

### *1) D is to Blame for the Delay*

50 This is not as such a cause of suspension, since prescription cannot be suspended, but it may be argued that the victim did not 'know' and therefore, as in the previous case, prescription does not start running for want of actual discovery.

### *2) Admission by D of P's Right or Partial Performance of P's Right by D*

51 Any act of debt recognition by the debtor – in this case, the tortfeasor – interrupts or renews prescription (pursuant to art 1973 CC).[101] Recognition will have to be proved by the party alleging it, eg by providing the accounting books of the debtor where such a debt is acknowledged (as in STS 14 February 2011 [RJ 2011\443]). Recognition by a solidary co-debtor also interrupts prescription (arts 1973 and 1974 para 1 CC), but as a rule recognition by the guarantor (*fiador*) does not interrupt prescription as regard the main debtor (STS 23 February 2011 [RJ 2011\2474]). Whether partial performance amounts to debt recognition may depend on the circumstances, in particular on whether it may be assumed that the paying debtor acknowledge the existence of the remaining debt.

### *3) Special Relations between D and P*

52 The mere fact that some specific kind of legal relations exists between the parties does not affect prescription. However, it has been noted by a scholarly opinion that in the case where the parties are bound by some kinds of legal relationships – in particular, familiar ones – it does not seem reasonable from an objective perspective to request that the right at stake is exercised. This is specially the case where the parties are the members of a couple, the parent and the son or daughter under him or her, or the holder of guardianship and the pupil. Certainly, the Spanish Civil Code does not allow suspension of the prescription period as a rule, but in those scenarios, it seems unreasonable to say

---

101 See *supra* 40.

that the person affected by prescription could exercise the right during the time in which that legal relationship was existing. Therefore, it has been argued that a solution should be found by way of suspension (pursuant to art 1969 CC).[102] But again this is more a proposal for statutory reform than a description of current legal practice.

53 As regards relationships between parents/children, spouses, guardian/ward, attorney/client, partners in partnership, legal entity/organs, employer/employee, and physician/patient, there are no rules of prolongation.[103] However under Catalan law there is suspension as regards the parents/children relationship (under art 121-16.d) CCCat).

### 4) *P's Lack of Legal Capacity*

54 Prescription takes place both against capable persons and persons with disabilities, adults or minors, natural or legal persons. This is so because under Spanish law prescription may take place against 'any kind of persons' (art 1932 CC).[104] Such an approach means a rejection of the Roman criterion expressed by the maxim *contra non valentem non currit praescriptio* (among others, see STS 27 November 1992 [RJ 1992\9597] and Court of Appeal of Madrid, 9th Section, 10 November 2005 [JUR 2006\10128]).

55 *Minor with representative*: To this regard, Spanish law does not make any distinction regarding whether the disabled person has a representative or not. The prescription period thus starts running irrespective of whether the person affected by it has a legal representative or custodian, an administrator or an organ which supplements its lack of full capacity, as well as if they lack it at all. In the latter case, the person affected by the disability, minor, etc, may file a claim against those persons who should have requested the appointment of a legal custodian (a tutor, for instance) and negligently failed to do so, but prescription will be unaffected by that.[105]

56 Whether P has a representative does matter in a different sense, though. In the case where the legal representative negligently failed to interrupt prescription, the person affected by it may sue the former for damage caused (pursuant to

---

[102] See *Díez-Picazo*, *supra* fn 2, 135.

[103] See also *infra* 54.

[104] Prescription also takes place against those who have not been legally deprived of their capacity but are nevertheless prevented from acting legally (for instance, because they lack the necessary authorisations). See *Díez-Picazo*, *supra* fn 2, 119.

[105] See *Díez-Picazo*, *supra* fn 2, 119. This is in contrast with the solution adopted by succession law with regard to the case in which a minor was forgotten by the testator. In that situation the time period accrues from the moment in which the minor reaches majority (STS 10 December 2014 [RJ 2014\6842], according to which this is a caducity period, not a prescription one).

art 1932.2 CC). When assessing damage, one has to pay attention not only to the fact that the right was extinguished by prescription, but also the viability of a hypothetical exercise of such a right had it not been extinguished that way.[106]

57 *Minor without representative*: As pointed out above, whether there is a representative or not makes no difference under Spanish law (unlike under Catalan law, art 121-16.2) CCCat, which lays down a suspension rule).

58 *Adult with mental disability with representative.*[107]

59 *Adult with mental disability with no representative.*[108]

### *5) Absence of Parties from the Jurisdiction*

60 It does not affect prescription (Decision of the Superior Court of Justice of Catalonia [*Sentencia del Tribunal Superior de Justicia de Cataluña*, STSJC] of 19 March 2009 [RJ 2009\4004]).[109]

### *6) Former Legal and Other Proceedings between the Parties*

61 *Before a court*: As a general rule, every litigation must end by a final ruling under Spanish law, since the court is obliged to pronounce itself on the subject matter. If the claim suffers from formal deficiencies and the claimant fails to correct them within the period of time given to that effect, the court will as a rule issue a decision declaring that the claim is not admitted. Even in those cases, the filing of the defective claim may have an effect on prescription, namely interrupting (ie renewing) it.[110]

62 As to litigation on a close matter, it will as a rule be irrelevant as regards prescription of the claim in tort. For instance, litigation on liability for the breach of a contract between the same parties will leave prescription of the claim in tort unaffected. However, it must be noticed that during the time in which criminal litigation for the same facts takes place and until it ends with a final decision it is not possible to file any other claim (art 114.1 LECrim). Once the criminal procedure has ended, the victim will be able to file the claim in tort and the prescription period will be renewed.[111] To that regard, the relevant moment

---

106 See *Díez-Picazo*, *supra* fn 2, 120.

107 See *supra* 54.

108 See *supra* 54.

109 See, with regard to prescription interruption, *Díez-Picazo*, *supra* fn 2, 143.

110 See *infra* 70.

111 See *R Juan Sánchez*, Nueva doctrina constitucional sobre la prescripción del delito y su incidencia en el ejercicio de la acción por responsabilidad civil ex delicto (2009) 1 InDret 1, 10.

is the one in which the decision by the criminal court is notified to the victim (STS 11 April 2002 [RJ 2002\3382] and Decision of the Court of Appeal of Pontevedra of 17 November 1992 [AC 1992\1582]).

*ADR*: The fact that the parties attempt to solve their issues by way of ADR or a settlement reveals that the potential claimant is willing to enforce her right to compensation and therefore such an attempt may amount to an interruption (thus a renewal) of prescription out of court.[112] 63

As has also been noted above, the application to initiate a mediation procedure suspends prescription.[113] This is a departure of the general principle that prescription cannot be suspended. The legislature aimed at avoiding that a perverse incentive was given to the parties, who could start a mediation procedure without any real will of reaching an agreement and with the sole intent of purging the part of the prescription period already elapsed.[114] 64

*Arbitration*: In the case of arbitration, the arbitration award has the effect of *res judicata* (pursuant to the Arbitration Act [*Ley de arbitraje*, LA], art 43) and therefore the parties will not be allowed to re-open the liability issue before a court at a later stage – except where the award is void and its annulation is requested (art 45 LA). 65

*Negotiations*: Something similar can be said with regard to negotiations. If the parties engage in negotiations between them, it may not be possible to say that the victim dropped her claim and therefore prescription will not accrue until the moment in which negotiations ended (STS 15 July 2005 [RJ 2005\9624]). In fact, conversations and negotiations may have taken place with the precise aim of establishing damage (as pointed out by STS 20 November 2017 [RJ 2008\19]). In a similar vein, case law focuses on whether the victim has the will to preserve the action or not, what is called the *animus conservandi* (STS 18 September 1987 [RJ 1987\9982] and 15 July 2005 [RJ 2005\9238]). 66

As regards settlements, the parties may settle tortious liability out of court, even in the case of *ex delicto* liability (art 1813 CC), and the settlement produces a *res judicata* effect (art 1816 CC). For this reason, it seems hardly probable that a party has to rely on a previous settlement to argue for prolongation or suspension of prescription. 67

---

112 See *supra* 41.

113 See *supra* 38.

114 See *E Serrano Gómez*, Artículo 4, in: L García Villaluenga and C Rogel Vide (eds), Mediación en asuntos civiles y mercantiles. Comentarios a la Ley 5/2012 (2012), 67.

Table 2. Prolongation

| Former proceedings | Prolongation | Rule | Comments |
|---|---|---|---|
| Legal | No | | No prolongation but interruption |
| ADR | It depends | Suspension (in the case of mediation only) | No prolongation but interruption (except for mediation) |
| Administrative | No | | It would actually depend on whether initiation of such proceedings reveals an intention to enforce claim valid. For instance, a claim filed before the EU Commission in an intracommunity dumping case was deemed to interrupt prescription (STS 2 October 2008 [RJ 2008\5588]) |
| Settlement | No | | No prolongation but interruption |

### 7) *Victim's Death*

68 The mere fact that the victim dies has no effect on prescription, since prescription may also take place or be effective against the potential heir. Therefore, it may happen that an heir acquires the inheritance and prescription has taken place between the death and the acceptation of the inheritance (pursuant to art 1934 CC).

### 8) *Victim's Bankruptcy*

69 If the victim cannot afford filing the claim for lack of resources, this is a merely material difficulty which does not prevent prescription from taking place. As a matter of fact, she may apply for free legal aid. By contrast, if it is the defendant who becomes insolvent, prescription against her will be interrupted as regards rights previous to the declaration of insolvency (pursuant to art 60.1 of the Insolvency Act).[115]

### *9)* Force Majeure

70 As has been pointed out before, prescription starts running from the moment in which the exercise of the right is possible from a legal perspective. Therefore, merely material impediments or obstacles (eg being in jail) are irrelevant. Unlike what happens in other legal systems, *force majeure* as such is irrelevant

115 Act 22/2003, of 9 July, *Concursal* (BOE no 164, 10.7.2003).

to this regard.[116] Nevertheless, it may be noted that after the Spanish Civil war the legislature passed an Act to suspend prescription, due to the difficulties of finding many people as a result of the conflict.[117] Suspension of prescription is therefore a very exceptional phenomenon, which takes place only in the cases provided for by the legislature under unusual circumstances.

*Natural disaster*: As pointed out above, it is not relevant. 71

*Wars*: The Commerce Code[118] provides that the government may suspend prescription in the case of war (art 955 CCom). 72

*Military service*: It is not relevant. Compulsory military service was actually suppressed in Spain in 2001. 73

*Imprisonment*: As pointed out above, it is not relevant. Imprisoned persons preserve the right to communicate with their lawyers, although it may be suspended or restricted under certain circumstances such as terrorism (art 51.2 of the General Penitentiary Act).[119] Therefore it may be assumed that they keep the ability to act in order to prevent prescription from happening, etc. 74

*Legal inability to file a claim*: If there is a legal inability to file a claim prescription cannot take place. So, for instance, if a criminal proceeding is pending no separate civil proceeding may be started by the victim, as pointed out above.[120] Legal impossibility to sue may derive from a material (substantive) or procedural reason, as the Spanish Supreme Court has acknowledged (STS 14 October 1991 [RJ 1991\6919]). 75

*Closed courts*: According to the general rules on deadlines, when a deadline is fixed in months or years the dates are counted from date to date (art 5.1 CC). Therefore, if the courts are closed on the very last day of the prescription deadline, the victim may not be able to file the claim. 76

*Other*: The Commerce Code provides that the government may suspend prescription in the case of epidemics or a revolution (art 955). Such a provision does not seem to have been applied by Spanish courts so far. 77

---

116 See *Díez-Picazo*, *supra* fn 2, 133 and 143.

117 Act of 1 April 1939, *que suspende plazas para prescripción y caducidad de acciones, delitos, instancias, etc*, (BOE no 97, 7.4.1939). From a criminal law perspective, it was later provided that liability arising from any crime committed before that same date would be deemed as time barred, see Decree-Act (*Decreto-Ley*) 10/1969, of 31 March, *por el que se declara la prescripción de todos los delitos cometidos con anterioridad al 1 de abril de 1939* (BOE no 78, 1.4.1969).

118 Royal Decree of 22 August 1885, *por el que se publica el Código de Comercio* (BOE no 289, 16.10.1885).

119 Organic Act 1/1979, of 26 September, *General Penitenciaria* (BOE no 239, 5.10.1979).

120 See *supra* 40.

## IX. CEILINGS ON THE EFFECTIVE TIME OF PRESCRIPTION

78 The general rules on prescription laid down by the Civil Code do not include any ceiling on the effective time of prescription. However, some special statutes exceptionally provide for such a ceiling when setting a separate liability regime in specific areas, as is the case of environmental liability (art 4 para 1 LRM),[121] nuclear energy (art 67 Nuclear Liability Act [LEN][122]), or products liability (art 144 Recast Text of the General Act for the Protection of Consumers and Users).[123] However, such ceiling rules are alien to the Spanish legal culture and result from the influence of international conventions or European Directives. An exception to that regard is the special liability rule applicable to damage caused by a Land Registrar, in which case the one-year period is to be counted from the occurrence of the negligent conduct irrespective of knowledge of the victim (pursuant to art 311 of the Land Registry Act).[124] There is a 30-year ceiling period under the Catalan Civil Code, though (art 121-24 CCCat).

79 Ceiling periods are not prescription periods, but have a different nature, since they cannot be interrupted and for this reason, they are similar to caducity periods.

**Table 3. Ceilings**

| Scope | Commencement | Length | Prolongation |
|---|---|---|---|
| Product liability | D's conduct – putting into circulation | Ten years | No |
| Bodily injury | No | | |
| Medical malpractice | No | | |

## X. STATUTE INTERPRETATION, JUDICIAL DISCRETION AND LACHES

80 In Spanish law two different perspectives coexist as to the nature and the interpretation of prescription. The traditional point of view, which is still

121 The period is 30 years from the emission, the event or the incident which caused damage.

122 Act 25/1964, of 29 April, *sobre energía nuclear* (BOE no 107, 4.5.1964). The period is ten years if damage is immediate, and 20 years if damage occurs on a delayed basis. Damage is 'delayed' if it occurs after ten years since it was caused, it was noticed, or the liable person was known (pursuant to art 46 of the same Act).

123 Royal Legislative Decree 1/2007, of 16 November, *por el que se aprueba el texto refundido de la Ley General para la Defensa de los Consumidores y Usuarios y otras leyes complementarias* (BOE no 287, 30.11.2007). The period is ten years since the product was put into circulation.

124 Decree of 8 February 1946, *por el que se aprueba la nueva redacción oficial de la Ley Hipotecaria* (BOE no 58, 27.2.1946). Also see to that regard STS 21 October 2013 [RJ 2014\435].

endorsed by case law, states that prescription is contrary to natural law, and should therefore be handled from a restrictive stance (*in dubio, contra praescriptio*). This is so because, as has been explained above, prescription is seen as an institution which restricts the possibilities of exercising a right. As a result, (a) prescription cannot be applied in an extensive way since that would cause uncertainty and a lack of security, and (b) if a court has doubts as to whether prescription has taken place or not, the criterion to be adopted is a restrictive one, by which the court will allow the right to be exercised unless it is clear that the claim is time barred. According to a statement which has been repeated many times by case law, prescription creates a conflict between legal certainty and so-called 'intrinsic justice', and since prescription is not based on intrinsic justice, it has to be dealt with from a restrictive stance.[125] From this perspective, the courts emphasise the importance of interpreting prescription rules according to the principles of good faith[126] and *pro actione* interpretation (STS 15 July 2005 [RJ 2005\9624]).

A manifestation of such an approach can be found in connection with the contract/tort divide. As has been shown, the prescription period in contract (five years, pursuant to art 1964 CC) is much longer than in tort (one year, pursuant to art 1968.2 CC). Therefore, the restrictive stance towards prescription leads to arguing that in case of doubt as to whether liability is in contract or in tort, the first option has to be adopted for the sake of restricting prescription.[127] 81

That point of view contrasts with the one adopted by modern legal scholarship. According to the prevailing view, prescription fulfils a prophylactic role, by keeping legal traffic clean of waste as if it was some sort of necrophagic species.[128] According to this other point of view, it is incorrect to point out that prescription is unjust; quite to the contrary, it is necessary and this is why all legal systems have rules to this regard. In particular, it has been noticed that the arguably unjust effect of prescription is contrary to the cogent nature of its statutory regime in many legal systems.[129] Moreover, it is incorrect to assume that prescription rules have to be interpreted as if they were special of different from other legal rules. The general criteria of interpretation, as laid down by the Civil Code (art 3 CC), should be adopted instead.[130] 82

It is noteworthy however that case law stresses the apparently unjust nature of prescription in cases of tort liability claim where, as has been shown, the 83

---

125 See STS 8 October 1982 [RJ 1983\401], 2 February 1984 [RJ 1984\570] and 22 March 1985 [RJ 1985\1197], followed by many others.

126 STS 11 December 2012 [RJ 2013\4350] and 19 January 2015 [RJ 2015\2325].

127 See *Albaladejo*, *supra* fn 5, 201.

128 See *Cavanillas*, *supra* fn 4, 13274 with further references.

129 See *Díez-Picazo*, *supra* fn 2, 48.

130 See *Díez-Picazo*, *supra* fn 2, 36 and 48.

legal period to file the claim is particularly short. It has been thus suggested that the case law doctrine is merely a device by which the courts try to alleviate the rigour of the statutory criterion and thereby expand the time for the victim to sue.[131] Such stance has led to some confusion in practice, since case law has not always been consistent with the restrictive approach which it repeatedly states. It is particularly striking that according to case law the causes of prescription interruption have to be interpreted in a restrictive way, although an extensive interpretation of the same would obviously make prescription more difficult to occur and is therefore more consistent with the idea of prescription as an unjust institution. As a scholarly opinion has pointed out, the two strands of case law collide, since if interruption of prescription is restricted, one favours prescription, whereas it is precisely prescription which should be restricted according to the other strand.[132] Apart from that, case law has made clear that restrictive interpretation cannot lead to an extension of the statutory time periods (STS 15 July 2005 [RJ 2005\9238] and 16 April 2008 [RJ 2008\4357]). Be it as it may, the fact is that recent case law seems to be abandoning the theory of the restrictive interpretation of prescription and adopting a more neutral stance.[133]

84 Although these kinds of divergences in judicial interpretation do indeed occur, Spanish courts are bound to apply the law and lack any discretionary power to depart from the same or not to apply a prescription period if prescription has already taken place.[134]

85 Under Spanish law it is considered that allowing a claim to be filed under certain circumstances is contrary to the general principle of good faith, in particular when the defendant could rely on the fact that the claim would never be filed. This may be so because the claimant behaved in such a way so as to create the impression that she waived the right to claim, for instance where the victim has let a long period of time to elapse without adopting any active steps to file the claim. Even though the prescription period may not be fully elapsed, it would be against good faith to file a claim when one has allowed the other party to assume that the claim would not be filed.[135] Such a doctrine, generally known as 'disloyal delay' (*retraso desleal*), has been influenced by the German doctrine on

131 See *Cavanillas, supra* fn 4, 13275, with further references.

132 See *Albaladejo, supra* fn 5, 13 and 225 and *Díez-Picazo, supra* fn 2, 139.

133 See *Cavanillas, supra* fn 4, 13275.

134 Courts are also not allowed to prolong prescription on mere grounds of justice. Under Spanish law, a court decision may only be based exclusively on justice when the law expressly allows this (art 3.2 CC).

135 However, the mere fact that some time has elapsed is not sufficient *per se* to that regard (STS 2 March 2017 [RJ 2017\846]). In addition to that an objective circumstance is required, namely, that the passive stance of the victim has led the defendant to the belief that the claim would no longer be filed (STS 12 December 2011 [RJ 2012\32]).

*Verwirkung* (forfeiture). Such a doctrine can be connected to the prohibition to act against one's own acts (*venire contra factum proprium*) and is described as a particular instance of abuse of a right.[136] The ultimate statutory basis for these doctrines is the general principle of good faith, as laid down by the Civil Code (art 7.2).[137] Case law has pointed out at the similarities of such an institution with laches in two decisions (STS 19 December 2008 and 25 January 2007 [RJ 2007\2778]), and Spanish legal scholarship has also compared it to estoppel by acquiescence.[138]

## XI. CHANGE OF PARTIES

### A. THE PLAINTIFF IS A TRANSFEREE OF THE VICTIM'S CLAIM

86 If the claim is transferred by the claimant to another party, the latter will be affected by prescription in the same way in which the transferor would have been but for the transfer. Such transfer may happen on a voluntary basis (so-called *cesión de crédito*, arts 1526 ff CC) or may be provided for by a statutory rule (so-called *subrogación*). Therefore, in the case of transfer of a personal right, the defendant will be able to rely on prescription, since the origin of the latter is previous to the act by which the right at stake was transferred.[139]

87 An example of subrogation is to be found in the insurance law, in the case in which the insurer pays compensation to the victim in lieu of the defendant. According to the Spanish Insurance Contract Act[140] subrogation by the insurer affects 'the rights and actions which belonged to the insured because of the accident' (art 43). Therefore, subrogation is merely change a in the persons of the legal relationship, which leaves the object of the same unaffected. This is a key difference with the right of recovery (*derecho de repetición*), in which case the person who paid another one's debt has a new right, separate from the victim's one. As a result, in the case of subrogation prescription accrual takes place when the victim knew the accident.[141]

88 If transfer occurs as a result of inheritance, the heir will succeed the deceased victim in the same right of action which belonged to the latter (pursuant to

136 See *Díez-Picazo*, *supra* fn 2, 85.

137 In this sense, STS 21 October 2005 [RJ 2005\8274], 28 November 2005 [RJ 2005\1233], 23 November 2007 [RJ 2007\8516] and 19 December 2008 [RJ 2009\24].

138 See *Díez-Picazo*, *supra* fn 2, 89.

139 See *C Cuadrado Pérez*, La cesión de créditos (2014), 143.

140 Act 50/1980, of 8 October, *de Contrato de Seguro* (BOE no 250, 17.10.1980).

141 See *JM Paniagua Manchado*, El derecho de subrogación de las aseguradoras en el seguro de daños (2014) 51 Revista de la Asociación Española de Abogados Especializados en Responsabilidad Civil y Seguro (RAEAERCS), 51, 64.

art 661 CC). Prescription may take place and is therefore not interrupted or suspended even though the right at stake may temporarily 'belong' to the heritage, which happens while the heir has still not accepted it (pursuant to art 1934 CC), so in the meantime no one may have been able to exercise such a right.

## B. THE DEFENDANT IS A TRANSFEREE OF THE TORTFEASOR'S OBLIGATION

89 As in the reverse situation described above, the change in the person of the tortfeasor is a merely subjective modification of the legal relationship which does not affect its object. For this reason, the change in the person of the defendant leaves prescription unaffected. Such specific change is not provided for by Spanish law, but it may be assumed that it is possible under the general rules on the modification of obligations (art 1203 CC). If transfer takes place on a hereditary basis, the heir will be placed in exactly the same position which the deceased person occupied, as her successor (art 661 CC). Therefore, it is considered that the heir inherits the same liabilities that the deceased person had – save for those which extinguish themselves upon death (art 659 CC), such as criminal liability (art 130.1.1 CP).[142] and that the prescription period is not interrupted by the mere fact that hereditary succession takes place. For the same reasons, the same rules of prolongation which were applicable to the deceased person will be applicable to the heir.

## C. CONTRIBUTION CLAIMS

90 The tortfeasor who is liable on a solidary basis has an action in contribution (or 'recourse action', *acción de regreso*) against the other such tortfeasors (pursuant to art 1145 para 2 CC). This is a separate action with regard to the one of the victims (since payment by one of the solidary tortfeasors extinguishes the obligation, art 1145 para 1 CC; STS 28 October 2015 [RJ 2015\4788]) and has also a different nature, since it is not an action in tort (and thus based in the causation of damage by another) but a personal action for the reimbursement of what has already been paid (STS 13 May 2011 [RJ 2011\3860]). As such, the action in contribution lacks a specific prescription period and therefore it is governed by the longer, general five-year prescription period (pursuant to art 1964 CC) – except in some particular cases, as in the one of motor vehicle

[142] Therefore, the culprit's death will extinguish criminal, not tortious liability, which may be claimed against the culprit's heirs (art 115 LECrim).

liability, in which case the period is one year.[143] Thus, the period may be longer than, or the same as, the one applicable to tort claims in general, depending on the kind of accident. Apart from that, the other solidary tortfeasors will be liable in contribution among them, but not on a solidary, but on a proportional or separate basis (STS 6 March 2015 [RJ 2015\836]). The accrual of the contribution claim starts on the payment to the victim (STS 28 October 2015, mentioned above). In conclusion, the joint and several tortfeasor who pays the victim has a separate claim in contribution against the other joint and several tortfeasors which prescribes independently from the original claim by the victim.

### D. DEPENDANT'S CLAIM

From a Spanish perspective, one should distinguish between two different actions. One is the action which the victim of an accident could have filed before dying, and the other one the action belonging to other persons depending from the former. If the victim had filed her claim timely, and death occurred after that, her successors could continue the same action as heirs. However, as already pointed out, if a person is claiming for her own damage, on the basis that she was depending on the primary victim, this is a different action and, according to the general rules, the prescription period starts running after the victim's death, from the moment in which the claimant 'knew it'.[144] From this perspective, it does not make any difference whether the victim dies before or after the prescription period. 91

## XII. OTHER ASPECTS OF PRESCRIPTION LAW

### A. STIPULATION

Prescription rules are traditionally considered mandatory under Spanish law. For that reason, the parties lack autonomy to modify or exclude them, since private autonomy is limited by imperative law (art 1255 CC). This is explicitly provided for by the regional law of Navarre. The Navarrese legislation provides that the agreements aimed at modifying the statutory periods of prescription will have no effect (art 27 FN). According to legal scholarship, such a prohibition to modify the statutory rules includes not only the prescription periods as such, 92

[143] See Royal Legislative Decree (*Real Decreto Legislativo*, RDL) 8/2004, of 29 October, *por el que se aprueba el texto refundido de la Ley sobre responsabilidad civil y seguro en la circulación de vehículos a motor* (BOE no 267, 5.11.2004) [hereinafter, LRCSCVM], art 7.

[144] See *supra* 15 and 16.

but also any other circumstances provided for by the law, such as causes of suspension or the ways of interrupting prescription.[145] This contrasts with the approach adopted by the Catalan Civil Code, according to which the parties may agree upon the prescription period, so as to shorten or expand them (art 121-3).

93 However, it has also been pointed out that the mandatory nature of the law of prescription can only be maintained if one starts from the premise that prescription as such serves the goal of providing legal certainty and social utility. Though, one may also see prescription as a way of protecting the obliged person, who may actually rely on the benefice of prescription or renounce to it. For this reason, the interest which is protected by prescription is a merely private one, and it is for this reason that one should not close the door to the possibility that the parties themselves provide what they find most appropriate on a voluntary basis as regards prescription. It may be noted that there is no statutory basis to forbid such agreements.[146] Even the rule which bans a beforehand waiver to future prescription (art 1935 CC) is deemed a merely blurry limit to those agreements.[147]

94 Spanish case law has indeed admitted some of them, in particular those by which the parties extend or reduce the prescription period or agree on the suspension of the same.[148] The parties may also agree upon a different rule of accrual, provided that prescription is not hindered in an extraordinary manner. Moreover, agreements on the causes of interruption are deemed also valid.[149] As regards agreements on suspension, legal scholarship has held that their validity depends on the purpose of the parties. If they aim at avoiding prescription because they need more time in the course of ongoing negotiations, the agreement is valid. However, it would be invalid if the parties merely aimed at adjourning prescription in an indefinite way.[150] Apart from that, it seems that the parties cannot agree that a right which may be the object of prescription will not be affected by it, since that would imply a waiver to future prescription contrary to art 1935 CC, mentioned above.[151]

95 In spite of the preceding remarks, Spanish legal scholarship rejects modification of caducity time periods, whenever they are established by a statute.[152]

---

145 See *Albaladejo*, *supra* fn 5, 330.
146 See *Díez-Picazo*, *supra* fn 2, 37.
147 See *Díez-Picazo*, *supra* fn 2, 43.
148 See *Albaladejo*, *supra* fn 5, 330–331; also in favour of such agreements, see *Díez-Picazo*, *supra* fn 2, 44 and 45.
149 Again, see *Díez-Picazo*, *supra* fn 2, 45.
150 See *Díez-Picazo*, *supra* fn 2, 144.
151 See *Díez-Picazo*, *supra* fn 2, 44.
152 *Díez-Picazo*, *supra* fn 2, 71.

## B. MEANING OF 'FILING A CLAIM' THAT INTERRUPTS THE RUNNING OF PRESCRIPTION

96 Although prescription is usually alleged by way of defence or exception, it could at least in theory be raised in the claim as well.[153] At any rate, prescription has to be alleged on an explicit basis. Therefore, it is not sufficient for the party who would be benefited by it to merely establish the facts from which prescription could be deduced and rely that the judge will dismiss the claim on such a basis (STS 12 May 2003 [RJ 2003/3898]).

## C. WHEN SHOULD THE DEFENCE BE RAISED AND DECIDED?

97 The defendant must allege prescription when replying to the claim (*contestación a la demanda*), pursuant to the Civil Procedure Act (art 405). If she alleges it at a later stage, it will be dismissed as a 'new issue' (*cuestión nueva*) which unduly alters the terms of the object of the judicial procedure (so-called *mutatio libelli*, thereby infringing art 456.1 LEC), or it may be considered that the party at stake renounced to it on an implicit basis.[154] It is sufficient that the defendant includes the prescription exception in the reply to the claim, without having to repeat it again when she explains what she demands (so-called *suplico*) (STS 15 October 2009 [RJ 2009\5574]).

98 Prescription is considered a 'peremptory exception' (*excepción perentoria*, eg STS 31 October 1995, mentioned above), ie one which has to be solved as part of the substance matter of the case, and not a 'dilatory exception' (*excepción dilatoria*), ie one which has to be solved before entering the matter of the case. The reason is that prescription is deemed to affect the subject matter of the case, in that it has an extinctive effect on the right or action at stake. In practical terms, that means that prescription has to be alleged, as has been pointed out above, in the reply to the claim. Therefore, it cannot be raised on appeal, not even by the defendant who was absent during the first instance.[155] There is no sanction for the failure to plead prescription but, as has been said before, the party who could have been benefitted from such an allegation will lose such a possibility.

99 The court will have to decide on prescription on the final decision of the case. In some judicial procedures (in particular, in the so-called *juicio ordinario*) there is a previous audience before entering to decide the matter of the case. It is not possible to discuss prescription in such a previous audience, since it

[153] See *Cordón*, *supra* fn 26, 86.

[154] See *Cordón*, *supra* fn 26, 90–91.

[155] See *Cordón*, *supra* fn 26, 91–92.

is not included in the kind of issues to be dealt with at such a procedural stage (art 416 LEC). Therefore, the court cannot decide on the basis of prescription at that stage, since it would deprive the parties of the right to discuss the matter of the case, or allege that prescription has been interrupted, or that a different period of prescription is applicable (Decision of the Court of Appeal [*Auto de la Audiencia Provincial*, AAP] Granada 16 February 2007 [JUR 2007\175286]).[156] Therefore, as a rule prescription has to be pleaded in the claim or in the reply to the same, and it is not allowed to plead it in later occasions – as, eg in the résumé of the pieces of evidence (STS 12 May 2003 [RJ 2003/3898]).

## D. WHO MAY RAISE THE DEFENCE?

100 As noted above, the defence may be raised in the claim or the reply to the claim, therefore it could be raised by any of the parties, although it will normally be by the defendant.[157]

101 According to the Spanish Civil Code, prescription of actions takes place 'by the mere lapse of time established by the statute' (*por el mero lapso del tiempo fijado por la ley*, art 1961). Such a provision may give the impression that prescription thus takes place automatically and does not need to be pleaded by the party benefitted by it. However, legal scholarship explains that what the legislature really means by this provision is that – in contrast to adverse possession, as has been pointed out – for prescription to take place possession, a just title, or good faith are not required. Prescription merely attributes the party who may plead it a legal power, the so-called 'legal power of prescription' (*facultad de prescripción*). All its other effects therefore depend on the exercise of such a power by the party at stake.[158]

102 From a procedural perspective, the allegation of prescription by the defendant is considered an exception (*excepción*) and not a counterclaim (*reconvención*).

103 If the defendant fails to allege prescription, such an omission cannot be replaced or saved by the court *ex officio*.[159] If it were, then the court decision could be deemed to infringe the adversarial principle and violate the right of the affected party to a fair process.[160] According to case law, prescription may be waived, and therefore cannot be applied without having being alleged by the party

---

156 In legal scholarship, see *Cordón*, *supra* fn 26, 91.

157 See *supra* 96.

158 *Puig*, *supra* fn 9, 32; *Díez-Picazo*, *supra* fn 2, 95–96, 107 and 109; *Cavanillas*, *supra* fn 4, 13279.

159 See *Albaladejo*, *supra* fn 5, 22.

160 See *Cordón*, *supra* fn 26, 88.

benefited by it. So, for instance, if only one of the co-defendants raises the prescription exception but not the other, and there is no solidarity among them, prescription will not benefit the first but only the second (STS 31 October 1995 [RJ 1995\7654]). This is a difference with regard to caducity which, according to the prevailing view, can be applied *ex officio*.[161] However, a scholarly opinion is that this is not an essential feature of all caducity periods.[162] In particular, one may distinguish between those cases in which there is a reason of *ordre public* or public interest – in which application of caducity *ex officio* is justified – and those in which such public interest is lacking – with regard to which caducity should be accepted on request by the party benefitted by it only.[163]

A different question is whether the defence may be raised by a third party. If prescription had taken place and thus the defendant D was not legally obliged to pay the plaintiff P, but D nevertheless paid, the legal effect of such a payment is that D cannot claim the sum paid back, and therefore P can retain it on the basis of a so-called natural obligation – as explained above.[164] It is usually said that one cannot be forced to pay a natural obligation, since the claim has been extinguished by prescription. Therefore, it seems that the third party may also rely on such basis to refuse to pay contribution to D. At any rate, as pointed out above, the party benefited by prescription bears the burden to plead it, and it is not sufficient that it has been pleaded by another party, unless they are bound by solidarity (joint and several liability).[165] 104

The most controversial issue to this regard has been determining whether interruption of prescription against one person has any effect against other persons to whom the former is linked in some way. In the case where prescription has been interrupted against one of several co-owners, it has been argued that such interruption does not affect the remaining members of the co-ownership, unless such an interruption has been done in a way which 'breaks the silence of the legal relationship' as regards such other members. For instance, this is the case if they knew about interruption, so if they tried to rely on prescription they would be acting in bad faith.[166] 105

If prescription has been interrupted against one of the solidary debtors, it has effect against the other debtors as well (pursuant to art 1974 CC). Such a rule is consistent with the idea that the solidary debtors act as some sort of agents of all the others – an idea which prevailed during French codification and seems 106

161 STS 26 November 1997 [RJ 2002\10383], 26 November 2002 [RJ 2002\10383] and 17 July 2008 [RJ 2008\4382. In legal scholarship, see *Puig*, *supra* fn 9, 35 and *Cordón*, *supra* fn 26, 92 and 95.

162 See *Cavanillas*, *supra* fn 4, 13293.

163 See *Díez-Picazo*, *supra* fn 2, 83.

164 See *supra* 10.

165 See *supra* 103.

166 See *Díez-Picazo*, *supra* fn 2, 154.

to have had an influence on Spanish law even though it was not accepted in an explicit way. However, it has been suggested that such a paradigm is no longer valid, since in most cases solidary debtors have nothing in common apart from the fact that they are solidary debtors. So, the Spanish Supreme Court has stated that the interruptive effect (pursuant to art 1974 CC) happens only where solidarity is provided by a statute or as a result of an agreement of the parties. By contrast, where case law speaks of solidarity in an improper sense (or obligation *in solidum*, as is also called) – ie where the defendants have acted independently from one another or a 'community of interests' among them is lacking – such interruptive effect against the other solidary debtors does not take place (so the very important STS 14 March 2003 [RJ 2003\3645] and 17 March 2006 [RJ 2006\5637]; also STS 25 November 2016 [RJ 2016\5643]).[167] In particular, solidarity *in solidum* requires that it is not possible to individualise who did what or define the responsibilities of each defendant (among others, STS 18 July 2011 [RJ 2011\6123]). However, one may argue – in contrast to such case law – that the legislature has not distinguished between different kinds of solidarity and therefore one should not make any distinctions as to the effects of interruption.[168] At any rate, the 'improper solidarity doctrine' actually leads to a considerable amount of complexity in those cases where a statute lays down a solidary liability rule as regards some kind of persons but not others, as happens in the case of the so-called construction process. Pursuant to the Act on Edification, the developer is liable on a solidary basis with all the other parties involved in a construction, but all the other parties have statutorily defined roles. Therefore, a claim filed against any of the other construction parties – eg an architect – interrupts prescription as regards the developer, but not the other way around).[169]

## E. BURDEN OF PROOF (OF ELEMENTS AND OF RULES OF PROLONGATION)

107 According to the general rules on civil procedure, the claimant bears the burden of proving the elements which ground up her claim, whereas the defendant bears that of proving those facts which hinder, extinguish or paralyse the claim (art 217 LEC). Therefore, the burden of proof of prescription lies on the defendant (in case law, see STS 10 March 1989 [RJ 1989\2034]). This does not need to prove a negative fact, as is the so-called 'silence of the legal relationship', but merely the facts which, in each case, give start to the prescription time period. The burden

167 In legal scholarship, see in favour of such an approach *Díez-Picazo*, *supra* fn 2, 152.
168 See *Albaladejo*, *supra* fn 5, 282.
169 STS 16 January 2014 [RJ 2015\277] and 20 May 2014 [RJ 2015\2256].

of proving the interruption of prescription lies however on the claimant.[170] The court may establish that prescription was interrupted for a cause other than the one alleged by the claimant, and the decision will not be inconsistent for that mere reason.[171]

## F. WAIVER

Under Spanish law (pursuant to art 1935 CC), it is only possible to waive prescription once it has taken effect, ie once it has been obtained or 'won' by the defendant (*prescripción ganada*). 'Won prescription' is therefore the situation in which the whole prescription period has elapsed and it is no longer possible to interrupt it.[172] Before that, waiver is excluded, and it is therefore not possible to renounce to a future prescription (*prescripción futura*). The reason given for such exclusion is that by waiving a future prescription the party at stake is not renouncing a subjective right but trying to modify the law in an objective sense.[173] Consequently, a court would probably give no effect to a waiver to future prescription and in the case at stake the victim would still be able to file the claim before the court. Nevertheless, as has been explained above, it could be considered that under certain circumstances such a victim would be behaving against the principle of good faith, since the apparent waiver may make the defendant assume that the claim will indeed never be filed. In that case, the effect would be the same as in the case a waiver had been done validly. At any rate, waiver to prescription – which may take care even implicitly[174] – rarely happens in practice.[175] 108

As regards caducity periods, it may be remembered that they cannot be interrupted. However, waiver to caducity may be admitted once caducity has taken place.[176] Before that, waiver is not admitted. However, some legal scholars support the view that caducity could be waived under certain circumstances even then. In particular, one should look at whether the right at stake is one of which its holder may be dispose freely – in which case there is less trouble in admitting waiver – or there are restrictions for public reasons.[177] 109

---

170 See *Cavanillas*, *supra* fn 4, 13285.

171 See *Díez-Picazo*, *supra* fn 2, 139.

172 See *Díez-Picazo*, *supra* fn 2, 191.

173 See *Puig*, *supra* fn 9, 113.

174 See *Díez-Picazo*, *supra* fn 2, 193. For that to happen, it is required that it may be deduced under the circumstances that the claim at stake has been renounced at (STS 12 December 2011 [RJ 2012\32]).

175 As noted by *Albaladejo*, *supra* fn 5, 304.

176 See *Cavanillas*, *supra* fn 4, 13293 and *Albaladejo*, *supra* fn 5, 315.

177 This point of view is held by *F Rivero Hernández*, ¿Apreciación de oficio de la caducidad en todo caso? (2001) 85 Revista de Derecho Privado 465, 482 ff.

# PRESCRIPTION IN TORT LAW: SWITZERLAND

Frédéric KRAUSKOPF and Bénédict WINIGER

## I. INTRODUCTION

1 Before the first Swiss Code of Obligations was drafted in the late 19th century, civil law was regulated by cantonal law. Prescription rules differed from canton to canton, depending on the influences (eg of the French Code Civil) they had been exposed to. It must also be noted that some Swiss legal scholars provided for an important advancement of the Swiss civil law during the 19th century.[1] The first prescription rules at federal level were those found in the first Swiss Code of Obligations of 1881 that was later replaced by the Swiss Code of Obligations of 1911 which is still in force today. They are to be seen as the result of a mixture of rules and ideas that were received from abroad and rules born out of domestic ideas and concepts at cantonal and federal level. Consequently, Swiss prescription law resembles the law of its European neighbours (especially France and Germany) but also exhibits some coining features that are genuinely 'Swiss made'.

2 Today, the *sedes materiae* of prescription law is still embedded in the Swiss Code of Obligation of 1911 (arts 60, 67 and 127–142). In the last 50 years, numerous special legislative acts containing liability and prescription rules came into force, so today's prescription law in Swiss civil law is highly dispersed and heterogeneous. Endeavours to reform and modernise the prescription law were repeatedly

1 Just to mention the four-volume 'Privatrechtliche Gesetzbuch' for the Canton of Zurich that was enacted between 1853 and 1856 and attracted international attention.

undertaken in the last decades but failed.[2] The latest legislative draft containing a revision of the prescription rules was (temporarily) turned down by the Legal Affairs Committee of the National Council on 4 September 2017. On 15 June 2018, however, the federal Parliament eventually adopted revised prescription rules of arts 60, 67 and 127 et seq. CO which entered into force on 1 January 2020.

## II. DEFINITION OF PRESCRIPTION

Under Swiss civil law, prescription (or statute of limitation) is a legal institution that prevents the creditor from enforcing an alleged right against the debtor because of the running of a specified period of time on a specific right.[3] Prescription does not extinguish the right;[4] however, it provides the debtor with a substantive defence that prevents the creditor from enforcing the right. Article 142 CO[5] provides for an important procedural rule: The court may not consider the prescription *ex officio*. 3

A harmed party can base its claim for compensation on any contractual or statutory (non-contractual) liability if the conditions for a particular liability are fulfilled. If more than one basis for liability exists, then the harmed party may assert competing claims (eg contractual and statutory claims) with distinct prescription periods.[6] 4

Regarding other modalities of prescription (reasons for prevention, suspension or interruption of the prescription period) the general clauses set out in arts 127 et seq. CO are to be applied also for tort claims.[7] 5

## III. THE NATURE OF PRESCRIPTION AND ITS EFFECTS

In Swiss law the institution of prescription is a matter of substantive law and not procedural law.[8] The defendant has the right to refuse to compensate the plaintiff by invoking the prescription defence.[9] The duty to invoke and to prove 6

---

2 Reference is made to the abandoned Swiss Draft Project on the Revision and Unification of Civil Liability of 2000 authored by Pierre Widmer and Pierre Wessner (for the explanatory report, see <https://www.bj.admin.ch/dam/data/bj/wirtschaft/gesetzgebung/archiv/haftpflicht/vn-ber-d.pdf>).

3 Federal Supreme Court Decision 119 III 108/110 consid. 3a.

4 Federal Supreme Court Decision 133 II 366/368 consid. 3.3.

5 Swiss Code of Obligations of 30 March 1911.

6 Federal Supreme Court Decision 4A_ 656/2011 (12.3.2012) consid. 2.2; 120 II 58/61 consid. 3a; 113 II 246/247 consid. 3; 112 II 138/142 consid. 3b; 99 II 315/321 consid. 5.

7 Federal Supreme Court Decision 123 III 213/219 consid. 6a; *RK Däppen*, in: Basler Kommentar Obligationenrecht I, Art. 1-529 OR (7th ed, Basel 2019), fn 1 ad art 60 CO.

8 Federal Supreme Court Decision 75 II 57/66 consid. 3a; 119 III 108/110 consid. 3a; 118 II 447/450 consid. 1b/bb.

9 Federal Supreme Court Decision 137 III 16/18 consid. 2; 133 III 6/26 consid. 5.3.4.

the prescription defence lies with the defendant. The court may not consider the matter of prescription *ex officio* (art 142 CO).[10] The expiry of the limitation period does not lead to a claim being extinguished; it just means that it cannot be enforced against the will of the defendant. In other words, prescription does not affect the existence of a claim but its enforcement.[11] The plaintiff's claim remains an *obligatio naturalis*, however, it can be burdened by invoking the prescription defence.

7 Forfeiture deadlines are not common in Swiss liability law. However, a very few special legal provisions contain periods that are expressly denoted as forfeiture deadlines[12] or interpreted as such by the courts.[13] If a right connected to a forfeiture deadline is not exercised within the forfeiture deadline, it is lost. This is why forfeiture deadlines have to be considered by the court *ex officio*.[14] Forfeiture deadlines cannot be suspended or interrupted.[15] Passed deadlines can only be restored under certain circumstances – so for instance if the entitled person was unable to act due to unsurmountable reasons that are not self-inflicted like, eg illness, accident or natural disasters.[16]

## IV. CONSIDERATIONS FOR AND AGAINST PRESCRIPTION OF TORT CLAIMS

8 In the first place there are *two opposing key arguments* which are being put forward when discussing the justification and legitimacy of prescription: The right of the creditor to enforce this right to performance towards the debtor on the one hand and the protection of the debtor from the creditor who remained inactive for a long time before initiating any demand for performance against the debtor. But there is a *third element* which became increasingly important in the discussion: According to the Federal Supreme Court, the prescription aims at protecting the public order and legal peace.[17]

---

10 Federal Supreme Court Decision 137 III 16/18 consid. 2; 134 V 223/227 consid. 2.2.2; 129 V 237/241 consid. 4.

11 Federal Supreme Court Decision 137 III 16/18 consid. 2; 133 III 6/26 consid. 5.3.4.

12 Eg art 10 Federal Act on Product Liability of 18 June 1993.

13 Eg former art 20 para 1 Federal Act on the Liability of the Confederation of 14 March 1958 (Federal Supreme Court Decision 136 II 187/192 consid. 6; 133 V 14/18 consid. 6; 126 II 145/159 consid. 2a. The revised art 20 para 1 now expressly qualifies this period as a prescription period.

14 Federal Supreme Court Decision 136 II 187/192 et seq. consid. 6; 133 II 366/369 consid. 3.4; 113 V 180/181 consid. 2; 112 V 6/8 consid. 4c; 111 V 135/136 consid. 3b.

15 Federal Supreme Court Decision 119 II 429/432 consid. 3b; 104 II 357/358 consid. 4a; 102 II 193/196 consid. 2b; 98 II 176/181 consid. 10; 74 II 97/100 consid. 4.

16 Federal Supreme Court Decision 136 II 187/193 consid. 6; 114 V 123/124 consid. 3b.

17 Federal Supreme Court Decision 137 III 16/18 et seq. consid. 2.1.

## A. AGAINST

The most important argument against the institution of prescription is found in the fact that the establishing of prescription periods constitutes a weakening of the creditor's legal positions, since it hinders his/her claim for performance which is deemed to be particularly unacceptable when it comes to claims for compensation.[18] The prescription is seen as an unjustified weakening of enforceable claims. For some, the interest of the creditor to be able to use the state's legal protection apparatus for the enforcement of his or her claim for an indefinite period should always be more important than the interest of the debtor to be protected against a late claim. 9

## B. FOR

The main argument in favour of the prescription pertains to the public interest of legal certainty and social peace which require that after a certain time claims cannot be brought forward anymore.[19] Generally, it can be said that the further in the past the relevant facts lie, the more difficult it becomes to reliably establish and assess them (because evidence is difficult or impossible to obtain).[20] Therefore, it is legitimate that the prescription of claims spares courts from having to assess facts that happened a long time ago.[21] Prescription also serves the need for regulation of certain issues in particular: Unresolved claims burden relationships between individuals. In this respect prescription also protects the debtor from having to secure evidence for an unlimited time (for instance by saving receipts). The plaintiff shall be encouraged to initiate litigation proceedings in a timely manner. In the context of disputed or uncertain claims, the plaintiff's lack of action over a longer period of time makes it seem likely that the claim is unfounded, has been redeemed or that the plaintiff is waving his or her right to assert the claim.[22] 10

---

18 Cf Federal Supreme Court Decision 119 II 216/220 consid. 4a/aa.

19 Federal Supreme Court Decision 90 II 428/437 consid. 8; 137 III 16/18 consid. 2.1.

20 *K Spiro*, Die Begrenzung privater Rechte durch Verjährungs-, Verwirkungs- und Fatalfristen, Bd. I: Die Verjährung der Forderungen (Bern 1975), 8.

21 *SV Berti*, Kommentar zum Schweizerischen Zivilgesetzbuch, Band V: Obligationenrecht, Teilband V 1h: Das Erlöschen der Obligationen, Zweite Lieferung: Art. 127–142 OR (Zurich 2002), n 11 zu Vorb. arts 127–142.

22 Federal Supreme Court Decision 137 III 16/19 consid. 2.1; 134 III 294/298 consid. 2.1; 90 II 428/437 consid. 8.

## V. ELEMENTS OF PRESCRIPTION – AN OVERVIEW

11 All four elements of prescription law – that is the starting point, the prescription period, rules of prolongation, and rules of upper limit – are regulated by Swiss statutory law. Whereas there is a large number of scattered statutory provisions that regulate the beginning and the duration of the prescription period; the suspension, the renewal and the extension of the prescription period as well as the waiver of the right to invoke the prescription are uniformly regulated for all claims in arts 129 and 134–141 CO.

## VI. THE STARTING POINT OF THE PRESCRIPTION PERIOD

12 The regular prescription period for *contractual liability* is ten years (art 127 CO), starting as soon as the debt is due (art 130 CO).[23] In cases of professional malpractice, the starting point is considered to be the moment when the malpractice happens or ends, even if the damage occurs later.[24] Besides the regular prescription, numerous legal provisions set the beginning and duration of the prescription period from claim to claim in a different way.[25] On 1 January 2020, the prescription period for contractual liability for bodily injury and death was amended. Now, the prescription includes a relative prescription period of three years and an absolute prescription period of 20 years (art 128a CO).[26] The *non-contractual liability* is also governed by two prescription periods: a relative prescription period of three years starting from the moment the victim is aware of the damage and the identity of the person liable for it and an absolute prescription period of ten years starting from the date on which the harmful conduct or event took place or ceased (art 60 para 1 CO). In cases of personal injury and death the absolute prescription period is 20 years (art 60 para $1^{bis}$ CO).[27]

### A. THE MEANING OF 'ACTION' AND 'CAUSE OF ACTION'

13 In Swiss law one would not speak about cause of action, but rather about conditions which need to be fulfilled for a successful action. The *non-contractual liability* is subject to two prescription periods: A relative prescription period that

---

23 This prescription period applies to the liability for medical and legal malpractice.

24 Federal Supreme Court Decision 137 III 16/20 consid. 2.3.

25 Cf also arts 210 and 371 CO regarding the prescription periods for warranty claims in purchase and work contracts.

26 Federal Journal 2018 3538 (German version) and Federal Journal 2018 3656 (French version).

27 Federal Journal 2018 3537 (German version) and Federal Journal 2018 3655 (French version).

only begins once the plaintiff is sufficiently aware of the whole damage and the identity of the liable person. The beginning of the prescription period can be determined as the point in time where the entire (actual and future) damages can be sufficiently estimated. For example, if three mistakes (A, B and C) are distinct mistakes, then the relative prescription period starts to run for every mistake separately once the harm appeared to the plaintiff and the damage is known to him. The absolute ten-year prescription period begins on the date on which the harm that gives rise to liability was caused,[28] that is, *in casu*, the day the three mistakes happened (see also *infra* Case 2).

## B. BROAD OR NARROW CONCEPTION OF 'CAUSE OF ACTION'?

**Case 1** – *D, a ski instructor, negligently fails to make sure that all skiers in her 'off-piste' group wear helmets. P, a skier in the group, hits a tree. P immediately suffers head injury X, and years later another head injury Y that developed from the same accident.* 14

In this case, the professional malpractice leads to a contractual as well as to a non-contractual liability of the ski instructor. Since 1 January 2020, the *contractual liability* as well as the *non-contractual liability* are subject to two prescription periods: A relative prescription period of three years that only begins once the plaintiff is sufficiently aware of the whole damage. The beginning of the prescription period can be determined as the point in time where the entire (actual and future) damages can be sufficiently estimated. If the professional malpractice of the instructor led to different harms, then the relative prescription period starts to run only once the different injuries appeared to the plaintiff and the entire damage is known to him (= one cause of action). In addition, an absolute 20 -year prescription period begins on the date on which the harm that gives rise to liability was caused,[29] that is, *in casu*, the day when the plaintiff suffered the accident on the slope.[30] 15

**Case 2** – *Physician D treats patient P negligently and performs three mistakes on the day of the treatment: A, B and C. Mistake A causes harm X after a year. Mistake B causes harm Y after two years. Mistakes A and C together cause harm Z after three years.* 16

Medical malpractice often triggers a contractual as well as a non-contractual liability of the physician (or the clinic that employs him or her). The *contractual liability* as well as the *non-contractual liability* for medical malpractice is subject 17

28 Federal Supreme Court Decision 127 III 257/269 consid. 2b/aa; 119 II 216/219 consid. 4a/aa.

29 Federal Supreme Court Decision 127 III 257/269 consid. 2b/aa; 119 II 216/219 consid. 4a/aa.

30 Federal Journal 2018 3537 et seq. (German version) and Federal Journal 2018 3655 et seq. (French version).

to two prescription periods: A relative prescription period of three years that only begins once the plaintiff is sufficiently aware of the whole damage and the identity of the person liable for the damage. The beginning of the prescription period can be determined as the point in time where the entire (actual and future) damages can be sufficiently estimated. If the three mistakes (A, B and C) are distinct mistakes, then the relative prescription period starts to run separately for every mistake once the harm appeared to the plaintiff and the damage is known to him. The absolute 20-year prescription period begins on the date on which the harmful conduct occurred or ceased,[31] that is, *in casu*, the treatment day when the three mistakes happened.

18 **Case 3** – *Builder D lays down defective foundations for a building thereby creating the risk of future collapse. As a result, the value to the owner of the building (P) decreases (harm A). Two years later the foundation subsides and requires fixing paid by P (harm B). Three years later cracks appear in the building fixed by P (harm C). Four years later the building collapses (harm D).*

19 If builder D was obliged by contract with P to build the foundations of the building, then he is subject to contractual liability towards P. According to art 371 para 2 CO, the customer's claims in respect of defects of an immovable work against both the contractor and any architect or engineer who rendered services in connection with such work prescribe five years after completion of the work. This also applies to claims for compensation for damages that resulted from defects. In case of maliciously concealed defects the prescription period is ten years. These prescription periods apply to all four harms (A, B, C and D) even if the harm occurs after their expiry. The prescription of the non-contractual liability is set in art 60 CO: For all four harms (A, B, C and D) the absolute prescription period starts with the harmful conduct or event – *in casu* the completion and delivery of defective foundations – and the relative three-year prescription period starts only once P becomes aware of the (whole) damage and of the identity of the person liable for the damage. The absolute prescription period is ten years for claims for damage to property and 20 years for claims for personal injury or death.

## C. THE STARTING POINT – BREACH OF DUTY OR OCCURRENCE OF DAMAGE?

20 The absolute prescription period of ten or 20 years that applies likewise to contractual and non-contractual liability starts with the occurrence of the potentially harmful (damaging) conduct or event. In case of a continuously

[31] Federal Supreme Court Decision 127 III 257/269 consid. 2b/aa; 119 II 216/219 consid. 4a/aa.

harmful conduct or event, the absolute prescription period starts when the behaviour or event ends. This applies also to cases where the harm (eg personal injury) and the resulting damage occur only after a latency period.[32] The relative three-year prescription period that applies to the non-contractual prescription starts to run when the injured person becomes aware of the damage and of the identity of the person liable for the damage. A relative prescription period of three years also applies to the contractual liability in cases of personal injury and death (see *supra* 12).

**Case 4** – *D enters P's premises without P's permission, thereby committing a tort of trespass, but without causing damage. P can file a claim against D asking for the remedy of D's eviction but fails to do so. A year later D causes physical harm to P's premises. P files a claim to compensation for the loss.* 21

In Swiss law, the fact as such to enter P's premises against his will is considered as an illicit act, but not as a tort. P has the possibility to file a claim against D based on property law, but not in tort law. A tortuous situation occurs only at the moment when D causes damage. Prescription of the tort claim starts at the moment, when P is aware of the damage and of D's identity (art 60 CO). 22

## D. WHAT IS CONSIDERED 'HARM' FOR PRESCRIPTION PURPOSES?

In Swiss law material harm is mainly defined according to the theory of difference, ie a diminution of the victim's patrimony (*damnum emergens*) or the absence of an augmentation considered as certain (*lucrum cessans*). For personal damage the law also enumerates homicide, personal injury and injury to personality rights (arts 45–49 CO).[33] 23

**Case 5** – *In an accidental event, D negligently caused an explosion that damaged P's ears. During the first two years P has to raise the volume to enjoy music. During the following three years P needs a hearing device. After a further five years P becomes deaf.* 24

According to Swiss law, each of the three states, partial loss of hearing, need of a hearing device and total loss of hearing would be considered as damage, each of them offering to P the possibility to file a claim against D. For each of the three states, a three-year prescription period starts at the moment when P is aware of the damage and the person who caused it. As the whole process occurs within the absolute prescription period of 20 years, none of the three events would be time-barred after five years when the victim becomes deaf. 25

---

32 Federal Supreme Court Decision 137 III 16/20 consid. 2.2 and 2.3.

33 For the whole see *B Winiger et al* (eds), Digest of European Tort Law 2: Essential cases on damage (Berlin 2011).

26 **Case 6** – *Builder D lays down defective foundations for a bridge, thereby creating the risk of future collapse if heavy rain falls. Two years later heavy rain indeed falls and the collapse becomes only a matter of time, as indeed happens four years after the laying of foundations.*

27 In contract between customer P and contractor (builder) D: According to art 371 para 2 CO, customer P has a claim during five years against contractor D for defects in an immovable work. The prescription period starts at the moment of the completion of the work (*réception de l'ouvrage*). *In casu*, customer P can file a claim after the collapse of the bridge.

In tort: According to art 58 CO a third person damaged by the collapse of the bridge has a claim against the property owner; the absolute prescription of ten years for property damage and 20 years for damage to persons starts with the damaging event (collapse) and the relative prescription of three years at the moment when the victim is aware of the damage and the identity of the liable person.

## E. THE STARTING POINT (ACCRUAL) IN CONTINUOUS TORTS

28 Swiss statutory law does not define or use the notion of 'continuous tort'. However, in several areas of the law this notion is relevant and being used in doctrine and practice, so for instance in insurance law when it comes to the question whether a sequence of tortious acts that led to damages is to be considered one damaging event or several distinct events. With respect to prescription, the notion of continuous tort is relevant for the beginning of the absolute prescription period of ten years provided for in art 60 para 1 CO (cf *supra* 13 ff). The same applies to the 20-year prescription period for cases of personal injury or death provided for in arts 60 para 1$^{bis}$ and 128a of the Swiss Code of Obligations. Whereas distinct (separate) tortious acts trigger separate and independent prescription periods for every claim that arises from each act, the absolute prescription period for the compensation claim arising from one continuous act begins to run only when the act has ended.[34] The same applies also to the three-year relative prescription period (art 60 para 1 CO) that requires the plaintiff's awareness of the damage: As long as the damaging *action* is still going on, the plaintiff will not be able to assess his/her damage and the relative prescription period will not start to run.[35]

[34] Federal Supreme Court Decision 127 III 257/260 consid. 2b/bb; 81 II 439/445 et seq. consid. 3 and 4.

[35] Federal Supreme Court Decision 2P.168/2003 (9.2.2004) consid. 2.3; 126 III 161/163 consid. 3c; 112 II 118/123 consid. 4; 109 II 418/421 et seq. consid. 3 and 4.

A harmful action that consists of the same (harmful) conduct or event that is directed against the same person and that lasts or is constantly repeated over a period of time (like continued or repeated exposure to harmful substances, defamation, etc) is considered to be a *continuous tort*.[36] If a harmful conduct or event meets the criterion 'continuous', both the contractual and the non-contractual liability arising from it is subject to ten-year prescription periods that begin to run only when the harmful conduct or event ends.[37] 29

**Case 7** – *Every week, during a month, D1 publishes a defamatory article on P1, each time in another newspaper and on a different topic. During the same period D2 publishes a defamatory article on P2, every second day, on the same topic and in the same newspaper.* 30

In the event that D2 publishes defaming articles periodically – *in casu* every second day during a month – in the same newspaper and if the articles are always directed against the same person, these defaming actions must be considered a continuous tort.[38] The consequence is that neither the relative[39] nor the absolute[40] prescription periods for non-contractual liability start before the end of the continuous tortious act. If the defaming articles are directed against the same person but published in different newspapers (that are directed to a different audience) then the question whether D1's behaviour is a continuous act or not is controversial. 31

**Case 8** – *D, a landowner, negligently exposes P, a neighbour, to unreasonable noise for three years. P's hearing is thereby weakened on a daily basis, gradually restricting P's ability to communicate and enjoy music.* 32

This is to be considered a continuous tort (same harmful conduct or behaviour committed by the same person against the same person in a lasting or frequently repeated way). The prescription period starts at the end of the damaging act. 33

**Case 9** – *A waste management company digs bins of toxic content into the soil. Toxic substance leaks into the soil and ground water, causing an apparent damage to crops and expenditure on cleaning on a daily basis. After two years the bins are removed from the soil.* 34

---

36 Federal Supreme Court Decision 92 II 1/7 consid. 5b.

37 Cf *F Werro*, in: Commentaire Romand (2nd ed, Basel 2012), fn 26 ad art 60 CO; *P Pichonnaz*, in: Commentaire Romand (2nd ed, Basel 2012), fn 21b ad art 127 CO.

38 Cf Federal Supreme Court Decision 126 III 161/163 et seq. consid. 3c, Pra 2001 Nr. 80 p. 470 et seq. consid. 3c.

39 Federal Supreme Court Decision 2P.168/2003 (9.2.2004) consid. 2.3; 126 III 161/163 consid. 3c, Pra 2001 Nr. 80 p 471 consid. 3c; 112 II 118/123 consid. 4; 109 II 418/421 et seq. consid. 3 and 4.

40 Federal Supreme Court Decision 81 II 439/445 et seq. consid. 3 and 4; 127 III 257/260 consid. 2b/bb.

35 This would be considered as a continuous tort. Concerning the crops, the absolute prescription period of ten years starts at the end of the damaging act and the relative prescription of three years at the moment the victim is aware of the damage and the identity of the person liable. Concerning the ground water, the absolute prescription starts at the moment the polluting effect on the water stops and the 'relative prescription' at the moment the victim is aware of the damage and of the liable person's identity.

### F. IS THE LATE DISCOVERY RULE A RULE OF THE STARTING POINT (ACCRUAL) OR A RULE OF PROLONGATION?

36 Unawareness basically does not influence the prescription, neither its onset nor its duration.[41] Some (short) prescription periods, however, only start once the plaintiff becomes aware of the damage he/she suffered and of the person who is liable for this damage. Such 'relative' prescription periods are always combined with a longer absolute prescription period that already starts to run with the damaging event or action (cf eg art 60 para 1 and $1^{bis}$ CO).

## VII. PRESCRIPTION PERIODS

37 The regular prescription periods for non-contractual liability are defined in art 60 paras 1, $1^{bis}$ and 2 CO: A claim for damages or satisfaction prescribes three years from the date on which the injured party became aware of the loss or damage and of the identity of the person liable for it but in any event ten years (or 20 years in case of personal injury or death) after the date on which the loss or damage was caused.

38 The relative prescription period of three year begins once the plaintiff is sufficiently aware of the damage he/she suffered and the identity of the person liable for the damage.[42] A plaintiff is considered to be aware of the damage, if he/she knows about the existence, the nature and the features of the damages in a way that allows him/her to file and substantiate a suit.[43] In other words, the plaintiff must be aware of the basis and the extent of the claim to such a

---

41 Federal Supreme Court Decision 137 III 16/18 et seq. consid. 2.1.

42 For more details cf *F Krauskopf*, Die Verjährung von haftpflichtrechtlichen Ansprüchen wegen Personenschäden unter Berücksichtigung der aktuellen Reformbestrebungen im Inland und in Europa, in: S Weber (ed), Personen-Schaden-Forum 2011 (Zurich 2011), 120 et seq.

43 Federal Supreme Court Decision 96 II 39/41 consid. 2a.

degree that he/she can assert the claim successfully.[44] In order to determine the awareness of the plaintiff the actual awareness (subjective standard) is relevant and not a state of awareness that could have been reached provided that due diligence (objective standard) would have been applied. The plaintiff must have command over the facts so he/she is able to estimate the damages.[45] In addition, so that the plaintiff can broadly estimate the damages, the damaging event must be concluded.[46] Depending on the circumstances, the plaintiff must have enough time to estimate the definitive extent of the damages either alone or with the help of third parties.[47] But the plaintiff may not wait to assert his/her claim up to the point in time where he/she knows the exact extent or amount of the damages. A basis that allows the plaintiff to estimate the damages suffices, particularly as art 42 para 2 CO provides that in cases where the damages cannot be numeralised, the court shall assess the damages at its discretion.[48] Frequently, the extent of the entire damage is definite only after a longer period of time. Where the extent of the damage is continuing to develop (namely the case with bodily injuries), the damages are to be considered a unit and not a sum of individual damages.[49] Since the relative prescription period only begins once the plaintiff is sufficiently aware of the whole damage, the beginning of the prescription period can be determined as the point in time where the entire (actual and future) damages can be sufficiently estimated.[50] Sufficient awareness of the person liable for the damages can be assumed once the plaintiff is aware of the elements necessary to assert the claim. The mere assumption that a person could potentially be held liable does not suffice to establish awareness of the identity of the person.[51] It is, however, not required that the plaintiff is aware of the exact legal bases that enable him/her to claim damages (principle of *iura novit curia*).[52]

The absolute prescription period of ten years (or 20 years in case of personal injury or death) pursuant to art 60 para 1 CO (art 60 para $1^{bis}$ CO) serves the interest of legal certainty as it is meant to prevent the defendant from being sued for damages which – ten years after the date on which the damaging act or event happened – have not yet arisen. Relevant for the beginning of the absolute prescription period 39

44 Federal Supreme Court Decision 2A.553/2002 (22.8.2003) consid. 4.3; 2A.29/2000 (12.5.2000) consid. 3a; 111 II 55/57 consid. 3a; 109 II 433/435 consid. 2.

45 Federal Supreme Court Decision 111 II 55/57 consid. 3a; 108 Ib 97/99 consid. 1b.

46 Federal Supreme Court Decision 126 III 161/163 et seq. consid. 3.

47 Federal Supreme Court Decision 111 II 55/57 consid. 3a; 96 II 39/40 consid. 2.

48 Federal Supreme Court Decision 131 III 61/67 et seq. consid. 3; 114 II 253/255 consid. 2a.

49 Federal Supreme Court Decision 4A_454/2010 (6.1.2011) consid. 3.1; 114 II 253/255 consid. 2a; 112 II 118/123 consid. 4; 108 Ib 97/100 consid. 1c.

50 Federal Supreme Court Decision 2P.168/2003 (9.1.2004) consid. 2.3; 111 II 55/57 consid. 3a; 92 II /4 consid. 2.

51 Federal Supreme Court Decision 4C.234/1999 (12.1.2000) consid. 5c/cc.

52 Federal Supreme Court Decision 131 III 61/68 consid. 3.1.2.

is the date on which the loss or damage was caused that gives rise to liability.[53] If the damaging event or act is a continuing one or consists of a sequence of actions, the prescription period only begins when the event or act ends.[54] Consequently, a claim can be (absolutely) prescribed before the plaintiff was ever even aware of it.[55]

40 Pursuant to art 60 para 2 CO, if the action for damages derives from an offence for which criminal law envisages a longer prescription period, that longer period also applies to the civil law claim instead of the relative and absolute prescription periods set in art 60 para 1 and $1^{bis}$ CO.[56] Article 60 para 2 CO requires that the harmful act of the defendant falls within the scope of a crime listed in the Swiss Criminal Code[57] and that there is an adequate causal link between the harmful act and the damage.[58] This special provision is of considerable importance especially for claims that result from personal injury. The prescription periods for felonies and misdemeanours are stated in arts 97 and 101 Swiss Criminal Code and the prescription periods for contraventions in art 109 Swiss Criminal Code (the beginning of prescription periods is regulated in art 98 Swiss Criminal Code).

41 Numerous legal provisions regarding non-contractual liability set the beginning and duration of the prescription period (ranging from two to 30 years[59]) which substantially differ from art 60 CO.

42 There are no statutory rules that specifically deal with the problem of late damage that occurs only after a long latency period. Thus, it is possible that damage claims prescribe before the plaintiff even becomes aware of the damage or before the damage becomes identifiable. In 2014, the European Court of Human Rights condemned Switzerland because of a violation of art 6 para 1 ECHR (right to a fair trial).[60] The case concerned a worker who had been diagnosed in 2004 with

---

53 Federal Supreme Court Decision 127 III 257/269 consid. 2b/aa; 119 II 216/219 consid. 4a/aa.

54 Federal Supreme Court Decision 127 III 257/260 consid. 2b/bb; 126 III 161/163 et seq. consid. 3; 119 II 216/220 consid. 4a/bb; 109 II 418/421 consid. 3; 107 II 134/140 consid. 4; 81 II 439/448 consid. 4.

55 Federal Supreme Court Decision 126 II 145/151 consid. 2b; 119 II 216/219 consid. 4a/aa; 92 II 1/7 consid. 5b.

56 Federal Supreme Court Decision 106 II 213/215 consid. 1 and 2.

57 Swiss Criminal Code of 21 December 1937.

58 Federal Supreme Court Decision 127 III 538/540 consid. 4b; 122 III 5/8 consid. 2c; 118 V 193/197 et seq. consid. 4; 4A_459/2009 (25.3.2010) consid. 3.2.

59 Eg art 32 para 1 Federal Act on Non-Human Gene Technology of 21 March 2003.

60 *Howald Moor and Others v Switzerland*; application no 52067/10 and 41072/11; cf also *F Krauskopf*, EMRK-widriges Verjährungsrecht! – Die Schweiz muss die Verjährung im Schadensrecht überdenken, in: Jusletter vom 24 März 2014; *C Müller*, Commentaire d'arrêt de la Cour européenne des droits de l'homme dans l'affaire Howald Moor et autres c. Suisse du 11 mars 2014 in: Newsletter responsabilité civile, assurances sociales et assurances privées de l'Université de Neuchâtel d'avril 2014.

an asbestos-related tumour caused by his exposure to asbestos in the course of his work in the 1960s and 1970s. The Swiss courts had dismissed the claims for damages on the grounds that the prescription period (of ten years) had expired. The European Court of Human Rights held that the relevant prescription rules violated the right of persons suffering from diseases that typically could only be diagnosed more than ten years after the event which caused the disease.[61]

# VIII. RULES OF POSTPONEMENT, SUSPENSION, RENEWAL AND EXTENSION

## A. UNAWARENESS – THE LATE DISCOVERY RULE

Modification (extension) of the prescription period: According to art 129 CO, the parties may not alter the prescription periods contained in the third title of the CO (arts 127–142 CO). However, the parties can shorten or lengthen any prescription period that is situated outside of the third title of the CO. The possibility to lengthen prescription periods of tort claims is, however, limited to ten years (art 127 CO).[62] 43

Prevention and suspension of the prescription: In art 134 CO the law provides for an exhaustive list of facts that cause the prescription period not to commence and, if it has begun, to be suspended.[63] Such facts pertain to: 44

(1) claims of children against their parents, for the duration of parental responsibility;
(2) the claim of person lacking capacity of judgement against his or her carer, for the duration of the advance care directive;
(3) claims of spouses against each other, for the duration of the marriage;
(3$^{bis}$) claims of registered partners against each other, for the duration of the registered partnership;
(4) the claim of an employee against his or her employer with whom he or she shares a household, for the duration of the employment relationship;
(5) the debtor who has the usufruct of the claim;
(6) claims that cannot be brought before a court for objective reasons.

The limitation period begins or resumes at the end of the day on which the cause of prevention or suspension ceases to apply (art 134 para 2 CO).

61 Federal Supreme Court Decision 136 II 187/198 et seq. consid. 7.4.4; 126 II 145/151 consid. 2b; 119 II 216/219 consid. 4a/aa.
62 Federal Supreme Court Decision 99 II 185/189 consid. 2a.
63 Federal Supreme Court Decision 100 II 339/344 consid. 4.

45 Interruption of the prescription period: art 135 CO names the actions that interrupt the prescription period. First: if the debtor acknowledges the claim and in particular if he makes interest payments or part payments, gives an item in pledge or provides surety (art 135 sec 1 CO). Second: by debt enforcement proceedings, an application for conciliation, submission of a statement of claim or defence to a court or arbitral tribunal, or a petition for bankruptcy (art 135 sec 2 CO).[64] Article 136 CO regulates the effect of interruption on co-obligors: Where the prescription period for one person who is jointly and severally liable for a debt or jointly liable in respect of an indivisible performance is interrupted, it is likewise interrupted for all other co-obligors, provided the interruption is due to an act by the creditor (art 136 para 1 CO). Where the prescription period for the principal debtor is interrupted, it is likewise interrupted for the surety (art 136 para 2 CO). Contrariwise, where the prescription period for the guarantor is interrupted, it is not interrupted for the principal debtor (art 136 para 3 CO). All prescription periods are subject to interruption,[65] even the absolute ten-year prescription period.[66] Since a prescription period can be interrupted repeatedly and unlimitedly,[67] there is basically no upper limit set to the prescription period. The plaintiff is allowed to exhaust the prescription period of his or her claim and to interrupt it as many times as he/she wants.[68] However, under certain circumstances, it can be considered an abuse of the law to deliberately wait too long to assert a claim (eg if the plaintiff wants to bring about collusion of evidence unfavourable for the defendant).[69]

46 Start of a new limitation period: According to art 137 para 1 CO, a new prescription period (with the same duration) commences as of the date of the interruption. If the claim has been acknowledged by public deed or confirmed by court judgment, the new limitation period is always ten years (art 137 para 2 CO). Article 138 CO contains in its three paragraphs three special rules:

(1) Where the prescription period has been interrupted by an application for conciliation, or the submission of a statement of claim or defence, a new prescription period commences when the dispute is settled before the relevant court.

---

64 This list is exhaustive (Federal Supreme Court Decision 132 V 404/411 consid. 5.2).

65 The only exceptions relate to the very few forfeiture periods.

66 Federal Supreme Court Decision 123 III 213/219 consid. 6a; 117 IV 233/243 consid. 5d/aa; 112 II 231/233 consid. 3e/aa.

67 Federal Supreme Court Decision 4C.9/1998 (14.5.1998) consid. 4a.

68 Federal Supreme Court Decision 137 III 16/18 et seq. consid. 2.1.

69 Federal Supreme Court Decision 131 III 439/443 consid. 5.1; 95 II 109/115 et seq. consid. 4; 94 II 37/42 consid. 6c.

(2) Where the prescription period has been interrupted by debt enforcement proceedings, a new limitation period commences as of each step taken in the proceedings.
(3) Where the prescription period has been interrupted by a petition for bankruptcy, a new limitation period commences as of the time specified by bankruptcy law at which it once again becomes possible to assert the claim.

Waiver of the right to invoke the prescription defence (see *supra* 11). 47

Unawareness basically does not influence the prescription, neither its onset nor its duration.[70] Some (short) prescription periods, however, only start once the plaintiff becomes aware of the damage he/she suffered and of the person who is liable for this damage. Such relative prescription periods are always combined with a longer absolute prescription period that already starts to run with the damaging event or action (cf eg art 60 para 1 and $1^{bis}$ CO) (see *supra* 13). 48

**Case 10** – *Chemical plant D negligently exposes bordering lands to toxic substances. As a result P, a nearby resident landowner, contracts a lung disease. P failed to sue in time because his former lawyer told him that the exposure was not tortious, and only his new lawyer told him, after the running of time, that it was tortious.* 49

The awareness of the legal situation has no incidence on the prescription of the claim. Article 60 CO requires only the factual awareness of the damage and the identity of the person liable for it. However, P has the possibility to file a claim against his incompetent lawyer for legal malpractice. 50

- Objective or subjective unawareness? (see *supra* Section VII).
- What is considered awareness of an element of liability (see *supra* Sections VI and VII).
- How heavy is the burden to acquire knowledge? (see *supra* Sections VI and VII).

**Case 11** – *Chemical plant D negligently exposes bordering lands to toxic substances. As a result P, a nearby resident landowner, contracts a lung disease, but is unaware of the causal link between exposure and disease because his physician fails to detect it. P does not seek a second opinion. After the prescription period runs on the disease P consults his new physician that tells him about the link. Did P's claim against D prescribe?* 51

In this case, P has a *non-contractual* claim (art 41 para 1 CO[71]) for compensation against D. According to art 60 para $1^{bis}$ CO, non-contractual claims prescribe 52

70 Federal Supreme Court Decision 137 III 16/18 et seq. consid. 2.1.

71 'Any person who unlawfully causes loss or damage to another, whether willfully or negligently, is obliged to provide compensation.'

three years from the date on which P (actually) became aware of the loss or damage and of the identity of D's liability for it but in any event 20 years after the date on which the loss or damage was caused. If more than 20 years passed since the last exposure to toxic substances, then the prescription periods for the non-contractual claims is expired. There are no statutory rules that specifically deal with the problem of late damages that occur only after a long latency period. Thus, it is possible that damage claims prescribe before P even becomes aware of the damage or before the damage becomes identifiable.

## B. OTHER RULES OF PROLONGATION

### 1) *D is to Blame for the Delay*

53 Deceiving or threatening behaviour of the defendant basically has no influence on the onset or the duration prescription period. If, however, the defendant (intentionally or involuntarily) induced the plaintiff to refrain from proceeding within the prescription period or from taking the adequate measures to interrupt the prescription, then the court may qualify the calling of the expiry of the prescription period by the defendant as an abuse of law and disregard it. The court will only proceed this way if the plaintiff's omission was effectively caused by the defendant's behaviour and is, from an objective (reasonable) standard, comprehensible.[72] The sole fact that the defendant offered to start negotiations or engaged in negotiations with the plaintiff is not sufficient for the latter to refrain from ensuring that the prescription period does not expire.[73]

### 2) *Admission by D of P's Right or Partial Performance of P's Right by D*

54 According to art 135 sec 1 CO, if the debtor acknowledges the claim and in particular if he/she makes interest payments or part payments, gives an item in pledge or provides surety, then the prescription period is interrupted and starts to run again from the beginning (with the same duration). Any behaviour of the defendant that the plaintiff may, in good faith, regard as an affirmation of a legal obligation that the defendant expresses to the plaintiff, is considered to be an acknowledgement of the debt.[74]

---

72 Federal Supreme Court Decision 131 III 430/437 consid. 2; 4A_516/2009 (11.12.09) consid. 4.1; 4A_224/2007 (31.8.2007) consid. 5.1.

73 Federal Supreme Court Decision 128 V 236/241 et seq. consid. 4a.

74 Federal Supreme Court Decision 134 III 591/594 consid. 5.2.1; 119 II 368/378 et seq. consid. 7b; 110 II 176/180 et seq. consid. 3; 5C.98/2004 (6.10.2004) consid. 4.4.1; 5C.41/2002 (17.6.2002) consid. 2.1.

### 3) *Special Relations between D and P*

Article 134 para 1 sec 1 CO imposes the suspension of the prescription period with respect to claims of children against their parents, for the duration of parental responsibility. Article 134 para 1 sec 3 and $3^{bis}$ CO provide for the same with respect to claims of spouses against each other, for the duration of the marriage, and of claims of registered partners against each other, for the duration of the registered partnership (see also *supra* 44 (1)). 55

See *supra* 44 (3).

Minority does not influence prescription.[75] The question whether a minor has a legal representative or not is not relevant for prescription.[76] 56

Erroneous legal advice does not affect the prescription periods in any way but the lawyer could be held liable for damage resulting from legal malpractice.[77] 57

See *supra* 44 ($3^{bis}$).

- Article 26 of the Swiss Merger Act[78] regulates the prescription of the personal liability of members of the transferring legal entity (if there is any): claims based on personal liability of the members for debts of the transferring legal entity prescribe three years after the merger becomes legally effective. If the claim only falls due after the publication of the merger resolution, then the three-year prescription period starts to run from the date when the claim becomes due. This time limitation does not apply to members who are also personally liable for the debts of the acquiring legal entity.
- Article 75 of the Swiss Merger Act sets forth a three-year joint and several liability of the transferring company with the new debtor acquiring company for claims arising before the transfer of assets. Claims against the transferring company prescribe three years after the publication of the transfer of assets. If the claim falls due only after this publication, then the three-year prescription period starts to run from the date when the claim becomes due (see also *infra* Section XI.B).

Basically, employment relationships do not affect prescription, but there is one exception: art 134 para 1 sec 4 CO imposes the suspension of the prescription 58

---

75 Federal Supreme Court Decision 5A_708/2007 (7.2.2007) consid. 3.

76 Federal Supreme Court Decision 5C.122/2006 (6.10.2006) consid. 3.3.

77 Cf Federal Supreme Court Decision 4A_103/2009 (27.4.2009) consid. 2.2.2; *F Krauskopf*, Zur Verjährung von Schadenersatzforderungen bei Haftung aus positiver Vertragsverletzung, in: HAVE/REAS (Zurich 2009), 273 et seq.

78 Federal Act on Merger, Demerger, Transformation and Transfer of Assets of 3 October 2003 (LFus).

period with respect to claims of an employee against his or her employer with whom he or she shares a household, for the duration of the employment relationship.[79] (See also *supra* 44 (4)).

*4) P's Lack of Legal Capacity*

59 So-called 'subjective facts' inherent in the person of the plaintiff are not considered to be able to influence prescription.[80] Article 134 para 1 sec 2 CO imposes the suspension of the prescription period with respect to claims of a person lacking capacity of judgement against his or her carer, for the duration of the advance care directive.

- *Minor without representative (see supra)*
- *Adult with mental disability with representative (see supra)*
- *Adult with mental disability with no representative (see supra)*

*5) Absence of Parties from the Jurisdiction*

59a No incidence.

*6) Former Legal and Other Proceedings between the Parties*

60 According to art 135 CO the prescription period is interrupted by debt enforcement proceedings, an application for conciliation, submission of a statement of claim or defence to a court or arbitral tribunal, or a petition for bankruptcy (art 135 sec 2 CO).[81] Where the prescription period has been interrupted by an application for conciliation, or the submission of a statement of claim or defence, a new prescription period only commences when the dispute is settled before the relevant court (art 138 CO). That means that prescription is suspended as long as the claim is pending in court.

61 Article 135 sec 2 CO names *exhaustively* the actions the creditor may take that interrupt the prescription period: debt enforcement proceedings, an application for conciliation, submission of a statement of claim or defence to a court or arbitral tribunal, or a petition for bankruptcy.[82] (See also *supra* Section VII.)

79 Federal Supreme Court Decision 95 II 126/128 et seq. consid. 1; 90 II 443/447 et seq. consid. 2.

80 Federal Supreme Court Decision 134 III 294/297 consid. 2; 5A_708/2007 (7.2.2007) consid. 3; 5P.203/2006 (6.10.2006) consid. 2.3.8.

81 This list is exhaustive (Federal Supreme Court Decision 132 V 404/411 consid. 5.2).

82 Federal Supreme Court Decision 132 V 404/411 consid. 5.2.

The sole fact that the defendant offered to start negotiations or engaged in negotiations with the plaintiff is not sufficient for the latter to refrain from ensuring that the prescription period does not expire.[83] But note that the law offers the option for the parties to conclude a written agreement concerning dispute resolution efforts in order to prevent or suspend prescription (art 134 para 1 sec 8 CO). 62

### *7) Victim's Death*

If persons entitled to support toward the deceased person (dependants) are deprived of their means of support as a result of homicide, they have an own claim – and not a derivative right – for compensation for that loss (art 45 para 3 CO).[84] The prescription period for this claim is regulated in art 60 para $1^{bis}$ CO (see *supra* 12). 63

### *8) Victim's Bankruptcy*

No incidence. 63a

### *9)* Force Majeure

No incidence.[85] 63b

Judicial vacations do not affect the beginning and duration of prescription periods. In particular, they do not suspend or interrupt prescription 64

According to art 134 para 1 sec 6 CO, the prescription period is suspended with respect to claims that cannot be brought before a court.[86] A creditor can only invoke art 134 para 1 sec 6 CO if neither a domestic nor a foreign court is available to him or her to assert his or her claim. 65

### *10) Other*

There are a few other facts that cause the prescription period not to commence and, if it has already begun, for it to be suspended, so for instance if the debtor 66

83 Federal Supreme Court Decision 128 V 236/241 et seq. consid. 4a.

84 Federal Supreme Court Decision 101 II 257/260 consid. 1a; 129 II 49/51 consid. 2; 112 II 87/92 consid. 2b; 108 II 434/436 consid. 2a; 102 II 90/93 consid. 2b.

85 Federal Supreme Court Decision 88 II 283/290 consid. 3.

86 Cf the latest case law with *F Krauskopf*, in: Präjudizienbuch OR. Die Rechtsprechung des Bundesgerichts (1875–2015) (9th ed, Zurich 2016), n 4 ad art 134 CO.

has the usufruct of the claim (art 134 para 1 sec 5 CO). Cf also art 1166 para 3 CO.[87]

## IX. CEILINGS ON THE EFFECTIVE TIME OF PRESCRIPTION

67 Prescription periods range from two to 30 years. It is a disputed question whether in cases where the Swiss criminal law provides for imprescriptibility for certain criminal acts[88] this also means that claims arising from such acts should also be considered imprescriptible (art 60 para 2 CO).[89] Since all prescription periods are subject to interruption, even the absolute prescription periods,[90] and since prescription periods can be interrupted repeatedly and unlimitedly,[91] there is *no upper limit* (ceiling) set to the prescription period. The plaintiff is allowed to exhaust the prescription period of his claim and to interrupt it as many times as he/she wants.[92] However, under certain circumstances, it can be considered an abuse of the law to deliberately wait too long to assert a claim (eg if the plaintiff wants to bring about collusion of evidence unfavourable for the defendant).[93] A very few legal provisions regulate the time period within which tort claims have to be asserted not as prescription periods but as *forfeiture deadlines*. Forfeiture deadlines cannot be suspended or interrupted.[94] Passed deadlines can only be restored under certain circumstances – so for instance if the entitled person was unable to act due to unsurmountable reasons that are not self-inflicted like, eg illness, accident or natural disasters.[95]

---

87 Swiss Civil Code of 10 December 1907.

88 Pursuant to art 101 para 1 Swiss Criminal Code there is no limitation of the right to prosecute the offences of: *a.* genocide, *b.* crimes against humanity, *c.* war crimes, *d.* felonies that have caused or threatened to cause danger to life and limb to a large number of persons as a method of extortion or duress, in particular through the use of means of mass destruction, the causing of catastrophes, or as part of a hostage taking offence, *e.* sexual acts with children, indecent assault, rape, sexual acts with persons incapable of judgement or resistance, sexual acts with persons in institutional care, prisoners and persons on remand and exploitation of a person in a position of need or dependency if committed against children under the age of 12.

89 Cf eg *AF Rusch*, in: Strassenverkehrsrechts-Tagung 2012 (Bern 2012), 227.

90 Federal Supreme Court Decision 123 III 213/219 consid. 6a; 117 IV 233/243 consid. 5d/aa; 112 II 231/233 consid. 3e/aa.

91 Federal Supreme Court Decision 4C.9/1998 (14.5.1998) consid. 4a.

92 Federal Supreme Court Decision 137 III 16/18 et seq. consid. 2.1.

93 Federal Supreme Court Decision 131 III 439/443 consid. 5.1; 95 II 109/115 et seq. consid. 4; 94 II 37/42 consid. 6c.

94 Federal Supreme Court Decision 119 II 429/432 consid. 3b; 104 II 357/358 consid. 4a; 102 II 193/196 consid. 2b; 98 II 176/181 consid. 10; 74 II 97/100 consid. 4.

95 Federal Supreme Court Decision 136 II 187/193 consid. 6; 114 V 123/124 consid. 3b.

# X. STATUTE INTERPRETATION, JUDICIAL DISCRETION AND LACHES

## A. STATUTE INTERPRETATION

Swiss prescription law is shaped in a way to leave only little room for judiciary discretion. On the one hand, when it comes to short (relative) prescription periods, courts seem to be more inclined to be generous towards plaintiffs (cf *supra* the comments regarding the required awareness of the damage in art 60 para 1 and $1^{bis}$ CO). On the other hand courts are often criticised for protecting economic interests by cutting off plaintiffs who claim for compensation for late damage (eg asbestos-related damage, cf *supra* the comments regarding late damages). The harshest criticism pertains to the Federal Supreme Court's interpretation of art 130 para 1 CO which sets the beginning of the regular prescription period for contractual claims (art 127 para 1 CO: ten years) for compensation by stating: 'The limitation period commences as soon as the debt is due'. According to the Federal Supreme Court, the injured party is entitled to ask for compensation once the damaging event or action took place, even if the damage occurs only later.[96] This seems out of touch with reality or even cynical, given the fact that no plaintiff will ever be awarded compensation by a Swiss court for a possible future damage of which it absolutely cannot be said whether it will occur or not. Ironically, it is the Federal Supreme Court itself which made it clear that a plaintiff's claim cannot succeed as long as it is not established that a damaging event or action will most probably lead to an actual damage.[97] But if the damage occurs more than ten years after the damaging exposure to asbestos, then the plaintiff will only be able to detect his/her disease and consequently assess his/her damages after the expiry of the prescription period. The Federal Supreme Court identified this problem but yet refused to postpone the starting point of the ten-year prescription period until the occurrence of the damage (which would better correspond to the wording of art 130 para 1 CO). In 2014, the European Court of Human Rights condemned this jurisdiction on the grounds that it violates the plaintiff's right to a fair trial guaranteed in art 6 para 1 ECHR (see *supra* Section VII). In response to this criticism, the absolute limitation period for contractual liability in cases of bodily injury and death was extended to 20 years. However, this still does not cover those cases in which the damage occurs after a latency period of more than 20 years since the harmful conduct or event. 68

96 Federal Supreme Court Decision 137 III 16/20 consid. 2.3.

97 Federal Supreme Court Decision 137 III 16/22 consid. 2.4.4.

### B. JUDICIAL DISCRETION

69 Swiss prescription law does not refer to open terms such as 'reasonableness' or 'good faith'. Also, no prescription or prescription-related rule explicitly authorises the courts to make use of discretion in any direction whatsoever. However, some terms like 'awareness', even if they leave less space for discretion than the mentioned terms, must still be interpreted (see also *supra* Section VIII). In addition, the courts may reject the defence of prescription in a case-by-case decision when this defence is deemed to be abusive (see *supra* Section VIII).

### C. LACHES

70 There is no such thing as laches in Swiss prescription law. Under reservation of the abuse of rights,[98] the plaintiff is free to exhaust the prescription period before filing a claim.

## XI. CHANGE OF PARTIES

### A. THE PLAINTIFF IS A TRANSFEREE OF THE VICTIM'S CLAIM

71 The assignment of a claim has basically no impact on the prescription period, neither does it interrupt the current prescription period nor does the nature and the duration of the prescription period change.[99] There is, however, a special legal provision that applies to social insurances only. According to art 72 para 3 of the Federal Act on the General Part of Social Insurance Law[100] the relative prescription period only starts to run once the insurer becomes aware of its insurance benefit and of the person which is liable for the insured event.

72 Inheritance (arts 560 et seq. CC) does not affect the prescription period of claims of the testator.[101]

### B. THE DEFENDANT IS A TRANSFEREE OF THE TORTFEASOR'S OBLIGATION

73 There are mainly three ways a liability debt can be transferred from the tortfeasor to another person with different impacts on the prescription:

---

98 Cf eg Federal Supreme Court Decision 127 III 257/266 consid. 6c.

99 *F Krauskopf*, in: Zürcher Kommentar zum Schweizerischen Zivilgesetzbuch, Kommentar zu Art. 143–150 OR (3rd ed, Zurich 2016), n 181 et seq. ad art 148/149 CO.

100 Federal Act on the General Part of Social Insurance Law of 6 October 2000.

101 In the contrary situation, where the testator was the debtor of a third party, the prescription period is suspended for a certain time (art 586 para 2 CC).

(1) Inheritance (arts 560 et seq. CC): According art 580 para 1 CC, any heir entitled to disclaim his or her inheritance has the right to request a public inventory. Article 134 para 1 sec 7 CO regulates the situation of the heirs during the inventory and states that the prescription periods are suspended. According to a doctrine, in certain cases the prescription periods shall be suspended from the moment of the death until the time limit for the disclaimer or acceptance of the inheritance by the legal and named heirs (art 567 CC).[102]
(2) Contractual assumption of debts (arts 175 et seq. CO): has no effect on prescription. However, if the debt acceptor acknowledges the debt assumed vis-à-vis the creditor, this shall result in the interruption of the limitation period pursuant to art 135 sec 1 CO.
(3) Merging or acquiring of companies (Swiss Merger Act).
   - Article 26 of the Swiss Merger Act[103] regulates the prescription of the personal liability of members of the transferring legal entity (if there is any): claims based on personal liability of the members for debts of the transferring legal entity prescribe three years after the merger becomes legally effective. If the claim only falls due after the publication of the merger resolution, then the three-year prescription period starts to run from the date when the claim becomes due. This time limitation does not apply to members who are also personally liable for the debts of the acquiring legal entity.
   - Article 75 of the Swiss Merger Act sets forth a three-year joint and several liability of the transferring company with the new debtor acquiring company for claims arising before the transfer of assets. Claims against the transferring company prescribe three years after the publication of the transfer of assets. If the claim falls due only after this publication, then the three-year prescription period starts to run from the date when the claim becomes due.

## C. CONTRIBUTION CLAIMS

The contribution claim of a tortfeasor against jointly and severally liable third parties is an independent claim with its own limitation period. However, it is often reinforced by a legally stipulated subrogation (art 149 CO).[104] The subrogation claim is a derived claim and is subject to the same prescription 74

[102] *RK Däppen*, in: Basler Kommentar Obligationenrecht I, Art. 1-529 OR (7th ed, Basel 2019), n 12 ad art 134 CO; *P Pichonnaz*, Commentaire Romand (2nd ed, Basel 2012), n 18 ad art 134 CO.

[103] Federal Act on Merger, Demerger, Transformation and Transfer of Assets of 3 October 2003.

[104] *F Krauskopf*, in: Zürcher Kommentar zum Schweizerischen Zivilgesetzbuch, Kommentar zu Art. 143–150 OR (3rd ed, Zurich 2016), n 22 and 189 et seq. ad art 148/149 CO.

as it existed before subrogation.[105] The legal assignment therefore does not change the prescription.

### D. DEPENDANT'S CLAIM

75 If persons entitled to support toward the deceased person (dependants) are deprived of their means of support as a result of death, they have an own claim – and not a derivative right – for compensation for that loss against the person liable for the death (art 45 para 3 CO).[106] The prescription period for this claim is regulated in art 60 al 1^bis CO: The three-year relative prescription period starts only when the dependents are aware of their damage and of the person who is liable for the damage, at the earliest at the moment of the provider's death. It has not been settled yet whether the absolute prescription period of 20 years starts with the damaging event that led to provider's death or only which is the death of the provider.[107]

## XII. OTHER ASPECTS OF PRESCRIPTION LAW

### A. STIPULATION

76 According to art 129 CO, the parties may not alter the prescription periods contained in the third title of the CO (arts 127–142 CO). However, the parties can *shorten or lengthen any prescription period* that is situated outside of the third title of the CO, which is the case for all non-contractual claims for compensation.[108] The possibility to lengthen prescription periods of tort claims is, however, limited to ten years (art 127 CO).[109] An agreement to shorten a prescription period is only valid under the reservation that the shorter period does not unduly impede the plaintiff to assert his/her claim.[110]

77 Another way to influence the prescription period (without interrupting it) is the defendant's declaration to *waive the defence of prescription*. This waiver is not subject to any formal requirement and is also valid when declared orally.[111]

---

105 Ibid.

106 Federal Supreme Court Decision 101 II 257/260 consid. 1a; 129 II 49/51 consid. 2; 112 II 87/92 consid. 2b; 108 II 434/436 consid. 2a; 102 II 90/93 consid. 2b.

107 *A Kottmann*, Schadensberechnung und Schadensschätzung bei Körperverletzung und Tötung, Notwendigkeit der Bildung von Regeln (Bern 2012), n 635.

108 Federal Supreme Court Decision 112 II 231/233 consid. 3e/bb; 99 II 185/191 consid. 2a.

109 Federal Supreme Court Decision 99 II 185/189 consid. 2a; 56 II 424/430 consid. 4.

110 Federal Supreme Court Decision 108 II 194/196 consid. 4b.

111 Cf the references to case-law with *F Krauskopf*, in: Präjudizienbuch OR. Die Rechtsprechung des Bundesgerichts (1875–2015) (9th ed, Zurich 2016), n 3 ad art 141 CO.

According to the Federal Supreme Court, the waiver shall not exceed ten years.[112] Pursuant to art 141 para 1 CO the defence of prescription may not be waived in advance. According to the Federal Supreme Court the waiver is only valid if the claim to which the prescription periods relate has already arisen.[113] The waiver can be validly declared by the defendant during the pending prescription period as well as after the expiry of the prescription period.[114] As of 1 January 2020, art 141 CO in its new version reads as follows: From the beginning of the prescription period, the debtor may waive the plea of limitation for a maximum of ten years. The waiver must be made in writing. In general terms and conditions, only the user may waive the raising of the defence of prescription. The debtor's waiver may be invoked against the insurer and vice versa, provided there is a direct right of claim against the insurer.

## B. MEANING OF 'FILING A CLAIM' THAT INTERRUPTS THE RUNNING OF PRESCRIPTION

Article 135 sec 2 CO names *exhaustively* the actions that interrupt the prescription period: debt enforcement proceedings, an application for conciliation, submission of a statement of claim or defence to a court or arbitral tribunal, or a petition for bankruptcy.[115] 78

## C. WHEN SHOULD THE DEFENCE BE RAISED AND DECIDED?

The question of when the latest possible moment has come for raising the defence of prescription in civil proceedings is subject to controversy. According to the prevailing opinion, all means of defence such as the defence of prescription must be put forward by the defendant within the time limits set by the procedural rules for the submission of new facts or evidence (nova).[116] Pursuant to a dissenting opinion, the exercise of a right to invoke the prescription is not 79

---

[112] Federal Supreme Court Decision 132 III 226/240 consid. 3.3.8; 4A_221/2010 (12.1.2010) consid. 3.

[113] Federal Supreme Court Decision 132 III 226/238 consid. 3.3.7.

[114] Federal Supreme Court Decision 99 II 185/188 et seq. consid. 2.

[115] Federal Supreme Court Decision 132 V 404/411 consid. 5.2.

[116] Federal Supreme Court Decision 4A_305/2012 (6.2.2013) consid. 3.3; *F Bohnet*, Les exceptions en procédure civile suisse, in: Procédure Civile Suisse: Les grands thèmes pour les praticiens, CEMAJ – Faculté de droit de l'Université de Neuchâtel (Neuchâtel 2010), n 22; *RK Däppen*, in: Basler Kommentar Obligationenrecht I, Art. 1-529 OR (7th ed, Basel 2019), n 4 ad art 142 CO; *P Reetz and S Hilber*, in: Kommentar zur Schweizerischen Zivilprozessordnung (ZPO) (3rd ed, Zurich 2016), n 31 ad art 317 CPC; *R Klingler*, Die Eventualmaxime in der Schweizerischen Zivilprozessordnung (Basel 2010), n 205 et seq.; *B Seiler*, Die Berufung nach der Schweizerischen Zivilprozessordnung (Zurich/Basel/Geneva 2013), n 1234 et seq.

subject to the nova-limitations.[117] The question whether the defence of prescription was timely raised, is a question of facts.[118] The defence must be raised before the main hearings which basically means within the exchange of written submissions. Article 229 CPC[119] determines that new facts and evidence are only admissible at the main hearings if presented immediately and if they occurred or were discovered after the exchange of written submissions or after the last instruction hearing (proper nova) or if they existed before the close of the exchange of written submissions or before the last instruction hearing but could not have been submitted despite reasonable diligence (improper nova) (art 229 para 1 CPC). If there was neither a second round of written submissions nor an instruction hearing, the defence of prescription can be submitted without limitation at the beginning of the main hearing (art 229 para 2 CPC).

80 The court may decide to limit the proceedings to the question of prescription for the time being (art 125 lit. a CPC). If the defence of prescription proves to be justified, a judgment is passed and the action is dismissed. This judgment may be brought before the court of appeal as an independent decision.[120] If, on the other hand, the defence of prescription is dismissed, the court can make an interim decision which can be independently challenged by appeal (art 237 CPC).[121]

## D. WHO MAY RAISE THE DEFENCE?

81 The expiry of the prescription period provides the debtor with a substantive defence that prevents the creditor from enforcing the right. Article 142 CO states an important procedural rule: The court may not consider the prescription *ex officio*.[122]

## E. BURDEN OF PROOF (OF ELEMENTS AND OF RULES OF PROLONGATION)

82 It is the defendant who has to establish that the prescription period passed since the accrual of the plaintiff's right to remedy and it is the plaintiff who has to establish that the running of time was or has been postponed, renewed or that the period has been extended.

---

117 *S Moret*, Aktenschluss und Novenrecht nach der Schweizerischen Zivilprozessordung (Zurich 2014), no 973.

118 Federal Supreme Court Decision 138 II 169/170 consid. 3.1.

119 Civil Procedure Code of 19 December 2008.

120 Federal Supreme Court Decision 97 II 136/137 consid. 1.

121 Federal Supreme Court Decision 5D_160/2014 (26.1.2015) consid. 2.4.

122 Federal Supreme Court Decision 137 III 16/18 consid. 2; 134 V 223/227 consid. 2.2.2; 129 V 237/241 consid. 4.

# PRESCRIPTION IN TORT LAW: UNITED STATES

Michael D Green*



* The author is grateful to Libby Casal, Wake Forest School of Law, class of 2018 and Ashley DiMuzio, Wake Forest School of Law, class of 2019, for their indefatigable and extensive research assistance.

## I. INTRODUCTION

1 In the US, the substantive rules of tort law are primarily determined by state courts and legislatures.[1] As well, prescription[2] of those claims is a matter for each state. Thus, different prescription rules and periods exist throughout the US, although there are some central tendencies among the states along with variations. In addition, tort claims against the US are governed by federal law, which provides its own statute of limitations.

1 See *AJ Levy*, Solving Statute of Limitations Problems (Kluwer 1987).

2 The most commonly used terms in the US to describe prescription of claims are 'statutes of limitation' and 'limitation of actions'. These terms will be used interchangeably along with prescription in this Report.

In what follows, this report aims to address the issues raised by the Questionnaire by reference to legal rules that have gained broad or substantial acceptance across the different US jurisdictions, and will also try to note areas in which the law varies significantly among jurisdictions. 2

## II. DEFINITION OF PRESCRIPTION[3]

Prescription in tort law is a legal institution that prevents P from enforcing an alleged right against D because of the running of a specified period of time on the tort claim. 3

The subject of prescription, as can be seen from the above definition, is usually the right of P to tort remedy from D, mainly the right to damages for harm caused. This right to remedy comes into being once a right protected by tort law, such as the right to bodily and property integrity, or the right to reputation, is breached. To the extent that one conceives of the latter right (not to be harmed by tortious conduct) as a primary right, and of the former right (to tort remedy) as a secondary right, it is the secondary right which is the subject of prescription. 4

Only the first sentence is a definition of prescription. That sentence comports reasonably well with the understanding in the US, although the author would replace 'institution' with 'rule' and substitute 'between accrual of the tort claim and initiation of legal action' for 'on the tort claim.' 5

The remainder of the definition above explains a tort claim and adds professional malpractice as a claim within the scope of this project and, although using terms unfamiliar to a US attorney, expresses ideas roughly compatible with US law of prescription. 6

## III. THE NATURE OF PRESCRIPTION AND ITS EFFECTS[4]

There are different ways by which prescription prevents P from enforcing an alleged right of remedy against D. Its effect may be: (a) to extinguish P's right to remedy; (b) to provide D with a substantive defence that prevents P from 7

3 The text in paras 3 and 4 contain excerpts from the Questionnaire and Analytical and Comparative report in this book.

4 The text in paras 7, 8 and 9 contain excerpts from the Questionnaire and Analytical and Comparative report in this book.

enforcing the right to remedy although it is not extinguished; (c) to provide D with a procedural defence that bars P's ability to enforce the alleged right to remedy through judicial proceedings before an authorised court.

8 To illustrate the difference between prescription that extinguishes the right (a) and prescription that provides a substantive defence against its enforcement (b), assume that D mistakenly compensates P for damage tortiously caused by D, although the prescription period elapsed and the claim is prescribed. Under the extinction effect (a) D would have the right to restitution under the law of unjust enrichment because P's right to compensation was extinct before payment. In contrast, under the substantive defence effect (b) D will have no right of restitution because P's right to compensation still exists.

9 To illustrate, on the other hand, the difference between the substantive effect of prescription (b) and its effect as a procedural bar (c), assume that P can enforce the alleged right to tort compensation upon D without judicial proceedings, for example by way of offset, or by other ways of self-help (such as selling or confiscating D's property). Could P do that after the prescription period elapsed? The answer would be negative under prescription as substantive defence (b) because P's substantive right to remedy is blocked. In contrast, under the procedural bar concept of prescription (c) the answer would be in the affirmative because only enforcement through judicial proceedings in court is barred, while P can enforce the right outside the court.

10 Concepts (a) and (b) exist in US law. Statutes of limitations in the US are traditionally characterised as a procedural defence that bars a plaintiff's ability to recover on a claim.[5] The expiration of the statute of limitations usually does not extinguish the right or cause of action but instead makes the remedy unavailable.[6] As affirmative defences, they require that the defendant plead that the plaintiff's claim for relief is barred because the statute of limitations has run and prove that the defence is applicable. Affirmative defences can be waived by failing, intentionally or otherwise, to assert them. This is most compatible with version (b) above.

11 However, there is also some modest authority that holds that the expiration of the statute of limitations extinguishes the right as well as the remedy.[7] For example, Wisconsin treats statutes of limitation as substantive rules instead of as a procedural defence.[8] Other jurisdictions that have treated limitations

5 See *JD Lee and BA Lindahl*, Modern Tort Law: Liability and Litigation §13:14 (2nd ed, Clark Boardman Callaghan 1990).
6 See *Ex parte HealthSouth Corp.*, 974 So. 2d 288 (Ala. 2007).
7 See *Ginkowski v Ginkowski*, 137 N.W.2d 403 (Wis. 1965).
8 See *Malone v Corr. Corp. of Am.*, 553 F.3d 540 (7th Cir. 2009).

periods as substantive defences include Puerto Rico[9] and California.[10] This difference between procedural limitations that only affect the availability of a remedy and substantive limitations that instead eliminate any right to relief was explained by one federal court that used 'statute of limitations' to refer to the former and 'statute of repose' to cover the latter:

> In contrast to statutes of limitation, statutes of repose serve primarily to relieve potential defendants from anxiety over liability for acts committed long ago. *Statutes of repose make the filing of suit within a specified time a substantive part of plaintiff's cause of action.* In other words, where a statute of repose has been enacted, the time for filing suit is engrafted onto a substantive right created by law. The distinction between statutes of limitation and statutes of repose corresponds to the distinction between procedural and substantive laws. Statutes of repose are meant to be 'a substantive definition of rights as distinguished from a procedural limitation on the remedy used to enforce rights.' Statutes of limitation serve interests peculiar to the forum, and are considered as going to the remedy and not the fundamental right itself [...]. Because of the substantive nature of statutes of repose, courts have treated the effect of the period expiring to be jurisdictional. Consistent with this view, other courts have expressly held that the running of a statute of repose creates a vested right not to be sued.[11]

In these instances, courts often speak of statutes of limitations as substantive, 12
rather than procedural, which has important implications for choice of law. A legislature may also expressly state in a statute providing a right of action that the right as well as the remedy is extinguished upon expiration of the statute of limitations.[12] Thus, where a statute of limitations is found to be substantive, it often is in the context of specific statutorily created causes of actions, rather than statutes of limitations applicable generally or to common law tort claims.[13]

Some jurisdictions regard statutes of limitation as a mix of both procedural 13
and substantive. For example, Missouri regards some statutes of limitation as

---

9 See *Medina v Toledo*, 718 F. Supp. 2d 194 (D.P.R. 2010), *aff'd sub nom. Moreno-Medina v Toledo*, 458 F. App'x 4 (1st Cir. 2012).

10 See *Ctr. for Self-Improvement & Cmty. Dev. v Lennar Corp.*, 94 Cal. Rptr. 3d 74 (Cal. 2009).

11 *Wenke v Gehl Co.*, 682 N.W.2d 405, 425 (Wis. 2004) (citations omitted) (emphasis added) (quoting *Goad v Celotex Corp.*, 831 F.2d 508, 511 (4th Cir. 1987).

12 See Okla. Stat. Ann. tit. 42 §23 (West 2016); *Baccus v Banks*, 192 P.2d 583 (Okla. 1947) (statue extinguishing a lien once the period for its enforcement has expired).

13 See *Frabutt v New York*, C. & St. L. R. Co., 84 F. Supp. 460 (W.D. Pa. 1949) (Federal Employers Liability Act provision requiring action to be brought within a specified amount of time bars remedy and eliminates liability if suit is not brought timely); *Zellmer v Acme Brewing Co.*, 184 F.2d 940, 942 (9th Cir. 1950) (statutorily created liability not known at common law, such as wrongful death, intended to affect the right and not merely the remedy); *M Joyce*, Tolling of Substantive Statutes of Limitation – White v. Violent Crimes Compensation Board, 32 Rutgers. L. Rev. 95, 95 (1979).

procedural, and others, such as those regarding wrongful death, as substantive.[14] Other courts have stated that the characterisation depends on the context of the issue before the court.[15] Therefore, whether a statute of limitations is characterised as procedural or substantive varies from state to state, and also according to the type of claim that is being asserted.

14 Some states divide statutorily created limitations periods into two categories: statutes of limitations and statutes of repose,[16] with statutes of repose barring the right and statutes of limitations barring the remedy.[17] Therefore, generally (although not exclusively as revealed above), the expiration of a statute of limitations has to do with the availability of the remedy, while statutes of repose affect the availability of the underlying right.[18] In other jurisdictions, statutes of repose are treated as procedural: an affirmative defence that must be timely raised; failure to do so waives the defence.[19]

15 Another variation exists for certain specific claims. A legislature can declare that compliance with the statute of limitations is a jurisdictional matter. Such a declaration removes adjudicatory authority of courts over the claim and that barrier to adjudication cannot be waived, even by agreement of the parties. Contract claims against the US (but not tort claims[20]) are subject to this jurisdictional barrier if the plaintiff does not comply with the statute of limitations.[21]

16 This report cannot answer the question of whether prescription falls into category (b) or (c) in this inquiry, as the author is unaware of any procedure

---

14 See *Messner v Am. Union Ins. Co.*, 119 S.W.3d 642, 647 (Mo. Ct. App. 2003) (describing prescription rule for uninsured motorist benefits as procedural and prescription period for wrongful death claims as substantive).

15 See *McConnell v Thomson Newspapers, Inc.*, 802 F. Supp. 1484 (E.D. Tex. 1992) (explaining that whether the claim is a common law or statutory claim and whether the prescription period is specified in law creating the substantive claim are important to determining whether a limitations period is procedural or substantive).

16 'Statute of repose' or, as used later in the prompts in this Report, 'long-stop' periods are most frequently distinguished from statutes of limitations based on when the clock for the period begins to run. Statutes of repose can begin to run before the victim has been harmed and hence expire before the victim has a valid legal claim to pursue. See *infra* 101–102.

17 See *Sprowles v Thompson*, 239 P.3d 981, 984 (Okla. 2010); *Jones v Methodist Healthcare*, 83 S.W.3d 739, 743 (Tenn. Ct. App. 2001).

18 See *CW Corman*, Limitation of Actions §1.1 (Little, Brown 1991); *Am. Fed'n of Teachers, AFL-CIO v Bullock*, 605 F. Supp. 2d 251, 261 (D.D.C. 2009) (statute of repose barring certain claims against banks asserting unauthorised signatures on customer's account was not a procedural defence that had to pleaded but instead extinguished customer's claim).

19 See, eg *Hess v Philip Morris USA, Inc.*, 175 So. 3d 687, 694 (Fla. 2015); *Pratcher v Methodist Healthcare Memphis Hosps.*, 407 S.W.3d 727, 739 (Tenn. 2013).

20 See *United States v Kwai Fun Wong*, 575 U.S. 402 (2015).

21 See *John R. Sand & Gravel Co. v United States*, 552 U.S. 130 (2008) (holding that the jurisdiction of the Court of Federal Claims is limited by the six-year statute of limitations

that would entitle a tort victim to sell another's property without having a court judgment authorising such.

## IV. CONSIDERATIONS FOR AND AGAINST PRESCRIPTION OF TORT CLAIMS

### A. THE QUESTION[22]

17 Prescription of a tort claim, as this report explained above, prevents P from enforcing a tort claim against D because of the running of a specified period of time (the prescription period or the upper time limit if earlier) on P's tort claim. That may deprive Ps from pursuing and enforcing their alleged rights against Ds. In other words, prescription actually closes the doors of courts and may significantly limit the (constitutional?) right to 'open courts'. As the ability to vindicate rights in courts empowers individuals and strengthen their trust in the state and in society, closing the doors of courts may undermine this empowerment and trust and even encourage people to bypass the legal system by methods of 'self-help'.

18 Given these negative effects of prescription, what are the considerations that nevertheless counterbalance the negative and justify prescription law?

19 Before proceeding to the cons and pros of prescription rules, a comment on the explanation in the Comparative Report on reasons for prescription is appropriate. This author does not find the explanation that they protect Ds from belated claims persuasive. It may be that there are reasons for protecting Ds from claims, timely or not, but on its face this justification is general and facile. Whether or not prescription periods do anything (and, if so, how much) to screen good claims from bad claims is an empirical matter. The Comparative Report cites no evidence on this matter (and the author knows of none). Without such evidence, the author finds the claim that '[t]ime limits on the filing of claims are a major factor in the ability of courts to distinguish between good claims and bad claims' to be unjustified. Finally, the deterioration of evidence can affect the plaintiff as much as the defendant. It is, after all, the plaintiff who must make out a case. When evidence necessary to do so is in the hands of others, plaintiffs will be negatively affected by deterioration due to the

encompassed in 28 U.S.C. §2501); *Rocky Mountain Helium, LLC v United States*, 2016 WL 6775965 (Fed. Cir. 2016) (contract claim dismissed on jurisdictional grounds because it was brought outside of the six-year limit).

22 The text in paras 17 and 18 contain excerpts from the Questionnaire and Analytical and Comparative report in this book.

passage of time. Plaintiffs may also be negatively affected by time passage even when they possess the necessary evidence if they are unaware of their claims and the preservation necessity.

## B. COMPARATIVE PERSPECTIVES

20 This report sets forth below the standard litany of cons and pros to statutes of limitations that are commonly asserted in the US.

21 *Cons:* There are a number of potential disadvantages to statute of limitations that are identified by courts and commentators:

(1) They preclude consideration of the merits of a suit and may result in barring meritorious claims.[23] Adjudication of a suit on its substantive merits, as a matter of public policy, is preferable to resolution on procedural grounds.[24]
(2) The inflexibility of statute of limitations can be seen to be arbitrary or unjust by failing to take into account facts and considerations that would justify excusing the plaintiff from complying with their requirements.[25] Thus, they may bar claims where the claimant was not at fault for the delay in filing suit or even had good reasons for failing to meet the deadline for filing.[26]
(3) Statues of limitations may be overbroad and bar claims where evidence remains fresh and indeed may have improved with the passage of time.[27]
(4) A bright line application, barring legitimate claims, may leave some claimants disillusioned with the legal process.[28]
(5) Access to the courts discourages people from resorting to unsanctioned mechanisms of recourse, such as self-help.[29]

---

23 See *James v Montoya*, 963 P.2d 993 (Wyo. 1998) (statutes operate regardless of merits, and courts have no right to deny their operation or discriminate between just and unjust claims).

24 *TT Ochoa and AJ Wistrich*, The Puzzling Purposes of Statutes of Limitation, 28 Pac. L.J. 453, 500 (1997).

25 See id. at 511.

26 See id. At fn 24, 486 (presenting an example where a defendant may be aware of a defective product because of experience with previous customers while a plaintiff is not).

27 See *MD Green*, The Paradox of Statutes of Limitations in Insidious Disease Litigation, 76 Cal. L. Rev. 965 (1989).

28 See id. at 983–84; *SM Malveaux*, Statutes of Limitations: A Policy Analysis in the Context of Reparations Litigation, 74 Geo. Wash. L. Rev. 68, 76 (2005).

29 See *Ochoa and Wistrich*, *supra* fn 24, 503.

*Pros:* US courts and commentators provide a number of justifications for statutes of limitations:[30] 22

(1) Assuring that evidence is available and fresh. Physical evidence may disappear, and memories may fade so that they can no longer be used or tested, and statutes of limitations, by encouraging diligent prosecution of claims, can avoid this problem.[31]
(2) At some point, potential defendants are entitled to peace of mind (often expressed as an interest in 'repose') in knowing that they are no longer subject to suit for an occurrence in the past.[32] An individual's (or an entity's) ability to manage his or her affairs may also be diminished by the uncertainty about, or unawareness of, potential lawsuits, and if they do not know about potential claims against them, they may make ill-considered decisions because of ignorance of the claim.[33]
(3) Statutes of limitations save public resources required to resolve stale claims.[34] Society is therefore better off if these costs can be avoided by requiring prompt assertion of claims.[35]
(4) Stability of transactions and relationships are important to society, and these are affected by looming potential litigation.[36]
(5) Society's legal standards and expectations change over time, so without a limitations period, judges and juries might apply modern legal standards to events that took place when different legal standards and sensibilities prevailed.[37]
(6) Being rule-based, statutes of limitations are relatively easy to apply and therefore minimise the administrative-transaction costs to adjudicate them.
(7) A short statute of limitation may express the legislature's ambivalence about the substantive right it has created.[38]
(8) Courts sometimes express or imply that those who do not pursue their rights promptly are slothful and therefore less deserving of a recovery. This justification tends to merge with one that suggests that when a

---

30 This report should not be understood as endorsing any or all of these advantages or disadvantages; rather, it simply reports on what courts and commentators have expressed.

31 See *DB Dobbs, PT Hayden and EM Bublick*, The Law of Torts §241 (2nd ed, West Group 2011); *Malveaux, supra* fn 28, 76; See *Ochoa and Wistrich, supra* fn 24, 471–472.

32 See *Dobbs, Hayden and Bublick*, id, §241; *Malveaux, supra* fn 28, 75–76.

33 See *Dobbs, Hayden and Bublick*, id, §241; *Ochoa and Wistrich, supra* fn 24, 464.

34 See *Dobbs, Hayden and Bublick*, id, §241; *Malveaux, supra* fn 28, 79 ('Statutes of limitations are justified as efficient because they: (1) reduce costs; (2) clear dockets; and (3) simplify judicial decisions.').

35 See *Dobbs, Hayden and Bublick*, id, §241.

36 See *Dobbs, Hayden and Bublick*, id, §241; *Ochoa and Wistrich, supra* fn 24, 466.

37 See *Dobbs, Hayden and Bublick*, id, §241; *Ochoa and Wistrich supra*, fn 24, 493–494.

38 See *Malveaux, supra* fn 28, 80.

claimant delays bringing a claim, it is likely less meritorious than those that are brought in timely fashion.[39]

(9) Statutes of limitations reinforce and strengthen institutional legitimacy, as they permit or bar claims on the basis of a bright-line rule, rather than judicial discretion.[40]

(10) Statutes of limitation serve to place plaintiffs and defendants on equal footing by preventing plaintiffs from gaining an advantage by gathering evidence while it is fresh, and then bringing suit against a defendant at a later date after the defendant would have impeded access to favourable evidence.[41]

## V. ELEMENTS OF PRESCRIPTION – AN OVERVIEW[42]

23 Analytically, there are four elements – four sets of rules – that together comprise prescription law: the starting point, the prescription period, rules of prolongation and rules of upper limit.

(1) *The starting point* – the date on which P's cause of action against D, claim which is subject matter of prescription, matures so that the prescription periods starts to run on this claim (unless its running is postponed by a rule of prolongation). In terms of the common law, the starting point is the date on which the cause of action accrues.

(2) *The prescription period* – the statutory period of time that after its running (from the starting point – from the date of accrual) the cause of action is prescribed.

(3) *Rules of prolongation* – rules that prolong the actual time that passes between the starting point (accrual) and the expiry of the prescription period on P's cause of action. There are four kinds of rules of prolongation: postponement, suspension, renewal and extension. When these rules apply, the effective time of prescription, namely, the actual time that passes from the starting point (accrual) to expiry of the prescription period, is longer than the prescription period.

Rules of prolongation usually apply in cases where P's delay to file a claim against D originates in contingencies that caused the delay, such as P's unawareness of relevant facts, mental disabilities, special relation between

39 See id.

40 See id., 81–82.

41 See *Ochoa and Wistrich*, *supra* fn 24, 483–484.

42 The text in para 23 contain excerpts from the Questionnaire and Analytical and Comparative report in this book.

P and D, *force majeure* and so on. When such reasons for the delay render it justified, the effective time of prescription is accordingly prolonged by rules of postponement, suspension, renewal and extension.

- Rules of postponement postpone the running of the prescription period, before it starts to run, beyond the starting point (accrual of cause of action), until the reason for postponement ceases to exist. For example, to the extent that D's mental disability at the starting point and afterwards is recognised as justifying postponement of the running of the prescription period, the period does not start to run until mental disability ends.
- Rules of suspension suspend the running of the prescription period as long as the reason for suspension exists. For example, to the extent that arbitration proceedings between P and D, that began after the starting point, justify the suspension of the prescription as long as they are conducted, the prescription will cease to run while these proceedings are conducted.

The difference between a rule of postponement and a rule of suspension is the following. A rule of postponement applies, where its reason exists, only where the period has not yet started to run. In contrast, a rule of suspension applies, where the reason for suspension exists, regardless of whether the period has not yet started to run or after it has begun to run. This is illustrated by the following example. Assume that the prescription period is five years, that at the starting point (date of accrual) P suffers from mental disability for one year, then becomes mentally able for two years, and then again becomes mentally disabled for additional four years until regaining ability. P's claim is filed seven years after the starting point. If mental disability is considered a rule pf postponement, P's claim would be prescribed since a period of six years ran over P's claim. But if mental disability is considered a rule of suspension, P would have three years to sue as only two years ran over P's claim. In such cases a rule of suspension actually 'swallows', overtakes, the parallel rule of postponement and is accordingly more favourable to Ps. Another illustration is EW law, which states that once the prescription period starts to run, its running cannot be stopped. This statement means that EW law allows only rules of postponement but not rules of suspension.

- Rules of renewal (also referred to as rules of interruption) restart the running of the prescription period in the sense that a new period of prescription starts to run afresh when the reason for renewal occurs. For example, where D admits P's right to torts compensation from D, this admission, if recognised as a rule of renewal, 'deletes' the period that ran until admission, and a new count of the period begins.

- Rules of extension, unlike the former rules, do not affect the running of the period, but rather extend the period itself. For example, if the victim of a tort (V) dies six months before the period expires vis-à-vis D, and the law provides that the derivative claim of the heirs (the estate) against D shall not prescribe within one year after V's death, this is a rule of extension that in this case extends the prescription period by six months.

(4) *The upper time limit* – the above rules of prolongation may indeterminately prolong the effective time of prescription to an extent that frustrates the goals of prescription law discussed below. To avoid such indeterminate prolongation the law may set an upper limit to the effective time of prescription, a ceiling period, that after its running the cause of action is prescribed even though the prescription period has not yet expired because of rules of prolongation. This upper time limit, the ceiling period, should be distinguished from the prescription period. As later explained, it may and actually should start earlier than the prescription period, namely, before the starting point (date of accrual) and it may and actually should be much less susceptible to rules of prolongation if at all.

24 Rules of accrual of a claim,[43] rules providing the prescription period itself,[44] rules of suspension,[45] postponement,[46] and extension of the prescription period,[47]

---

43 See generally *J Bordeau*, Law Governing Accrual of Cause of Action Under Statutes of Limitations, 5 Cyc. of Federal Proc. §15:465 (3rd ed, updated 2016).

44 See generally *infra* text accompanying fn 148.

45 See, eg NYCPLR §208 (infants and insane persons given additional time after the statute of limitations would ordinarily run in which to file suit); Wis. Stat Ann. §893.16 (suspending the running of the statute of limitations for a person with mental illness for two years after the disability ceases and extending the statutory period for up to five years); See generally *infra* text accompanying fn 212–275.

46 See, eg *Martinez v United States*, 333 F.3d 1295, 1319 (Fed. Cir. 2003) ('The "accrual suspension" rule is "strictly and narrowly applied: [...] [The plaintiff] must either show that defendant has concealed its acts with the result that plaintiff was unaware of their existence or it must show that its injury was 'inherently unknowable' at the accrual date."') (quoting *Welcker v United States*, 752 F.2d 1577, 1580 (Fed. Cir. 1985)); see generally *infra* text accompanying fn 212–275.

47 See, eg 28 U.S.C. §1367 (suspending the statute of limitations for state claims asserted in federal court based on supplemental jurisdiction that are later dismissed for lack of jurisdiction during the time the claim was pending in court and extending the limitations period for 30 days after dismissal); *Poland v Porter*, S.W. 214, 218 (Tex. Civ. App. 1906) (discussing suspension of the statute of limitations for making a claim related to ownership of real property); see generally *infra* text accompanying fn 212–275.

and rules of repose[43] all exist in the US. The author is unsure what additional information this prompt seeks to elicit.

# VI. THE STARTING POINT OF THE PRESCRIPTION PERIOD

## A. THE MEANING OF 'ACTION' AND 'CAUSE OF ACTION'[49]

The cause of action is the source, the root, of a particular action. Usually a particular action arises from, or originates in, an occurrence such as an accident, professional malpractice, defaming publications, etc. When an occurrence contains a multiplicity of conducts and/or of caused harms which are tortious under tort rules, it may produce a variety of particular tort actions, tort claims, which differ from each other in the facts regarding D's conduct, caused harms and applicable torts. Yet, when a group of particular actions, claims, has a common factual/legal source, it is said that all these particular actions belong to the same source, the same cause of action. So, the cause of action may be the occurrence as a whole or part of it. 25

This is exemplified by the following illustration: Physician D treat patient P negligently and performs three mistakes on the treatment day: A, B and C. Mistake A causes harm X after a year. Mistake B causes harm Y after two years. Mistakes A and C together cause harm Z after three years. The occurrence is the medical treatment. This occurrence contains a multiplicity of facts regarding D's conduct (three different mistakes A, B, C) and a multiplicity of harms (X, Y, Z). It accordingly raises a multiplicity of particular actions, particular claims (for harms X, Y and Z). Yet, to the extent that these actions, or some of them, have a common factual/legal source, they may be regarded as originating in the same cause of action – the medical treatment in this case. 26

Please discuss the concept of cause of action for prescription purposes in your jurisdiction referring to the above analysis (of A, B, C), or presenting another one. 27

The scope of a cause of action for statute of limitations purposes is that it generally encompasses all injuries suffered in a 'transaction or occurrence or a series of transactions or occurrences'[50] and any consequential future harms. Moreover, it includes all legal theories that might be asserted to provide a remedy 28

---

48 See *infra* text accompanying fn 276–284.

49 The text in paras 25, 26 and 27 contain excerpts from the Questionnaire and Analytical and Comparative report in this book.

50 *Sopha v Owens-Corning Fiberglas Corp.*, 601 N.W.2d 627, 633 (Wis. 1999).

for those injuries. The inclusion in a cause of action of all injuries suffered in a series of transactions both expands the scope of causes of action and adds an element of discretion in determining when multiple injuries are part of the same series of transactions. The Restatement (Second) of Judgments provides, albeit with regard to the scope of a claim for *res judicata* purposes, that it encompasses all rights to remedies against a defendant with respect to a transaction or series of transactions and goes on to explain the meaning of 'transaction':

> What factual grouping constitutes a 'transaction,' and what groupings constitute a 'series,' are to be determined pragmatically, giving weight to such considerations as whether the facts are related in time, space, origin, or motivation, whether they form a convenient trial unit, and whether their treatment as a unit conforms to the parties' expectations or business understanding or usage.[51]

While this definition is for purposes of *res judicata* and preclusion, it is often assumed that the definition for purposes of preclusion is co-extensive with the definition for purposes of prescription.[52] A narrower conception of the scope of a claim exists when harm is determined to be continuing, as occurs in nuisance. If the nuisance is not found to be permanent but instead to be continuing, each increment of harm is treated as a separate claim.[53]

## B. BROAD OR NARROW CONCEPTION OF 'CAUSE OF ACTION'

**Case 1** – *D, a ski instructor, negligently fails to make sure that all skiers in her 'off-piste' group wear helmets. P, a skier in the group, hits a tree. P immediately suffers head injury X, and years later another head injury Y that developed from the same accident.*

29 The statute of limitations period traditionally begins, and the clock begins to run, when the plaintiff's claim accrues.[54] This means the time when the defendant's tortious act resulted in a legally cognisable harm.[55] Thus, P's cause of action would accrue with the occurrence of injury X. Based on the transactional analysis of the scope of a cause of action discussed above,

---

51 Restatement (Second) of Judgments §24 (Am. Law Inst. 1982).

52 An important contemporary exception to the breadth of a claim for statute of limitations periods exists in the latent disease context when exposure to a toxic agent creates a risk of multiple diseases, such as is the case with asbestos. Courts have ruled that each different disease is a distinct claim for statute of limitations purposes. See *infra* text accompanying fn 65–69.

53 See *Meyers v Kissner*, 594 N.E.2d 336, 340 (Ill. 1992).

54 See *Dobbs, Hayden and Bublick, supra* fn 31, §242.

55 See id.

P's cause of action would include injury Y. Thus, one statute of limitation would be applicable to both injuries X and Y and would accrue on the occurrence (or discovery) of X. Damages for the future injury Y, subject to the qualifications stated in the discussion of Case 1, could be recovered in the suit filed based on injury X. Also, if P missed filing the claim for injury X in timely fashion, a claim for injury Y would also be barred on prescription grounds because X and Y are components of the same transaction.

If P sues for injury X and a final judgment is entered in that suit, the doctrine of *res judicata* would bar a second suit for injury Y based on the *res judicata* single judgment rule.[56] The single judgment rule declares that once a final judgment is entered on a cause of action, no further action may be pursued even if later harm occurs. A British case, *Fetter v Beale*,[57] graphically illustrates this principle. P sued D and recovered £11 for bruises suffered from D's battery. Thereafter, 'part of [P's] skull by reason of the said battery came out of his head,' and he brought a second suit to recover damages for that injury. The court dismissed the second action based on the single judgment rule. Note that, in *Fetter*, the second injury was far more serious than the first. The order in which the injuries occur and the differences in the seriousness of the harm do not affect the analysis. 30

An exception has formed when a plaintiff has developed a disease and is at risk of developing a different disease in the future due to the same toxic exposure. Under this exception, an earlier-discovered disease does not trigger the statute of limitations for a lawsuit based on a later 'independent' latent disease caused by the same exposure.[58] This exception was created in asbestos litigation where there are at least three different diseases caused by asbestos – asbestosis, lung cancer and mesothelioma – each with a different latency period. Thus, a victim who is diagnosed with asbestosis and who does not bring suit is not barred from a later suit to recover for mesothelioma that is filed after the prescription period for asbestosis expired.[59] Recently, the California Supreme Court extended this exception to diseases arising out of tobacco use.[60] 31

A federal appeals court used the reasoning of this latent disease exception to hold that two separate fires that resulted from an allegedly defective sauna 32

56 See id, at §248.

57 *Fetter v Beale* [1697] 91 Eng. Rep. 1122 (King's Bench).

58 See *Pooshs v Philip Morris USA, Inc.*, 250 P.3d 181, 183 n.1 (Cal. 2011) (listing other courts that have adopted this exception). But see *Kiser v A.W. Chesterton Co.*, 770 F. Supp. 2d 745 (E.D. Pa. 2011) (applying Virginia law), *aff'd*, 517 F. App'x 109 (3d Cir. 2013).

59 See, eg *Wilson v Johns-Manville Sales Corp.*, 684 F.2d 111 (D.C. Cir. 1982); *Potts v Celotex Corp.*, 796 S.W.2d 678 (Tenn. 1990).

60 See *Pooshs v Philip Morris USA, Inc.*, 250 P.3d 181, 183 (Cal. 2011) (requiring that later disease for which suit is brought is 'separate and distinct from an earlier-discovered disease').

heater constituted two different causes of action for prescription purposes.[61] No suit was filed after the first fire, and although the statutory period had expired when the plaintiff sued for damages caused by the second fire, the court held that although a single tortious act occurred, there were two causes of action with two different accruals if the harms were 'separate and distinct.'[62]

33 It would not matter whether injury Y is causally connected to injury X with regard to the basic principle of the scope of a cause of action and the single judgment rule. It might, however, matter for the latent disease exception as courts have insisted that, for the exception to apply, the second disease must be 'independent' or 'separate and distinct.' Where the two diseases are causally related, the author thinks a court would be considerably less likely to conclude that they were independent or separate and distinct.

**Case 2** – *Physician D treats patient P negligently and performs three mistakes on the day of the treatment: A, B and C. Mistake A causes harm X after a year. Mistake B causes harm Y after two years. Mistakes A and C together cause harm Z after three years.*

34 The author has been unable to find any law directly addressing this question.[63] The author is inclined to think that, as a first step in analysing this question, a court might conclude that all of the harms arose from the same transaction or series thereof because all of the acts of malpractice occurred on the same day and arose from the same treatment provided by D. That multiple harms result would ordinarily not mean that there were separate claims as P could recover in her first action for the future harm (at least to the extent that the risk of such harm was known) and, in most jurisdictions, that the future harm was more likely than not to occur. Thus, the statute of limitations would

61 See *Cigna Ins. Co. v Oy Saunatec, Ltd.*, 241 F.3d 1, 9 (1st Cir. 2001).

62 See id., 10.

63 A smattering of case law has been found that addresses factually similar situations to Case 1 but in which the issue is not how many claims exist for prescription purposes but how many occurrences of malpractice have occurred for purposes of medical malpractice reform statutes that, for example, limit the recovery of a patient to a specified amount for each occurrence of malpractice or for purposes of determining how much a provider must reimburse a state compensation fund. In those cases, courts have ruled that there are multiple occurrences, thereby enabling victims or the state compensation fund to recover greater amounts from the provider committing multiple acts of malpractice. See *Dawson v United States*, 2013 WL 3187078 (W. Va. 2013); *Medical Assurance of Indiana v McCarty*, 808 N.E.2d 737 (Ind. Ct. App. 2004). Similar issues arise in determining how many occurrences took place for purposes of insurance coverage with occurrence-based triggers of recovery. Nevertheless, the author does not think that the outcome in these cases has much predictive power for how courts would rule for statute of limitations purposes. See *Beckley Mech., Inc. v Erie Ins. & Cas. Co.*, 374 Fed. App'x 381, 384 (4th Cir. 2010) (recognising a distinction 'between the continuing tort theory for purposes of a statute of limitations analysis and a "series of acts" under an insurance policy for purposes of coverage.').

begin to run from the date that harm X occurs. Having said this, there is a fair amount of parallel in Case 2 with the latent disease cases in which the same exposure creates a risk of different diseases, each of which has a different latency period. In that instance, as noted above, courts have carved out an exception to the accrual analysis just stated and treated the occurrence of each disease as a separate claim for purposes of the statute of limitations.[64] The author is, however, unaware of that exception, which courts adopting it often comment is a narrow one,[65] being applied in the medical malpractice context.[66]

**Case 3** – *Builder D lays down defective foundations for a building thereby creating the risk of future collapse. As a result, the value to the owner of the building (P) decreases (harm A). Two years later the foundation subsides and requires fixing paid by P (harm B). Three years later cracks appear in the building fixed by P (harm C). Four years later the building collapses (harm D).*

First, limitations on recovery of pure economic loss in tort would substantively 35
bar claims for the decrease in the value of the building (harm A).[67] At that point, there has been no physical impairment to the building. Purely economic losses resulting from D's negligence are ordinarily unrecoverable in tort absent property damage. The author notes that a few courts, nevertheless, have declined to adopt the economic loss rule for negligence in residential construction.[68]

For the subsequent harms, the economic loss doctrine may or may not apply. 36
The economic loss doctrine has been held to apply to negligent design and installation in construction,[69] the situation invoked in Case 3. 'The economic loss doctrine limits the recovery of damages in tort for product defects when the defect has caused neither a personal injury nor any damage to property other than the manufacturer's work itself.'[70] Thus, the economic loss rule does not apply when a defect in a house causes damage to other property.[71] Whether a defect in a house has caused damage to other property is controversial.[72]

---

64 See *supra* text accompanying fn 65–69.

65 See *Pooshs v Philip Morris USA, Inc.*, 250 P.3d 181 (Cal. 2011) (expressly limiting its holding adopting this exception to latent disease cases).

66 One court has applied outside the latent disease context to a heater that allegedly caused multiple fires. See *infra* text accompanying fn 68–69.

67 See *FMR Corp. v Boston Edison Co.*, 613 N.E.2d 902 (Mass. 1993).

68 See *David v Hett*, 270 P.3d 1102 (Kan. 2011); *Kennedy v Columbia Lumber & Mfg. Co., Inc.*, 384 S.E.2d 730 (S.C. 1989).

69 See *Berish v Bornstein*, 770 N.E.2d 961 (Mass. 2002).

70 See *SR Barrett, Jr.*, Recovery of Economic Loss in Tort for Construction Defects: A Critical Analysis, 40 S.C. L. Rev. 891, 892 (1989).

71 See Restatement (Third) of Torts: Products Liability §21 (Am. Law Inst. 1998).

72 See Restatement (Third) of Torts: Liability for Economic Harm §2 (Am. Law Inst., Tent. Draft No. 1, 4 April 2012).

Some courts have held claims are not barred by the economic loss doctrine when the negligence in construction causes harm to other parts of the building.[73] However, other courts have held that negligence in construction that causes damage to other parts of a building does not come within the damage-to-other-property principle.[74]

37 Many states have statutes that specifically establish the limitations period for construction defects.[75] There is no uniform view among courts of when a claim accrues for a construction defect. Observe that none of the harms caused by B–D appear to have been latent and thus we omit discussion of discovery rules for construction defects, which some jurisdictions employ.[76] For harm B, plaintiff may pursue a breach of contract or perhaps a negligence action.[77] A cause of action for damage to property accrues when the damage occurs.[78] A cause of action for negligent injury to real property due to construction mis-design accrues when the harm to the property is sufficiently significant to put the plaintiff on notice that a defect exists.[79]

38 Thus, under these theories, the causes of action in tort for harms B, C, and D would accrue when the foundation subsides and harm B occurs. Under a breach of contract theory, the cause of action accrues at the moment the contract was breached, so the cause of action would have accrued when the defective foundation was laid.[80]

---

73 See *Harris v Suniga*, 149 P.3d 224 (Or. Ct. App. 2006) (negligent construction of apartment building that caused dry rot to wooden beams), *aff'd*, 180 P.3d 12 (Or. 2008).

74 See *Ass'n of Apartment Owners of Newtown Meadows ex rel. its Bd. of Directors v Venture 15, Inc.*, 167 P.3d 225 (Haw. 2007) (citing and discussing other cases that reached the same conclusion); *Redarowicz v Ohlendorf*, 441 N.E.2d 324 (Ill. 1982).

75 See, eg Colo. Rev. Stat. §13-80-104 (West 2016); Cal. C.C.P. §337.1 (West 2016).

76 Some courts apply the discovery rule to claims against a builder for foundation deterioration. See *S Larsen*, Modern Status of the Application of 'Discovery Rule' to Postpone Running of Limitations Against Actions Relating to Breach of Building and Construction Contracts, Annot., 33 A.L.R.5th 1 (originally published in 1995); *Anderson v Brouwer*, 160 Cal. Rptr. 65 (1979). Thus, under this approach the limitations period begins to run when the defect would be discoverable by reasonable inspection. See *Lantzy v Centex Homes*, 73 P.3d 517, 522 (Cal. 2003); *Scully v First Magnolia Homes*, 614 S.E.2d 43 (Ga. 2005). Or in some other iterations of the discovery rule, when the defect, the negligence of the contractor, and the causal connection between the two were discovered or should have been discovered.

77 See generally, *MM Schneier*, Post-Construction Contract Claims: Statutes of Limitations and the 'Discovery Rule', 29 No. 9 Const. Lit. Rep. 1 (Sept. 2008).

78 See 54 C.J.S. Limitations of Actions §234; *Alabama Power Co. v Cummings*, 466 So. 2d 99 (Ala. 1985).

79 See *Tallmadge v Skyline Const., Inc.*, 272 N.W.2d 404 (Wisc. Ct. App. 1978).

80 See *Anderson v Brouwer*, 160 Cal. Rptr. 65 (Cal. Ct. App. 1979); *S Larsen*, Modern Status of the Application of 'Discovery Rule' to Postpone Running of Limitations Against Actions Relating to Breach of Building and Construction Contracts, Annotation, 33 A.L.R.5th 1 (originally published in 1995); *MM Schneier*, Post-Construction Contract Claims: Statutes of Limitations and the 'Discovery Rule', 29 No. 9 Const. Lit. Rep. 1 (Sept. 2008); *CLL Assocs. L.P. v Arrowhead Pac. Corp.*, 497 N.W.2d 115 Wis. (1993).

## C. THE STARTING POINT – BREACH OF DUTY OR OCCURRENCE OF DAMAGE?

**Case 4** – *D enters P's premises without P's permission, thereby committing a tort of trespass, but without causing damage. P can file a claim against D asking for the remedy of D's eviction but fails to do so. A year later D causes physical harm to P's premise. P files a claim to compensation for the loss.*

Because, as stated, trespass does not require a showing of harm, the claim for trespass would accrue upon D's entry on the land. P would be entitled to nominal damages, but eviction would likely require an action provided by property law rather than tort law. One assumes from the prompt that D remains on P's premises as a trespasser for a year. If that is the case, this situation would constitute a continuing tort – that of trespass, and P could file suit at any point and recover damages at least for the length of prescription prior to filing suit.[81] 39

## D. WHAT IS CONSIDERED 'HARM' FOR PRESCRIPTION PURPOSES?

**Case 5** – *In an accidental event, D negligently caused an explosion that damaged P's ears. During the first two years, P has to raise the volume to enjoy music. During the following three years P needs a hearing device. After a further five years, P becomes deaf.*

Many progressive diseases are the basis for tort claims in the US and virtually all are handled by the discovery rule, which is addressed below.[82] 40

A limitation on plaintiff's bringing suit for progressive injury is the 'single injury rule' employed by multiple states. The 'single injury rule' states that all damages for past, present, and future injury stemming from the same negligent action must be resolved in one suit.[83] As seen in Case 5, sometimes harm can cause both acute and chronic injury, with the later onset of injuries occurring after the statute of limitations has expired. In these cases, some jurisdictions adhere to the 'single injury rule,' allowing the statute to start running when the plaintiff first knows or reasonably should have known about the initial injury, the hearing loss.[84] 41

---

81 See, eg *Woldson v Woodhead*, 149 P.3d 361 (Wash. 2006); *Breiggar Properties, L.C. v H.E. Davis & Sons, Inc.*, 52 P.3d 1133 (Utah 2002); see also *infra* text accompanying fn 99–137.

82 See *infra* text accompanying fn 173–198.

83 *MA Searcy*, A Guide to Toxic Torts, §9.01(1) (2017).

84 Id. at §9.01(5)(a).

42 In reaction to the unfairness the 'single injury rule' created for plaintiffs with progressive or latent diseases, many jurisdictions have developed a 'separate injury rule.'[85] However, this exception is only applicable when the continued injuries or diseases are 'separate and distinct' from each other.[86] Under the fact pattern of Case 5, the injuries P sustained seem all to be related, and therefore P would have difficulty invoking the 'separate injury rule.'

43 Of course, the initial injury must be one that is legally cognisable. Some courts have ruled that pleural plaque, an abnormal condition of the lungs that develops from asbestos exposure but which has no clinical symptomology, does not constitute legally cognisable injury.[87] Damage to the ears combined with some hearing loss is not comparable to pleural plaque, however. If the ears were visibly damaged that would constitute a cognisable harm, as would hearing loss.

**Case 6** – *Builder D lays down defective foundations for a bridge, thereby creating the risk of future collapse if heavy rain falls. Two years later heavy rain indeed falls and the collapse becomes only a matter of time, as indeed happens four years after the laying of foundations.*

44 There are two different statute of limitations that could apply to Case 6. If there were a written contract between the parties, then the state statute concerning contracts will apply.[88] On the other hand, a tort action can also be filed if the defective work results from negligence. Certain states also have separate statutes of limitations for injury to real property and injury related to unwritten contracts.[89] This report limits discussion of Case 6 to the applicable tort claim.

45 In cases where negligent construction causes a building defect that eventually leads to physical damage of property, there are multiple interpretations about what is considered 'harm' for the purposes of prescription. Some states begin the statute running upon the 'project's substantial completion,'[90] while others require the plaintiff to have actual or constructive knowledge of the defect.[91] In either case, the defective construction constitutes the harm, rather than

---

85 Id. at §9.01(5)(c).

86 Id.

87 See *Giffear v Johns-Manville Corp.*, 632 A.2d 880 (Pa. Super Ct. 1993), *aff'd sub nom. Simmons v Pacor, Inc.*, 674 A.2d 232 (Pa. 1996); *Ford Motor Co. v Miller*, 260 S.W.3d 515 (Tex. App. 2008). But see *Ackison v Anchor Packing Co.*, 897 N.E.2d 1118 (Ohio 2008).

88 *EL Kellett*, Annotation, What Statute of Limitations Governs Action by Contractee for Defective or Improper Performance of Work by Private Building Contractor, 1 A.L.R.3d 914 (2018).

89 Id.

90 See *Brisbane Lodging, L.P. v Webcor Bldg., Inc.* 157 Cal. Rptr. 3d 467, 469 (Cal. Ct. App. 2013); see also *Palisades at Fort Lee Condo. Ass'n, Inc. v 100 Old Palisade, LLC*, 169 A.3d 473 (N.J. 2017).

91 See *Romeo & Sons v P.C. Yezbak & Son*, 652 A.2d 830 (Pa. 1995).

the injury that occurs due to the defect. However, if the collapse causes personal injury to an individual, that person would have his or her own tort claim which begins running at the time the injury occurs.

## E. THE STARTING POINT (ACCRUAL) IN CONTINUOUS TORTS

There is a notion of continuous tort in the US, often referred to as the 'continuing tort doctrine' or 'continuing violation doctrine.'[92] A continuing tort is one that cannot be defined by a specific time and place of tortious conduct and injury, and requires continuous tortious conduct,[93] not merely continuous injury.[94] Typically, this occurs in the nuisance and trespass context when a defendant's continuous behaviour interferes with another's use of the land or a trespasser remains on another's property. Continual torts can also occur in defamation, invasion of privacy, and environmental torts, among others. It includes not only a continuous tortious act, but also a series of distinct yet related tortious acts that are together treated as one, as might occur with intentional infliction of emotional distress in the employment context.[95] A significant body of commentary critical of the continuous tort doctrine has developed.[96] 46

There are two versions of the continuous tort doctrine. Under one version, the so-called 'forward condensing model,' the cause of action accrues and the limitations period does not begin to run until the tortious conduct ceases.[97] Because the statute of limitations does not begin to run until the tortious conduct ends, one claim can cover the entirety of the harm that occurred.[98] Thus, under this version, the plaintiff has the option to file suit immediately for legally cognisable harm or may wait until the harm has ceased and then 47

---

92 See *E Peled*, Rethinking the Continuing Violation Doctrine: The Application of Statutes of Limitations to Continuing Tort Claims, 41 Ohio N.U. L. Rev. 343, 343 (2015). See also *EC Surette*, Accrual of Claims for Continuing Trespass or Continuing Nuisance for Purposes of Statutory Limitations, 14 A.L.R. 7th 8 (2015).

93 See *United Air Lines, Inc. v Evans*, 431 U.S. 553, 558, 560 (1977); *Christian v Atlantic Richfield Co.*, 358 P.3d 131, 140 (Mont. 2015).

94 See *Maslauskas v United States*, 583 F. Supp. 349, 351 (D. Mass. 1984).

95 See *JR MacAyeal*, The Discovery Rule and the Continuing Violation Doctrine as Exceptions to the Statute of Limitations for Civil Environmental Penalty Claims, 15 Va. Envtl. L.J. 589, 618 (1996); *K Graham*, The Continuing Violations Doctrine, 43 Gonz. L. Rev. 271, 280–81 (2008).

96 See *Peled, supra* fn 92, 346 and n 8.

97 See id., 353; *Rentas v Ruffin*, 816 F.3d 214 (2d Cir. 2016) (under New York law, cause of action for intentional infliction of emotional distress does not accrue until conduct ceases); *Effs v Sony Pictures Home Entm't, Inc.*, 197 So. 3d 1243 (Fla. Dist. Ct. App. 2016) (recognising that for a continuing tort, the cause of action accrues when the tortious conduct ceases).

98 See *Peled, supra* fn 92, 352; *Wilson v Giesen*, 956 F.2d 738, 743 (7th Cir. 1992).

seek to recover for all damages once the injury is complete.[99] In neither case will the statute of limitations be an impediment to recovery.

48 Under the second (termed the 'recurrent') version, sometimes referred to as the 'rule of separate accrual,' each combination of tortious conduct and harm constitutes a distinct cause of action and only harm that occurs within the limitations period is recoverable.[100] This second version permits a plaintiff who has not filed an action in timely fashion based on when harm first occurred, which ordinarily would prevent recovery for any harm related to the defendant's tortious conduct, to have separate claims and accruals during the entirety of the period of defendant's tortious acts. To recover for all harm caused, the victim may need to bring successive actions for damages if the harm continues for a longer period than the statute of limitations provides.[101] In each action, recovery is limited to the harm suffered within the limitations period prior to commencement of each action.[102] The rule of separate accrual has been applied to statutory antitrust claims as well as common law nuisance and trespass claims[103] and occupational injury claims.[104]

49 One should distinguish between continuous and permanent trespass or nuisance, although courts have had trouble in determining which of these doctrines is appropriate to any given factual scenario.[105] A permanent trespass or nuisance exists when the initial trespass or nuisance is treated as the source of all of the plaintiff's damages.[106] When that is the case, there is a single cause of action, and the plaintiff may recover all damages, including ones that will occur in the future, in a single suit. The Second Restatement of Torts identifies a permanent trespass or nuisance as one where 'it appears that the invasions will continue indefinitely,'[107] which provides justification for awarding damages for all future harm.[108]

---

99 See *MacAyeal*, *supra* fn 95, 618; *Miller v Cudahy Co.*, 858 F.2d 1449, 1454 (10th Cir. 1988).

100 See *MacAyeal*, *supra* fn 95, 618; *Zenith Radio Corp. v Hazeltine Research, Inc.*, 401 U.S. 321, 338 (1971).

101 Alternatively, the plaintiff may be able to recover for future harm if she can meet the requisite proof requirements for such.

102 See *Christian v Atlantic Richfield Co.*, 358 P.3d 131, 141 (Mont. 2015).

103 See *MacAyeal*, *supra* fn 95, 620; *Meyers v Kissner*, 594 N.E.2d 336, 340 (Ill. 1992).

104 See *MacAyeal*, *supra* fn 95, 620; *Santiago v Lykes Bros. S.S. Co.*, 986 F.2d 423, 428 (11th Cir. 1993) (seaman suffered hearing loss from continual exposure to loud noise).

105 See *Graham*, *supra* fn 95, 301–311.

106 See *Walker Drug Co. v La Sal Oil Co.*, 902 P.2d 1229, 1232 (Utah 1995); *Graham*, *supra* fn 95, 310; Restatement (Second) of Torts §899 cmt. d (Am. Law Inst. 1977).

107 Restatement (Second) of Torts §930 (Am. Law Inst. 1977).

108 One court distinguished continuing torts from permanent ones by stating that continuing torts are ones in which the situation has 'stabilized' or the damage is 'reasonably certain'. *Haugen Trust v Warner*, 665 P.2d 1132, 1135 (Mont. 1983) (observing that the situation had not 'stabilized' where a basement continued periodically to flood and the extent of damage to the basement from the flooding varied from occurrence to occurrence).

**Case 7** – *Every week, during a month, D1 publishes a defamatory article on P1, each time in another newspaper and on a different topic. Is this a continuous tort? During the same period, D2 publishes a defamatory article on P2, every second day, on the same topic and in the same newspaper.*

The defamatory article published by D1 in a different newspaper each week would likely not be considered a continuous tort.[109] This would be true of D2's conduct as well. The defamatory conduct of D1 and D2 is discrete rather than continuous. Moreover, although the harms to reputation of these discrete publications may overlap, each publication would cause some harm that the others did not. And, the harms suffered by both Ps are 'lumpy' rather than continuous because each publication may cause a different magnitude of harm, depending on its content and its readers. 50

Under the multiple publication rule, each communication of printed matter gives rise to a distinct and separate cause of action.[110] The multiple publication rule has been modified by characterising any printing of a book or multiple editions of the same newspaper as a single publication for defamation purposes.[111] However, this rule has no application to Case 7 as each publication was in a distinct issue of the newspapers involved. 51

Today, a majority of states now use the single publication rule.[112] The single publication rule provides at least that any one edition (in some versions, even multiple editions) of a newspaper or magazine, or any one printing of a book, represents a single publication no matter the number of copies involved. The Uniform Single Publication Act, recommended legislation for states to adopt, provides that there is only one cause of action for any tort based on any single publication, such as an edition of a newspaper.[113] Courts have also held that copies or reprints of libelous material do not constitute a single publication, and thus each copy or reprint of the alleged defamation would give rise to a new cause of action, each with the statute of limitations running from the time of reprinting.[114] However, whether treated as a single publication or multiple publications, this would not be a continuing tort. Regardless of which approach is applied, an article printed in different newspapers would 52

---

109 See *AG Nadel*, Annotation, What Constitutes 'Single Publication' Within Meaning of Single Publication Rule Affecting Action for Libel and Slander, Violation of Privacy, or Similar Torts, 41 A.L.R.4th 541 (originally published in 1985); see also Restatement (Second) of Torts §577A (Am. Law Inst. 1977).

110 See id.

111 See *Lee and Lindahl*, *supra* fn 5, §36:35.

112 See *Lee and Lindahl*, *supra* fn 5, §36:35; see also *Ogden v Association of United States Army*, 177 F. Supp. 498 (D.D.C. 1959); *Wright v Bachmurski*, 29 P.3d 979 (Kan. Ct. App. 2001).

113 See Uniform Single Publication Act §1, 14 U.L.A. 377 (1990).

114 See, eg *Barres v Holt, Rinehart & Winston, Inc.*, 330 A.2d 38, 52 (N.J. Law. Div. 1974), *aff'd*, 359 A.2d 501 (N.J. App. Div. 1976), *aff'd*, 378 A.2d 1148 (N.J. 1977).

give rise to a separate publication and therefore separate causes of action, each with its own statute of limitations. Courts have also held that copies or reprints of libellous material do not constitute a single publication, and thus each copy or reprint of the alleged defamation would give rise to a new cause of action, each with its own statute of limitations running from the time of reprinting.[115] However, whether treated as a single publication or multiple publications, this would not be a continuing tort.

53 It is important to note that the Internet has created interesting challenges for the application of the continuing tort doctrine, for example when the statute of limitations begins to run on defamation claims arising from multiple posts made on a social media website.[116] In *Laughland v Beckett*, the posts made were continuously updated and the author sought new audiences for his posts.[117] The court held that the statute of limitations did not begin to run until the last publication was made. Thus, while the newspaper examples would likely not be considered continuous torts, defamation actions relating to social media pages have been considered continuous torts in at least one jurisdiction.[118]

**Case 8** – *D, a landowner, negligently exposes P, a neighbour, to unreasonable noise for three years. P's hearing is thereby weakened on a daily basis, gradually restricting P's ability to communicate and enjoy music.*

54 The continuing tort doctrine has been most commonly applied to nuisance actions by landowners against their neighbours. As explained above, there are two approaches to the continuous tort doctrine.[119] Under the 'forward condensing model,' the tolling would not begin until the unreasonable noise ceases. Therefore, P would be able to bring her suit immediately, assuming that the harm to her hearing is legally cognisable. P could also wait to bring her suit until the noise stops in order to recover for all of the damages once the injury is complete. Unless P waits too long after the noise ceases, the statute of limitations will not bar recovery.

55 Under the 'rule of separate accrual,' every time the unreasonable noise causes harm to P's ears, P has a separate cause of action. Any claim P brings can include any harm that occurred within the statute of limitations period.

---

115 See *Nadel*, *supra* fn 109; *Jackson v Ideal Pub. Corp.*, 274 F. Supp. 318 (E.D. Pa. 1967) (separate cause of action each time photograph was reprinted in publication); *Dodd v Harper & Bros.*, 3 A.D.2d 548 (N.Y. App. Div. 1957), *appeal dismissed*, *Dodd v Harper & Bros.*, 151 N.E.2d 622 (N.Y. 1958) (reprinting constituted a separate and distinct publication).

116 See *Laughland v Beckett*, 870 N.W.2d 866 (Wis. 2015).

117 See id.

118 See id. The author has been unable to find cases from other jurisdictions addressing this matter.

119 See *supra* text accompanying fn 104–115.

However, if P waits too long to bring the claim, some of the original damage may be barred.

**Case 9** – *A waste management company digs bins of toxic content into the soil. Toxic substance leaks into the soil and ground water, causing an apparent damage to crops and expenditure on cleaning on a daily basis. After two years the bins are removed from the soil.*

In this case, harm appears continuous in that cleaning is required on a daily basis, which implies additional harm occurs each day. Indeed, even the harm to crops may be continuous if the toxic waste spreads over time to consume additional crops. Under the 'recurrent' version of prescription, P could recover harm incurred prior to filing suit back for the time of the prescription period. Under the 'forward condensing' version, P would be able to recover for all harm if she filed suit within the prescription period after the bins were removed and harm was no longer occurring. It would make no difference for prescription purposes that the harm in this case involves property damage and pure economic loss,[120] although there may be other impediments to recovery for the economic loss. Limitations periods are based on the type of tort[121] not the type of harm.[122] 56

## F. IS THE LATE DISCOVERY RULE A RULE OF THE STARTING POINT (ACCRUAL) OR A RULE OF PROLONGATION?

This is not a question for which the author has found US courts or commentators to have given much (any?) thought. The author finds the analysis in the Analytical and Comparative report persuasive, although one might contend that the time when suit might first be brought could be a different one from when the claim accrues for prescription purposes.[123] Canvassing cases reveals that most courts describe the discovery rule as delaying 'accrual.'[124] 57

---

120 Pure, despite the property damage, because the economic loss was not a consequence of the property damage.

121 Or sometimes a single period for all torts is prescribed. See *supra* text accompanying fn 104–115.

122 See text accompanying *supra* fn 51–53.

123 That is the case, for example, when the statute of limitations begins to run at the time of the tortious act by the defendant.

124 See, eg *Fox v Ethicon Endo-Surgery, Inc.*, 110 P.3d 914, 922 (Cal. 2005) ('[i]n order to employ the discovery rule to delay accrual of a cause of action'); *Trinity River Auth. v URS Consultants, Inc.-Texas*, 889 S.W.2d 259, 262 (Tex. 1994) ('The discovery rule, under which the cause of action is deemed not to accrue until the injury becomes discoverable, is merely an exception to this general rule.'). But see *In re Processed Egg Prod. Antitrust Litig.*, 931 F. Supp. 2d 654, 656 (E.D. Pa. 2013) ('the discovery rules of 16 states should toll their claims arising under the laws of those jurisdictions').

However, in none of these cases was the implication between delayed accrual and tolling addressed by the court nor did it make any difference in the resolution of the case. Indeed, one court described discovery as delaying accrual and tolling in the same paragraph without any appreciation for the difference between the two.[125] One court explicitly distinguished equitable tolling from the discovery rule:

> Equitable tolling serves to pause the running of a statute of limitations where a party '"has pursued his rights diligently but some extraordinary circumstance" prevents him from meeting a deadline.' 'It differs from the [discovery rule] in that the plaintiff is assumed to know that he has been injured, so that the statute of limitations has begun to run; but he cannot obtain information necessary to decide whether the injury is due to wrongdoing and, if so, wrongdoing by the defendant.' While the discovery rule governs the time when the limitations period begins, 'equitable tolling instead halts the running of the clock' in cases where the clock has started.[126]

## VII. PRESCRIPTION PERIODS

### A. THE PRESCRIPTION PERIOD AND THE EFFECTIVE TIME OF PRESCRIPTION

58 The pattern in the US is as described in the draft report. When it is thought that claimants need more time, specific doctrinal rules that prolong the period in which suit must be brought are employed. For example, many state legislatures have enacted statutes that toll or suspend the running of the statute of limitations for children while under the disability of minority.[127] The effect of the statute may be that the time of the person's disability is not counted as part of the limitations period.[128] Thus, the statute may not run during the time that the person is underage.[129] There is a specific tolling provision for the military

---

125 '[M]ost of the tort claims enumerated in that statute have been considered to be subject to tolling until the plaintiff learns of (or with reasonable diligence should have discovered) his or her injury. The appellate court explained that the discovery rule has been characterized as applying to delay the accrual [...]'. *Shively v Bozanich*, 80 P.3d 676, 681–82 (Cal. 2003). Another court used 'tolling' and 'delayed accrual' as equivalents. *Hartz v Diocese of Greensburg*, 94 F. App'x 52, 55 (3d Cir. 2004) 'the principle of delayed accrual under the discovery rule to toll the statute of limitations').

126 *Morales-Melecio v United States*, 190 F. Supp. 3d 249, 258 (D.P.R. 2016) (citations omitted); see also *Cada v Baxter Healthcare Corp.*, 920 F.2d 446, 451 (7th Cir. 1990).

127 See, eg 735 Ill. Comp. Stat. Ann. 5/13-211 (West 2016); 9 R.I. Gen. Laws §9-1-19 (2016); S.D. Codified laws §15-2-22 (2016).

128 See, eg Ariz. Rev. Stat. Ann. §12-502 (2016); Tex. Civ. Prac. & Rem. Code Ann. §16.001 (West 2015).

129 See, eg Or. Rev. Stat. §12.160 (West 2016); Utah Code Ann. §78B-2-108 (West 2016).

under the federal Servicemembers Civil Relief Act.[130] It suspends the running of the statute of limitations for the period of military service and applies to actions in both federal and state court.[131]

## B. ONE, FEW OR MANY PRESCRIPTION PERIODS?

There are diverse prescription periods for different kinds of torts in the US. Limitations periods vary both by state and by tort. For example, prescription periods for certain intentional torts range in length from one year[132] to four years[133] depending on the state. The statute of limitations for breach of warranty under the Uniform Commercial Code, which addresses warranty recovery for product defects, is four years, but the claim accrues on tender of delivery rather than when harm occurs.[134] 59

There are often different periods for different types of tort claims. However, if a state has not defined a limitations period for a specific tort, then a general civil-limitations statute will apply.[135] The statute of limitations period for negligence actions for personal injury or property damage generally ranges from two to three years across US jurisdictions.[136] There is usually a shorter time period for intentional torts.[137] Perhaps this is because most intentional torts are 'snapshot torts' in which all relevant events occur in a short period of time, and the victim is acutely aware of those events. Specific statutes of limitation also exist for fraud,[138] trespass,[139] and libel and slander.[140] Libel and slander periods vary in length from one[141] to three years.[142] 60

130 See 50 U.S.C.A. §3936.

131 See id.

132 See, eg Ark. Code Ann. §16-56-104 (West 2016) (one year for assault, battery, false imprisonment, and slander); Colo. Rev. Stat. Ann. § (West 2016) (one year for all intentional torts and for defamation).

133 See Fla. Stat. Ann. §95.11(3)(o) (West 2016) (four years for all intentional torts).

134 See U.C.C. §2-725 (the claim accrues at the time of 'tender of delivery', unless the warranty is for future performance).

135 See *50 State Survey, Civil Statutes of Limitation*, Westlaw (2016).

136 See *Dobbs, Hayden and Bublick, supra* fn 31, §241.

137 See *SM Speiser, CF Krause and AW Gans*, The American Law of Torts §5:34, at 455 (Thomson Reuters 2013).

138 See Neb. Rev. Stat. Ann. §25-207 (West) (four years); Idaho Code Ann. §5-218 (West) (three years).

139 See Colo. Rev. Stat. Ann. §13-80-102 (West) (two years); Mo. Ann. Stat. §516.120 (West) (five years).

140 See S.D. Codified Laws §15-2-15 (actions for libel and slander must be commenced within two years).

141 See 735 Ill. Comp Stat. Ann. 5/13-201.

142 See Vt. Stat. Ann. tit. 12, §512 (West).

Additionally, many states have specific statutes of limitations periods for different types of professional malpractice.[143] Courts generally look to the actual nature of the tort, rather than the label employed by the pleader in determining which statute of limitations applies.[144]

## C. ACTUAL PRESCRIPTION PERIODS IN TORT CLAIMS

61 Prescription periods, their ranges and typical periods are addressed in Section B above. Prescription period shopping could be an issue as there are different statute of limitations periods for different torts and contract claims. Joinder rules generally permit a plaintiff to assert all legal claims against the defendant so long as they arise from the same transaction or occurrence or series thereof.[145] Thus, a plaintiff could join a breach of warranty (contract), negligence, and strict liability (both tort) claim for harm caused by a product in the same action. However, period shopping with multiple claims joined in the same action is generally not a problem. Each claim is subject to the applicable statute of limitation for that claim.[146] Under this view, the plaintiff may choose his or her claims and recover when at least one claim is not barred by the statute of limitations and the plaintiff is successful on the merits of that claim.[147]

62 Another form of 'shopping' for favourable statutes of limitations occurs with forum shopping. Because statutes of limitations are procedural,[148] the forum jurisdiction ordinarily applies its own statute of limitations. Thus, a plaintiff whose claim has expired in his home court may attempt to bring suit in a state with a longer statute of limitations.[149] Many states have responded to this forum shopping by enacting 'borrowing statutes.'[150] Borrowing statutes provide that a cause of action arising in another jurisdiction, which would be barred by the prescription period in that jurisdiction, will be barred in domestic courts, notwithstanding the domestic forum's longer prescription period.[151]

---

143 See *50 State Survey, Civil Statutes of Limitation*, Westlaw (2016).

144 See *Speiser Krause and Gans, supra* fn 137, §5:34, 455.

145 Fed. Civ. Pro. 20.

146 See *Speiser Krause and Gans, supra* fn 137, §5:34.

147 See id.

148 51 Am. Jur. 2d, Limitations of Actions §11 (updated 2018).

149 See, eg *Ferens v John Deere Co.*, 494 U.S. 516 (1990).

150 See *Executone of Columbus, Inc. v Inter-Tel, Inc.*, 665 F. Supp. 2d 899 (S.D. Ohio 2009).

151 See *FM Dougherty*, Annotation, Validity, Construction, and Application, in Nonstatutory Personal Injury Actions, of State Statute Providing for Borrowing of Statute of Limitations of Another State, 41 A.L.R. 4th 1025 (originally published in 1985).

Period shopping also occurs in the context of nuisance and trespass, which have, in recent years, tended to overlap. This occurs when a plaintiff brings one claim because the other would have been time barred. For example, in *Martin v Reynolds*, the plaintiff brought a trespass action, which had a six-year statute of limitations.[152] The defendant contended that the conduct at issue constituted nuisance, which had a shorter statute of limitations, and thus would have been time barred.[153] In that case, the court agreed that the conduct at issue constituted a trespass, and thus plaintiff could proceed on that claim.[154] 63

## VIII. RULES OF POSTPONEMENT, SUSPENSION, RENEWAL AND EXTENSION

### A. UNAWARENESS – THE LATE DISCOVERY RULE

Courts have held the discovery rule applicable to professional malpractice, products liability, toxic tort, defamation, and construction claims.[155] The first invocation of a discovery rule was in medical malpractice cases in which the physician left a foreign object in the patient during surgery.[156] Courts, generally, have embraced the discovery rule across most tort claims[157] and when a court does not do so, it appears largely adventitious or the result of the difficulty of discovery for that claim rather than the result of a particularly long prescription period.[158] However, there are specific courts for specific types of claims that have declined to adopt a discovery rule.[159] 64

152 See *Martin v Reynolds Metal*, 342 P.2d 790 (Or. 1959).

153 See id.

154 See id.

155 See *Corman*, *supra* fn 18, §11.1.2, at 141–42.

156 See id., §11.1.2.1, at 136.

157 See id., §11.1.2.3, at 140.

158 See *Hood v McConemy*, 53 F.R.D. 435, 445 (D. Del. 1971) (stating that discovery rule is unavailable for legal malpractice claims and distinguishing medical malpractice where it is available as involving 'inherently unknowable' aspects of the latter). Similarly, courts are split on whether the discovery rule applies in wrongful death cases. See 25A C.J.S. Death §166 ('other authorities have declined to extend the statute of limitations by adopting the discovery rule in wrongful death cases'). Courts that deny discovery rule application in death cases rely on the conclusory and unpersuasive ground that there 'can never be an issue since the action accrues at the time of death.' Id.

159 See generally *Gates Rubber Co. v USM Corp.*, 508 F.2d 603, 610 (7th Cir. 1975) ('With the possible exception of New Jersey, Iowa and Arizona, we do not find any jurisdiction in which the discovery rule has been adopted for all tort claims, or even for all negligence claims.'). The *Gates* decision is now over four decades old; nevertheless, there remain some states that do not apply the discovery rule to all tort claims. See *Doe v Archdiocese of Cincinnati*, 849 N.E.2d 268, 284 (Ohio 2006) ('Today's holding makes inapplicable to alleged victims of clergy sexual abuse the discovery rule.'); *Specialized Loan Servicing, LLC v Jan.*, 119 So. 3d 582, 590 (La. 2013) ('the discovery rule does not apply in La. U.C.C. conversion cases').

In addition, at least one state, Virginia, does not employ a discovery rule for any claim.[160]

65 There is no pattern that this author is aware of in the US in which discovery rules are adopted more frequently for claims for which there is a short prescription period. Indeed, what pattern there is seems more closely connected to claims in which the claimant is unlikely to know of injury or its causal connection with the defendant's tortious conduct. Thus, toxic torts are one sort of claim for which courts have embraced the discovery rule.[161]

*1) Unawareness of what Elements of Liability?*

66 Some versions of the discovery rule only require knowledge of injury. For those, unawareness of other facts supporting the claim would be irrelevant to the invocation of the discovery rule. Some versions of the discovery rule do, in addition, require knowledge of both the injury and the causal connection to the source of that harm.[162] Thus, a lung cancer victim would have to have knowledge not only of his cancer but also that it was the result of asbestos exposure for a suit against an asbestos product manufacturer. Finally, the most demanding version of the discovery rule requires knowledge of both injury and cause as well as the facts that would support a claim of tortious conduct by the defendant.[163]

67 Why do courts and legislatures not require knowledge of all of the elements of a mature tort claim? The author is unsure as courts simply tend to articulate whichever version of the discovery rule is employed in that jurisdiction and proceed to apply it. Nevertheless, it might be speculated that two factors are at work. First, when discovery rules were first adopted, they were in medical malpractice cases in which a surgeon left a foreign object behind in the patient's body.[164] Once the patient discovered injury from that foreign object, all of the other requisites for a tort claim fell into place – the harm was a result of a foreign object and the existence of such strongly suggested negligence by the surgeon. Once that version was established, *stare decisis* may have entrenched it even though other tort areas did not have such a tight connection of discovery of these elements. Second, the author suspects reluctance by

---

160 See *Blankenship v Consolidation Coal Co.*, 850 F.3d 630, 635 (4th Cir. 2017).

161 See *DB Dobbs*, The Law of Torts §218, at 557 (West Group 2000) ('The discovery rule is especially appealing for victims of toxic torts, the effects of which may not appear for many years or even generations.').

162 See *Dobbs, Hayden and Bublick, supra* fn 31, §243; *Rathje v Mercy Hospital*, 745 N.W.2d 443 (Iowa 2008).

163 See *R Craig et al.*, Toxic and Environmental Torts 609 (West 2011); *Dobbs, Hayden and Bublick, supra* fn 31, §243; *Lagassey v State*, 846 A.2d 831 (Conn. 2004).

164 See *Corman, supra* fn 18, §11.1.2, at 136–137.

courts to embrace an 'all elements' discovery rule because of concern that such an extension of the time for suit would unfairly burden defendants.[165]

**Case 10** – *Chemical plant D negligently exposes bordering lands to toxic substances. As a result, P, a nearby resident landowner, contracts lung disease. P failed to sue in time because his former lawyer told him that the exposure was not tortious and only his new lawyer told him, after the running of time, that it was tortious.*

Dan Dobbs reports on how courts deal with P's knowledge of a valid legal claim against D:[166] 68

> [A]ccording to some authority, [the plaintiff must know] that the defendant may have been negligent or otherwise legally responsible, or that there was enough chance that defendant was legally responsible that a reasonably diligent person would further investigate the facts showing the defendant's responsibility.[167] Other authority, however, starts the statute running upon discovery of injury and causation without discovery of facts suggesting the defendant's fault.[168]

Dobbs adds 'Some cases emphasize that the discovery rule does not depend upon discovery of legal rights as distinct from discovery of facts; if the plaintiff discovers the facts, her ignorance of legal rules that give her a claim 69

---

165 In addition, the US Supreme Court rejected an all-elements version for tort suits against the government based on language in the statute authorising such suits. See *United States v Kubrick*, 444 U.S. 111 (1979).

166 *Dobbs, Hayden and Bublick, supra* fn 31, §243.

167 *McRae v Group Health Plan, Inc.*, 753 N.W.2d 711 (Minn. 2008); *Walk v Ring*, 44 P.2d 990 (Ariz. 2002); *Lagassey v State*, 846 A.2d 831 (Conn. 2004) (statute does not begin to run until the plaintiff discovers or should have discovered all the elements of a cause of action, including the defendant's breach of duty and causation); see also *Norgard v Brushwellman, Inc.*, 766 N.E.2d 977 (Ohio 2002) ('when the employee discovers, or by the exercise of reasonable diligence should have discovered, the workplace injury and the wrongful conduct of the employer'). Under the reasonable-diligence test, if the defendant or other apparently reliable sources assures the plaintiff that the defendant has not acted wrongfully, the plaintiff may well be reasonable in relying on those assurances and in not investigating further. See *Walk v Ring*, 44 P.2d 990 (Ariz. 2002); *Kitzig v Nordquist*, 97 Cal. Rptr. 2d 762, 771 (Cal. Ct. App. 2000).

168 See *Rotella v Wood*, 528 U.S. 549 (2000) (RICO claim; discovery of injury sufficient to start the clock; discovery of a pattern of racketeering activity required to establish a cause of action is not required); *United States v Kubrick*, 444 U.S. 111 (1979); see also *Poole v Coakley & Williams Constr.*, Inc., 31 A.3d 212 (Md. 2011) (statute of limitations accrued on the date that plaintiff fell on black ice, which gave him sufficient notice of the 'nature and cause of his injury'; he was thus under a duty 'to acquire the identities of all potential defendants before the running of the limitations period'); *Sherrill v Souder*, 325 S.W.3d 584 (Tenn. 2010) (statute of limitations in medical malpractice case began to run when the plaintiff gained knowledge that would be sufficient to place a reasonable person on notice that the injury was the result of the doctor's conduct, so that the wrongfulness of his conduct could have been discovered through reasonable diligence).

has no effect to postpone running of the statute.'[169] There is a subtle difference between knowing the facts of the defendant's actions and knowing that they amount to a breach of duty that will support a legal claim, and in some more extreme cases the difference may disappear.

70 With regard to Case 10, first, the author thinks that P did not have the requisite knowledge of a viable claim because of the incorrect advice of the first lawyer. Clients do not act unreasonably by relying on the advice of counsel. But only in those jurisdictions requiring knowledge of legal responsibility would this matter for purposes of application of the discovery rule.

71 Equitable tolling is applied when the plaintiff has been lulled into inaction or been prevented from asserting her rights.[170] However, courts are reluctant to apply the doctrine to error by a client's attorney because parties are bound by the acts of their lawyer.[171] In *Lee v Cook County, Ill.*, the court said that the ineptitude of an attorney does not support equitable tolling.[172] The client's remedy was a malpractice action against the lawyer.[173]

72 Courts do not require discovery of all consequences of the injury or the full extent of damages.[174] So long as P knows that she has suffered legally compensable harm, that is sufficient to satisfy that element of the discovery rule.

*2) Objective or Subjective Unawareness?*

73 Regardless of which version is applicable, the second issue identified above now arises: is discovery based subjectively on the knowledge of the plaintiff or objectively based on what a reasonable person would know, including the knowledge gained by reasonable investigation? The discovery rule in the US consists of a dual subjective-objective standard: whether the plaintiff has discovered, or should have discovered, by reasonable diligence, the requisite facts.[175] Thus, accrual occurs when the plaintiff subjectively knows the relevant facts or (objectively) when a reasonable person would know the facts. Where the plaintiff does not have sufficient information to know a matter

---

169 *Dobbs, Hayden and Bublick, supra* fn 31, §243.

170 See *Nicks v Department of Business and Professional, etc.*, 957 So. 2d 65 (Fla. Dist. Ct. App. 2007).

171 Courts may be more forgiving when the claimant or attorney has exercised due diligence in pursuing his or her rights. See *Granger v Aaron's, Inc.*, 636 F.3d 708 (5th Cir. 2011); *Lee v Cook County, Ill.*, 635 F.3d 969 (7th Cir. 2011).

172 See *Lee*, 635 F.3d. at 969.

173 See id.

174 See *Dobbs, Hayden and Bublick*, supra fn 31, §243; *Larson & Larson, P.A. v TSE Industries, Inc.*, 22 So. 3d 36 (Fla. 2009).

175 See *Dobbs, Hayden and Bublick*, id, §243; *Hanson v Singsen*, 898 A.2d 1244, 1249 (R.I. 2006); *BASF Corp. v Symington*, 512 N.W.2d 692, 695–696 (N. Dak. 1994).

but has a reasonable basis for suspicion, she must conduct an investigation into the facts.[176]

Inquiry notice is another way the discovery rule's tolling ends. Inquiry notice occurs when 'a plaintiff knows or should know of facts that would lead an ordinarily prudent person to investigate the matter further, or inquire into whether actionable conduct was involved.'[177] Essentially, once a plaintiff has access to facts that would inform him of the injury, the discovery rule's tolling ends, and the limitations period begins running.[178] This is a form of objective notice, as described in the above paragraph. 74

In instances in which the existence of any of these matters is reasonably in dispute, resolution is a matter of fact for the jury. 75

### 3) *How Heavy is the Burden to Acquire Knowledge?*

For inquiry notice to trigger the discovery rule, all that is required is 'sufficient information to put plaintiffs on notice to make further inquiry if they harbor doubts or questions'[179] To avoid inquiry notice ending discovery-rule tolling, it is the plaintiff's burden to show that she either (1) diligently investigated her symptoms or injury and was unable to discover the cause, or (2) if she did not diligently investigate, that the cause of the injury would still have been unknown even after a diligent investigation.[180] 76

**Case 11** – *Chemical plant D negligently exposes bordering lands to toxic substances. As a result, P, a nearby resident landowner, contracts a lung disease, but is unaware of the causal link between exposure and disease because his physician fails to detect it. P does not seek a second opinion. After the prescription period runs on the disease, P consults his new physician who tells him about the link. Did P's claim against D prescribe?*

Whether or not P's claim against D is barred by the statute of limitations depends on which version of the discovery rule P's jurisdiction adheres to. If tolling of the statute only requires knowledge of injury, then P's limitations clock began ticking as soon as he discovered the lung disease, and thus his claim has prescribed. If tolling of the statute requires knowledge of the D's harmful actions or of the causal link between D's actions and P's injury, then tolling 77

---

176 See *Dobbs, Hayden and Bublick*, id, §243; *Taygeta Corp. v Varian Assocs., Inc.*, 763 N.E.2d 1053 (Mass. 2002).

177 *LR Frumer et al.*, Products Liability, §26.04(e) (2017).

178 Id.

179 *Ziots v Stryker Corp.*, 655 Fed. Appx. 622, 625 (10th Cir. 2016) (quoting *Macris v Sculptured Software*, 24 P.3d 984, 990 (Utah 2001)).

180 See *Frumer et al.*, *supra* fn 177.

would only start once it was reasonable for P to have known about D. Absent further facts, P would have no basis on which to disbelieve his doctor and conduct any further investigation into the cause of his disease. Therefore, inquiry notice is not applicable to Case 11. Rather, the tolling of the prescription period would begin when P consulted the new physician, who informed P of the causal link.

## B. OTHER RULES OF PROLONGATION

### *1) D is to Blame for the Delay*

78 Generally, fraud, misrepresentation, or deception has been held to estop defendants from employing the statute of limitations as a defence.

79 Thus, when the defendant has misrepresented the duration, applicability, or operation of the statute of limitations, inducing the plaintiff to delay taking action until after the statute of limitations period expired, estoppel may apply.[181] Equitable-estoppel tolling prevents the defendant from employing the statute of limitations defence when that defendant took active steps to prevent the plaintiff from suing in a timely manner.[182] Some courts use the terms equitable estoppel and fraudulent concealment interchangeably.[183]

80 When not used interchangeably, fraudulent concealment and equitable estoppel are differentiated on the basis that while both involve the defendant doing something to induce the plaintiff to delay filing her claim, equitable estoppel may apply even when the defendant's conduct was unintentionally deceptive.[184] Fraudulent concealment 'occurs when the defendant suppresses or misrepresents facts that are the basis of the plaintiff's cause of action' with the intent to deceive the plaintiff.[185] Connecticut, for example, has a statute that provides that if a person fraudulently conceals the existence of a cause of action, then such cause of action accrues at the time when the person entitled to sue discovers the existence of the claim.[186] With regard to fraudulent concealment,

---

181 See *AE Korpela*, Annotation, Fraud, Misrepresentation, or Deception as Estopping Reliance on Statute of Limitations, 43 A.L.R.3d 429 §2[a] (originally published in 1972).

182 See *id*; see also *Webb v Gardner, Carton & Douglas LLP Long Term Disability Plan*, 899 F. Supp. 2d 788, 794 (N.D. Ill. 2012) (threats to retaliate do not constitute conduct sufficient to invoke equitable estoppel); *Tenamee v Schmukler*, 438 F. Supp. 2d 438 (S.D.N.Y. 2006).

183 See *Guerrero v Gates*, 442 F.3d 697, 706 (9th Cir. 2006); *Molina v OneWest Bank*, FSH, 903 F. Supp. 2d 1008 (D. Haw. 2012).

184 See *Cangemi v Advocate S. Suburban Hosp.*, 845 N.E.2d 792, 810 n.4 (Ill. App. Ct. 2006).

185 See *Corman, supra* fn 18, §9.7.1, at 55–56 and 61; *Jones v ConocoPhillips*, 130 Cal. Rptr. 3d 571 (Cal. Ct. App. 2011); *Hamilton v Smith*, 773 F.2d 461, 468 (7th Cir. 1985).

186 See Conn. Gen. Stat. §52-595 (West 2016).

the statute of limitation is tolled, or postponed, 'until the cause of action is, or should have been discovered by the plaintiff.'[187] Thus, after postponement, the statute of limitations starts to run from the time when the right of action is discovered by the plaintiff or when a person in the exercise of ordinary diligence should have discovered it.[188]

### *2) Admission by D of P's Right or Partial Performance of P's Right by D*

Admission by D of P's right does not toll the statute of limitations. Partial performance, however, has been recognised as a basis for tolling the statute of limitations.[189] For example, in *Jackson v Costa Lines, Inc.*, the court determined that defendants waived the statute of limitations defence encompassed in a federal statute[190] based on their partial performance of the contractual agreement with the plaintiff after he had rendered salvage services under the contract.[191] The court tolled the statute of limitations until it became reasonably apparent to the plaintiffs that defendant would not adhere to the terms of the agreement as plaintiff believed them to be.[192] 81

### *3) Special Relations between D and P*

Legal relations, alone, between D and P are not grounds for tolling the statute of limitations.[193] However, a claimant may be more justified in relying on a fiduciary for purposes of equitable tolling.[194] 82

### *4) P's Lack of Legal Capacity*

'There is no general doctrine of the law according persons under the disability of minority, or infancy, an exemption from the operation of the statute of 83

---

187 See *Corman, supra* fn 18, §9.7.1, at 56; *United Fid. Life Ins. Co. v Law Firm of Best, Sharp, Thomas & Glass*, 624 F.2d 145, 149 (10th Cir. 1980) (quoting *Farmers' State Bank v Keen*, 167 P. 207, 209 (Okla. 1917)).

188 See *Paine v Jefferson Nat. Life Ins. Co.*, 594 F.3d 989, 992 (8th Cir. 2010) (applying Arkansas law).

189 See *Jackson v Costa Lines, Inc.*, 490 F. Supp. 393 (S.D. Fla. 1980), *aff'd*, 667 F.2d 97 (11th Cir. 1981); *Miller v Super Seal Container Corp.*, 62 F. Supp. 578, 579 (D.D.C. 1945).

190 *See Jackson v Costa Lines, Inc*, id.

191 See id. at 396.

192 See id. at 397.

193 See *McBroom v Child*, 392 P.3d 835 (Utah 2016) (equitable discovery rule did not apply to toll ward's breach of fiduciary duty claim against guardian).

194 See *Weiss v Swanson*, 948 A. 2d 433, 451 (Del. Ch. 2008). Delaware, an important state for corporate matters because most public companies are incorporated there, appears to be the most devoted adherent to this principle.

limitations applicable to their causes of action.'[195] Many states have enacted statutes that toll or suspend the running of the statute of limitations while the claimant is under the disability of minority.[196] Under a tolling theory, the statute does not run during the time that the person is underage.[197] Another means for dealing with minority is for the statute to provide a specified amount of time to bring the action after the removal of the disability.[198] The limitations period then starts running after the child reaches majority.[199] Some state tolling statutes specifically provide that the statute runs against a minor who has a legal representative as it would if the minor were not under the disability.[200] However, most state minority-tolling statutes do not expressly address this issue.[201] Some courts have held that the appointment of a legal representative triggers the running of the limitations period[202] based on the logic that a representative has the capacity to protect the interests of a minor, including filing of lawsuits. Other courts that have addressed the issue have determined that the appointment of a legal guardian does not affect the tolling of the statute during minority.[203]

84 The basis for tolling prescription for those with mental disabilities is similar to that for minors. Numerous states have enacted statutes that provide for tolling based on mental disability.[204] As with minority, the effect of the statute may be either to toll the running of the statute during the disability[205] or to provide a certain (and different) amount of time to bring action after the removal of the disability.[206] The general rule is that the disability must exist at the

195 *MM McCarthy*, Effect of Appointment of Legal Representative for Minor on Running of State Statute of Limitations Against Minor, 1 A.L.R.6th 407 (originally published in 2005).

196 See, eg 735 Ill. Comp. Stat. Ann. 5/13-211 (West 2016); 9 R.I. Gen. Laws §9-1-19 (2016); S.D. Codified laws §15-2-22 (2016); see generally id. §1.

197 See eg Or. Rev. Stat. §12.160 (West 2016); Utah Code Ann. §78B-2-108 (West 2016).

198 See eg Ark. Code Ann. §16-56-116 (West 2016); Wis. Stat. Ann. §893.16 (West 2016).

199 See eg Minn. Stat. Ann. §541.15 (West 2016); Neb. Rev. Stat. §25-213 (West 2016).

200 See eg Va. Code Ann. §65.2-528 (West 2016); Colo. Rev. Stat. Ann. §13-81-103 (West 2016).

201 See *McCarthy*, *supra* fn 195.

202 See *Johnson ex rel. Johnson v Blackwood*, 919 So. 2d 1053 (Miss. Ct. App. 2005); *Anderson v Canipe*, 317 S.E.2d 44 (N.C. 1984). For extended discussion of the reasoning of courts that have determined that appointment of a guardian triggers the running of the limitations period, see *McCarthy*, *supra* fn 195.

203 See *Luchini ex rel. Luchini v Harsany*, 779 P.2d 1053 (Or. 1989); *Strahler v St. Luke's Hosp.*, 706 S.W.2d 7 (Mo. 1986).

204 See *MM McCarthy*, Effect of Appointment of Legal Representative for Person Under Mental Disability on Running of State Statute of Limitations Against Such Person, 111 A.L.R.5th 159 (originally published in 2003).

205 See eg D.C. Code Ann. §12-302 (West 2016); Haw. Rev. Stat. Ann. §657-13 (West 2016).

206 See eg Ind. Code Ann. §34-11-6-1 (West 2016); Mont. Code Ann. §72-14-302 (West 2015).

time the action accrued,[207] and any disability arising after the statute has started to run will not suspend its running.[208]

There is no consensus in the US on the effect of a guardian on the tolling of the statute.[209] Some courts hold that the appointment of a representative does not trigger the running of the statute of limitations[210] while other courts hold that the appointment of a representative does trigger the running of the statute.[211] 85

Physical disability does not toll the statute of limitations.[212] A small minority of jurisdictions hold otherwise.[213] 86

### 5) *Absence of Parties from the Jurisdiction*

Tolling the statute of limitations due to the absence of a party from the jurisdiction is a rule that developed historically because of limits on courts' ability to exercise personal jurisdiction over defendants who could not be served within the state. This tolling was also applied to corporations that had no presence or authorised agent within the state.[214] The advent of broader provisions for obtaining jurisdiction over foreign individuals and corporations ('long-arm statutes') has largely, but not entirely, removed the rationale for 87

---

207 See eg S.C. Code Ann. §15-3-40 (West 2016).

208 See *McCarthy, supra* fn 195. For example, Texas's tolling statute specifically states that a disability that arises after a limitations period starts does not suspend the running of the limitations period. See Tex. Civ. Prac. & Rem. Code Ann. §16.01 (West 2016). But see Vt. Stat. Ann. tit. 12, §551 (West 2016) (if person entitled to sue becomes unable to protect their interests due to mental condition after cause of action accrues but before statute has run, time of incapacity does count as part of limitations period).

209 See *McCarthy, supra* fn 195, §2[a].

210 See *Pardy v United States*, 548 F. Supp. 682 (S.D. Ill. 1982); *Emerson v S. Ry. Co.*, 404 So. 2d 576 (Ala. 1981).

211 See *Smith v Kelley*, 643 N.Y.S.2d 764 (N.Y. App. Div. 1996); *Zator v State Farm Mut. Auto. Ins. Co.*, 752 P.2d 1073 (Haw. 1988).

212 See 1 Defense Against a Prima Facie Case §1:14 (rev. ed, 2009); see, eg *Wiggins v Edwards*, 442 S.E.2d 169 (1994); *Phillips v Adams*, 436 S.E.2d 567 (Haw. 1993); *Whisnant v Coots*, 337 S.E.2d 766 (1985).

213 See Cal. Civ. Proc. Code §340.6 (West 2016) (statute of limitations for attorney malpractice claim is tolled while plaintiff is under a legal or physical disability that restricts the plaintiff's ability to commence legal action); *Dove v Fordham Univ.*, 56 F. Supp. 2d 330 (S.D.N.Y. 1999) ('The availability of a toll based on a mental disorder or physical disability is limited to exceptional circumstances'), *aff'd sub nom. Dove v O'Hare*, 210 F.3d 354 (2d Cir. 2000).

214 See, eg *Bratton's Estate v Trojan Boat Co.*, 172 N.W.2d 457 (Mich. Ct. App. 1969), *aff'd*, 189 N.W.2d 206 (Mich. 1971) (statute of limitations was tolled although the defendant was out-of-state and unable to be served personally because the plaintiff in good faith delivered the summons and complaint to the sheriff for immediate service). See also *CR McCorkle*, Annotation, Absence of Judgment Debtor from State as Suspending or Tolling Running of Period of Limitations as to Judgment, 27 A.L.R. 839, §3[b] (originally published in 1953).

these tolling provision.[215] Some courts hold that the long-arm statute of a state supersedes the tolling of the statute for foreign defendants.[216] Today, the absence of a defendant from the jurisdiction is still recognised as a justification for tolling the statute by most states.[217]

88 P's absence from the jurisdiction is irrelevant for prescription as jurisdiction is obtained over a plaintiff by virtue of implied consent from filing a claim in that jurisdiction.

*6) Former Legal and Other Proceedings between the Parties*

89 'Savings clauses' are quite common and designed to avoid forfeiture of a claim when the plaintiff has timely filed an action but it is dismissed on grounds other than the merits after the statute of limitations has run.[218] These savings statutes typically extend the statute of limitations for a period after the dismissal of the first action. Without such a savings clause, the prescription period would continue to run during the pendency of the suit, and if it expired during that time, a second suit would be prescribed.[219]

90 Generally, the conduct of settlement negotiations or discussions does not provide a basis for suspending the statute of limitations or for estopping the defendant from relying on it.[220] Courts frequently assert that there is no application of equitable estoppel precluding the defendant from asserting statute of limitations as a defence in the absence of a promise to settle, pay, or perform, or absent fraudulent concealment or misrepresentation.[221] Although a

---

215 *KJ Rampino*, Tolling of Statute of Limitations During Absence from State as Affected by Fact that Party Claiming Benefit of Limitations Remained Subject to Service During Absence or Nonresidence, 55 A.L.R.3d 1158[2a] (2017); cf See *Burger King Corp. v Rudzewicz*, 471 U.S. 462 (1985).

216 Id.; see *Meyer v Paschal*, 498 S.E.2d 635 (S.C. 1998) (tolling statute does not apply when court could have acquired personal jurisdiction through notice and publication or long-arm statute).

217 See *WW Heiser*, Can the Tolling of Statutes of Limitations Based on the Defendant's Absence From the State Ever Be Consistent With the Commerce Clause?, 76 Mo. L. Rev. 385, 385 (2010); see, eg Alaska Stat. §09.10.130 (West 2016); Idaho Code Ann. §5-229 (West 2016); Me. Rev. Stat. Ann. tit. 14, §866 (West 2016).

218 See *Speiser, Krause and Gans, supra* fn 137, §5:32; *Allen v Greyhound Lines, Inc.*, 656 F.2d 418 (9th Cir. 1981).

219 *Elmore v Henderson*, 227 F.3d 1009, 1012 (7th Cir. 2000) ('If the suit is dismissed without prejudice, meaning that it can be refiled, then the tolling effect of the filing of the suit is wiped out and the statute of limitations is deemed to have continued running from whenever the cause of action accrued, without interruption by that filing.').

220 See *AE Korpela*, Annotation, Settlement Negotiations as Estopping Reliance on Statute of Limitations, 39 A.L.R.3d 127 (originally published in 1971); *Howard University v Cassell*, 126 F.2d 6 (D.C. Cir. 1941); *Foresman v Eastern S.S. Corp*, 177 So. 2d 887 (Fla. Dist. Ct. App. 1965).

221 See *Korpela, supra* fn 220; *Caledonia Sand & Gravel Co. v Campbell*, 260 A.2d 221 (Vt. 1969).

great deal of Alternative Dispute Resolution (ADR) is conducted after suit is filed, for pre-suit ADR the result would be the same.

### 7) *Victim's Death*

When a victim dies in the US,[222] there are two claims that may be made: (1) a wrongful death action that is brought on behalf of dependants and close family members for their losses due to V's death; and (2) a survival action that permits recovery for the damages that the decedent could have recovered at the time of death. This includes medical treatment, lost past and future wages, and pain and suffering, all discounted by the living expenses that the decedent would not incur due to death. Logically, the survival action claim accrues at the time of initial harm to the victim, which of course may precede death. 91

In the case of survival actions, courts, as suggested above, start with the principle that the statute of limitations continues to run, and death does not suspend the statute's operation.[223] Some states have granted additional time for the commencement of actions by executors and administrators.[224] For example, under the Uniform Probate Code, when a decedent passes away before the statute of limitations bars the claim, the cause of action surviving the decedent cannot be barred sooner than four months after death.[225] 92

In the case of a wrongful death claim, the earliest it accrues is at the time of death of the victim. When a person dies before a cause of action in the decedent's favour has accrued, and there has not been an administrator or other representative appointed, courts are faced with determining whether the cause of action commences to run from the date of the accrual of the action or as of the date of the appointment of the administrator.[226] Some courts have followed the rule that the statute of limitations does not commence to run until the appointment of an administrator.[227] In some cases not decided 93

---

222 One assumes in the text that the death is a result of D's tortious conduct. If that is not the case, then only the survival action would be available after death.

223 See Am. Jur. Limitation of Actions §219; *Griffin v Hannan*, 93 P.2d 1078 (Okla. 1939).

224 See Am. Jur. 2d, Executors and Administrators §1128.

225 See Unif. Probate Code §3-109 (amended 2010), 3 U.L.A. 1 (2016).

226 See *FV Lapine*, Annotation, Statute of Limitations: Effect of Delay in Appointing Administrator or Other Representative on Cause of Action Accruing at or After Death of Person in Whose Favor it Would Have Accrued, 28 A.L.R.3d 1141 (originally published in 1969).

227 See id.; *Collins v Jamaica Hosp.*, 158 A.D.2d 649 (N.Y. App. Div. 1990) (wrongful death action was untimely because county public administrator was eligible to act as administrator at time of patient's death); *Matthews v Matthews*, 177 So. 2d 497 (Fla. Dist. Ct. App. 1965) (action against decedent's daughter for fraudulently inserting name as assignee of certificate, lack of personal representative capable of suing on behalf of decedent imposed impediment to the running of the statute of limitations).

under statutes setting out the time from which the action accrues, courts have recognised that the statute of limitations runs from the date of the accrual of the cause of action.[228] Therefore, in this scenario, the statute could continue to run or, alternatively, the claim could accrue upon the appointment of an administrator or executor.

*8) Tortfeasor's Bankruptcy*

94 During the period of legal proceedings that are of such a character that the law forbids one of the parties to exercise a legal remedy against another, such as bankruptcy, the running of the statute of limitations is postponed, or if it has started to run, then suspended.[229]

*9)* Force Majeure

95 Damage caused by a natural disaster has been recognised as a justification for tolling the statute of limitations.[230] Natural disasters have also been recognised as grounds for extending the period to file suit.[231]

96 There is a specific tolling provision for servicemen under the Servicemembers Civil Relief Act.[232] It suspends the running of the statute of limitations for the period of military service and applies to actions in both federal and state court.[233] The period of military service is included in the computation period for bringing the suit.[234]

97 Some states have enacted statues that state that if a person is in prison at the time the cause of action accrues, then he or she may bring the action after the disability is removed.[235] However, some states do not recognise a tolling provision on behalf of an imprisoned person.[236]

---

228 See *Lapine, supra* fn 226; *Haney v Old Equity Ins. Co.*, 295 N.E.2d 828 (Ind. Ct. App. 1973) (representative could not bring action on behalf of decedent to recover under health and accident policy long after period required under the policy had expired).

229 See *West Coast Fruit Co. v Hackney*, 136 So. 699 (Fla. 1931); *Gibbs v Lester*, 41 S.W.2d 28 (Tex. Comm'n App. 1931).

230 See *Assoc. Drs. Cuidado Salud Visual v Morales*, 124 D.P.R. 591 (1989) (period of time during and immediately after a hurricane was excluded from calculation of statute of limitations because of damage caused by the natural disaster).

231 See *State v All Prop. & Casualty Ins. Carriers Authorized & Licensed to do Bus. in the State of La.*, 937 So. 2d 313 (La. 2006) (statutes extending prescriptive period for filing insurance claims from Hurricanes Rita and Katrina were constitutional).

232 See 50 U.S.C.A. §3936.

233 See id.

234 See id.

235 See *Dobbs, Hayden and Bublick, supra* fn 31, at §246; Vt. Stat. Ann. tit. 12, §551 (West 2016).

236 See Md. Code Ann. Cts. & Jud. Proc. §5-201 (West 2016).

Courts have tolled the prescription period when there is a pending class action suit on the same subject matter.[237] For example, in *Stevens v Novartis Pharmaceuticals Corp.*, the court decided that the statute of limitations in the plaintiff's action against a drug manufacturer was tolled by the filing of a separate and earlier class action suit by other individuals, which included the plaintiff as a member of the class, against the manufacturer.[238] Such suspension is only necessary when the class is not certified or if the plaintiff chooses to opt out of the class and pursue her own individual action.[239] 98

Statutes of limitations are suspended between citizens of countries at war and begin to run again once peace is restored.[240] Even if there is no statutory provision, this suspension is judicially provided.[241] 99

There is little case law on whether closed courts prolong the statute of limitations, perhaps because courts are rarely closed for extended periods.[242] What precedent has been found does not extend the statute in this circumstance,[243] except for when war is responsible for the closing of the courts.[244] 100

## IX. CEILINGS ON THE EFFECTIVE TIME OF PRESCRIPTION

There are ceiling periods, known in the US as 'statutes of repose,' as opposed to 'statutes of limitations.' Under statutes of repose, the right is no longer available after the specified period of time has passed.[245] 'Final repose', 'cut-off,' or 'ceiling' statutes have the effect of establishing an absolute bar to the maintenance of any action for the tort specified by the legislation.[246] Statutes of repose have been 101

---

237 See *Dobbs, Hayden and Bublick*, *supra* fn 31, at §246; *Stevens v Novartis Pharm. Corp.*, 247 P.3d 244 (Mont. 2010).

238 See *Stevens*, 247 P.3d at 244.

239 Similarly, a court in one jurisdiction may toll the applicable statute of limitations based on the filing of a class action in another jurisdiction, which is known as 'cross-jurisdictional tolling.' See *Patterson v Novartis Pharms. Corp.*, 909 F. Supp. 2d 116, 122 (D.R.I. 2012); *Staub v Eastman Kodak Co.*, 726 A.2d 955 (N.J. Super. Ct. App. Div. 1999).

240 See *Lipmanowich v Crookston Lumber Co.*, 210 N.W. 47 (Minn. 1926); see generally Note, Does War Toll the Statute of Limitations?, 57 Colum. L. Rev. 1140 (1957).

241 See *MC Dillon*, An Overview of Tolls of Statutes of Limitations on Account of War: Are They Current and Relevant in The Post-September 11th Era? 13 N.Y.U. J. Legis. & Pub. Pol'y 315 (2010).

242 The outbreak of the coronavirus as this report was going to press may challenge the claim in the text about courts being rarely closed for any length of time.

243 See *Ramirez v McCravy*, 4 So. 3d 692 (Fla. Dist. Ct. App. 2009) (holding that a series of administrative orders closing the courts during hurricanes did not toll the running of the statute).

244 See *Hanger v Abbott*, 73 U.S. (6 Wall.) 532 (1867).

245 See *Corman*, *supra* fn 18, §1:1, at 4.

246 See *Speiser, Krause and Gans*, *supra* fn 137, §5:29.

passed in some states relating to claims for products liability,[247] against those making improvements to real estate,[248] for medical malpractice, and generally for negligence.[249] However, latent injury exceptions are generally built into products liability statutes of repose in recognition of the long latency period between exposure and development of disease.[250] Under this exception, the plaintiff's cause of action is not extinguished by a statute of repose when the injuries are latent and undiscoverable during the repose period.[251] Some states provide for this exemption by statute.[252] Some exemptions focus on a particular type of product.[253]

102 The critical feature of statutes of repose is that they begin to run at a time other than when the claim accrues. Thus, in the products liability area, the period would begin to run at the time the product was manufactured or first sold. In the case of medical malpractice, it would be at the time of the negligent act by the physician. Because these events occur before any claim has accrued, they can bar claims before the victim has been injured and thus prevent any claim from being asserted by the victim.

## X. STATUTE INTERPRETATION, JUDICIAL DISCRETION AND LACHES

103 It would be inappropriate for a judge to ignore a statutorily created statute of limitations. In 'grey areas' judges may exercise discretion, such as determining when a claim accrues, for example, although in most such instances resolution would be a matter for the jury rather than the judge.[254] The author does not

---

247 See *Chang v Baxter Healthcare Corp.*, 599 F.3d 728 (7th Cir. 2010) (statute of repose for products-liability suits cuts off liability after a fixed number of years regardless of whether plaintiff has been injured or discovered the claim).

248 See *Dziewiecki v Bakula*, 824 A.2d 241 (N.J. Super. Ct. App. Div. 2003), *aff'd*, 853 A.2d 234 (N.J. 2004) (New Jersey statute imposes ten-year statute of repose for improvements to real property).

249 See *Columbia/CSA-HS Greater Columbia Healthcare Sys., LP v S. Carolina Med. Malpractice Liab. Joint Underwriting Assn*, 769 S.E.2d 847 (S.C. 2015) (medical malpractice statute of repose created under South Carolina statute).

250 See *DM Holliday*, 13 American Law of Products Liability 3d §47:80; *Pulmosan Safety Equipment v Barnes*, 752 So. 2d 556 (Fla. 2000).

251 See *Holliday*, *supra* fn 250, §47.80.

252 See Colo. Rev. Stat. §13-80-107(1)(b) (West 2016) (claims from prolonged exposure to hazardous material are exempted from repose statute); Conn. Gen. Stat. §52-577c (West 2016) (exemption for claims from exposure to hazardous pollutants).

253 See Neb. Rev. Stat. Ann. §25-224 (West 2016) (exception to repose for cause of action accruing from exposure to asbestos); Or. Rev. Stat. Ann. §30.908 (West 2016) (action resulting from breast implants exempt from general repose statutes).

254 For example, when it is uncertain whether P had or should have had the requisite knowledge for purposes of the discovery rule.

think that there is a universal or even strong tilt in the way judges exercise their discretion. The author suspects that judges who are more 'rule-bound' are less likely to be swayed by their assessment of the merits of the case in exercising discretion. On the other hand, judges who are more sympathetic to flexible standards are more likely to be influenced by their assessment of the merits of the claim.

Open terms, such as 'reasonableness' or 'good faith,' are not used in prescription law, although they do play a role for purposes of laches. 'Good faith' has been used in the context of the equitable tolling doctrine, which protects the claim of a plaintiff who has several legal remedies and pursues one in good faith, thus tolling the statute of limitations for the other remedies.[255] 104

There is a doctrine of laches in the US. The doctrine of laches is an affirmative defence that denies relief to a plaintiff who has unreasonably delayed in asserting a claim.[256] Laches is limited to claims in equity[257] and does not apply to legal claims where statutes of limitations have been prescribed by legislation. Thus, laches is not applied to ordinary tort claims.[258] Unlike the 'rule' approach of prescription, laches entails a flexible standard that considers the relevant facts and circumstances. 105

For laches to be applicable, the plaintiff must cause unreasonable delay in bringing the claim. In determining whether the plaintiff's delay was unreasonable, courts consider the length of the delay, the reasons for the delay, the effect of the delay on the defendant, and overall fairness.[259] In determining whether the period of delay is unreasonable, some courts give no accord to the applicable statute of limitations while others look to it for guidance.[260] 106

When unreasonable or inexcusable delay is shown, the second element of laches must be proven: that the delay by plaintiff has prejudiced the defendant.[261] Prejudice results when the defendant's position is adversely affected in a way that would not have occurred if the plaintiff had promptly brought the action.[262] 107

---

255 See *Oakland v Bowman*, 840 N.W.2d 88 (N.D. 2013) (quoting *Grand Forks Homes, Inc. v State ex rel. State Bd. of Equalization*, 795 N.W.2d 335 (N.D. 2011)).

256 See Corman, *supra* fn 18, §3.3.2, at 181–182.

257 'Equitable claims' are predominantly ones that seek injunctive relief, although the full rules on the equity/law distinction are quite complicated.

258 The exception might be a nuisance claim in which the only relief sought is injunctive.

259 See id. §3.3.2., at 183–184; *Bevelheimer v United States*, 4 Cl. Ct. 558 (1984) (citing *Goodman v McDonnell-Douglas Corp.*, 606 F.2d 800 (8th Cir. 1979)).

260 *See Corman, supra* fn 18, §3.3.2, at 185; *Foster v United States*, 733 F.2d 88 (Fed. Cir. 1984) (omitting discussion of the underlying statute of limitations period when ruling on the applicable laches issue).

261 See id., §3.3.2.2, at 186; *Alberico v United States*, 7 Cl. Ct. 165, 168 (1984).

262 See *Corman, supra* fn 18, §3.3.2, at 187; *Alberico*, 7 Cl. Ct. at 168.

# XI. CHANGE OF PARTIES

## A. THE PLAINTIFF IS A TRANSFEREE OF THE VICTIM'S CLAIM

108 One scenario in which a claim would be transmitted by law would be the death of the victim. Generally, once a cause of action has accrued, the statute of limitations continues to run, and death does not suspend the statute's operation.[263] Some states have extended the time for the commencement of actions by executors and administrators after the death of the victim.[264] For example, under the Uniform Probate Code, no statute of limitations running on a cause of action of a decedent, which had not been barred at the date of death, shall apply to bar a cause of action surviving the decedent's death, sooner than four months after death.[265] As is evident from the above, the substitution of an executor or administrator does not commence a distinct action for which the statute begins to run anew.

109 Generally, the statute of limitations begins to run against heirs to enforce rights and causes of action belonging to their ancestors at the same time that the statute of limitations would begin to run against their ancestors.[266] As a theory, heirs and their ancestors are regarded as one person, with one cause of action that accrued during the lifetime of the ancestor.[267]

110 Where the claim is transferred to heirs who are minors, rather than an administrator or executor, their disability will suspend the running of the statute until the disability is resolved.[268]

## B. THE DEFENDANT IS A TRANSFEREE OF THE TORTFEASOR'S OBLIGATION

111 Ordinarily the death of the defendant does not affect the running of the statute of limitations. One important exception to this rule is when the death prevents

---

263 See Am. Jur. Limitation of Actions §219; *Griffin v Hannan*, 93 P.2d 1078 (Okla. 1939).

264 See Am. Jur. 2d, Executors and Administrators §1128; 50 Tex. Jur. 3d Limitation of Actions §114 ('In the case of the death of any person against whom or in whose favor there may be a cause of action, the running of the applicable statute of limitations is suspended for 12 months after death, unless an administrator or executor is sooner qualified, in which case, the statute of limitations begins to run at the time of the qualification.'). For an example, see *supra* fn 233 and accompanying text.

265 See Unif. Probate Code §3-109 (amended 2010), 3 U.L.A. 1 (2016).

266 See *Tarnavsky v McKenzie Cty. Grazing Ass'n*, 665 N.W.2d 18, 23 (N.D. 2003).

267 See *Scallon v Manhattan Ry. Co.*, 185 N.Y. 359, 367 (1906).

268 See *Switzer v Reynolds*, 606 P.2d 244 (Utah 1980); *Neal v Butler Aviation Int'l, Inc.*, 422 F. Supp. 850 (E.D.N.Y. 1976); *CT Drechsler*, Annotation, Change in Party After Statute of Limitations Has Run, 8 A.L.R.2d 6 (originally published in 1949).

the victim from being able to bring an action, ie until the estate has been probated and an administrator or executor is in place.[269]

An insurer's claim by subrogation derives from that of the insured.[270] Thus, it is subject to the same statute of limitations as though the insured were suing.[271] The statute of limitations begins to run from the date of accrual of the subrogor's claim, rather than the date of the accrual of the insurer's subrogation claim.[272] An insurer's subsequent subrogation to the rights of the insured does not extend the period during which a suit can be brought.[273] 112

## C. CONTRIBUTION CLAIMS

The generally recognised rule is that a claim for contribution based on tort does not accrue, and the statute of limitations does not begin to run, until the time of accrual of the cause of action for contribution, which occurs when a party seeking contribution makes payment to plaintiff in excess of the party's share of liability.[274] Therefore, the court would generally hold that the payment by defendant to plaintiff starts the running of the statute of limitations. A minority of courts have decided that the statute of limitations begins to run from the time judgment is entered against defendant or when the claim is settled.[275] 113

## D. DEPENDANTS' CLAIM

For a discussion of wrongful death and loss of consortium, see the discussion above.[276] 114

---

269 See *JB Glen*, Application and Limits of Rule that Death of Person Liable does not Interrupt Running of Statute of Limitations, 174 A.L.R. 1423 (Originally published in 1948).

270 See *S Plitt et al.*, 17 Couch on Ins. §236:8; *Employers Mut. Liability Ins. Co. v Brown Wood Preserving Co.*, 182 S.W.2d 30 (Ky. 1944).

271 See *Plitt et al.*, id; *Great American Ins. Co. v U.S.*, 575 F.2d 1031 (2d Cir. 1978); *Underwriters at Lloyd's Under Policy No. LHO 10497 v Peerless Storage Co.*, 404 F. Supp. 492 (S.D. Ohio 1975).

272 See *Plitt et al.*, id; *Aetna Cas. & Sur. Co. v Windsor*, 353 A.2d 684 (D.C. 1976); *Southeastern Fidelity Ins. Co. v Porter*, 457 So. 2d 298 (La. Ct. App. 1984).

273 See *Plitt et al.*, id; *St. Paul Fire & Marine Ins. Co. v Glassig*, 887 P.2d 218 (Mont. 1994); *Indiana Lumberman's Mut. Ins. Co. v Curtis Mathes Mfg. Co.*, 456 So. 2d 750 (Miss. 1984).

274 See *MT Brunner*, Annotation, When Statute of Limitations Commences to Run Against Claim for Contribution or Indemnity Based on Tort, 57 A.L.R.3d 867 §3[a] (1974); *Hammond v Toy Indus. Ass'n, Inc.*, 8 F. Supp. 3d 484 (S.D.N.Y. 2014); *Reddy v PMA Ins. Co.*, 20 A.3d 1281 (Del. 2011).

275 See *Brunner*, id §3[b]; see, eg *Bonfield v Jordan*, 560 N.E.2d 412 (Ill. App. Ct. 1990); *Kala Investments, Inc. v Sklar*, 538 So. 2d 909 (Fla. Dist. Ct. App. 1989).

276 See *supra* fn 263–265 and accompanying text.

# XII. OTHER ASPECTS OF PRESCRIPTION LAW

## A. MEANING OF 'FILING A CLAIM' THAT INTERRUPTS THE RUNNING OF PRESCRIPTION

115 State law defines commencement for the purpose of tolling the state statute of limitations even for diversity actions in federal court.[277] In most states, the statute of limitations is tolled when a complaint is filed.[278] In a few states, the statute of limitations is not tolled until the defendant is served with process.[279]

## B. WHEN SHOULD THE DEFENCE BE RAISED AND DECIDED?

116 The defence must be raised in the responsive pleading to the complaint – the answer – where affirmative defences are pled. Failure to assert the statute of limitations in the answer would waive it, although there are provisions that permit amendment of pleadings when the opposing party would not be prejudiced, and the amended pleading would not interfere with efficient court processes.[280]

117 If the statute of limitations issue can be resolved based on the facts pled in the plaintiff's complaint and the law, it can be resolved early on a motion to dismiss the complaint. More often resolution is delayed until the defendant can establish facts that are required to resolve the statute of limitations issue, and this would typically occur after discovery on a motion for summary judgment. Where the facts relevant to the defence are in genuine dispute, resolution will be delayed until trial where a jury can resolve the disputed facts.

## C. WHO MAY RAISE THE DEFENCE?

118 'Ordinarily, the statute of limitations defense is personal and cannot be asserted for someone.'[281] If the parties are not in privity, the statute of limitations may not be used by someone who has no relation.[282] Therefore, a third party would not be able to raise an unrelated defendant's statute of limitations defence.

---

277 See *MN Parry*, Commencement Rules and Tolling Statutes of Limitations in Federal Court: Walker v. Armco Steel Corp., 66 Cornell L. Rev. 842, 842 (1981).

278 See *Dobbs, Hayden and Bublick, supra* fn 31, §241; Cal. Civ. Proc. Code §350 (West 2016).

279 See *Dobbs, Hayden and Bublick, supra* fn 31, §241; N. Dak. R. Civ. P. 3.

280 See Fed. R. Civ. Pro 15; *Speiser, Krause and Gans, supra* fn 137, §5:30.

281 See *Kobbeman v Oleson*, 574 N.W.2d 633, 640 (S.D. 1998).

282 See id. For a discussion of contribution, see *supra* fn 274–275 and accompanying text.

## D. BURDEN OF PROOF (OF ELEMENTS AND OF RULES OF PROLONGATION)

In the US, the general principle that one who makes a claim bears the burden of proof regarding all facts necessary to satisfy the prima facie elements of the pled claim. However, it is the defendant, asserting the statute of limitations as an affirmative defence, who has to establish that the prescription period passed since the accrual of the plaintiff's right to remedy.[283] When the statute of limitations would otherwise bar the action, the plaintiff bears the burden to assert and prove an exception to the statute of limitations.[284] 119

283 See *Corman*, *supra* fn 18 §16.2.1, at 360; *Patrick v City of Chicago*, 103 F. Supp. 3d 907 (N.D. Ill. 2015); *Bradford-White Corp. v Ernst & Whinney*, 872 F.2d 1153, 1161 (2d Cir. 1989).

284 See *Corman*, *supra* fn 18 §16.2.1, at 361–62; *Cannonball Fund, Ltd. v Dutchess Capital Mgmt., LLC*, 993 N.E.2d 350 (Mass. App. Ct. 2013) (once defendant has established that statute of limitations has run, plaintiff bears the burden of alleging facts which would permit his or her claim proceed despite the running of the statute).

## D. BURDEN OF PROOF OF ELEMENTS AND DEFENCES OF PROLONGED [illegible]

119 In the US, the general principle is that the one who makes a claim bears the burden of proof regarding the facts necessary to satisfy the prima facie elements of the pleaded claim. However, [illegible] the defendant asserting the statute of limitations or an affirmative defence [illegible] has to establish that the prescription period passed since the accrual of the plaintiff's right to remedy.[93] Where the statute of limitations would otherwise bar the action, the plaintiff bears the burden to assert and prove an exception to the statute of limitations.[94]

93 See [illegible]

94 [illegible]

# PRESCRIPTION IN TORT LAW: EUROPEAN UNION

Nina BARANOWSKA* and Piotr MACHNIKOWSKI



* The analysis of prescription of non-contractual claims against the EU was part of Nina Baranowska's research supported by the National Science Centre, Poland (2014/13/N/HS5/03519).

## I. INTRODUCTION

1 As concerns the issue of limitation periods on claims in tort, there are three dimensions in EU law. First, limitation of claims brought against the EU itself has been regulated. This is the primary subject matter of the present report. Second, in striving to harmonise national laws and ensure the functioning of the common market, the EU enacts directives requiring the implementation of specified regulations into domestic law. At times these directives concern tort law, and make reference in some scope to the issue of limitation periods. Third, the issue of expiry of claims appears in conjunction with the liability of a Member State for damage caused by a violation of EU law; such liability is subject to a mixed set of regulations, both national and European. The second and third issues are the focus of the last fragment of the report.

## II. DEFINITION OF PRESCRIPTION

2 Expiry of a claim for damages against the EU[1] is regulated in art 46 of the Statute of the Court of Justice of the European Union.[2]

> Article 46 Proceedings against the Union in matters arising from non-contractual liability shall be barred after a period of five years from the occurrence of the event giving rise thereto. The period of limitation shall be interrupted if proceedings are instituted before the Court of Justice or if prior to such proceedings an application is made by the aggrieved party to the relevant institution of the Union. In the latter event the proceedings must be instituted within the period of two months provided for in Article 263 of the Treaty on the Functioning of the European Union; the

1 Article 340(2) TFEU in reference to art 268 TFEU (Treaty on the Functioning of the European Union, OJ C 326, 26.10.2012, pp. 47–390).

2 Article 281 TFEU states that the Statute of the Court of Justice of the European Union shall be laid down in a separate Protocol.

provisions of the second paragraph of Article 265 of the Treaty on the Functioning of the European Union shall apply where appropriate. This Article shall also apply to proceedings against the European Central Bank regarding non-contractual liability.

The Statute constitutes an annex to the treaties in the form of Protocol no 3, and enjoys the status of primary law, setting out the procedure for proceedings before EU courts and the fundamental rules of their functioning. 3

The case law of the Court indicates that the time limit is a fundamental principle of law. 'The limitation period for bringing an action fulfils a generally recognized need, namely the need to prevent the legality of administrative decisions from being called in question indefinitely, and this means that there is a prohibition on reopening a question after the limitation period has expired'.[3] 4

## III. THE NATURE OF PRESCRIPTION AND ITS EFFECTS

The article under discussion here sets out the rules according to which damages claims against the EU shall be time-barred. A claim brought after the expiry of that time is inadmissible and leads to a formal plea of inadmissibility.[4] The provision thus sets out *the time which the injured party has the possibility of pursuing claims*, while at the same time not setting out the effects of the completion of that time period on the right to remedy itself. This may mean that its purpose is to provide a procedural defence that bars the ability of the aggrieved party to litigate the right before European courts. However, it cannot be conclusively resolved whether the aggrieved will continue to enjoy the substantive right following the expiry of action ability. The case law of the Court has yet to address the possibility of setting off an expired claim in damages or demand by the EU for the refund of a satisfied claim (if the EU were to pay damages in spite of having employed a time-limit defence), which would allow for a determination of the effect made by the expiry of the limitation period. EU case law regarding the limitation period generally covers the right to remedy in connection with a procedural element. The focus of analysis is 5

---

3 Case 3/59, *Government of the Federal Republic of Germany v High Authority of the European Coal and Steel Community* [1960] ECR 53, p. 61.

4 See art 130 Rules of Procedure of the General Court (OJ L 105, 23.4.2015, pp. 1–66) and art 151 Rules of Procedure of the Court of Justice (OJ L 265, 29.9.2012, pp. 1–42), and, eg joined cases 256, 257, 265 and 267/80 and 5/81, *Birra Wührer and others v Council and Commission of the European Communities* [1982] ECR 85, pp. 105–107. See *B Wagenbaur*, Court of Justice of the European Union: Commentary on Statute and Rules of Procedure, C.H. Beck-Hart-Nomos (2013), p. 138.

thus not a substantive right that may exist as actionable or not, but rather the potential to seek damages in court. The Court, however, has determined that the limitation period is a substantive one, although in this case the context of the case and criteria adopted in making the distinction. The issue of whether the five-year limitation period is a procedural or substantive matter arose out of doubts associated with the question of potentially extending that period by the ten-day grace period allowed for distance (art 51 Rules of Procedure of the Court of Justice and art 60 Rules of Procedure of the General Court; the extension came about in conjunction with art 57(6) and (7) Rules of Procedure of the Court of Justice, pursuant to which in determining whether the time limit has been observed, exclusively the date on which correspondence was lodged at the Registry of the Court is taken into account). Initially in the *Lefebvre* case it was held that the time limit could be extended by an additional grace period accounting for distance,[5] but this position was not accompanied by any justification. In turn, in the case of *Evropaïki Dynamiki* the Court held that because the five-year period is an issue of substantive, rather than procedural, law, the ten-day period allowing for considerations of distance is not included in it, a position which is presently the dominant point of view.[6] In the *Evropaiki* case the Court drew a distinction between procedural time limits and limitation periods, claiming that procedural time limits are supposed to ensure the proper functioning of the justice system, as well as clarity and certainty of legal situations.[7] Their objective is to ensure that administrative decisions and judicial rulings become final, by which they serve the public interest. As a result, they are not subject to the discretion of the parties or the Court, and EU courts should examine *ex officio* whether they have been observed.[8] Procedural time limits include the limit for bringing an annulment application (art 263(6) TFEU), or appeal (art 56 of the Statute). Distinct from procedural time limits, limitation periods are intended to regulate the performance of a subjective right, as upon their expiry the entitled party can no longer invoke that right before a court. The Court has included in these substantive regulations both the limitation period and the time limit for revision of a judgment in art 44 of the Statute (the latter of which, however,

---

5 Case T-571/93, *Lefebvre frères et soeurs and others v Commission of the European Communities* [1995] ECR II-2379, para 26.

6 Case C-469/11 P, *Evropaïki Dynamiki – Proigmena Systimata Tilepikoinonion Pliroforikis kai Tilematikis AE v European Commission* [2012] ECLI:EU:C:2012:705, paras 49–59; See *K Lenaerts, I Maselis and K Gutman*, EU Procedural Law, Oxford University Press (2015), p. 544.

7 Case C-469/11 P, *Evropaïki Dynamiki*, para 50. See also: case 227/83, *Sophie Moussis v Commission of the European Communities* [1984] ECR 3133, para 12; case 191/84, *Jean-Pierre Barcella and others v Commission of the European Communities* [1986] ECR 1541, para 12.

8 See also case C-246/95, *Myrianne Coen v Belgian State* [1997] ECR I-403, para 21 and the case law cited.

is examined *ex officio*).[9] However, it remains undetermined whether the expiry of the limitation period results in the loss of the right itself.

## IV. CONSIDERATIONS FOR AND AGAINST PRESCRIPTION OF TORT CLAIMS

The Court emphasises that the objective of the limitation period in art 46 of the Statute is, on the one hand, to ensure protection of the rights of the aggrieved party and to give that party sufficient time to file a claim, while on the other hand to prevent a situation in which the aggrieved party could endlessly delay pursuing the right to damages. Thus, the limitation period is intended to encourage the aggrieved to take action, and after its expiry, to stabilise the legal situation. In the Court's judgment, the limitation period gives protection to both the aggrieved party and the individual liable for the damage.[10] 6

The Court somewhat reluctantly makes the claim that the primary objective of the institution of the limitation period is the more general protection of the interests of the EU as the obliged party. In conjunction with the fact that claims for damages can involve a financial burden on the EU, the five-year period is directly associated with the necessity of solicitude about public finances.[11] The limitation period thus allows the EU to protect its finances from the demands of individuals who have not displayed the necessary diligence and failed to take advantage of their rights in the time provided.[12] 7

In the case law of the Court one may also encounter the opinion that the limitation period is intended to harmonise protection of the aggrieved party with the principle of certainty of law.[13] On the one hand, this may mean the 8

---

9 Cf *Lenaerts, Maselis and Gutman, supra* fn 6, p. 749. See art 44(1) of the Statute of the Court of Justice of the European Union: An application for revision of a judgment may be made to the Court of Justice only on discovery of a fact which is of such a nature as to be a decisive factor, and which, when the judgment was given, was unknown to the Court and to the party claiming the revision. (2) The revision shall be opened by a judgment of the Court expressly recording the existence of a new fact, recognising that it is of such a character as to lay the case open to revision and declaring the application admissible on this ground. No application for revision may be made after the lapse of ten years from the date of the judgment. According to Lenaerts, the aforementioned three-month time limit is a procedural one, while the ten-year limit is substantive.

10 See, eg case T-247/08, *C-Content BV v European Commission* [2010] ECR II-205, para 54; Also case T-140/04, *Ehcon BV v Commission of the European Communities* [2005] ECR II-3287, para 57; case C-469/11 P, *Evropaïki Dynamiki*, para 53.

11 See case T-45/01, *Sanders and others v Commission of the European Communities* [2004] ECR II-3315, para 59. The case concerned a labour dispute, but remarks concerning prescription from the Staff Regulations were useful in explaining the function of prescription in general.

12 Case T-45/01, *Sanders*, para 69.

13 Case T-140/04, *Ehcon*, para 57.

stabilisation of social relations based on long-standing factual circumstances, and thus generally understood protection of public order.[14] On the other hand, this may have something to do with a sort of legal security expressed in protecting the EU budget against expenses resulting from an event causing damage in the distant past, and therefore protecting the EU as a whole.[15]

9 Among the shortcomings in the regulation of claims in damages, insufficient protection of aggrieved parties in the event of personal injury, as well as in the event of violation of human rights must be mentioned. Violations of human rights are not encompassed by separate regulation and should be decided on the basis of art 340(2) TFEU, by which the limitation period set out in art 46 of the Statute will also apply. In the case of the limitation period under discussion here, it would seem that fears as to the deterioration of the evidence over time are unfounded. It should be observed that the liability in question concerns broadly understood public authority. A large number of cases heard by the Court are related to legislative activity, and in such cases the potential for deterioration of evidence is far less than in other types of cases.

10 The scope of protection of the aggrieved party's interests depends on the length of the limitation period, the manner in which its inception is determined, and the possibilities for its interruption and/or suspension. Taking into account the complicated, multi-aspectual nature of matters brought before the CJEU, doubts may arise as to whether regulations concerning these elements establish the appropriate scope of protection for aggrieved parties.

## V. ELEMENTS OF PRESCRIPTION – AN OVERVIEW

11 Article 46 of the Statute of the Court of Justice of the European Union allows for distinguishing two main elements of prescription: starting point and period. The provision in question also addresses the issue of prolongation but does it in a very limited way – by stating only which procedural actions lead to the interruption of the prescription period.

12 According to the said provision, prescription period starts at the occurrence of the event giving rise to liability.

13 The length of the period has been set to five years, with no regard to matters such as the aggrieved person's awareness of the claim and his or her diligence in finding facts that constitute the basis for the claim.

---

14 *A Knade-Plaskacz*, Zasada odpowiedzialności pozaumownej Unii Europejskiej, Towarzystwo Naukowe Organizacji i Kierownictwa 'Dom Organizatora' (2011), p. 189.

15 Case T-45/01 *Sanders*, para 64.

# VI. THE STARTING POINT OF THE PRESCRIPTION PERIOD

## A. GENERAL REMARKS

Pursuant to art 46 of the Statute, the limitation period runs from the moment of the event that led to liability being incurred (*from the occurrence of the event giving rise thereto*). The Court has held that the earliest moment from which the limitation period can run is from the concretisation of the damage, *id est* the materialisation of the effects of unlawful action taken by EU institutions. It is only then that the cause of action comes into being for prescription purposes. 14

## B. CONCRETISATION OF THE DAMAGE

In joined cases 46 and 47/59 *Meroni* the Court held that the limitation period cannot expire prior to the occurrence of damage.[16] In later cases the Court accepted that the existence of the right of the aggrieved party to pursuing a claim for remedy of damage depends on the fulfilment of certain conditions: unlawful measures adopted by the community institution, real damage, and a causal nexus between the activity of the institution and the damage.[17] 15

---

[16] Joined cases 46 and 47/59, *Meroni & Co., Erba – Meroni & Co., Milan v High Authority ECSC* [1962] ECR 783, pp. 419–421. Although the decision concerns a matter adjudicated on the grounds of the Treaty establishing the European Coal and Steel Community, it can also be applied to the EEC and then to the EU. However, as P. Olivier rightfully notes, the content of art 40 ECSC Statute, itself the counterpart to art 43 EEC Statute, does not have exactly the same wording in its German and Dutch language versions (p. 12). *P Oliver*, Limitation of actions before the European Court (1978) 3 ELRev., p. 12. See also: joined cases 9 and 25/64, *Acciaieria Ferriera di Roma (FERAM) and others v High Authority ESCS* [1965] ECR 401, pp. 320–321.

[17] Case 51/81, *De Franceschi SpA Monfalcone v Council and Commission of the European Communities* [1982] ECR 117, para 9; case C-104/97 P, *Atlanta AG and others v European Community* [1999] ECR I-6983, para 65; case C-146/91, *KYDEP v Council of the European Union and Commission of the European Communities* [1994] ECR I-4199, para 19; case T-106/98, *Fratelli Murri SpA v Commission of the European Communities* [1999] ECR II-2553, para 25; case C-257/90, *Italsolar SpA v Commission of the European Communities* [1993] ECR I-9, para 33; case T-199/96, *Laboratoires Pharmaceutiques Bergaderm and Jean-Jacques Goupil v Commission of the European Communities* [1998] ECR II-2805, para 48; case C-51/05 P, *Commission of the European Communities v Cantina sociale di Dolianova Soc. coop. arl and others* [2008] ECR I-05341, paras 52–54; case T-247/08, *C-Content BV*, para 53; case 4/69, *Alfons Lütticke GmbH v Commission of the European Communities* [1971] ECR 325, para 10; case T-478/93, *Wafer Zoo Srl v Commission of the European Communities* [1995] ECR II-1479, para 47; joined cases 197 to 200, 243, 245 and 247/80, *Ludwigshafener Walzmühle Erling KG and others v Council and Commission of the European Communities* [1981] ECR 3211, para 18; joined cases T-481/93 and T-484/93, *Vereniging van Exporteurs*

The limitation period can only begin to run when all conditions giving rise to the obligation to remedy the damage are met, in particular when the concretisation of the damage occurs.[18]

16 The literature indicates certain problems arising out of this understanding of the provision,[19] but they do not seem to be overly serious. First, mention is made of the excessive burden placed on the EU to foresee the effects of legislative solutions adopted. When considering, however, that the EU is liable not for all activities, but only for unlawful activities, it may be assumed that institutions are sufficiently aware of the consequences of their decisions. Second, difficulties may arise in determining when damage was in fact suffered. The fact of damage occurring is, however, one of the conditions of liability which the aggrieved party must always prove in order to pursue a claim against the EU. Third, the damage may arise much later, even years after the event causing it. Essentially, a situation in which a single incidence of injury occurred after a very long period of time had elapsed has not yet come before the Court. In the case of damage stretching over a period of time, the limitation covers the period of five years, counted backwards from the day the action is brought. However, it cannot be excluded that the damage arises a significant length of time after the event causing it. This is most likely in the case of personal injury caused by factual actions of the EU, which may make the absence of a long-stop justified.

17 In the case of damage brought about by legislative measures, the limitation period cannot begin running prior to the occurrence of the injurious effects of such measures, and thus until the damaging effects of that act have arisen and hence until the time at which the persons concerned were bound to have suffered certain damage.[20] The beginning of the limitation period will

---

*in Levende Varkens and others and Nederlandse Bond van Waaghouders van Levend Vee and others v Commission of the European Communities* [1995] ECR II-2941, para 80; case T-332/99, *Paul Jestädt v Council of the European Union and Commission of the European Communities* [2001] ECR II-2561, para 40; case T-20/94, *Johannes Hartmann v Council of the European Union and Commission of the European Communities* [1997] ECR II-595, para 107; case T-28/03, *Holcim (Deutschland) AG v Commission of the European Communities* [2005] ECR II-1357, paras 59, 86; case T-174/00, *Biret International SA v Council of the European Union* [2002] ECR II-17, paras 38, 45; case T-138/03, *É.R. and others v the Council of the European Union and the Commission of the European Communities* [2006] ECR II-4923, paras 49, 99; case C-136/01 P, *Autosalone Ispra dei Fratelli Rossi Snc v European Atomic Energy Community* [2002] ECR I-6565, para 29.

18 Joined cases 256, 257, 265 and 267/80 and 5/81, *Birra Wührer*, paras 9–11; Case T-140/04, *Ehcon*, para 39; case C-51/05, *Cantina sociale*, para 54; case C-136/01, *Autosalone*, para 30.

19 See *A Biondi and M Farley*, The right to damages in European Law, Kluwer Law International (2009), pp. 93–94.

20 See *inter alia* joined cases 256, 257, 265, 267/80 and 5/81, *Birra Wührer*, para 10; case C-282/05 P, *Holcim (Deutschland) AG v Commission of the European Communities* [2007] ECR I-2941,

not therefore be calculated as the day on which the unlawful legislation was adopted or promulgated, but from the moment its effects were felt by the aggrieved.[21] The mere publication of the act should be held as the event giving rise to damage. The beginning of the limitation period is also not dependent on ascertainment of the unlawfulness of measures taken by EU institutions in other proceedings.[22] Unlawfulness of measures is an issue examined in the course of reviewing the claim for damages.

As in the case of individual acts, the limitation period begins with the moment at which the injurious effects of the individual act are felt by the entity that act concerns.[23] 18

The beginning of the limitation period for personal injury was examined by the Court in the case of *É.R.* The matter concerned remedy for damage allegedly suffered by the applicants as a consequence of the infection and subsequent death of members of their families who developed a new variant of Creutzfeldt-Jakob disease (mad cow disease). The CFI determined that it was not appropriate to rely on the moment when the first clinical symptoms characteristic of the disease suffered by their relatives appeared as the beginning of the limitation period for their action. At the same time, it held that before the victims' deaths that damage cannot be regarded as having fully materialised. The Court therefore held that the limitation period is not to begin before the respective dates of the death of each of the victims or, if it is later, of the establishment of a definite diagnosis.[24] 19

## C. CONTINUOUS DAMAGE

Establishing the moment of materialisation of damage as the beginning of the limitation period is problematic when it comes to continuous damage. 20

para 29; case 51/81, *De Franceschi SpA Monfalcone*, para 10; case C-51/05, *Cantina sociale*, para 54; How to calculate limitation period to each of the applicants see: joined cases 256, 257, 265, 267/80 5 and 5/81, *Birra Wührer and others v Council and Commission of the European Communities* [1984] ECR 3693, paras 15–24.

21 Case 51/81, *De Franceschi SpA*, para 12; case C-51/05 P, *Cantina sociale*, paras 54–55; case C-282/05 P, *Holcim (Deutschland)*, para 29; case T-76/94, *Rendert Jansma v Council of the European Union and Commission of the European Communities* [2001] ECR II-243, para 76.

22 See case C-282/05, *Holcim*, paras 29–31.

23 Case C-282/05 *Holcim*, paras 29–30; case C-335/08 P, *Transports Schiocchet Excursions SARL v Commission of the European Communities* [2009] ECR I-104 (Pub somm), para 33; case T-367/08, *Michel Abouchar v Commission of the European Communities* [2009] ECR II-128 (Pub somm), para 23; case T-280/08, *Claude Perry v Commission of the European Communities* [2009] ECR II-36 (Pub somm), para 36.

24 Case T-138/03, *É.R.*, para 50.

The Court does not focus on the construction of continuous tort (continuous activity). It is irrelevant whether the source of the damage is a single event or a continuous one. What is important is whether the damage is of a continuous nature. Continuous damage should be understood as damage that does not arise in the course of a single event, but emerges and develops over time. Its dimensions grow proportionally to the passage of time in defined units: daily, monthly or annually. Because it is dynamic in nature, and not a one-off event, it is not possible to determine *a priori* the value of the general damage.[25] If the damage arose in an immediate fashion, even when its full extent can be understood only after the event giving rise to it has concluded, this is not continuous damage.[26] For example, in the *Inalca SpA* case the Court held that the damage comprised of costs of assistance and legal advice, as well as of personnel, incurred on the day domestic proceedings were initiated constituted a one-off event. Even if the extent of the damage could not be definitively determined at the moment of commencement of domestic proceedings, it is certain that the damage resulted from the fact of their commencement.[27]

21 In conjunction with the fact that art 46 of the Statute does not lay down a maximum period after expiry of which a claim for damages cannot be pursued, and also does not allow for the possibility of awarding an annuity as damages, the problem arises of the temporal scope of the EU liability for continuous damage. The Court has limited liability for such damage, holding that a limitation applies with its start as the day on which the action was submitted (the event interrupting the period of limitation), and it encompasses a period exceeding the five years before the submission of the claim, without prejudice to other rights which arose at a later time.[28] To put it differently, the five-year period establishes the maximum length of time during which the EU can be held liable for damage, even if that damage develops over time. If in the course of the five-year period preceding the submission of the claim the damage ceased expanding (and it began prior to that period), consideration should

25 See case T-20/94, *Hartmann*, paras 132–133; case T-76/94, *Jansma*, paras 78–79; case T-201/94, *Erwin Kustermann v Council of the European Union and Commission of the European Communities* [2002] ECR II-415, paras 63–64; case T-332/99, *Jestädt*, paras 44–45; case T-174/00, *Biret*, paras 41–42; case T-28/03, *Holcim*, paras 69–70.

26 Case T-140/04, *Ehcon*, para 67. In the opinion of the Court, continuous damage is not damage incurred as a result of one's good name being impugned, nor reduction in the amount of work, the absence of opportunity to expand expertise or develop expertise in a new area, as it was not renewed on a daily basis after the occurrence of the circumstances that caused it. The various types of damage were caused directly and immediately by the fact of rejection of an offer submitted by the complainant in the scope of the discussed public procurement, even if the full dimension of the damage could only be assessed after rejection of the discussed offer.

27 Case C-460/09 P, *Inalca SpA – Industria Alimentari Carni and Cremonini SpA v European Commission* [2013] ECLI:EU:C:2013:111, paras 79–81.

28 Case T-20/94, *Hartmann*, paras 132–133.

be given only to the scope of damage which arose in the five-year period preceding the interruption of the period of limitation.

Among examples of continuous damage in the case law one may cite: damage arising in conjunction with fees calculated proportionally to the number of days for which a bank guarantee was issued,[29] damage arising as a result of the prohibition on the importation into the community of beef and veal treated with certain hormones,[30] and damages arising by reason of being prevented from marketing milk pursuant to Council Regulation (EC) No 857/84.[31] 22

## D. FUTURE DAMAGE

The Court has allowed for the possibility of pursuing damages for future damage. Bringing an action prior to the occurrence of damage is possible when: the damage is imminent (*coming or likely to happen very soon*) and there is a high degree of certainty that it will occur (*the damage must already be in existence when the action is brought*), even if the extent of the damage is not known.[32] The aggrieved party is, therefore, in a somewhat deleterious situation, but its dimensions are not yet known, and these will depend on factors which cannot be foreseen at the moment the action is brought.[33] 23

This does not, however, mean that the limitation period begins to run earlier in the event of future damage.[34] Rather, the Court has granted the aggrieved an additional right consisting in the possibility of bringing an action earlier, with the objective of challenging illegal action. The running of the period of limitations for claims in damages should still be calculated from the moment in which the damage materialised.[35] Otherwise, this period could expire before the damage in fact arose, and thus before a condition of liability came about. It thus means that in the case of future damage, two moments must 24

29 Case T-28/03, *Holcim*, paras 69–70.

30 Case T-174/00, *Biret*, para 41.

31 Case T-20/94, *Hartmann*, paras 132–133; case T-76/94, *Jansma*, paras 78–79; case T-201/94, *Kustermann*, paras 63–64; case T-332/99, *Jestädt*, para 45.

32 Joined cases 56-60/74, *Kurt Kampffmeyer Mühlenvereinigung KG and others v Commission and Council of the European Communities* [1976] ECR 711, para 6; See Opinion of Advocate General Reischl of 2 June 1976 in case 56-60/74, *Kampffmeyer* [1976] ECR 748, p. 752.

33 *T Hartley*, Non-contractual liability: Future Loss and Actions for a Declaration (1976) 1 ELRev., pp. 555–556.

34 Case C-282/05, *Holcim*, para 33. The ECJ held that in the decision of the Court of the First Instance in the matter of T-28/03, *Holcim*, para 68, the determination of the beginning of the running of the limitation period in respect of future damage as the day it became possible to file an action for declaration is incorrect and constitutes a violation of the law. Cf. *P Oliver*, The action for damages: when does the time begin to run? (1982) 7 ELRev., p. 186.

35 See Opinion of Advocate General Reischl in case 56-60/74, *Kampffmeyer*.

be distinguished: that from which an action can be brought (the earlier one, from the moment of existence of the conditions for pursuing a claim arising from future damage) and that from which the limitation period is calculated (the later one, from the moment the damage materialised).

25 Furthermore, it can be seen that art 340(2) TFEU performs an additional function – it can serve as the basis for bringing an action for declaration of a claim, which prevents the negative effects of the passage of time between the event giving rise to the damage and the emergence of the damage itself. The declaration allows for the determination that the EU is obliged to make good damage that the aggrieved will suffer. The CJEU has held that the declaration is a remedy available in community law with regard for policy – to prevent greater damage, and for national law – declaration exists in the majority, if not in all Member States' laws.[36]

## VII. PRESCRIPTION PERIODS

26 The length of the limitation period is five years from the moment of the event giving rise to liability. The Court's case law indicates that the length of that period has been determined with a view to the necessary amount of time that the aggrieved party needs to collect the relevant information in order to submit a claim, and to review the facts that are to be invoked in support of that claim.[37]

27 The limitation period for damages claims is not differentiated by the events for which the EU bears liability (eg legislative, administrative, or factual measures), nor by the type of damage (personal injury, property damage) or type of good violated.

28 Although the time limit is not differentiated, in practice problems have appeared with distinguishing actions for annulment under art 263 TFEU and actions under art 340(2) TFEU. This distinction is significant if one takes into account that actions for annulment shall be instituted within two months of the publication of the measure, or of its notification to the plaintiff, or, in the absence thereof, of the day on which it came to the knowledge of the latter, as the case may be. The Court resolved the question of the relation between the actions in the following manner: The fact that a claim for annulment is held to be inadmissible renders the claim for damages inadmissible where the

---

36 Case 56-60/74, *Kampffmeyer*, paras 5–9. See also *Hartley*, *supra* fn 33.

37 Case C-136/01 P, *Autosalone*, para 28; case T-247/08 *C-Content BV*, para 54; also case T-140/04, *Ehcon*, para 57.

action for damages is actually aimed at securing withdrawal of an individual decision which has become definitive and would, if upheld, have the effect of nullifying the legal effects of that decision.[38] In the *Cobrecaf* case the Court invoked the actual purpose of the applicants' alternative claim for damages, which was secure payment of a sum corresponding exactly to the amount denied to it by reason of the disputed decision. On these grounds it declared that it is designed to secure indirectly annulment of the individual decision rejecting the applicants' request for financial aid and declared the action inadmissible.[39]

## VIII. RULES OF POSTPONEMENT, SUSPENSION, RENEWAL AND EXTENSION

### A. INTRODUCTION

Article 46 of the Statute sets out two events which interrupt the running of the period of limitations: bringing an action before the Court of Justice, and prior submission by the aggrieved of an application to the relevant EU institution. 29

### B. SUBMISSION OF AN ACTION TO THE COURT

The Court applies a strict understanding of the concept 'bringing an action before the Court' and holds that the running of the limitation period can only be interrupted by bringing an action for damages under art 340 TFEU.[40] This means that the running of the limitation period is not interrupted by the submission of an action other than one for damages, nor through commencement of proceedings before a national court, and this regardless of whether the proceedings are solely dedicated to the claim for damages or such a claim were to be advanced during a different phase of proceedings, such as an application for relief,[41] as well as regardless of the identity of the parties and the subject-matter 30

---

38 See case 175/84, *Krohn & Co. Import-Export GmbH & Co. KG v Commission of the European Communities* [1986] ECR 753, paras 32–33.

39 Case T-514/93, *Cobrecaf SA, Pêche & Froid SA and Klipper investissements SARL v Commission of the European Communities* [1995] ECR II-621, paras 58–62.

40 Case C-282/05, *Holcim*, para 36.

41 See case C-136/01 P, *Autosalone*, paras 56–57; case T-246/93, *Günther Bühring v Council of the European Union and Commission of the European Communities* [1998] ECR II-171, para 72; case C-51/05 P, *Cantina sociale di Dolianova*, para 69; case C-335/08 P, *Transports Schiocchet*, para 30; see also joined cases T-457/04 and T-223/05, *Camar Srl v Commission of*

of the proceedings (relief requested, evidence).[42] The absence of knowledge or certainty on the part of the aggrieved as to the selection of the appropriate procedure (type of proceedings), regardless of how complicated the matter is, does not justify submission of a claim to the wrong organ.[43]

31 The action must be submitted to the Court in the course of the limitation period. The moment of submission is decisive, *id est* the moment in which the procedural act is undertaken, in respect to which provisions concerning procedural time limits are applied. These are calculated taking into account exclusively the date on which a given letter was served to the secretariat of the Court.[44] For observance of the time limit it is sufficient to send the letter via telefax (from the moment the fax is sent, the party has ten days to submit originals of the action and any attachments), or bring the submission directly to the Court (an action can be submitted at any time, and a guard will make a note of the date of submission in accordance with the principal that 'The Court is never closed').[45]

## C. PRIOR SUBMISSION OF AN APPLICATION TO THE APPROPRIATE INSTITUTION

32 The second event interrupting the course of the limitation period is submission of an application to the appropriate EU institution, insofar as the aggrieved then brings an action to the Court within the time limits determined by reference to art 263 TFEU or art 265 TFEU, depending on the case.[46] This should be understood as follows: The aggrieved, prior to bringing the matter before the Court, may submit an application to the relevant EU institution for restitution. In the event of a negative decision, the aggrieved should

---

*the European Communities* [2008] ECR II-215 (interruption in connection with the lodging of an action for damages), paras 73–81.

42 Case C-136/01 P, *Autosalone*, para 57: 'It should also be pointed out that [...] neither the Commission's conduct before the national court nor the fact that the subject-matter of the proceedings before that court is identical to the subject-matter of the action dismissed as inadmissible by the order under appeal can be relevant to the outcome of the case.'

43 See, eg case C-282/05, *Holcim*; case C-51/05 P, *Cantina sociale di Dolianova*.

44 Article 57(6) and (7) Rules of Procedure of the Court of Justice; arts 72(2) and 73(3) Rules of Procedure of the General Court.

45 See: *Lenaerts, Maselis and Gutman*, *supra* fn 6, 751, 753 and 754.

46 Case 11/72 *Luigi Giordano v Commission of the European Communities* [1973] ECR 417, para 6; case T-222/97, *Alfons Steffens v Council of the European Union and Commission of the European Communities* [1998] ECR II-4175, paras 35–37, 42; case T-76/94, *Jansma*, paras 80–81; case T-167/94, *Detlef Nölle v Council of the European Union and Commission of the European Communities* [1995] ECR II-2589, para 30; case T-261/94, *Bernhard Schulte v Council of the European Union and Commission of the European Communities* [2002] ECR II-441, paras 68–71; case T-140/04, *Ehcon BV*, para 47.

bring the matter to the Court within two months of the date of receipt of the decision (by reference to art 263 TFEU).[47] If the aggrieved does not receive a decision from the institution within two months of the submission of this application, an action should be brought before the Court within the following two months (by reference to art 265 TFEU). In the event the aggrieved receives a response from the institution within those two months, a new two-month period for submitting an action is initiated.[48] Observance of these time limits means that the day on which the application to the EU institution is filed is considered the day on which the limitation period was interrupted.[49]

After the expiry of the aforementioned time-limits, it is still possible to file an action,[50] considering that the time limits referred to in art 46 of the Statute are not intended to shorten the limitation period, but merely define the moment of interruption. Otherwise, an aggrieved party that submitted an application to an institution and then failed to submit an action would be in a worse situation than one who submitted the statement of claim directly to the Court.[51] Submission of an action to the Court after the expiry of these time limits only means that the interruption of the limitation period should be considered as the moment when the action was submitted to the Court, and not the application to the institution.[52] 33

The application referred to here should be submitted to the relevant EU institution, *id est* to the institution which the aggrieved is accusing of unlawful activity (potentially liable), and from which remedy of damage is being demanded.[53] Submission of the application to an inappropriate institution does not interrupt the running of the limitation period. 34

47 See, eg case T-332/99, *Jestädt*, paras 47–50.

48 Joined cases T-195/94 and T-202/94, *Friedhelm Quiller and Johann Heusmann v Council of the European Union and Commission of the European Communities* [1997] ECR II-2247, para 132: 'Since the Commission's reply was given more than two months after the applicant's letter, but within the period for challenging an implied rejection, that reply caused a new period to start to run (see also Case C-25/91, *Pesqueras Echebastar*). Since the action was brought before the end of that second period, the interruption of the limitation period took place on 12 January 1994'.

49 Case T-140/04, *Eacon*, paras 28, 39, 46–48; case 11/72, *Giordano*, paras 5–6; case T-167/94, *Nölle*, paras 30–31; case T-332/99, *Jestädt*, paras 47–55; case T-28/03, *Holcim*, paras 73–74.

50 Case 11/72, *Giordano*, paras 5–7.

51 Joined cases T-8/95 and T-9/95, *Wilhelm Pelle and Ernst-Reinhard Konrad v Council of the European Union and Commission of the European Communities* [2007] ECR II-4117, para 75.

52 Case T-28/03, *Holcim*, paras 73–74.

53 Case T-76/94, *Jansma*, paras 80–96; case T-261/94, *Schulte*, paras 68–71; case T-246/93, *Bühring*, paras 71–75. See more *M Broberg*, The calculation of the period of limitation (2001) 26 ELRev., p. 284.

35 The claim filed after previous submission of an application should be a claim for damages, and not a grievance against the decision of the organ refusing to award damages (action for annulment) nor one for failure to respond (action for failure to act).[54] The subject of the action and the application should thus be identical and encompass a claim for damages.

## D. EFFECT OF INTERRUPTION OF THE LIMITATION PERIOD

36 Article 46 of the Statute does not set out the legal effects of interruption of the limitation period, nor does it distinguish the effects indicated previously of the two manners of interrupting that period. When taking into consideration that the five-year period of limitation applies to the period during which the aggrieved may institute proceedings before the Court,[55] it should be considered that the effect of interrupting the limitation period is simply ruling that an application is permissible. In practice, submission of an application to an institution sometimes leads to the aggrieved receiving additional time to engage in other action,[56] but this is not always done by suspending the prescription of the limitation period, rather by defining another moment of its expiry. In practice this does not always entail the extension of the time limit by two months.

37 There is essentially no need to calculate the limitation period anew. Restarting the limitation period is justified when it can be interrupted by various juridical or procedural acts (eg initiation of mediation or acknowledgement of a claim), and thus the course of a single claim's limitation period can be interrupted multiple times by acts other than the submission of a claim. The effect of interrupting the limitation period again after an interruption is also important for the potential to enforce the claim after it has been adjudicated. These problems do not seem to affect expiry of a claim for damages against the EU. Interruption occurs only by the submission of a claim to the Court, and the five-year period counted from the materialisation of the damage is the maximum period within which the EU may be liable. After submission of a claim, the Court resolves the matter and any judgments are considered *res judicata* in respect of the

---

54 Cf *H Schermers and D Waelbroeck*, Judicial Protection in the European Communities, Kluwer Law International (1992), p. 473; *Oliver*, *supra* fn 16, p. 13; *G Bebr*, Development of Judicial Control of the European Communities, Martinus Nijhoff Publishers (1981), p. 266.

55 *Broberg*, *supra* fn 53, p. 287.

56 Joined cases T-8/95 and T-9/95, *Pelle*, para 75. The Court held that the fact of filing an application for damages to a community institution can only lead to extension of the five-year limitation period set out in art 43 of the Statute, but not its shortening. See case 11/72, *Giordano*, paras 6 and 7; case T-167/94, *Nölle*, para 30; joined cases 5, 7 and 13 to 24/66, *Kampffmeyer*, p. 260.

parties to the proceedings; they cannot submit the same claim invoking the same facts and circumstances.[57] In respect of enforcement of an award of damages art 280 TFEU is applied, which refers to art 299 TFEU. Under para 2 of art 299, enforcement proceedings are regulated by the civil procedure in force in the country where the enforcement is taking place. Thus it may be concluded that the temporal limits of the possibility to enforce a claim after it has been judicially ascertained are subject to national law.

## E. SUSPENSION OF THE RUNNING OF THE LIMITATION PERIOD

Article 46 of the Statue only regulates the rules governing interruption of the running of the limitation period, but not of its suspension. The potential to suspend the running of the limitation period has been taken up by the Court in respect of two situations. 38

The first is a consequence of the Court's case law allowing for renouncing the defence of prescription. This is associated with the issue of liability on account of Regulation No 857/84 for damage incurred by producers of milk or milk products who, pursuant to non-marketing or conversion undertakings given under Regulation No 1078/77, were precluded by Regulation No 857/84 from receiving a reference quantity and who were unable, as a result, to market any quantity of milk exempt from additional levy.[58] In these cases it was held that EU institutions can renounce the defence of prescription, including prior to the expiry of that period, in respect of a specified group of entities as well as a specified period (which essentially took place).[59] Waiver of the defence of prescription in the discussed cases came first in the form of a Communication of the Commission, and then as a Regulation. This should be understood as an EU institution undertaking an obligation to refrain from 39

---

57 See case T-341/07, *Jose Maria Sison v Council of the European Union* [2011] ECR II-7915, paras 17–25; case T-164/01, *Arnaldo Lucaccioni v Commission of the European Communities* [2003] ECR FP-I-A-67, FP-II-367, para 28; case C-462/05, *Commission of the European Communities v Portuguese Republic* [2008] ECR I-4183, para 23. It results from the case law that *res judicata* encompasses the factual and legal circumstances which in reality and in the necessary manner were resolved in a given judicial ruling (see joined cases C-238/99 P, C-244/99 P, C-245/99 P, C-247/99 P, from C-250/99 P to C-252/99 P and C-254/99 P, *Limburgse Vinyl Maatschappij et al v Commission of the European Communities* [2002] ECR I-8375, para 44).

58 Case T-246/93, *Bühring*, paras 2–8.

59 Eg case T-222/97, *Steffens*, paras 37–41; joined cases T-195/94 and T-202/94, *Quiller*, para 136; See: *T Heukels and A McDonnell*, Limitation of the Action for Damages Against the Community: Considerations and New Developments, in: T Heukels and A McDonnell, The Action for Damages in Community Law, Kluwer Law International (1997), pp. 217, 239 et seq.

raising the defence of prescription. This obligation was of a political nature and its objective was to encourage producers to refrain from bringing claims for damages. As a result, institutions would gain the time needed to find appropriate solutions, and producers would not bear the negative consequences of waiting for them.

40 The Court set out the consequences of renouncing the defence of prescription prior to the expiry of the limitation period (when a community institution invoked expiry of a claim before the Court in spite of having renounced it) in the case *van den Berg*. This type of renouncement was held to be a voluntary unilateral obligation, the result of which was that institutions cannot invoke the defence of prescription during the period the renouncement concerns in a given case. In the *Quiller* case the Court held that the defendants cannot rely on the fact that the applicant behaved in a manner which worked exclusively to their benefit, because undertaking was a unilateral act of the institutions only intended to discourage the applicant from bringing an action.[60] If, therefore, in spite of the temporary renouncement of the prescription defence the institution were to invoke expiration in the course of proceedings, the Court should be bound by the renouncement. The period encompassed by renouncement of the defence is not counted to the running of the limitation period. Renouncement of the defence therefore leads to suspension of the running of the limitation period.[61] After the obligation not to set up the defence of prescription has itself expired, the limitation period continues where it was stopped and does not begin anew.[62] It is true that suspension of the running of the limitation period was not foreseen in art 46 of the Statute, but this possibility to suspend the running of the limitation period is not based so much on the provisions of art 46 of the Statute, as much as it is on renouncement of the right to invoke that article by a given party against whom a claim has been brought; suspension of the running of the limitation period is not prevented by the fact that this article makes mention only of interruption of the course of the limitation period.[63]

---

60 Joined cases T-195/94 and T-202/94, *Quiller*, para 138.

61 See *inter alia* decisions of the Court of First Instance in joined cases T-195/94 and T-202/94, *Quiller*, paras 137–142, and in case T-20/94 *Hartmann*, paras 135–140; see also *S Hackspiel*, commentary to art 43, in: H von der Groeben, J Thiesing and C Ehlermann (eds), Kommentar zum EU-/EG-Vertrag, Nomos (5th ed 1997), vol 4, p. 858 (para 6); *M Núñez Müller*, Die Verjährung außervertraglicher Schadenersatzansprüche gegen die EG (1999) 20 EuZW, p. 611 (pp. 614 et seq.).

62 Joined cases T-8/95 and T-9/95, *Pelle*, para 71; C-164/01 P, *G. van den Berg v Council of the European Union and Commission of the European Communities* [2004] ECR I-10225, para 100.

63 Opinion of Advocate General Christine Stix-Hackl of 20 November 2003 in case C-164/01 P, *G. van den Berg v Council of the European Union and Commission of the European Communities* [2004] ECR I-10225, paras 91–111.

The Court's case law has not yet addressed the renouncement by an institution of the defence of prescription without a time limitation, which would lead to the potential to pursue claims on the part of the aggrieved without any limitation in time. The effectiveness of such an obligation is, however, doubtful, as it would run contrary to the essence of expiry as an institution. 41

The second circumstance leading to suspension of the running of the limitation period is submission by the aggrieved of an application for legal aid prior to submission of a claim to the Court.[64] This is associated with the fact that in proceedings before EU courts, parties other than Member States and EU institutions must be represented by a lawyer (art 19(3) of the Statute). In the case of *Lallemand-Zeller* the Court awarded legal aid to the applicant, while at the same time remarking that the time for bringing an action does not run from the date of submission of the application for legal aid to the date on which the applicant is served with the order granting him legal aid and appointing his lawyer.[65] In the literature the argument is raised that because the Court did not directly express what types of action were referred to, submission of an application for legal aid leads to this effect in respect of claims in damages as well. Suspension ends in the moment the aggrieved is informed of the awarding of legal aid and is assigned counsel.[66] The case law of the Court does not provide grounds for solving a situation in which the aggrieved has not received legal aid but nevertheless submits a claim using the help of counsel that has agreed to undertake the matter. 42

## F. UNAWARENESS (LATE DISCOVERY)

The issue of whether the limitation period can begin running if the aggrieved did not have knowledge of the event giving rise to the damage, and thus was in fact deprived of the time necessary to pursue the claim, was addressed in the case 145/83 *Adams*.[67] In that case, events impacting the EU incurring liability in damages occurred at various moments, and the aggrieved became aware of those events at different times. Prior to obtaining that knowledge the aggrieved could not have suspected that the actions of EU institutions were the cause of the damage. In conjunction with this fact, the expiry of the limitation 43

---

64 See: *Broberg, supra* fn 53, p. 287.

65 Case T-92/92, *Loic Lallemand-Zeller v Commission of the European Communities* [1993] ECR II-31 (main proceedings case T-27/93).

66 *Broberg, supra* fn 53, p. 287.

67 Case 145/83, *Stanley George Adams v Commission of the European Communities* [1985] ECR 3539. The *Adams* case has been widely discussed in the literature, see, eg *AIL Campbell*, Confidentiality and EEC Law (1986) The Journal of the Law Society of Scotland, pp. 125–126; *N March Hunnings*, The Stanley Adams Affair or the Biter Bit (1987) 1 CMLRev. pp. 65–88.

period cannot constitute a valid defence to a claim by a person who has suffered damage where that person only belatedly became aware of the event giving rise to it and thus could not have had a reasonable time in which to submit his application to the Court or to the relevant institution before the expiry of the limitation period.[68]

44 In the *Autosalone* case, however, the Court rejected the view that the limitation period does not run until the moment in which the aggrieved obtained precise information about the facts of the case. Specific knowledge of the facts is not among the conditions which must be met for the limitation period to begin running.[69] Otherwise, '[...] a confusion would arise between the procedural criterion relating to the commencement of the limitation period and the finding that the conditions for liability were satisfied, which can ultimately be made only by the court before which the matter has been brought for final adjudication on its substance'.[70] The five-year period is thus a time for determining the responsible party and the precise causes of the damage, as well as for gathering and verifying evidence. The aggrieved's level of certainty as to the circumstances of the case is insignificant, which the aggrieved may not even attain in the course of judicial proceedings (eg in the event the claim is held impermissible).

45 As for the aspect of knowledge of the aggrieved in respect of the scope of the damage, in the *Cantina* case the Court held that in determining the beginning of the running of the limitation period, it is not permissible to take into account the subjective assessment of its existence.[71] In the alternative case, the aggrieved would be able to decide about the moment at which a claim arising out of liability in damages would expire, which would contradict the requirement of legal certainty vital in application of limitation periods[72] and would lead to evidentiary difficulties. The beginning of the running of the limitation period is thus associated with an objective injury to the property interests of the aggrieved party.[73] The Court even declared more generally that the rules for expiry of claims for the remedy of damage may only be based on strictly objective criteria.[74] A certain lack of consistency, however, found its way into the justification of the verdict. The Court held that the aggrieved were fully aware of the circumstances responsible for the damage they incurred, and as a result the conditions set forth in the *Adams* case were not met.

68 Case 145/83, *Adams*, para 50; Cf case T-138/03, *É.R.*, para 50.
69 See determination in the case C-136/01 P, *Autosalone*, paras 31–33.
70 Case T-124/99, *Autosalone Ispradei Fratelli Rossi Snc v European Atomic Energy Community* [2001] ECR II-53, para 24.
71 Case C-51/05 P *Cantina sociale di Dolianova*, paras 58–59.
72 Ibid, paras 45, 59, 60.
73 Ibid, para 63.
74 Ibid, para 62.

At the same time, the Court did not negate the possibility of taking into account the element of knowledge on the part of the aggrieved, and even confirmed its position expressed in the *Adams* case, but held that it was not relevant to the case at hand.

The element of knowledge held by the aggrieved party can be taken into consideration when calculating the limitation period, but only applying an exclusively objective perspective. As a rule, the limitation period cannot begin until the emergence of the conditions constituting grounds for a claim in damages and the damage itself materialises, unless the aggrieved party could not be aware of them. The moment of becoming aware of those conditions should be considered the earliest moment at which the aggrieved could have learned of them.[75] In the Court's case law, awareness on the part of the aggrieved as to the conditions for liability can impact the running of the limitation period only in exceptional situations, and it would seem that this can occur primarily when the event giving rise to the damage consists of factual actions of EU institutions. 46

## G. OTHER CASES

In the *Ehcon* case the Court indicated that supplying incorrect information to the other party deprives the party supplying such information of the right to set up the defence of expiry of the claim made against it. Strict application of the limitation period in such a situation would be incompatible with certainty of law and the proper performance of justice.[76] 47

With regard to the specificity of EU liability, some circumstances simply cannot exist and influence the running of the limitation period (medical treatment relation, family relations). Others which are possible (the aggrieved being a minor,[77] mental disability, physical disability, physical absence from the jurisdiction, *force majeure*, court's ruling or law that prevent from litigating the claim) have not been reviewed by the Court in the context of their influence on the running of the limitation period. It would seem that the running of the limitation period is not impacted by employment relations,[78] negotiations,[79] 48

---

75 Case T-140/04, *Ehcon*, paras 43–45.

76 Case T-140/04, *Ehcon*, paras 64–65. Cf case C-326/96, *B.S. Levez v T.H. Jennings (Harlow Pools) Ltd.* [1998] ECR I-7835, paras 21–34.

77 See, eg joined cases 169/83 and 136/84, *Gerhardus Leussink and others v Commission of the European Communities* [1986] ECR 2801.

78 See, eg joined cases 169/83 and 136/84, *Leussink* and case 58/75, *Jacques Henri Sergy v Commission of the European Communities* [1976] ECR 1139.

79 See *A Pereira*, Limitation Periods in EC Law, in: H Koziol and R Schulze (eds), Tort Law of the European Community, Springer (2008), p. 302.

evidential difficulties for the claimant who needs time to gather evidence,[80] financial difficulties of the claimant in raising money required for litigation[81] nor closed courts.[82]

## IX. CEILINGS ON THE EFFECTIVE TIME OF PRESCRIPTION

49 The time limit for the expiry of a claim in damages against the EU is not limited by 'ceiling periods', under which a claim is prescribed after the ceiling period expires even if the prescription period has not yet expired because of the prolongation, rules of postponement, renewal and extension. Article 46 of the Statute does not foresee a maximum time limit after which damages may not be pursued, which results in part from the manner in which the remaining elements of the limitation period are regulated. First, the beginning of the limitation period is counted from the materialisation of the damage (not from the moment of awareness of the damage). Second, there is no detailed regulation addressing postponement, which would facilitate significant extension of the running of the limitation period. Third, to date the possibility of suspension of the running of the limitation period has only been acknowledged by the Court in the event of a temporary renouncement of the defence of prescription (in the relevant cases the renouncement of the prescription defence was effective for a relatively short time), and in the event an application for legal assistance is submitted (which also has a relatively short-term effect). Fourth, even in the event of continuous damage, five years (counted back from the event interrupting the running of the limitation period) is the maximum period for EU liability.

## X. STATUTE INTERPRETATION, JUDICIAL DISCRETION AND LACHES

50 Article 46 of the Statute is formulated quite generally, and it does not set precise criteria for applying a limitation period to claims in damages against the EU. The rules addressing calculation of the limitation period, including determining the beginning of the running of that period, interruption and suspension of

80 See, eg case C-136/01 P, *Autosalone*, which confirms that the five-year limitation period is the time granted to the aggrieved for determining the responsible party and precise causes of the damage, as well as for gathering and examining evidence.

81 See case T-140/04, *Ehcon*, paras 68–69.

82 See *Lenaerts, Maselis and Gutman*, *supra* fn 6, pp. 751, 753 and 754.

its running, and special cases for calculating the limitation period in respect of continuous and future damage have been created in judicial decisions of the Court of Justice. The case law of the Court itself does not, however, refer to abstract legal constructions, but is rather based on a flexible, case-by-case approach.

As a general observation, in resolving issues associated with limitation periods 51
the Court applies the rules in a manner which is harsh on the aggrieved (eg calculating the beginning of the limitation period from the first moment when the damage occurred; limiting the EU's liability to five years in the case of continuous damage), which means that a claim may be held inadmissible even when it constituted good claim.[83]

The present rules governing the limitation period are the result of a long 52
period of evolution in the case law, which does not mean that all elements of the issue are clarified. There remain problems in such areas as the effects of the absence of knowledge on the part of the aggrieved of the event giving rise to damage. Furthermore, certain issues associated with the limitation period have not yet been addressed by the Court, which does not exclude the possibility of their being resolved in the future (eg the meaning of a mental disability of the aggrieved, or *force majeure*).

In respect of resolving matters concerning liability in damages on the part 53
of the EU, the Court does not apply the doctrine of laches.

## XI. CHANGE OF PARTIES

The issue of change of parties and how it affects prescription period has not 54
been discussed in the CJEU jurisprudence, while the problem of multiple tortfeasors and their contribution claims cannot arise because of the nature of liability in question, that is liability of a single international organisation.

## XII. OTHER ASPECTS OF PRESCRIPTION LAW

### A. STIPULATION

The possibility of temporary renounciation of the defence of prescription has 55
already been discussed. To date, the case law of the Court has not addressed the issue of shortening or lengthening the limitation period by way of mutual agreement between the parties.

---

83 See, eg case C-136/01, *Autosalone*.

## B. PROCEDURAL ASPECTS

56 The case law of the CJEU is clear that the expiry of the limitation period is not taken into account *ex officio*, but only when invoked by the party against whom a claim for damages has been brought. There are two arguments in support of this position. In the *Roquette Frères* case the Court invoked the 'general principles common to the laws of the Member States', deduced from a comparison of national legal systems (the verdict, however, contains no detailed comparative legal analysis, which is merely referred to).[84] In the *Evropaiki Dynamiki* case the Court indicated that the expiry of the limitation period cannot be considered *ex officio* as this is a question of substantive law that influences the performance of a subjective right and is not a matter of public interest.[85] Such a justification does give rise to certain doubts as the time limit for resumption of proceedings, itself a matter of substantive law, is taken into account *ex officio*.

57 Taking into consideration the expiry of the limitation period solely when raised as a defence by the debtor enhances protection of aggrieved parties and requires greater procedural engagement on the part of EU institutions, which should be assessed as an appropriate solution.

58 The defence of prescription should be raised (at the written procedure) in response to a claim, not later than in the second exchange of briefs. Pursuant to art 84 Rules of Procedure of the General Court and art 127 Rules of Procedure of the Court of Justice, no new defences may be set up during the course of proceedings unless they are based on legal or factual circumstances coming to light after their commencement.[86]

---

84 Case 20/88, *SA Roquette Frères*, paras 11–13.

85 Case C-469/11 P, *Evropaiki Dynamiki*, paras 50–52. See also: *Heukels and McDonnell, supra* fn 59, p. 239; *Broberg, supra* fn 53, p. 289.

86 Under art 84(2) of the Rules of Procedure of the General Court, any new pleas in law shall be introduced in the second exchange of pleadings and identified as such. Where the matters of law or of fact justifying the introduction of new pleas in law are known after the second exchange of pleadings or after it has been decided not to authorise a second exchange of pleadings, the main party concerned shall introduce the new pleas in law as soon as those matters come to his knowledge. According to art 127 Rules of Procedure of the Court of Justice (1) No new plea in law may be introduced in the course of proceedings unless it is based on matters of law or of fact which come to light in the course of the procedure. (2) Without prejudice to the decision to be taken on the admissibility of the plea in law, the President may, on a proposal from the Judge-Rapporteur and after hearing the Advocate General, prescribe a time-limit within which the other party may respond to that plea.

European law contains a general principle that the party which makes a claim incurs the burden of proof (proves the fact) regarding that claim. This is also applicable to a defence.[87] As a result, in the case of prescription it is the defendant which bears the burden of proof that the prescription period has passed. The complainant, however, bears the burden of proving a different moment for the beginning of the running of the period or its suspension. 59

The defence of prescription is examined during review of permissibility of the claim, and thus during the formal phase of proceedings. As a result, allowing the defence of prescription leads to impermissibility of the claim, not its dismissal as groundless.[88] 60

## XIII. PRESCRIPTION TIME LIMITS IN EU DIRECTIVES AND CJEU *FRANCOVICH* CASE LAW

### A. INTRODUCTION

Apart from the aforementioned limitation periods on claims directed against the EU, to a quite limited extent EU law, through directives, impacts national law systems in the area of prescription of claims in tort. As it is known, the directive is an instrument for harmonisation of law within the EU. It establishes rights and (more frequently) duties for Member States. These states are under an obligation to implement a directive within the time limit stated therein, *id est* to achieve in national law the effect set out by the directive, usually through the adoption of appropriate domestic legislation. The form and the means of achieving the objective set out in a directive are, however, left up to the discretion of the Member State (art 288(3) TFEU). The impact of directives on national law varies, and generally depends on the level of detail and character of rules contained in it. If it is sufficiently high so as to essentially deprive domestic legislators of freedom in their choice of the 'forms and means' of implementation, then the force of the impact exerted by the directive on national law differs little from the direct effect of an EU regulation. This impact is also dependent on the nature of the rules set out in the directive. Several types of 61

Article 124(1) of the same act states that within two months after service on him of the application, the defendant shall lodge a defence, stating: '[...] b) the pleas in law and arguments relied on [...]'.

87 *Lenaerts, Maselis and Gutman*, *supra* fn 6, p. 765. See: *K Lenaerts*, Some Thoughts on Evidence and Procedure in European Community Competition Law (2007) Fordham Inter. L.J., pp. 1463–1495.

88 *Wagenbaur*, *supra* fn 4.

harmonisation can be distinguished. From the perspective of the private law, distinctions of particular importance are:

- comprehensive and partial harmonisation – the former serves to regulate a given area of social relations in its entirety, while the latter does not encompass all matters which usually comprise the scope of the relevant national regulations;
- full (maximal) and minimal harmonisation – the former consists in establishing a state of law which is to be achieved by Member States without the possibility of adopting solutions more beneficial for any of the particular parties to the regulated legal relations, while the latter involves indicating a minimal standard of protection for the entity whose interests are supposed to be protected by the implementation of the directive; Member States retain the possibility to adopt a higher level of protection (implementation of solutions more beneficial to the protected entity);
- fully-binding harmonisation and optional harmonisation – the former does not leave Member States with any choice as to the adoption of certain solutions set out in the directive, while the latter leaves some freedoms of decision as to transposition of particular provisions in the directive, or freedom of choice between two or more possible solutions.

Tort law is encompassed by partial harmonisation, and in a very narrow scope – it encompasses only two areas of that law, *id est* product liability and liability for damage resulting from violation of competition law.[89] In the former, one deals with a case of maximum harmonisation,[90] whereas in the latter a mixed approach has been taken in which regulation of prescription is of a minimal character.

## B. PRESCRIPTION IN PRODUCT LIABILITY LAW

62 Council Directive of 25 July 1985 on the approximation of the laws, regulations and administrative provisions of the Member States concerning liability

---

[89] The issue of damage is also addressed by Directive 2004/35/CE of the European Parliament and of the Council of 21 April 2004 on environmental liability with regard to the prevention and remedying of environmental damage. It cannot, however, be considered an act of tort law, as it does not award claims in damages to individual entities, but merely gives the competent authority the right to recover from the entity who has caused the damage or the imminent threat of damage, the costs it has incurred in relation to the preventive or remedial actions taken under the directive. According to art 10 of the directive, the competent authority is entitled to initiate cost recovery proceedings within five years from the date on which preventive or remedial measures have been completed or the liable operator, or third party, has been identified, whichever is the later.

[90] See *G Howells*, in: P Machnikowski (ed), European Product Liability, Intersentia (2016), pp. 25 ff.

for defective products (85/374/EEC) in its art 10 obliges Member States to provide in their legislation that a limitation period of three years applies to product damages claims covered by the Directive. The limitation period begins to run from the day on which the plaintiff became aware, or should reasonably have become aware, of the damage, the defect and the identity of the producer. Regulation of suspension and interruption of the limitation period remains in the Member States' sphere of competence. Furthermore, art 11 of the Product Liability Directive requires Member States to make product liability claims subject to a cut-off period. The claims are to be extinguished after ten years from the date on which the producer put into circulation the actual product which caused the damage, unless the injured person has in the meantime instituted proceedings against the producer.[91]

## C. PRESCRIPTION OF COMPETITION DAMAGES CLAIMS

Before liability for claims caused by damage arising out of violations of competition law was regulated in a directive, the case law of the CJEU has essentially determined the existence of such liability, while leaving a wide range of more detailed issues, including the limitation period and the law of Member States, with the standard disclaimer that principles of equivalence and effectiveness must be observed.[92] This situation changed with the entrance into force of Directive 2014/104/EU of the European Parliament and of the Council of 26 November 2014 on certain rules governing actions for damages under national law for infringements of the competition law provisions of the Member States and of the EU. The principal objective of the directive is to guarantee the right to damages for parties injured by actions in violation of European and domestic competition law while at the same time ensuring the effectiveness of public-law programmes for protection of competition (in practice achieved to a large extent through relaxation of penalties against enterprises that admit to engaging in infringements). National laws on prescription are perceived by the Directive as a potential limitation of the right to damages, and also a threat to the effectiveness of non-judicial dispute resolution procedures.[93] This is why the directive regulates minimal prescription time limits, determines the beginning of their running, and defines the circumstances which must result in their suspension or interruption. 63

91 For a more detailed discussion see *A Janssen, P Machnikowski and R Schulze*, in: P Machnikowski (ed), European Product Liability, *supra* fn 90, pp. 88 ff and the literature cited therein.

92 Joined cases C-295/04 to C-298/04, *Vincenzo Manfredi v Lloyd Adriatico Assicurazioni SpA, Antonio Cannito v Fondiaria Sai SpA and Nicolò Tricarico and Pasqualina Murgolo v Assitalia SpA* [2006] ECR I-6619.

93 See recitals 36 and 49.

64 According to art 10 of the directive, Member States are entitled to lay down rules applicable to limitation periods and to determine when the limitation period begins to run, its duration and conditions of interruption and suspension. The Member States' freedom in this respect is, however, limited. Limitation periods cannot begin to run before the infringement of competition law has ceased and before the claimant knows, or can reasonably be expected to know of the behaviour and the fact that it constitutes an infringement of competition law, the identity of the infringer and the fact that the infringement of competition law caused harm to the claimant. The length of the prescription period has been set at no less than five years. The Member States must also ensure that a prescription period is suspended or interrupted if a competition authority starts an investigation or proceedings in respect of an infringement causing damages and that the suspension does not end earlier than one year after the infringement decision has become final or after the proceedings are otherwise terminated.

65 Furthermore, art 18 of the Directive requires Member States to ensure that the limitation period is suspended for the duration of a consensual dispute resolution process (which is understood broadly as any mechanism enabling parties to reach an out-of-court resolution of a dispute concerning a claim for damages) in which the claimant and defendant were involved or represented.

66 As can be seen, provisions of the Directive regulate only the prescription period starting with knowledge (or constructive knowledge) of the infringement, damage, causal link and the liable person. The Directive does not introduce any long-stop period and it expressly states (in its recital 36) that Member States are allowed to maintain or introduce such a period that is of general application, if only it does not render practically impossible or excessively difficult the exercise of the right to compensation.

## D. LIMITATION PERIODS FOR LIABILITY OF STATES FOR VIOLATIONS OF EU LAW

67 European law establishes the rule of liability of public authorities for damage incurred by such an authority as a result of a violation of that law.[94] In proclaiming that rule the Court has set out the basic conditions of liability, establishing a minimal level of protection for the injured. Detailed rules of liability are shaped by the Member States, but they cannot be less favourable for the injured than

[94] Joined cases C-6/90 and C-9/90, *Andrea Francovich and Danila Bonifaci and others v Italian Republic* [1991] ECR I-5357; joined cases C-46/93 and C-48/93, *Brasserie du Pêcheur SA v Bundesrepublik Deutschland and The Queen v Secretary of State for Transport, ex parte: Factortame Ltd and Others* [1996] ECR I-1029.

those related to violations of domestic law (principle of equivalence) nor be shaped so as to render the collection of damages impossible or excessively difficult (principle of effectiveness). In assessing national regulations on the expiry of claims from the perspective of the principle of effectiveness, the Court has stated that the setting of reasonable limitation periods for bringing proceedings, after which claims are forfeited, inasmuch as it constitutes an application of the fundamental principle of legal certainty, in principle satisfies the requirement in question. In this context the Court pointed out that the limitation period it had placed under review enabled the beneficiaries to ascertain the full extent of their rights and specified the conditions under which loss sustained as a result of the breach of community law will be made good.[95]

In another ruling the Court stated that in order to serve their purpose of ensuring legal certainty, limitation periods must be fixed in advance and the harmed individuals must be able to determine the applicable limitation period with a reasonable degree of certainty.[96] Settling more detailed issues that arose in relation to the specific facts of the case, the Court held that EU law does not require the limitation period for damages claim to be interrupted or suspended during infringement proceedings against the State brought by the EU Commission, and lack of such effect of infringement proceedings does not make it impossible or excessively difficult for individuals to exercise the rights to damages. Furthermore, it has held that EU law does not preclude the limitation period from beginning to run on the date on which the first injurious effects of the incorrect transposition have been produced and the further injurious effects are foreseeable, even if the infringement of the EU law (failure to correctly transpose the directive) has not ceased yet.[97] 68

95 Case C-261/95, *Rosalba Palmisani v Instituto nazionale della previdenza socaile (INPS)* [1997] ECR I-4025.

96 A similar view has been expressed in the public procurement case C-406/08 *Uniplex (UK) Ltd v NHS Business Services Authority* [2010] ECR I-817.

97 Case C-445/06, *Danske Slagterier v Bundesrepublik Deutschland* [2009] ECR I-2119.

# APPENDIX: QUESTIONNAIRE

In the course of the analytical and comparative discussions following this Questionnaire some changes were made in the cases, in the order of the topics discussed and in the suggestions made. Therefore there are some differences in this regards between the Questionnaire and the final reports.

## I. INTRODUCTION

The aim of the project is to explore how (and why) the passage of time on an alleged tort law claim affects (and should affect) the claim, the parties (P the plaintiff and D the defendant) and other parties through the defence of *prescription* (limitation of actions).

## II. DEFINITION OF PRESCRIPTION

Prescription in tort law is a legal institution that prevents P from enforcing an alleged right against D because of the running of a specified period of time on the tort claim. In the context of tort law the subject of prescription is usually the right to tort remedy, mainly the right to damages for harm caused. This right to remedy is a right that comes into being once a right imposed by tort law, such as the right to bodily and property integrity, and the right to reputation, is breached (some jurisdictions distinguish in this regard between a *primary* right and a secondary right to remedy). For the purpose of this project, claims for professional malpractice are also considered as tort claims, although in some jurisdictions they are treated as contractual claims, as long as they are based on grounds of tortious conduct (eg breach of a standard of care).

**Question** – *Does this definition suit your jurisdiction? Other definitions?*

## III. THE NATURE OF PRESCRIPTION AND ITS EFFECTS

There are different ways by which prescription prevents P from enforcing an alleged right of remedy against D. Its effect may be: (a) to extinguish P's right to remedy; (b) to provide D with a *substantive* defence that prevents P from enforcing the right to remedy although it is not extinguished; (c) to provide D with a *procedural* defence that bars P's ability to litigate the right in courts.

To illustrate the difference between (a) and (b) assume that D mistakenly compensates P for damage tortiously caused by D, although the prescription period elapsed. Under (a) D would have the right to restitution under the law of unjust enrichment because P's right to compensation was extinct before payment. In contrast, under (b) D will have no right of restitution because P's right to compensation still exists.

To illustrate the difference between (b) and (c) assume that P can enforce a right to tort compensation on D by selling D's property with no need to apply to court order. Could P do that after the prescription period elapsed? The answer would be negative under (b) because P's substantive right to remedy is blocked. In contrast, under (c) the answer would be in the affirmative because only litigation in court is barred and P can enforce the right outside the court.

**Question** – *What is the nature of prescription of tort claims in your jurisdiction (a, b, c)? Other concepts regarding the nature of tort prescription? Are there varieties of concepts so that different concepts (a, b, c, or others) apply to different areas of tort law?*

## IV. CONSIDERATIONS FOR AND AGAINST PRESCRIPTION OF TORT CLAIMS

Prescription of tort claims prevents P from enforcing an alleged tort right against D because of the running of a specified period of time on the tort claim. That may deprive Ps from pursuing and enforcing their alleged rights against Ds. In other words, prescription actually closes the doors of courts and may significantly limit the (constitutional?) right to 'open courts'. As the ability to vindicate rights in courts empowers individuals and strengthen their trust in the state and in society, closing the doors of courts may undermine empowerment and trust.

Given these negative effects of prescription, what are the considerations that nevertheless counterbalance the negative and justify the operation of prescription law? The answer is that the major consideration that justifies prescription is the protection of Ds, actual and potential, from the costs and wrongs of belated claims, and that public interests and even the interests of Ps also provide justifications for prescription. These considerations are presented below, preceded by the distinction between 'good' claims and 'bad' claims.

## 'GOOD' CLAIMS AND 'BAD' CLAIMS

Not all tort claims made by Ps are necessarily 'good' claims in the sense that they are meritorious claims that should be recognised and enforced by courts. Some claims are 'bad' in the sense that they are non-meritorious and should be denied by the courts. Claims are 'bad' when the alleged facts pleaded do not represent the truth, or because the relevant combination of facts and law does not constitute a right recognised by tort law. 'Bad' claims may be filed by Ps either in bad faith – false, vexatious, extortionist – or in good faith being based on misconception of facts and mistakes of law. Obviously, Ps do need a reasonable period of time to detect and learn the facts, gather evidence and prepare their claims. Therefore, a very short period of prescription may have a negative effect in this regard – the denial of 'good' claims. Yet, after this reasonable period elapses and no claim is made, the court may lose the ability to distinguish between good and bad claims, and recognise and enforce bad claims due to deteriorating evidence and change of moral and social norms. Therefore it is important that the prescription period and the effective time of prescription (see *infra* Section VI) should be set at a length that bars, if at all, few 'good' claims" but does screen most bad claims.

## PROTECTION OF POTENTIAL Ds

A major goal of prescription law is to protect *potential* Ds against the burden and costs of preserving evidence and financial reserves by limiting the period in which they are subjected to legal risks of litigation and resultant uncertainties. It should be stressed that the number of *potential* Ds protected by prescription is huge: Producers are exposed to numerous tort claims of consumers, and the same applies to medical institution and their patients, employers and employees, insurance companies and their insureds and so on.

## PROTECTION OF ACTUAL Ds

- Prescription protects actual Ds against bad claims that may be enforced upon them by courts due to the deterioration of their ability to defend caused by the passage of time.
- Prescription also protects actual Ds against frustrated expectations not to be sued and their reliance on these expectations.

## PROTECTION OF SOCIAL INTERESTS

- It is against public policy to allow bad claims to succeed because of the passage of time.
- Society's limited resources should not be spent on stale, 'rusty' claims that are more costly to adjudicate and may even disrupt 'public peace'.
- The costs of preserving evidence and financial reserves for pending claims in particular, and the costs of legal uncertainty in general, are not only private costs of Ds but also social costs (eg malfunction of capital markets due to difficulties in assessing market value of bodies exposed to future claims). Prescription reduces these costs.

Considerations of fairness between actual Ps and Ds support prescription. On the one hand delay on Ps' part may be a kind of neglect, or an indication of waiver, or even an intentional misuse of right, that weakens their late claim to enforce an alleged right. On the other hand this delay may do injustice to Ds who are unable to defend due to the passage of time and whose legitimate expectations are frustrated. Moreover, as moral and social norms may change over the years (eg required standard of safety), and as courts are not always able or willing to adjudicate an old case according to old norms rather than present norms, it may be unfair to adjudicate old cases according to such present norms.

## PROTECTION OF Ps

- Although prescription bars Ps' claim, it also protects them in the sense that it encourages Ps to file their claims within a reasonable time and thereby protects them against failure of good claims to succeed due to the deterioration of their evidence over time.
- Prescription also promotes justice among Ps as adjudication of belated claims may often consume more judicial resources than timely claims. Such allocation of resources is unfair as Ps who act reasonably are deprived of societal resources consumed by other Ps who act unreasonably.

**Question** – *What are considered to be the major pros and cons of prescription in your jurisdiction?*

## V. ELEMENTS OF PRESCRIPTION – AN OVERVIEW

Analytically, there are four elements – four sets of rules – that together comprise prescription law:

(1) *Rules of accrual* that determine the date in which the cause of action accrues *for prescription purposes* – the date the prescription period starts to run (unless postponed under element 3).

(2) *The prescription period* – the statutory period of time that after its running the cause of action is prescribed.

(3) *Rules of prolongation: postponement, renewal and extension* – Rules of prolongation are rules that prolong the actual time that passes between accrual of cause of action and its prescription beyond the prescription period. When these rules apply, the *effective time of prescription* is longer than the *prescription period*. There are different rules of prolongation: postponement and suspension, renewal and extension:

   (a) When rules of postponement or/and suspension apply, the prescription period does not run. The difference between postponement and suspension is the following: a rule of *postponement* prevents the running of the prescription period *before it started to run*, although the cause of action already accrued. A rule of *suspension* stops the running of the prescription period after it began (ie there is a *break*). Possibly, a rule may combine postponement and suspension. To illustrate, assume that time does not run when P suffers from mental illness. If P was mentally ill when the cause of action accrued for one year, mental illness would be a rule of postponement – time would run only after a year. If time had run for two years and only then P became mentally ill, for three years, in which the running stopped, mental illness would be a rule of suspension. If P were ill for one year after the cause of action accrued, recovered for two years and then became ill again for three years, mental illness in this case would be a rule of both postponement and suspension (for a combined period of four years in which the prescription period did not run).

   (b) When rules of renewal apply, the count of the prescription period starts afresh. For example, if D admitted P's right three years after the period began to run on P's claim, and admission is a rule of renewal, the three years are 'deleted' and the count of the prescription period starts afresh.

(c) When rules of extension apply the prescription period is extended by the specified period. For example, if the law provides that heirs (the estate) P of the victim V who died would have at least one year to sue the tortfeasor D, and V dies six months before the period expires, the period for P would be extended by six months so that P would have one year to sue.

These rules of prolongation (postponement and suspension, renewal, extension) usually apply in cases where P's delay to file a claim against D originates in difficulties, such as unawareness of relevant facts, mental illness, death or *force majeure*, that justify the prolongation of the effective time of prescription.

(4) *Ceiling on the effective time of prescription* (rules of 'long-stop' or 'repose') – Rules of postponement, renewal and extension may indeterminately prolong the effective time of prescription to an extent that frustrates the goals of prescription law (*infra* Section IX). To avoid such indeterminate prolongation the law may set ceiling periods that after their running the cause of action is prescribed although the prescription period has not yet expired because of postponement, renewal or extension.

**Question** – *What are the elements of prescription in your jurisdiction? How are the above four elements treated in your legal system?*

## VI. THE STARTING POINT OF THE PRESCRIPTION PERIOD

The starting point of the prescription period is the point in time in which P's cause of action is borne (accrues). So what exactly is the cause of action? And what are the relations between the 'action' and its 'cause'? It should be stressed that the notion of 'cause of action' may have different meanings or different interpretations in different contexts: civil procedure, *res judicata* and prescription. The focus here is on its meaning for prescription purposes in tort claims (including contractual claims of malpractice based on negligence).

### THE MEANING OF 'ACTION'

An action in tort alleging entitlement to tort remedy should usually contain the following ingredients: facts regarding D's tortious conduct (act or omission) and its circumstances, harm caused in-fact to P by D's conduct, applicable tort that renders D's conduct tortious and entitles P to tort remedy against D for the harm caused. Every combination of these facts, harm caused and applicable tort constitutes a particular action in tort.

## THE MEANING OF 'CAUSE OF ACTION'

The *cause* of action is the source, the root, of a particular action. Usually a particular action arises from, or originates in, an 'occurrence' such as an accident, professional malpractice, defaming publications, etc. When an occurrence contains a multiplicity of conducts and/or of caused harms which are tortious under tort rules, it may produce a variety of particular tort actions which differ from each other in facts, harms and applicable torts. Yet, when a group of particular actions has a common factual/legal source it is said that all these particular actions belong to the same source, the same cause of action. The cause of action may be the occurrence as a whole or part of it.

This is exemplified by the following illustration. Physician D treats patient P negligently and performs three mistakes on the treatment's day: A, B and C. Mistake A causes harm X after a year. Mistake B causes harm Y after two years. Mistakes A and C together cause harm Z after three years. The occurrence is the medical treatment. This occurrence contains a multiplicity of facts (three different mistakes A, B, C) and multiplicity of harms (X, Y, Z). It accordingly raises multiplicity of particular actions (for harms A, B and C). Yet, to the extent that these actions, or part of them, have a common factual/legal source, they may be regarded as originating in the same cause of action – the medical treatment in this case.

## HOW BROAD SHOULD THE CAUSE OF ACTION BE FOR PRESCRIPTION PURPOSES?

The subject of prescription, it should be stressed, is not *a particular action* but rather its *cause of action*, the source from which the particular action originates. Once a cause of action prescribes with a particular claim that originates from it, all other particular claims that originate in the same cause of action also prescribe. In the above illustration, if all three particular claims belong to the same cause of action, when this cause of action prescribes because the particular claim for harm X prescribed, then the particular claims for harm Y and Z would also prescribe. But if claims for harms X, Y and Z belong each to a different cause of action, then the prescription of the claim for X would not lead to the prescription of other claims. The prescription period has to run separately on each cause of action before it prescribes.

It therefore follows that a *broad* definition of a cause of action, namely, as one that includes many particular claims (eg X, Y and Z belong to the same cause of action) would be detrimental to Ps and beneficial to Ds because prescription of one particular claim would lead to the prescription of all claims belonging to the broadly defined cause of action. In contrast, a *narrow* definition of a cause of action, namely, as one that includes few particular claims or just one (eg X, Y and Z each belong to a different cause of action) would be beneficial to Ps and detrimental to Ds because prescription of one particular claim would not lead to the prescription of other claims, although emerging from the same occurrence, because they belong to narrowly defined different causes of action.

Since the decision as to how broad or narrow the cause of action should be defined for each particular claim is vested with the courts, it appears that courts have a wide discretion in deciding whether a particular claim has prescribed or not. In the above illustration, they would have a wide discretion to decide, where claim for X prescribed, whether claims for Y and Z would also prescribe (broad definition of cause of action) or not (narrow definition).

*In the following questions and cases, we want you as precisely as possible to describe what would constitute the first point in time that a prescription period may start running. In other words: when does the cause of action come into being for prescription purposes?*

**Question** – *How broad is the notion of cause of action for prescription purposes in your jurisdiction?*

Under the strict and narrow sense of the notion 'cause of action' any change in any of the above ingredients of an action – facts, harms, tort – forms a different cause of action. In contrast under a broader sense of the notion different claims may belong to the same cause of action even if they differ in facts, harms and tort.

**Case 1** – *Physician D treats patient P negligently and performs three mistakes on the day of the treatment: A, B and C. Mistake A causes harm X after a year. Mistake B causes harm Y after two years. Mistakes A and C together cause harm Z after three years. For the purposes of prescription – are X, Y and Z three different causes of action (narrow sense), so that the cause of action for each damage accrues at a different date with the occurrence each damage, or do X, Y and Z belong to the same cause of action (broader sense) so that they are all accrue (and are prescribed) with X?*

**Case 2** – *D, a ski instructor, negligently fails to make sure that all skiers in her 'off-piste' group wear helmets. P, a skier in the group, hits a tree. P immediately suffers head injury X, and years later another head injury Y that* *developed from the same accident. Does the cause of action for injury Y accrue with injury X (one cause of action) or with injury Y (two causes of action)? Does it matter whether Y is much more severe than X or vice versa? Does it matter whether Y is causally connected to X or rather causally independent of X?*

**Note** – for each of the harms in the above two cases assume that action can be filed only for harms that *actually occurred*. The question of 'when does the harm occur?' for prescription purposes is discussed below.

**Case 3** – *Builder D lays down defective foundations for a building, thereby creating the risk of future collapse if heavy rain falls. As a result, the value to the owner of the building P decreases (harm A). Two years later heavy rain indeed falls. Three years later the foundation subsides and requires fixing paid by P (harm B). Three year later cracks appear in the building fixed by P (harm C). Four years later the building collapses (harm D). Given the four harms, at which date did each harm occur in your jurisdiction for prescription purposes?*

**Note** – The question whether the four harms belong to the same cause of action for prescription purposes should not be addressed here. It is discussed above.

## CONTINUOUS TORT?

Another major question regarding the notion of 'cause of action' is whether and to what extent the law recognises the notion of 'continuous tort'. The question arises where the D's tortious conduct can be characterised as 'continuous'. Prominent examples in common-law countries are trespass and nuisance but other forms of harm infliction can also be characterised as 'continuous' – exposure to harming substances, medical treatment, failure to recall a product, defamation, etc. Once the law characterises continuous harm infliction as 'continuous', the question is whether the cause of action accrues at *the end* of the period or at its *beginning*.

**Question** – *Is there a notion of continuous tort in your jurisdiction? When is a sequence of tortious acts and ensuing harms considered 'continuous' rather than a series of distinct torts? How similar, and how close in time and space, should tortious acts be in order to be considered 'continuous'? When does the cause of action accrue in continuous torts – the beginning or end of the series of tortious acts or in-between?*

**Case 1** – *Assuming that in the above physician illustration the three treatment mistakes (A, B, C) were performed in three consecutive weeks and not on the same day – would the three mistakes be considered 'a continuous tort' rather than* *three individual torts (A, B, C)? And if so, what would be the accrual date of this continuous tort (harm X, harm Z or another date?).*

**Case 2** – *Every week D publishes a defamatory article on P, each time in another newspaper. Is this a continuous tort? Would it matter if D publishes the same defamation every week in the same newspaper owned by him or defames P differently in different newspapers each time in the same jurisdiction?*

**Case 3** – *Employer D negligently exposes employee P to unreasonable noise at the workplace for three years. P's hearing is thereby weakened on a daily basis, gradually restricting P's ability to communicate and enjoy music. Would this exposure be considered continuous tort?*

**Case 4** – *Is a continuous failure of producer D to recall a defective product that causes harm to consumer P regarded as a continuous tort?*

## WHEN DOES THE HARM OCCUR?

A third major question regarding the notion of 'cause of action' is what exactly is the meaning of 'harm' for prescription purposes? Where the cause of action accrues only when D's tortious conduct causes harm to P, as is often the case, is the *risk* of harm to P considered a harm or should harm actually occur? Obviously, if a risk of harm is considered a harm the cause of action will accrue earlier than if actual harm is required.

There are several options in this regard:

- *Risk* of harm *per se* would be considered as harm for limitation purposes. But if so, there should be a minimal probability threshold, as otherwise every remote and speculative risk would be considered harm.
- Only risk of *certain* future harm (100% probability – 'doomed from the start') will be deemed as 'harm' for accrual purposes.
- Only actual materialisation of the harm can be considered 'harm'.

Two points should be made in this regard.

Firstly, if risk of harm is considered 'harm' for prescription purposes, but P cannot actually succeed in a tort claim before the risk materialises, then there would be a problematic gap in time between the accrual of a cause of action for prescription purposes and the ability of P to succeed in an actual tort claim.

Secondly, a future risk of one kind of harm may be considered a materialised harm of another kind. For example, defective foundations of a building generate a future risk of collapse and physical harm to buyers but at the same time they already cause pure economic loss to buyers as the value of the building diminishes.

**Question** – *In your jurisdiction what is considered the occurrence of the harm for prescription purposes (running of the prescription period): actual accrual (Realisation of the risk? Certainty that the risk will materialise? Only probability that the risk will materialise (which degree of probability is required))?*

This above is illustrated by the following case examples.

**Case 1** – *A negligent medical treatment by physician D more than triples the probability that patient P will contract a disease. P indeed contracts the disease after five years. When does the cause of action accrue?*

Sometimes it is known that the harm was caused (and the cause of action accrued) within a given period. Yet, it is unknown when exactly the damage occurred. The question is how should the court determine the date of accrual? Should it be the beginning or the end of the period? Or somewhere in between?

**Case 2** – *Employer D negligently exposes employee P to toxic radiation at the workplace for ten years. It is known that during this period P's lungs were injured by the radiation, but because P is a heavy smoker, it is unknown when exactly. When does P's cause of action accrue?*

**Case 3** – *A concert pianist is injured by a reckless cyclist, during his summer holiday (1 July). His fingers are broken, and he can no longer play. His financial loss occurs only in August, at the time of the first planned concert. When does the cause of action for the financial loss accrue?*

## VII. PRESCRIPTION PERIODS

The time that has to run on the accrued cause of action from the date of its accrual to the day of its prescription is the *prescription period*. Notably, rules of postponement, renewal and extension of the prescription period may prolong the *effective time of prescription*, namely, the actual period of time that passes between accrual and prescription. These rules of prolongation are discussed in the next section (VIII). This part deals only with the statutorily specified periods of prescription.

A major question regarding the prescription period is whether there should be a *general* period that applies to a variety of claims (tort, contract, unjust enrichment, etc), or instead various, differentiated periods tailored each for specific causes of action (different periods for tort and for contract, etc), or even different periods for different torts within tort law. The pros of diversified periods are basically better adjustment of the periods to the goals of prescription law. The cons of diversified periods are complexity and uncertainty resulting from the need to classify causes of actions according to prescription periods, and from a phenomenon of 'period shopping' by Ps who try to present their claim as belonging to a branch of law where limitation is longer.

**Question 1** – *In your jurisdiction, is there: (a) a general period of prescription common to all private law claims?; (b) Few general periods for different fields of private law? (eg different periods for torts, contracts and unjust enrichment)?; (c) Diversity of prescription periods for different kinds of claims? Is there a special period for the prescription of judgments?*

**Note** – In case of multiplicity of periods for claims other than tort claims major examples will do. No need to go into details.

**Question 2** – *Are there different periods for different tort claims (eg different periods for different kinds of damage? Special long periods for intentional or reckless wrongdoing)? Please specify the different periods for the different tort claims. What explains these differences where they exist?*

**Question 3** – *In case of diversified periods adjusted to different kinds of tort claims, or different periods for tort claims and other claims that concur with tort claims (malpractice), are there problems of classification of claims or of 'period shopping' where D tries to classify her claim as belonging to claims with a longer limitation period? How are these problems handled by courts? In jurisdictions where contractual claims concur with tort claims, and there are different periods of prescription for contract and tort, how do courts treat such attempts of 'period shopping'?*

## VIII. RULES OF POSTPONEMENT, SUSPENSION, RENEWAL AND EXTENSION

Sometimes Ps fail to file claims in time but present subjective/objective justifications for the delay such as being unaware of the claim, minority, illness, other disabilities, special relations with D (family, treatment, employment, etc), staying abroad, previous litigation, admission by D, *force majeure*, etc.

There are various ways to treat these contingencies in a fair manner:

(1) Set a very long basic limitation period (see Section V).
(2) Postpone the running of the prescription period before it begins to run and/or postpone its continuation if already begun (suspend its running) – while justification exists.
(3) Renew (restart) the running of the whole period once the justifying event occurs.
(4) Extend the basic limitation period so that it will not end while justification exists or before P is given a reasonable time to file claim after justification expires.

Combinations are also possible such as 2+4.

All the above legal techniques actually prolong the time in which claims can be filed, and as a result the *effective time of prescription, namely, the actual period of time that passes between accrual and prescription* may be longer than the *prescription period*. For example, if the prescription period is five years, but the running of this period is postponed for three years because of late discovery in the specific case, the effective time of prescription would be eight years.

**Question** – *Please indicate whether in your jurisdiction the following contingencies are recognised as justifications for prolongation of the effective time of prescription and what legal techniques are used for each (postponement, renewal, extension or combinations). Please specify which are statutory and which are judicial.*

(1) Unawareness – non-discovery of facts constituting the claim (the late discovery rule).
(2) D is to blame for the delay – misleading P, threatening P, etc.
(3) Admission by D of P's right or partial performance of P's right by D.
(4) Legal relations between D and P – D is P's custodian, D is P's trustee, etc.
(5) Medical treatment relations.
(6) Employment relations.
(7) Family relations – marriage, parents and children.
(8) P's minority – does it matters whether P has a representative?
(9) P's mental disability – does it matters whether P has a representative?
(10) P's physical disability.
(11) P's and/or D's physical absence from the jurisdiction.
(12) *Force majeure*.
(13) Former litigation between the parties that ends without final ruling or ongoing litigation?

(14) ADR and settlements proceedings.
(15) Court's ruling or law that prevents P from litigating the claim.
(16) Evidential difficulties of P who needs time to gather evidence.
(17) Financial difficulties of P in raising the money required for litigation.
(18) Closed courts.
(19) Prolongation by courts on grounds of justice.
(20) Any other recognised justifications?

With regard to *unawareness* (late discovery):

**Question 1** – *Is this justification subjective or objective? (Where it is subjective, the running of time is postponed, or suspended (if already begun), until P actually, subjectively, becomes aware of the facts constituting the claim. Where the justification is objective, the running is postponed or suspended only until a reasonable person would have discovered the relevant facts even if P did not).*

**Question 2** – *What are the facts that P must be unaware of leading to postponement or suspension? (D's tortious conduct? P's harm? Causal link between the two? D's identity?)*

**Question 3** – *Is unawareness of the fact that tort law provides remedy in P's case considered a justification for postponement until discovery of this 'legal fact'?*

**Case 1** – *Employer D's negligence exposes employee P to toxic substances. As a result, P contracts a lung disease, but is unaware of the causal link between exposure and disease because his physician fails to detect it. P does not seek a second opinion. After the prescription period runs on the disease P consults his new physician who tells him about the link. Did P's claim against D prescribe?*

**Case 2** – *As in Case 1 except that P, being aware of the causal link, failed to sue in time because his former lawyer told him that the exposure was not tortious, and only his new lawyer told him, after the running of time, that it was tortious.*

## IX. CEILINGS ON THE EFFECTIVE TIME OF PRESCRIPTION

Rules of postponement, renewal and extension, that prolong the effective time of prescription, may prejudice Ds by making it difficult for them to defend claims filed many years after the cause of action accrued. For example, if P was harmed at birth, allegedly by D's negligence, and the running of time is postponed until majority (18), and the prescription period is five years, the effective time of prescription would be 23 years after birth. Moreover, Ds are often unaware of whether Ps have a recognised justification that prolongs the effective time of prescription beyond the prescription period.

All the above generate much uncertainty which may conflict with the goals of prescription law. To retain a minimum degree of certainty, the law of prescription may employ 'ceilings periods' under which a claim is prescribed after the ceiling period expires even if the prescription period has not yet expired because of the prolongation rules of postponement, renewal and extension. If the ceiling period, for example, is 20 years, D's claim in the above example would prescribe 20 years after birth and not after 23 years.

As its major aim is to restore or secure some certainty for Ds, the ceiling period may start running not from the date the cause of action accrued, but from the date of D's act or omission (taking into account continuous conduct), as this date is known to D. For example, in product liability cases while the prescription starts to run (unless postponed) from the date P was harmed by the product (accrual), the ceiling period may run from the day the product was marketed by D. Alternatively, the ceiling period may run from the date the cause of action accrued, like the prescription period.

Another question is whether the ceiling periods, although aimed to counterbalance the prolonging effect of rules of postponement, and extension (Section VI), are nevertheless subjected to any of these prolonging rules. That could be the case, for example, where the delay was caused by D's misconduct that caused P's delay.

**Question** – *Are there 'ceiling periods' in your jurisdiction? To which kind of claims do they apply? What is their length? When does each period start to run? Are there any prolongations of the ceiling periods by rules of prolongation?*

## X. STATUTE INTERPRETATION, JUDICIAL DISCRETION AND LACHES

Given the pros and cons of prescription (see *supra* Section III), both the legislature and the courts are required to seek what they view as the right balance between the diversified and often conflicting considerations. The legislature strikes this balance while enacting the statutory rules of prescription and amending them. The courts strike the balance when interpreting the statutory rules. They also do it in exercising judicial discretion to the extent that such discretion, explicitly or implicitly, is vested in them. This complicated balancing should be made with regard to each of the four elements of prescription, and, most importantly, with regard to their combined effect.

## INTERPRETATION

In balancing the pros and cons of prescription judges may differ as to where the right balance lies. Some judges, for example, may be hostile to prescription because it closes the courts' doors and deprives Ps of their rights, while others may be more sympathetic to prescription given its goals. These differences in approach may lead to different schools of interpretation of the statutory provisions: one that favours interpretations restricting the scope of prescription and another, more 'neutral', that seeks to achieve the goals of prescription regardless of whether its scope is narrowed or widened.

**Question** – *Are judges in your jurisdiction hostile, neutral or sympathetic to prescription, or differ in their approach? Is it in any way regarded unethical to reject a claim on the basis of rules of prescription?*

## DISCRETION

Judicial discretion, which transcends mere interpretation of statutory provisions regarding prescription may be, as mentioned, implicit or explicit.

Judicial discretion is *implicit* where the statute uses general, open terms or concepts, without providing any real guidelines as to how to implement them in specific cases. Prominent examples are the concepts of 'reasonableness' or 'duty' in negligence law and of 'good faith' in contract law. Some of these wide, open concepts, may be referred to as *standards* that call for judicial discretion in their application on specific cases as opposed to *rules* that require 'only' interpretation in their application. In prescription law such implicit discretion can be found, for example, where the court has to decide when the cause of action accrues for prescription purposes. As shown (Section VI), absent statutory guidelines the court may need to exercise discretion to determine how broad the cause of action is, whether a tort is a continuous one, and when the damage occurs. Another example is where the court has to determine whether the non-discovery of facts by P is 'reasonable' so that it triggers a rule of postponement.

**Question** – *Does your prescription law use general, open terms such as 'reasonableness' or 'good faith'? In which contexts of prescription?*

Judicial discretion is *explicit* for our purposes where the statute explicitly authorises the court to accept or reject the defence of prescription, on a case-by-case basis, with regard to specified claims. The discretion can be limited to types of damage (eg bodily injury), to types of Ps (eg minors) or to types of conduct (eg intentional or reckless wrongdoers). The discretion may be either fully open or provided with statutory guidelines and considerations that should be accounted for and balanced by the court.

At first sight discretion may look more attractive than the statutory regime. Given the pros and cons of prescription one may wonder why the desired balance between the two should be struck by the statutory rules discussed above and not be left to judicial discretion on a case-by-case basis. After all, is it not preferable that the court will strike the balance between the conflicting considerations in the specific circumstances of the litigating parties, and then decide whether to accept or reject the defence? Assume, for example, that the court finds that in the circumstances of the case that bar D's ability to defend and introduce evidence was increased by the passage of time rather than diminished, that P's claim looks like a 'good claim', and that P did not neglect his claim. Is it not preferable that the court will be authorised to reject the prescription defence rather than obliged under the statutory rule to accept it?

On the other hand, it should be stressed, that the major goals of prescription law are not to do justice between the litigating parties but rather to protect the vast groups of *potential* Ds and society at large from the costs of preserving evidence and financial reserves indefinitely, and from other costs of uncertainty regarding legal risks. Granting wide discretion to courts on a case-by-case basis to accept or reject the defence will unavoidably generate such a degree of uncertainty that may undermine and frustrate the ends of prescription. Indeed, the perspectives behind the design of statutory rules are wider and more balanced than the judicial perspectives in a case-by-case decision. While the court naturally concentrates on doing justice between the few litigating parties, the legislature is more sensitive to the interests of the huge group potential Ps and to the interest of society at large.

**Question 1** – *Does your law explicitly allow or even mandate judicial discretion on a case-by-case basis to accept or reject the prescription defence in tort claims? If so, with regard to which kinds of tort claims? (Types of harm? Of Ps? Of Ds? Of the nature of the tortious conduct? Otherwise?) Does the statute set parameters and guidelines for the exertion of this discretion? What are they?*

**Question 2** – *Do judges interpret the rules of prescription differently from other rules within private law?*

## LACHES

A legal doctrine parallel to prescription that calls for judicial discretion is laches. It allows courts to reject P's claim because of the passage of time since its accrual if the delay in filing harmed D because she legitimately relied on P's omission to file during that period. The doctrine of laches can function as a judicial, discretionary, alternative to prescription or as additional defence. As an additional defence it may bar P's claim before the expiration of the prescription period and such an outcome may be considered undesirable as it undermines prescription law (claim may be subjected to laches before it is subjected to prescription).

**Question** – *Does the law in your jurisdiction authorise courts to reject a claim, including a tort claim, on the ground of laches or of a similar doctrine? What are the conditions for such rejection of tort claims?*

## XI. CHANGE OF PARTIES

### VICTIMS

Sometimes the claim of the victim of tort (V) against the tortfeasor (D) is either transmitted (by law) or transferred by agreement (if the law allows) to another person (P). The question in such cases is whether and how such change affects prescription. Does it renew, start afresh, the running of the prescription period between P and D, or does the running of the period on V continue on P? And do rules of prolongation (postponement, renewal and extension) apply to P in the same way that they apply to V?

**Case 1** – *V's right against D is subrogated to insurer P that compensated V under the insurance policy for harm caused by D. Does the running of time on P's subrogation claim start afresh when P acquires the right of subrogation, or does the running on V's claim continue on P's claim?*

**Case 2** – *V dies and his rights against D are transmitted by the law of inheritance to P. When V died, only one month remained of the prescription period. P sues after two months but argues, alternatively, that: (a) when V died a new count of the prescription period starts afresh for P; (b) that even if the running of time continues it is postponed by rules of prolongation because P was unaware of the claim against D (V was aware) or because P suffers from mental disability (V did not).*

Similar questions arise where P's claim against D actually substitutes V's claim although P's right against D is not formally transmitted from V to P but is considered an independent claim. A prominent example is the contribution claim of one tortfeasor (P) against a tortfeasor D where P and D are jointly liable to V. Another example are claims made by the dependents (Ps) of the deceased V, against D who injured V, injury that later caused V's death, for loss of financial support that D would have otherwise provided. Such claim actually substitutes V's claim for loss of earnings.

*Joint Tortfeasors*

**Case 1** – *V dies due to injury caused by D. At his death only one month remained of the prescription period. P, a dependent, sues after two months for loss of support but argues that the running of the prescription period on her claim starts only with V's death. D argues that P's claim as a dependent substitutes V's claim for prescription purposes and is therefore prescribed.*

**Case 1a** – *The same as Case 1 except that V dies after the expiration of the prescription period.*

**Case 2** – *P and D are jointly and severely tortfeasors vis-á-vis V. A month before the prescription period on V's claims against P and D expire, P compensates V. Two months later P sues D for contribution. P argues that the running of the prescription period on her claim starts only with the payment to V. D argues that P's contribution claim substitutes V's claim for prescription purposes and is therefore prescribed. What would the court decide in your jurisdiction?*

**Case 2a** – *The same as Case 2 except that P compensated V after the expiration of the prescription period on V's claim against P and D. What would the court decide in your jurisdiction?*

*Dependants*

**Question** – *If in your jurisdiction dependants Ps of a deceased victim V have an independent claim against D who tortiously injured V, injury that later caused V's death, does Ps' cause of action accrue with V's injury or with V's death? May this problem be treated by other rules than those concerning prescription?*

## CHANGE OF PARTIES – TORTFEASORS

**Question** – *To the extent that liabilities of tortfeasors may be transferred to others (eg by inheritance law to the estate of the tortfeasor), does such a change start a new period of prescription? Do rules of prolongation (postponement and suspension, renewal and extension) apply to the transferee? For example, if mental illness is a rule of suspension, would mental disability of the transferee D stop the running of the prescription period although the original tortfeasor was not mentally ill?*

# XII. OTHER ASPECTS OF PRESCRIPTION LAW

## STIPULATION AND WAIVER

**Question 1** – *Can the parties to potential proceedings validly agree in advance on rules of prescription different from the statutory rules? Is there a difference in this regard between tort law and other fields of law or between different kinds of torts? Can the parties agree to shorten the period (is there a threshold)? To extend it (indefinitely)? To disapply or change rules of prolongation (postponement, renewal), extension)? Are there formal requirements to such an agreement (separate contract, writing, signature)?*

**Question 2** – *If D informs P before trial, by a unilateral act, that she waives her prescription defence, can she nevertheless raise the defence at court?*

## PLEADINGS BY THE PARTIES

**Question 1** – *What is the procedural act by P that stops the running of the prescription period? Is it the filing at the court office of a form of claim by P? A written notice or demand sent by P to D or some other act?*

**Question 2** – *Is prescription a defence that has to be pleaded by D or may the court raise it at its own initiative – ex officio?*

**Question 3** – *At which procedural stage should the defence be pleaded by D? Should it be raised at the beginning of the proceedings? Is there a sanction for failure to do so? When should the court decide the prescription issue? Is it a preliminary issue that requires preliminary decision or can it be decided with the other pleadings made by the parties?*

**Question 4** – *Can the defence be raised by a third party, T, who claims, for some reason, that D's claim against P is prescribed? (eg can T, a joint tortfeasor with D, refuse to pay contribution to D on the ground that D paid P after the prescription of P's claim against D and T)?*

## BURDEN OF PROOF

**Question** – *According to the general principle that one who makes a claim incurs the burden of proof regarding that claim, it is D who has to establish that the prescription period passed since the accrual pf P's right to remedy and it is P who has to establish that the running of time was or has been postponed, renewed or that the period has been extended. Is this the case in your jurisdiction?*

# ABOUT THE EDITORS

Israel Gilead is Bora Laskin (Emeritus) Professor of Law at the Hebrew University of Jerusalem, where he was Dean of the Faculty of Law between 1999 and 2002. Since 2016, he has been a Professor and Head of the Advanced Legal Studies program at The Academic Center for Law and Sciences. Professor Gilead is a member of the Israeli Council of Higher Education and chairs its committee in charge of social sciences, law and business administration. He is a member of the European Group on Tort Law, of the American Law Institute, of the Codification Committee established by the Israeli Ministry of Justice, and also of the board of Directors in a major bank and insurance company. Professor Gilead is the author of numerous publications on tort law, law and economics, prescription and corporate law.

Bjarte Askeland is an Appeal Court Judge in Gulating lagmannsrett, Bergen, Norway and was, until 2019, Professor of Private Law at the University of Bergen. He has led a Norwegian law committee on the assessment of personal injury awards (2008–2011) and a research project on 'the temporal dimension of tort law' funded by the Norwegian Research Council (2008–2012). He is a Member of the European Group on Tort Law and the author of monographs and numerous articles on tort law.

# ABOUT THE EDITORS

Israel Gilead is [illegible] Emeritus Professor of Law at the [illegible] of Jerusalem, where he [illegible] of the Faculty of Law [illegible] 1999 and 2002. Since 2018, he has [illegible] Professor and Head of the [illegible] Legal Studies program at The [illegible] Center for Law and Society. Professor Gilead is a member of the [illegible] Higher Education [illegible] its committee in charge of [illegible] and Business Administration. He is a member of the European Group on [illegible] of the American Law Institute, the Codification Committee established by the Israeli Ministry of Justice, and also of the Board of Directors in a [illegible] bank and insurance company. Professor Gilead is the author of numerous publications on tort law, law and [illegible], possession and corporate law.

[illegible] Askeland is [illegible] Court Judge in [illegible], Bergen, Norway and [illegible] Professor of Private Law at the University of Bergen. He has [illegible] law committee on the assessment of personal injury [illegible] (2008) [illegible] research project on the temporal dimension of tort law funded by the Norwegian Research Council (2008–2012). He is a Member of the European Group on Tort Law and the author of a monograph and numerous articles on [illegible].